FROM MIGRANT TO ACADIAN

From Migrant to Acadian

A North American Border People
1604–1755

N.E.S. GRIFFITHS

Canadian Institute for Research
on Public Policy and Public Administration
University of Moncton

McGill-Queen's University Press
Montreal & Kingston • London • Ithaca

Legal deposit first quarter 2005
Bibliothèque nationale du Québec

Printed in Canada on acid-free paper

This book has been published with the help of a
contribution from Lord Black of Cross Harbour.

McGill-Queen's University Press acknowledges the
financial support of the Canada Council for the Arts
for its publishing program. We also acknowledge the
financial support of the Government of Canada
through the Book Publishing Industry Development
Program (BPIDP) for our publishing activities.

Library and Archives Canada Cataloguing in Publication

Griffiths, N.E.S. (Naomi Elizabeth Saundaus), 1934–
    From migrant to Acadian : a North American border
people, 1604–1755 / N.E.S. Griffiths.

Includes bibliographical references and index.
ISBN 0-7735-2699-4

    1. Acadia – History.   2. Acadians – History.
3. Acadians – Ethnic identity.   I. Title.

FC2043.G74 2005   971.6'004114   c2004-903565-7

This book was typeset by True to Type in 10/12 Baskerville

In Memoriam

R.L. Griffiths, 1893–1970
A.M. Griffiths, 1901–63
K.M. Griffiths, 1938–66
J.M. Griffiths (Nell-Nichols), 1928–75
Mme Edna (LeBlanc) Dionne, 1898–1979

Contents

Maps

The location of settlements, physical features, and other information portrayed on these maps has been compiled from a variety of sources, including comtemporary eighteenth-century maps and the *Atlas of Canada*. Major sources are acknowledged in the captions of each map. A uniform map base was newly created to display the information on this series of maps. The maps were compiled by Larry McCann, University of Victoria, and drafted using computer technology by Michael Fisher, University of Alberta. The spelling of French words is based largely on contemporary usage and thus can vary from map to map.

Acknowledgments

So many people have given me aid and comfort over the past decades, as I have studied and written about the history of the Acadians, that my greatest fear, as I write these words, is that I will forget to acknowledge someone's particular contribution to my work. Friends and colleagues, librarians, archivists, research assistants, other scholars I have known only through correspondence, my own university as well as Mount Allison University and the Université de Moncton, the Social Sciences and Humanities Research Council (SSHRC) – I want to record my gratitude to all these people and institutions who have helped to make my studies possible.

The idea for this particular book has been in my mind since 1970 but it was not until 1988 that I was able to begin steady work on it. Much of the delay was due to administrative responsibilities, including eight and a half years as dean of the Faculty of Arts at Carleton University. However, in 1988 I was appointed to the Winthrop Pickard Bell Chair in Maritime Studies at Mount Allison University, and I spent from July to December of that year in Sackville, New Brunswick. To Mount Allison University and its then vice-president, Sheila Brown, I owe a great debt of gratitude. Without her support, the transition from administrative life to that of full-time scholarship and teaching would have been much more difficult. These months gave me time to consider what issues of importance I wanted to stress in a narrative of Acadian experience and to read extensively in the fields of seventeenth- and eighteenth-century North American history. The result was the publication, in 1992, of *The context of Acadian history, 1604–1755*, based on four public lectures given in 1988 at Mount Allison, in which I outlined the major questions that I wanted to explore.

But this summary of the help that renewed my interest in writing the present work omits by far the most important result of the six months I spent in Sackville. This was the refreshing of old friendships and the making of new ones among scholars of Maritime history. I had time for long talks with George Rawlyk, whose untimely death has been a great loss to

those of us working in the field of Maritime history, and to have the pleasure of equally lengthy discussions with Larry McCann, then head of the
Institute of Canadian Studies at Mount Allison, which gave me a height-
ened perception of Maritime geography. During the fifteen years that have
elapsed since my sojourn at Mount Allison University, the continued
friendship and help of scholars has been of crucial importance for my
work. The interest of Georges Arsenault, Neil Boucher, Margaret Conrad,
Gwen Davies, David Frank, Gerry Hallowell, Barry Moody, John Reid, and
Brook Taylor, whose capacity to listen to me and ask useful questions has
been inexhaustible, has cheered me on in moments of discouragement.
Further, the generosity with which all have sent me copies of their own
writings that were relevant to my purposes has been a great help.

I was also able, during my time at Mount Allison, to spend unhurried
days at the Centre d'Études Acadienne at the Université de Moncton. I
had known francophone scholars of the Acadian experience since my
studies for my MA at the University of New Brunswick in 1956–57, when
A.G. Bailey, who was my supervisor there, sent me to Moncton to meet with
Father René Baudry. Baudry guided me through the documents held in
the archives of what was then Saint-Joseph's College at Memramcook. I
owe much to these two distinguished scholars: Dr Bailey gave me some
indication of the way in which the outside world regarded Acadian history,
and Father Baudry introduced me to the way in which Acadians regarded
their own experience. Thirty-two years later, my extended and leisurely stay
in Sackville allowed me to become well acquainted with those working at
Centre d'Études Acadiennes and the resources being gathered there. Maurice Basque, Regis Brun, Jean Daigle, Ronald Labelle, and René-Gilles
Leblanc answered questions and queries with great patience. Faculty members in other departments, in particular Muriel Roy of the sociology
department, and Léon Theriault of the history department, also added a
great deal to my knowledge of the extensive research which resulted in the
publication of the invaluable overviews of Acadian matters edited by Jean
Daigle at the Centre in 1980 (followed by a second edition in 1993).
Other scholars at the Université Sainte-Anne and St Francis Xavier University also made me aware of their interests and invited me to discuss my
ideas with them. This broad net of acquaintanceship among both francophone and anglophone scholars working in Maritime history has been
both a help and a pleasure through the years.

Also in 1988, on the insistence of Mme Beaulieu, at that time head of
the department of continuing education at the Université de Moncton, I
gave an introductory course on Acadian history to a class of Acadian and
English-Canadian students. Their passionate interest in the subject, diverse
points of view, and penetrating questions made me consider carefully why
I envisaged Acadian history as having followed a particular pattern of
development. On my return to Carleton University, the students who took
courses with me in Acadian history reinforced this need to explain the

assumptions with which I worked. In fact, it is probably because of this shrewd questioning by the young that I was able to write a successful application for an SSHRC grant in 1988.

Students demand answers to why one has embarked on a particular field of study and how one's interest relates to the general concerns of the discipline. Teaching them is an extraordinary aid to clarity of thought. Colleagues, for their part, most frequently question research techniques and modes of analysis while also offering suggestions about archival and library resources and ideas about how issues can be better explored, or more succinctly expressed. Throughout my career at Carleton University, I had the great good fortune of finding my colleagues in the university in general, and in the history department in particular, generous in discussion of their own research and mine. I had the privilege of joining a young and growing university in 1962, when the whole academic staff numbered no more than eighty-five (with five full-time professors in the department of history) and the student body barely reached two thousand. The history department was then chaired by David Farr, who hired me as a sessional lecturer and who gave me continued support over the ensuing decades. Stan Mealing was also on staff at this time and his wise, kind advice was of inestimable value to a young academic. Nostalgia plays a part but I remember with gratitude that, during the first twenty years I spent at Carleton, there was an absence of cynicism about the value of scholarship and its rewards as well as a respect for the way in which one chose to formulate the particular questions worked upon. The particular disciplines that made up the faculties had not yet erected priestly walls and the open-mindedness of political scientists such as Ken Macrea and sociologists such as Bruce MacFarlane made not only for wide reading but also for a constant awareness that different perspectives could produce radically different interpretations of the same phenomena.

More than anything else, my colleagues in these decades constantly emphasized that the basis of their work was a fascination with the realities of human experience. The curiosity that they showed about one another's research was probably the result of this fascination and it was a curiosity that was immensely attractive to me, since it led to endless discussions about each individual's projects, over coffee and tea, beer and wine, and, when finances really improved, single-malt scotch. Inevitably, as both the university and the department grew, friendships tended to become greater with those whose fields of study were cognate. This led to the emergence of a small group whose interest was in eighteenth-century history on both sides of the Atlantic, a group that included historians working in the National Archives of Canada, in the Department of National Defence, and at the University of Ottawa. Meetings among us were haphazard but the discussions were not and my thanks go out to its members: Carmen Bickerton, Julian Gwyn, Peter King, Stan Mealing, Fred Thorpe, and Syd Wise. But those of my colleagues whose main interests were in other fields also gave me ideas and encouragement: conversations with Keri Abel, Marilyn Barber, Peter Brown, David Dean, Bruce Elliott, Peter Fitzgerald, Robert Goheen, Fred Goodwin, Deborah Gorham, Norman Hillmer, Brian McKillop, Del Muise, Blair Neatby, Rod Phillips, and John Taylor stand out in my memory.

The months I spent at Mount Allison University led to my involvement with the publication of a volume of essays, edited by Phillip A. Buckner and John G. Reid, entitled *The Atlantic region to Confederation: A history* and published by the University of Toronto Press in 1994. This meant that I had the pleasure of listening to the ideas of, in particular, J.M. Bumsted, Rosemary E. Ommer, Ralph Pastor, and Graeme Wynn. The year 1994 also brought me a Research Achievement Award from Carleton University and a further grant from the SSHRC. The former meant a year's release from teaching and the latter allowed me to work at the Public Record Office in London on British naval records relating to the years 1740–60 and on United Kingdom newspaper records for the same years. It also meant a short research stint at the Archives Nationales in Paris and a second, longer visit to the Centre d'Études Acadiennes in Moncton. By 1996, when I took early retirement, I was in a position to begin writing. This appalling stage, when one ruffles through the files of rough drafts, considers earlier attempts at presenting particular episodes in articles, wonders whether another two or three years reading and research would not be the proper course to follow, was made easier by two invitations, both of which I gladly accepted. The first was to give the Standard Life Lecture at the Institute of Canadian Studies, University of Edinburgh, in 1998. I chose as my subject "The formation of community and the interpretation of identity: The Acadians, 1604–1997," which allowed me to think about the way in which the events of the seventeenth and early eighteenth centuries marked the later development of Acadian history. The comments made by Colin Coates and Ged Martin were not only shrewd but particularly encouraging.

The second invitation I received was from Donald Savoie, the director of the Institut Canadien de recherche sur le développement régional at the Université de Moncton, who offered me a continuing appointment as a senior visiting research at the institute, beginning in 1999. The result has been, for me, a most joyous and fruitful relationship with the institute, the university, and the surrounding countryside. Being able to spend unhurried periods of time in a major Acadian university and to enjoy the warm hospitality of old friends and new colleagues enriched the last years of work on *From migrant to Acadian* immensely. In particular, the efforts made by the Honourable Roméo Le Blanc to introduce me to people he thought I would enjoy knowing provided me with a much deeper knowledge of the political concerns of the Acadians than I had previously had. Two new friends in particular, Claude Bourque and Robert Pichette, have a particularly subtle understanding of the extent to which current interpretations of Acadian history have influenced present Acadian politics. I think that their questions and comments have made me present my ideas of the past much more fully than I might otherwise have done, clarifying as much as possible my assumptions about Acadian society.

Throughout these years, too, the unfailing assistance of librarians and archivists has made my work possible. At Carleton University the inter-library loan department worked valiantly and courteously to produce books from other libraries and Francis Montgomery did more than anyone could expect to guide me through government documents. Lois Yorke of the Public Archives of Nova Scotia, Karen Smith, special collections librar-ian at Dalhousie University, Felicity Osepchook, head of archives at the New Brunswick Museum, Saint John, Camilla Bourgeois of the Centre d'Études Acadienne, and Charlotte Dionne Labelle of the library of the Université de Moncton all provided me with invaluable aid when I needed it. I would also like thank Joan White of the history department at Carleton University and Ginette Benoit of the Institut de recherche at the Univer-sité de Moncton for helping me collate receipts for grant monies, a most necessary task. As well, I owe a particular debt of gratitude to Dan Benoit, who for more than ten years has acted as my computer "guru," sorting out my self-inflicted difficulties with those extraordinarily exasperating and invaluable machines.

Finally, I want to thank those whose efforts have helped in the transfor-mation of an author's manuscript into a published book. Philip Cercone and Joan McGilvray of McGill-Queen's University Press withstood the arrival of a lengthy manuscript without losing their enthusiasm for publi-cation; Curtis Fahey, as my editor, made every effort to ensure that the work contained a minimum of errors, labouring over the footnotes with great fortitude, while, at the same time, cleverly and ruthlessly trimming my prose and, on top of everything else, producing the index. Henri Pilon worked equally nobly in overseeing the accuracy of citations from French sources. Tim Krywulak, a doctoral student at Carleton University, strug-gled, even before the editing stage, to corral the endnotes into some order and then correlated them with the Bibliography.

Finally, I must thank, with considerable warmth, those who have provid-ed funds for the publication of the work: Lord Conrad Black, for his con-tribution to the costs of the English version; and Donald Savoie and the Institut Canadien de recherche sur le développement regional and Sheila Copps and the Heritage Department of the Government of Canada, for defraying the costs of the forthcoming French translation.

Introduction

My introduction to Acadians came even before I immigrated to Canada in 1956. In 1953 I met students from New Brunswick at the University of London, students who spoke French as a mother tongue and who saw themselves as Canadian but for whom that identity was coloured by the sense of a strong Acadian heritage. I learned from them that the history of Acadia reached back to the seventeenth century and was marked by drama, complexity, and endurance. In their telling, it was the history of a people who had never had political independence but had developed a strong, unique identity nonetheless. It was also a history, apparently, that was dominated by events in the eighteenth century, a deportation of the majority of the community in 1755 from their ancestral lands, an incident of the world war being waged at that time between England and France. I was unclear, in 1953, as to the number of those who, after being deported, returned to Acadia – as well as to how they managed to do so – but what was very clear to me was that a sense of Acadian identity was as important to my new acquaintances as a sense of Welsh identity was to my father's family.

My formal study of the Acadians began in 1956 when, as explained in the Acknowledgments, I went to the University of New Brunswick to work with A.G. Bailey for my master's degree. Under his guidance, and with the help of Father René Baudry, then teaching at the Collège Saint-Joseph of Memramcook, I began to understand what the deportation of 1755 had actually involved and also what historians had thought about the subject. I came to the realization, too, that the history of Acadian identity is anything but simple, although it can be made to appear so. At the opening of the seventeenth century there were no Acadians, but by the close of that century there were people, living in territory known internationally as "Acadia or Nova Scotia," essentially present-day Nova Scotia, New Brunswick, and Prince Edward Island, who considered themselves to be first and foremost Acadians rather than members of any other group. In 1755 the majority of this community was sent into exile; however, by the close of the eighteenth century, a sufficient number had returned to lands close to those on which their ancestors had first established themselves. There they once more asserted their identity as a separate and distinct people. Today, the Acadians form the bulk of the French-speaking population of the Maritime provinces and number around 300,000. Those are the basic facts. By the conclusion of the work for the master's degree, however, I realized that behind this account of Acadian history lie innumerable disputes, arguments over "what" happened "when" being as fiercely waged as ones concerned with final results.

The Acadians have always had trouble convincing people that they are a truly distinctive community, not merely a small colony of expatriate Frenchmen or an appendage of Quebec. One of the major determinants in the chain of events that resulted in the deportation of 1755 was the refusal of both English and French to accept the Acadians' definition of themselves as "les français neutres." Nor were the Acadians much more successful during the nineteenth and twentieth centuries in asserting their identity. They did not evince an interest in provincial and federal politics until after Confederation, and, in the twentieth century, as Antonine Maillet has remarked, they have often been regarded as a people whose best characteristics derive from strong French cultures rooted elsewhere and whose worst are the result of an innate Acadian weakness. They are, for many people, not a significant living culture but an oddly persistent folk society, with attributes that are often seen as charming rather than valuable. But there is far more to Acadian history than this and since 1957 that history has been for me as much an avocation as a professional concern.

I worked at the Collège Maillet in northern New Brunswick immediately after graduation. Circumstances then interrupted my Acadian studies but in 1964, after I had joined the history department at Carleton University, I registered for my doctorate as an external student at the University of London; my thesis topic was the causes and aftermath of the deportation of the Acadians and I was awarded my PHD in 1970. Since then, I have had the great good fortune to find that the subjects I chose for graduate study have continued to fascinate me.

Acadian history has many attractions as an area of enquiry. In the first place, it has a marked beginning. There was no community of Acadians before 1604 and the foundation of Acadian society was built during the seventeenth century by people with a variety of European backgrounds, mainly French but with an admixture of some others from the British Isles as well as a seasoning of Amerindians. Acadian history, therefore, is that of a relatively small group of people, and, while its understanding obviously demands knowledge of the history of much larger political and cultural entities, it is a history that provides a manageable field of study. One can examine in detail the Acadian experience and begin to answer some of the questions about the ways in which human communities produce a sense of "national" identity that retains importance for those who come after, people whose problems and difficulties are very different from those confronted by their ancestors.

Furthermore, while Acadian history involves a relatively small group of humanity, its course has been sufficiently complex and intricate that it warrants, and requires, sustained and detailed scholarly investigation. In 1988, as holder of the Winthrop Pickard Bell Chair of Maritime Studies at Mount Allison University, I had a magnificent opportunity to outline in some detail, and for four specific periods, the intricate nature of the history I wished to write. For me, the 1680s, the years when migration from France to "Acadie" added to an existing population rather than created a new colony, and when European heritage interacted with the North American environment, seemed a reasonable starting place for Acadian history. Above all, the history of these years provided an opportunity to show the way in which seventeenth-century national ideologies were quite different, both in importance and in content, from their counterparts in the nineteenth and twentieth centuries. The second era chosen, the 1730s, is one in which one can see an Acadian community flourishing economically, politically, socially, and culturally. Elsewhere I have described it as the golden age of Acadia.[1] It is important to understand what happened in these years because it was then that the Acadian vision of life began to take shape. They were the years that would be imagined by Longfellow in his poem and that would be remembered as a time of innocence and plenty, the formative era of the Acadian community. The third and fourth periods were almost self-defined: they encompass the years leading up to the deportation and the immediate period of exile. Questions about the why and how of the deportation may never find answers agreeable to all. Yet, in my 1988 lectures, I tried to present what I still believe are the most important questions to discuss and an overview of the evidence that must be considered.[2]

This present work represents a development of the ideas presented at that time. What has made Acadian history of such vital interest to me is that it is about men and women who decided to identify their sense of community by the word "Acadia" and in so doing created a people where none had been before. How did this occur? What were the important points in the evolution of the society of migrants into a polity, a polity that has endured in spite of extraordinary trials? At the same time, the growing debate during the last half of the twentieth century and beyond regarding the capacities of the state to respond to the challenge of differing local identities among its citizenry has sharpened my interest in the Acadian experience. Given the destructive force of the politics of national identity over the last two hundred years, it is not surprising that even the terms of this debate are contentious. Is the debate a matter of discovering the best way for a state to integrate its minorities?[3] Does it involve a logical development of world politics at the close of the twentieth century and the opening of the twenty-first, a reaction to the globalization of economic and political power?[4] Or is it an argument between an evil tribalism and a rational globalization?[5] Whatever the argument is about, one thing seems clear: all sides use ideas of what happened in the past to bolster arguments about what is happening in the present and what ought to happen in the future. It is in this context that Acadian history appeals to me since it provides a concrete example of the capacity of small communities to retain a distinct sense of local identity in the face of powerful forces of assimilation, and to do so without political autonomy.

I have chosen to present my ideas in the form of a critical narrative of Acadian experience. Chronology is the backbone of the work because I want to give pride of place to the sequence of events and to show how the complicated patterns of the political struggles between and within the governments of the British and French monarchies had an impact on the development of the Acadians. It is the Acadians' own unique historical experience that is the foundation of their identity but this has often been overlooked by historians who have concentrated on broad issues of imperial policy, with Acadian matters considered as an example rather than interesting in their own right, or who have adopted a comparative approach in which the experience of others is as important as that of the Acadians. Since 1956, when I began my studies on the Acadian deportation, writings about Acadian history have proliferated but the majority have been dedicated to nineteenth- and twentieth-century Acadian history, to examinations of a specific problem in Acadian life, or to the presentation of a particular interpretation of the events of 1755.[6] Works devoted to tracing the slow development of settlement over one hundred and fifty years in Acadia have been few. What is attempted here, in contrast, is an account centred upon the vicissitudes of the European settlement of the area, from its beginning in 1604 until the summer of 1755 when Colonel Charles Lawrence and the Council of Nova Scotia decided to deport the Acadians. The way in which European politics affected the development of the colony decade by decade, and the impact of transatlantic events as well as events in the immediate area of Acadian settlements, are examined in the context of the Acadians' creation over time of their own particular identity. It is hoped that this history of Acadia will lead not only to an understanding of Acadian life during these decades but also to the realization that there is much more to Acadian heritage than the catastrophe of the deportation.

Throughout the more than three decades that I have spent working in this field, many people have provided support and advice that has been valuable beyond measure to me. A number of these are thanked in the Acknowledgments, but here I wish to single out the contributions of a few dear friends. Winifred Dionne, one of the first Acadians I met, continues to give me aid and counsel as I try to understand the ways of Acadians. Enid and Peter King have listened to me talk about my work much more than they might have wished, while wining and dining me almost weekly. Sheila Brown and Donald Wylie have continuously urged me on. Margaret Wade Labarge, the distinguished medieval historian, has read the chapters as they hobbled, more often than flowed, from my computer, providing me with a viewpoint of one interested in Acadians but not intimately familiar with their history. John Reid has been the expert reader, also ploughing through each chapter and making certain that I would revise the manuscript in the light of the latest scholarship. Sydney Francis Wise, whose scholarly writings are primarily in the fields of Upper Canada and Canadian military history, has also read all the chapters, some of them twice, and given me invaluable advice. To these cheerful souls, I owe an immense debt of gratitude. The flaws of this work are all my own but there would have been many more had I not had the help of those named here.

FROM MIGRANT TO ACADIAN

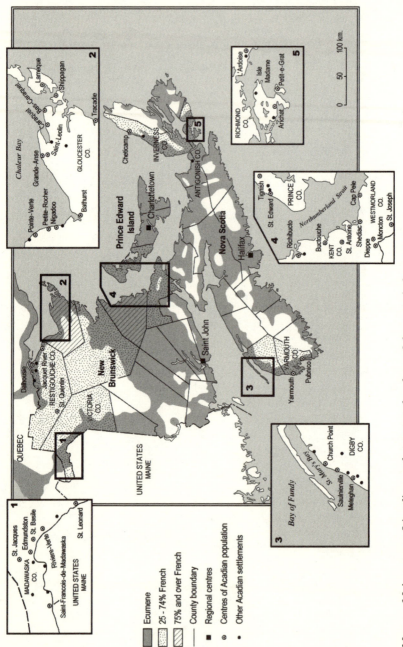

Map 1   Major areas of Acadian settlement at the close of the twentieth century.

CHAPTER ONE

Exploration for Settlement and Trade

Europe's exploration of the world's oceans during the sixteenth century, and the way in which its peoples then sailed these waters, is the context for the settlement of the French and English on the northwestern shores of the Atlantic during the first half of the seventeenth century. The quest of some for adventure and others for fame and fortune, some for knowledge and others for political power, fuelled the development of better and better seagoing vessels by the Europeans from the mid-fourteenth century onwards.[1] It was, however, the continual search for protein in the shape of fish that pushed men in small ships farther and farther across the grey seas of the North Atlantic. The success that attended their efforts meant that, by 1600, the Atlantic realm of what is now Canada had become part of the European economy and fishermen from many European ports came to catch and process cod there. The emergence of established French and English settlement near the fishing grounds was based, in large part, upon the differing ways in which fishermen incorporated fur-trading activities into their ventures. At the same time, those who ruled the sea coasts of western Europe developed a strong political interest in these newly revealed and sparsely inhabited lands.

Throughout the sixteenth century, France was, more often than not, embroiled in civil war but French fishing ventures across the Atlantic prospered. This was due, in the most part, to the individual efforts of people based in the ports on the Atlantic and Channel coasts rather than to any initiatives by the central government. However, the explorations of Jacques Cartier took place with the blessing of the crown, partly because of the desire of the French monarchy to find a counterbalance to the American ventures of Spain and Portugal. By the end of the sixteenth century, European expansion into the Americas had become a matter of interest and concern to both France and England.[2] When Henri IV came to power in 1589, he was convinced that a strong French presence in North America was important for French prestige in Europe, quite apart from any economic advantages that might accrue. He dispatched the first major French expedition intended to settle Acadia with a charter of commission, issued in 1603, for "the colonization of the lands of La Cadie, Canada and other places in New France."[3] The charter noted that "ships-captains, pilots, merchants and others have for many years visited frequented and trafficked" with the people who lived there and the time had now come to bring some order into the process.[4]

This commission was given to Pierre Du Gua, Sieur de Monts, a Protestant nobleman, and pronounced him viceroy and captain-general "tant en la mer qu'en la terre au pays de la Cadie, du Canada et autres terres de la Nouvelle France au 40° au 46°."[5] It was a lengthy document, spelling out in great detail the need for formal recognition of French authority "in and about the said country of La Cadie."[6] This involved not just developing "the friendship already begun with some of the tribes found there" in order to exploit commercial relations and spread Christian beliefs but also preventing English incursions in the area.[7] The commission noted explicitly that "certain strangers design to go to set up colonies and plantations in and about the said country of La Cadie, should it remain much longer as it has hitherto remained, deserted and abandoned."[8] De Monts's mission was the settlement and defence of these unmapped lands in the name of France and, not incidentally, the conversion of their indigenous inhabitants to Christianity. But it was clearly specified that the whole of the work was to be carried out without any royal subvention – "sans rien tirer des coffres de Sa Majesté." The crown wanted the expansion and protection of French interests in North America but wished this to be done without expense.

For a generation, all efforts to fulfil these commissions, whether by de Monts or his successors, met with little success. This was due, in part, to the internal state of France at the time. The accession of Henri IV had brought an end to three generations of bitter and almost continuous fighting within the country, the result not only of religious strife and dynastic rivalries but, as well, uprisings by the poor and dispossessed against the powerful. The provinces that, later on in the seventeenth century, would provide a considerable number of migrants for both the valley of the St Lawrence and Acadia were, in the last decade of the sixteenth century, the very places where the struggle was most bitter, where war and its aftermath, plague and famine, devastated the countryside. There would be no pressure of surplus population in Normandy and Brittany for more than a generation after 1589, the year that Henry IV had made his decision that "Paris was worth a Mass" and converted to Catholicism. Similarly, the southwest, Poitou, Saintonge, Angoumois, Marche, Limousin, and Perigord, which would be almost as important as a source of migrants for New France, needed time to recover from devastation. Further, while the peace crafted by Henry IV, sealed by the Edict of Nantes in 1598, ended overt civil strife, it did not wipe out religious hatreds or extinguish political enmities and only worsened the economic situation of the poor. As the seventeenth century opened, France was still divided by bitter dynastic and religious intrigues, often leading to local outbreaks of armed revolt against the crown.

In these conditions, there was little possibility of state aid for overseas colonization. There were just too many urgent domestic problems demanding money. But Henry IV and his advisers, struggling to make certain that France had a powerful central government, could not ignore the need to claim jurisdiction over all forms of colonial development. Thus, a commission to a man like de Monts, someone who had fought for the king during the recent hostilities, made a great deal of sense. First, it stamped colonial activity as a matter of the crown's authority, an issue of state policy. Secondly, it rewarded men, to whom Henry IV owed a debt, with the possibility of making their fortunes. While no state money would be provided, de Monts's commission was accompanied by the granting of royal monopolies for the exploitation of both the fisheries and the fur trade. Providing such monopolies could be enforced, de Monts would be able to finance his enterprise. Finally, the awarding of the commission to de Monts, a Huguenot,[9] was a demonstration that Henry IV intended religious toleration to be observed, at least as far as government patronage was concerned.

De Monts had crossed the Atlantic once or twice before and had been part of Pierre de Chauvin de Tonnetuit's expedition to Tadoussac in 1600. These voyages had given de Monts some understanding of the difficulties that he would encounter in implementing his commission, the problems of raising money against hoped-for profits, of finding reliable partners to go with him, of recruiting men who understood the risks of the venture. From 1603 to 1607, in the face of such obstacles, he worked to establish the base for a continuous French presence in Acadia. These were almost the only years in which Acadia was the most important focus of French colonization efforts in North America. In 1608 the valley of the St Lawrence became the centre of French attention and de Monts himself would give up his interest in Acadian development and turn to the exploration of the land along that great river. However, his work between 1603 and 1608 not only resulted in the accumulation of a large body of dependable information about Acadia but also helped to establish the region as a site for future French activity.

De Monts's decision to turn his attention to the St Lawrence was a matter of business, based upon opposition to his activities from commercial interest in ports from Dieppe to Saint-Jean-de-Luz. According to Samuel de Champlain, the geographer on de Monts's first expedition to Acadia, Basque and Breton merchants had opposed de Monts on his earlier voyages to the St Lawrence and were now determined to stop this latest undertaking.[10] They had written to the king, claiming that de Monts "prevented them from carrying on their fishing, depriving them of the use of things which had always been free" so that soon "their wives and children would become poor and destitute, and be obliged to beg their bread."[11] For at least two generations, the people of the Atlantic ports – Dieppe, Rouen, Honfleur, Saint-Malo, Nantes, La Rochelle, Bordeaux, and Saint-Jean de Luz – had exploited their links to North America with minimal interference from any central authority. The ideal, for these towns, was a series of individual ventures which would bring fur and fish back to France and the profits back to the French. Now de Monts, backed by Henri IV, was proposing, one more time, to prevent honest townsfolk from pursuing their own initiatives and to use the wealth generated by such voyages to develop settlements abroad, settlements that would siphon off monies due to the ports themselves. This tension between endeavours backed by royal authority and the customs of the people of Atlantic ports was to prove an ongoing handicap for French colonial development in North America. Throughout the seventeenth century, the independence of the people of the Atlantic coast from the central government meant constant challenges to those armed with the authority of the king, be it Henry IV or Louis XIV, to establish settlement in North America.

The city of Rouen fired the first shot in 1604. Early in January, de Monts arrived in that city carrying letters patent from the king, which granted him a ten-year monopoly over trade with "les sauvages des dites terres [Acadia]."[12] On 13 January 1604 the Parlement of Rouen, the law court of the city, refused to recognize any of de Monts's patents and wrote a remonstrance to Henri IV which outlined its concern for the interests of the Catholic religion and for free trade.[13] Taking the city at its word, that the cause for anxiety was primarily religious, the king replied on 17 January to the effect that the several gentlemen of the Catholic Church, of good faith, morals, and "edification," who were sailing with de Monts would be well able to ensure the propagation of the true religion.[14] Rouen continued obdurate, despite a further letter from the king requiring its compliance. The city dispatched its advocate general to argue its cause in person. The king reaffirmed de Monts's patents by letter, on 25 January, asserting royal authority and the needs of the kingdom as a whole. Early in February, the patents were finally registered. Of course, Rouen's defeat did not end the opposition of other Atlantic ports. Barely had this opposition been countered than there was a general petition, signed by the respective mayors and councillors, bailiffs, and prominent citizens of Bayonne, Saint-Jean-de-Luz, and La Hendaye, demanding the right to trade with North America, as they were wont to do, without let or hindrance from de Monts. Again, the petition was denied but the demand of the ports for complete freedom in the exploitation of transatlantic connections was to be reiterated time and again.[15] Hostility towards the very idea of a permanent settlement colony led to all types of intrigues against those who wanted migration as much as exploration and trade.

Despite these obstacles, by the second week of February 1604, de Monts had set up a trading company to back his venture. On the 10th of that month, he signed, before lawyers in Rouen, an agreement with merchants of that city and others from Saint-Malo, La Rochelle, and Saint-Jean-de-Luz. The expedition was to organized with the help of Samuel Georges and his brother-in-law, Jean Macain of La Rochelle,[16] and it was hoped that the venture would be supported by as many people as possible to avoid complete ruin for any single person should it fail. Corneille de Bellois, a Rouennais,[17] would keep accounts and de Monts himself put up some two thousand *livres* towards general equipment, food, and arms.[18] We have no idea how de Monts raised this money. Champlain remarked that de Monts's earlier voyages to the St Lawrence had brought him to the edge of bankruptcy.[19] In any event, the sum was raised and was sufficient to persuade the merchants of the various ports to subscribe the rest of the funds necessary to equip two small ships.

It was early spring before the ships set sail, one of 120 tons, on which de Monts himself embarked, and one of 150 tons, the *Bon Renommé*.[20] They were heavily loaded, carrying wine and cider, salted meats, dried fruit, and grain as well as ready-cut timber for the intended settlement.[21] Henri IV had told the truth when he assured the burghers of Rouen that the expedition was to be more than just a Huguenot venture. Champlain noted that de Monts had "collected a number of noblemen and all kinds of artisans, soldiers and others of both religions, priests and ministers."[22] Not only was Champlain himself a devout Catholic but so was Jean de Poutrincourt, next to de Monts himself the most well-connected member of the expedition. Poutrincourt's father had been ambassador to the Emperor Charles V and his sister a maid-in-waiting to Mary Queen of Scots.[23] The family had fought against Henry IV until 1693.[24] Perhaps more than any other of the leaders of the expedition, Poutrincourt dreamed of establishing a new society in a new land. Marc Lescarbot, the Paris lawyer who arrived in Acadia in 1606 and whose writings on the early French exploration of North America would become classics, wrote that Poutrincourt was "desirous to see these lands of New France, there to choose a spot to which he might retire with his household, his wife and children ..."[25] Poutrincourt, and his son, Biencourt, would play significant roles in the development of Acadia over the next twenty years.[26]

Whether Catholic or Protestant, the men who set sail with de Monts were veterans of the civil wars, and a number of them had been soldiers in Poutrincourt's own regiment. Several had sailed to the St Lawrence before. Champlain had fought against the Catholic League and had sailed the Caribbean as well as to the St Lawrence before this expedition in 1604. François Gravé Du Pont,[27] de Monts's second-in-command and captain of the *Bon Renommé*, had been a soldier before he turned to venturing in North America. Catholic himself, he had accompanied the Huguenot Chauvin de Tonnetuit, and de Monts, on his expedition to the St Lawrence in 1600.[28] Very little, except their names, is known of most of the others. But Jean Ralluau, who served as de Monts's secretary, the Sieur d'Orville, the Sieur de Beaumont, Fougeray de Vitré, and La Motte Bourgjoli were of an age to have fought in the recent battles.[29] The presence of two Catholic priests, one unknown, the other called Nicholas Aubry,[30] as well as an anonymous Protestant minister, provided the expedition with some of its intellectual entertainment. Champlain wrote about their fierce and lengthy arguments over religion.[31] As to the generality of the company, some sixty men, there were two ships' surgeons and an apothecary, masons, cooks, pilots, a smith, and carpenters, as well as others with no specific trade or occupation.[32] There were no women, but this does not reflect any attempt (such as the English were making in Newfoundland at much the same time) to exclude them.[33] The majority of those who sailed with de Monts considered the expedition just a stage in their lives, a view made explicit in the contracts they signed, which guaranteed them return passage to France. Some, such as Daniel Boyer and François Rocques, who were tile makers and roofers, and Robert Lescuyer, a mason, bound themselves for only one year.[34] Most committed themselves for three years, a term of service that would improve their standing in the various craft guilds in France and, perhaps, allow them to save money.

The expedition was, above all, a venture into the barely known, planned only in the most general terms. While the previous hundred years had seen ever-increasing contact between Europe and the Americas, both sides had less than clear-cut images of each other, composed as much of ignorance and prejudice as of knowledge and empathy. To de Monts and his companions, in common with most of his countrymen as well as the majority of other Europeans, the indigenous people of the Americas were unquestionably without enduring political rights to the lands in which they lived.[35] Further, the assumption behind the commissions and patents which de Monts had received was that the culture of those natives in the lands now claimed by France was unarguably inferior to that of Europe. The term generally used by the French to refer to such peoples was *les sauvages*. The missionary activity envisaged by members of de Monts's expedition, like similar activity carried out by other Europeans elsewhere on the continent, was undertaken in an unquestioned faith that Christianity embodied a greater truth than that of any native religion. While de Monts and his companions might, now and then, be brought to concede that an individual native was as good, or even better than, any individual European, there was no doubt in their minds that the complex patterns of European life were much in advance of the social norms of the strangers they met in Acadia.

The ancestors of the Mi'kmaq and the Malecite-Passamaquoddy had lived in what is now Nova Scotia, Prince Edward Island, New Brunswick, southeastern Quebec, and eastern Maine for at least two and a half millennia and had named the various regions. There is debate among present-day writers about what names covered what territories but it is generally agreed that Unimake would become Cape Breton Island; Kmitkinag,

Nova Scotia; and Ebegweit, Prince Edward Island.[36] Over all, Esisgeoagig was the word that the Mi'kmaq applied to the territory claimed by France as "Acadie."[37] In 1600 they numbered about three thousand, living in an area of roughly 30,000 square miles. To the north they clashed with the St Lawrence Iroquois over the Gaspé; to the west they had ongoing skirmishes with the Malecite and the Penobscot; and their influence on the Atlantic coast stretched to Anticosti Island, Newfoundland, and Labrador.[38] The Malecite and the Passamaquoddy are virtually identical people, but the Malecite lived along the Saint John River drainage basin and the Passamaquoddy were mostly to be found at the mouths of the Saint John and St Croix rivers.[39] Together, by 1600, they numbered about 1,000.[40] Ethnologists group Mi'kmaq and Malecite-Passamaquoddy with other peoples of the Eastern Woodland culture.[41]

Over the previous century, contact between native North Americans and Europeans had become commonplace and the immediate dangers involved in the process, as well as the benefits to be obtained, were well known to the aboriginal population. Episodic violence, the kidnapping of women and children, and the goods Europeans offered for trade were part of the known – if not everyday – experience of the coastal peoples of Atlantic North America. Until 1600, they had been capable of adopting European goods, notably iron and copper tools and utensils, without catastrophic disruption of their own ways. The quantity of new goods, at this period, was insufficient to make the production of the old unnecessary, and, besides, the greater efficiency of the European tools was not something that would cause, of itself, a major strain on the traditional fabric of Amerindian society. The arrival of de Monts, however, signalled the beginning of revolutionary change. He and his successors, La Tour, d'Aulnay, and de Razilly, were set on the establishment of permanent European settlement in Acadia and the building of this society would result in a radical transformation of aboriginal life. But in the spring of 1604 all this lay in the future.[42]

That year it took de Monts's ships two months to cross the Atlantic.[43] On 1 May 1604 Cap Sable was sighted by de Monts's vessel, the two ships having separated during the ocean voyage. Champlain noted that the sandy soil supported no full-grown trees, "only underwood and grasses whereon pastured the bullocks and cows taken there over sixty years ago by the Portuguese."[44] Within the week, the de Monts party had reached the mainland and anchored, for four days, off a headland they baptized Cap de la Have.[45] De Monts then sailed on, looking for a better place to establish a temporary headquarters while he waited for Gravé to arrive. On the 12 May, de Monts seized a ship whose captain, Jean Rossignol, was illegally trading for furs.[46] The fury of both captor and captive on this occasion was a presage of many similar confrontations in the future. De Monts, and later leaders of official expeditions, displayed righteous indignation in defence of their legal authority; Rossignol, and later transgressors of monopolies, blustered about their traditional rights.

The next day, the ship sailed into a beautiful, sheltered bay, which de Monts named Port Mouton because the carcass of a sheep that had fallen overboard and drowned was rescued and roasted.[47] The name still persists. Here, de Monts set up a temporary camp, dispatched Champlain, Ralluau, and ten men to explore,[48] and waited for Gravé. Since the latter's ship carried most of the supplies for the expedition, its non-arrival would force the rest of the company to return to France. Champlain was away for three weeks and, during his absence, de Monts established shelters on shore and sent a small shallop with one of the crew and "some Indians as guides ... to search along the coast of Acadia for Pont-Gravé."[49] Neither Champlain nor Lescarbot comment upon this helpful action by the Mi'kmaq but it was indicative of the relatively peaceful relations between natives and newcomers that would prevail in this region for the next one hundred and forty years. During all that time, there would be only rare attacks on Acadian settlements by the Mi'kmaq, although after 1700 Mi'kmaq hostility towards the British was evident.

Gravé and the *Bon Renommé* finally arrived, having captured four Basque ships trading for furs. At the end of the second week of June 1604, as Lescarbot wrote, "the whole of New France being at length assembled in two ships,"[50] they weighed anchor at Port Mouton to pass the time before the winter in exploring the country as far as they could. They investigated St Mary's Bay and afterwards sailed farther along the waters which they named French Bay, now called the Bay of Fundy.[51] The ships then entered, in Champlain's words, "one of the finest harbours I had seen on all these coasts, where a couple of thousand vessels could lie in safety."[52] Champlain went on to describe the rivers that entered the bay, the wooded hills, and the way oaks and other trees came down to the edge of water meadows. He considered that "the place was the most suitable and pleasant for a settlement we had seen,"[53] and, for its beauty, the area was given the name Port Royal (Annapolis Royal, N.S.), by which it was known exclusively until 1713, when the English renamed it Annapolis Basin.

Poutrincourt was much attracted by the land and asked de Monts to grant him the site. In return for a promise to establish a settlement there, de Monts agreed, according Poutrincourt fishing and fur monopolies within the area as well. All of this was confirmed by Henry IV on 23 February 1606.[54] Poutrincourt's grant was the first to be made by de Monts, and it signified one of the ways in which contemporary French practices of property ownership and central authority were to organize life in Acadia. Proprietorship over the land was to be directly dependent on the king and grants; the latter were made by those who held royal commissions and were to be ratified by the crown. Ownership was not outright but dependent on the fulfilment of particular conditions. At the same time, the rights of the proprietor included privileges of exploitation which would, it was expected, fund the obligations incurred. For more than two generations, the rights and land accorded Poutrincourt would make him and his heirs the most important landowners in the colony.

This grant also made clear that there would be no recognition of any prior rights of the Mi'kmaq or other native peoples. The avoidance of immediate conflict between French and Mi'kmaq over land ownership was due, first, to a lack of Mi'kmaq knowledge as to what, precisely, the French actions meant; secondly, to the migratory nature of Mi'kmaq society; and thirdly, to the minuscule number of French actually present at this point in Acadia. The second point requires elaboration. The Mi'kmaq's lives were bound by seasonal wanderings and "marked by diffuse and compact settlement."[55] In the winter, the Mi'kmaq exploited the land in small migratory kin groups; in summer, they congregated in much larger communities at river mouths along the seashore. In neither phase was agricultural activity a major enterprise. Thus, there was no immediate conflict with the newcomers over land use.

As is so often the case, then, an occasion from which would flow momentous consequences passed by with little drama or ceremony and even less introspection on the part of those involved. In fact, de Monts was not particularly impressed by Port Royal and he sailed on, looking for a more favourable site to establish his headquarters. On 24 June the ships passed the mouth of a broad, deep river that the French named the "Saint-Jean," in honour of the saint whose day it was.[56] From there, the ships continued southwest to Passamaquoddy Bay and up the broad estuary of what became known as the St Croix River.[57] Here, on a small island named by de Monts "Île Sainte-Croix," now called Dochet Island, they decided to settle for the winter.

It proved a disastrous choice. Lescarbot, who did not arrive in Acadia until 1605, reported accounts about the lack of drinking water and the scarcity of firewood on the island.[58] But in early July 1604 the decision seemed reasonable. Champlain, who was there at the time, wrote of the good anchorage, a supply of clay for brick making, and the island's security from attack.[59] At any rate, de Monts now set the company to work to build the settlement, according to a plan drawn up by Champlain.[60] The buildings were enclosed within a barricade, gardens being planted outside. There was a storehouse, separate quarters for de Monts, single rooms for the other gentlemen who were going to remain over the winter, and dormitory rooms, sleeping five or six, for the rest. As well, a small chapel, a kitchen, and a forge were built. The kitchen had an oven as well as an open fire and space was provided for a hand-mill. The men worked hard, even though tormented by black flies and mosquitos, both pests much more vicious and infinitely more numerous than their European relations. Many of the men suffered from a migrant's susceptibility to the bites, and "their faces were so swollen that they could scarcely see."[61] Nevertheless, partly because of the sawn timber brought from France, which provided window frames and door frames, the work proceeded apace. By the end of August, good winter quarters had been built on the island and a barn and a mill on the mainland.

At this point, the two large ships departed for France, under Poutrincourt's command, with orders to report on the expedition's progress. Ralluau and Gravé also went back, but they were instructed to return in the spring of 1605 with additional stores as well as recruits for settlement. Return they did, to find that the winter had been unusually severe, and the consequences for the men no less so. The temperature dropped so low that "the cider froze in the casks and each man was given his portion by weight."[62] Scurvy struck and, of the seventy-nine men who had remained, thirty-six died before spring.[63] Most of the rest suffered a milder form of the disease, which was the result of a lack of vitamin C, their diet being mostly salt meat and bread. (Even the flour for the bread was in short supply, because, as was the case in contemporary Europe, grain had to be ground daily by hand, and most of the company did not even have the strength for that task.) Not only were they weakened by scurvy, they were further debilitated by the cold, for ice made trips to the mainland for firewood few and far between. No one had been prepared to endure the rigours of a winter like that of 1604–5 in Acadia. As Champlain wrote, "it is difficult to know the country without having wintered there."[64]

Spring came at last and, an hour before midnight on 15 June 1605, Gravé arrived.[65] Over the next two months, de Monts sailed the coast as far as the south as Nausett Bay, beyond Cape Cod and Plymouth harbour. Despite what might be thought of as more attractive sites for settlement, and despite the absence of any sign of English claims, de Monts returned to the Bay of Fundy and decided to move his establishment just across the water from Port Royal, having, as Champlain wrote, "found no port that appeared to us suitable."[66] Considering the impact the selection of this site would have on the development of French colonization and the later choices made by the English, Champlain's brief comment raises questions. This is particularly so since Lescarbot remarks that de Monts had earlier wished to move some six degrees south of Sainte-Croix Island.[67] We have no record of how the decision was made. Perhaps de Monts was swayed by encounters with the coastal peoples they had met travelling south; these were Abenaki, much more numerous than either the Mi'kmaq or the Malecite-Passamaquoddy. Even more important, the Abenaki were a settled, agricultural people. Further, while there were some French speakers among the Mi'kmaq and Malecite-Passamaquoddy, no such individuals were to be found among the Abenaki and communication between newcomer and native would be difficult. Finally, the Bay of Fundy was close to the traditional fishing grounds of the French in North America. Each spring brought boats from France to fish off the coast and thus there was always the possibility of settlers crossing the Atlantic as passengers in such vessels, should this be necessary. The Bay of Fundy area was also not that far away from the entry to the St

Lawrence, the river which, from the time of Cartier, had captured the imagination of French explorers.

At any rate, August 1605 saw almost all the buildings, so painstakingly erected on Sainte-Croix Island, transferred to the sheltered eastern coast of the Bay of Fundy and rebuilt on the site of Port Royal. As the cold weather closed in, the situation was much better for the settlers than it had been a year before. The site was far more pleasant to the eye, the long sweep of the bay a different vista from the tree-enclosed inlet of Sainte-Croix, and the buildings were arranged with more attention to consider-ations of comfort and defence – instead of being scattered across the site, they were organized as an enclosed square, with living quarters and store-houses making up a single defensible structure. This plan was to become known as that of a "habitation" and it was developed as a pattern for the French trading settlements on the St Lawrence. The water supply at Port Royal was good, by well within the walls. There was also a plentiful supply of firewood close at hand. The dormitories were built with some sense of space, and public rooms, the kitchens, and the chapel gave even the least of the company a place to be alone. Towards the end of September 1605, de Monts sailed back to France. All but three of those who had survived the ordeals of the previous winter returned with him; the ones who remained were the Sieur de Vitre, the pilot Pierre Angibault *dit* Champ-doré, and Champlain.[68] This trio had some forty or so companions, men who had arrived with Gravé in the spring. They would find the weather much more clement and scurvy much less of an affliction. Nevertheless, twelve men died from that sickness, among them both the priest and the minister. These two were buried together, it is recounted, in a common grave because they had been notoriously argumentative with one another during their lives and the company wished to see whether in death they could be at peace.[69]

The most significant event of this winter, 1605–06, was the establish-ment of amicable relations with the Mi'kmaq. Port Royal was much more central to these people than Sainte-Croix had been and Lescarbot record-ed that "when winter came the savages of the country assembled at Port Royal from far and near to barter what they had with the French, some bringing beaver and otter skins, which are those held of most account in that country, and also moose skins, of which excellent buff-jackets may be made, others bringing fresh meat ..."[70] The leader of the Mi'kmaq in the area was Membertou, reported to have been a strikingly handsome man although of advanced years. His political control over his people was enhanced by his role as a shaman, which gave him considerable authority as a healer and spiritual adviser. When he died in September 1611, the Jesuit Pierre Biard wrote that "this was the greatest, most renowned and most formidable savage within the memory of man; of splendid physique, taller and larger-limbed than is usual among them; bearded like a French-man, although scarcely any of the others have hair upon the chin; grave and reserved; feeling a proper sense of dignity for his position as commander."[71] During this first winter of European settlement in the Port Royal region, Membertou and his people became familiar with daily life of the newcomers, sharing in the banquets of fresh meat, much of which the Mi'kmaq themselves provided.

Champlain spent the winter organizing the notes he had made of the New England coast and preparing for further exploration in the spring. By 16 March, he was ready to set out with Gravé to explore the coast to the south in a pinnace. They had hardly left, however, when a storm drove them ashore on White Deer Island, off Grand Manan. The damage to the small craft forced them to turn back at the mouth of the St Croix River and head for Port Royal. They set forth again in the first week of April but this voyage proved equally unfortunate, the pinnace being wrecked before they had reached the passage to the Bay of Fundy.[72] Once more, the company settled down to wait for ships from France. Champlain passed the time gardening and traces of his work are still visible at Port Royal today. By midsummer, plans were made to go in search of French fishing vessels along the Atlantic coast, from Canso to the Baie des Chaleurs, in order to secure passage back to France.[73] Without new supplies of foodstuffs, particularly of flour, grain, and oil, and of dry goods, such as gunpowder, bullets, and replacements for tools broken or lost, surviving another winter would be difficult for the Europeans. In mid-July all but two men, whose names are recorded as La Taille and Miquelet, set off in two tiny craft along the coast. They were off Cap Sable on 24 July when they were hailed from a shallop by Ralluau. He told them that Poutrincourt was on his way, in the *Jonas*. Ralluau had been sent to skirt the coast in case the men, who had over-wintered, had left to find fishing vessels to take them aboard. The late arrival of new supplies was due primarily to adverse winds. The *Jonas*, out of La Rochelle, had run aground in a spring gale, just before she was due to sail. She had finally set out on 11 May and took two and a half months to make the voyage, a long time for a spring sailing.

Plans were now made to continue the settlement. Poutrincourt was in charge because de Monts had encountered growing opposition to his venture when he had landed in France the previous winter. His very success, in bringing back a good quantity of furs, raised as much envy from those opposed to his monopoly as it did support from those he had involved in his enterprise.[74] As a result, he had decided to remain in France to deal with the opposition and delegated his authority to Poutrincourt. Despite the difference of religious belief, Poutrincourt and de Monts were friends of long standing, brought together in their support for Henry IV, as the only man capable of ending France's bloody civil war. Jean de Poutrincourt, at this time forty-nine years old, was the fourth son of Florimond de Biencourt and Jeanne de Salazar and his links to other members of the French nobility were of great value at this time. The year before, Poutrincourt had been able to recruit both soldiers and arms for de Monts.[75] Now he had brought back with him an interesting company of men, among them his own fifteen-year-old son, Charles de Biencourt, as well as the twenty-year-old son of Gravé, Robert. These two would be involved throughout their lives in the development of Acadia, and, during their first months in the settlement, they both set about learning Mi'kmaq.[76] As well, Poutrincourt recruited Louis Hébert, the apothecary who later established himself and his family in Quebec, and Marc Lescarbot. As for the rest of the company, Marcel Trudel writes that there were more applicants than places for the positions as carpenters, masons, stone-workers, locksmiths, toolmakers, and wood-workers.[77] Lescarbot thought that the ease of recruitment was due to the force of Poutrincourt's name.[78]

The day after he landed at Port Royal, Poutrincourt set the company to work, half to till the land and the rest to improve the buildings. A lime kiln was built, charcoal made for the forge, and pathways cut to the cultivated land. The *Jonas* had been fully loaded, and her cargo included a variety of grains, cabbage, lettuce, turnips, and onion seeds as well as a considerable amount of wine. Lescarbot, who enjoyed what he called "September liquor," considered that de Monts and his partners had made "an honourable provision for us."[79] The supply of foodstuffs, for those who would remain in Acadia, included peas, beans, rice, prunes, and raisins as well as oil and butter.[80] Further, the *Jonas* had brought pigs, chickens, pigeons, and a sheep. The cows had died on the voyage because, it was felt, there had not been a woman on board to care for them, and no man could be expected to have such knowledge.[81] Finally, there was the usual supply of goods designed specifically for the fur trade – axes, kettles, ironware, and textiles.[82]

On 25 August 1606, barely a month after her arrival, the *Jonas* set sail for France. Again, only three of the company who had passed the previous winter at Port Royal remained: Champlain, who wanted to complete his survey of the Atlantic coast, Champdoré, and Fougeray de Vitré. The life of the settlement after the departure of the *Jonas* was occupied with making preparations for the winter and with continuing the exploration of the coastline. Carpenters, joiners, stone-cutters, masons, locksmiths, tailors, and a wood-sawyer worked at their crafts some three hours each day, spending the rest of the time hunting and fishing.[83] On 5 September 1606 Poutrincourt and Champlain set out in the pinnace to visit Sainte-Croix and then explore the coast farther south. Champlain wanted to sail directly to that point where they had turned back the previous year, but Poutrincourt overruled him. An American historian, Samuel Eliot Morrison, agrees with a Canadian, Morris Bishop, that this was a crucial decision, since it effectively prevented the French from exploring what would be, but was not at that time, the focus of English and Dutch colonization: Rhode Island and New Amsterdam.[84] At Sainte-Croix, Champlain recorded that they were cheered by finding wheat that "had come up as fine as one could desire and a quantity of garden vegetables which had grown up large and fair."[85] By the beginning of October, the little company had reached Stage Harbour, south of Cape Cod, where the present village of Chatham now stands. They stayed there for two weeks, setting up an oven to bake fresh bread.[86]

This sojourn ended with a scuffle with the Nauset, a people used to fighting for their territory. Poutrincourt had warning of trouble to come, when, on 14 October, he noticed the Nauset women and children leaving the area. He attempted to bring all his company on board but some five or six young men disobeyed and were attacked during the night. Three died immediately, one on the voyage back to Port Royal, and another on arrival there.[87] After this skirmish, Poutrincourt continued to sail southward but returned to Stage Harbour on 20 October, hoping to capture some of the Nauset and use them at "forced labour at the hand-mill and at wood-cutting."[88] This plan failed, but some five or six Nausett were killed and a number of the French wounded.

Poutrincourt then decided to return to Port Royal, where, after a stormy passage, they arrived to a cheerful welcome on 14 November. As they prepared to disembark, Lescarbot and six companions, dressed as Neptune and Tritons, and accompanied by Membertou and his family, came to the shore to greet them. Then followed the first entertainment, written by a European and presented by both French and Mi'kmaq, in Acadia. It was a pageant, celebrating the French exploration of the New World, and trumpets sounded at the conclusion.[89] All then walked up the hill to the habitation and entered under the gateway, newly decorated with the French fleur-de-lis and the personal coats of arms of de Monts and Poutrincourt. The cooks set about preparing a splendid meal: roast chickens, copious wine, fresh-baked breads. This was typical of Lescarbot. Even Champlain, who had no great fellow feeling for him, was grateful for these "sundry jollities."[90]

During the winter months, the company took heart from such entertainments and the Order of Good Cheer was founded. This order, in Champlain's words, "consisted of a chain which we used to place with certain little ceremonies about the neck of one of our people, commissioning him for the day to go hunting. The next day it was conferred upon another and so on in order."[91] Lescarbot recounted the pride with which each one took the assignment, the result being varied fare, which included ducks, geese, partridge, moose, and caribou, as well as good entertainment at meals. When Lescarbot's turn came, the menu was built around fresh-caught salmon, fresh-killed hare, and a play written specially for the occasion. Lescarbot also noted that Membertou and other leaders of the Mi'kmaq "who came from time to time ... sat at table, eating and drinking like ourselves." He added: "And we were glad to see them, while, on the contrary, their absence saddened us."[92]

As mild winter gave place to an early spring, the little company set about gardening, expanding the living accommodations in expectation of the arrival of new recruits, and beginning the construction of a water mill. Everything looked set for the future development of the settlement. But when the *Jonas* arrived on 24 May 1607, it brought the news that de Monts had lost his monopoly and all were to return to France. The barrage of complaints by the merchants of the Atlantic ports, especially those of Brittany, had been joined by equally vociferous complaints from the Hatters Corporation of Paris. They informed Henry IV's chief minister. The Duc de Sully, that the price of fur had risen steeply because of de Monts's privileges and asked that these be ended.[93] The king acquiesced and the attempt at a permanent settlement in Acadia was brought to a halt. Poutrincourt was exasperated. So much had been gained – experience of the realities of year-long living in the new land, good relations with and some understanding of the native peoples, the possibilities of commerce, and, above all, accurate cartographical knowledge of a considerable stretch of the Atlantic coast. All this was now to be lost because of intrigues at court, the connivances of profiteering merchants, and the trade in smuggled furs.

This hiatus in the development of a permanent French settlement on the Atlantic coast came at the very time that the English arrived there in some strength. At the end of July 1607, just when Poutrincourt and Champlain were gathering themselves to leave Port Royal, Raleigh Gilbert and George Popham, sponsored by the Plymouth Company, arrived off Canso. The expedition comprised two ships, the *Mary and John* and the *Gift of God*. They went to trade at La Hève (present-day Upper La Have) and thence to the coast of what would become Maine. On 9 August 1607, on the site of present-day Monhegan, the first Protestant service was celebrated in what would become known as New England.[94]

In early October 1607 Poutrincourt had an audience with Henry IV and presented him with five Canada geese, one very sick caribou, and fine examples of grain: wheat, rye, barley, and oats.[95] Over the next weeks, Poutrincourt began to appreciate de Monts's situation and thus his own. The central government clearly wished to establish a formal and continuous French presence in North America, but it did not have the means to ensure that monopolies, granted to those commissioned to achieve this end, would be respected. Nor was the government willing to invest directly in the enterprise. Finally, it quickly became apparent that even those who were committed to the establishment of a permanent French settlement in North America were split as to whether it should be planted in Acadia or in Canada, the name that was now being given exclusively to the St Lawrence valley. Champlain opted without hesitation for the latter and de Monts supported him.

Poutrincourt remained true to his vision of establishing himself and his family in Acadia. However, the splintering of the efforts of the small handful of Frenchmen interested in year-round settlement in North America – as opposed to the number concerned with the maximization of the fur trade for the minimum of investment and effort – would severely hamper his endeavours. Acadia quickly began to be seen, not only in the eyes of government officials but also in those of merchants and moneylenders, as secondary to the developments on the St Lawrence. The reasons for the greater interest in the latter are many: the imposing majesty of the river and its obvious connection to a massive hinterland, coupled with the possibility that it might very well be a route to Asia; clear evidence that the fur trade could be greater and more easily organized from there[96]; the belief that it would easier to protect the Gulf of St Lawrence from other Europeans than it would be to defend the indented Atlantic shoreline; and the argument that there were more peoples to be converted to Christianity along the St Lawrence than on the Atlantic coast. For all these reasons, after 1607, Acadia would become of much less importance for French colonial interests than the valley of the St Lawrence.

In fact, for the next twenty-five years, until the aftermath of the Treaty of Saint-Germain-en-Laye of 1632, French officials paid only minimal attention to Acadia. Yet the French presence in the area was constant, despite incursions by the English in 1612 and claims by the Scots after 1621. Thus, when France did send a substantial expedition to Port Royal in 1632, led by a cousin of Richelieu, de Razilly, it came to lands where Frenchmen had not only traded for more than a generation but where a number had established a permanent year-round presence. While there are perhaps two or three years during this period when no one from France is known to have wintered in Acadia, from 1614 onwards there was almost always some young man, born in France, who spent the winter months with the Mi'kmaq or the Malecite. Certainly, every summer, including that of 1608, there were ships from France, not only at Canso but in the Bay of Fundy.

De Monts did not just abandon Acadia in 1607. Henry IV had been much impressed by the grain brought back from Acadia, and on 7 January 1608, he renewed de Monts's commission for the establishment of colonies in "la Cadie and Canada." As well, de Monts was granted the unenforceable fur-trade monopoly, this time for one year.[97] In Champlain's judgment, this was "luy donner la mer a boire," utterly worthless,[98] but it proved enough to bring some funding to de Monts. In April 1608 he was able to dispatch three ships, two under the command of Champlain, whom he ordered to build a fort at Quebec, and one with Ralluau and Champdoré to trade with the Mi'kmaq and to continue to explore Acadia.[99] This was the last time that de Monts would be directly involved in Acadian matters. Earlier that same year, on 2 February, he had appointed Poutrincourt as his second-in command to develop Port Royal. In future, de Monts would limit his own activities and personal interests to the St Lawrence.

French ventures in Acadia over the next five years consisted of the work of settlement undertaken by Poutrincourt, growing missionary activity, and, above all, semi-legal trading. Throughout the seventeenth century, but particularly during these early decades, ships slipped out of the French Atlantic ports carrying iron goods, in particular kettles and knives, as well as textiles and peas, beans, prunes, and tobacco.[100] Few of them were completely legal enterprises; for the most part, these ships were engaged in breaking someone's fur monopoly. Such ventures added up to a considerable trade between France and Acadia, a trade that resulted in important and continuing contact between French and Mi'kmaq.[101] Consider the case of Robert Gravé Du Pont. This young man, who had been in Acadia for the winter of 1606–07 and had had his hand blown off during the skirmishes with the Nausett, was now in his mid-twenties. He was bilingual, Mi'kmaq and French, and in 1610 he had sailed from Saint-Malo, a port notorious for backing free enterprise if not outright smuggling, to trade at the mouth of the Saint John River.[102] His enterprise was certainly an infringement of the monopolies that had been issued by the crown to de Monts and Champlain. And there were many like him. For these men, the profits from a successful voyage were more than enough to offset the fines levied if they were caught breaking laws which the Atlantic ports considered pernicious and were less than enthusiastic about enforcing.[103] Gravé himself occasionally spent the winter in the Saint John valley and from 1613 to 1618 he lived there, sending major consignments of furs back to his partners in France annually. At one point, the Mi'kmaq complained of his treatment of women. Biencourt, Poutrincourt's son, then the official head of the colony, felt bound to investigate. In Gravé's view, however, he was a trader not a settler and completely independent of someone whose business was the organization of a colony.[104] His attitude was typical of those who were involved in Acadia as fishermen and traders, and the result, inevitably, was clashes with those who arrived with commissions from the king. The only way such traders could be brought to submit to those who carried the king's commission was through force. Gravé surrendered to Father Biard, who brokered a shaky peace with Biencourt for him, but only after the latter had captured Gravé's second-in-command and his fort on the Saint John.

Like all of those who struggled to impose some structure upon French efforts in Acadia between 1610 and 1632, Poutrincourt was beset with difficulties. His personal fortune was not particularly great and he had a family to keep, six daughters and two sons. He had intended to return to Acadia quickly but it took him over two years to find the money to support the expedition in 1610. Further, if de Monts had had problems with Catholics in general, Poutrincourt faced much more complicated problems within the Catholic Church, which, at the opening of the seventeenth century, was deeply divided. The divisions were rooted in the quarrels among the different religious orders, such as the Jesuits and the Recollets, and between such orders and the secular priests. All groups had their own allies at court and all sought the right to dominate, if not monopolize, the conversion of the North America's indigenous peoples. As a Catholic,

Poutrincourt was susceptible to a great deal of pressure to back the claims of either the Jesuits or the Recollets for the right to exclusive missionary activity in Acadia.

Poutrincourt's tardiness in returning to Acadia earned him a stinging reproach from Henry IV, who met him in Paris in late 1609.[105] But the king offered no funding and so Poutrincourt had to turn elsewhere for assistance, a task made more difficult because of parallel ventures by Champlain and de Monts to the St Lawrence. Poutrincourt sought loans from both Protestant and Catholic merchants; however, the growing animosity between Catholics and Protestants in France, which would reach a new level of intensity after the assassination of Henry IV on 14 May 1610, meant that even the unsuccessful request by Poutrincourt for loans from the Huguenot merchants in Dieppe[106] was enough to raise questions about his suitability for the leadership of the enterprise among those closest to the king. The interdenominational character of de Monts's first voyage was a thing of the past. French overseas expansion was, even before the end of Henry IV's reign, becoming predominantly Catholic. Those of Reform (Protestant) beliefs who would be involved would be so without either official approval or recognition.

Ostensibly, therefore, Poutrincourt's expedition was Catholic, and, when he finally embarked on 25 February 1610 aboard the *Grâce-de-Dieu*, he took with him a priest, Jessé Fléché. Fléché was neither a Jesuit nor a Franciscan but a secular priest with an enthusiasm for missionary work. Within three weeks of his arrival at Port Royal, on 24 June, he had baptized Membertou's entire family, some twenty people.[107] Poutrincourt's hand in this activity has been much criticized but Lescarbot defended him, on the grounds that Membertou and his family had had plenty of time, during the earlier French sojourns, to become acquainted with the basic precepts of Christianity.[108] Further, there is no doubt that Poutrincourt wanted to report to the king, through messages sent back with the *Grâce-de-Dieu* in the autumn, that he had had some success in spreading the Catholic faith. Fléché spent a year in Acadia and during that time baptized some hundred Mi'kmaq.[109] However, when the Jesuits Pierre Biard and Enemond Massé arrived a year later, they were highly critical of what had been achieved, noting that the unbaptized had as much knowledge of Christianity as those who allegedly had been converted.[110] Poutrincourt was about to find out that growing interest in converting native Americans to Christianity was to became part and parcel of the development of the French settlement of Acadia, in a way that it had not been earlier.

At the time of the de Monts expedition, the religious differences between Mi'kmaq and French had been accepted as a fact of life. Now, in addition to the general development of French activity within their territory, a specific and continuing effort was undertaken to change the religious beliefs of the Mi'kmaq. The job was made difficult, however, by the huge variation in the way the newcomers practised their religion. For

example, while Poutrincourt was a devout Catholic, he distrusted all members of the Jesuit order, and, at a broader level, the piety of the Catholic
settlers contrasted greatly with the behaviour of traders, such as Gravé,
who had little or no attachment to Catholicism. In fact, it soon became
obvious to those primarily interested in missionary activity among native
Americans that the behaviour of the average migrant from France was a
major stumbling block in their work. As Biard wrote, the Mi'kmaq considered themselves better than the French, "for," they say, "you are always
fighting and quarrelling among your selves; we live peaceably. You are envi-
ous and are all the time slandering each other; you are thieves and
deceivers; you are covetous, and are neither generous nor kind; as for us,
if we have a morsel of bread we share it with our neighbour."[111]

As far as Poutrincourt was concerned, the religious issue affected not
only the way in which he obtained support for his ventures but also the way
in which he established his settlement. This was due, in large measure, to
the presence in Acadia of priests belonging to missionary orders. As long
as the institutions of Catholicism were represented by secular clergy, that
is to say, men linked directly to a bishopric, Poutrincourt's leadership within the settlement was relatively unchallenged. During the winter of
1610–11, there had been grumbling at some of his orders, particularly
those relating to the grinding of grain, but he faced no arguments over
major policy issues.[112] The arrival of missionaries who belonged to a religious order such as the Jesuits or the Franciscans, however, meant the
arrival of men whose ambitions were centred upon something other than
the establishment of a settlement. Since their prime concern was the conversion of the Amerindian, both Jesuit and Franciscan were ready to argue
that this objective must take precedence over all else. The actual impact
that a missionary could have on civil policy of the settlement depended as
much on his personality, and on the general reputation of his order, than
it did upon the influence of his order in France. Yet, at the very least, missionaries added another layer of complexity to the task of governance in
the settlement. At the worst, they presented an outright challenge to secular authority.

Thus, Poutrincourt was less than enthusiastic when, in the spring of
1611, two Jesuits turned up with his son, Biencourt. This young man, who
was about twenty at the time, had returned to France with the *Grâce-de-Dieu*
in early July 1610, less than six weeks after the ship had brought the expedition to Acadia. He was expected to be back before the onset of winter,
but it was not until 21 May 1611 that he greeted his father at Port Royal.
His tardiness was due in part to the weather, in part to the normal aggra-
vations attendant on selling furs and provisioning the ship, but, above all,
to the attitude of Antoinette de Pons, the Marquise de Guercheville, wife
to the then governor of Paris and chief lady-in waiting to the queen mother, Marie de Médicis, now regent of France.[113] The Marquise de
Guercheville[114] was typical of that group of devout, aristocratic French

Catholic women who interested themselves in missionary work during the seventeenth century. To a large extent, such women provided aid and comfort to the work of religious orders rather than to the activity of the secular clergy in any particular diocese. The marquise was a benefactor both for individual Jesuits and for the order as a whole. She met had Biencourt when he arrived at court to report on Acadia and decided to invest in the colony. She was not just a silent partner, however, providing funds for others to disperse. Her aim was to keep Acadia for the Indians but Indians converted to Christianity by the Jesuits. She supplied the sum of four thousand *livres* under a contract, signed 20 January 1611, which entitled the Jesuits not only to undertake missionary work in Acadia but to a share in the profits of the monopoly of the fur trade granted to Poutrincourt.[115] It was her hope that the Jesuits would become self-financing through this provision and, at the same time, gain considerable influence over the way in which the settlement developed.

The backing of the Marquise de Guercheville allowed Biencourt to provision the *Grâce-de-Dieu*, to recruit thirty-six newcomers for the settlement, and to leave Dieppe on 26 January 1611. This was accomplished in spite of much acrimony at the port. Dieppe itself was a centre of Reform beliefs and the greater part of the ship's crew, including its captain, Jean Daune, and the pilot, David de Bruges, were Huguenot.[116] The knowledge that there would be two Jesuits on board caused difficulties with the Dieppe merchants who, for a time, swore "with their loudest oaths, that, if the Jesuits had to enter the ship, they would simply put nothing in it ..."[117] Matters were smoothed over and finally the Huguenot merchants Abraham Duquesne and Jean Dujardin also invested 1,200 *livres* in the venture.[118] After setting sail, the *Grâce-de-Dieu* experienced a fierce voyage, the passage through the Grand Banks being strewn with icebergs. Fathers Biard and Massé, the first Jesuit missionaries in Acadia, disembarked at Port Royal in third week of May 1611.

Poutrincourt was content enough to see the *Grâce-de-Dieu*, although the ship's arrival would not solve all his problems. The past winter had not been easy, despite the continued support of the Mi'kmaq. Game had been scarce and the supplies brought from France had run short.[119] All of the new recruits were migratory workers, with no intention of settling permanently in the colony. Again, there were no women.[120] Commenting on this particular point, Lescarbot bluntly remarked that "in any settlement whatsoever, nothing will be accomplished without the presence of women."[121] Because of the unexpectedly long crossing, the stores intended for Port Royal had been broached, meaning that supplies for the coming winter were liable to run out. As a result, Poutrincourt decided to leave for France as soon as possible, in the hope that, unlike his son, he could make a return voyage within four months. It was a hope rather than a belief and only twenty-three people were left behind to continue the settlement, under the leadership of Biencourt.

Poutrincourt did not find that the political situation in France had become less complicated, or less tense, since the spring. The regency of Marie de Médicis was under attack, the great nobles were vying among themselves for power and influence, and the nobility as a whole was at odds with the emerging urban middle class. The religious debates, too, were growing more complicated, more bitter, and more deeply embroiled with questions of status and power. Poutrincourt arrived at court on 10 August 1611, in debt and desperate for funds to send help to Port Royal. Once more, Madame de Guercheville came to the aid of the colony but insisted on an even more stringent contract, one that included land concessions within Acadia. Further, she demanded that the monies she granted be controlled by a brother in the Jesuit order, Gilbert du Thet.[122] Poutrincourt saw no alternative but to agree. Within two years this agreement would embroil his family in a bitter and lengthy lawsuit with the Jesuits.[123]

If matters were difficult for Poutrincourt in France during the winter of 1611, they were no easier for his son, Biencourt, in Acadia. The arrival of Gilbert du Thet with supplies in January 1612 helped the colony survive the winter but exacerbated the problems that Biencourt had already had with Biard and Massé. Du Thet was about thirty-five at the time and took it upon himself to advise the much younger Biencourt on how to administer the colony.[124] By spring, Biencourt, officially the vice-admiral of France in Acadia, was at loggerheads with the Jesuits, who, among other things, had taken a liking to Robert Gravé Du Pont and were considering moving their work to the Saint John River under his guidance. Matters worsened to such a pitch that the Jesuits threatened Biencourt with excommunication. Tempers calmed a little over the weeks, but du Thet left for France in late June, on board a fishing vessel. He took it upon himself to inform Madame de Guercheville of how unreliable the Poutrincourt family was as a partner for those interested in missionary work.

Du Thet's report led Madame de Guercheville to buy out de Monts's residual rights in the colony and help to arrange for the title of viceroy of Canada to be given to Henri de Bourbon, the Prince de Condé. This meant that the rights of the Poutrincourt family were, in theory, now restricted to the grant of Port Royal. It also meant, in practice, that official French efforts in Acadia were split. On 23 January 1613 a ship arrived at Port Royal, carrying supplies that helped that settlement but also carrying du Thet and the news that the Poutrincourt family had lost its official status within the colony. In mid-May 1613 the *Jonas* appeared, well laden with supplies and with new recruits, but stopped only to pick up the Jesuits before proceeding southward to found a new settlement. This was the short-lived Saint-Sauveur establishment, built at the mouth of the Pentagöuet (Castine, Maine). It was short-lived because, less than two months later, on 2 July 1613, Samuel Argall, a Virginian, arrived on the board the *Treasurer*. A brief skirmish took place, resulting in a number of French casualties – two dead and four wounded. One of those badly wounded was du Thet, who would die within twenty-four hours.[125] The rest of the company, some twenty in all, including Biard and Massé, were taken prisoner. About half the company, including Massé, were allowed to make their way back to France by using the longboat of the *Jonas* to reach fishing ships off Canso. Two of these took them aboard and they reached Saint-Malo in mid-October 1813.[126] The rest, with Biard, were divided between the *Jonas,* which had been retaken by the English, and the *Treasurer* and brought to Jamestown.[127] In October 1613 Argall returned to Saint-Sauveur and cut down the cross the Jesuits had planted, replacing it with a Protestant version that also proclaimed the sovereignty of James I over the territory. He then set fire to the few buildings that had been erected and went on to do the same to the old buildings that remained on Sainte-Croix. Finally, on 1 November 1613, Argall arrived at Port Royal, gathered up most of the livestock, and burnt the settlement to the ground, save for the mill that had been built farther up the basin.[128] Biencourt and the rest of the settlers had been out hunting when Argall arrived, and they found the habitation in ashes on their return.

Argall's actions made clear that English claims in North America were certainly as definite as they had been when Henry IV first commissioned de Monts. In the same way, in the same years, that the activities of the French fishermen and fur traders been expanded through settlement projects, so too had those of England. English establishments in Newfoundland might seem to be precarious but those engaged in their development were quite as tenacious as those attempting to make Acadia a permanent settlement.[129] Further, while Europeans established at Quebec numbered less than twenty in 1610, those at Conception Bay numbered a good forty. Finally, England's Atlantic adventures in these early years included Virginia, whose English population was more than 200 in 1612 and which at that time was the base for English claims to extensive rights in North America. Whatever else Argall's actions implied, they were an explicit statement about English territorial ambitions – he did indeed act under a commission of the governor of Virginia to expel the French from all territory claimed by England.[130] It also has to be borne in mind that at this time, from the viewpoint of the European powers, rivalry for sovereignty over lands in the New World was a logical extension of their rivalry elsewhere.

Argall left Port Royal on 9 November 1613. On 17 March 1614 Poutrincourt arrived there to find his son, and a handful of companions, living in the shelter of the mill. At first sight, ten years' effort to bring about a permanent settlement of Frenchmen in Acadia seemed to have come to an unsuccessful end. For Poutrincourt, this was indeed the last time he would be in Acadia. But the disaster he faced, while considerable, did not end his, or his son's, involvement in Acadia and it certainly did not mean the end of a French presence there. Poutrincourt himself returned home almost immediately, this time with a fair cargo of furs to cover his expenses,[131] leaving Biencourt once more in charge. And it was through this man that the "official" French presence was maintained in the colony during the next decade. Within the year, Poutrincourt died in battle in Champagne, aged fifty-eight. Biencourt inherited his rights and titles and spent the rest of his life attempting to build on the foundations of his father's work.

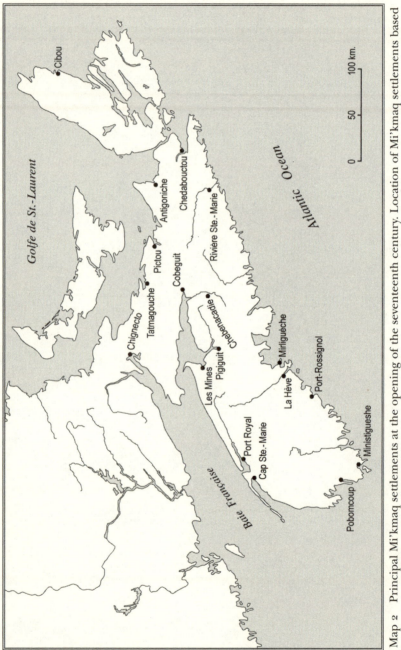

Map 2 Principal Mi'kmaq settlements at the opening of the seventeenth century. Location of Mi'kmaq settlements based on Wicken, "Encounters with tall sails."

CHAPTER TWO

"Acadie" or "Nova Scotia"

At the opening of the seventeenth century, the establishment of European settlement in North America was a slow business driven, above all, by the actions of individuals.[1] De Monts, Poutrincourt, and Champlain had taken the initiative and persuaded Henri IV and his chief adviser, the Duc de Sully, to grant them the right to organize French settlement in North America.[2] Institutional structures, governmental regulations, the theoretical underpinnings of the legal rights of the monarchs of England and France, all these followed the enterprising efforts of individuals, organized and financed by the establishment of private companies. But, if it was the relatively uncoordinated activities of individuals that established and developed the connection between Europe and North America, both France and England sought to exercise a minimum of authority and control over what was happening. As de Monts's contract had explicitly stated, a major reason for his being commissioned was to bring order into the French fishing activities in the North Atlantic.[3]

To a great extent, what made it possible to finance and pursue visions of North American settlement was the continuing need for fish and the growing demand for furs in both countries. These were the profitable enterprises that pulled small ships across the Atlantic ocean during the first decades of the seventeenth century and transformed that huge body of water from a barrier between the continents into something more like a bridge. There are countless contracts in the archives of the French Atlantic ports between a ship's captain and his crew plus one or more young men, willing to borrow to buy trade goods, and a couple of merchants, themselves willing to give credit against future profits.[4] France had no tradition of joint-stock companies, something that greatly facilitated money-raising for similar ventures at this time in England, where it was not only an accepted and familiar mechanism but also one that spread the risks among a much greater number of backers.[5] But the absence of such a mechanism, while it handicapped the French, was not an insurmountable obstacle to their North American enterprises. A web of connections between the

French Atlantic ports and North America developed throughout the seventeenth century, rooted in innumerable individual contracts for particular voyages that brought together lawyers, merchants, ships' captains, and their crews with those actually interested in exploration and settlement. Though such documents have been a matter of much study, only rarely have they been integrated into the many accounts of early Acadian history.[6] This is due, in part, to the ambiguous legality of much of the activity, whether it was primarily a matter of fish or of the fur trade itself. It was seldom one or the other exclusively and the existence of monopolies meant that the majority of transatlantic ventures were, in whole or in part, on the shady side of the law. The entwining of all these differing enterprises into the pattern of legal activities concerned with French settlement in North America creates a complex picture.

One way of disentangling events is to begin by looking at Acadia as the location of one of the most highly successful French Atlantic fisheries as well as a centre for profitable fur-trade operations. Such an approach makes clearer the links between the attempt to establish French settlement in Acadia, the European search for protein, and the Amerindian demand for European goods.[7] It also provides the necessary understanding of what was involved in the seventeenth-century shipping industry that carried explorers and settlers across the ocean. The knowledge acquired by those who sailed with the fishing fleet – knowledge both of the vessels themselves and of the kind of training needed for their crews – was to prove an invaluable resource for men such de Monts and Champlain. French and English techniques of ocean fishing had developed to an impressive level of competence. It was a highly labour-intensive occupation, however, and required a skilled workforce as well as some sort of land base for its success.[8] This inevitably brought the crews into contact with the Amerindians and increased the Europeans' store of information concerning the surrounding lands, something that in turn further increased the importance of the fishermen for those who sought to establish permanent settlement. In sum, the European exploitation of the Atlantic fisheries of the seventeenth century was not a passive background to exploration and settlement efforts but something without which the latter would never have occurred.

Fish were caught either inshore or offshore, that is, either close to land or on the Grand Banks, those relatively shallow waters off the coasts from Maine to Labrador. The fish could be brought back to a home port in two forms: as "wet," also known as "green" or salted cod, and dry, which was precisely what its name suggests. Dry cod also demanded salt for its processing, but by no means the quantity that "green" cod demanded. In the "wet" or "green" fishery, lines were cast over the side of the ship and the fish so caught were taken to narrow tables on the deck to be cleaned and filleted. The salter would then layer them in the hold, head to tail and each layer well salted. In the late sixteenth century, ships sent out from France for this activity were, on average, according to Harold Innis, around one hundred tons and carried a crew of some fifteen to eighteen men. The ships would be out of their home port from late January or early February until the end of May or the beginning of June, depending on the weather and the state of fishing that year. Loaded with salt on the outward voyage, they returned with holds filled with fish. A vessel of some 100 to 150 tons could bring back some 20,000 to 25,000 fish. This fishery did not absolutely demand a land base for its prosecution, but those engaged in it would often repair to land for supplies of wood and water.

The dry fishery required more equipment, more labour, and larger ships. The product was worth more than that of the "wet" or "green" fishery because the dried fish offered better food value and sold at higher prices in the market. For the dry fishery, the use of the shore was a necessity and it meant temporary settlements, the seasonal establishment of communities of European men on what, for them, was the coast of a new world. Those who worked the dry fishery required good beaches, big enough to allow the fish to be processed and for the men engaged in the work to be housed for the season. Ships for the dry fishery would seldom leave their home port before February and often did not return until the late summer. The technique was to catch fish close to the shore from shallops with three-men crews. Thus, small craft had to be brought out from Europe as part of the cargo of the larger vessels. Once the fish were brought to shore, they were cleaned and split before being lightly salted. After a few days, the fish were washed, drained, and then spread out on flakes, wooden structures much like large open-slat draining boards, to dry for some ten days, depending on weather conditions. This process was labour-intensive and men and boys were brought out from the home ports for "rigid specialized work in what were virtually unmechanized seasonal factories."9 Ships of no more than 60 tons did engage in dry fishing but the average vessel engaged in this pursuit was at least 100 tons and could bring back to Europe as much as 200,000 cod a season. The financial rewards for such a venture would bring a fair profit not only to the owners but also to those who provisioned the ship and to the fishermen themselves.10

As the European fishing fleets established their presence along the Atlantic coast of North America, trading was already under way between Amerindians and Europeans, thus adding another incentive for Atlantic crossings. By the opening of the seventeenth century, the fur trade was an established feature of the relationship between the two continents, facilitated and fostered by the growing native demand for the iron pots, guns, and cloth brought by Europeans.11 Those engaged in the manufacturing and marketing of fur products in Europe became equally involved in the process of obtaining the furs from North America, the Hatters Corporation of Paris being a good example.12 The forces bringing about the expansion of the fur trade were thus twofold. In France, businesses developed with the dual purpose of processing and marketing

North American furs and of producing goods – hatchets, ironware, clothing materials, and some foodstuffs – specifically designed for the trade in
furs. In North America, native peoples from the Atlantic coast to the
heart of the continent gathered the furs that would be traded in
exchange for such products.

The French Atlantic ports from Dieppe to Saint-Jean-de-Luz were, by
1600, thoroughly engaged in every aspect of this economy. All of them
sent ships out to the coastline of Acadia – the Atlantic shore from northern Maine to the Gaspé peninsula – in pursuit of fish and furs. Ventures
might be risky but the *Jonas*, which brought back the colonists from Port
Royal in 1607, also brought back to Saint-Malo 100,000 cod, green and
dry,[13] worth some 10,000 *livres*.[14]

Catholics and Protestants were rivals, in any given port, for the control
of such ships, their provisioning, and their considerable profits. This
intense competition had, of course, been a contributing factor to the troubles that Poutrincourt endured as he sought backing for his undertakings.
Partnerships were almost always put together just for the one voyage and,
as often as not, dissolved in an atmosphere of legal wrangles and court proceedings. At the same time, ports often fought among themselves for the
right to develop each new commercial venture. In this sense, La Rochelle
and Dieppe were bitter enemies, since transatlantic endeavours meant that
a port benefited not only from the trade in fish and fur but also from all
the advantages of building and provisioning the ships themselves.[15] There
were alliances forged among the ports, especially by the fishing interests,
to block the granting of monopolies, but the majority of such alliances
were of short duration.[16] It is this reality that has led K.G. Davies to suggest
that the sectional interests of the varying regions of France were such that
it is almost impossible to speak of France itself founding colonies in the
seventeenth century.[17]

But, although France was far less of a structured, coherent, and unified
country under Louis XIII than it would be under Napoleon, or even under
Louis XIV, it did have a central government and that government was
intent on increasing its authority. Government officials struggled to bring
some order into transatlantic ventures and divert some of the profits of the
fish and fur trades into the tax system. While there was no effective
machinery to enforce the commissions and monopolies the crown issued,
and penalties for non-compliance were inconsistent and unpredictable,
the existence of king, court, and councils had to be acknowledged. In the
final analysis, Louis XIII and his ministers would prove capable, when they
wished and when their attention could be brought to bear upon the issues,
of exercising a commanding influence on the way in which colonial ventures developed.

All of this activity, the rivalry between different ports, the bitter parti-
sanship of Catholic and Protestant, and the evolving nature of power of
the French crown, is the context of early French efforts in Acadia. But it

was the realities of the profits from the fisheries and the fur trade that played the crucial part in the process of settlement, however much individual aspirations were hindered or helped by other factors. When de Monts arrived in Acadia in 1604, his presence was both an important new departure in French-Mi'kmaq relations and, at the same time, merely a logical development of a well-established relationship that had gone on for three generations. Fishing vessels arrived each spring off Cape Breton; both Champlain and Lescarbot had noted their presence without surprise.[18] The development of what was then known as English Harbour (later Louisbourg) and of the beaches of Canso was well under way. A Basque ship was reported in the latter region in 1607, and Lescarbot reckoned that the profits would be about 10,000 *francs* a day.[19] In 1609 there were a number of ships catching and curing fish in the Baie des Chaleurs, off the south shore of the Gaspé peninsula.[20] Lescarbot noted that men from Saint-Malo and La Rochelle were engaged in the fur trade off Port Royal in 1611 and in 1613 and that two ships from Saint-Malo were trading off Port Mouton.[21] In short, the growth of a permanent French settlement in Acadia is only one element in the complex process of French expansion across the Atlantic.

In this context, Argall's raid, however devastating in its immediate effects for the development of such a settlement, was no more than a skirmish between England and France, a signal that the demarcation of their relative spheres of influence in North America had became a matter of acknowledged dispute. In fact, there is evidence that Claude de La Tour immediately challenged the English action by re-establishing a fur-trading post in the neighbourhood of Saint-Sauveur in the wake of Argall's raid.[22] However, in 1614 it was Biencourt's ability to remain in Acadia, pursuing a dream of a continuous and permanent French settlement there, that was of crucial importance in staking out French territorial claims. His success in this enterprise was due entirely to the existence of the fur trade and the fishery.

Biencourt's activities established a continuing link with the political realities of France and provided a focal point for the interests of La Rochelle merchants in the development of Acadia. Inheriting his father's rights to Port Royal and environs, Biencourt faced problems on both sides of the Atlantic. In Acadia there was the question of where he, and those he recruited, would establish themselves. In France, there was the matter of the rights of himself and his family, as opposed to the rights claimed by the Jesuits. And in both places there were those others who were engaged in the fishery and the fur trade. Overall, too, the matter of financing for whatever projects Biencourt envisaged was just as pressing as ever. These were considerable challenges and, in 1614, Biencourt was no more than twenty-four years old.

We know only a little about who his companions were and not a great deal more about his living arrangements in Acadia. One of his companions, however, was definitely Charles de La Tour, who had arrived as a teenager with his father, Claude de La Tour, in 1610[23] and who had stayed on with Biencourt when his parent wandered elsewhere after the Argall raid.[24] The leaders of the first attempt at French settlement in Acadia had been a middle-aged group of veterans of the French civil wars. Those who succeeded them were much younger men, a post-war generation. Exactly how many others there were, besides Biencourt and the younger La Tour, is unknown, nor is it clear how many European companions Robert Gravé Du Pont had on the Saint John River at this time. But at any given point there were probably no more than twenty Frenchmen who wintered over in Acadia. The absence of struggles among the neighbouring indigenous peoples, as well as the open support and friendship of the Mi'kmaq for the French, were major factors in the day-to day lives of the newcomers and in the actual fur trading that Biencourt oversaw.

Biencourt made a living but no great fortune.[25] Yet, while his financial success might have been moderate, he still dreamt of the establishment of a permanent settlement colony. In September 1618 he wrote about his hopes and fears in a letter to the mayor and aldermen of Paris, with whom he had some connections through his mother's family. The letter is written in good, clear French, with style and intelligence.[26] He opened by stating how he and his father had been engaged in attempting to bring about a flourishing French settlement in Acadia for fourteen years. Now, he wrote, he was particularly concerned because, unless something was done, he believed that Acadia would soon end up as an English colony, or at least become wholly dependent on the English. People from that country, he remarked, had already shown the French outright hostility. They had banished the Jesuits from their location (at Saint-Sauveur), burnt his own settlements (at Sainte-Croix and Port Royal), and recently taken prisoner a ship out of Dieppe. Further, Biencourt continued, the English were settling Bermuda and Virginia apace and just recently he had seen a convoy of five hundred men, accompanied by a number of women and children, putting in for wood and water in his neighbourhood.[27] Biencourt's conclusion was that if nothing was done to aid French settlement in Acadia, the English, having established themselves farther down the Atlantic coast, would find no difficulty in coming north and taking over.

To counter this possibility, Biencourt suggested that three forts be established along the coastline claimed by France. More particularly, he proposed that Paris could easily help prevent further English expansion at little expense and to its own advantage. Biencourt urged the city councillors to hire a couple of ships and send to Acadia able-bodied beggars, the poor, and the needy, "all those who suffered in secret, not daring to let their misery show."[28] He considered his ideas eminently feasible because the soil was good, game plentiful, and fish abundant. Paris should support such a venture, he went on, for the glory of God, because of the traditional role Paris had always played in trade, and because the enterprise would return considerable profits. Biencourt believed that, once established, the settlers would be self-supporting in terms of the provision of leathers, fats, meats, and milk products. They would then be able to provide Paris with wood for ships, charcoal, and building materials generally, all of these goods now being imported from countries over distances quite as long and perilous as the ocean voyage between Acadia and France.[29]

His vision went unanswered and his fears were quickly justified. Within two years, on 3 March 1620, a petition was presented to James I of England (and James VI of Scotland) requesting authority to establish the "Council for New England."[30] The request was granted, on 3 December 1620, by royal patent. The territory claimed, and awarded by the authority of the English crown, was that between latitudes 40° and 48°, limits that clashed with those already claimed by France for Acadia.[31] The voyage of the *Mayflower*, carrying the Pilgrim fathers,[32] began before the patent was actually issued. That ship's arrival, on 11 November 1620, at the place that Champlain had named Port Saint-Louis fifteen years earlier, and that would now be named Plymouth Bay, marks the beginning of the successful English colonization of what would become Massachusetts and Maine. There was no immediate challenge to Acadia from this venture but within less than a generation the matter of Massachusetts policy towards the latter was an issue for both colonies.

Nor was this initiative the sole challenge to French ambitions. Within the year, on 10 September 1621, a Scotsman, William Alexander, later the Earl of Stirling, was granted a charter to "Nova Scotia" by James I.[33] The lands granted in this charter were described as extending along the length of the St Croix River as far as the St Lawrence – in other words, the Gaspé region and the present-day Maritime provinces. Most of this territory was, indeed, land already claimed by France as Acadia and by the end of the decade the phrase "Acadie ou la Nouvelle Ecosse" – Acadia or Nova Scotia – was used in all international documents referring to the area. It was asserted, at the time, that this grant to Sir Willaim was better made than any other European title for North America, since it was a grant limited by landmark rather than by latitude. In fact, the distinction mattered little. As the seventeenth century progressed, Europeans established other major settlements on either side of "Acadia or Nova Scotia," all with boundaries equally as vague, and extraordinarily complex disputes arose over the limits of the lands claimed.

As was the case with the arrival of the Pilgrim fathers, the grant to Sir William Alexander made no immediate difference to the lives of Biencourt and his companions. John Reid has pointed out that "this first New Scotland scheme suffered from the same defects in theory and practice as had that of de Monts some eighteen years earlier; the granting of a large colonial area to a single promoter offered little chances of effective colonization."[34] Alexander had as much trouble as de Monts had had in raising support generally, and money in particular, for his venture. His attempts at establishing colonists failed.[35] The first expedition, in 1622, never reached

Nova Scotia and wintered in Newfoundland, while the second, in 1623, barely surveyed the southeastern shore of Nova Scotia before returning. Jules de Menou, a nineteenth-century historian, considered that the expedition did not land because of the obvious presence of the French.[36] Alexander would make no further attempts until 1628.

In the meantime, the French presence in Acadia continued to be a matter of Catholic missionaries, Biencourt and his companions, and the fishing fleets. After the collapse of Saint-Sauveur, the Jesuits had, for the moment, turned its attention to the St Lawrence valley. It was the Recollet fathers, Franciscans, who next took up missionary work in Acadia.[37] This order became interested in the colony partly because of a direct request of Jesuits and partly because, although Biencourt's main business was still carried on through La Rochelle, he had some connections with Bordeaux where the Recollets had significant strength. It was in response to the demands of a merchants' association in that port that the Recollets sent missionaries to Acadia.[38] Sometime in 1620, three or four priests arrived and established themselves on the Saint John.[39] The mission was short-lived. From 1620 to 1624, these men wandered through the colony, from the Saint John River to Miscou on the Atlantic coast, as well as from Port Royal to the Cap Sable area. They came with no knowledge of the Mi'kmaq or Malecite, either their customs or their languages. One of the priests died from exposure during the winter of 1623 in what is now central New Brunswick. The following year the survivors left for Quebec.

Contemporary comments on the existence led by Biencourt and his companions are ambivalent. As early as 1611, the Jesuits had remarked that men sent out to establish a colony of France had often sought a different life among the Mi'kmaq: "most marry with the savages and pass the rest of their lives among them, adopting their way of life."[40] The assumption behind this judgment is that European settlement should be organized apart from the indigenous inhabitants. Within five years, the comments would be more acerbic. The young men were accused of living lives given over to immorality in general and debauchery in particular.[41] By 1624, the commentary was openly censorious and it was asserted that Biencourt's company was a disorganized group of some eighteen or twenty men "mingling with the savages and living an immoral and infamous life as dumb beasts without any practice of Religion, not even taking care to have those children they fathered on the poor miserable women baptized but abandoning them to their mothers ..."[42]

Historical opinion has tended to accept this view and the conclusions offered by Rameau de Saint-Père, a nineteenth-century French historian, are representative of the view of a fair number of historians. "The eastern shores of Acadie," he wrote, "have always been a place of half-wild, half civilized life, where half-breed families come together, their roots growing back to the companions of Biencourt and La Tour."[43] This view has all the force of a good half-truth: the strict moral codes of an ideal Catholic bourgeois life were certainly not a major concern in the lives of most of the young Frenchmen in Acadia in the 1620s. This did not mean, however, that they had no love for the children they fathered or that, when priests were available, they did not solemnize their relationships with Mi'kmaq women, according to European cultural norms.

Marriage was important for both Europeans and Amerindians. The majority of those who lived in Acadia during the seventeenth century, Europeans and Amerindian, had their sexual activity shaped by marriage. There was, of course, sexual activity outside marriage in both societies, but both Mi'kmaq and Europeans had developed customs and institutions that made marriage part of the normal life experience of the majority of adults, men and women alike. In both societies, marriage meant the acknowledgment by some public ceremonial of the commitment to a partnership that was expected to endure, if not until death intervened, at least for some considerable period of time. There were significant variations in the actual experience of marriage, not only from one society to the next and from one generation to the next but also between couples within the same society and within the same generation. Whatever the variation in custom, however, there was always an essential and important similarity: a major component of the sexual life of the individual flowed within the bounds established by the society in which that person had lived as a child.[44]

As far as the records of marriage according to Catholic rite are concerned, material is sparse but does exist. There are two cases where documents attest to the care of Frenchmen for their children and, at the same time, imply Christian marriage. The first is that of André Lasnier, whose baptismal record is preserved in the municipal archives of Libourne, a village near Bordeaux. It affirms that he was born at Port la Tour, the son of Loys Lasnier and "une femme Canadienne."[45] While it is possible that the child was born outside marriage, the probability is that the parents had had their union blessed by one of the Recollets and registered it as soon as possible. At any rate, the charge that the French had no care for their children certainly cannot be proved in the case of Lasnier. The second set of records relates to the first of three marriages of one of the most important men in early Acadian history, Charles de La Tour.[46] In his late twenties or early thirties, he married a Mi'kmaq woman with whom he had three daughters. There is both direct and circumstantial evidence for this. The direct evidence is contained in declarations of one of his daughters who married a Basque fur trader, Martin d'Arpentigny, Sieur de Martignon, who later owned land at the mouth of the Saint John.[47] The circumstantial evidence comes from the careers of the other two daughters, both of whom joined religious orders in France for which documentation of legitimate birth was a necessity.[48] One of the daughters is reputed to have had such a magnificent voice that she was brought to sing before members of Louis XIII's court.

This particular marriage was important, beyond the lives of the individuals concerned, in that it attested publicly to a belief in the social justifiability of such a relationship among the European community. The very eminence of Charles de La Tour served as an argument in favour of the practice and his example was to be followed during the 1630s and 1640s by members of the Lejeune, Thibodeau, and Martin families.[49] Such marriages are a clear indication of the measure of worth accorded by the early French explorers to their sexual relationships with Mi'kmaq women. Intermarriage according to European rites was sought by men who obviously valued both their sexual partners and their offspring. In comparison with what occurred along the St Lawrence, moreover, Catholic-Mi'kmaq intermarriage in Acadia is particularly significant. A.G. Bailey unearthed only three church marriages of French and Amerindian along the St Lawrence between 1608 and 1667, in a population that was considerably larger than the Acadian community.[50]

There were also marriages between European and Mi'kmaq according to Mi'kmaq rite, whereby the couple lived among the Mi'kmaq. This assertion is based upon contemorary descriptions – by Champlain, Nicolas Denys, the Jesuits, and others – of Mi'kmaq rites and customs, and upon the interpretation of that evidence in the light of analogous situations in the later history of the fur trade.

The Mi'kmaq were hunter-gatherers and, while they came together in gatherings of two hundred or more in spring and summer, they spent a fair part of the year separated into small groups. Custom required that the groom, usually a man in his twenties, spend about two years in the tent of his prospective father-in-law. During this time, sexual relations between the intending partners were forbidden. The actual marriage, the public recognition of the union, was celebrated by several days' feasting and long speeches of advice to the couple from parents and elders of the group and by the shaman. If in later years the couple wished to separate, this was not difficult to arrange.[51] Property and children were not matters that were settled entirely on the basis of power of one sex over the other. Since the woman drew the man to her family, she would not be left destitute with no blood-relation support if he left her. Moreover, illegitimate children were considered a sign of fertility rather than of shame. The major social demand on the family was for the unit to be capable of self-support whenever possible, as well as a source of aid to others in emergencies. Within this context, the relationship of individuals was subject to all the realities of human affection.[52]

In my view, marriages according to Mi'kmaq rite occurred although written evidence is subject to more than one interpretation. At least some of the unions, reported by both Jesuit and Recollet as involving French men living immorally among the Mi'kmaq, would have been considered by those involved as formal marriage. Because such marriages would not have been recognized by the priests, and thus would not have been registered, the existence of Mi'kmaq-European marriages is a matter of speculation. One of the main arguments that could be advanced against the occurrence of marriages according to Mi'kmaq rite is the Mi'kmaq attitude towards illegitimate children. If such offspring carried no stigma, either for themselves or for their mother, the need for legitimization of the union was obviously less. That said, however, one should bear in mind Sylvia van Kirk's statement that Indian women in western Canada, "even more than the men ... welcomed the advent of European technology. Items such as kettles, knives, awls and woollen cloth considerably alleviated their onerous domestic duties. The notable instances that can be cited of the Indian woman acting as ally or peacemaker to advance the cause of the trader suggests that it was in the woman's interest to do so."[53] Partly as a consequence of this state of affairs, native women married European fur traders according to "the custom of the country" – traditional native marriage customs – and, says van Kirk, "distinct family units" developed.[54] There is a strong possibility that similar unions occurred in Acadia.

At any rate, by the time that Biencourt died in 1623, it is clear that the Mi'kmaq had come to a generally friendly accommodation with the French among them. It is also clear that the French expected that the Mi'kmaq would actively support their endeavours to establish a permanent presence. Charles de La Tour, whom Biencourt had appointed as his successor, wrote to France in 1627, pleading for help to strengthen the settlement and asking that he be given a commission to defend the Acadian coast.[55] He stated that he was confident that he had the strength to defend the king's interests with some hundred families allied to his interests and his small, determined group of Frenchmen. In fact, the Mi'kmaq were the most effective support that La Tour had. He also wrote to Richelieu in much the same terms. In both letters, he remarked that he had to combat not only the English – "who are bound and determined to seize the country of New France and appropriate both the dry and green cod and the fur trade"[56] – but also other Frenchmen. He complained bitterly that he had "only three small vessels against the strength of the French from the great river who to this instant have pursued me to the point of death."[57]

Charles de La Tour's letters show the chaotic state of the France's North American enterprise in the early seventeenth century as well as his particular problems in Acadia. The venture along the St Lawrence had developed almost as slowly as had Acadia. In terms of settlement, Quebec in 1627 was certainly the more successful colony, but it was no flourishing concern. The population of Europeans there was only seventy-two, mostly male but including three families.[58] Acadia could claim some thirty Europeans who wintered there, all male. The English in Newfoundland were more firmly established at this time than the settlers of either French colony, despite an active policy by London of discouraging settlement. Both Cupids Cove and Ferryland had been established by 1625.[59] The first had a population of "fifty-four men, six women and two children in 1612 and Lord Baltimore's settlement at Ferryland a hundred in 1625." Trading in New France, however, had clearly flourished, legal business alone bringing an estimated 150,000 *livres* to its participants in 1627.[60] But Champlain was always beset with financial problems, constant challenges to his authority, and only desultory support for settlement itself.

Champlain received, in 1612, a commission as lieutenant from Henri de Bourbon, Prince de Condé, whom Louis XIII had recently named as the viceroy of New France. This commission gave Champlain real powers over treaties with the natives, the administration of justice among the French, and the restraint of illegal trade.[61] Like de Monts and Poutrincourt before him, however, he was faced with interminable wrangling among those backing his ventures and continuous poaching upon the monopolies granted to support his endeavours. On 7 May 1620 Louis XIII confirmed Champlain's right to administrative authority in the colony but provided little precision about the limits of his territorial responsibilities. To add to the general confusion, Champlain discovered, on 8 November 1620, that the Sieur Dolu, acting as the agent of the Duc de Montmorency, the new viceroy, had cancelled all previous monopolies to those who had heretofore supported Champlain and given them to the Caën family, merchants based in Rouen.[62] In the spring of 1622 an agreement between those newly appointed to trade in New France and those who had formerly been licensed to trade there was carpentered together as the Compagnie de Montmorency (sometimes known as the United Company).[63]

Conflict between Acadia and the St Lawrence had already occurred in 1616, when Biencourt had seized a ship, the *Ange-Saint-Michel*, whose provenance was Rouen, legally trading for those engaged in claiming the St Lawrence for France.[64] Now, ships sailing for the Montmorency company caught fish off the Gaspé coast and traded furs around Miscou. In fact, in 1626 the ranking officer for the French fishing fleet, La Ralde, established quarters at Miscou[65] and left a small number of his men to spend the winter there. Inexperienced, they almost fell victim to the weather – according to Champlain, there were eight feet of snow at Miscou – and to scurvy.[66]

It was this southeastern expansion of interest, coming in the main from an alliance between the fishing vessels plying the Atlantic coasts and the ongoing development of Tadoussac as a crossroads for the fur trade, that led to trouble from the "French of the great river" for Charles de La Tour. Uncertainty about the limits of his authority led him to ask for aid, not only against the English encroachments on his colony but to prevent French intrusions on rights he considered that he held as an inheritance from Biencourt. His letters arrived just months after Richelieu had, in fact, taken steps to organize French colonial policy, in North America and elsewhere. While La Tour's plea had no influence on Richelieu's proposals, the reverse was certainly not true. Acadia, and La Tour, would be greatly affected not only by the ideas that the cardinal brought to French colonial development but by the way in which he oversaw the implementation of those ideas. Richelieu had become Louis XIII's chief adviser in 1624 and his attention turned to trade and colonial matters in 1626. That year the king signed an edict outlining proposals for the organization of commercial and colonial matters and added to Richelieu's titles that of surintendant general of trade.[67] The following year the Compagnie de La Nouvelle-France, more commonly known as the Compagnie des Cent-Associés, took shape. It embodied not only the ideas of the cardinal and king but also those of Isaac de Razilly, a long-time naval commander and Richelieu's cousin.[68] He would be appointed to the governorship of Acadia in 1632.

Razilly had sent Richelieu a long memorandum in November 1626 on the need to exploit the advantages of French access to both the Mediterranean and the Atlantic.[69] One of the points he made was one that Champlain had long voiced: the lack of concern that the merchants of the Atlantic ports had for settlement. Richelieu incorporated several of Razilly's ideas in the organization of the new company, especially those relating to funding and the organization of settlers. However, the cardinal was also much influenced by reports from religious who had served in New France, both Jesuits and Recollets. It took Richelieu from the spring of 1627 to that of 1628 to decide what policy he should follow. Under its official name of the Compagnie de La Nouvelle-France, the new body was granted the monopoly for trade and settlement in all North America, from the St Lawrence to Florida, without any recognition being given to prior claims of the original inhabitants or of the English and the Dutch, not to mention the residual rights stemming from de Monts's efforts in Acadia.[70] Its funding was to come from the hundred members, each of who would invest 3,000 *livres*, for a combined capital of 300,000. There was to be free trade between France and New France for fifteen years.[71] The company would be managed by a committee, established in Paris, of twelve directors, only a third of whom were to be merchants.[72]

Louis XIII's full support for the enterprise was shown by particular privileges granted to those willing to back the new initiative. The king attempted to ensure the participation of the French elites by formally and explicitly exempting all who became engaged in the enterprise from the possibility of losing their status as members of the nobility. In the seventeenth century, France was still a society where social status was reflected in a legal social hierarchy of three orders: the First Estate, which was restricted in the main to high-ranking members of the Catholic priesthood and to some members of male Catholic religious orders; the Second Estate, which included those who could show patents of nobility; and the Third Estate, which embraced the rest of the population. The importance of membership in a particular estate was, above all, a matter of privilege, and there was a long-standing prohibition against members of the nobility engaging in trade.[73] But this prohibition, while it undoubtedly stopped some members of the nobility from commercial activity, was by no means uniformly observed.[74] The king's decree removed any possibility that a noble might lose the rights associated with his membership in the Second

Estate if he became involved with the Compagnie de La Nouvelle-France.

Louis XIII did not pay attention only to the particular social conventions of the nobility. He also gave his attention to the circumstances of the Third Estate, many of whose members were subject to the guild system, which continued to rule many of the trades and professions in France at this time. It was proclaimed that all artisans – men who were coopers, dyers, weavers, ironworkers, and so on – and who spent six years in New France would be accorded the rank of master in their respective guild on returning to France.[75] Interest in linking the development of the colonial society to that of the metropolitan was also emphasized in provisions concerning citizenship. It was stated that the descendants of the French who settled in North America would have the rights and privileges of those born in France itself.[76]

Neither Richelieu nor Louis XIII overlooked the issue of religion. The second clause of the edict establishing the company stated that none but Catholics were to be taken to New France as settlers.[77] Such a provision was only to be expected in the climate of the late 1620s in France. As Richelieu made clear in his *Mémoires,* his ambition was to create a strong central power by curbing all opposition to the crown, whether it came from the nobles or elsewhere.[78] The popularity of the Reform church in the ports on the Atlantic coast, and in particular the position of La Rochelle as a major centre of the Reform religion and as a stronghold of opposition to a whole slew of royal policies, resulted in open warfare between that city and the central government in 1625. It was in the aftermath of the defeat of La Rochelle, on 6 May 1628, that the king signed the letters patent establishing the Compagnie des Cents-Associés.[79] The attempt to exclude Huguenots from becoming a significant group within New France was thus a logical development both of Richelieu's own ideological beliefs and of circumstances of civil unrest in France.

The translation of new colonial policy into action had already begun in late 1627, as Richelieu tidied up the majority of the claims of those who asserted they held rights, granted in previous years, to trade with New France. Various settlements were made with a number of individuals, including Madame de Guercheville's claims in Acadia, and by 1628 almost all rivals to the new company had been suppressed. It looked as if a new day had dawned for French migration to North America. But the three ships that left Dieppe on 28 April 1628, carrying supplies and settlers for Quebec and Acadia, never reached their destinations. They were captured by the Kirke brothers of Dieppe, sailing under letters of marque.[80] Miscou was also taken and within the year Quebec itself fell to the English. It would not be returned to French control until after the Treaty of Saint-Germain-en-Laye in 1632.

There were five Kirke brothers, David, Lewis, Thomas, John, and James, and their quasi-official actions were rooted in the shifting domestic and international politics of Europe.[81] In the late 1620s, Anglo-French relations were governed by the needs of the monarchs in both countries to consolidate their own respective power bases. Louis XIII was faced with governing a polity where many powerful players were reluctant to admit the rights of any central government and Charles I ruled lands where argument raged over the limits of the power of the crown itself. Both countries had an established church but neither country was without believers, accorded at least some rights, in institutions of Christianity outside those supported by the state. France was primarily, but not exclusively, Catholic; England was predominantly but not exclusively Protestant. Both countries had accepted, at this point, the need for some degree of religious toleration, although in neither country was it practised with much enthusiasm. Further, in the tangled web of international affairs in Europe in 1625, Catholic France and Protestant England were allies against the Catholic powers of Spain and Austria. At the same time, while the marriage in 1625 of Charles I with Henrietta-Maria, the sister of Louis XIII, pointed to some agreement between England and France, there was considerable opposition in both countries to particular policies of the other. Thus, the revolt of La Rochelle, against Richelieu and Louis XIII, had led to an English attempt to help the port in 1627, an attempt that signally failed. The Kirke brothers' raid in 1628 was part of a wider English movement to help the Huguenot cause and, simultaneously, gain personal advantage in so doing. For Acadia, the results of the Kirkes' exploits meant only the usual lack of supplies and information from France.

But these same years also saw a renewed effort by Sir William Alexander to pursue his schemes for the colonization of Nova Scotia. After the reverses suffered by his earlier expeditions, Sir William had looked for different ways of financing his enterprise. In 1624, with the support of James I, who much favoured the idea of a Scottish colony, it was decided to raise the necessary backing through the institution of an order of knights-baronets.[82] As John Reid has pointed out, the baronetcies would serve three purposes. First, money would be raised because each baronet would be obliged to pay roughly sixty pounds sterling to Alexander "for his past chargeis in the discoverie of the said cuntrey and for surrendering and resigning his interest to the saidis lands and barronies."[83] A further financial obligation was to send and support "sex sufficient men, artificers or laboureus" to the colony or pay another one hundred pounds sterling. Secondly, the baronies would change the basis of colonial settlement from the development of communal organization to that of fiefs, for each baronetcy was to be based upon 30,000 acres of land, of which more than half would be held by the baronet directly from the crown, the rest being reserved for common purposes. Finally, it was expected that a number of the knights-baronets would be resident within the colony and would, like the resident patentees of New England, give advice in matters of government. In 1625 a new charter was issued by Charles I to Alexander, confirming the rights granted in 1621.[84] Eight actual baronies were established by 1626 and provisions were made to incorporate Nova Scotia into the kingdom of Scotland "in order that Sir William and the baronets could take seisin of their distant lands in the castle of Nova Scotia without the necessity of going to Nova Scotia."[85]

It took until the spring of 1628 for Sir William Alexander to assemble ships, supplies, and colonists at Dumbarton and it was early summer before the expedition actually sailed. It was under the command of his son, also named Sir William Alexander. Little is known about this expedition, save the fact of its existence. It never reached Nova Scotia, probably wintering in Newfoundland, and its members suffered greatly from scurvy.[86] The next year, however, another attempt was made and ships left under the dual command of James Stewart, Lord Ochiltree, and, once more, the younger Sir William. The fortunes of these men divided, with Lord Ochiltree establishing a short-lived community on Cape Breton and Sir William Alexander building a much longer-lasting settlement in the vicinity of Port Royal. Lord Ochiltree's ship arrived off Cape Breton in the first week of August and established Fort Rosemar, some ten miles from where Louisbourg would be established in the eighteenth century.[87]

However, within six weeks Captain Charles Daniel, fresh out of Dieppe, arrived. He had already joined the Compagnie des Cent-Associés and had supported a number of fishing ventures off Cape Breton over the past three or four years.[88] Daniel besieged and captured the fort that was in process of being built, sailed to Bras d'Or and founded Fort Sainte-Anne there, and then returned to France with his captives.[89] According to an account purporting to be that of Lord Ochiltree, Daniel captured the latter by treachery and "expulsit the poor people outt off the forth and exposed them, without schelter, or cover, or clothis, to the mercy of the rayne and cold wind, wch did exceed att that tym, so thyat the poor people (wheroff ane greatt number of them wer old men and women, wemem w^t chyld, and yong childrein att thair breasts) they, i say, wer forced to turne downe the face of ane old schallope and to creepe in uynder itt to save thayr lyffs from the bitternes off the cold and rayne, wch was most extream in thatt place."[90] However highly written this account may be, it includes some information about the make-up of the community: there were "too or thrie Ingliss gentlemen and thair wyffs," part of total company of "fyfty men, wemem and childrein." French contemporary accounts estimate the number of colonists to be much the same but assert that only seventeen were taken back to France, whereas Ochiltree suggests that all were "imbarked in the said captane Danyell ship, fyfty men, wemem and childrien being inclosed in the hold of the schipe in so little bound that they wer forced to ly upon other as they hayd beein so mony fisshis, lying in thair awin filhe and fed upon bread and water that by famine and the pestiferus smell of thair awin filth many of them wer throwin in the sea, throw famin the mothers lossing thair milk, the poor foukis childreein lost thair lyff and wer throwin in the sea."[91] Meanwhile, the young Sir William

Alexander had arrived before Port Royal and had been as impressed as Poutrincourt with its anchorage, its "fruitfull vallies adorned and enriched with trees of all sorts."[92] A site was chosen for a fort, located close to what would be the site of the later Fort Anne, on the banks of what would be named the Allaine (or Lequille) River. The colonists found their first winter, 1629–30, as bitter as that experienced by de Monts: Champlain was told that, of the seventy who wintered there, thirty had died.[93]

The source of this news was Claude de La Tour and it is his life that binds together the Scots and French efforts in Acadia at this time. It seems fairly clear that it was Claude de La Tour who returned to France in 1627, taking with him the letters his son had written to Louis XIII and Richelieu. It is also certain that Claude de La Tour was on board one of the ships that left Dieppe in 1628, as part of the first efforts of the Compagnie des Cent-Associés. He was one of those captured by David Kirke that year[94] and sent to England in the spring of 1629. On arrival, he went to London and attached himself to the court, where he met and married one of the queen's ladies-in waiting.[95] He also met Sir William Alexander the elder and obtained from him knights-baronets for himself and for Charles, on the understanding that they would be good and faithful subjects of the king of Scotland and work to bring Acadia to the same state of loyalty.[96] He seems to have accompanied Sir William Alexander later that same year but returned again to Scotland before the winter. In 1630, accompanied by his wife, Claude de La Tour returned to Acadia, with supplies intended for the support of the Scottish settlement. Precise details about the number of ships and their cargo are scarce. We know that it was early spring when two ships, on one of which Claude de La Tour was a passenger, arrived off Cap Nègre, where Charles de La Tour still remained.[97] Charles de La Tour was less than pleased when he was apprised of the arrangements that his father had concluded with Sir William Alexander. In spite of considerable argument from his father, the son remained firm in his allegiance to France and the result was a skirmish between the parties, lasting about forty-eight hours. At its conclusion, the ships departed. There is disagreement as to whether Claude de La Tour, with his new wife and four servants, decided at this point to disembark and remain with Charles de La Tour on the latter's terms or whether the ships with the elder La Tour on board sailed on to Port Royal.[98] Denys has the father disembarking and the ships returning directly to England, whereas Champlain has Claude de La Tour among the English at Port Royal in the summer of 1630.[99] Champlain also recounts that Charles de La Tour sent messages to his father at Port Royal, attempting to "bring him back to his duty [and] also for the purpose of learning from him the state of the English, and their plan of action, so as afterwards to take the course that might seem best in the light of his report."[100] What is clear is that, within a fairly short space of time, Claude de La Tour was living in a house just outside his son's fort.[101]

Charles de La Tour's decision, at this time, to turn down the offer of becoming a Scottish baronet (he would think better of it some twenty years later) was rewarded by the appearance within weeks of two ships from Bordeaux, provisioned with supplies, more itinerant workers, and three Franciscans.[102] In charge was Bernard Marot, a man in his forties who had been part of the Poutrincourt expedition to Port Royal in 1610.[103] He carried with him letters from the Compagnie des Cent-Associés, addressed to Charles de La Tour, appointing him one of their number, urging him to continue loyal to Louis XIII, and informing him that the supplies, arms, and men had been sent to help him build a habitation wherever he thought best.[104] Charles de La Tour set about the deployment of these new resources by making preparations to establish a fortified trading post at the mouth of the Saint John, to be known as Fort Sainte-Marie. If successful, such an action would confine the Scottish colonists within narrow boundaries. When Marot returned to France, he carried with him a good cargo of furs, a request for support for this project, and a glowing report of the younger La Tour.[105] It was this commendation, rather than his letters of 1627, that gained Charles de La Tour the title of lieutenant general of Acadia in February 1631. News of this commission reached him in the spring of the year, along with more materials and men for his Saint John River initiative.[106] That venture was proving more successful than the establishment made by Captain Daniel on Cape Breton, which had been struck by scurvy. The Scots who had settled across the bay from Port Royal had also suffered over the winter. According to Champlain, of the thirty settled at Fort Sainte-Anne in 1629, twelve died because of poor lodging.[107] But then, having weathered their first winter, they were in better shape and were reported as going from strength to strength.[108]

By 1631, the French presence in Acadia was still a matter of a tiny handful of traders and missionaries, scattered from Cape Breton to the mouth of the Saint John and reinforced by the French fishing fleet. It had been challenged by the Kirke brothers, the wavering political allegiance of the elder La Tour, and, recently, the arrival of Scottish colonists. At the same time, the English presence in the region had been strengthened by the activities of the Massachusetts Bay Company, which became a legal entity on 4 March 1629.[109] Five ships left London in late April and early May that year and crossed the Atlantic within two months. The *Mayflower*, which had carried colonists in 1620, was again in service for this new enterprise. Some three hundred men, women, and children disembarked in Massachusetts Bay in June 1629, intent on building their lives anew, and they were followed the next year by a further thousand. This was a migration bound together with a clear purpose and organized to achieve it. No comparable effort had been made, between 1627 and 1631, by the Compagnie des Cents-Associés, partly because of the activities of the Kirke brothers but also because the French had yet to produce any method that would encourage a comparable migration of family units. This was about to change, after the provisions of the Treaty of Saint-Germain-en-Laye, signed on 29 March 1632, restored French authority to both New France and Acadia. At long last, French expansion across the Atlantic was now to become something more than the probing efforts of a diverse group of individual entrepreneurs.

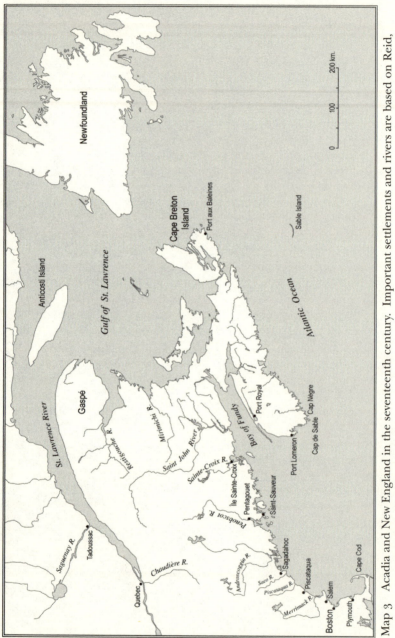

Map 3   Acadia and New England in the seventeenth century. Important settlements and rivers are based on Reid, *Acadia, Maine and New Scotland*.

CHAPTER THREE

The First Acadian Community

With the international situation of Acadia firmly established under the Treaty of Saint-Germain-en-Laye, France began a determined effort to develop the colony and between 1632 and 1654 a permanent population of Europeans was established there. Although small – by 1650 it numbered no more than three hundred – it represented the crucial beginning of the Acadian community. Later Acadian identity was greatly influenced by the way in which the migrants, who formed the basis of this sparse population, were brought to Acadia and settled. The individuals who made up the first "founding migration" to Acadia, that is, the men and women who, to a great extent, founded the large families that were to make up the nucleus of the Acadian population, had much in common with those who would play a similar role in Quebec.[1] The backgrounds of those who crossed the Atlantic to either destination were similar, representing all the regions of France but coming predominantly directly from the cities.[2] However, Acadia's experience also differed from Quebec in important respects.

For most of the 1630s, Acadia, unlike Quebec, had two legitimate lieutenant governors, both commissioned and recognized by Louis XIII, because the rights of Charles de La Tour were not revoked when Isaac de Razilly received his appointment. Moreover, the Compagnie des Cent-Associés never had the dominant control, let alone the monopoly of trade, in Acadia that it had along the St Lawrence. Despite the vast proprietory rights granted to the company in 1627, it was only one partner among many in Acadian affairs and, as the years went on, it became of less and less importance to those engaged in establishing a French settlement there. Further, from the outset, while the fur trade was of major importance to the entrepreneurs behind Acadian settlement projects, just as it was along the St Lawrence, fish was almost as significant as fur in the lives of those who actually settled in the more southerly colony. Finally, as Leslie Choquette has pointed out, Acadia's political and economic situation favoured, to a greater extent than in Quebec, "short-term movements of

population, whether of fishermen, merchants, soldiers, or building workers for the fortifications." Throughout these twenty-two years, the colony
"accommodated a significant if difficult to quantify contingent of particularly mobile Frenchmen."[3]

It was as much because of absence-of-mind and ignorance of geography
as of anything else that Acadia ended up with two concurrent and legitimate lieutenants governor after 1632. There is no doubt that this did, in
fact, happen, despite the efforts of some historians to deny the legitimacy
of Charles de La Tour's appointment.[4] In late March 1632 Razilly signed
an agreement with Richelieu to "receive restitution [of Acadia] at the
hands of the English and put New France in possession of it,"[5] and on 10
May 1632 he received a royal commission naming him lieutenant governor of the king in New France and requesting him to "take possession of
Port-Royal."[6] His reward, much of his support, and a certain amount of
control over his actions would come through the Compagnie des Cent-
Associés. Unfortunately for the peaceful development of Acadia, just over
a year earlier, on 8 February 1631, Charles de La Tour had been also been
named "governor and lieutenant-general of His Majesty's shore and the
places which depend upon it." On 19 January 1633, eight months after
Razilly's appointment, La Tour is referred to by these same titles in an
agreement he signed with the Compagnie des Cent-Associés.[7]

And so Acadia was a colony in 1632 not only with ill-defined borders but
also with a divided command and a multiplicity of companies interested in
trading supplies for its fur and fish rather than in establishing settlers.
Razilly's commission was to remove the colonists sent out by Sir William
Alexander and establish French settlers in their place. Richelieu and the
Compagnie des Cent-Associés provided some financial assistance for the
enterprise, contributing 10,000 *livres* and a ship, *L'Espérance de Dieu*. However, Razilly raised the greater amount of money himself for his expedition, some 150,000 *livres*, through a company he established with his
brother, Claude de Launay-Razilly. One of their most important agents was
Nicolas Denys, who worked in La Rochelle for the provisioning of the venture and would himself cross the Atlantic to seek his fortune in the colony.[8]
The *Gazette de Renaudot* reported that Razilly left the port of Auray, on the
south shore of Brittany, on 16 July 1632,[9] with three ships in all, "loaded
with all kinds of necessaries and three hundred gentlemen." Neither passenger lists nor detailed provision lists have yet been discovered for these
ships. There is other, mostly later, evidence but the absence of anything
comparable to Champlain's diaries for these years has spawned a great
deal of speculative debate.[10] The writings of Nicolas Denys, who arrived in
Acadia in either 1632 or 1633 and spent the next forty years in the colony,
are memoirs written in old age rather than a meticulous account composed at the time of events recorded. So there is considerable conjecture
about details of the expedition, in particular about whether the "trois cens
hommes d'élite" included women and children; whether there were three

Capucins on board, or six; and whether Razilly made landfall at Cap Sable before sailing to La Hève.[11]

Razilly, who came from a solidly established family among the minor nobility and had had a distinguished naval career, mostly in the Mediterranean and along the Atlantic coast, was certainly acquainted with both Champlain and Lescarbot and had used their writings as references for the report on colonial development he wrote for Richelieu in 1626.[12] When he arrived off the coast of Acadia, in the region of La Hève, on 8 September 1632,[13] he had four important objectives to pursue simultaneously: the repossession of Port Royal and the removal of the English and Scottish from the colony; the establishment of his own headquarters; the organization of his own authority within Acadia in light of the claims of La Tour and others; and the economic development of the colony. The easiest task was that of ousting the Scots, which Razilly accomplished during his first months in the colony. There was one last outbreak of hostilities. In 1632 Andrew Forrester was in charge of Port Royal for Sir William Alexander. It is a moot point as to whether the former had received notice from the latter of the peace settlement between England and France by the summer of that year. In any case, on 18 September 1632 Forrester sailed to the mouth of the Saint John River with a force of some twenty-five men and captured Fort Sainte-Marie by treachery.[14] He and his men were welcomed by Jean-Daniel Chaline, the young man whom Charles de La Tour had left in charge, but they turned on their hosts as soon as they had entered the fort, pulling down the cross and the arms of the king of France and, on their departure for Port Royal, taking with them a number of prisoners and a considerable cargo of furs.[15] This was the last fighting, between the Scots and the French, before Port Royal changed hands. Sometime in the last week of November or in early December 1632, forty-two erstwhile Scottish settlers were put on board the *Saint-Jean*, to be returned to England.[16]

Razilly's choice of La Hève, rather than Sainte-Croix or Port Royal, as the site of his headquarters has been seen as a sailor's decision, with the good harbour and its position in terms of transatlantic shipping considered to be the determining factors.[17] But in fact the decision was as much that of a soldier and of a colonial entrepreneur as of a sailor. Razilly had no way of knowing, at the time, whether he might have to fight for Port Royal, even though he would arrive there with a quantity of official English and Scottish documents giving him the power to repossess the settlement.[18] As to Sainte-Croix, while obviously a holding that Razilly considered capable of being developed, it was also the site of the disastrous first year of the de Monts expedition, a generation earlier. The question of the fisheries must have played a part in his decision, for not only were the "bancs la Hève" recognized at that time as good fishing grounds but the renowned Canso fishing stations were much closer to La Hève than either Port Royal or Sainte-Croix. This meant assured communication with France, should the expedition run into difficulties with its own supply ships. But whatever the major reason, La Hève was Razilly's choice for his headquarters and he administered his affairs from this base for the next three years, until his death, at the age of forty-nine, on 2 July 1636. Writing to Lescarbot in the early spring of 1634, Razilly was full of enthusiasm, remarking that the soil was amazingly fertile, with both wheat and vines flourishing. The crops that had been sown and were now thriving, Razilly continued, included "melons, cucumbers, peas, beans, lettuce, purslane, cauliflower ..." Further, "roses, raspberries, gooseberries, small cherries and strawberries grew naturally," and the pasturage was excellent, the milk yielding butter quite as good as anything produced in Brittany. Fish was abundant, in lakes and streams as well as off the coast, where "turbot paved the sea."[19] Razilly also reported that good forts had been built, capable of standing against all enemy action, and that he had the military supplies necessary to withstand a six-month siege. He named his fortifications Fort Sainte-Marie de Grâce and a few traces of the buildings can still be seen today.

Razilly had considered at length what had caused the failure of earlier expeditions, from illness to uncertain supplies and wretched living conditions. He brought with him lime, plaster, bricks, and some 2,000 sawn planks as well as a sufficiency of tools and capable workmen so that reasonable living quarters could be quickly established. He also ensured a good food supply, making certain that "neither wheaten bread, nor three kinds of wine, nor beef, milk, butter, oil, vinegar, spices, rice, sugars and jams were lacking." Once spring arrived, "dairy products, fresh butter, game and eggs became common."[20] Nevertheless, the first year was hard, and of those who stayed, one-fifth of them died – forty out of two hundred – more from inadequate housing than from scurvy.[21] Within two years of his arrival, however, Razilly had built himself reasonable quarters as well as a chapel, a store, and houses for his workmen.[22] Nicolas Denys had been granted land by Razilly on the opposite shore from La Hève, at Port Rossignol, now Liverpool Bay. He was as equally enthusiastic about the land and its prospects. He wrote in his memoirs that he had "a dozen men with me, some labourers, others makers of planks or staves for barrels, [others] carpenters, and others for hunting. I was provided with all kinds of provisions, [and] we made good cheer for the game never failed us."[23] When Razilly visited Denys some time in 1634, he was served pigeon soup, wild geese, duck, teal, snipe and plover "in pyramids," raspberries and strawberries for dessert, and both white wine and claret.[24]

Some historians are convinced that a number of women sailed with Razilly in 1633.[25] The fact that the *Gazette de Renaudot* does not mention women and children is not conclusive: as always, past reality is more than just what is included in the preserved written records – in this case, for example, Capucins were definitely among the passengers but went unreported at the time. Considering that Razilly's first priority was the repossession of much of the colony, he might well have limited membership in this expedition to men. Denys's description of La Hève does not help. It refers to 1635 and is not explicit about whether the farming community of some forty "habitans," which he reported as then in existence at Petite Rivière – perhaps a mile from La Hève – included both men and women.[26] In his letter to Lescarbot, Razilly had commented on the fact that his own celibate state, as a Knight of Malta, had probably hindered the recruitment of married couples, something that must change, he wrote, if the colony was to flourish.

There is no doubt that women, as well as men, in seventeenth-century France sought better lives through migration. Travelling, while less comfortable, more difficult, and more dangerous than in later ages, was, nevertheless, a constant element in the experience of both rural and urban peoples. Though the majority of the population lived and died in the place where they were born, a large and significant minority, both men and women, old and young, journeyed, permanently or for a season, to another town, another province, another country. But French migration, even if relatively common, was more often within a region, or from the rural areas to the city, or to Spain and the Rhineland than across the Atlantic. That journey was, in the first half of the seventeenth century, most often undertaken by men, single or without their families, and for a relatively short period of time.[27] Of the three hundred who sailed to Acadia in 1633, barely two-thirds remained there over the winter.[28] It seems most unlikely that women were part of this particular expedition.

The sailing of 1633 was the first of a series, all aimed, first and foremost, at establishing a strong administrative and trading centre for the colony. No women are reported as passengers on any of these ships. Razilly's brother, Claude de Launay-Razilly, embarked fifty-eight men for the colony, on board the *Catherine*, out of Auray, in March 1634.[29] Later sailings that year from La Rochelle are recorded as carrying more than another hundred men, expressly bound to winter over in Acadia. Within twelve months of Razilly's arrival, La Hève was a thriving trading post, the centre for a small farming community in the area, and, above all, a major port of call for a large fishing fleet. At one point during the summer season, there were more than five hundred transient fishermen ashore in the fledgling settlement.[30] It was, however, an overwhelmingly male world and the female presence was provided through contact with the Mi'kmaq. Its main activities thus involved sailors and fishermen, traders and craftsmen, all occupations that encouraged seasonal migration. Settlement was not yet the establishment of families, whether with European or Amerindian partners, and agriculture was a supplement to European supplies, not yet a means of permanent sustenance.

The third problem that Razilly faced was that of organizing the chain of command within the colony and establishing its frontiers, not only with New England but also between Acadia and Quebec. Razilly had arrived in Acadia with a solid reputation as an efficient administrator, a

skilful commander of men, and, rare indeed, someone who understood
the needs of commerce as much as the needs of the military.[31] But he
faced a complex reality of conflicting jurisdictional claims. The creation
of the Compagnie des Cent-Associés in 1627, despite the clearly stated
wishes of both Richelieu and Louis XIII for a single, unified North American colonial policy, had resulted neither in the cancellation of all previous grants to particular individuals nor in the disbandment of all other
trading companies. It had, instead, created an overarching structure
which, in theory, would coordinate all French activities in North America, sometimes by extinguishing prior rights, at other times by accepting
them, as well as by developing new contracts and agreements. The difficulty with this scheme, however, was that regardless of how logical it was
on paper, translation into action took time and was, inevitably, accompanied by court challenges. It was clear that Charles de La Tour had a certain authority within the colony: the question was how much, and where
did its geographical writ run? Similarly, it was clear that the coastal
boundary between Acadia and northern Maine was located somewhere
south of Pentagöuet, and that between Acadia and Quebec in the region
of the Baie des Chaleurs, but precisely where should such lines be drawn?
Further, there were other companies legally active on Cape Breton.[32]
Thus, Razilly had to recognize not only that there was more than one
"lieutenant-general du Roi" in Acadia but also that there was more than
one trading company with rights to the development of markets and
expectations of promoting settlement.

Over the next three years, Razilly avoided outright confrontation with
other interested parties within Acadia, first, by concentrating on the establishment of his authority in the vicinities of La Hève, Port Royal, and
Sainte-Croix, and, secondly, by exercising his commission and patents
without undue rigour. He made no attempt to extend his authority to Cape
Breton, although he had been granted the right to do so. There, the
efforts of Captain Daniel had resulted in the establishment of Fort Sainte-
Anne in 1629.[33] Razilly allowed Daniel and later his partner, Pierre
Desportes de Lignères, to function without interference. Nor did Razilly
attempt to exercise any authority over Charles de La Tour and his establishments at Cap Sable and the mouth of the Saint John River. Indeed, he
backed La Tour's efforts to confine the English trading ventures to the
area west of the Penobscot.[34] In 1633 the latter had had a skirmish with
Isaac Allerton[35] and the Plymouth colony at Machias. In 1635 La Tour
informed Allerton that "he had authority from the king of France, who
challenged all from Cape Sable to Cape Cod, wishing them to take notice,
and to certify the rest of the English, that, if they traded to the east of
Pemaquid, he would make prize of them."[36] Later that year, Razilly sent
Charles de Menou d'Aulnay, whom he had appointed as his second-in-
command, to reinforce the French claims by seizing the trading post of
Pentagöuet, situated at the edge of the territory claimed by Massachusetts.

Yet there was little immediate reaction to this move from the Massachusetts colony.

While Razilly managed to keep his own chain of command reasonably organized, he was not able to ensure that those whom he commanded worked smoothly with one another. Razilly obviously thought a great deal of Charles de Menou d'Aulnay, who was the complete opposite of Charles de La Tour. In many ways the clash between the two men was typical of the rivalry in early-seventeenth-century France between two competing and overlapping social systems: "a society of orders, based on traditional social-legal classifications, and a society of classes, based on economic activity and wealth."[37] La Tour had lived from early adolescence in North America, had married a woman native-born to the continent as his first wife, and had had his ideas shaped by those from France who were determined to build new communities in Acadia. Charles de Menou d'Aulnay had been shaped by adolescence and early manhood in Europe. Born in the early years of the century, probably in 1604, he was of much the same social status as Razilly and had served under him in the Mediterranean. D'Aulnay's father was a distant cousin of Cardinal Richelieu and, from all accounts, d'Aulnay himself considered status conferred by birth of major importance.[38] His aim was the exploitation of Acadia, as a development of his family's fortune in France, while La Tour's was the development of Acadia, as the place where he would found his own fortune. Even before he had arrived in Acadia, d'Aulnay had clashed with La Tour. In late 1632 d'Aulnay, acting as one of Razilly's agents, had arrived in La Rochelle with a ship, loaded with lumber from the St Lawrence, which he needed to unload and sell immediately. The official he chose to take inventory of the cargo, a certain Gaigneur, informed d'Aulnay that he had no authority to do any such thing and besides which he was already busy with a suit against some Basques, on behalf of Charles de La Tour.[39] He flatly refused to leave this work and accommodate d'Aulnay. From this crossing of interests, the relationship of d'Aulnay and La Tour never recovered. Razilly continually employed d'Aulnay as one of his agents in France for the marketing of furs, fish, and lumber as well as the acquisition of supplies, recruits, and ships for the colony.[40] D'Aulnay would find himself constantly running up against the interests of La Tour, whose titles and commissions for settlement in Acadia were clearly superior to his own. Razilly was able to keep the hostility between d'Aulnay and La Tour under control but on his death in December 1635 the rivalry between the two men erupted, to the detriment of the colony.

At that point, d'Aulnay began acting as his sole legitimate heir and openly challenged La Tour for exclusive control of the colony. Whether or not Razilly had willed d'Aulnay such rights as were in his power to bestow – for the actual authority and title of governor were a matter of the crown's choice, not of inheritance – is debatable.[41] It seems clear that d'Aulnay was supported by Razilly's brother, Claude de Launay-Razilly, and that d'Aulnay acted on Isaac de Razilly's death as if he had been left such rights. The result was that the work of establishing a settlement in Acadia, supported by both the fur trade and the fishery, was to be both slowed and subtly changed: slowed, because over the next fourteen years both d'Aulnay and La Tour spent almost as much time fighting one another as they did developing the colony; changed, because d'Aulnay had, by the end of 1636, moved the greater part of the settlement at La Hève to Port Royal, where the economy would be as much a matter of agriculture and the fur trade as of the fishery. Razilly's firm belief in the value of the fishery to the colony had been much the same as that of Nicolas Denys and d'Aulnay would soon be at odds not only with La Tour but also with Denys. D'Aulnay obviously envisioned Port Royal as the nucleus of the colony. Thus, from his point of view, enterprises centred either on the eastern Atlantic coast or along the southwestern boundary would, if unsuccessful, dissipate resources unnecessarily. It would be worse, of course, if such ventures were to succeed, since this would challenge his overall authority in the colony.

It is a tribute to Razilly that, at his death, Acadia was a colony that could endure a vendetta among its leaders. It was his administration that prepared the ground for the arrival of the first recorded migrant families on board the *Saint Jehan,* which left La Rochelle on 1 April 1636.[42] While there are records of a number of sailings from the French Atlantic coast to Acadia between 1632 and 1636,[43] this is the only one for which a detailed passenger list has survived. Nicolas Denys acted as agent for the *Saint Jehan,* registering the ship's roll thirty-five days after its departure, on 6 May 1636.[44] With this ship, Acadia began a slow shift from being primarily a matter of explorers and traders, of men, to a colony of permanent settlers, including women and children. The roll of the seventy-eight passengers and eighteen crew members of the *Saint Jehan* gives the provenance of the individuals as well as an idea of their trades. The document begins by listing the one extended family among the group, that of Nicolas Le Creux, who came from Breuil and travelled with his wife, Anne Motin, two of her brothers, Claude and Jehan, the latter probably a priest, and a sister, Jeanne, who would marry d'Aulnay soon after her arrival and, when he was drowned in 1650, his rival, Charles de La Tour. She had eight children with her first husband, none of whom had children themselves, and five with Charles de La Tour, two boys and three girls, all of whom would play a role in the future development of the Acadian community. With the family travelled a cousin, Jacqueline de Glaisnee, and another young girl, Jehanne Billard. Le Creux was certainly the most socially prominent of the company and he is credited with having brought with him thirteen other migrants – farmers, carpenters, someone with a particular knowledge of how to construct a mill, and one lumberman (*fauder de bois*). Seven of the group are listed as having come from the Dijon area; an Isaac Pesselin came from Champagne; the two carpenters came from Paris; and Jehan

Donno, the man credited with knowing how to construct mills, was listed as ordinarily living in Paris, although originally from Angers.

The other passengers were listed under four headings. The first was a group of people from Anjou; some of these were farmers but others were craftsmen, including a cooper, a cobbler, a master gardener, a gunsmith and lockmaker, a miller, four tailors, a toolsmith, and a vintner. The toolsmith, Guillaume Trahan, brought not only his wife and two children but also a valet. He would become a prominent member of Acadian society and a political leader in Port Royal. Another married man, who travelled with his wife and son, was Pierre Martin. Like Trahan, Martin and his family would become rooted in Acadia.[45] Among this group, five men had brought wives and children, but we know little about their lives after 1636. There was one widow, a Madame Perigault, who came with her two sons, described as farmers. In all, this group included twenty-three men, six women, and eleven children. In the next category were twelve men, nine of them carpenters from the Basque country, who had been hired specifically to build small seagoing vessels and launching docks. The others included with this group were sailors. A small number of salt makers were grouped together on the list; Jehan Sandry was named as the master salt maker and he brought his wife. The final category was the crew, all described as having come from the "Auray river." While the presence of European women is a signal that settlement was seriously contemplated, there were yet so few of them in this group of migrants that they did not immediately affect the status of Acadia as basically a colony of European transients.

Razilly had died before the *Saint-Jehan* arrived at La Hève and by the fall of 1636 d'Aulnay had established the immigrants at Port Royal. While there is no written record of why d'Aulnay decided to quit La Hève, the establishment of Port Royal as his headquarters had a great deal to be said for it. It linked him to the previous efforts to establish the colony by de Monts and Poutrincourt while, at the same time, it heralded a difference in his policies from those of his predecessor. It also brought him much closer to the main source of furs, which were gathered on the mainland – present-day New Brunswick – rather than on the peninsula. D'Aulnay believed that it was in the profits from fur that the economic future of the colony lay. The move, as well, brought d'Aulnay much nearer to both La Tour's operations at the mouth of the Saint John River and the disputed border between Acadia and Maine. D'Aulnay was thus able to oversee more closely both the activities of his major rival for the control of Acadia and the attempted incursions of his most important opponent into the territory claimed by France. Finally, while the agricultural potential of Port Royal was not, at that time, obviously superior to that of La Hève, given seventeenth-century farming techniques, there was no doubt that the site had proved to be good farming land earlier in the century and was capable of considerable development.[46]

For the future of the colony, the move was particularly important, in that it drew Amerindian and European into much closer contact than the development of coastal enterprise, dependent on the fisheries, had done. While the emergence of a coherent Acadian identity was shaped by the geography of the land settled as well as the political, social, and economic situation of the immigrants themselves, the importance of another factor – aboriginal goodwill – cannot be underestimated.

As has been suggested, in the early decades of European settlement, the natives received the newcomers with wary friendliness rather than belligerence. There was no need for the early settlers to carry guns with them as they began to farm, as their contemporaries had to do along the St Lawrence. The Mi'kmaq shared their knowledge of the environment, their incomparable skill in winter travel, and their knowledge of seagoing canoes with the Europeans. They were also quite willing to trade.[47] The fur trade in "Acadia or Nova Scotia" was so much smaller, in comparative terms, for the Europeans than the enterprise of New England or New France that its vital importance for those engaged in it has often been overlooked. It was the most important source of funds for the Europeans attempting to settle there and the cause of the bitter conflicts between those seeking its profits. It could not have functioned without the cooperation of the Mi'kmaq, as people wanting European iron goods and guns, as hunters themselves, and as traders in their own right, middlemen between Europeans and people farther west. There have been acrimonious debates about the impact of such trade on Mi'kmaq society,[48] but it seems clear that, at this time, the middle decades of the seventeenth century, the Mi'kmaq facilitated its operation and that the trade itself resulted in "the establishment of kinship ties between individual traders and Mi'kmaq villages."[49]

Then there was the question of religious belief. This was a less thorny problem for Mi'kmaq and settlers in Acadia than it was either in New England or in New France, where there is no doubt that religion occupied centre stage; missionary activity among the Amerindians and religious observances among the settlers were constant issues of concern for the elites of these societies.[50] There was no comparable phenomenon in "Acadia or Nova Scotia." This means, not that there were no attempts to convert the Mi'kmaq or that those who came did not have Christian beliefs, but that the issues of conversion of the Mi'kmaq and of Christian observance among the settlers did not hold the same measure of intensity as elsewhere. The Mi'kmaq neither burnt nor tortured those who came among them. There were no saints, by martyrdom or through the practice of heroic virtue, among the seventeenth-century settlers in the colony. The indigenous religious beliefs of the Mi'kmaq reflected the importance to them of the environment in which they lived. Such an orientation would not have been alien to the many Franciscans who worked among them, whose lives were governed by a discipline established by a man who talked to the birds and called the moon his sister, the sun, his brother.[51] Further, the Jesuit missionaries who did work among the Mi'kmaq seem to have been more closely connected to the colonists than they were in New France and much less likely to emphasize the necessity of cultural change for their converts.

Yet, if Acadia was fortunate to enjoy the goodwill of the aboriginal inhabitants of the area, it also had a heavy burden to carry in the form of the rivalry between d'Aulnay and La Tour. This progressed – or, perhaps more accurately, degenerated – from claim and counter-claim to outright warfare. Whatever hopes La Tour might have cherished that d'Aulnay would return to France on Razilly's death, and continue his career there as a naval officer, were ended when d'Aulnay's married the twenty-one-year-old Jeanne Motin, who had newly arrived from France.[52] This was a clear indication that d'Aulnay intended to continue his career in Acadia.

He began as he would go on, by ending the arrangement that Denys had had with Razilly, to ship timber back to France in the latter's ships.[53] It was obvious that d'Aulnay intended to establish his authority as the sole legitimate authority in the colony; he would rather stand the financial loss of his ships sailing in ballast than aid someone who claimed rights, both of fishing and settlement, obtained without his favour. And so it is not surprising that matters quickly worsened with La Tour. A decree intended to regulate their dispute was issued by Louis XIII on 10 February 1638. It named d'Aulnay as Razilly's successor but enjoined him to maintain a good understanding with La Tour.[54] Any chance of this happening, however, was minimized because the decree gave d'Aulnay authority over much of the northern shore of the Gulf of Maine and the Bay of Fundy but not its only fort at the mouth of the Saint John River. La Tour, on the other hand, was given the present-day peninsula of Nova Scotia but not Port Royal. The personal antagonism between the two men, exacerbated by their commercial rivalry for the fur trade, was now fuelled by political arrangements that gave each man a legal foothold in the other's territory. From this point, until the death of d'Aulnay in 1650 and the subsequent marriage of La Tour to his widow in 1653, there was almost continual fighting between the two men in North America and incessant politicking in France between their rival supporters.[55]

Quite apart from the hindrance that such a feud posed for French immigration to Acadia, it had a significant impact upon the relationship of Acadia with the English colonies of Maine and Massachusetts. Contact between the Europeans attempting to establish colonies on the northeastern seaboard of the American continent was inevitable and, given the way in which religious antagonisms were linked to national rivalries at that time, tended to be hostile more often than not. The relationship between Acadia and Massachusetts was, from the beginning, one of inequality. Massachusetts was always the more populous, in terms of European settlers, and the stronger, in terms of commercial activity, and it was also much more important to England than Acadia was to France. From the beginning, Massachusetts recognized the need to pay attention to Acadian affairs. On 17 January 1633 John Winthrop, then governor of that colony, wrote in his diary "that the French had bought the Scottish plantation near Cape Sable, and that the fort and all the ammunition were delivered to them, and that the cardinal, having the managing thereof, had sent some companies already, and preparation was made to send many more the next year and divers priests and Jesuits among them." Winthrop believed that the French "were like to prove ill neighbours being Papists" and he set about strengthening the defences of Boston.[56]

The skirmishes of the 1630s, which took place in the general area of Pentagöuet, did nothing to lessen Boston's wariness. Nevertheless, George Rawlyk points out that, as Massachusetts strengthened and the possibility of a major military challenge from Acadia diminished, "anti-Catholicism became much less intense" and while "prejudice remained ... it was never strong enough to preclude commercial or diplomatic relations."[57] So when, in 1642, La Tour decided to seek help from Massachusetts in his struggle with d'Aulnay, his request was received courteously, if not with great enthusiasm. In early July 1642 John Winthrop noted in his journal the arrival of emissaries from Acadia in Boston. "Here come in a French Shallop with some 14 men, wherof one was La Tour his lieutenant."[58] This was Nicolas Gargot de La Rochette, whose family was Huguenot, and he proved a skilful diplomat.[59] Winthrop continued: "They brought letters from La Tour to the governour, full of compliments, and desire of assistance from us against Monsieur D'Aulnay. They staid here about a week, and were kindly entertained, and though they were papists, yet they came to our church meetings." Winthrop concluded this entry by saying that "the lieutenant seemed to be much affected to find things as he did, and professed he never saw so good order in any place."[60] The following year, La Tour himself came to Boston, on board the *Saint Clement*. To Winthrop's consternation, the ship was able to sail right into Boston harbour, without let or hindrance. "If La Tour had been ill minded towards us," Winthrop wrote, "he had an opportunity as we hope neither he nor any other shall ever have the like again."[61] Winthrop was somewhat reassured by the fact that La Tour had brought his wife with him – in 1639 he had married, for a second time, Françoise-Marie Jacquelin, who was connected to La Rochelle commercial interests.[62]

La Tour informed Winthrop that "d'Aulnay his old enemy, had so blocked up the river to his fort at St. John's as his ship could not get in."[63] Taking care always to go to church with the governor, La Tour attempted to persuade the people of Massachusetts in general, and Boston in particular, to give him aid. This resulted in a meeting, of those of the magistrates and deputies of the colony as were in town, to discuss "whether it was lawful for Christians to aid idolators ..." and "whether it was safe for our state to suffer him [La Tour] to have aid from us against d'Aulnay. " Winthrop went on to summarize the discussion in his journal. It is worthwhile to examine it in some detail since its conclusions encapsulate the attitude of Massachusetts to Nova Scotia over the next thirty years. The religious issue was dealt with summarily enough and its discussion concluded with the pious hope that "such aid may as well work to the weakening of popery by winning some of them to the love of truth" and the cynical thought that "by strengthening one part of them against another, they may both be more weakened in the end."[64] The attitude was typical of the accommodation between Catholics and Protestants that was beginning to emerge in the seventeenth century: persecution to the point of murder, of either by the other, was being replaced by a reluctant acceptance of divergence. It was not so much a question of toleration as an understanding that the eradication of differing beliefs was not immediately possible. However intolerant the rhetoric of the varying Christian denominations would be after 1600, the bitter religious anarchy of the sixteenth century would rarely be repeated.

Nevertheless, the political leaders of Massachusetts debated the situation presented by La Tour mostly in religious terms. Winthrop thought that "Papists are not to be trusted, seeing it is one of their tenets that they are not to keep promise with heretics,"[65] but it was generally agreed that La Tour's interest would keep him honest. The question of whether France would be provoked by any action taken by Massachusetts was analysed without biblical references, but with the comment that "it is usual in all states in Europe to suffer aid to be hired against their confederates, without any breach of the peace, as by the states of Holland against the Spaniards, and by both out of England, without any breach of the peace, or offence to either." Solomon's wisdom was quoted when the question of meddling in the La Tour-d'Aulnay dispute was discussed and the conclusion was that d'Aulnay had to be stopped before he became too powerful. It was decided that "d'Aulnay is a dangerous neighbour to us; if he have none to oppose him, or to keep him employed at home, he will certainly be dealing with us, but if La Tour be not now helpen, he is undone, his fort, with his wife, children and servants, will all be taken, he hath no place to go unto – this ship cannot carry back him and all his company to France, but will leave them on the shore here, and how safe it will be for us to help them it is doubtful, but to let them go will be more dangerous, for they must go to d'Aulnay, and that will strengthen him greatly, both by their number, and still also by their present knowledge of our state and place ..."[66]

This did not mean that Massachusetts allied itself unequivocally with La Tour. Instead he was given the "liberty to hire for his money any ships in our harbour, either such as came to us out of England or others."[67] What was at work here was shrewd political judgment allied with commercial interests. Winthrop himself was clear that, however much it might be wished otherwise, Massachusetts was involved in Acadian affairs and so a policy that avoided outright war was essential. While there was opposition within the colony to support for La Tour, particularly from those who feared that d'Aulnay might launch an attack on isolated settlements below Pentagöuet, the governor's policy stood. It was a policy that had the support of his son, John Winthrop, Jr, and two other Boston merchants, Thomas Hawkins and Edward Gibbons, all three of whom had a considerable interest in developing the fur trade north and east of Penobscot.[68] Hawkins and Gibbons provided La Tour, at the cost of £940, with fifty crewmen and thirty-eight cannon.[69] On 14 July 1643 La Tour left for the Saint John River with four ships and a complement of 270 men to repossess Fort Sainte-Marie. That objective was quickly achieved but then La Tour went on to attack Port Royal, d'Aulnay's headquarters. This was no more than a marauding expedition: three of d'Aulnay's men were killed, the mill was set on fire, and one of d'Aulnay's ships, carrying a good quantity of furs, was captured.[70] La Tour then retreated and the Massachusetts volunteers returned to Boston, with their wages paid and a share of the captured supplies.

There were two serious consequences of this skirmish. First, Winthrop was less than pleased when informed of it, calling the action "offensive and grievous."[71] He had expected La Tour to regain his own territory and restore the status quo, not to increase tension in the area. Secondly, d'Aulnay was sufficiently incensed to ensure that the news of the matter reached France, through reports sent back by the Capuchins who were living at Port Royal.[72] He himself set out for France, with his wife, in October 1643 and was in Paris until the early spring of 1644. The death of Louis XIII in 1642, and the accession of his five-year-old son as Louis XIV, had led to considerable jockeying for power and political life was, even more than before, a matter of conspiracies, plots, and intrigues. In this situation, d'Aulnay, with aristocratic connections, stood a greater chance of success than La Tour and his wife, whose supporters were not only mainly merchants but also often allied with Protestant interests. Early in 1644, a major writ was issued by king in council, which began by summarizing the course of the dispute between d'Aulnay and La Tour since 1640. It concluded by confirming d'Aulnay's rights, ordering La Tour to return to France to answer the charges against him, and forbidding Madame La Tour to leave the country.[73]

In the meantime, La Tour had not been idle. He had spent considerable time in Boston, asking for further aid, on the grounds that his father had purchased Port Royal from Sir William Alexander.[74] Once more, the governor and council of Massachusetts debated the question in terms of theology and of practical politics. Winthrop records the questions discussed: "was it lawful for true christians to aid an antichristian" and "whether it were safe ... in point of prudence." The decision was to write to d'Aulnay, enclosing a copy of the order by the governor of Massachusetts that forbade anything but the strictest neutrality on the part of the inhabitants of the commonwealth. This letter, which was sent in the early spring of 1644, concluded with a reference to "a course of trade our merchants had entered into with La Tour, and our resolution to maintain them in it."[75] With this assertion of neutrality, La Tour had to be content, although he remained in Boston seeking greater support until early July. It was not until the autumn of that year that d'Aulnay sent a lengthy reply to the dispatch he had received from Boston. In it he was courteous to the extreme and stressed "that civillity which is naturall to you, as allso your generousness towards all your Neighbours." In closing, d'Aulnay proposed that "whatever troubles may fall out ... between the two Crowns of ffrance and England (which I heartily pray God not to grant) to keep inviolably with you and those which are under your Authority that peace and intelligence which is requisite in these beginnings ..."[76] As John Reid has commented, this is an extraordinary offer, "from one American colonizer to others, that peace should be maintained in all circumstances to facilitate the vital task of colonial development." [77]

D'Aulnay reinforced his message by dispatching his own emissary to Boston. This was a Capuchin brother, François-Marie Ignace de Paris.[78] As a result of his work, a treaty was signed on 18 October 1644. It recognized Acadia as "a province of New France," and although no specific boundaries were mentioned, it was implicitly assumed that Pentagöuet and points northeast would remain to the French and Pemaquid and points southwest to the English.[79] The treaty also specified that "it shall be lawful for all men, both French and English, to trade with each other."[80] This was the critical issue for Massachusetts: the primacy of trade, and thus the need of Massachusetts not to be seen as bound exclusively to the interests of either La Tour or d'Aulnay.

Over the next two years, Massachusetts continued to offer some aid to La Tour, despite the relationship entered into with d'Aulnay. When Madame La Tour, who had ignored the prohibition against her leaving France, appeared in Boston in late 1644, complaining that the ships she had hired had not been worked according to contract, her plea was heard and damages awarded in her favour.[81] She left for the Saint John River in late December 1644. The spring of 1645 saw the low point of La Tour's fortunes and the beginning of the considerable, if brief, success of d'Aulnay, before the latter's death in 1650. La Tour had left Fort Sainte-Marie in the late winter of 1645 to seek, yet again, supplies in Boston, and in the early spring Madame La Tour was there alone. D'Aulnay arrived at the Saint John River on 13 April 1645 with a force of some two hundred men. Madame La Tour surrendered on 18 April and "all the soldiers captured [there] were hanged, except for one man ... who had agreed to be the executioner of his comrades."[82] Three weeks later, Madame La Tour died.[83] La Tour spent the winter of 1645–46 in Boston and then left for Quebec. He did not return to Acadia until 1653, after d'Aulnay had drowned in a canoe accident on the Saint John.

With La Tour out of the colony, d'Aulnay was able to consolidate his position, backed by powerful friends at court. Earlier, in the fall of 1645, the queen mother, Anne of Austria, regent for her young son, Louis XIV, wrote to him promising him a fully equipped ship for his future endeavours.[84] One of d'Aulnay's first actions was to gain control over the fur trade on the Saint John River. He was succesful in this enterprise and traded over three thousand moose pelts the first year.[85] As he started to establish control over the rest of the colony, he was given complete authority to do so by the crown, which, however, did not consult the Compagnie des Cent-Associés in the matter even though that body was still, in law, the overarching authority for French actions in North America. In the spring of 1647 d'Aulnay received letters patent naming him "gouverneur et lieutenant-general" with far-reaching powers, both civil and military. He had the right to name officers, military and judicial, distribute patronage, establish laws, make treaties, build towns, and issue seigneurial grants. He was also given the exclusive monopoly of the fur trade in the colony.[86] As René Baudry remarks, this was the most sweeping delegation of vice-regal powers to any Acadian authority since the time of de Monts.[87]

D'Aulnay immediately set out to attack all others engaged in trade throughout the region, including the groups of settlers and, most particularly, Nicolas Denys. The latter had taken the precaution, in 1645, of obtaining rights to exploit Miscou and Nipisguit (present-day Bathurst) directly from the Compagnie des Cent-Associés.[88] In 1647 d'Aulnay raided these establishments, making off with supplies worth some 8,343 *livres*.[89] But his opponents were beginning to counter-attack in France. A court challenge was instituted by the Compagnie des Cent-Associés, which, in late 1647, drew up a factum. This was a bill of particulars against d'Aulnay, alleging that he had fraudulently obtained power on the death of Razilly, that he had obtained his position of lieutenant-general by an illegal procedure, without consulting the company, and, finally, that he had done nothing over the years either for the settlement itself or for the conversion of the Indians.[90] Over the next months, as he fought a swarm of legal challenges, d'Aulnay plunged ever deeper in debt.[91] He had still to pay the 14,000 *livres* he owed Launay-Razilly, Isaac de Razilly's brother, when he acquired rights for the latter's shares in the Launay-Razilly-Cordonnier company.[92] By 1644, d'Aulnay's debts to his major supplier, Emmanuel Le Borgne, had reached 81,000 *livres*, and, by 1650, Le Borgne had presented d'Aulnay with a bill which amounted to 260,000 *livres*, including interest and capital.[93] D'Aulnay's death that year left his financial problems to his widow, Jeanne Motin.

Within the year, La Tour had once more regained the title of governor and lieutenant-general of Acadia, the letters patent of February 1651 granting him exactly the same powers that d'Aulnay had received four years earlier.[94] As he began to re-establish himself, La Tour found one of his major problems to be Emmanuel Le Borgne, who, on 9 November 1650, two months before La Tour was recognized by the French crown, had gained legal rights not only to d'Aulnay's property in France but also to "all the dwellings of La Heve, Port Royal, Pentagoet, the St. John river as well as Miscou, the island of Cape Breton and other dependencies."[95] Meantime, Jeanne Motin, now in her mid-thirties with eight children (four sons and four daughters), had sought the protection of the Duc de Vendôme. The latter drove a hard bargain for his patronage and she surrendered not only half the properties to which she had some title in the areas of Port Royal and La Hève but also those on the Saint John River – claimed by La Tour – and those on Cape Breton, claimed by Nicolas Denys.[96] Since this action produced no immediate help, she turned to La Tour, now a widower in his mid-fifties. Signing an agreement to keep their financial affairs separate, the couple were married in the summer of 1653, the contract being signed on 24 February of that year.[97] La Tour agreed to look after d'Aulnay's eight children: the four girls would enter convents and the four boys, the military. None maintained any connection with Acadia and the boys left no issue. The couple would have five children of their own, two boys and three girls, four of whom would build their lives in Acadia and the fifth, a girl, would marry one of Le Borgne's sons.[98]

It is at this point that the Le Borgne family became one of the major players in Acadian affairs. Over the next twelve months, from the moment he heard of d'Aulnay's death, Emanuel Le Borgne set out to gain control of the colony. Le Borgne had been born in Calais in 1610 and had moved to La Rochelle sometime before his marriage there in 1635 to the daughter of a well-connected family, that of Jacques Françoys, noble "de la robe" and widely related to others of similar circumstance.[99] Le Borgne himself became not only a prosperous merchant but also an important official, serving as the consular magistrate of La Rochelle from 1643 to 1672. The father of twelve children, whose godparents were, almost without exception, well placed in the service of the crown, he himself became sufficiently wealthy to support d'Aulnay's activities for almost a decade, before pressing for repayment. When the news of d'Aulnay's death reached him, however, he had set about protecting the substantial investments he had made in the latter's endeavours. He arrived in Port Royal just after the marriage between La Tour and Jeanne Motin had taken place, at a moment when La Tour had left for the Saint John River. Le Borgne brought with him on board the *Chateaufort* more than a hundred men, as well as munitions and supplies.[100] Jeanne Motin signed papers, recognizing her obligations for debts of 200,000 *livres*.[101] Le Borgne then went on to subdue the post at Pentagöuet, capture the property of Nicolas Denys at Saint-Pierre on Cape Breton, burn the buildings that remained at La Hève, and, as the *coup de grâce*, destroy almost all of what d'Aulnay had left of Denys's property at Nipisguit. It was Nicolas Denys who first attempted to challenge Le Borgne's actions in France. He managed to have the Compagnie des Cent-Associés grant him seigneurial rights from Canso to the Gaspé, as well as the monopoly of the fur trade from Newfoundland to Virginia.[102] All of these activities, however, became moot when, on 14 July 1654, a New England expedition led by Robert Sedgwick captured La Tour's fort on the Saint John.[103] With this action, the fortunes of Acadia became definitely those of a border community, considered by two powerful states as rightfully theirs.

At this point in its history, Acadia was, first and foremost, a commercial enterprise, spread over an extended territory, capable of showing considerable profit, and attracting competing interests. There were continual, if not continuous, sailings of ships from the French Atlantic ports, for different places in Acadia, some involved primarily with the fisheries, others engaged in the fur trade, and yet others in support of the settlements.[104] The categories were never mutually exclusive and shipowners often sailed with more than one of these objectives in view. Those engaged in the fisheries were usually the most single-minded, following the most traditional and least innovative course, with fur trading a minor, if profitable, sideline. By 1650, Canso had become one of the most well-known and best-organized fishing areas, with gravel beaches for drying the cod. But the whole of the continental coast, from present-day Guysborough (Chedabuctou) to Miscou at the entrance of the Baie des Chaleurs, provided harbours nearly as good. Perhaps a hundred and fifty ships a year might be involved in fishing off these shores.

The fur trade was the riskier matter, since, while it could yield even greater profits, it involved heavy overhead costs and frequently resulted in litigation because of competing claims about monopoly rights. Further, it demanded a sophisticated sense of merchandising in both French and Amerindian societies.[105] It was this activity of the newcomers that was most deeply intrusive into the lives of the Mi'kmaq and the Malecite, altering the basis of much of their material culture. There has been little attempt to trace the overall value of the Acadian fur trade as a commercial enterprise during these years and any estimation of what it was worth would be little more than a guess. Nevertheless, it was this trade that financed both La Tour and d'Aulnay, allowing them to raise money for the provisions for the settlements, to pay the soldiers they recruited, and to borrow on the expectations of profit. For the development of Acadia, the link between the fur trade and the slowly growing settlements was of first importance. It meant the continued association with the European world, a conduit not only for European goods but also for news of political events, ideas, and people. While crossing the Atlantic was still a hazardous and lengthy voyage in the mid-seventeenth century, the ocean was no longer the barrier to communication that it had been fifty years previously.

The slow growth of the European population in the colony since 1636 was partly the result of French migration patterns and partly of the strife between the Acadian leaders, which had affected the pace and manner of settlement of the colony, its religious life, and its attitude towards its English Protestant neighbours. Both d'Aulnay and La Tour had organized the passage of quite a considerable number of people across the Atlantic between 1636 and 1650. However, the majority were men brought over primarily for military purposes, whether as soldiers or as craftsmen, and for limited service contracts. A few, particularly craftsmen, determined to settle after their contract was ended, but the majority were part and parcel of those who saw the Atlantic as something that did not pose much greater dangers than a long journey overland – a dangerous passage, perhaps, but one they intended to cross in both directions. Such were the craftsmen recruited by La Tour's agent, Guillaume Desjardins, whose contracts still exist: gunsmith and carpenter in 1640;[106] nail maker and blacksmith, wood sawyer, baker, and mason in 1641.[107] Similarly, d'Aulnay brought over such craftsman through Emmanuel Le Borgne.[108] There is no evidence to suggest that any of these individuals remained after their contracts were ended.

It is generally considered that the Acadian population, estimated at some 120 colonists and 40 soldiers in 1640,[109] had reached no more than 300 people, or some fifty families, in 1650.[110] A.H. Clark judged that it was made up of some forty-five to fifty European households, established at Port Royal and La Hève, with perhaps some sixty single men elsewhere in the colony.[111] John Reid is of the opinion that the population was at least 400.[112] Clark seems to have omitted from his calculations the households of the chief men of the colony. D'Aulnay, both La Tours, and Denys usually had their wives with them as well as servants. Further, the continued European settlement of the Cap Sable area, not to mention the settlements of Nicolas Denys, have been ignored. At much the same time, 1652, Trudel has estimated that the population of European descent in the St Lawrence area was five times as great, approximately 1,500,[113] while Reid has estimated that Maine had about 1,000 settlers in 1650.[114] Although "Acadia or Nova Scotia" did not have anywhere near these numbers of colonists that year, more Europeans were present than has been generally acknowledged.

Geneviève Massignon, writing at the opening of the 1960s, considered that a significant majority of Acadia's early population had roots in the Loudunais district of France. Recent work has called this assertion into question.[115] This is not say that no one from the Loudunais area, where d'Aulnay had considerable holdings, settled in Acadia. It is, however, to suggest that those who came to Acadia, especially in the years before 1650, were more broadly representative of the various regions of France. In other words, those who came were not part of a concerted migration from any particular area in France, and although many arrived as part of a group, that group was normally assembled in the port from which it sailed. People drifted to the coastal towns, migrating in incremental steps from small village to inland town and then to the ports. While the northwest of France contributed significantly to transatlantic emigration, there was also considerable migration from elsewhere. However, tracing those who left the centre and southwest of France for North America is a more complex task, because they are the more likely to have wandered within France for a greater length of time before emigrating than those of the northwest.[116] Marcel Delafosse, the archivist who worked for many years among the notarial records in La Rochelle, considered the destination of most migrants, Acadia or the valley of the St Lawrence, to be a matter of chance: what was the destination of the next ship to sail? Certainly, the evidence that does exist, about particular individuals who came to the colony before 1650, rarely links these migrants to each other or to the same regions of France. Even groups of migrants, brought together for the express purpose of emigration, were usually recruited from more than one region of France. The list of the *Saint Jehan* brought together people reported as coming from the valley of the Loire, from La Rochelle, and from Brittany. But we have little evidence that these were, in fact, their places of birth and childhood. The Acadian genealogist Stephen White rarely hazards a guess at the regional descent of those Acadian families he has studied, whose ancestors are recorded as arriving before 1650.[117]

At the time of Sedgewick's raid, there were six major seigneurial grants and three smaller subgrants within the colony. In considering their importance, Clark wrote that Acadian seigneuries were as large as the Canadian ones and "infinitely less practical."[118] "Seigneurial grants in the 'greater Acadian area,' Clark continued, "may have been intended to be of the same general kind as those in Canada but the majority of the grants remained paper entities and, of those which had more or less reality, we are poorly informed about their actual operation, the payment of dues of various kinds, the geographical limits of the individual *rotures* or seigneurial 'domains,' and the processes of granting, inheriting or transferring the rights to either." During these early years, the seigneuries were basically statements of administrative rights and responsibilities rather than blueprints for action. Joan Bourque Campbell has described those who held them as "land settling agents."[119] This is a good description of their main purpose, as far as French officialdom was concerned. The immensity of the land, combined with the importance of the fur trade and the fisheries as the chief economic pursuits in the colony, greatly lessened the possibility of rigid landowning controls over settlement patterns. The preoccupation of La Tour and d'Aulnay with fighting each other meant a further lack of outside authority over the settlements. All that said, however, there is no doubt that the existence of the seigneuries implied social divisions within the emerging communities and that this greatly influenced the structure of their political life.

Nicolas Denys had been given land stretching from the Baie des Chaleurs to Canso, including much of Cape Breton; the area around Port Royal belonged to d'Aulnay's heirs, as did that around La Hève and the St Croix River; La Tour's grants included Cap Sable and land on the Saint John. Philippe Mius d'Entremont had obtained land from La Tour around

Pobomcoup, as had Antoine Hervieux and Amand Lalloue, who had been granted islands in the same area.[120] There is only conjecture as to the conditions which La Tour attached to these grants, and, to a great extent, their importance lies in the legal battles to which they gave rise later in the century. Litigation is one of the more far-reaching results of a great many seventeenth-century grants, cases lasting well into the middle of the eighteenth century. It is from the evidence presented in these cases, often a generation or more later, that what was given and to whom, and on what conditions, is known.[121]

All the seigneuries had trading posts, and by 1640 most of these were occupied year-round. One of the most significant was that of Pentagöuet. Here d'Aulnay had been active since 1635 and established a fort, with gardens, an orchard, a farm, and a grist mill.[122] It is believed that at least one seventy-ton ship had been built there.[123] Usually there was a resident garrison of eighteen. La Tour's fort on the Saint John would have been of much the same type but, at present, we have little knowledge of how it was built. The establishments at Cap Sable and at La Hève remained occupied throughout this period. While some cultivation was carried on in both places, they appear to have functioned more as trading posts than as settlements. Nicolas Denys built fortifications wherever he roamed, from La Hève to Saint-Pierre and from Chedabouctou (present-day Guysborough) to Miscou, but, again, these turned out to be linked primarily to commerce rather than to settlement, they were highly vulnerable to attacks from his rivals, and we have little record of what was actually constructed. In all of these establishments, the presence of European women was minimal, consisting of the wives of La Tour and Denys and, perhaps, some servant girls. D'Aulnay's decision to move to Port Royal in 1636 had led to that settlement becoming the most important agricultural development within the colony. The best contemporary description of what had been developed by 1650 is that of Denys, who admitted, despite his dislike of d'Aulnay, that the latter had "a fine and good fort." Further, Denys wrote, "there is a great extent of meadows which the sea used to cover, and which the Sieur d'Aulnay had drained." This land, the account continued, "bears now fine and good wheat."[124] The question of how the settlers turned to dyking land has been much discussed. Was it a question of salt needs? Or was it, from the first, linked to agriculture?

A great deal is known about the history of salt making and marsh draining in France. It is a long and complicated story which has attracted the attention of a considerable number of historians and geographers.[125] It begins around the eleventh century with the work of the Benedictines, but by the end of the sixteenth century the low-lying areas at the mouth of the Charente and the Gironde "presented scenes of desolation."[126] Restoration attempts were begun by Henry IV and carried on by Louis XIII, particularly in the areas around Bordeaux and in Poitou. One of the most redoubtable Dutch experts, a man named Bradley, came to France in 1597 and received large concessions of land in the Marais Poitevin. A compatriot, Conrad Glassen, drained the marshes of Blanquefort, Bordeaux, and Bruges in the first decade of the seventeenth century. Within a generation, these men had local apprentices and in 1639 Louis XIII "granted privileges for 20 years to Pierre Siette from La Rochelle, who held the position of 'engineer and geographer to the court,' in order to drain marshes and flooded land in the provinces of Aunis, Poitou, and Saintonge."[127]

Razilly had considered that Acadia would be partly sustained by the cod fishery and had foreseen the need to find some way of producing salt locally. No matter whether it was to be transported as "wet" or "dry," getting the fish back to Europe demanded great quantities of salt. If salt could be produced locally, the ships could bring provisions for the settlers and, even more important, the salt used would not be taxed to the same extent as it was in France. In 1636 Jean Cendre and Pierre Gaboret, from the Bordeaux area,[128] were brought out under contract to Razilly to construct salt marshes. There is no written record of their moving from La Hève to Port Royal, but with Razilly's death it seems probable. There, the step from dykes for drainage to dykes for salt production would have been a relatively easy one to take. Agricultural trades in seventeenth-century France, while often guild-controlled, were not rigorously separated. While we know nothing of the capabilities and training of Cendre and Gaboret, it seems likely that they would have been well aware of the differing methods of marsh drainage between the mouth of the Loire and that of the Gironde.

However the knowledge came to the colony, the making of dykes, either for salt production or for drainage, was part of the resources of Acadian communities by the middle of the seventeenth century. For either purpose, their construction with the agricultural technology of seventeenth-century Europe was a labour-intensive activity, requiring a great deal of organized manual labour. The dykes established at Port Royal before 1650 could not have been built without the full support of the tiny community. There were, after all, at the most generous of estimates, no more than thirty families actually settled there by d'Aulnay. Even the smallest of dykes would require, at some point in its construction, participation by all those physically capable of hard labour. It could only be begun when the tides were low and it required both a carefuly prepared foundation and a well-established bank. The size of the early dykes at Port Royal has not yet been fully established but later Acadian dykes were between six and twenty feet, with a breadth of ten to twelve feet.[129] While the tides at Port Royal are not as forceful as those in the Minas Basin, they are, nevertheless, still very powerful. Even small dykes required considerable labour to dig out the foundations, to line the trenches either with tree trunks, interlaced branches, and smaller saplings or with a combination of branches and sod, and to build up the banks with earth and wood. Once the dyke was built, it would continue to demand a major commitment of time and energy by the majority of the settlers. It required close surveillance to ensure that any breaches made by general wear and tear were quickly repaired. Maintenance work in the fall to prepare it for the ravages of winter cold and spring storms also had to be carried out. The emergence of marshland agriculture necessarily implied the development of a strong sense of community among the settlers, most of whom would not have known one another before they arrived.

The impact of the sea upon the Acadian community was not confined to development of the salt marshes alone. For much of the seventeenth century, Acadian settlements were built at river mouths. Fish was an important part of the diet. Its harvest for commercial purposes was a major factor in the Acadian economy, although the major part of such harvesting was the business of fishing fleets from elsewhere. Their arrival off the Acadian coasts meant at least, minimal trade and, at best, considerable profits from the sale of furs and fresh food. The sea was a highway within the colony, as easy, if not easier, than any provided by the land. The building of boats at Pentagöuet under d'Aulnay's auspices presaged the later construction of any number of small craft capable of exploiting the coastal waters, crossing the Bay of Fundy, and linking the mouth of the Mirimachi, Canso, Cape Breton, and Port Royal. The sea was the constant background of early Acadian life and often enough a crucial food source when there was a poor harvest, followed by a severe winter and poor hunting.

While Acadia territory was the crossroads of the exploitation of the fur trade and the fisheries,[130] it was the success of agriculture, an occupation dominated by the climate of any given year, that would make or break the colony. The establishment of farms, with harvests that would mean food self-sufficiency for the newcomers, was the necessary foundation for permanent settlement. Farming, as ever, was labour-intensive and demanded attention to numerous tasks simultaneously. Shelter for livestock, chickens, cattle, pigs, and horses had to be built and maintained. The daily food and water needs of each species had to be met and modified with attention to their breeding cycles. At the same time, vegetable gardens had to be sown and attended, orchards established, and grain fields ploughed and seeded. The tools for all these tasks were part of each well-equipped expedition from Europe but their repair and maintenance became the business of those who used them. In Port Royal there were some specialized craftsmen, especially smiths and carpenters, but all settlers would find it useful, if not imperative, to have some knowledge of woodwork and smithing. Hard and fast categories of occupation, exclusive reliance upon one activity, would be a great handicap in the early decades of the colony. Most men would hunt, fish, farm, carpenter, and repair tools.

Similarly, women were fully occupied. Domestic tasks were their domain, food and clothing the major products. Women had primary responsibility for the preparing and preservation of food, and, as often as not, the responsibility for dairy and poultry products. As well, the care of the garden, once the land had been dug, was theirs. The preservation of food, both long and short term, meant the preservation of meat, by salting and drying. It involved the making of all forms of preserves, jams, and jellies and the storing of vegetables and fruits for the winter. At the same time, while tailors had come out to the colony, the majority of textiles were spun, woven, dyed, and sewn at home. More than anything else, however, children ensured that women's lives were centred upon the household. By 1650, the newcomers in Acadia were by no means a self-generating community, one that could sustain itself demographically without additional migration. In fact, by 1650, families were just coming into being among the settlers, the first recorded birth of European parentage in Port Royal being that of Mathieu Martin in 1639.[131] At this time, there were no three-generational families among the settlers in Acadia. It is true that the people of pre-industrial world had such short lifespans that most children had lost one of their parents by the time they reached marriageable age. But most rural communities had a number of older inhabitants, above all women, capable of giving advice about childrens' ailments and household tasks. Even in Newfoundland, families had been established much earlier, the first birth being recorded in 1611. Along the St Lawrence, not only had close to four hundred children of European parentage been born by 1653, but a number of them had parents who, themselves, had been born in the colony.[132] The absence of a cohort of older women, experienced in child rearing and able to counsel and support young mothers, added to the burdens of the young women in Acadia. Finally, the growth of the families also meant that the physical demands of pregnancy, after the first successful birth, had to be endured while caring for one or more children. The home was not a place of leisure but one where the necessities of daily life were provided, to a large extent, by women.

Evidence about the operation of the seigneurial system, in terms of the granting of land to those intending to bring settlers to the colony, is scanty but there is even less evidence about the terms granted to the settlers themselves at this time. There is no doubt that d'Aulnay did establish a number of families at Port Royal. His own evidence, given in 1644 in the middle of legal wrangles with La Tour, was that he had established some "two hundred men, as many soldiers and workmen as craftsmen, not counting women and children, the Capucins nor the children of savages. Further, there were twenty French households, who have come with families ..."[133] But there is no record of the terms on which the land was actually worked. Comments were made by Denys to the effect that d'Aulnay treated the settlers as "serfs, without allowing them to make any gain."[134] There is some evidence, from a generation later, that the terms might have been those of sharecroppers, ownership of the land being retained by d'Aulnay and rent paid in the form of a percentage of the crop harvested. Equipment, seed, and animals would be provided as well by d'Aulnay against this share in the products.[135] Certainly, despite his preoccupation with fighting La Tour and raiding Denys, d'Aulnay attempted to settle Port Royal with himself as the holder of major seigneurial power. It is clear that the communal buildings, including a church, a grist mill, and a saw mill, as well some of the houses, were built as the result of d'Aulnay's efforts. With the arrival of English control in 1654, however, which would continue for the next fifteen or so years, whatever landholding regulations had been established were significantly changed.

Sedgewick's raid did not only interrupt the establishment of a seigneurial system in Acadia, it also modified the influence of Catholicism within the community. There is no evidence, at this point, of the extent to which Catholicism was a matter of personal devotion, as opposed to social convention, among the Acadians. Priests had always been part of the French attempts to establish settlement in Acadia. They were most often members of either the Jesuit or a Francisan order, for the religious orders had greater resources to spend on ventures abroad than did the average diocese. It was not until 1657 that the archbishopric of Rouen became responsible for the administration of the institutional structure of the Catholic Church in French North America. Rome had established the Sacred Congregation for the Propagation of the Faith to oversee the activities of the Catholic Church outside Europe in 1622.[136] But, for the next thirty or so years, this body was much more interested in Asia than in North America and there was no overall structure to Catholic expansion in North America. The priests sent to Acadia and New France by the Jesuits and the Franciscans before 1657 were often more interested in the conversion of the aboriginal peoples than in the souls of the newcomers.

After 1612, the Jesuits' role in Acadia, in particular, was focused upon the Mi'kmaq, although the Jesuit presence on Cape Breton originated as a chaplaincy to the trading post established by Daniel at Sainte-Anne's in 1629.[137] In 1642 it was decided to make Nepissiguit (present-day Bathurst), at the mouth of the Miramichi, the headquarters of Jesuit activity in Acadia and it retained this distinction for the next twenty years.[138] While Denys had a continuing interest in this area, the main concern of the priests there was the Mi'kmaq.

D'Aulnay and La Tour had Franciscan priests in their entourage. Known officially as the Order of the Friars Minor, the Franciscans had divided more than once since the death of their founder, St Francis of Assissi, in 1225. In 1525 the Capucins, so called because of the deep hoods they wore on their gowns, came into being, dedicated to a strict observance of the vow of poverty. In 1606 the Recollets were born out of this branch of the Franciscans. They placed an emphasis on quiet meetings of their communities for meditation about the demands of the religious life. Members of the Recollet order were most often attached to La Tour and those of the Capucin observance to d'Aulnay, thus adding yet one more complication to the politics of Acadian life.

In sum, Acadia at the time of Sedgewick's raid was a place where a small handful of French migrants had staked a claim to establish a settlement, where competing French interests fought with one another over the lucrative fur trade, where French fishing vessels congregated for the season, and where the native Mi'kmaq had established trade relations with the newcomers. The raid itself reaffirmed the interest of the neighbouring English colonists in the area. The next decades would see the development of Acadian life under the influence of Massachusetts, as well as through the continuing activities of the French.

CHAPTER FOUR

The Establishment of a Border Colony

Neither France nor England accorded North America a great deal of time and attention in the middle decades of the seventeenth century. It was not that the chief men involved in the government of either state ignored overseas developments, but rather that, for both states, matters nearer home were of more pressing importance. France, in the mid-1650s, was coping with the consequences of the end of the Thirty Years' War and the civil unrest of the Fronde, an abortive revolt against the crown. Five years of intermittent civil war had resulted in no major gains for those who wished to curb the power of the young king, just sixteen in 1654, and his chief minister, Mazarin. It had, however, meant considerable hardship for much of rural France, dislocation of urban development, and increased taxes. The attention of the French government was focused on the task of re-establishing working relationships with the great nobles, the provincial authorities, and the developing urban centres, as well as on the need to alleviate the misery of those areas of the country, particularly the north-eastern and southwestern provinces, where fighting had been long and savage. Further, the economic life of seventeenth-century France revolved to an overwhelming degree around agriculture; what foreign trade there was centred primarily upon the Mediterranean, Asia, and the West Indies.[1] In these circumstances, the problems of the French colonial efforts in North America were addressed on a piecemeal basis. The fisheries would always command attention, the fur trade only sporadically. As to other North American issues, they were noticed if they were presented through the particular interests of someone with influence in court circles or if they were part and parcel of some more immediate problem with another European power. In the final analysis, in 1653 Mazarin had to govern a vast land with a population of twenty million; across the Atlantic, the French population along the St Lawrence was barely 1,500 and that of Acadia perhaps 300.[2]

In England, the situation was somewhat different. As late as 1688, 88 per

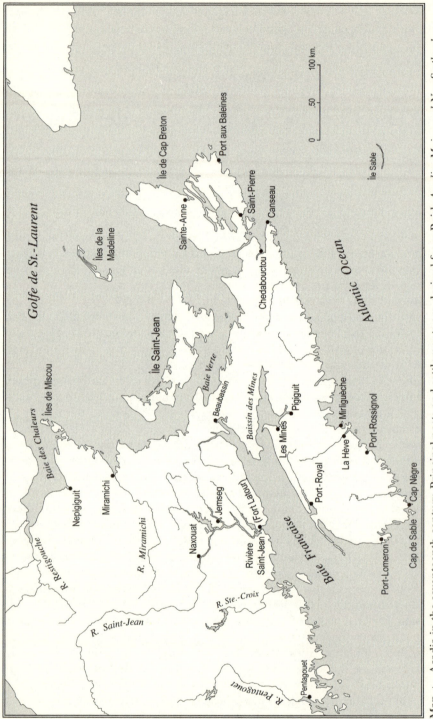

Map 4   Acadia in the seventeenth century. Principal posts and settlements are derived from Reid, *Acadia, Maine and New Scotland*.

cent of the population was still engaged in agriculture.[3] Yet, long before the seventeenth century, external trade had been much more important to England than it was to France, though it was centred upon European countries, Russia, the Mediterranean, and the Far East rather than North America. The West Indies gained considerable importance by the middle of the seventeenth century,[4] and the English colonies in North America were of more significance to Oliver Cromwell and his government than Acadia and New France were to Louis XIV and his counsellors. Permanent immigration to North America was, both proportionately and in round numbers, much greater from the British Isles than from France. By 1650, when the population of England and Wales was between five and six million,[5] the British population of North America was over 50,000. By that date, too, Massachusetts had emerged as a significant partner in the development of England's lucrative transatlantic trade. This has been described as "a polygon formed by lines drawn between port towns in the British Isles, Newfoundland, the American mainland, the West Indies, the Wine Islands [Canaries], and the continent of Europe. Outward from the larger ports in the British Isles flowed shipping, manufactures, and investments in colonial property, the enhanced value of which returned as colonial products to be sold at home or abroad."[6] Nevertheless, the impact of imperial questions on Cromwell's government still took second place to matters relating to Scotland, Ireland, and Wales.[7]

The English attack on Acadia in 1654 was not the result of any carefully planned policy on the part of London but an initiative taken by the leader of expedition, Robert Sedgwick. That year, England and France were at peace with one another. In 1652 France had recognized the protectorate of Cromwell and the commonwealth government, and, within three years, the two countries would be allies against Spain. Since 1652, however, England had been at war with the Dutch. Hostilities between these two countries had broken out that year, partly because of trade rivalry and partly from the sheer exasperation of each country with the other.[8] In particular, the English complained that the Dutch refused to acknowledge the English mastery of the seas in order to obtain control of the North Sea fisheries. Further, it was contended that the Dutch had decided to challenge the Navigation Act of 1651, which forbade the importation into the British Isles of "the produce of Asia, Africa, and America except in British ships or those belonging to the plantations, and required that majority of the crews should be the subject of the Commonwealth."[9]

Sedgwick arrived in London sometime in 1653. He had originally migrated to Massachusetts in 1636, at the age of twenty-five, and had become both a successful merchant and an active member of his church. He had been chosen the major-general of the colony, thus the man in charge of the colonial militia, in 1652. He resigned the post the following year, however, partly because he wished to go to London. At that time he had major interests in the New England fisheries[10] and was heavily involved in the trade between London, Boston, and either the Azores or Spain. By the late 1640s, his ships brought manufactured goods to Massachusetts and then took fish to either Spain or the Wine Islands and semi-tropical products back to London.[11] His visit to London resulted in his return to Massachusetts with a military commission from Oliver Cromwell to attack New Netherlands.[12]

Sedgwick was given charge of three ships, the *Augustine,* the *Church,* and the *Hope,*[13] with his son-in-law, John Leverett, a distinguished veteran of the parliamentary army and an important political figure in Massachusetts,[14] as second-in-command. They had barely arrived in back in Boston, in early June 1654, when word was received that peace had been negotiated between England and Holland. Sedgwick, with Leverett's support, decided to take advantage of the vague instruction at the end of Cromwell's commission which stated that, once the foray against the Dutch had been successfully concluded, "if tyme permitt and opertunitye be presented, you are to proseed to the gaineing in any other places from the Enemie who upon advise with a counsell of warr may be judged feizeable and conduceing to the settlement of the peace and saiftye of the English plantations." It seems clear that, for Sedgwick, "the Enemie" were French ships, possibly pirates, and he decided to "spend a lyttle time in ranging the coast against the French, who use tradeinge and fishinge hereabouts."[15] Meanwhile, Leverett would remain in Boston to arrange a cargo of masts in order that the ships need not return to London in ballast. When the small fleet sailed out of Boston, at least one of the captains considered that its aims were strictly limited, the intention being only to take the time "we are forced to stay for our masts,"[16] perhaps two months in all.

Once arrived at the mouth of the Saint John River, in the second week of July 1654, Sedgwick proceeded to take full advantage of the quarrels between Le Borgne and La Tour. The former had returned to France in late 1653, but it was only to register Jeanne Motin's acknowledgment of debt and to reprovision his ship, the *Chateaufort.* By the late spring of 1654, Le Borgne was again at Port Royal, with considerable provisions, merchandise worth 75,000 *livres,* and a force of more than a hundred men.[17] His intention was, in the words of Nicolas Denys, to make good his claim "to be the Seignior of all the Country as creditor of Sieur d'Aulnay."[18] Le Borgne hoped to establish a de facto control of the colony, since he had no authority from France for any such political pretensions, by capturing La Tour's establishment, Fort Sainte-Marie, on the Saint John. But when he arrived there, La Tour was strong enough to repel him, having a force of seventy men and seventeen pieces of ordnance.[19] On 13 July, Le Borgne left to regroup at Port Royal. The next day, Sedgwick began a siege which led a few days later to La Tour's surrender and the capture of a "considerable quantitie of moose skins."[20] La Tour's descendants would claim, in 1701, that Sedgwick had plundered their ancestor to the tune of 200,000 *livres.*[21] Sedgwick then went on to Port Royal, where, after a brief skirmish,

Le Borgne surrendered on 8 August. On 2 September, Pentagöuet was also captured, Sedgwick remarking that it was "a small Fort, yet very strong and a very well composed peece with eight peece of Ordnance one brass, three murthers, about eighteen Barrels of powder, and eighteen men in garrison."[22]

Success required terms of surrender and Sedgwick came to different arrangements with each of the captured forces. La Tour managed to negotiate some freedom of movement, and before the year's end, had arrived in London to present his case. At Pentagöuet, there was no one of rank and importance for Sedgwick to consider. He left a small garrison there but allowed Peter Crushett, who had managed the collection of furs in the region for d'Aulnay, to remain in charge of that operation.[23] At Port Royal, the situation demanded much more political subtlety than had been the case at La Tour's fort or at Pentagöuet. The military surrender was the same accorded La Tour. The commander, La Verdure, and his "soldiers and domestics" were also allowed to "leave the fort with their arms, drums beating, flags displayed, fusil on shoulder ..."[24]

There were at least three major issues requiring attention now that Sedgwick had established his control over the most populous community in the colony. Two of these were closely interrelated and had implications for future trading relations between Massachusetts and Acadia, should Sedgwick's conquests not be confirmed by an international agreement: What was to be the fate of Le Borgne, who was present at Port Royal, with no official authority but an obvious financial interest in Acadian affairs? And, similarly, what was to happen with d'Aulnay's children, some, if not all, of whom were still resident in the fort? Le Borgne received kid-glove treatment, so good, in fact, that there were murmurs that he had made some sort of secret deal with Sedgwick.[25] Le Borgne was allowed to return to France in the *Chateaufort* but required to leave his eldest son, Emmanuel Le Borgne Du Coudray, behind as a token of good faith. The children of d'Aulnay were guaranteed their property – furniture, buildings, and cattle – although what this actually meant would become a matter of much debate. Nicolas Denys reported that these youngsters (it is unclear how many were then at Port Royal) took shelter with him in 1655.[26] That left the question of the settlers and the missionaries. This was a matter of discussion, if not outright negotiation, between Sedgwick, Le Borgne, the Capucin Léonard de Chartres, and two of the leading settlers. Both settlers and missionaries were offered a choice, depending on whether they wished to remain in Acadia or to return to France. If the settlers chose the former, they were granted freedom of conscience and the right to remain in their own homes, with whatever possessions they held, on the condition that they recognized whatever seigneurial obligations they owed. Otherwise, should they wish to return to France, they would be provided with passage at their expense and they would have with the right to sell whatever they wished of their property, providing it was to people who would remain in the colony. These same articles stated that there would be no compensation for cattle that had already been requisitioned by the soldiery. As to the priests, they also would be given passage to France should they wish; otherwise they might remain, providing they did not settle within two or three leagues of the fort itself. These terms and conditions were signed by six people, who were, in order of their signatures on the document, Jacques Bourgeois, Robert Sedgwick, Robert Salem, Mark Harrison, Richard Mors, Emmanuel Le Borgne, Guillaume Troum, and Father Léonard de Chartres.[27] Bourgeois and Troum (more commonly Trahan) were related by marriage and both would establish their families in the colony. Guillaume Trahan had arrived in Acadia as an associate of Charles d'Aulnay, on board the *Saint Jehan*. He was then in his mid-twenties and was accompanied by his first wife and his daughter, Jeanne. Jacques Bourgeois was some years younger than Trahan, having been born around 1619. He was a surgeon and arrived in 1641 on board the *Saint-François*. Sometime during the next two or three years, he married Jeanne Trahan, with whom he would have ten children.[28]

On one copy of the documents, Trahan is referred to as a "sindic."[29] This position was a long-standing institution of French civic government but in spite of, or perhaps, because of this heritage, its attributes changed, according to time and place. By the sixteenth century, syndics were basically people elected by their local community, for a limited period, to take care of some matter that demanded both time and attention.[30] In many respects, the position was that of secular churchwarden. Marcel Marion, the authority on French seventeenth-century institutions, wrote that it was a position that was neither agreeable nor profitable.[31] It was, however, an important element in the development of village politics since it was a definite counterbalance to the influence of the outside authority, whether local seigneur, churchman, or royal official. The position was established by 1647 in Montreal, Trois-Rivières, and Quebec.[32] Trahan's signature on the agreement, together with that of Jacques Bourgeois, is an indication of the extent to which the settlers were regarded as something more than colonists with no political identity, under the absolute control of officials dispatched from France.

Thus, the agreement brought together the views of the colonial administrator, merchant adventurer, missionary, and settler. While his was the position of immediate, military strength, Sedgwick was well aware that what was behind him was not the colony of Massachusetts but the politics of an imperial power, and those none too clearly expressed. As later correspondence by him and his son-in-law makes clear, Sedgwick had stretched Cromwell's commission to its limits.[33] Indeed, when Sedgwick returned to Boston, the General Court of Massachusetts ordered him to explain "by what authority or Commission, of which they are yet altogether ignorant, they have surprised the ffrench and possess'd their forts."[34] After all, the commonwealth had just annexed Maine and further expansion was not an immediate priority. As well, in March 1651 Massachusetts authorities had been at considerable pains to emphasize, in a letter to Jeanne Motin, then the widow of d'Aulnay, that they neither knew nor intended "anything but all neighbourly, loving and friendly compliance with you, unless ought shall proceed from yourselves towards us contrary thereto."[35] While French activity in Acadia was always of concern to Massachusetts, at this point the commonwealth was much more interested in peaceful conditions for trade, both in terms of supplies for the settlers and for goods for the fur trade. Sedgwick's answer to his questioners was the declaration of his accomplishment, rather than any argued reply. He had gained, first, the recognition of military control over French-claimed territories, from the La Hève to Pentagöuet. This implied, secondly, the right to pursue the fur trade both from Pentagöuet and on the Saint John River. Thirdly, these terms meant the recognition of some level of English authority over the most populous settlement of the colony. Sedgwick did not achieve control of anything much farther east and his command over the La Hève area would be challenged within two years. Nicolas Denys was left, more or less untroubled, both at Saint-Pierre and along the Atlantic coast.

Emmanuel Le Borgne, for his part, managed to return to France with most of his men and his ship, and with his major rivals for the French development of the colony, Jeanne Motin and Charles de La Tour, apparently vanquished. Given that his position was only that of a creditor, albeit one recognized in France as implying certain legal claims to d'Aulnay estates, this was no mean achievement. The position of the Capucins was less clear-cut. Most accounts of the battle for Port Royal speak of the destruction of the church and monastery. There was certainly no attempt made to ensure that the institutions of Catholicism should be protected. The provision that no priest should live within three miles of the settlement seems both a recognition by Sedgwick of the impossibility of preventing missionary activity among the Mi'kmaq and a wish to diminish the influence of Catholicism within Port Royal. At the same time, the provision that the settlers should have "liberty of conscience" argues that conversion was not a major priority for Sedgwick.

We have no records of what the settlers thought either about the defeat of French arms in general or about the curtailment of religious life in particular. They were used to life in which pitched battles between rivals over land rights and the fur trade were commonplace, if not everyday, occurrences. While few in number, most of the settlers had established families. Now that the fighting was over, they were officially guaranteed the ownership of their property, both land and moveable possessions, with the sole restrictions being on its resale. Further, there was no attempt to interfere with the conditions on which they held their land, and it was specifically stated that their tenure should continue as it had in the past and that, where appropriate, they should fulfil their "seigneurial dues for which they are obliged [by the terms] of their grants."[36]

We have little idea what these duties were because there are no surviving written records from this period detailing such matters. In theory, the settlers established at Port Royal would have paid the *cens* on receiving the land from either d'Aulnay or La Tour. This was a token sum, probably no more than a *denier* an acre, and was a recognition that the title to the land still rested, to a limited extent, in the hands of the person who granted it to the inhabitant. The settlers would also have been liable for the *rente*, usually an annual payment, a combination of money and kind, and for the *banalités*, charges made for the use of the mill and any other common services the seigneur provided for the community. The other main obligation that was levied, in most seigneuries along the St Lawrence, was the *lod et ventes*, sums approximating a twelfth of the sale price, and was paid when land was sold outside the line of direct succession.[37] In circumstances where settlers were at a premium and seigneurs were more interested in the fur trade than in agriculture, neither d'Aulnay nor La Tour seem to have made any serious efforts to collect monies from those they had helped settle.

What is clear from these terms is that, as far as Sedgwick was concerned, military control would not necessarily imply major alterations in the civil affairs of the settlers. This decision was the easier to make because of the colony's small population. While we have no reliable population data for 1654, it is plain, both from the evidence in the papers of d'Aulnay, Denys, Le Borgne, and La Tour and from a census taken sixteen years later, that European settlers in the colony then numbered between 250 and 300. This figure would translate into roughly a hundred or so adults.[38] Such a number, especially if it was made up of smalll groups only loosely connected and in process of growing, would obviously benefit from clear norms of political and legal behaviour. However, such a small population would find it easy enough to rely on oral traditions and the customs that had evolved over the past twenty years. At any rate, the settlers did not face a major challenge from the imposition of New England practices. The Massachusetts system of distributing ownership of land, on terms of free tenure, through the authority of the General Court, was not brought into operation. Such a profound change would have meant a deliberate choice of some form of government that granted political rights to the settlers within English law, rather than an interpretation of their rights from French law. Given the variation of government within the English colonial system in North America and the tensions between the various regimes, it is likely that Sedgwick decided to postpone a consideration of change until English settlers should arrive. The policy he pursued meant that Port Royal faced no immediate reorganization of either landholding conventions or political institutions at this time. Nevertheless, the fact that there would be no attempt whatsoever either to reinforce French customs or to introduce English practices meant that Acadian land tenure began to resemble the traditional English freehold system rather than a seigneurial system.

As far as the general political situation of the colony was concerned, what was at work, in the agreement by all parties to these terms, was the tension between the politics of a region and the interests of empires, mediated by the presence of men well aware of the realities of both. On the one hand, there was the knowledge and interests of those whose lives were bound up in the political geography of the region, what John Reid has described as that of the northeastern maritime colonies established in North America by Europeans.[39] On the other hand, there was the fact that, behind such local concerns was the reality of European state power. "Acadia or Nova Scotia" was in process of becoming what J.B. Brebner would describe as "a continental cornice ... the eastern outpost and flank for both French and English in North America."[40] Sedgwick's raid and its aftermath confirmed Acadia's place in the political geography of North America as a border colony between two great empires. It was of only occasional importance to either, but the fortunes of its communities were as much subject to the sudden shifts of European diplomacy as they were to the dictates of the specific regional politics. In the mid-1650s, however, it was as much the influence of particular individuals as the designs of greater political entities that determined the course of events both in, and for, the colony. Neither La Tour nor Le Borgne were about to concede Sedgwick the last word, for both men had considerable financial interests bound up in the future of the region. La Tour sought redress in London and Le Borgne gathered support in France. For the next fourteen years, the actions of these men and their associates had a major influence on Acadian development.

La Tour's arrival in London was reported to Mazarin by the French ambassador, Antoine de Bordeaux, on the last day of December 1654.[41] In his letter, Bordeaux referred to La Tour as "the Governor of the forts which the English have taken"[42] and considered that their restoration to French control would be swift and easy. In this he was much mistaken, and part of his error arose from a lack of appreciation of the impact of Massachusetts interests on English policy. The relationship between Massachusetts and the English authorities differed in three major ways from that of the French authorities and their North American colonies. First, as has already been noted, the settler population of Massachusetts was already large: somewhere around 20,000 by 1654.[43] Secondly, New England in general, and Boston in particular, had begun to supply England with tar, timber, and turpentine, essentials for the maintenance of a navy, whether merchant ships or men-of-war.[44] Further, many successful New Englanders had crossed to England to fight with Cromwell in the 1640s and later occupied high positions in his government.[45] This meant not only a considerable understanding of the interests of Massachusetts among Cromwell's advisers but an informed knowledge of the needs of the colony. It is thus not surprising that when La Tour presented his claim for powers of government and trade in the "region of Nova Scotia, on the basis of the baronetcies conferred upon himself and his father," the question was considered in the light of representations made by Massachusetts.

These were brought forward by Leverett, who had been appointed the agent for Massachusetts in London in November 1655, with instructions to protect the colony's interests "before the Lord Protector and his honorable council in England."[46] Additionally, should Cromwell show "propensities ... to gratifie New England," Leverett was enjoined to "improve your best interest and opportunitie for the obtayning thereof, provided they be free from charges and other ingagements."[47] There was sufficient tension between London and Boston over how far Massachusetts could act independently of England to make the former consider at length and, in the end, to turn down the proposition.[48] La Tour's rights were recognized but only on the condition that he pay his New England creditors. His debts were considerable, including more than £3,000 to the widow of Marie Gibbons and more than £4,000 to Joshua Scottow, his agent in Boston,[49] but he was able to discharge his obligations by going into partnership with Thomas Temple and William Crowne. Temple, then in his forties, was the nephew of William Fiennes, the Viscount Saye and Sele, who was member of Cromwell's Council of State. He was suspected of being a Royalist while his uncle was a long-time opponent of the Stuarts.[50] It was Fiennes who brought La Tour and Temple together and arranged their meeting with Thomas Crowne, who had allied himself with the parliamentary cause in 1641. Some scholars have considered Crowne as above all a merchant though most emphasize his service to the Earl of Arundel and his election to the House of Commons.[51] The salient fact about him was his wealth, for not only were there La Tour's debts to be taken into account in the disposition of Nova Scotia but Leverett was pressing for the unpaid balance of the expenses he had incurred for Sedgwick's expedition, amounting to more than £4,000.[52]

The solution arrived at included, first, the recognition of La Tour's claim, which allowed the English government to reinforce its title to the area. The French did not accept this but agreed that the final disposition of "the Acadian forts" should be settled after a report by special commissioners.[53] Secondly, on 9 August 1656, a patent issued to La Tour, Temple, and Crowne granted them "the country and territory called Acadie, and part of the country called Nova Scotia ... from Merliguesche on the Eastorn coast ... as far as Pentagoet ... and within the lands along the said coast to one hundred leagues in depth."[54] On 17 September 1656 letters were dispatched to Leverett informing him that Thomas Temple was to be governor of the forts of Acadia and that he was to have delivered to him "on his arrival in Acadie, commonly called Nova Scotia, possession of the forts of St. John and Pentagoet, with the magazines, powder, vessels ammunition, etc."[55] Within the week, on 20 September 1656, La Tour signed a contract with Temple and Crowne, ceding all his rights and interests in Nova Scotia, excluding those previously granted to Amand Lalloue,[56] in exchange for the immediate payment of the claims of Marie Gibbons and the future payment of 5 per cent of the profits from the fur trade, agriculture, and mines within the colony.[57]

La Tour had spent his adult life in Acadia. He now retired there, his debts paid, and lived with his increasing family until his death in 1663. Temple seems to have paid monies regularly to Joshua Scottow. As well, the family traded furs independently, Madame La Tour sending a "scroll" of Beaver skins, weighing about eighteen pounds, to Scottow in 1657.[58] It is probable, given the status of Jeanne Motin, that the Motin-La Tour family lived in the accommodation in Port Royal that d'Aulnay had built. Scottow corresponded with both husband and wife and sent letters and supplies to them. The goods ordered between 1657 and 1660 argue a fair standard of living for the Motin-La Tour family, whether the household included some of the Motin-d'Aulnay children or only the five Motin-La Tour children. Some of the objects purchased, such as the "6 looking glasses" or the "two dozen knives," were likely for trade. The household also imported a fair amount of food, including flour, bread, butter, peas, and pork as well as wine and rum. The following year, 1659, the list was longer. As well as the above provisions, it included salt, a bushel of "Indian corn," a runlet of vinegar, and three jars of oil. Tobacco was ordered annually, white sugar less frequently. Luxuries on the list included twenty stone of prunes and eight stone of raisins. The following year, 1660, a quarter of a pound of nutmeg was added. Each year, nails, powder and shot, knives, and fish-hooks were ordered as well as pots and pans. Clothing was bought, on one occasion four pairs of children's shoes and on another a yard of silk. Woolen cloth, canvas, ribbons, and buttons appear annually and now again stockings and combs.[59]

These accounts give only a glimpse of the lifestyle of one of Port Royal's more prominent settlers, a lifestyle that was not typical of the average colonist. But the accounts also show that the inhabitants of Port Royal obtained goods from Boston easily enough and that frontier living had some possibility of both leisure and comfort. The back-breaking toil of clearing land, farming, and household work could be mitigated for those who had money. The purchase of a fair amount of meat, bread, and flour outside the colony suggests either an unwillingness on the part of the local populace to sell their surplus to their neighbours or the lack of same. There is not really a sufficiency of evidence to decide the matter.

On 6 November 1663 a certain Michel Dantez wrote to Colbert that he had recently returned from a voyage that had taken him to Newfoundland and to New England, "where I learnt of the death of Monsieur de la Tour, formerly King's lieutenant in this country."[60] *Plus ça change, plus c'est la même chose*: over the next fifteen or so years, France continued to claim sovereignty over the area, and there continued to be pitched battles among rival claimants for the control of the Acadian fur trade. The permanent communities of European settlers developed slowly, while itinerant soldiers and traders from that continent were more than common in the region. France continued to press for rights to ownership of the territory through diplomatic channels and the Le Borgne family continued to dispatch armed expeditions to enforce their trading claims. England's interests were of minor concern in London but a matter of considerable attention and concern for merchants and policy makers in Boston. The Mi'kmaq continued to participate in the fur trade and to develop links with the newcomers.[61] Towards the end of November 1657, the Compagnie des Cents-Associés granted to Le Borgne the area from the Sainte-Marie River, on the far eastern tip of the peninsula, to the Maine border, explicitly excluding previous grants to La Tour and Nicolas Denys,[62] and taking for granted that the Maine border was along the St George River.[63] At much the same time, on 10 December 1657, the French government revoked the patents to La Tour and appointed Emmanuel Le Borgne as "gouverneur en Acadie," with the usual lack of precision as to borders and plenipotentiary powers. Within the year, in November 1658, the French ambassador delivered a strongly worded complaint to the English government to the effect that the English had attacked Port Royal, Saint John, and Pentagöuet, burned the church, and committed other damage.[64] These actions demonstrated that, in the eyes of France, the results of Sedgwick's raid had yet to be determined and that, while La Tour's rights were not fully abrogated, nor his arrangements with Temple disputed, there still remained a French colony south of the Gaspé peninsula.

Both Le Borgne and Temple were primarily interested in the fur trade, Le Borgne in order to recoup and develop the investments he had by way of loans to d'Aulnay, Temple in order to establish a personal fortune. The same year, 1657, that Le Borgne received official recognition for his Acadian ambitions from the French government, Temple arrived in Boston on board a borrowed naval vessel, the *Sparrow*, armed and provisioned.[65] His partner, William Crowne, arrived shortly afterwards and the two joined forces with three Boston merchants, Thomas Breedon, Hezekiah Usher, and Thomas Lake, to exploit the Nova Scotia fur trade.[66] That trade's profits, however much they were squandered in lawsuits, paid enough of both principal and interest to keep investors interested in funding ventures in Acadia. The reputation of its value was part of the reason that Temple was willing to buy La Tour's rights, for an outlay of 52,000 *livres*, at a time when the average wage for an established craftsman was 80 *livres* a year.[67]

The Acadian fur trade was one of the major reasons why Europeans came to the area between 1604 and 1672, and its profits covered the costs of transportation of those few people intending to settle, their immediate provisioning, and trade goods for the Mi'kmaq. Even after that date, the year in which direct action by the French government meant greater support for the settlement in the colony, the fur trade continued to be of considerable importance for both Acadians and Mi'kmaq. Relatively little work has been done on the specific accounts for ships taking goods and people directly to Acadia, rather than to the St Lawrence. It seems clear, however, that there was not much difference in cost of passage, for both provisions and passengers, between the two destinations.[68] Trudel has estimated that it cost between 66 and 80 *livres* for a transatlantic passage in 1653, 75 *livres* in 1655 and 1658, 91 *livres* in 1661, and 108 *livres* in 1662.[69] The cost of moving goods was similar: 60 *livres* per ton for passage east to west, and 50 *livres* for the return journey. If the profit from goods, in both directions, was considerable, so was the outlay needed to finance the movement of the migrants and the goods. The cost of credit was another variable: it ran somewhere between 22 per cent and 30 per cent per annum for most of the century.[70] Even Nicolas Denys, although he financed some of his endeavours through the fisheries, depended on the fur trade, and it was the financial backbone of the activities of both La Tour and d'Aulnay.

The native peoples were, of course, crucial for the fur trade, and in this regard the colony continued to be blessed. Not only did Acadian-Mi'kmaq relations remain peaceful, but rivalries between the native groups themselves never spilled over into full-scale war. The fighting that did occur during these years was both brief and localized. It has been suggested that, during the sixteenth century, the Mi'kmaq had developed communication and trading networks with other peoples in the hinterland and so had sufficient prestige and power to play an effective role as middlemen in the seventeenth century.[71] Be this as it may, because there was no major dissension among the native peoples in the area at the time of the Europeans' arrival, the newcomers were not entangled in local wars.

The battle for control of the fur trade between Temple and the Le Borgne family erupted quickly, once they had had their ventures blessed by their respective European governments. In early May 1658 the latter set out to repossess La Hève. The expedition was masterminded by Emmanuel Le Borgne's eldest son, Emmanuel Le Borgne Du Coudray, and led by his second son, Alexandre Le Borgne, then no more than eighteen, with further backing by a merchant from Bordeaux named Guilbaut. It arrived off La Hève in early summer 1658[72] and captured stores and pelts stored there to the value of some £2,000.[73] Temple took effective counter-measures: Le Borgne and company were captured and taken to Boston, and spent some time in prison both there and in London.[74] The following year, another attack from the Le Borgne family was also beaten back but such skirmishes occurred most years until Acadia was, once again, considered part of the French empire.[75] Yet, despite these difficulties, as well as his own inexperience in colonial ventures and lack of knowledge of Boston business practices, Temple was able to profit from Nova Scotia. He might often have been in debt but the cash flow of trade, in furs and provisions, allowed him to keep his creditors at bay between 1658 and 1667, whether in Boston or in London.[76] His annual receipts from Acadia were sufficient for him to live well and continue to pursue his fortunes there. While he complained that his net income from Nova Scotia never amounted to more than £120 a year, as George Rawlyk has pointed out, Temple "was able to accumulate a great deal of valuable property in Boston and along the Kennebec River."[77]

Throughout the period in which he held the colony for the English, Temple was plagued by competition, in much the same way as La Tour had been encumbered with the claims of d'Aulnay and Le Borgne. Partnerships, such as that established with Thomas Breedon, a Boston merchant, ended in litigation. Breedon, who had arrived in Boston in 1648, was primarily interested in the acquisition of wealth and a return in style to the land of his birth. He seems to have had few, if any, religious convictions.[78] He acted as Temple's mentor in Boston society and was his banker, business manager, and general contractor. Another challenge came from Thomas Elliott, a member of the court of Charles II, who began to take an interest in the colony at the time of the Restoration.[79] His case was based upon nothing more than court politics. The repudiation of the grants given by the Cromwell's government led to a general scramble for preferment by those now in power. Elliott managed to gain title to the governorship of Acadia but Temple retrieved his position by agreeing to pay Elliott £600 pounds a year.[80] The Kirke family, associated with the efforts of the Alexanders in the 1620s, also advanced claims.[81] By 1662, however, Temple had managed to consolidate his position as the appointed English authority for Acadia, albeit at some financial cost, and had been granted a knight baronetcy.[82]

But all these political hassles did not mean the end of French activity in the area nor the establishment of English settlers there. Temple concentrated his efforts on the area from Merligueche to Pentagöuet, including the development of the trading posts on the Saint John River and the exploitation of Port Royal. He certainly made continuous efforts to discourage the activities of the Le Borgne family along the coastline adjacent to La Hève, but the very fact that these efforts had to be continuous is an indication of their lack of success. He attempted to tax French fishing vessels around Merligueche and Port Rossignol, at a rate of 10 per cent of their catch.[83] This, of course, implied the presence of something taxable. But Temple never really made any attempt to extend his authority to the land beyond Merligueche and left Nicolas Denys undisturbed. The latter had received, on 1 January 1654, a wide-ranging grant as "Governor and Lieutenant-General" over "the coast and islands" from the Gaspé to Canso and with fishing rights "as far as Virginia."[84] Denys never attempted to carry his ambitions southwards but he and his family continued to develop his establishments at Saint-Pierre and Nipisiguit (present-day Bathurst, N.B.), making a living by fur trading, fishing, and some lumbering. He managed to establish a few settlers, perhaps some seven families in all. The extent of his grants were contested both by the reality of English occupation, south of Merligueche, and by expeditions that arrived from closer to home, sent out by competitors from Dieppe and Honfleur. Inevitably, there was also a challenge from the indefatigable Le Borgne family. They made an appearance in 1658, claiming fishing rights at Canso.[85] Another couple of adventurers, A.M. de Canger and Charles Baye de La Giraudière, attempted to establish an inshore fishery at Chedabouctou, probably in early 1660. This expedition had been well financed, for Denys reported that La Giraudiere had built on St Mary's River a fortified house "with two pieces of brass cannon and some swivel guns."[86] It entangled Denys in litigation but matters were settled in his favour in 1667.[87] In 1663 François Doublet, a Norman who became involved in trade along the St Lawrence in 1659, managed to acquire the right to exploit the Îles-de-la Madeleine and Île Saint-Jean (Prince Edward Island).[88] Doublet visited Denys and outlined his plans. The latter accurately predicted failure for these projects within three years.

These ventures, and one or two others that were even more ephemeral, were attempts to establish settlement based on the development of inshore fishing as well as the fur trade. They failed to flourish for any length of time, to some extent because they were made up, almost exclusively, of men with little interest in permanent migration. Denys owed at least part of his success to his wife, Margeurite Lafitte. We know almost nothing about her except that she was the daughter of a Bordeaux merchant and they were married in La Rochelle in 1642.[89] They seem to have had three children, one son, Richard, and two daughters. Richard was born at Saint-Pierre, probably in 1654. He spent his life along the shores of Cape Breton Island and present-day New Brunswick.[90] That Nicolas Denys was able to keep two widely separated posts, Saint-Pierre and Nipisiguit, in operation was due, in large measure, to the fact that he was a permanent, if peripatetic, resident. While the raids and skirmishes by d'Aulnay and Le Borgne meant that Denys often lost the furs at one of his posts, he was always able to replace them with those stored at the other. On his fairly frequent voyages to France, needed to ensure that his rights were recognized by successive generations of French officials, Denys left his wife to manage his affairs. He and his family developed cordial relations with the Mi'kmaq and his son married Anne Parabego, herself a Mi'kmaq, in 1681.[91]

Thus the continuing interests of the French, whether the relatively distant activities of Denys or the projects of the Le Borgnes, were the unchanging context for Temple's endeavours. Further, Temple showed no real interest in establishing an English settlement. He put his energies and those of his partners into the development of the fur trade, making Pentagöuet his main establishment but also repairing La Tour's old fort at the mouth of the Saint John and establishing another upriver at Jemseg. These posts were staffed solely by men, recruited, as far as is known, in Massachusetts. The relative closeness of large communities, such as Boston, meant that it was possible for men to be recruited for relatively short periods of time. Temple might have taken steps to encourage English-speaking migrants but in 1666 war broke out again between the English and the

Dutch. Once more, the hostilities quickly involved the English with the French. While the fighting was confined to Europe and the West Indies, Massachusetts shipping, especially that engaged in trade with Nova Scotia, faced increased activity from French privateers. The Treaty of Breda brought matters to an end in 1667 but its terms spelled ruin for Temple. The peace that was signed on 21 July had, as one of its principles, the surrender of conquests. France restored to the British St Christopher's, Antigua, and Montserrat; England, Acadia to France.[92] On 17 February 1667/68[93] Charles II issued letters patent for the return of all Acadia to France, naming specifically "the forts and habitations of Pentagoet, St. John, Port Royal and Cape Sable."[94]

This exchange was bitterly resented in Massachusetts and tenaciously fought by Temple, so that although the agreement was signed in 1667, the actual handover of the colony did not take place until nearly three years later. When it became plain in Boston that Acadia would definitely be returned to France, the General Court sent a strongly worded remonstrance to London. It was pointed out that "should the French have that country it would not only obstruct the trade of peltry, but of fishing which is most considerable." Further, such an accommodation would mean "a reviving of the French King's withering interest in North America, but a very large augmentation of advantage to their settlement at Kebeck."[95] Temple's strategy, while much more subtle, was equally fruitless and laid the groundwork for considerable international wrangling in the eighteenth century. In a letter to the Privy Council of November 1668, he argued that Pentagöuet really belonged to New Plymouth and that "Acadia is but a Small part of the country of Nova Scotia."[96] The view found some support in London[97] and would be argued strongly by the French after 1713, when the question as to what the boundaries of Acadia were became of major strategic importance. However, this opinion was not seriously pursued and in August 1669 a sharp order was sent to Temple, ordering him to comply with the terms of the peace treaty and deliver the colony to the French.[98] The following year, Hector d'Andigné de Grandfontaine arrived in Boston on board the *Saint Sebastien*, armed with copies of the orders sent by Charles II as well as a commission from Louis XIV, dated 22 July 1669, empowering him to take possession of Acadia.[99] On 7 July 1670 Temple finally wrote to Richard Walker, whom he addressed as "captain Walker, my deputy governor of the said parts, actually upon the place."[100] Temple signed this missive as "Sir Thomas Temple, knight baronet, lieutenant for his majesty of Great Britain, of the countries of Nova Scotia and Acadie." In it he directed Walker and all other officers to deliver "Acadie and the forts of Pentagoet, St. John, Port Royal, Laheve and Cape Sable to M. Grandfontaine, the representative of His Most Christian Majesty, Louis XIV."[101] Temple and Grandfontaine had also reached an accord whereby the former was granted permission to remove both material – "shallops, merchandise and trade goods, livestock and furs" – and men from the colony.[102]

Hector d'Andigné de Grandfontaine was forty-three years old when he was named governor of Acadia and had served with the Carignan-Salières regiment at Quebec since 1665.[103] Armed with Temple's directive, he left Boston for Pentagöuet. There, on 5 August 1670, he took possession of a well-built fort of stone, which enclosed barracks, a storehouse, a guard-house, central dwelling quarters, and a chapel.[104] Having been instructed to make Pentagöuet his headquarters, in order to establish the boundary as effectively as possible, Grandfontaine settled in. He sent his second-in command, Pierre de Joybert de Soulanges et de Marson, to oversee the sur-render of the other posts. He, too, was a member of the Carignan-Salières regiment and had served with Grandfontaine at Quebec.[105] On 27 August 1670 the surrender of "fort Gemisick, on the Saint John river" took place. This wooden building had been established by Temple more than ten years earlier. It was "forty paces long by 30 wide, enclosed all round by new stakes of 18 feet high." Inside these walls there was "a house 20 paces by 10, two chimnies and two sheds, a forge, a ton of coals, a table with draw-ers , and two wooden chairs." As well, there was a storehouse, which had a large closet for goods and four mounted iron guns.[106] On 2 September 1670 the surrender of Port Royal took place, an announcement to that effect being made "publicly and aloud, in the presence of all the inhabi-tants, assembled for that purpose."[107] Joybert also took charge of La Hève and Fort La Tour but there are no surviving accounts of these actions.

The arrival of Grandfontaine, with some forty soldiers, thirteen officers, and eight aspiring colonists, marked a new era for Acadia. In the orders Grandfontaine had received on his appointment, he was commanded to send a detailed description of the state of the colony to France, including a census of the buildings and their state of repair, the number of settlers, and their pursuits.[108] Requests for such reports were typical of French sev-enteenth-century bureaucracy.[109] It is interesting that no request was made for information regarding the seigneurial grants per se, since the registering of landholdings with government authorities is one of the fun-damental legal functions of a state. Grandfontaine's report, which he duti-fully had compiled, has been the foundation of most writing about what Acadia was like in 1671.[110] The survey was brought together by a Recollet, Laurent Molin, and included information about Pentagöuet gathered by the engineer Hugues Randin.[111] There is general agreement that it erred by omission, though probably not by commission. As A.H. Clark wrote, "the census was most nearly complete in the Port Royal area; it clearly was both incomplete and ambiguous in the outlying settlements." Robert Rumilly has also pointed out several specific omissions, including mem-bers of both the La Tour and Le Borgne families who were known to be in Port Royal at that time.[112] It is not surprising that the census is probably correct in those it lists but does not include all who were in the colony. Census takers were viewed with considerable suspicion in the seventeenth century. Most Europeans were convinced that if someone wanted to know details about your family, land, houses, and other possessions, the information would, almost certainly, result in more taxes or the imposition of some other irksome obligation. As well, the settlers in Acadia had had remarkably little interference from outside authority during the past thirty years and had little taste for officials of any stripe. At the close of his report, Molin wrote that Pierre Melanson refused to give either his age or details about his cattle and landholdings and that his wife asked him "whether I was mad, to run about the streets on such a matter."[113] Two other families, that of Estienne Robichaut and Pierre Lanoue, were equally uncooperative.

While statistical data had begun to be valued in seventeenth-century Europe, its compilation was often haphazard, subject to the whims of the people who gathered it. Molin's census of the Acadian colony is clearly the product of an age much less interested in, and knowledgeable about, statistics than late-twentieth-century Western society. Without confirmation from parish registers, the ages given cannot be relied upon as being much more than approximate. Even the overall summaries of information appended to the report by its author are sometimes incorrect. Further, the small size of the population recorded makes much statistical analysis, such as average age of marriage, of family size, and so on, impossible. Whatever its shortcomings, however, this first survey of Acadia provides provide a great deal of information about the texture of the community life of those whose descendants, traced through the male line, make up two-thirds of those who identify themselves as Acadian more than three centuries later.[114]

Molin recorded a total of 302 men, women, and children of European descent, living in six different locations. The numbers given for amount of land cleared and cattle, sheep, goats, and pigs owned are inconsistent, but the overall figures suggest some 419 acres of land cleared and farmed and around five hundred cattle in pasture, along with more than five hundred sheep, three dozen goats, and at least thirty pigs. Port Royal was reported as having sixty-eight families, the population of Pobomcou as being three men, three women, and eight children, and that of Cap Nègre as being a man, a woman, and two children. At Pentagöuet, Molin listed one family and twenty-five soldiers and noted that Mouskadabouet had thirteen residents. In conclusion, he reported Saint-Pierre, on Cape Breton Island, as having three families with five children. These different descriptions of family groupings are an indication of the variation of terminology within the document. It is, in fact, much less a nominal census than a survey of families and households, and these last two categories are not always explicitly differentiated. Also, there is no conformity in the way which the information is recorded, either for the families or for the landholdings. Adult offspring are sometimes reported twice: as the children of one household and as adults in a separate dwelling, on occasion in a different settlement. Sometimes land held is reported as land cleared, other times just as land held. The shortcomings of the survey reveal more than just an absence of statistical sophistication. Those who set it in motion were also unclear on exactly what the boundaries of the colony were. The survey is restricted to the area from Cape Breton Island to Pentagöuet. No attempt was made to include the settlement of Denys at Nepisiguit, let alone European activities around Miscou.

However, the document provides an extraordinary amount of information which, if it cannot yield the accurate statistical tables of a present-day census, does provide a sense of early settler life in Acadia. Used as descriptive material, one can build portraits of the various communities, their daily lives, their interactions, and the differing family structures within the colony. Looking first at the data for the the tiny communities on the shorelines, one immediately appreciates that whether the settlers were relatively wealthy, such as the Mius d'Entremont family at Pobomcoup, or on the edge of poverty, such as the Poulet family at Cap Nègre, the daily round would be arduous. The Mius d'Entremont family were the only recorded setters at Pobomcoup, the father being Philippe Mius d'Entremont, then sixty-two years old, who had come to the colony three years earlier with Charles de La Tour, a childhood friend. In 1653 the latter accorded him patents to the Pobomcoup fief, as a barony, a territory that stretched from Cap Nègre to Cap Fourchu (Yarmouth).[115] His household consisted of himself; Madellene Ellie, his wife, who was forty-five; three sons, Jacques, seventeen, Abraham, thirteen, and Philippe, eleven; and a daughter, Marie, just two. The survey reported, as well, that d'Entremont's eldest daughter, Marie-Marguerite, was living in the Mius d'Entremont household, but it also has her living with her husband at Port Royal. The family had six acres of cleared land, twenty-six cattle, twenty-nine sheep, twelve goats, and twenty pigs. It is probable that there were chickens as well.

Philippe Mius d'Entremont had been the king's attorney in 1670 and this suggests some status and resources. Nevertheless, no servants, either for the household or on the farm, are recorded. Within the household, work would fill the day for Madellen Ellie, managing a kitchen without running water and only a rudimentary fireplace chimney, with two adults and four children to feed and the two year old around her feet as often as not. Clothing had to be assembled, washed, and mended. If there was a garden, for onions, lettuce, carrots, and cabbages as well as herbs, it would have been her province. Given the flock of sheep, she might very well have spun and woven as well. Certainly, she would cope with fresh-butchered meat, including smoking parts of the animals for the winter. Outside, her husband had to ensure the care of animals and the nurturing of the land. The two eldest boys would help and the youngest would probably have been part shepherd, part cowherd. The pigs could forage for themselves for most of the year but the grazing animals would need care, especially in the winter. Even if none of the land was planted for grain, the cattle and sheep would need to be moved once or twice a week so that they would not

over-graze and to make certain they would manure the fields more or less
evenly. In the summer, wood for cooking and heating had to be cut, and
enough stored to season for the winter. Hay would also have to be gathered
for the winter. Some of the cattle and goats would have been in milk at
least some of the time. When an animal was butchered, its skin would need
tanning and cleaning. Further, hunting and fishing would have been pursued in particular seasons. Finally, at least some of the time the father
would have been away, obtaining goods to trade with the Mi'kmaq or buying provisions in Port Royal. Undoubtedly, the occasional ship called in
and some provisions, condiments (salt, sugar, vinegar), and tools and textiles as well as ammunition would be bought. The appointment of Mius
d'Entremont as a representative of the crown and the marriage between
his daughter and Pierre Melanson of Port Royal indicates a certain level of
contact with that community.

Neither of the two households that were reported at Cap Nègre, that of
Armand Lalloue, the Sieur de Rivedon, and of Guillaume Poulet, were as
well established as that of the Mius d'Entremont family. Lalloue was fifty-
eight years old and his wife, Ellisabeth Nicolas, forty. Again, an eldest son is
reported, aged twenty-four, but not named. Lalloue had four more children: two sons, Amant, fourteen, and Amand, twelve; and two daughters,
Jeanne, twenty years old, and Elisabeth, whose age was given as the same as
that of Amand. The family had two acres of cleared land, twenty goats, and
twenty-nine pigs. For the Poulet family, the name and age of Guillaume's
wife are not given, nor, if there were any children, is there any indication of
their names and ages. It was noted, however, that the family had roughly an
acre of cleared land and perhaps half a dozen pigs. In the summary of the
report, the cleared land is called a garden. While the lack of cleared land
and livestock might seem to reduce the workload, this would be more
apparent than real. What was not herded or cultivated would have to be
sought by hunting, fishing, and gathering. Nor was the work within the
house liable to be much less; clothing would have to patched and mended
to last as long as possible. Skinning and tanning of furs and hides would
probably be a major domestic task, since textiles were an expensive item.

The most important settlement, and the most fully described, was Port
Royal. The families there brought together just over 250 individuals: 65
men, 67 women, and 125 sons and daughters. Over the past twenty years,
the community had become multi-generational and contained people of
all ages. Its youngest inhabitant was the two-day-old daughter of François
Perlerin and Andrée Martin, too young even to be officially accorded a
first name. Jehan Gaudet was the oldest settler and he asserted his age as
ninety-six. There were fifteen sets of grandparents, including Jacques
Bourgeois, fifty, and Jeanne Trahan, forty, who had ten children, the
youngest only four in 1670. Two of their children were already married
and there were two grandchildren. Several grandparents had children of
their own who were younger than one or more of their grandchildren.

Such a couple was Abraham Dugas, fifty-five, and Marguerite Doucet, forty-six, who had eight children, the two youngest being girls aged seven and six. Their two eldest daughters were married and Marie, who was twenty-three and the wife of Charles Melanson, had four children, the eldest of whom was seven. The oldest grandparent was Pierre Commeaux, who was seventy-five. His wife was Rose Bayou, thirty-five years younger, and they had eight children, aged between seven and twenty-one. Their sole grandchild was the three-week-old daughter of their eldest, their son Estienne. Jehan Terriau, seventy, and his wife, Perrine, sixty, had the greatest number of grandchildren – thirteen grandchildren by eight children.

But if Port Royal could boast three generations among its settlers in 1671, it was very much a youthful community, with 114 children aged ten or under, of whom 19 were less than a year old. When those aged between ten and fifteen are included, the total reaches 162. While the evidence does not allow any conclusions about fertility rates per se, it does permit a comment on the standard of living. Conception does not take place if a woman is exhausted or underfed. There were eighteen households in which the wife was twenty-five years or younger; more than half of the women had borne their first child before they were eighteen, four of them at the age of sixteen, five at seventeen. Further, not only did these women begin their families at a young age, they also had a number of children. Among them, nineteen women accounted for thirty-one youngsters. Four had borne a child roughly every two years. One of these was the wife of Michel de Forest, Marie Hebert, who had three children under five by the time she was twenty: a four year old, Michel; Pierre, aged two and a half; and René, who was a year old. The seventeen women living in the colony who were forty-six years and over had borne ninety-three children between them. Their family size ranged from the childless state of Clément Bertrand and his wife, Huquette Lambelot, to the three families of eleven children: that of François Gauterot and Edmée Le Jeune; that of Michel Boudrot and his wife, Michelle Aucoin; and that of Anthoine Bourc and his wife, Anthoinette Landry. Genetic endowment and lack of disease obviously affected both birth and survival rates, but a good food supply was a necessary factor for the bearing and rearing of so many young. It is clear that Acadia had had no major food shortage for over two decades nor any major epidemic of measles or chickenpox or smallpox. These were the childhood illnesses which, with others, such as typhoid, whooping cough, and the plague, kept the death rate among children so high in seventeenth-century France. There, at the same period, "out of every hundred children born, twenty-five died before they were one year old, another twenty five never reached twenty and a further twenty-five perished between the ages of twenty and forty-five."[116]

Another indication of the standard of living in the community was the distribution of property.[117] Two of the five widows, Perrine Landry, sixty

years old, and Marie Sale, sixty-one, had neither land nor animals. We have
no other information about their circumstances, whether they lived alone
or as boarders. All other adults surveyed had property of some sort. Several phrases about the state of the landholding are used. Some holdings are
described as "terres Labourables et en valeur," that is, "cleared and farmed
land." Other terms are "terre en labour" ("land being farmed") and "terres Labourables." This last phrase has the implication that the land was
workable but nothing had yet been done. Some households are reported
as having "point de terre en Labour" ("no land being farmed"). This does
seem to mean no land held, since four married men, one bachelor, and
one of the widows are reported quite definitely as having "point de terre."
All of the men without land, however, unlike the two widows, are reported
as having cattle and sometimes sheep as well. This well-nigh universal ownership of animals was much like the situation of similar communities in
Massachusetts, where most owned both cattle and swine.[118] In fact, settlers
such as Edward Johnson considered the growth of flocks and herds there
a sure mark of divine favour; his accounts showed that villages half the size
of Port Royal had almost as much livestock.[119] New England, indeed,
reversed the English practice of fencing cattle and instead fenced the cultivated land, allowing the animals to roam free.[120] It is probable that Port
Royal pastured animals on common-water meadows but we have no contemporary evidence about this practice.

It is also unclear whether all those people listed separately actually were
in different dwellings, although most historians have assumed that this was
so. The widow Barbé Baiolet, with a cow and six sheep but no land, was
sixty-three years old and was reported as having eight children, two married daughters in Port Royal and the other six children "either in France
or elsewhere."[121] She might very well have lived with one of her daughters.
Two of the men are called "laboureur," meaning farm labourer. One was
Michel Poirier, one of the two bachelors recorded in Port Royal, a young
man of twenty. He had two cows and he might have been a part of a larger household. The other so designated was Jacques Girouard, twenty-three,
with a seventeen-year-old wife and a young son, Alexandre. This small family had seven cattle and three sheep. The final two reporting no landholdings were a cooper and a gunsmith. It is probable that both these families
had their own dwelling. Jacques Belou the cooper was thirty and had a
twenty-year-old wife and a baby daughter of eight months. He owned seven
cattle and one sheep. The gunsmith was Jehan Pitre, aged thirty-five, with
a wife, Marie Peslet, twenty-six years old, who was one of the daughters of
the widow Baiolet. This family had three children, daughters aged five and
three and an eight-month-old son. They had a single cow.

There was obviously a considerable difference in the circumstances of
those with lands and herds and those with little or no land and few animals. But a number of factors mitigated against the immediate development of strong social and economic divisions within the community. Coop-

erative work was crucial if the migrants were to survive the first years in their new circumstances. Whether shared or single-family dwellings, the housing in Port Royal would have been built cooperatively. Even the simplest of shelters, whatever the material used, whether logs, planks, or stone, demanded a great deal of physical labour for its construction. We know more about the building of the forts and trading posts in the colony at this time than we yet do about the construction of the average house. Ongoing archaeological work in the Annapolis valley, however, indicates that the average dwelling of the early settler was sturdily constructed with a good cellar and chimney structure. The materials used included stone and sawn planks more often than logs. Chinks in the walls were filled in with tamped clay and grasses.[122]

However simple such dwellings might seem, a man and his wife needed their neighbours to help. Further, the need to build the dykes and establish the physical environment of barns and wharfs, not to mention the church and the fort, made all members of the community interdependent. Demography, too, reinforced connections between people. The smallness of the population, limited immigration, and the social demands of lives lived in relatively immobile circumstances meant that the pool of available marriage partners for young adults between 1654 and 1671 was more or less restricted to their neighbours.

In sum, the early years of settlement demanded a general civility in the community, if a reasonable standard of living for any and all was to be achieved. This last factor has been variously described by historians. E.P. Thompson has named it "mutuality,"[123] while Thomas Hubka considers it "a pervasive ethic of mutual aid between farm families," something that became "so deeply ingrained into farm life that it assumed a quasi-religious role." Hubka points out that early farming communities developed a long list of cooperative activities which included "work sharing (particularly the exchange of labor, animals, tools and machinery); health care (the assistance in sickness birth and death) ... artisan skills (blacksmith, herbalist, carpenter); disaster relief (sudden death and fire); building construction ... road maintenance."[124] Keith Wrightson, examining early-seventeenth-century England, details the dimensions of what he terms "a moral community," standards of behaviour enforced by social pressure within a village or small town, along with a basic recognition of the need for some standard of accord between individuals and of the need to accept obligations for seasonal help at times of seeding and harvesting as well as in times of crisis.[125] Across the Atlantic, Darett Rutman considers that such values gained a further imperative; he writes that "the small place of early America was ... a congeries of interacting neighbours – more of *good* neighbours – but only because it had to be that way."[126] In other words, those who settled Port Royal, having left differing circumstances of life in the various regions of France, were now constrained to accept one another and set about the establishing of a community.

When examining social stratification among the Acadian community in 1671, one must remember that most of the community had only just migrated to the colony and family relationships through the marriages of the second generation were of major importance. Social stratification would sharpen over the next decades, with the growth of the colony, but any analysis of relative wealth at this point must pay considerable attention to family relationships and whether or not there was a marketable skill in the family. The position of Charles Bourgeois, twenty-five, and Anne Du Gast, seventeen, with a daughter aged one and a half, was not really similar to that of Jehan Corporon, twenty-five, his eighteen-year-old wife, Françoise Scavois, and their six-week-old daughter. The first couple was well established with twelve cows, seven sheep, and two acres of cleared land. As well, both sets of in-laws were in comfortable circumstances. The husband's father was Jacques Bourgeois, who had eight children at home, was the surgeon in the colony, and had thirty-three head of cattle, twenty-four sheep, and twenty acres of cleared land. The wife's father was Harbraham Du Gast, fifty-five, with six unmarried children, nineteen head head of cattle, three sheep, and sixteen acres of cleared land. The other couple, however, Jehan Corporon and Françoise Savoie, had only a cow and a sheep and no cleared land. Further, the husband was, apparently, the first of his family to immigrate and he had no relatives in Acadia. His wife's family was much less well positioned than the family of Anne Du Gast. Françoise Savoie's father was a farmhand and he and his wife had eight children at home, four head of cattle, and six acres of cleared land.

But the caution that Rutman has emphasized in his work, that the small settlement communities of Europeans in seventeenth-century North America were always in process of changing, either growing or dimishing, enlarging their own area or budding off other settlements, limits the validity of the statisitical analysis of any one year. The economic divisions within the Acadia of the early 1670s reveals less about relationships between people and more about the possibilities of the economic development of Port Royal. It was clearly possible, with good fortune and a good family partnership, to cultivate a fair-sized landholding and reasonable flocks and herds, certainly more than the average family of five would need for a year's sustenance. A family of four adults (people over sixteen years old) and four children would need about five cattle and another five sheep, with the same number of pigs and somewhere to pasture them, to feed themselves for a year.[127] Seven other families at Port Royal had holdings and herds that rivalled those of Jacques Bourgeois: Anthoine Gougeon and his wife, Jeanne Cherbrat, had one daughter, aged fourteen. They had twenty head of cattle, seventeen sheep, and ten acres of cleared land. Jean Labatte and his nineteen-year-old wife, Renée Gauterot, had no children but twenty-six head of cattle, fifteen sheep, and fifteen acres of cleared land. Daniel Leblanc and his wife, Françoise Gaudet, had six sons and one daughter. They had eighteen head of cattle, twenty-six sheep, and ten acres

of cleared land. Their daughter was already well married. Her husband was
Martin Blanchard and they had no children at the time of the survey but
five head of cattle, two sheep, and fifteen acres of cleared land. The six
Leblanc sons gave their parents fifty-two grandchildren in all, thirty-five of
them being grandsons.[128] Charles Melanson, who was just twenty-eight,
and his wife, Marie Dugas, who was twenty-three, had four children by
1670. He had the largest herd of cattle reported: forty animals. As well, he
had six sheep and twenty acres of cleared land. Claude Petitpas and his
wife, Catherine Bagard, had seven children under twelve. They had twenty head of cattle, twelve sheep, and the largest amount of cleared land
reported: thirty acres. Michel Richard and his wife, Magdeleine Blanchard,
had seven children, fifteen head of cattle, a flock of fourteen sheep, and
fourteen acres of cleared land. In other words, Acadians in these years
obviously found the colony to be a place where, with hard work and good
fortune, a reasonable living could be made. Not surprisingly, it was from
among the descendants of this last group of settlers that future leaders of
the community came. But the functioning of such a small settlement
meant that "neighbourliness" was of greater value in these early years than
recognition of social status.

Almost no written records have survived that provide information
about the terms on which land had been granted, by anyone of official
standing, to the settlers of Port Royal and there is even less information
about the way in which the labour resources of the colony were organized. That land had been distributed conditionally is certainly implied
by the terms of capitulation that were signed in 1654. As has already
been noted, reference in a court document of 1675 suggests that the system d'Aulnay established at Port Royal was a form of sharecropping,
where land and tools were provided by the seigneur in return for rent,
either in money or kind, and a percentage of the year's crop.[129] There
are also references in later documents of the 1680s to leases being granted and rents paid.[130] It seems clear that the terms on which the settlers
held their lands were observed by them if the seigneur was present to
enforce his rights. But control of settlement can be really effective only
when land is scarce or where land and climate combine to make subsistence farming difficult. None of these conditions obtained in Port Royal.
After 1640, dwellings were established further inland, quite some distance from the original Champlain-de Monts habitation. This was in part
due to the much better, and more abundant, agricultural land to be
found along the river valley. D'Aulnay had definitely moved down to the
present site of Annapolis Royal by the opening of the decade.[131] During
Temple's time, the settlers had begun to establish themselves even farther along the Rivière-du-Dauphin (Annapolis River).[132] This made
them considerably more independent of whatever authority was in place
at Port Royal.

If there are few records detailing the conditions surrounding land title and usage for the settlers of Port Royal in 1670, there are even fewer shedding light on how the economic and social institutions of the colony operated. There are no accounts of the way in which the community set about organizing the labour necessary for building the dykes, who planned and took charge of their construction, or how rights of cultivation or pasturage were accorded. The fact that those with no lands possessed animals would argue for some type of common grazing rights. There is no information as to whether those with less land and fewer animals worked for wages, whether in specie or in kind, for those who had more. Quite apart from the general level of cooperation established among the settlers, some of the families would clearly need weekly, if not daily, assistance. The workload of a young couple, such as Jean Labatte and Renée Gauterot, with no children but with a herd of twenty-six cattle and a flock of fifteen sheep as well as fifteen acres of cleared land, would imply some such help. While it was predominantly an agricultural settlement, or perhaps because it was such a settlement, Port Royal had a number of craftsmen, including the surgeon, Jacques Bourgeois, one of the wealthiest men in the village. Apart from the young weaver and one of the coopers, all those who cooperated with the survey were reported as possessing animals, if not land, and most had both land and animals. Coopers and barrel makers were of considerable importance at a time when boxes and barrels were vital for storing food and dry goods, and there were four of them in the community. One was clearly well situated: Anthoine Hébert was fifty and his wife fifty-eight. They had three grown children, a herd of eighteen cattle, fourteen sheep, and six acres of cleared land in two separate locations. The two others were of such different ages and family circumstances that it is not easy to say who was the better situated. Jacques Belou was thirty years old with a wife ten years younger than himself and a daughter of eight months. The family had seven head of cattle and one sheep but no land. The other was Pierre Commeaux, seventy-five years old, with a wife, Rose Bayou, thirty-five years younger, and nine children, eight still living at home. He had a herd of sixteen cattle, a flock of twenty-two sheep, and six acres of cleared land. Their trades must have earnt them, in specie or in kind, additional resources but we can deduce little from the census data about their relative circumstances. Two other men whose trade also involved woodwork were carpenters. Again, their two situations were dissimilar. Clément Bertrand was fifty and and his wife, Huquette Lambelot, forty-eight. They had no children and no cleared land but ten head of cattle and six sheep. Thomas Cormier, thirty-five years old with a seventeen-year-old wife, Magdeleine Girouard, had a two-year-old daughter. He had seven head of cattle, seven sheep, and six acres of cleared land. Nor are the circumstances of the two gunsmiths any more alike than those of the two carpenters and the barrel makers. The younger, Pierre Sire, aged twenty-seven, had an eighteen-year-old wife and a three-month-old son, Jehan. He had eleven cattle and six sheep and an indeterminate amount of uncleared land. The other was Abraham Dugas, with six children living at home, nineteen cows, three sheep, and sixteen acres of cleared land. All other trades reported had but one practitioner. There was no blacksmith but one tool maker in metal, capable of producing and caring for saw, scythes, axes, and ploughshares. He was Jehan Pitre, married to Marie Peslet. They had three children, five and under, one cow, no sheep, and no cleared land. There was one mason, Pierre Doucet, married to Henriette Peltre. The couple had five children ten and under; they had seven cows and six sheep as well as four acres of cleared land. There was a weaver, the bachelor Mathieu Martin, living on his own, with four cows and three sheep but no land. Pierre Melanson was reported as a tailor but he gave no details of his circumstances.[133] Finally, one man gave his occupation as sailor: this was Laurent Grange, married to Marie Landry, with two children, six cattle, six sheep, and four acres of cleared land.

In sum, Port Royal in 1671 was an agriculturally based community, with a standard of living that supported family growth. Its livestock holdings compared favourably with those of similar communities elsewhere, both along the St Lawrence and in Massachusetts. But it was also more than this. It was a developing community, embedded in the larger society of transatlantic European migration. The settlement was also linked to the activities of other settlers and traders within the colony, and, above all, it had established trading patterns with Boston merchants. The perception that Port Royal was somehow a sleepy gathering place of peasants, relocated from one static cultural tradition to begin another, cannot be substantiated. At a most elemental level, the small community had to have regular contact with larger centres. It was not, as this point in time, capable of sustaining itself without trade, whether with other settlements in North America or with Europe. The settlers imported goods both for trade with the Mi'kmaq and as necessities in their own lives: textiles and tools, guns, shot and powder. They also bought a variety of articles that, if not strictly necessary, were of great importance: shoes and stockings, tobacco, and foodstuffs, such as sugar, wine and spirits, oil and vinegar. Between 1654 and 1671, the majority of such goods came from Boston. French officials were appalled to discover that this trade was not significantly altered by the arrival of Grandfontaine.

Port Royal had become the most significant European settlement in an area of interest to fishermen, fur traders, and would-be migrants from both England and France. This meant the presence in the region of a highly mobile population of speculators and a steady trickle of official military and political personnel from across the Atlantic. The local governance and politics of Port Royal were, however intermittently and haphazardly, part and parcel of a more general structure. Thus, Guillaume Trahan, recognized as a syndic in 1654, was reported in 1671 as a *marechal*, someone who represented, at the very least, a delegated authority for law and order. Fishing vessels brought news and ideas to the area, as well as the occasional migrant. Those few priests who visited the colony, even during the years of English control, were another source of information. Nor were the inhabitants themselves people inclined to accept, without question, official directives. Migrants are often people who have already displayed a great deal of initiative in the organization of their lives, having usually left the countryside for the town as a first step towards migrating across the Atlantic. Even those migrants who came directly from the countryside were people who sought a better life than the one they had known, one that would improve both their economic standard of living and their position within the social structure. The general temper of the early settlers was one of independence, something that officials, sent out from France to North America, would frequently deplore in the coming decades.

CHAPTER FIVE

Acadia: A Colony of France

Grandfontaine's assumption of control in Acadia was the beginning of forty years of French administration for the territory. They were years in which a continuous effort was made to provide the settlers with an institutional structure for their lives, one that was linked to both Quebec and Paris. But they were also years when that effort was often weak: there were eleven different governors and/or commanders during those decades.[1] Further, from 1670 until 1684, and again from 1691 to 1700, the administrative centre of the colony was not at Port Royal, the oldest and largest population centre of the colony, but variously at Pentagöuet, the Saint John valley, or the Chignecto isthmus, the bridge of land between present-day New Brunswick and Nova Scotia. During those years, there were frequent skirmishes between French forces and those of Massachusetts, as well as one foray by the Dutch against the main Acadian settlements. Whatever the causes of these armed disputes – the fur trade, the exploitation of the rich fisheries off the Acadian coasts, or the simple clash of Anglo-French imperial expansion – Acadia endured the consequences of conflict among parties essentially based elsewhere but with a strong interest in the colony. In these circumstances, the sense of France as an invincible imperial power had little chance of developing among the settlers. At the same time, in spite of all the obstacles, the Acadian population slowly grew and developed settlements over a wide area, fashioning institutions to cope with the political necessities of their lives. These forty years were also the decades in which, however important the economic pull of Massachusetts might be, the Acadian settlements created their own particular pattern of social relationships, bringing together a network of kin relationships, economic activity, political habits, and religious practices that would evolve over the succeeding generations into an enduring community identity.

The political context for the evolution of Acadian society during these years was, of course, French imperial designs in North America. There had been significant changes in the way in which France was governed, both domestically and in its overseas colonies, during the period when Temple controlled Pentagöuet and Port Royal. In the early spring of 1661, Louis XIV, then twenty-three, had initiated major administrative reforms, laying the foundation both for internal development and for overseas expansion. Building upon the work of the great cardinals, Richelieu and Mazarin, the monarch brought under his own supervision the authority previously vested in the major institutions of the state. He asserted control over all official government correspondence, and thus over most official government action, by announcing on 10 March 1661 that, in future, all ministers would "assist me with your counsels when I ask for them" but "not sign anything, not even a passport ... without my command."[2] He then went on to pare down the administrative centre of the government, the king's council. This body might not have been quite as chaotic as Louis described it later on in his memoirs, but there is no doubt that, by 1660, it had become unwieldy, sometimes attended by thirty or more, stuffed with the favourites of the powerful and men of noble birth. Louis cut its membership to three, excluding himself: François-Michel Le Tellier (as secretary of war), Hugues de Lionne (secretary of state for foreign relations), and Nicolas Fouquet, soon to be replaced by Colbert (as superintendent of finances). Presided over by the king, it became known as the "High Council," and all important matters of state were decided there. Its proceedings consisted not of conversations among equals but of the presentation and explanation of the king's ideas and policies.[3] The decision-making power in France was now, in theory, under the monarch's control, narrowing though not eliminating the field for competing and contradictory policies. It was from Louis XIV that colonial policy would be promulgated after 1661, even though both the intellectual underpinnings and the necessary bureaucratic infrastructure might be the work of his advisers.

Louis XIV had the industry, the talent, and the necessary physical energy to establish this personal rulership, which is generally known as "absolutism," as the central fact of political power in France, though it was a rulership mitigated by the communication capability of the time, land travel at the pace of a horse and sea voyages by sailing ship, as well as by the limitations of seventeenth-century bureaucracy (the keeping of records with quill pens and no carbon paper). In these circumstances, absolutism found its strength through the control of administrative and judicial authority and, above all, through the assertion of the supremacy of the royal prerogative against all challenge. Louis XIV had much of the pragmatic common sense of his grandfather, Henry IV, as well as much of the latter's attractiveness and charm, but the grandson was much less pragmatic, much more the ideologue. In many ways, their ambitions were similar: the unification of France. However, whereas Henry IV had sought to build a country on the reconciliation of differences, his grandson's ambition was to make his government reflect his singular and particular vision of what it was to be king, the representative of a unifying, and unified, society. To that end, Louis XIV sought to make the population, great and small, truly his subjects. France, as a state, was to be encapsulated in the reputation of its king, and thus his subjects must ever be solicitous of their monarch's "dignity, glory, greatness and reputation." These four words were those used most often by Louis XIV, in the memoirs he wrote for the instruction of his son, to describe the qualities to be emphasized in the public behaviour of the ruler.[4] With such aspirations, it was inevitable that his government would pay attention to overseas concerns as an unquestioned area for the crown's interests.

And, in 1661, French colonial activity across the Atlantic desperately needed attention. That year, in Acadia, only the settlements of Nicolas Denys remained outside English control, while along the St Lawrence the Iroquois continued their attacks, rural settlement was in disarray, and internal administration was rent by dissension. The total population of European descent in the St Lawrence valley was barely three thousand, as compared with the twenty thousand settlers at the same date in Massachusetts.[5] Pierre Dubois Davaugour had arrived as governor of New France on 31 August 1661. It was his reports of the state of the colony, along with letters of complaint about his harsh and unyielding character from many different sources – including Bishop François de Laval and the governor of Montreal, Paul de Chomedey de Maisonneuve – that helped shape the plans of Louis XIV and Colbert to bring about order in French colonial affairs. But it must be remembered that, to France, neither Canada nor Acadia were as important as the Caribbean and the Mediterranean.[6]

Colbert was the perfect complement for Louis XIV, and without him Louis XIV could neither have restructured French internal administration nor reformed French colonial institutions.[7] The king was clear about how he wanted to rule, and Colbert was able to provide the process that would make such rulership possible. Louis XIV had a vision of his kingdom, united and prosperous and the centre of expanding empire; Colbert knew how the administration should be structured to make such a vision a reality, in spite of opposition from towns, the nobility, and the peasantry and the slow pace of communication.[8] Colbert was almost twenty years older than the king, having been born on 29 August 1619. Both because of the situation of his family when he was born and his own career, he had the all important personal contacts that an administrator needed to function well during the reign of Louis XIV. Colbert had been part of court circles for nearly fifteen years. His family was one of those advancing through the ranks of the *noblesse de la robe,* that part of the aristocracy that gained its status through service in the judiciary and general administrative service to the crown.[9] The government of France in the 1660s was staffed through the direct patronage of the crown and acknowledged social status was of crucial importance for an individual's selection and promotion. Ministers and the staff employed by state institutions worked predominantly through the power they held because of their appointment by Louis XIV and the support they garnered from those to whom they were socially connected. Thus, Colbert's family connections, and those of his friends and acquaintances, were almost as important as his own social standing.[10]

On 28 November 1640 the future minister entered the Department de la Guerre. Colbert's advancement was slow but steady, much helped by the department's head, Michel Le Tellier, who made him one of his personal assistants in 1645.[11] In December 1648 Colbert married Marie Charron, the daughter of another well-placed functionary, who brought a considerable dowry with her. The events of the Fronde turned Colbert into a messenger between Cardinal Mazarin and the court, as it moved about the provinces. Despite an uneasy personal relationship between the two men, Mazarin was impressed by Colbert's efficiency, astute financial abilities, and devotion to the monarchy. With the end of the Fronde in 1652, Mazarin made Colbert his personal agent, responsible for the intricate details of his private fortune. Given the state of confusion between Mazarin's finances and those of the queen mother and the young king, as well as between all three and the monies of the great government departments, Colbert's duties gave him ample opportunity to observe the way in which the day-to-day business of France was carried on.

When Mazarin died, Colbert was someone known to the king, of proven loyalty and equally proven administrative competence. Where Louis saw the development of the French colonies as a necessary adjunct to his power, Colbert saw these colonies as an integral part of French development, a source of raw materials and a market for French industry. Quite apart from the representations made by the secular and religious authorities of New France, king and minister were convinced of the need to reorganize French expansion across the Atlantic, to bring it into some sort of orderly relationship with the crown. Both men, however, would and did sacrifice North American colonial needs to European demands, and the requirements of French trade elsewhere, whenever circumstances warranted. They saw the colonies primarily as some sort of appendage to France, not as the beginning of an independent French society.

In 1663, four years before the Treaty of Breda returned Acadia to France, and nine years before Grandfontaine arrived as governor, the question of French territorial claims in North America had been addressed. The charter of the Compagnie des Cents-Associés was revoked, with minimal and tardy recompense being given to its shareholders.[12] This did not signal the end of trading companies as an arm of French expansion in North America; in fact, such companies became both more numerous and larger over the next decades. It did mean, however, the curtailment of their role as an arm of government. Henceforth, until 1763, French affairs in North America would be the direct responsibility of the crown. In practice, "New France was now a province with the same royal administrative structures as the other provinces of the European homeland: a military governor, an intendant in charge of justice, public order and financial administration; and a system of royal courts."[13] Colonial affairs were now to be the business of the Ministry of the Marine in Paris, and, in 1663, this ministry was one of Colbert's responsibilities. The Counseil Souverain of New France acted much as the provincial *états* and *parlements* did: as a check on the power of the appointed officials.

In theory, instructions from France guided the actions of all officials in New France. Yet, in practice, there was great leeway for individual initiative, not least because the new system was at the mercy of the vagaries of transatlantic travel. A return voyage from La Rochelle to Quebec, during the favourable months of the year for Atlantic crossings, took a minimum of three months, and that does not include the week or so needed to travel between Paris and La Rochelle, nor the time needed to compose a reply to the letter in Quebec.[14] Voyages of over a hundred days were not unknown.[15] Should a ship's captain be courageous enough to sail with the gales of autumn or in winter weather, the passage would be longer and might very well end in disaster. But communication, if slow, did exist. Instructions were sent annually to Quebec and Acadia, and the collaboration between Louis XIV and Colbert gave French North American enterprise a firmer structure than it had had previously. Acadia came back into French colonial jurisdiction just on the eve of another change of policy by Louis XIV and Colbert as to the financial support to be given to colonial affairs, so that the organization of its administration followed their most recent thinking about such matters.

From the outset, when Port Royal and Pentagöuet were under the control of Massachusetts, Acadia was included in Colbert's plans. Jean Talon's commission as the first intendant under the new regime, dated 23 March 1665, stated explicitly that his authority included the supervision of financial and judicial matters throughout "Canada, Acadia, the island of Newfoundland and other countries of France in North America."[16] Thus, when Grandfontaine was appointed, Colbert explicitly informed him that he was subordinate to the governor and intendant of Canada.[17] The governor of Acadia was certainly considered worth less: his annual salary was 2,400 *livres*,[18] and he always had an argument over expenses, whereas the governor of Quebec received 12,000 *livres* as his annual salary and another 12,000, granted with little delay, for expenses.[19] There were three major drawbacks to this arrangement. First, Grandfontaine, like other governors after him, always received instructions directly from France, and, on occasion, these were inconsistent with those sent down from the St Lawrence. Grandfontaine's own instructions had been framed with question of the New England border with Acadia as the major concern, rather than the needs of developing the Port Royal area. This emphasis was definitely a matter of metropolitan politics rather than North American interests.[20] Secondly, the travel time between Acadia and Canada was as various a matter, if not quite as long, as that between Canada and France. Whether the journey was made via the Saint John River or by ship round the coast, a return trip, in the best of circumstances, was likely to take at least three months. Thirdly, while the situation of Canada had much improved over the past decade, its government had little time and energy, and even fewer resources, to spend upon settlements that were over a thousand miles from Quebec and not linked to Canada's primary paths of expansion.

At first, it looked as if the relationship between the two colonies would be of great value to Acadia. Grandfontaine and Jean Talon were much of an age; Grandfontaine had been born in 1627 and Talon in 1626. Although one had spent his life in military service and the other in administration, both were from established families and both were strongly committed to the visions of Louis XIV and Colbert. Grandfontaine was gifted enough in matters military but Talon was a brilliant administrator, passionately committed to the development of a country he believed could be built into a great realm if it had the attention it deserved.[21] Further, Grandfontaine was the first of a number of important public figures in Acadia who had seen service in Europe as well as in Canada. All had a fair knowledge of French imperial politics and were ambitious, interested in making a success, in financial and social terms, of their lives. Some, like two of Grandfontaine's officers, Pierre de Joybert de Soulanges et de Marson and Jean-Vincent d'Abbadie de Saint-Castin, fully intended to settle in North America, whether in Canada or Acadia. Others, like Grandfontaine himself and Jacques de Chambly, who succeeded the former as governor of Acadia, pursued careers elsewhere after service in North America.

There was no disagreement between Grandfontaine and Talon as to what Acadia needed if it was to flourish as a French colony: an increase in population, the reduction of Massachusetts's influence, and the development of strong links between Port Royal and Quebec. These ideas had the full support of Colbert, who instructed Grandfontaine to encourage the soldiers who accompanied him to settle there, writing that "the essential point on which you should concentrate is to work in every possible way for the establishment of soldiers and families at the settlements of Port-Royal, Pentagoet, the St. John River and throughout the length of the coastline belonging to His Majesty, helping them with every aid in your power that you can provide and guarding their peace and comfort, so that, on seeing how well treated and at ease they are, other Frenchmen will be convinced to go and live in that country."[22] Earlier that same year, Colbert had also written to Talon, telling him to consider the establishment of a major line of communication between the two colonies as "the best possible good that you could do for both of the lands."[23]

Grandfontaine served only three years service as governor, being recalled in the spring of 1673. He had barely enough time to become acquainted with the colony and its many problems. The governor had charge of a vast territory, comprising land now held by Maine, New Brunswick, and Prince Edward Island, and was expected to establish

French control over the coastline south of Pentagöuet to the Kennebec as well as the area northeast along the coast, across the Bay of Fundy to Cape Breton. He was also expected to oversee the Atlantic coast from Canso to the Gaspé peninsula, including what would become Prince Edward Island and all of present-day New Brunswick, as well as the area inland from the Bay of Fundy to the source of the Saint John, if not farther north. Within these lands the Mi'kmaq and the Malecite lived, convinced that they had never surrendered to the Europeans either permanent ownership of the land or sovereignty over their communities. Not only were they, at this time, much more numerous than the settlers but without their coopera-tion the fur trade, one of the major economic staples of the colony, would collapse. Finally, the arrival of Grandfontaine did not mean the disappear-ance of other interested parties, such as the Le Borgnes, with holdings in Port Royal, and Nicolas Denys and his family, with claims to property from the Baie des Chaleurs to Cape Breton Island.

It was clear from the instructions that Grandfontaine received that those who drew them up had little real understanding of the intricate relation-ship between Acadia and Massachusetts. In 1670 neither Canada nor France was in a position to supply Acadia with the dry goods that both the settlers and the fur trade needed. Talon, accordingly, had told Grand-fontaine to "build a link and communication structure with Boston to obtain necessities."[24] In his first year as governor, Grandfontaine sent to Boston for a carpenter to aid boat building,[25] and he may also have pur-chased miscellaneous supplies for the garrison and colonists.[26] But, in short order, Talon became convinced that the Port Royal-Boston relation-ship must be brought to a peaceful conclusion, though he offered no pro-posal as to how this might be accomplished.[27] The place of Massachusetts in Acadian affairs was not just a question of a small number of trading ves-sels and a disagreement over fishing rights. It was by far the most pressing and the most difficult of Grandfontaine's external problems, encompass-ing the fisheries, the fur trade and more general commerce as well as the matter of where exactly the boundary between Maine and Acadia ran.

Yet there was little the governor could do to resolve these problems, given the paucity of military resources at his command. He had arrived with about forty soldiers and thirteen officers to garrison Pentagöuet, the Saint John River fort of Jemseg, and Port Royal, and to make the French presence a reality elsewhere in the colony. He had no naval support what-soever, and had, in fact, purchased a ketch from Temple to give himself swift communication between Pentagöuet and Port Royal.[28] Grand-fontaine proclaimed French rights to oversee both the fisheries and the fur trade, announcing that English fishing vessels should put in at Pen-tagöuet and pay a licence fee of twenty-five crowns (*écus*), the same fee that had been enforced on French ships during Temple's tenure.[29] There are no records that anyone ever complied with this particular edict but over the next twenty years Acadian officials turned again and again to this device in order to establish at least some semblance of control over Acadian coastal waters.

The hope that the border of Acadia would be established at Kennebec also came to naught. The explorer Simon-François Daumont de Saint-Lusson had reported to Talon that the English settlers along the Kennebec and at Pemaquid "desired nothing more than to be subjects of Louis XIV," but Talon wondered whether this wish sprang from fear of the French as neighbours or from "a genuine desire to be ruled by his Majesty."[30] Grandfontaine was more sanguine about the matter and informed Colbert that these English settlers would take the oath to Louis XIV if they were accorded freedom of religion.[31] Talon's doubts proved to be well founded when, the following year, a petition from the Kennebec area "bearing ninety-six signatures from the various settlements of this area, requested that the General Court authorize the extension of the Massachusetts government north-eastwards."[32] In consequence, the county of Devon was created and, as far as Massachusetts was concerned, the southern boundary of Acadia was the Penobscot. In sum, the return of Acadia to French control neither ended the economic influence of Massachusetts on the colony nor established clear boundaries for the area.

Within the colony, Grandfontaine had some success in clarifying the role of the French government but little in terms of enticing and establishing settlers. He ended the pretensions of Emmanuel Le Borgne's family to any official status by instructing the inhabitants to consider him as having no more authority than they in the affairs of the colony. All other claims and counter-claims by the heirs of d'Aulnay and La Tour were referred to France for adjudication. Grandfontaine supported the appointment of Philippe Mius d'Entremont as attorney general (*procureur du roi*) in the colony, a position d'Entremont held for the next eighteen years.[33] This selection, for an important administrative post, of the head of a family that had been in the colony since 1650 and was related, by marriage, to both the La Tours and the Melansons was astute. It established an important link between the new administration and the settlers of Port Royal. The question of additional settlers proved disappointing, in large measure because of the vacillations of the French government. In 1669 Colbert had written to Talon that he was to consult the intendant of Rochefort, Charles Colbert de Terron, who was in charge of overseeing Grandfontaine's departure for Acadia, in order that everything possible might be done for the French establishment of Acadia and Cape Breton, in particular to encourage the development of trading posts there.[34] In 1671 the first and last group of settlers on Grandfontaine's watch arrived on board the *L'Oranger*: sixty in all including one woman and four girls.[35] We have no further information about these people as a group, although later documents occasionally provide enough information to suggest that an individual, or their ancestor, might have been on board this ship or part of the group of eight or nine colonists who sailed with Grandfontaine on the *Saint-*

Sebastien.[36] But in 1672, before assisted migration to Acadia had resulted in any considerable number of migrants, the financial pressures of Louis XIV's war against the Low Countries ended the royal subsidies for transporting migrants to Acadia and Quebec.[37] Further recruitment would be, in the main, a matter of individual enterprise with, occasionally, some assistance from a fishing company.

Given this lack of government-assisted migration, the extent to which new seigneurial grants could be employed to encourage settlement became important. During Grandfontaine's governorship, four new grants were made, all with frontage on the Saint John River. The possibility of this waterway becoming the major part of an effective route to Rivière-du-Loup and Quebec made it a significant area for immediate development. The establishment of settlements, rather than just fortified trading posts, along its banks would greatly help in achieving Colbert's wish for an effective link between Quebec and Acadia.[38] At the same time, such settlement would reinforce French claims to the Saint John River valley. All four grants were made during the third week of October 1672. The earliest, signed by Talon on the 17th of the month and issued to Martin d'Aprendestiguy de Martignon, was for land measuring six leagues by six leagues on the west bank of the river. Aprendestiguy, a Basque, had been involved in trade with Acadia out of Saint-Jean-de-Luz from the 1650s and had married one of the three daughters that Charles La Tour had been given by his first wife, the Mi'kmaq woman whose full name has not been preserved. In the document of concession, Aprendestiguy's long involvement with Acadian affairs is remarked upon, as is his position as an heir of his father-in-law, La Tour. Further, the concession recorded that d'Arprendestiguy asserted that he had the support of a number of Frenchmen who were willing to work with him to establish cattle farming well enough to supply beef to the French possessions in the Caribbean, as well as Quebec, and, at the same time, to begin an effective dry fishery. The grant did not spell out explicitly any obligation to establish settlers, as opposed to establishing residence – *feu et lieu* – on the land within the year. Fealty, of course, was owed to the king, in the person of the governor of the colony at Pentagöuet. The rest of the conditions in the concession were similar to those in Canada: the rights of seigneurial justice (judging disputes surrounding land usage and inheritance), the rights of transfer subject to the Coutume du Vexin Français, the preservation of oaks suitable for shipbuilding, and the obligation of informing either king or the Compagnie des Indes should mines be discovered.[39]

The following day a smaller grant, of some two leagues of river frontage, was granted to Jaques Potier, Sieur de Saint-Denis. It was noted in the concession that Saint-Denis was acting on what he had heard about the Saint John River: that the land was capable of providing good grain and that the fisheries were bountiful.[40] Like d'Arprendestiguy, Saint-Denis averred that he had the backing of others. Further, he stated that

he would bring settlers from France "the following year," sufficient to
establish a small settlement.[41] The conditions attached to this grant were
the same as those laid upon his neighbour, but whereas we have evidence
that d'Arprendestiguy at least lived on his seigneury for some years, Saint-
Denis appears to have been an absentee landlord from the outset. We
have little information about him, and whether or not he was a member
of the Nicolas Juchereau de Saint-Denis family, who were active at Tadoussac and Saint-Roch-des-Aulnaies, is open to question. At any rate, this concession seems to have had no more than a paper existence. The final two
seigneuries granted were to two brothers: Pierre Joybert, who had been
living at Fort Jemseg since late 1670; and his younger sibling, Jacques.
Grandfontaine had a quarrelsome relationship with Pierre, even though
the two had worked together previously in Canada. The brothers had
been born in Champagne. Pierre was twenty-three and had already served
in Portugal when he came with Grandfontaine to Quebec in 1665 as a
member of the Carignan-Salières regiment. In 1672, the year of this
grant, he married Marie-Françoise, the daughter of the then attorney general of New France, Louis-Théandre Chartier de Lotbinière.[42] Pierre's
concession emphasized the service he had given to France, both in
Europe and in the New World, and noted that he had been appointed by
Frontenac to control the Saint John River area. His seigneury ran north
four leagues from the mouth of the river and was one league in depth,
including the site of the present-day city of Saint John.[43] The younger
brother, Jacques, was given an adjacent grant, but there was no biographical evidence about his attainments or his plans for the concession.[44] The
conditions on which both these seigneuries were to be held were the same
as those stated in d'Aprendestiguy's grant.

These grants signify, among other matters, the reinforcement of French
land-ownership customs in Acadia. As suggested earlier, the turmoil of the
d'Aulnay-La Tour era, followed by the superficial control of Temple over
the settlers, worked against the establishment of a strongly hierarchical
seigneurial system. But it must be remembered that even along the St
Lawrence, as R.C. Harris has shown, the seigneurial system did not mean
a "feudal" society, one dominated by a landowning class, with the lives of
the majority of the settlers circumscribed by the privileges of a few.[45]
Throughout the seventeenth century, no French settler argued about the
final authority of the king, as the ultimate landlord of all territory governed by France, and thus the need to establish land ownership by grant
and to have such a grant recorded. Yet the existence of vast tracts of land,
in the eyes of Europeans, entirely open for settlement meant a fundamental change in the power of the seigneurs. In Europe, even in France, land
was scarce and people numerous. In North America, land was plentiful
and European subjects scarce. Almost endless litigation arose as settlers
challenged seigneurial control, arguing about what had been granted by
whom, to whom, when, and on what conditions. In both Canada and Aca-

dia, the settlers believed in private property and in land ownership regulated by the state. Until 1710, the seigneurial system remained the legal foundation of land titles for Europeans in Acadia, and even after that date it still held some legal force in the English courts.[46] Still, as will be seen later, the founding of settlements at Beaubassin, between 1672 and 1676, and at Minas in the early 1680s took place with a very minimal application of the classic seigneurial obligations, the payment of dues on the one hand and the provision of communal services, such as grist mills and sawmills, on the other.

For Grandfontaine, the question of seigneurial control within the colony was of much less importance than the need to organize immediate supplies for his headquarters and deal with argumentative subordinates. There were always quarrels among those administering colony, resulting as much from the difficulties inherent in a posting to a sparsely populated and poorly maintained border command as from personal antagonisms among individuals. Equally pressing was the need to persuade French authorities, in Canada as well as in Europe, to live up to their promises of support and to come to a reasonable accommodation with Massachusetts. Throughout the forty years of French government, both Quebec and Versailles consistently paid lip-service to the importance of supporting Acadia but only rarely provided significant help. As for the question of Acadian-Massachusetts relationships, whether it was part of the French or British empires, New England in general, and Massachusetts in particular, was the prevailing wind of Acadia's political and economic life. In terms of agriculture, fishing, and hunting, the Acadian economy was largely a matter of Acadian enterprise but in the area of commercial activity, whether the fur trade with the Mi'kmaq or the obtaining of supplies for the settlements or for trade, Massachusetts was a major and continuing influence. In some form or another, all these matters would be of equal import to those who followed Grandfontaine as governor.

While the question of support from Europe was always an issue, whether the governor was English or French, those French regimes that were based at Pentagöuet or Jemseg were always in a much more difficult position than those based at Port Royal, because neither fort could rely upon local agriculture for adequate supplies of cereals, fruit, and vegetables. The area around Pentagöuet had been farmed during d'Aulnay's tenure, and there had been a mill and an orchard at that time.[47] But the 1671 census reported neither cleared land nor animals at Pentagöuet. The correspondence between Quebec and Versailles gives contradictory information about the food supply available there. On 11 November 1671 Talon informed Colbert that the garrison was "the more easily provisioned because of the fish and shellfish that the proximity to sea made abundant." In the same letter, Talon also remarked on the quantity of meat sent annually to Boston from the colony, in exchange for cloth.[48] Yet, in November 1672, Frontenac – who had arrived in Quebec as the governor of Canada in April of that year

– wrote to Colbert about the miserable situation of Grandfontaine. Frontenac reported that he had dispatched provisions for the relief of the fort but it is not known what these were.[49] It is unlikely that the garrison was in danger of starvation, given the hunting possibilities. What was probably lacking was flour and peas, beans and lentils, particularly necessary in an age before the potato for any balanced diet, and perhaps reasonable clothing for the winter. At any rate, no reports have survived of either death or serious illness among the soldiers, such as scurvy, which would result from any serious lack of food.

Though the situation was probably one of uncomfortable scarcity that year, rather than one of dangerous shortages, there is no doubt that France sent only minimal aid to both Acadia and Canada in 1672. For Canada, this meant slower development in the 1670s than the colony had known in the previous decade. Frontenac, in the same letter in which he informed Colbert that he had sent aid to Grandfontaine, remarked that if the king "only wanted to do for the preservation of this country what he has done for the least of towns that he has taken in Holland, and send to Canada and Acadia what there is as a garrison in the smallest of these places, we would be protected from all sorts of insults and in a most favourable position for the development of a country that could become, one day, a very considerable kingdom."[50] Though it is true that Frontenac did not receive the level of subsidies for Canada that he wanted, it is also true that the situation along the St Lawrence had much improved during Talon's tenure as intendant. Enough had been achieved to ensure that Canada was able to expand, even after Colbert deliberately curtailed the funds allocated to the colony after 1672.[51]

The situation in Acadia was far worse. Indeed, the fundamental lack of commitment by Colbert and Louis XIV to the establishment of a strong French military presence in Acadia resulted in yet another successful raid on its settlements in the summer of 1674, this time by a Dutch-led force. Grandfontaine had left the colony in May 1673 and his replacement, Jacques de Chambly, arrived directly from Quebec, aboard the *Saint-Jean,* in the autumn of that year. Chambly was also a veteran of the Carignan-Salières regiment, and he had already obtained a seigneury on the banks of the Saint-Louis, his concession grant noting his service to France in Canada.[52] There is no record of his arriving at Pentagöuet with much in the way of new supplies, either of goods, soldiers, or colonists. The fort itself had had a fair complement of armaments when Grandfontaine took possession 1671: a minimum of eight iron guns and two small culverines within the walls of the fort, and two guns outside the walls.[53] There was also some ammunition: "200 bullets ranging in calibre from three pounds up to eight pounds." The amount of powder and shot that the fort held is not known.[54] The exact strength of the garrison is also a matter of dispute, the figures ranging from twenty-three to thirty men.[55] Whatever the size of the force, when Jurriaen Aenoutsz arrived off Pentagöuet in the *Flying Horse,* with at least fifty men and eight cannon, on 10 August 1674, Chambly surrendered after a short skirmish in which he was severely wounded.[56]

In its origin, this raid had a great deal in common with that of Sedgwick twenty years earlier. News of war between the United Netherlands and France (the latter allied briefly with England) had reached the Dutch governor of Curacao, who dispatched Aenoutsz to harass English and French settlements in North America.[57] When Aenoutsz latter reached New York, however, he discovered that peace had been made between England and Holland. Whereas Sedgwick, on arriving in Boston, had obtained the vague backing of the Massachusetts authorities for his subsequent decisions, Aenoutsz obtained only the support of a Massachusetts adventurer, John Rhoades, for his further actions. Rhoades took an oath allegiance to the Dutch and set forth with Aenoutsz to plunder as much of Acadia as possible. Together, they sacked Pentagöuet, so that it was "levell'd with ye ground,"[58] captured both Chambly and his lieutenant, Saint-Castin, and then went on to pillage Jemseg and capture its commander, Pierre Joybert. After formally claiming the territory between the west coast of the Bay of Fundy and Pentagöuet as New Holland, which he did by burying bottles with copies of his commission in them, Aenoutsz returned to Boston with the guns from Pentagöuet and his captives, Chambly and Joybert.[59] Saint-Castin had managed to escape, carrying a letter to Frontenac from Chambly relating what had occurred.

Neither Frontenac nor Colbert considered that the attack had been officially backed by Massachusetts, although the former was of the opinion that, unofficially, the authorities in Boston had done little to hinder the raid and much to encourage it. As George Rawlyk points out, the "plan was hatched in New York"[60] and the New Englanders who joined in were motivated by greed rather than politics. Chambly had written to Frontenac that he had been attacked by "Buccaneers coming from Santo Domingo via Boston."[61] When he wrote to Colbert, Frontenac stated that he had paid the ransom of 1,000 beaver skins that had been demanded for Chambly and Joybert. In response, Colbert approved payment of the ransom but suggested that there had been at least "some negligence" on the part of Chambly.[62] As soon as Rhoades began to take his commission from the Dutch seriously and to harass Boston merchants trading with the Acadians, the Massachusetts authorities moved quickly to bring the adventurers to heel.[63] By the end of April 1675, Rhoades was in jail in Boston and sentenced to death for piracy. He escaped this penalty, however, and by 1678 was in Delaware.[64]

From one point of view, this raid was no more than a minor irritant for the Acadian communities. The Treaty of Nimwegen in 1678, which ended the war between France and Holland, did not even mention the matter. But from another point of view, the raid was much more significant: it ended official French occupation of Pentagöuet and greatly weakened any claim for placing the boundary of Acadia much farther south than the

St Croix River. The success of this pirate's assault exposed the total inadequacy of the French military presence in Acadia, as well as the extent to which French forces along the St Lawrence were barely sufficient for the defence of Canada itself. The only action that Frontenac felt able to take was to dispatch a number of canoeists to discover the condition of the fort and to bring back members of Joybert's family to Quebec.[65] It was mainly through young Saint-Castin, who married the daughter of the Abenaki chief Madokawando, and his subsequent life with the Abenaki, that France was able to continue to exert any influence southwest of the Bay of Fundy after this raid.[66]

Massachusetts might have moved more vigorously to push northwards at this time but the simmering hostilities between settlers and Amerindians erupted into open warfare in southern Massachusetts in June 1675.[67] This was beginning of King Philip's War, which raged through southern Massachusetts over the next two years.[68] While it ended in victory for the colonists, it was a victory that was won at great cost: the Puritan colonies estimated their direct war expenses at about a hundred thousand pounds.[69] At the same time, the indirect cost to their economies was also great. There had been a major interruption to the fur trade, the loss of manpower as men were drawn to the militia had a great impact on the fishery and agriculture, and the destruction of buildings, cattle, and crops was considerable.[70] As important as these material losses were, however, the political and cultural effects were as great, if not greater. The conflict altered the relationship between Massachusetts and New York, which saw in the problems of Boston a golden opportunity to gain authority in the region of Pemaquid. It also greatly complicated the relationship of Massachusetts and Acadia.[71] New York was more inclined than Massachusetts, which had experienced more than a generation of commercial traffic between Port Royal and Boston, to take a hard line towards the Acadian communities. Finally, the war encouraged London to interfere more directly in the affairs of New England and entrenched fear and suspicion of Amerindians among the settlers.[72]

King's Philip's War was also the catalyst for the outbreak of war in Maine in September 1675 between the settlers and the Abenaki, a conflict that lasted until 1678.[73] As John Reid has pointed out, while King Philip's War undoubtedly exacerbated the tension between the Maine settlers and the Abenaki, there were local causes that added fuel to the more northerly conflict. The settlers in Maine lost "260 out of a population of perhaps 3,500,"[74] a somewhat higher proportion than those killed in southern New England. Property was destroyed and farms abandoned, and the settlers' bitterness against "the inconstant savage" deepened in both places. In southern New England, the aftermath of King Philip's War meant that Amerindian power in that region was fragmented. It never posed as strong threat in the future as it had in the past. In the north the result was much more ambiguous. There, the expansion of Maine was temporarily brought to a halt. In 1677, during the negotiations leading to the peace established in 1678, the Kennebec sachems warned the Massachusetts governor that they were the "owners of the country and it is wide and full of enjons and we can drive you out."[75] At the same time, the intervention of New York in the Pemaquid region meant the prosecution of an equally aggressive policy, articulated, in a council meeting held in that colony on 11 September 1677, as "no man to trust any Indyans."[76]

Together, these wars fundamentally changed the relationship between Acadia and New England by encouraging the belief in Massachusetts and Maine that the French-speaking and Catholic settlers of Acadia were the covert allies of the Amerindians. In 1676 Edward Randolph wrote to London that "the government of the Massachusetts hath a perfect hatred for the French, because of their too near neighbourhood ... and looke upon them with an evill eye, believing they have had a hand in the late warre with the Indians."[77] The fact that Saint-Castin had established himself within five miles of Pentagöuet, and married the daughter of an important and powerful Abenaki chief, increased English suspicions. Further, while the Mi'kmaq were not actively engaged with the Abenaki against the English settlers, a number of Mi'kmaq in the Cap Sable area had been captured by slavers from Massachusetts and sold in the Mediterranean,[78] which led to Mi'kmaq reprisals against Massachusetts fishing vessels the following year.[79] This raid and reprisal were small matters in comparison to the bloodshed of the more southerly conflicts. In terms of the relationship between Acadia and Massachusetts, however, they marked the beginning of a significant change. Over the next ten years, the relationship between the two colonies become increasingly tense. The obviously amicable connection between Mi'kmaq and Acadian, the Acadian role as middlemen in the fur trade between Massachusetts and the Mi'kmaq, and Acadian attempts to control both offshore fishing rights and the coal fields and gypsum deposits of Cape Breton led to growing exasperation in Boston with the Acadian communities. What had been a porous border on the northeastern approaches of New England was now becoming a much more impermeable frontier. This was due in part to the existence of an official French presence, however weak, and in part to the growth of Acadian settlements, however slow.

For a while, it seemed as if Acadian affairs might regain some tranquillity. There was little reaction from France to the 1674 raid, other than Colbert's comment, already cited, that the loss of the fort must have entailed at least some negligence on the part of Chambly.[80] But Acadia continued to be of major concern to Frontenac and he was happy to step into the breach. Chambly had retained the governorship but never returned to the colony. Pierre Joybert, who had also been taken prisoner, had returned to Quebec in 1675. Frontenac gave him command of the Saint John River area that year. The following year, Joybert was accorded a grant of Nachouac (Nashwaak) and also of land that included Fort Jemseg itself.[81]

For the next two years, he acted as governor of the colony, although his authority does not seem to have extended even as far as Port Royal, let alone to the Atlantic coast. His major source of supply for trading goods, fish hooks, hunting knives, axes, and tobacco, as well as supplies of cloth, flour, wine, pepper, and other comestibles, was Boston.[82]

On Joybert's death in 1678, Frontenac placed Michel Leneuf de La Vallière et de Beaubassin in charge. This man seemed the perfect choice: he was the third son of then governor of Trois-Rivières and he had both knowledge of and an interest in Acadia. La Vallière had been born in Canada in 1640 and sent to France for his education. He had returned in 1657 and sometime before 1666 had made his way to Cape Breton.[83] That year he married the daughter of Nicolas Denys, Marie. She bore him eight children before her death in 1683. Between 1666 and 1676, La Vallière lived a roving life, only occasionally centred upon the houses of his father-in law at Nipisguit and Miscou. He was involved in all the occupations that Denys pursued, fishing, agriculture, the fur trade. He also maintained his connections with Quebec and in 1670 was part of the expedition against the Iroquois in the Lake Ontario region.[84] At about the time that Denys returned to France in 1671, La Vallière arrived back in Acadia to support his young brother-in-law, Richard Denys de Fronsac, in the latter's attempts to ensure that Massachusetts recognized the rights of the Denys family to the coal and gypsum on Cape Breton Island.[85] It was under La Vallière's leadership that three Massachusetts vessels were captured in 1676, and later courts awarded him prize money for two of them.[86]

As well as involving himself deeply in the affairs of his wife's family, and continuing to maintain links with life along the St Lawrence, La Vallière sought to establish his own settlement in Acadia. His family was growing rapidly. In 1676 he petitioned for a seigneurial grant on the Chignecto isthmus. The Jesuit Pierre Biard had reached that area in 1612, along with Biencourt, and had described it as containing "many large and beautiful meadows, extending further than the eye can reach ... the country ... would be very fertile if it were cultivated."[87] There are no written reports of any attempt at either agriculture or the establishment of trading posts there in the intervening years, but it was merely unexploited territory, not unknown or unpopulated. The Mi'kmaq were certainly acquainted with the area, their familiarity with the whole Atlantic seaboard from the Gaspé to Maine being well known.[88] There seems no doubt that the family of Jacques Bourgeois helped to establish a settlement at Beaubassin, either immediately before or at the very time that La Vallière was granted his seigneury there.[89] Where La Vallière's settlement was situated, and its relationship to that of the settlers from Port Royal, is unclear. A number of writers quote La Vallière's concession as containing a clause that enjoined him not to disturb "inhabitants of the province that are to be found in possession of land and inheritances that they are cultivating, living on and working to increase its value," but documentation of this does not seem to have survived.[90]

La Vallière was granted his seigneury on 24 October 1676.[91] Its limits were extensive: on the Atlantic coast, roughly from just below present-day Shediac to the Philip River, including Baie Verte; on the west, from Memramcook as far south as Springhill. The original grant used some Mi'kmaq place names, drawing the boundaries on the Atlantic between the Kigiskouabougoouet River and the Kimongouitche. On the Bay of Fundy side, the landmarks used were Chignecto Bay and Cape Tourmentine. The grant was seen by his father-in-law as an infringement on his own rights. Nicolas Denys therefore sought, and received in 1677, a ruling from Jacques Duchesneau de La Doussnière et d'Ambault,[92] the intendant of New France, reaffirming the rights of the Denys family to the area first granted to Nicolas Denys in 1654, together with a licence, not only to charge a duty on all coal and gypsum exported from Cape Breton, but also to seize those taking furs in this area without permission from Denys.[93] Rivalry between various families, whose lands and rights were imprecisely defined, was to continue as the norm in Acadian life during the 1680s.

Frontenac's appointment of La Vallière to succeed Joybert in 1678 did little to limit such disputes in the colony. It was very much a matter of patronage, and it was challenged both in France and in Acadia.[94] In France the challenge was a matter of delay and deferral, while in Acadia the confrontation was only occasionally a matter of outright defiance; more often it was a question of recalcitrance and laggardly compliance. La Vallière was not confirmed as governor by Louis XIV until 1683, in spite of increasingly plaintive letters from Frontenac.[95] Until this confirmation was received, Duchesneau, the intendant, refused to pay La Vallière any monies as salary.[96] This delay in confirmation from France was of no help to La Vallière in his attempts to bring together the colony under a single administrative control, to cope with the incursions of Massachusetts fishing vessels in waters claimed by France, and to impose some sort of seigneurial system in Beaubassin and the settlements which developed in the Minas Basin after 1680.[97] In 1679 Frontenac summarized the extent to which the Acadians disliked official interference. In a dispatch to Louis XIV urging the confirmation of the appointment of La Vallière as the new governor of Acadia, Frontenac wrote: "M. de la Vallière ... has told me that he has been to Port Royal, where the inhabitants have shown little care for receiving his order, whether because they have been accustomed to be without a commander, or because of the divisions amongst them, or whether, indeed, from some tendency towards Englishness and parliaments, which has been brought [as] the result of the visiting and trade with Boston."[98] Frontenac continued by saying that the inhabitants were brought to a proper sense of their duty by La Vallière, who had managed to have sworn "a new oath of fidelity by all the inhabitants and had organized public celebrations, for the glorious victories that Your Majesty won last year."[99]

The attitude of the inhabitants was only one of three major problems facing La Vallière. But it was, if less dramatic, more important in the long run for the internal politics of the colony than the other two: the matter of the Acadian fisheries and the activity of Massachusetts. The nature of much Acadian political discourse has its roots in these years, when French authority was being re-established at the same time as the population was expanding and founding new settlements. The movement of families that had cultivated land and cattle, from Port Royal to Beaubassin and the Minas Basin, before 1686 was not only evidence of the growth of Port Royal families but also a mark of the initiative and energy of those who went to establish the new settlements. It was colonization by settlement of the land first, and the registration of ownership later. The absence of French officials for some sixteen to seventeen years after 1654, and the lack of interest shown by Temple in establishing formal institutions registering land ownership during this same period, has meant that the written records of the early expansion of the Acadians from Port Royal between 1671 and 1686 are few and far between. Those who settled on land without an obvious and recorded title of settlement during these years were understandably wary of any attempt to introduce formal registration practices to confirm titles to their holdings. Frontenac's judgment that Port Royal's opposition arose because it was a settlement unused to any outside official is astute. But in a small and closely related society, such as that which existed among those of European descent in the colony at this time, claims of land ownership would be a matter of communal memory, something to be registered with civic officials when such were in evidence. Certainly, once men were appointed to civic office by the new regime, the Acadians seem to have used their services without question.

Further, while the majority of written records concerning landholding practices in Acadia during the years 1670–1710 have been lost, enough remain to show that the Acadians, like other European settlers in North America, had a strong sense of the legal right to own land and, therefore, of the probable need to obtain some official documentation of ownership.[100] Port Royal paid at least minimal attention to seigneurial customs, as a process of record, if not an obligation to be fulfilled. For example, at this period, Le Borgne's son, Alexandre de Belle-Isle, was recognized as having rights to grant land in the area. He had taken the name Belle-Isle in 1667, when his father had claimed the governorship of the colony. While Grandfontaine had effectively challenged that pretension, he had not challenged the right of the Le Borgne family to hold land, as seigneurs, in the Port Royal area. In 1679 Belle-Isle granted land to Pierre Martin and his son, Mathieu Martin, who, the concession recorded, were already both farming it and living on it. The land is described not by length and breadth but by the local geography. It was said to be bordered on the east by "the big meadow, on the west by the Mill stream, on the south by the river Dauphin and in the north by the hills."[101] The annual *rentes* was a penny, a capon, and a barrel of oats, to be delivered to Belle-Isle's residence on 1 January.[102] The concession was witnessed by a number of citizens, including Pierre Melanson and Jacques de La Tour, in the presence of a notary.

However, while it is possible that Port Royal was reacting merely against the institution of new controls, it is also possible that La Vallière might have been attempting to regularize the ownership of land broadly and to impose strict seigneurial practices in the Port Royal area itself. There is sparse, but clear, evidence that he attempted something of the sort in the developing settlements of Beaubassin and Minas. In 1682 a case was brought before the Conseil Souverain of Quebec concerning a refusal by inhabitants of Beaubassin to accept contracts from La Vallière, a refusal that was apparently upheld by the council.[103] None of the settlers whom La Vallière had brought from Canada was party to this suit, which seems to have been the result of an attempt by La Vallière to extend his authority over the whole of the isthmus, in spite of the possible existence of orders against this. At any rate, La Vallière made little attempt to establish cordial relationships with the established settlers of the colony. This was to prove a great handicap to him, especially after 1682, when he faced increasing problems with Massachusetts, the emergence of yet one more fishing company intent upon exploiting Acadian inshore fisheries, and the recall of his chief supporter, Frontenac, to France.

From the outset of his command, La Vallière had to come to an accommodation with New England, an arrangement that would allow the continued exploitation of the fishing grounds of the colony by ships out of Massachusetts, New Hampshire, and, to a lesser degree, New York as well as Acadian commerce with Boston. The aftermath of King Philip's War and the Abenaki War made the New England fishermen the more eager for profit and the waters off the shore of Acadia were some of the richest fishing grounds available to them. Since 1661, New England had become a major supplier of dry and salt fish to the West Indies. Harold Innis writes that "the last English ships to engage in the New England fishery were said to have sailed in 1661,"[104] leaving the West Indian and, to some extent, the Spanish trade open to New England exports. The return of Acadia to France had made little difference to the fishing vessels that sailed from Boston to the rich fishing grounds off the coast between Cap Sable and La Hève. In the 1670s there were usually thirty or more shallops plying these waters each year, as well as a fair number of larger vessels, giving employment to more than five hundred men.[105] Some ships made two or three voyages and caught as much as 1,000 quintals of cod a season.[106] The French, for the most part, had turned their attention, after Sedgwick's capture of the colony in 1654, from the waters off Canso and the southwestern Atlantic coast to the Baie des Chaleurs, especially around Île Percé, and Newfoundland. In 1675 large French ships from Bordeaux and Saint-Malo concentrated on Plaisance (Placentia, Nfld.).[107] This practice not only left the New England fishing fleet almost unchallenged on the Acadian banks, it also meant that Acadian commerce was, inevitably, with Massachusetts, primarily Boston. There were occasional ships around Canso from France during these years but nothing to match the New England fishing fleet.[108] Whether directly tied to the fur trade or to the necessary provision of most manufactured goods, including guns, ammunition, and knives, as well as fine textiles and oil, sugar, spices, wine, and spirits, for the Acadians themselves, there was rarely any other alternative source for such goods but trade with New England. Over and over again this fact was underlined in letters to France, both from individual entrepreneurs and from officials.[109]

In coping with this situation, La Vallière, with the support of Frontenac, followed the precedent of Grandfontaine and issued licences to those New England fishermen willing to buy them, granting the right to fish in the coastal waters of the colony and access to Acadian beaches for drying the fish. Frontenac had written to the Massachusetts General Court in the fall of 1681, complaining that boats came without permits or licence to fish off the Acadian coast, take coal from Cape Breton, and trade with the Indians.[110] Frontenac's complaints were taken seriously by the court, which sent John Nelson to Quebec in the late summer of 1682 in order to discuss the issues raised. Over the next decade, Nelson became increasingly important for Acadian affairs and his career owed much to the position of the colony as a junction between two empires. Nelson, who had come to Boston in 1670 at the age of sixteen, was Thomas Temple's nephew and, on the latter's death in 1674, became his principle heir.[111] Sometime before 1684, he established himself in Boston society, marrying Elizabeth Tailer, who was connected with the Stoughtons, an important family in Massachusetts politics, and took over his uncle's quest for further compensation for the loss of rights in Nova Scotia and his business interests. While still in his early twenties, Nelson met and became fast friends with Saint-Castin, who was much the same age.[112] Partly because of this relationship and partly because of his decision to follow his uncle's former activities in Port Royal, as well as in the Pentagöuet area, Nelson quickly became recognized, in Boston, as someone well versed in Acadian affairs. His particular mission to Quebec in 1682 had little immediate impact on Acadian-Massachusetts politics because Frontenac was away in Montreal and the two men did not meet.[113] However, the very fact of the mission indicated the seriousness with which Massachusetts regarded the question of fishing rights off the Acadian shores and the new formality with which that colony would pursue matters relating to the practice.

On 11 October 1682 the General Court passed a resolution condemning "irregularities" on the part of the inhabitants of Massachusetts in "their trading, making of fish, fetching of coales within the territories belonging to the French."[114] As George Rawlyk writes, in essence this was a reiteration of the policy that had been established by Winthrop: "Massachusetts citizens operating in French territory had to be subject to French law in their relations with the inhabitants."[115] In any case, French law was not going to be all that onerous for the Massachusetts fishing fleet to observe. Permits were almost immediately available. In late October 1682 La Vallière had written to Nelson asking him to set about offering such permits for sale.[116] La Vallière, of course, had no resources to enforce compliance but the permit cost such a small sum that its purchase could be seen to be in the nature of good manners rather than a major recognition of political or economic control. Whether or not this system of licensing might have provided Acadian officials with a source of income for the colonies, and simultaneously entrenched the regulation of fishing along the Acadian banks in French hands, is open to debate. The arrangement was never really given a chance to work because other events intervened. Most important, Frontenac was recalled by an order of 7 May 1682 and embarked for France that autumn.[117]

His departure marked the beginning of a rapid turnover of both the governors and the intendants of New France, which lasted until his reappointment in 1689. During the same period, those appointed to Acadia served for equally short terms. To add to the uncertain nature of political affairs in Acadia, during the same months that Frontenac and La Vallière were corresponding with Massachusetts on the matter, Louis XIV granted a new French fishing company patents to exploit the Acadian fisheries, without any appointed official in either New France or Acadia being consulted. This company, called the Compagnie de la Pêche Sédentaire de l'Acadie, or simply the Compagnie d'Acadie, had the support of Bordeaux merchants but was primarily based in La Rochelle. Quite apart from the risks faced by any new enterprise attempting to exploit North Atlantic fishing grounds at this period, the Compagnie d'Acadie confronted particular problems: its very existence was a challenge to both the New England domination of the Acadian banks and La Vallière's conviction that he had the right to regulate the fishing industry, whether French or English, off the Acadian coast. Moreover, the new company was headed by Clerbaud Bergier, a Huguenot, at a time when both France, and New France, were becoming less and less tolerant societies. Louis XIV had grown increasingly impatient with Huguenot beliefs and had worked to limit both the participation of Huguenots in public life and their observance of their own religious practices. In 1681 he authorized the billeting of troops in the houses of Protestants, with the understanding that life would be made as difficult as possible for the householders unless, and until, they converted to Catholicism. Other brutal measures followed, culminating in the revocation of the Edict of Nantes in 1685.[118]

At the very least, the 1680s were not a decade that favoured Huguenot activity, and it is surprising that Bergier was able to find any support at all for his proposals. But Bergier had more than twenty years' experience in trading ventures linking New England and the Caribbean.[119] He had previously visited Acadia in 1680, through the good offices of Nicolas Denys, who had instructed his son to give Bergier every aid and assistance.[120] But

the possibility of Huguenot activity in the colony was fought in France by
Jean Dudouyt, vicar general of the Canadian church since 1671. He
believed that to allow Bergier to proceed would be contrary to the interests of France, of the king, and of God himself, and he wrote in these terms
in 1681 to the Marquis de Seignelay, Colbert's son, then minister of the
Marine.[121] In spite of this strong opposition, Bergier obtained the necessary concession from the king, on 28 February 1682,[122] through linking
himself with powerful Catholic allies, particularly Charles-François Duret
de Chevry, the Marquis de Villeneuve, who put up most of the initial
financing for the Compagnie d'Acadie.[123] However, objections on religious grounds continued. In particular, Bishop Laval of Quebec wrote to
France in November 1682 to point out that he considered it most important to observe the edict which forbade the establishment of Huguenots in
Canada and "above all, not to suffer them in Acadia."[124] Such hostility
meant that when the company ran into difficulties, which it did, officials
were hesitant to come to its aid.

Bergier made a good beginning. His grant was for land at Chedabouctou and he had established eighteen men and one woman there before
May 1682.[125] During the next months, Bergier sent out another ten or
eleven people, built shelters, and sowed crops (oats, rye, and barley) as
well as fruit trees and vines. Further, he persuaded men from Port Royal to
join with him in exploiting the Canso fisheries.[126] Six small boats set out
from that settlement in 1683 but were captured and destroyed by New
Englanders.[127] Licences might be acceptable to New England fishermen
but not Acadian fishing boats. Bergier immediately appealed to Versailles
for aid to protect his company. In March 1684 his company was given the
right to capture any foreign ships taking fur or fish along Acadian
shores.[128] It is possible that his success in this enterprise was due to letters
sent by one of his associates, Robert Challes, to the Marquis de Seignelay,
who was now in charge of North American matters.[129] Challes had accompanied Bergier to Chedabouctou in 1682 and in his memoirs Challes commented on the letters he wrote about Acadia to Seignelay.[130] At any rate,
on 10 April 1684 La Vallière was ordered to cease acting as commandant
and to desist from issuing fishing permits to foreigners. On the same date,
Bergier was appointed in his place as the king's lieutenant in Acadia and
François-Marie Perrot, then the governor of Montreal, as governor of Acadia.[131] The nomenclature becomes important here, because La Vallière
had been the "commandent du roi en Acadie" while Bergier was named
"lieutenant." Perrot's appointment as governor was due, to a large extent,
to pressure brought by the authorities at Quebec.

At the same time as Bergier was petitioning Louis XIV for extended powers, the authorities in Quebec were writing to both the king and the minister protesting his very presence in Acadia. Both the governor, Joseph-
Antoine Le Febvre de La Barre, and the intendant, Jacques de Meulles,
had been appointed in 1682, and both disliked Bergier's company. Their

grounds were twofold: first, Bergier's religious beliefs, and secondly, the fact that he and the company had been established without either of them being consulted or informed. There is no doubt that both men supported the policy of Louis XIV that Huguenot beliefs were to be suppressed wherever and whenever possible. Both also believed that Acadia was not a separate colony but part of New France and subject, if not to direct governance, to some kind of supervisory control from Quebec. On this issue, the king and his ministers were almost always ambivalent, sometimes making the Quebec authorities explicitly responsible for Acadian affairs, at other times intervening directly and supporting a certain independence from New France for Acadian officials. In November 1683 de Meulles had written indignantly to the minister, complaining that neither he nor La Vallière had ever been informed of Bergier's projects, the man himself being, de Meulles commented, "of the so-called reformed religion." Bergier's actions, de Meulles believed, were in direct conflict with the best interests of Acadia.[132] The same month La Barre wrote even more strongly to Seignelay.[133] He opened his letter by describing Bergier as an opinionated Huguenot who had twice declared bankruptcy. He went on to say that he found not being informed of Bergier's patents utterly bizarre, adding, "It is important, Monseigneur, not to allow the French Huguenots to build an establishment so close to the English of New England, who are also of the religion that is called reformed; and in a country where no ships come from France for trade and where for subsistence one must make do with the Bostonnais."[134] Bishop Laval joined his voice to the chorus of disapproval. In a letter written on 10 November, he deplored the presence of heretics in Acadia and asked the king to bring this to an end.[135] In a letter sent to La Barre on 10 April 1684, the king made it clear that Bergier was to command in Acadia until François-Marie Perrot, at that time still governor of Montreal, could take up his new appointment as governor of the colony.[136]

In the meantime, Bergier returned to Chedabouctou and began an aggressive campaign against New England fishing vessels. In July 1684 he seized seven ketches and a sloop off Cap Sable. He bore his prizes to La Rochelle, where it was discovered that all the vessels were from New Hampshire and that two had licences granted by La Vallière.[137] As was to be expected, these actions not only upset fishing vessels from New England but also enraged La Vallière and those who supported him. Within a year, four French ships, using Chedabouctou as a base, were captured by ships from New England.[138] Soon after this affray, La Vallière's son, Alexandre, attacked Bergier's fishing station. Bergier himself was absent but his son was briefly held captive and furs that allegedly belonged to the Compagnie de l'Acadie were confiscated.[139] About this time, Bergier disappears from the written record of Acadian affairs, being replaced by Charles Duret de Chevry de La Boulaye, the nephew of the Marquis de Neuville, as the appointed lieutenant for the king in Acadia.[140] The passage of the

Edict of Fontainebleau in October 1685, which revoked the Edict of
Nantes, had made Bergier's continued leadership of the company virtually
impossible.

On the surface, the rivalry between Bergier and La Vallière seems a
replay of that of d'Aulnay and La Tour, but the resemblance is no more
than superficial. D'Aulnay and La Tour were much more individually and
personally significant to the development of Acadia than either Bergier or
La Vallière and the colony itself was much stronger in the 1680s than it
had been in the 1640s and 1650s. We are fortunate to have a series of
reports, written by official commentators, about the state of the colony
between 1685 and 1689. François-Marie Perrot, who served as Acadia's
governor between 1684 and 1687, was resident in Port Royal in 1686 and
dispatched blistering commentary to France about the colony. As well, the
intendant Jacques de Meulles and Bishop Saint-Vallier[141] visited Acadia at
much the same time. De Meulles arrived in November 1685 and returned
to Quebec in the summer of 1686, and not only wrote dispatches about his
voyage but also left a diary recounting what he experienced.[142] Saint-Vallier spent the late spring and summer of 1686 in Acadia and included an
account of his experiences there in his general report on the state of the
Catholic Church in Canada.[143] These records together include, if somewhat idiosyncratically, information about sex distribution, family size, age
distribution, the location of communities, the number of livestock, and the
amount of land cleared, as well as judgments on what Acadian society was
like at this time.

The population had nearly doubled in the fifteen years since the previous census, from roughly five hundred to over nine hundred. Inevitably
there are differences in the totals given in the various reports, but these dis-
crepancies are minor and it is clear that there were least nine hundred people of European descent in Acadia by 1686.[144] There had been a certain
amount of migration since 1671, mostly, but not exclusively, male. Some
had arrived with Grandfontaine, and La Vallière, too, had brought some
settlers with him from Quebec. On the whole, however, the growth in population was due to natural increase. People were fertile and the children
lived. Throughout the settlements the average family size seems to have
been five or six children. In a study that covers a greater time span than the
three years of the census, and that uses as well the few available parish
records, Gysa Hynes found that the average number of children per family
was seven, with many families having ten and a few having fourteen or
more.[145] In common with the experience of much of New England, infant
mortality was low, at least 75 per cent of the children surviving to adulthood.[146] This was a very different reality from that of Europe. In France, no
more than 50 per cent of children born reached adulthood. Another 25
per cent died between the ages of twenty and forty-five.[147] Immigration
continued to Acadia during the next twenty-five years but, by 1686, the
colony was close to being self-generating demographically.

By comparison with Canada and Massachusetts, the Acadian population of European descent was minuscule: that of New France, at the same period, was close to ten thousand, and Massachusetts close to fifty thousand.[148] But it was large enough, and the settlements throughout the colony sufficiently interconnected, to allow us to consider Acadia at this time as a society in the making, not merely a trading outpost of Europe. Kinship structures within and between the differing settlements, established economic relationships, and legal, political, and religious customs are all to be found by the mid-1680s. Together, these networks built a pattern of social interaction which made Acadian society an entity that differed substantially from its neighbours. There are parallels in New England and New France for most, but not all, aspects of Acadian experience. It was, however, not only the particular combination of characteristics that developed in the colony which made it distinct from its neighbours but also the way in which each strand of Acadian life was bound into the whole. Acadia was a border colony, not only because it was situated at the meeting place of empires, or because it was ruled alternately by France and by England, but because its larger and more powerful neighbours treated it as such. Neither New England nor New France were ever able to assimilate Acadia fully into their own territory, and only occasionally attempted so to do. There was always a measure of independence accorded, willingly or unwillingly, to Acadia by its more powerful neighbours. And this independence was reinforced by officials in both London and Paris.

The dominance of Port Royal has overshadowed the fact that Acadia by 1686 was much more than just this particular community. There can be no doubt, of course, about the importance of Port Royal. It was the oldest settlement in the colony and was almost always linked to the other communities of the colony by kin ties. Until the founding of Halifax in 1749, it was most often the administrative centre of the colony and its population was the most varied. Its permanent settlers saw a greater number of transients – administrators, soldiers, ecclesiastics, and merchants – than did the settlements at Beaubassin and Grand Pré. As well, the visitors usually stayed longer at Port Royal than did similar transients elsethere in the colony. Finally, the attitude of those who lived at Port Royal was built on a greater awareness of the general politics of the region, the influence of both French and English upon events, than those who lived elsewhere in the colony exhibited. Few European or Mi'kmaq inhabitants of the colony would be unaware after 1670 of the fact that two powers considered Acadia a matter of a certain importance in their colonial designs. However, the opinions of those whose lives centred upon the sea as much as the land, settlers and those Mi'kmaq whose lives were particularly linked to the shores from Baie Verte to La Hève, were built on different assumptions than those of Grand Pré, for example, whose lives revolved around agriculture and trade rather than fish. Also, those who were not in daily contact with officials sent out from Europe, whether secular or religious, were more inclined to develop their own ways of solving community difficulties.

There is no doubt that in 1686 Port Royal was the most important population centre of the colony, with ninety-five families reported as settled in the town, making a population of 583 people, 197 adults and approximately 295 children.[149] It also was the most important centre for trade, both internally with other settlements and the Mi'kmaq and externally with Massachusetts, and the place where religious life was most often structured and a priest most frequently to be found. But the politcal life of the colony, as a whole, was profoundly affected by the other populated neighbourhoods, such as the Saint John valley and the area around Pentagöuet, which had long histories of trading with the Mi'kmaq and where people of European descent might be few in number but were continually present after 1670. For example, there were the outports, from the Baie des Chaleurs to Chedabouctou and from Cape Breton to Cap Sable, which had been settled by two or three families of European descent for more than a generation. In 1686 Jacques La Tour's establishment at Cap Sable had fifteen inhabitants, divided among four different families and including a black man called La Liberté. Only one family had been recorded there in 1670. They, and the people of other outposts, managed to survive and bring up children through a mixture of activities – farming, fur trading, hunting, and fishing. Marriage partners were usually found among the people of Port Royal. In all, including the establishment of Richard Denys on the Miramichi, the families established on seigneurial grants from the mouth of the Saint John to Jemseg, and those attached to Saint-Castin, around Pentagöuet, numbered roughly a dozen, adding perhaps seventy-five people to the total population of European descent present in 1686. Finally, by that year, both Beaubassin and Minas had been settled by out-migration from Port Royal and were themselves expanding communities of some size. Beaubassin, de Meulles reported, had a population of 129, divided among seventeen families, and Minas had 57 people, divided into ten families. Nor should the transient population of soldiers and fisherman be overlooked when considering the demographics of the colony: there were thirty soldiers stationed at Port Royal in 1686 and over fifty fishermen reported at Chedabouctou.[150]

The sense of the colony as a whole, rather than just a smattering of statistics, comes through in the accounts left by those who wrote in the 1680s. The early reports of Champlain and Lescarbot had conveyed the beauty of the lands and rivers they explored. These later reports are nowhere near as elegant or as evocative but they do convey a strong sense of the physical geography of Acadia, of what it meant to arrive there from New France, having travelled with difficulty from Quebec, and of how travel within Acadia was both commonplace and time-consuming, an everyday matter and yet an exhausting undertaking. De Meulles recorded that the journey from Beaubassin to Port Royal by sea could easily take twelve days in the best of circumstances and the overland route, during the winter, could well take a month and occasionally more. To journey from Port Royal to La Hève overland took most of a week. Champlain, Lescarbot, and Denys had waxed eloquent on the land, the beauty of its bays and rivers, its forests and lakes, the immensity of the landscape. These later reports talked of communities and settlements, sometimes approvingly, sometimes critically, and continuously emphasized the difficulties of moving from one place to another, whether by sea or overland.

De Meulles and Saint-Vallier came to the colony at different times of the year and by different routes from New France, and, once in the colony, followed different itineraries. The actual logistics of their journeys emphasize the enormous space that the Acadians confronted. Their small communities spun the necessary network of communications across distances that have to be measured in terms of time it took to travel them and the dangers that had to be faced. De Meulles came by sea from Quebec, leaving there on 11 October 1685. He arrived at Île Percé nineteen days later, on 30 October. Departing for Baie Verte and Beaubassin, he was wrecked off Miscou the next day, 31 October, but had the courage to continue, four days later, in one of the ship's small boats. He arrived on 12 November at the seigneury of Richard Denys de Fronsac, the son of Nicolas Denys, at mouth of Miramichi. It took de Meulles another ten days to journey to Beaubassin, by way of the coast and a bitter portage from Baie Verte. He arrived at his destination on 23 November, having been delayed by an early and severe frost, which made the terrain difficult both for canoes and for foot travel. In all, the voyage from Quebec to La Vallière's settlement had taken over six weeks. The absence of La Vallière himself, and the bitter weather, forced de Meulles to spend the winter there, rather than continuing immediately to Port Royal. He left for the mouth of the Saint John River on 20 April 1686. On 2 May he was at Port Royal, where he remained for two weeks before leaving to visit La Hève and Chedabouctou. Having visited both Canso and Saint-Pierre he left for Île Percé in early June, arriving there on the 19th of that month, stopping once more at the seigneury of Richard Denys. On 20 June, de Meulles left for Quebec and arrived there more than two weeks later, on 6 July.

Saint-Vallier came down through the river route, from Rivière-du-Loup, which he considered "the last habitation in Canada," to the mouth of the Saint John River.[151] He left the shores of the St Lawrence on 7 May 1686 to enter a countryside "where winter still held sway." He travelled with seven companions, two other priests and five experienced canoeists, and it took ten days to reach what is now called Grand Falls on the Saint John, referred to by the bishop as "le grand Sault saint Jean Baptiste."[152] To reach this point from the St Lawrence, Saint-Vallier had the choice of taking the route via Lake Temiscouta and the Madawaska River or voyaging by way of Lake Pohenegamook. It seems clear that he came by way of Pohenegamook. Continuing south to Meductic, Saint-Vallier sent all but one of the priests on to Port Royal, while he himself and a companion went to the coast, to visit the establishment of Richard Denys at the mouth of the Miramichi, a "small stone fort with four bastions, enclosing a house."[153] The bishop had journeyed just over seven weeks since leaving Quebec; de Meulles, in spite of the shipwreck, had taken roughly a month to reach the same destination from the same point of departure. But the bishop had stopped a number of times en route between Quebec and Riv-ière-du-Loup and from that point it took under three weeks to reach the Acadian coast. Along the way, Saint-Vallier had shown great interest in the Amerindians he had met, at Grand Sault and at Meductic. He spent a week in the vicinity of the Miramichi and Richibubouctou with the Mi'kmaq families that gathered to greet him. He then continued down the coast to Chedabouctou, by way of Richibucto, Shediac, and Île Saint-Jean. From Chedabouctou, Saint-Vallier returned to Baie Verte and complained bit-terly about the clouds of mosquitos he faced on the portage across to Beaubassin.[154] From Beaubassin he went along the coast to Minas and from there to Port Royal, mostly by water. The seas were rough and, after nine days on board the small ship, having run out of supplies, his party came to shore and walked the rest of the way overland, arriving there late on the evening of 25 July. The bishop returned to Quebec via Beaubassin, Baie Verte, and the sea route, ending his journey on 26 August.

The two men appraised the colony very differently. De Meulles was in his late thirties or early forties at this time and in his diary and dispatches comes across as cantankerous, critical, and self-important.[155] He reported that the colony was much in need of more effective government and its inhabitants of greater discipline, noting constantly in his diary the times he issued ordinances to regulate the lives of the inhabitants and the number of times he exhorted them to live in peace with one another. He had been monumentally bored by the life among the company he found at Beaubassin during the five months he stayed there and this may have made him more dour than usual.[156] Saint-Vallier, who would be thirty-six years old in November 1686, had a much different attitude: he was much more optimistic about people than the civil servant, even though some matters, such as the brandy trade with the Mi'kmaq, caused him similar concern. De Meulles agreed that the brandy trade was a problem and had published an ordinance against the practice when he was in Port Royal earlier in the year.[157] The bishop remarked often about the work of the four priests who were within the colony: two missionary priests from Normandy at Ched-abouctou, having as their cure the men of the French fishing fleet;[158] Louis Petit at Port Royal, where he had been resident since 1676; and Louis-Pierre Thury, who been working among the Mi'kmaq for about a year. De Meulles did not mention any of the clergy in the colony. Instead he reported his own efforts at Canso "to remedy the abuses which had crept in among" the recently converted Huguenots among the crews of fishing vessels, "who continued their public worship in the manner of their former religion." De Meulles "insisted upon their hearing Mass on feast days and on Sundays, and upon their working only on those days on which they were permitted to work."[159] No mention is made of who the priest there might have been. It is probable that he was one of those stationed at Chedabouctou. Civil servant and bishop seem to have been equally impressed by the beauty of the landscape, but the best that de Meulles could manage about Beaubassin was that its meadows could pasture more than 100,000 cattle. Saint-Vallier, however, called it charming and mentioned the many little streams that flowed through its broad meadows.

De Meulles's diary is only part of the record of his visit to Acadia; he was, of course, engaged in taking a census, of the people, the cleared land, and the animals owned. An interesting point is that he shows no historical sensitivity about his work, and perhaps he did not know about the 1671 census. Certainly he was less meticulous; daughters were not named and the reports of domestic animals were haphazardly recorded. The lack of historical reference is also apparent in the way in which he talks of the development of the colony. There is little appreciation that the colony had not only survived, in spite of continued neglect by France, but actually developed. Port Royal had endured while Beaubassin and Minas had been established, the acreage of land cleared throughout the colony had doubled, there had been close to a 50 per cent growth in the number of cattle reported, the number of sheep kept had approximately doubled, and the herds of goats and pigs had grown significantly.

As in Port Royal fifteen years earlier, cleared land and stock were unevenly distributed in these new settlements. The extent to which economic divisions were emerging among the settlers will be discussed in chapter 6, but it is clear that there were differences between those with few dependants, considerable cleared acreage, and reasonable numbers of animals and those with growing families, no land, and few animals.[160] As far as sheep and pigs are concerned, the size of the herds and flocks attributed to particular households is similar to that reported for the New England colonies, families having anywhere from three to a dozen sheep and much the same number of pigs in both places.[161] However, the Acadians owned more cattle than was common in New England at this time, where "a dozen cowkind, even when it included not only mature animals but younger ones from one, to three years old, was a large herd."[162] At Port Royal, almost 20 per cent of the families, eighteen out of ninety-five, had more than a dozen cattle. Of the ten families recorded at Minas, three had similar herds and at Beaubassin 50 per cent – eight out of sixteen families – were listed with more than a dozen cattle each.

Even though the settler population in Acadia was so much smaller that of New France and of the majority of the English-speaking colonies in North America, in all three areas the leadership for the establishment of new communities was provided by settlers who had already established themselves.[163] The question of land shortage has often been given as the motive for internal migration within a colony. But, in Acadia, the continued population growth of the older establishments would argue that this was only one of many reasons, including social, political, and religious tensions within the older communities as well as the lure of the frontier itself. In Acadia the family of Jacques Bourgeois and his wife, Jeanne Trahan, formed a strong link between Port Royal and Beaubassin. In the census of 1686 the family is divided between the two settlements, with the widow and children of the eldest son, along with the middle son and two of the seven daughters, established in the new community. The youngest son was settled at Port Royal but also farmed land at Beaubassin.[164] Pierre Melanson, who had refused to cooperate with the first census taker in 1671, was the prime mover behind the Minas Basin settlement.[165] He, too, had been reasonably situated in Port Royal in 1671 but was clearly someone who questioned controls. He might very well have moved for political reasons, although by 1686 he had mellowed somewhat. De Meulles reported that Melanson had nine children, ranging in age from twenty years to a newborn, and a herd of thirty-one cattle and eight sheep as well as twelve goats.[166] But the new communities were not just founded by one or two well-established families from Port Royal: the surnames of fifteen of the twenty adults listed at Minas in 1685 are to be found at the older settlement in 1671, 75 per cent of the population. At Beaubassin, where the impact of migration from Quebec was, at this time, significant, two-thirds of the surnames are similarly to be found in that census, twenty-three of the thirty three adults, more than 66 per cent. As well as people, Port Royal had also provided the new communities with stock, tools, and, perhaps as important as anything else, the knowledge of skills necessary to survive and prosper.[167]

Dykes were constructed at both Beaubassin and Minas. Saint-Vallier wrote that the first years at Beaubassin were particularly difficult because of the lack of dry pasture and the amount of work and resources it took to establish the dykes.[168] He is one of the few seventeenth-century commentators who seems to have realized how much work was involved in the building and maintenance of dykes. At Minas, too, the bishop reported that the community was draining the marshes.[169] Nor was the heritage of skills restricted to agricultural techniques: Saint-Vallier comments on the weaving done by the women in Beaubassin, although he considers it rough and insufficient to provide for all the needs of the community.[170] De Meulles wrote that skills had been handed on from one generation to the next and that there were weavers, masons, carpenters, woodworkers, and tool makers in the colony. He also noted that they built boats capable of coastal travel and that they made their own clothes, the women making stockings, gloves, and bonnets.[171] The bishop ended his account of Beaubassin by remarking that the settlers gathered grain and fished, for both salmon and cod. In fact, he judged, they would be above reproach if only they were a little more restrained in the matter of the brandy trade with the Mi'kmaq.[172]

In terms of the texture of Acadian life, the judgments of de Meulles and Saint-Vallier differed most over Port Royal. François-Marie Perrot, who had arrived as governor of Acadia in late September 1685, described Port Royal at this time as a straggly collection of houses with considerable distances between the buildings, in no way a compact village. Both he and de Meulles commented, adversely, on relations between Acadian and Mi'kmaq. Perrot was convinced that the very structure of Port Royal led to its people "taking to the woods and leading a scandalous life with the savages."[173] De Meulles wrote in his diary that he issued ordinances concerned "with ways of remedying the libertinism of several of His Majesty's subjects, who keep Indian women in their dwellings, who desert father and mother and follow these Indian women into the woods."[174] The bishop, on the other hand, endorsed the report given him by Louis Petit, the priest who had been appointed the vicar general of Acadia by Laval in 1676 and had lived since then in Port Royal. Petit had come to Canada as a captain in the Carignan-Salières regiment in 1665 and, when he decided to enter the priesthood, had studied at the seminary of Quebec. He was ordained by Bishop Laval in 1670.[175] In a letter that Petit had sent to Saint-Vallier in October 1685, there is no mention of loose living among his flock. Instead, Petit describes his congregation as sweet-natured, with a tendency to piety and not given to swearing or drunkenness, and the women as chaste.[176] He was pleased with their attendance at Mass on Sundays and holy days and their reception of the sacraments. Saint-Vallier, indeed, found the church at Port Royal pretty and adequately furnished.

The reports of Acadian religious practices at this time show that a significant proportion of the colonists gave considerable importance to the social observance of Catholic belief. Saint-Vallier speaks of the way in which the people of Beaubassin and Minas asked him to name a priest for their settlements. Petit comments on the way in which Saint-Castin arrived from the Pentagöuet area at least twice a year to attend Mass, and how he often gave generously to the church. Petit also writes about the way in which the Port Royal congregation supported not only High Mass but the celebration of Vespers. It is also clear that what formal education there was in the colony was the result of the activity of its priests. It was Petit who encouraged an unnamed colonist to give lessons to the boys of Port Royal and Petit himself taught the girls their catechism. Finally, there is evidence of the extent to which the women immediately baptized the newborn. This, for the bishop, was a practice that should cease. It can, however, be read as the result of strong convictions, held by the women, about the importance of the sacrament as the rite of admittance to membership in the Catholic Church.[177]

Together, these commentaries paint a picture of a society with a good relationship with the original inhabitants of the area. There are no reports of hostilities with the Mi'kmaq. The fur trade was obviously lucrative and a matter of common practice whereby guns, ammunition, axes, and brandy as well as other products were bartered by Acadians throughout the colony for furs, which were then traded to New England, particularly Massachusetts.[178] Not only did John Nelson have a year-round store in Port Royal but other merchants sent ships each year to Beaubassin and Minas, once these settlements were founded. De Meulles reported that every spring three or four English ships came, loaded with every necessity, bartering for furs and other goods.[179]

But, while the fur trade was important, it was not the staple of the Acadian economy – that was agriculture. Essentially, Acadian farming practices were those of seventeenth-century France and England, labour-intensive and limited by the few agricultural tools available: scythe, sickle axe, and rough ploughs. Until the end of the 1680s, no horses were reported in the colony, nor is there any evidence, in these early decades, of oxen as draft animals. The key to the obvious success of Acadian agriculture was the development of marshlands, drained by dykes, a practice that spread as the colony expanded and supported the growth of animal husbandry. The Acadians, in common with other European colonists in North America, gained their shelter, food, fuel, and clothing from the land through hard labour. Good hunting and fine fishing helped. Lumber, while available, was locally available but would also be imported as dressed planks for certain buildings, such as grist mills and sawmills, though not usually for boats.[180] Food grown was not restricted to wheat and peas, although Perrot reported that in 1686 these were in good supply at Port Royal. He also remarked on the abundance of apples and cherries.[181] Textiles were home-produced, if not exclusively at least to a considerable extent. Crops included hemp and flax.[182] This meant that spinning wheels and looms were also part of the technology available to the Acadians and that spinning and weaving were equally tasks for Acadian women. The sheep, too, provided wool. Nor should the fact that many Acadians made their own shoes, *souliers sauvages* (probably moccasins), be overlooked.

In sum, by 1686, against all odds, Acadia was not just a scattering of trading posts but an emerging society. The fifty years of experience of a common pattern of everyday life, the necessary interaction with neighbours, had resulted in economic, social, and political networks that provided the groundwork for a developing Acadian community. The Norwegian sociologist Fredrik Barth has pointed out that, whether people wish the result or not, continuous interaction among a small group develops a social and political community.[183] The years from 1671 to 1686 were, for Acadia, years when the colony established itself as a presence in North America, not strong, not powerful, but there, something that both New England and New France had to take into consideration. During the next twenty-four years, what had been built would grow and prove capable of enduring yet more attacks from the former and something less than fully committed support from the latter.

CHAPTER SIX

Acadia: Life in a Border Colony

It was not merely that Acadia had become a larger and more complex society, over the past several decades, that stopped the Bergier-La Vallière hostilities repeating the pattern of the La Tour-d'Aulnay rivalry. It was that this same passage of time had brought equally far-reaching changes throughout the transatlantic world. France, England, New France, and New England had altered at least as much as Acadia and so had their policies, both in terms of general international goals and alliances and in terms of Acadian issues. Both France and England had seen a major growth in national cohesion, owing largely to the greatly increased power of their respective monarchies. As a result, government action in both countries was beginning to be a matter of deliberate design for the state, rather than an issue of dynastic ambitions between monarchs in foreign affairs and aristocratic power politics in the domestic arena. Since 1620 there had been an emphasis on the development of the state itself, in the sense that the central government, in both countries, had evolved ways and means of bringing local and regional authorities under much greater control.[1] Both England and France were grappling with the problems of creating a sense of national interest within their realms, at the same time as the economic and political institutions necessary to do so were being put in place. Jeremy Black has written that, in the last decades of the seventeenth century, "there was no constitutional, political or confessional consensus [in France], and this lay behind the contentious politics" of the period.[2] But, while there was no all-embracing consensus, there is no doubt that governments sought the support of those ruled, however this might be obtained. Inevitably this meant an attempt, by both European powers, to influence, if not control, colonial activities more closely, since colonies were seen by them as an integral part of each realm. At the same time, the development of the New England colonies and of New France meant that these polities gave an equally increased attention to each other's ambitions and activities. Whereas Acadia had been of peripheral and episodic interest to both England and France, and to the other colonial societies, in the 1630s, it was a matter of continuous interest to all of them by the 1680s. Indeed, for New England and Newfoundland, Acadia sometimes became of major significance.

Thus, by 1680, France played a much more direct role in Acadian affairs than it had earlier. This did not mean that the connection between the authorities in France and colonial officials in Port Royal always followed the same pattern. Logically, after the restoration of French control over the colony in 1670, its administration should have been explicitly either under the control of the governor and intendant of New France or administered directly from France. In practice it was both and neither. Sometimes French authorities considered Acadia an appendage of the larger colony. At other times, as in the appointment of Acadian officials and the establishment of the Compagnie de la Pêche Sédentaire, it was treated as a direct responsibility of the crown. The officials in Acadia usually acted as if they were primarily responsible to France. Whether this was true or not, the presence of commanders and governors, salaried, appointed for fixed terms, and not always entangled in the politics of settlement and trade, added new players to the cast of squabbling characters. Even if the reports to France by these officials were biased in favour of one or other of the parties, such reports provided Louis XIV and his ministers with a much more detailed context for their decisions about Acadian matters. Partly as a result of this, and partly because of the growing importance of North American colonial matters in French government policy after 1680, Acadian questions received measurably more attention from the authorities than before. This resulted in a trickle of material support, which was important, and a considerable amount of diplomatic correspondence with London about Acadian concerns. The interest of the authorities on the St Lawrence in Port Royal and environs had been superficial fifty years earlier. Now, although there was little direct aid sent from Quebec to Acadia, the letters of the intendant and governors frequently commented on Acadian affairs. The visit of de Meulles is indicative of the extent to which Quebec officials had come to consider Acadian concerns within their purview, if not unquestionably within their jurisdiction.

Until 1690, England's interest in the colony was considerably less than that of France. The disposition of Acadia by the Treaty of Breda in 1667 had been accepted by Charles II and his advisers against the strenuous objections of Thomas Temple and his allies. The Lords of Trade and Plantations[3] had enough North American matters to think about without considering the issue of Acadia. To begin with, there was the continuing problem of Newfoundland[4] and the troublesome ten colonies on the continent itself. Indeed, what attention England did devote to Acadia during the 1680s was the direct result of pressure from New England. Whereas in the 1640s there had been considerable debate in Massachusetts as to the type and kind of aid that could be given to La Tour and d'Aulnay, in the 1680s ships left from New York and New Hampshire to join others from Maine and Massachusetts fishing off the Acadian coasts. It was no longer simply a matter of Port Royal and Boston, uneasy neighbours reaching an accommodation, essentially on their own, and relatively unrestricted by the considerations of the interests of anybody else. Acadian external relations now involved the developing border politics of burgeoning empires as well as the expressed concerns of their immediate neighbours. This became clear during the warfare of the 1690s, known in North America as King William's War and in England and Europe as the War of the League of Augsburg.

The regime of François-Marie Perrot, who had been appointed governor on 10 April 1684, was a period of transition for Acadia, between what might be called the period of neighbourhood politics and the era of major colonial strife between France and England in North America. Many of the old political patterns held sway for the three years of his appointment, to a large extent because of the suspension of the Massachusetts Charter in 1684. The subsequent administrative turmoil, before the emergence of the Dominion of New England in 1686 and its disintegration in 1689,[5] engulfed not only that colony but Maine, Rhode Island, New Hampshire, and the territory of the Duke of York in northern Maine as well, intensifying the rivalries and tensions among the colonies themselves. These events slowed the realization that major changes were occurring in Acadian–New England relations. There is no indication in any official correspondence, whether written in London, Boston, Paris, or Quebec, in September 1685, the date of Perrot's arrival in Acadia, that the recent clashes between the Compagnie de la Pêche Sédentaire and New England ships were more than a particularly violent eruption of a common enough happening.

Perrot was not a person of much political vision, although he had a certain shrewdness. He was Jean Talon's son-in law and had previously been the governor of Montreal, a post from which he had been dismissed because of general drunkenness and illegal fur trading.[6] It was almost certainly the influence of his father-in-law, who had been appointed, on his return from Canada, to the office of first valet of the king's wardrobe, that provided Perrot with another official appointment. Intelligent, energetic, and, above all, determined to become rich, Perrot wrote to the minister of the Marine, immediately after his arrival in Acadia, to ask for the grant of a large seigneury at La Hève.[7] His letter also solicited funds and supplies to establish a fort there, soldiers to provide the property with a garrison, a small vessel, cannon, and a missionary. These requests being refused, Perrot was soon engaged in trade with Boston, and, within the year, he is reported to have sent brandy, wine, and linen there.[8] His business seems to have flourished for, when he was dismissed from the governorship in April 1687, two years after his arrival, he remained in the colony, taking an active part in Acadian-Massachusetts affairs.

Perrot sent his first major dispatch to the minister on 9 August 1686.[9] It was highly critical of Port Royal. He considered that lands had been granted without due consideration; the concessions had been too extensive and too far apart from one another, thus allowing some of the settlers far too great a facility for licentious contact with the native population.[10] He believed that the situation was the fault almost entirely of Alexandre Le Borgne de Belle-Isle, now in his mid-forties, who claimed seigneurial rights over much of the Port Royal region[11] and who was, in Perrot's opinion, a drunkard who had granted the lands, with little or no thought, to the first comer.[12] Perrot did admit that the colony had a structure of regulations that could serve it well but he considered the officials then present in the colony either too old or too drunk to fulfil their functions properly. He did concede, however, that the countryside was pleasant enough and that one could easily exploit the fishery.

At much the same time as Perrot set out for Acadia, events in Europe took place which clearly signalled that, even though they might be far from a central consideration, North American matters were now of some importance in the minds of those engaged in the direction of high policy in London and Paris. In February 1685 James Stuart became James II of England and James VII of Scotland. He was determined to restore his realms to Catholic ways and a proper understanding of the rights of kings. That same year, Louis XIV had revoked the Edict of Nantes, thereby ending all pretense at religious toleration within his jurisdiction. The actions of the former would lead to the loss of his thrones, that of the latter to a major confrontation with the Protestant forces of Europe. In 1686 both kings understood that their policies required public support from their peoples and wished to resolve as many external matters as possible, in order to be free to concentrate on domestic affairs. One of the results of this mutual taking stock was the attempt to settle the questions of their North American interests in the treaty signed at Whitehall on 16 November 1686.[13]

Known as the Treaty of Neutrality, it was in force barely three years, but the ideas it embodied would be considered at varying times in the future. When the English Revolution of 1688–89 took place, and William of Orange replaced James II, however, the treaty itself became a dead letter. Much of its importance for North America lies in the very fact of its existence, testimony to the growing attention that was being accorded colonial matters by both England and France. Its negotiators, as John Reid has pointed out, knew that the only way to ensure peace in North America between France and England was "to regulate the limits of the lands which each of the two nations should possess."[14] Their perception marked the beginning of a slow realization by European governments that the problems of North America were of a different order than those posed by dissident regions within each European realm. However, the Treaty of Neutrality was firmly rooted in past practice and based upon the contemporary European perception of colonies as the extensions of the monarchs' realms. It embodied the idea that the wishes of the colonial elites, and their visions of the future, must, necessarily, give way to the policies of the imperial powers and the demands of European diplomacy.[15] Thus, the most obviously important provision of the treaty, in the minds of European officials, was at the same time its most inconsequential for North American colonies, because it implied a control of North American colonial politics by Europe which could not be practically enforced. This was the stipulation that, though the two countries might be at war in Europe, "their colonies in America should continue in peace and neutrality." The presumption is clear: warfare between the colonies in North America was subject to close control from the other side of the Atlantic – this at a time when the fastest crossing of the Atlantic, with the finest of weather throughout, on board the best of the tall ships, was forty-nine days.[16] As well, this provision implied that no local causes of dissension would provoke an outbreak of hostilities in North America, if peace held in Europe.

Further, as far as Acadia and New England were concerned, the treaty's provision on the Acadian fisheries was unworkable. As George Rawlyk writes: "What the treaty specifically prohibited was the drying of fish on Nova Scotia soil by Massachusetts fishermen, a drastic measure which, if enforced, would significantly affect the entire Massachusetts economy."[17] Leaving aside the question of how such a provision could, in fact, be enforced, given the geography of the coastlines involved and the technology of the sparse naval forces available,[18] those who wrote this clause had really no appreciation of the way in which the Atlantic fishery was pursued by those in the colonies, nor much sensitivity to the place of that fishery in the economy of Massachusetts in particular and New England in general. As has already been mentioned, in the 1680s at least thirty or forty small fishing boats each brought off a thousand quintals of cod from the Acadian banks annually.[19] A large proportion of this catch was then exported to the West Indies and to Bilbao. The merchants so engaged expected a 50 per cent profit on the fish sold and a further 100 per cent profit on goods bought and imported to New England.[20] The majority of those who fished took advantage of the sheltered coves and bays of Acadia to dry their catch and they fought against any disruption of this practice. The hostile reaction to the arrival of the Compagnie de la Pêche Sédentaire, which had resulted in the capture of the four French fishing vessels the following year, was a warning of more trouble ahead. However, because the Treaty of Neutrality did not recognize the serious nature of the Acadian-New England conflict over the Acadian banks, it provided no machinery for settling the inevitable disputes that occurred.

Similarly, the issue of the boundary between Maine and Acadia – an even more complex matter than the fishery dispute – was left unresolved. The area in question was extensive and geographically complex. The dominance of the St Lawrence River as a highway into a continent has often overshadowed the importance of the rivers to its south, especially those of present-day Maine and Massachusetts, as entry points. But these rivers, the Penobscot, the Kennebec, and the Saco, among others, are also pathways from the ocean to the hinterland. Inevitably, both Maine and Acadia claimed control of much of the area, arguing constantly over which river had been previously agreed upon as the boundary. More important, at this time the area was relatively unsettled by Europeans, although both French and English had established strong trading relations with the native Americans. These people, the eastern Abenaki, were militarily capable and had forced Massachusetts to recognize their claims over Maine in 1678 when that colony agreed to pay the tribes an annual quit-rent of "a peck of corn for every English family."[21] The Abenaki lived in small villages along the river valleys from the Penobscot to the Saco and were connected to one another by, above all, proximity and family relationships.[22] At the time of contact they were fundamentally hunter-gatherers, although they had developed some agriculture.[23] The sea was nowhere near as important to them as it was to the Mi'kmaq, with whom they had an uneasy relationship, occasionally peaceful, more often quarrelsome. Both peoples considered that they had a right to range widely as part of their hunting practices. While the contacts that the M'ikmaq developed with the newcomers from Europe were primarily with the French, the Abenaki developed relationships with both French and English.

In fact, as Kenneth M. Morrison has pointed out, as early as 1614, after Argall's attacks on Saint-Saveur and Port Royal, the Abenaki were aware of the implications of alliance with one or other groups of Europeans.[24] Over the next decades, both French and English sought to bring them into a firm alliance. On the whole, the French efforts were more effective, partly because of the development of common religious ties and partly because of the absence of any major French settlement pressure. It was through Quebec that the French relationship with the Abenaki was primarily orchestrated, and it was based upon effective Jesuit missionary activity and considerable secular respect for Indian rights.[25] At the same time, English settlement in Maine had been successful enough to establish a number of small communities, intent on further expansion but not able to produce a civil government of any great strength. As a result, lawlessness was rife and control by the appointed officials over the settlers, in particular over their hostile and belligerent responses to Abenaki activities, was weak.[26] From 1670 onwards, the Maine settlers showed increasing contempt for Abenaki ways. They refused to abide by the 1678 treaty terms or pay quit rents to the Abenaki. They paid no attention to Abenaki farming and fishing practices. Their cattle damaged the Abenaki's unfenced corn fields, and, on the Saco River, settlers placed nets that interfered with the spring runs of fish, an important Abenaki food source.[27] By the 1680s, Maine was attempting to assimilate land controlled by Abenaki, while the French were making every effort to ensure that these same Abenaki remained under their influence. Thus, any effort to draw a precise boundary between Acadia and Maine, in 1686, demanded an agreement on the control of territory which was not only in dispute between the two colonies but was also lived in, and claimed, by a people supported by the French secular and religious officials on the St Lawrence.

The complex nature of the Acadia-Maine border issue and the repercussions for Acadia began to emerge within months of the Treaty of Neutrality having been signed. In the summer of 1686 there was a raid by New York ships on a cache of supplies, dispatched by John Nelson to Saint-Castin, who lived and traded on the Penobscot.[28] The latter had remained in the general area of Pentagöuet ever since 1674, despite his inheritance of the family title and some property rights in Bearn, on the death of his elder brother in that year.[29] Perrot protested about the seizure to the governor of New York, Thomas Dongan, asserting that the Pentagöuet area had been ceded to France by the Treaty of Breda. Dongan replied rapidly, on 6 October 1686, remarking that he was "not aware that anything has been done to the French on their territories." But, he continued, "if you remained on the soil of the King of England's province, you cannot expect peace, nor can I give you any satisfaction."[30] He concluded by asserting that it was the French who had "broken the treaty [of] neutrality by your resting on the King of England's ground, and, so this is all I shall answer to your letter, though I am your obedient servant Thos. Dongan."

Perrot wrote a lengthy report on the situation to the minister of the Marine. In it he noted that it was John Nelson who had suffered the loss, taking the opportunity to praise the latter for having done much good for the Acadians, including providing them with credit in hard times.[31] Perrot went on to describe Saint-Castin in unflattering terms, considering that he had brought much of the trouble on himself and had done little to prevent the pillage. The governor of New France, Jacques-René de Brisay de Denonville, wrote to the minister at much the same time, on 10 November 1686. He did not mention the fracas but did praise Saint-Castin and suggested that, if Perrot wished to resign, Saint-Castin would make an excellent governor for Acadia.[32] Neither letter could have reached France much before January 1687 and the extent to which either played a part in Perrot's dismissal that year can only be imagined. What is known is that, once more, Louis XIV did not appoint as governor of Acadia the candidate proposed by the governor of Quebec but instead named Louis-Alexandre Des Friches de Meneval to this position on 1 March 1687.[33] Meneval was not a member of a great noble family, although he was considered to be of "good birth." Primarily he was a career officer in the army and had earned the good opinion of the Vicomte de Turenne. Now his task was to shore up a neglected outpost of empire and re-establish French prestige in an area where, officials thought, it had been deteriorating badly.

He received detailed instructions as to the nature of his task in April 1687.[34] The limits of his jurisdiction were described as lying between the Gaspé and the Kennebec River, the latter, it was stated, being the boundary between New France and New England. In terms of the policy aims of the French government for the colony, there was no substantial difference between that outlined for Meneval and that contained in the instructions given to every governor since Grandfontaine, a policy that all had found impossible to implement. Meneval, like Grandfontaine, was to prevent the English from trading and fishing in Acadia.[35] What was different, however, was the level of support with which Meneval was provided and the detailed commentary he was given on the internal problems of the colony. The terms on which Meneval served were a considerable improvement on those accorded his predecessors: his salary was set at 3,000 *livres* and he was given a further 1,000 *livres* for general expenses before he left.[36] Even taking into account the fluctuating value of the *livre* since Grandfontaine was paid seventeen years earlier, Meneval's emoluments were a considerable increase over those granted his predecessor. His salary, however, remained markedly below that accorded the governor general of New France. Denonville, appointed to that position on 1 January 1685, was paid 24,000 *livres* a year.[37]

Meneval also received a great deal more in terms of personnel and general supplies, and even intermittent naval backing, than his predecessors. Early in the summer of 1687, the naval transport *La Bretonne* was dispatched to Chedabouctou, arriving there in July. On board were Gargas, a clerk in the Ministry of the Marine, who was to serve as a record keeper in the colony for a year, and Miramont, an officer in charge of some thirty soldiers, munitions, and 4,000 *livres* to be spent on reconstructing the fort at Port Royal.[38] One of the king's frigates, the 150-ton *La Friponne*, which carried sixteen guns and about sixty men, was also sent early that summer to patrol Acadian waters and to drive away any foreign vessels attempting to fish or trade there.[39]

Finally, the detailed description of the internal situation of the colony, given to Meneval, owed much to Perot's reports. It was remarked in the former's instructions that the king had been informed of those who "claimed to have exclusive rights over vast stretches of the country, with the right to grant land to others, without having worked either to cultivate the land, animal husbandry, or at the fishery, occupying themselves exclusively with trade in the forest, with scandalous debauchery, and reacting violently against the French, on the pretext of the said rights."[40] The size of concessions had been a matter of long-standing concern to the French authorities and, throughout the 1670s, had been constantly criticized by the king.[41] But, as R.C. Harris has pointed out, Louis XIV "ratified almost all augmentations sent to him," that is, the increases to the small seigneuries granted by Talon.[42] The concern with the size of the Acadian seigneuries seems to have been as much a matter French preoccupation with the establishment of agriculture and the development of the fisheries as it was a question of the actual acreage granted. In any case, Meneval's instruction was to reimpose the authority of the crown and he was given the right to dispatch to France any who refused to reform their ways and accept the new dispensation.

Meneval needed all the help he could get because, even before he arrived in October, there was trouble, both on land and at sea, the former due to the ambitions of Governor Edmund Andros, who headed the new Dominion of New England, and the latter to French action. Both occurred at much the same time: the episode on land in late June 1687 and the clash at sea about a month later. The first was a continuance of New York action in the Pentagöuet area. Saint-Castin reported, in a dispatch to Denonville, that some eighty men had landed there and claimed the coast, as far as the St Croix River, as belonging to England.[43] It is clear that this was one more attempt by the English to establish that the Acadian boundary was the St Croix River. Similarly, the incident at sea was the French attempt to establish their authority over the Acadian fisheries, something that the fishing fleets of New England much feared. At the same time as Louis XIV issued Meneval with his instructions, in March 1687, Andros reported to the Lords of Trade and Plantations that there was considerable apprehension "among our fishing parties" as to what might occur in the coming season.[44] Two weeks earlier, Edward Randolph had written to the same body, observing that "our trade dayly decays and the prohibition to fish on the French coast of Nova Scotia ... will quite destroy our fishery."[45] These fears were justified when *La Friponne*, which arrived off Chedabouctou in early summer, captured two fishing ketches from Salem on 22 July 1687. One of them, the *Margaret*, owned and captained by Stephen Sewall, managed to escape but the other was taken to Port Royal and its master and crew kept prisoner.[46] Sewall and other Salem merchants wrote promptly to Governor Andros, relating what had happened and requesting action.[47] The matter was placed before the council in Boston on 4 August 1687 and Captain Francis Nicholson, a British army officer, was dispatched to Port Royal to make a strong protest over the matter and to learn what he could about the state of that settlement. Since Meneval had not yet arrived, Nicholson returned to Boston without the concessions Andros and the council desired, namely, the restoration of the ketch and its crew, compensation for the injury suffered, and assurances against such seizures in the future.[48]

Meneval reached Chedabouctou at the beginning of October 1687, on board a ship of the Compagnie de la Pêche Sédentaire. Thus, his introduction to his posting was through the enterprise managed by the nephew of his benefactor, Charles-François Duret de Chevry, the Marquis de Villeneuve, who had supported Meneval strongly for the governorship of Acadia. The marquis was of some importance in the political life of the court at Versailles and was the patron of a number of those who were appointed in Acadia, including the later commander, Joseph Robinau de Villebon, because of the interest of his nephew in the colony. This man, Charles Duret de Chevry de La Boulaye, had assumed full responsibility for the Compagnie de la Pêche Sédentaire when Bergier disappeared from the scene in 1685 and had been relatively successful in establishing an inshore fishery at Chedabouctou. By his own account, La Boulaye had worked to improve the site since the departure of de Meulles and to establish a year-round settlement to anchor the migrant labour demanded by the fishery. In a report he wrote for the minister of the Marine on 24 September 1687, La Boulaye remarked that the inshore fishery would finally be well established at Chedabouctou that year. He went to say that the *Saint Louis*, which had left the day before, carried on board not only twenty experienced fishermen but another ten men, among whom there were carpenters, barrel makers, locksmiths, masons, and surgeons.[49] Further, La Boulaye explained, he intended to build both a church and housing for the two priests, who had been sent to minister to the fishing fleet. Meneval was no doubt aware of La Boulaye's intentions but Chedabouctou would have appeared a mere halting place to him, a station with no European families and little agriculture.

Meneval went on to Port Royal on board the *Friponne*. His home for the next three years was, in terms of the landscape, as beautiful as ever it had been: a sheltered bay, ringed with forested hills, a fort, a church, and a sprinkling of houses built on the estuary, with farms stretching back along the meadowlands of the Rivière-du-Dauphin. The population was small, somewhere between four and six hundred, counting all those established within the valley and along the hillsides.[50] Nicholson, in the dispatch he sent to London in 1687, estimated that there were about eighty families in the region and in Port Royal itself perhaps fifteen houses, "all very mean ones." Gargas, Meneval's record keeper, reported fourteen houses and a mill in the statistical tables he attached to his report. In his description of the settlement, however, he wrote that Port Royal contained "only nine or ten dwellings, the other buildings being barns." He described the houses as "low, made of pieces of logs of wood, one on top of the other covered with thatch, that in which the Governor lives being the only one covered with planks."[51] Nicholson had included, as one might expect, a description of the military strength of Port Royal. He noted the "ruine of an old Earthern fortification" and had discovered that there were "about 40 soldiers whereof tenn were old ones, the rest came in the Man of Warr, withe the Lieut. a Comisary and two other Gentlemen." Finally, he mentioned that there "only three old Guns, but [they have] now brought 15 very fine and large ones."[52] Neither commentator mentioned the church per se, although Nicholson did note that he based his estimate of the population on the attendance at church and Gargas listed it among the buildings he tallied. Nor did either man make any commentary as to where Perrot or other notables, such as Villebon, the future commandant of Acadia, then lived. But Gargas did indicate that, after difficulties in finding accommodation, he and Miramont lived "in a kitchen belonging to M. Perrot, and this kitchen had to be bedroom, hall, study, kitchen, cellar and loft for both of us."[53]

To Meneval, his posting was to prove a mixed blessing. While it was a considerable advancement for one who had been just a company lieutenant when appointed, it was also an appointment to a very distant outpost of the French empire with a history of being the object of attack and counter-attack. The problems he faced were those his predecessors had found intractable. Moreover, the company of his fellow officials would prove to be little to his taste and that of the Acadians themselves even less so. He was fortunate that the first six months of his tenure were relatively peaceful. During this period, Meneval did little but see that monies owed to the soldiers by Perrot were paid, while also bewailing the indebtedness of the inhabitants to "les Anglois."[54] Meneval thought that this lamentable state of affairs resulted from the extremely high prices that the Acadians had to pay the latter for supplies, as a result of their "invasion."[55] It is difficult to understand which raid Meneval had in mind, since the last direct assault on Port Royal had taken place before 1671. In any case, he did not immediately set about reconstructing the defences at Port Royal and informed the minister of the Marine that he was considering establishing once more the fort at Pentagöuet.[56]

As the weeks went by, he and Gargas clashed continuously. Gargas returned to France in August 1688, having drawn up a statistical account of the colony and written a description of much of it. These he sent to the king, along with an account of his personal experiences during his stay in the colony. This account records every disagreement he had with the governor, from matters of minor bureaucracy to complaints that Meneval deliberately sabotaged his attempts to collect information. Gargas further complained of Meneval's refusal to counter-sign receipts provided by others and of forcing him to pay the soldiers while they were billeted among the inhabitants rather than lodged in the guardhouse. On the second point, Gargas considered the soldiers "on leave" and not entitled to wages. In the eyes of this scrupulous bureaucrat, the governor's antagonism to his activities was motivated, first, by his wish to replace Gargas with "a creature [une créature de] of Monsieur le Marquis de Chivry [sic]"; second, by his view that Gargas was "infringing on his authority" (j'enpiettons sur son autorité); and third, and most important, by the belief that Gargas "knew too much about what was going on in Acadie" (la trop grande connaissance que j'avais de toutes ce qui se passoit à l'Acadie).[57] Gargas associated Villebon with Meneval's attitude to him. The former had been in the colony since 1685 and would be appointed its commandant on 7 April 1691.[58] Gargas wrote that "truth forces me to say that the said Villebon is capable of destroying the best established colony and that his presence is an invincible object to its establishment."[59] He also accused Villebon of

stirring "up the greater part of the inhabitants to refuse me the information [needed to compile the general census], even to the point of advising
them (except for the respect due Your Highness) to chase me away when
I asked for the information."[60] It is hardly surprising to find that Gargas
also quarrelled with the settlers, in particular with the large and important
Bourque family, in this case over the loan and return of a canoe.

However querulous and self-justifying Gargas appears, however incomplete his statistical survey may be, his report on the colony is one of the
most interesting and useful in this period. It is interesting because it is, first
and foremost, the report of a cantankerous and curious mind, and it is particularly useful because it adds much to our knowledge of the colony on
the brink of two decades of war and rumours of war. Gargas seems to have
travelled almost the entire colony, except for the Miramachi and the Baie
des Chaleurs. His account traces a journey from Port Royal to the Saint
John River, via Minas and Beaubassin, and from there, first to Passamaquoddy Bay and then along the coast as far as Pemaquid. He also
went from Cap Sable via La Hève and Canso to Cape Breton. He wrote
short descriptions of most of the places, with acerbic comments on the settlements, and how they could be better managed. Above all, he counted,
although how and with what help we do not know. His was not a nominal
census. He collected numbers and these included totals for the Mi'kmaq
population as well as the Acadian, of wigwams as well as houses, of farm
buildings as well as land cleared and animals kept. He compiled tables that
gave numbers of enlisted men, guns and cannons, swords and pistols. As
ever, this work demands as much scepticism as it does acceptance. But
where it can be checked by later research, through the examination of
church registers and archaeology, for example, it is usual to find that while
data may have been omitted it has not been invented. The overall picture
is often dependable, the details unreliable.

The population estimates of Gargas can be considered in the light of the
nominal census made de Meulles two years earlier and a short numerical
census of the following year. Gargas reported a population of over eight
hundred settlers, approximately the same number as that given by de
Meulles. The 1689 census, however, reported the population as somewhere between nine hundred and nine hundred and fifty. What is clear,
both from Gargas and from the 1689 census, is that Minas had become a
growth centre, while Port Royal's population had fallen by some ten families, a loss of between fifty and a hundred people.[61] Given that Port Royal
was an inevitable source of supply for the new settlements, this is no surprise. Flocks, herds, and land cleared had increased for the colony as a
whole, and, although the number of cattle at Port Royal had diminished,
the number of sheep remained the same.[62] In attempting to gauge the relative wealth of farming communities, economists have worked with a ratio
of livestock units per capita. It is assumed that a farm family required one
livestock unit – a head of cattle or five sheep or five pigs – for each of its

members in order to live at a reasonable level. In this theoretical world, Clark has pointed out that a household composed of three generations, "two grand-parents, two parents, and four children, is considered to have been no more than self-sufficient in animals if it owned two oxen, four cows, five sheep and five pigs."[63] Any increase in the units per capita would mean that the family would be capable of some sort of commercial activity, such as the sale or exchange of live animals, preserved meat, wool, and hides. Gargas reported 998 cattle and 889 goats and sheep in 1688. He made no attempt to number the pigs, and no account was taken of poultry.[64] If we use his own estimate of a population of roughly eight hundred settlers, Gargas's figures argue that there was a good sufficiency of livestock units for the colony, when augmented by the uncounted swine. In other words, animal husbandry was flourishing by the end of the 1680s. When this data is looked at in the context of the hunting and fishing opportunities available, it is clear that the supply of protein in Acadia was plentiful by 1688.

But protein alone is not enough and the success of grain crops is more difficult to estimate. The various censuses, while usually listing cleared land, do not provide much information about acres sown and harvested. On occasion, it seems, there was enough grain for trade. Gargas mentions that Villebon, at that point Meneval's lieutenant, paid almost two hundred hogsheads of grain to ketches from New England in 1688.[65] Grain harvests, however, are much at the mercy of the weather, even more so than animals, and no reliance could be placed on a surplus in any given year. The combination of a late spring, a cold summer, and an early winter often enough caused grain crops to fail in France. Disease and pests, moulds and mice can produce a season of scarcity with little warning. From the census reports, the best that can be said of the progress that Acadian agriculture had made by 1688 is that the amount of acreage under cultivation had gradually increased. Gargas is at some pains to distinguish between uplands cleared and marshes dyked. Like many another French official, he criticized the Acadian reliance on the latter, commenting that "it would be a good plan to force the inhabitants to clear the higher ground. Most of them, as at Port Royal, Minas etc., take pleasure only in building levees in the marshes where they sow their wheat ... having already built the dykes, they do not wish to undertake new labours, and the country will always remain unchanged, especially if the Governor allows the young sons of the colonists to go and settle along the coast, where they do nothing but hunt or negotiate with the natives."[66] Quite how coercion could be applied to the settlers, Gargas does not say. Lastly, from Perrot onwards, comments are made about the wealth of vegetables in Acadian gardens: onions, cabbages, beets, peas, chives, turnips, parsnips, and salad greens. Orchards, too, are described, with good crops of apples, pears, and cherries reported.[67] Even if no other information were available, the survival rate of the children argues a good diet.

Gargas summarized the total Mi'kmaq population in the areas listed as 277 men, 270 women, and 572 children, living in 229 wigwams. In crude terms, this would mean that the ratio of children to adults was roughly half that of the neighbouring Acadian population. This is really no more than a supposition, however, because no indication is given of the age of the young ones, although, for the Acadians, Gargas distinguishes between boys who are younger or older than fifteen, and between girls who are older or younger than twelve. In considering the information that Gargas reported about the Mi'kmaq, we must bear in mind two caveats. First, although Mi'kmaq settlements were inhabited year-round, during the winter the population was generally greatly diminished, as "families who had been living together in one village divided into hunting/fishing groups of several households."[68] We have no knowledge of when, let alone how, Gargas assembled his information but his totals for Mi'kmaq population must be considered even more approximate than those he provides for the Acadians. Secondly, he did not visit the Atlantic coast between Baie Verte and the Baie des Chaleurs, thus omitting the considerable Mi'kmaq population in that area, particularly that reported by Bishop Saint-Vallier at Richibouctou and the mouth of the Miramachi. What can be drawn from the data, however, is an indication that the Acadians almost always had Mi'kmaq communities as close neighbours. In the immediate vicinity of Port Royal, for example, Gargas reported one village with twenty people, six men, six women, fourteen children, and four wigwams. Further inland at "Le Cap" he recorded three men, two women, five children, and one wigwam. At Minas, he reported fifteen men, fifteen women, twenty-two children, and fifteen wigwams, and at Beaubassin he listed four men, five women, twelve children, and five wigwams.[69] Gargas recorded other Mi'kmaq villages at Cap Sainte-Marie, Cap Sable, Port Rochelais, La Hève, Chedabouctou, and Canso. The largest concentration of population was found in villages on the St John River, around Pentagöuet and at Chedabouctou.

Thus, in 1688, Acadia was in the best condition it had ever been, boasting a growing population with an established subsistence economy, capable of some commercial enterprise, and a lucrative fur trade. But, at this very time, the Anglo-French struggle for the dominance of North America was beginning to take shape, a struggle consisting, as Brebner writes in *New England's Outpost*, "of raids on frontier villages, on trade depots, on Indian villages, and on formal fortresses; of fights between fishing vessels; of seizure of trading ships or looting of them; and finally, of semi-official piracy and privateering."[70] Somehow, though, the colony not only survived these troubles but grew stronger. Brebner claims that, in the 1671–1714 period, the population of Acadia quadrupled.[71] To explain this puzzle, he argues that "there were, in effect two Acadias, each important in its own way. The one was the Acadia of the international conflict, the other the land settled and developed by the Acadians."[72] The warfare of these years was above all "a French and Canadian affair rather than an Acadian one."[73] There is much truth in this, but the argument needs qualification. Closer analysis reveals that, while the Acadian population approximately doubled in the eighteen years between 1671 and 1689, almost twenty-five years would pass before it doubled again. In any event, arguments about the precise size of the population growth must be limited by the recognition of how subject to error the data from these decades is, even with the work that has been done since Brebner's time.

To appreciate fully the situation of Acadia in the late seventeenth century, the scholarship produced in the seventy-five years since the appearance of Brebner's seminal account – dealing with the forces that lay behind the actions of developing nation states, the nature of French policy in Acadia between 1689 and 1710, and, above all, the daily realities of Acadian life in this period – needs to be taken into account.[74] To begin with, the policy of France towards Acadia was an integral part of the policy of Louis XIV for the development of the French monarchy in Europe, not a policy centred upon the needs of the colony.[75] It therefore becomes vital to understand something of the nature of European international politics at the end of the seventeenth century. Paul Kennedy has pointed out that "the most significant feature of the Great Power scene after 1660 was the maturing of a genuine *multipolar* system of European states, each one of which increasingly tended to make decisions about war and peace on the basis of 'national interests' rather than for trans-national, religious causes."[76] He goes on to say that this change was neither instant nor absolute. In many ways, King William's War in North America – developing as it did out of the War of the League of Augsburg – is the watershed between the old system of long-term religious alliances and the new era of realpolitik. Its beginning was in the fear that swept the Protestant states, after the Revocation of the Edict of Nantes, that Europe was about to be plunged once more into religious strife.

It was clear by that year, 1685, that France was the foremost military power in western Europe, with an army that was better organized, better supplied, and larger than its rivals and a navy that was capable of matching the Anglo-Dutch fleet.[77] England, Brandenburg, the United Netherlands, and Savoy formed the League of Augsburg to defend the states of the upper Rhine, should France embark on a crusade of conquest and conversion. At the same time, however, this coalition had the support of Catholic Spain, and, even while Louis XIV continued his measures against the Huguenots, more than a tenth of the French army was made up of Protestant (mainly German) soldiers.[78] Further, when the fighting began with the French invasion of the Rhineland in late September–early October 1688, Louis XIV was influenced as much by the need to counter the successes of the Catholic Austrian empire against the Turks as by any newly aroused animus against the Protestant powers. But, nevertheless, over the next nine years, France confronted a basically Protestant alliance that, while not able to field quite as many troops, was capable of bringing Louis XIV to the negotiation of the Treaty of Ryswick in 1697.

In these circumstances, Louis XIV's attitude to his North American responsibilities was one of distracted concern. Obviously, both Acadia and New France were important colonial possessions in the mind of Louis XIV, not to be bargained away or surrendered through inattention. To a monarch for whom *La Gloire* – the reputation of his country for all things excellent – was a virtue, imperial prestige was to be preserved. But the urgencies of the European struggle consumed his government, and supplies were problematic. In 1690 the paper strength of the French army was 338,000,[79] of which barely one hundred were in Acadia and, at most, two thousand in Canada.[80] At the same time, France had a navy of more than two hundred ships of all sizes, of which only one frigate, *La Friponne,* regularly patrolled the Acadian fishing banks.[81] As the war in Europe developed over the winter and spring of 1688–89, relations between the English and French, and between Amerindian and European, were tense. In April 1689 Louis XIV recalled Frontenac, now sixty-seven, out of retirement and appointed him to replace Denonville as governor.[82] This proved to be on the eve of England's formal declaration of war against France on 7 May 1689. As a direct result of this, Frontenac was charged with mounting a major offensive against New York.[83] He arrived in Quebec to carry out his commission on 12 October 1689.

In the meantime, events in Acadia had also evolved. The summer of 1688 began peacefully enough. The *La Friponne* arrived in early summer with instructions to protect the Acadian fisheries. On board were thirty more soldiers for the garrison in charge of a Captain Soulogne, bringing the official tally to ninety.[84] As well, there was an engineer, Pasquine. He had instructions to report on how best to rebuild Port Royal and to provide something capable of providing shelter for soldiers and settlers in the case of a sudden attack; however, he was told that it was not necessary to consider fortifications to withstand a siege. He was also told to visit the Pentagöuet area, since it was proposed to build a fort at the limits of the territory claimed by France, in order to counter English claims in the area.[85] Mathieu de Goutin was also a passenger, yet another protégé of the Marquis Duret de Chevry. De Goutin would become the most important judicial official in the colony, serving as lieutenant general for justice in Acadia for most of the next twenty-two years. In this position he heard all civil and criminal suits as well as those directly associated with navigation and trade.[86] In early August *La Friponne* was probably somewhere in the region of Port Royal because, at that time, an effective raid was carried out by an English privateer on the *Saint Louis,* then at Canso.[87] The *Saint Louis,* which belonged to the Compagnie de La Pêche Sédentaire, was two hundred and fifty tons and had sailed from La Rochelle, arriving at Chedabouctou on 14 July 1688. It carried supplies to the value of 12,000 *livres* and was captured and pillaged at

Canso on the 9–10 August, along with another smaller company bar-que.[88] Its capture had significant consequences for it meant that Port Royal would need to continue to trade with New England for supplies. As well, it brought Saint-Castin into firm alliance with the French officials. Like John Nelson and others, as late as 1688 Saint-Castin had sought, in the words of Edward Randolph, to "live indifferent" to the conflicts of others.[89] That, however, proved untenable in the long run. Cotton Mather was appalled when Andros attacked Saint-Castin's property in 1687; he asked "whether the Indians, who were extremely under the Influence of St. Casteen ... did not from this very Moment begin to be obstreperous?"[90] After that incident, Saint-Castin reacted by refusing to submit to claims that he was in any way subject to New England authorities. Now, with the seizure of the *Saint Louis* – another affront that he saw as an official action of Governor Andros – Saint-Castin was forced to declare himself openly. Henceforth, he worked assiduously for France, and his hostility to New England was an important factor in the Abenaki's actions after 1688.[91]

In September of that year, 1688, Meneval dispatched a lengthy overview of the colony.[92] It has a dry tone and the text concentrates upon the need to delineate the boundary between Acadia and New England. Meneval related that he had stopped trade between Port Royal and the English. He admitted that this had "somewhat annoyed the inhabitants who have had help" from that quarter. "But," he added, "they will easily be consoled if the Company [de la Pêche Sédentaire] will continue to bring them the same supplies as it has done in the past."[93] It seems obvious that Meneval wrote while unaware of the raid on Canso that had taken place over a month earlier. Such lack of knowledge brings home the difficulties of travel within the colony at this time. No one, apparently, had thought it necessary to dispatch a specific messenger to inform the governor of what had occurred and the news must have been brought to Port Royal by someone journeying there for some other purpose.

In another report, written in the autumn of 1689, Meneval warned against the policy that France had pursued at the end of the summer. The representations of the Compagnie de la Pêche Sédentaire to the king, after the capture of the *Saint Louis,* had resulted in the dispatch of two more frigates, the *Embuscade* and the *Fourgon,* for temporary duty in Acadian waters. In the first week of September these ships had captured six fishing ketches out of Salem, as well as a large brigantine.[94] George Rawlyk points out that "this represented at least ten per cent of the Salem fishing fleet and was a serious blow to the entire Massachusetts fishery."[95] Predictably, outrage was voiced in the General Court and fears were expressed that "wheras we are Informed our said Ketches are Carried into Port Royall by two French Friggots of Considerable strength whereby we are discouraged from setting out our Vessels the next spring and the being of two such shipps on the Coasts may be of dangerous consequences to the whole

Countrye."[96] Meneval was apprehensive that this capture of fishing vessels would provoke retaliatory action and he was convinced that, should this occur, the colony would not be able to defend itself. He was right on both counts.

But there were other events on the periphery of Acadian life in 1689 which helped to bring about a massive attack by New England on Port Royal in 1690. First, official news of King William's accession had reached Massachusetts in early April 1689, thus bringing to an end the rumours that had been rife about political developments in London.[97] Within days, the Dominion of New England had come to an end, Andros had been replaced by eighty-seven-year-old Simon Bradstreet, and the General Court had set about calming internal political dissent. The strength of the new administration soon allowed attention to be given to the problems of the fishing fleet. At the same time, the Wabanaki began a series of raids on settlements from Maine to New Hampshire, taking Pemaquid in August 1689.[98] Finally, the news reached Boston in the first week of December 1689 that France and England were at war. This was the same week that the General Court was petitioned "to inquire into ye present condition of our said neighbours ye ffrench; & consider what may be proper and & necessary for us to doe respecting them, so as to prevent their being capable to make further depredations on us, & their assisting & supplying our Indian enemies."[99] The fishery interests were only a part, if an important part, of the reasons that persuaded Massachusetts to attack Port Royal. What tipped the balance were Abenaki-French raids in late February and early March 1690 on Schenectady, New York, and on Salmon Falls, New Hampshire.[100]

The man who was named major-general to lead the expedition against Acadia was Sir William Phips, born on the banks of the Kennebec in 1651. His appointment was not only a severe disappointment but also a political defeat for John Nelson, who had expected to be in charge of the venture.[101] Phips had began his life in poverty in Maine but he had made a fortune through recovering a sunken treasure ship in the Caribbean. Appointed by James II as provost-marshal for the Dominion of New England, he had been in London in 1688 but had returned to Boston in late winter 1689. Now he set about assembling the force he would lead to Acadia.[102] The soldiers were, in the main part, volunteers, attracted by the offer of the same wages that impressed frontier soldiers received and promised "the just Half of all Plunder taken from ye Enemy ... shared among the Officers and Souldiers, (Stores of Warr only excepted)."[103] Phips sailed from Boston on 23 April 1690, on board the *Six Friends*, and, after picking up the military contingent at Nantasket, he left on 28 April 1690 for Mount Desert Island with four other vessels.[104] At Mount Desert, the expedition was joined by two vessels from Salem, the barque *Union* and an unarmed ketch, carrying militia from Essex County. The total strength of the crews numbered 266, that of the soldiery 446.[105] After having stopped along the coast, at Saint-Castin's property and the settlements at Machias and Passamaquoddy, the ships anchored opposite Port Royal in the evening of 9 May 1690.

What then followed began civilly enough but quickly degenerated into a nasty affair of bad faith followed by plunder and pillage. Early on 10 May, according to a short English account of events, entitled *A Journal of the proceedings in the late expedition to Port Royal ...*, the "Flag of Truce" was sent a shore "with a demand for the Governour to surrender the Fort; and in Answer he sent on Board a Letter by one his Priests to aquaint our General that he [was] willing to surrender upon our Terms."[106] All accounts agree that Meneval immediately capitulated. He had under ninety soldiers in his command and was outnumbered nearly three to one. There were no French ships in the area, he was outgunned, and the defences of the fort were, as he had advised six months previously, in ill repair and in no shape to withstand attack. Louis Petit, the parish priest, went aboard the *Six Friends* to negotiate terms. These included, according to his report, the agreement to transport the garrison to either France or Quebec, and to allow the settlers to retain their property and remain in possession of their land and to be free to practise their religious beliefs.[107] On Sunday, 11 May, the *Journal* records that "Possession of the Fort was given; the Governour and Officers delivered their Swords to our General, who returned the Governour his Sword and likewise some of the Officers. The Soldiers laid down their Arms and were guarded to the Church, where they were kept as Prisoners."[108] The imprisonment of the soldiery was already a breach of the terms of capitulation and the next day matters worsened. The English and French accounts diverge over the cause. The *Journal* records that on the morning of Monday, 12 May, "we went a-shore to search for hidden goods (for during the time of Parley they had broken open the King's Store, and Merchant Stores, and convey'd sundry Wares into the woods). We cut down the Cross, rifled the Church, Pu'lld down the high-Altar, breaking their Images; and brought our Plunder, Arms and Ammunition into Mr. Nelson's Storehouse." An anonymous observer wrote that the first sign of trouble was the peremptory demand of Phips for Meneval's sword, when the two men met on the Monday morning.[109] Petit believed that Phips, once he realized quite how weak the garrison at Port Royal had been, "was disgusted with the honest compromise he had made" and set about looking for excuses to break it.[110] Emerson Baker and John Reid suggest, however, that Phips had intended the capitulation terms not so much as a "compromise ... as a convenience that could be dispensed with as soon as Port Royal had surrendered without a fight."[111]

Whatever might have been the immediate cause of Phips's action, there is no doubt that the capture of military supplies, foraging, and plunder had been planned from the outset. Meneval, indeed, had agreed as part of the terms of capitulation to give all up "all the great Artillery, small Arms and stores of War and whatever else belongs to the French King."[112] Nor is it surprising that some of the cattle were killed. Living off the country-side, whether friendly or hostile, was common practice for all armies at this time. While provisions – especially bread, biscuits, and flour – were part of an army's baggage train, the prospect of fresh meat would have delighted the heart of the quartermasters. But the actual degree of the slaughter of livestock cannot have been much more than that needed to provision the troops, given that the numbers of animals at Port Royal recorded in a 1693 census show an increase in both flocks and herds since 1689. In the earlier year Port Royal was reported as having 573 cattle; in 1693, 955. In 1689 sheep numbered 617; in 1693 the flocks had grown to number 1,279 animals.[113]

In considering the pillaging of the inhabitants, one has to bear in mind, too, that plundering was accepted in the late seventeenth century as a nor-mal activity for the soldiery, and that it was as much a method of making up for unpaid wages and uncertain provisions as a matter of acquiring wealth.[114] While there were generally agreed upon "rules of war" at this time, these were, as ever, more often honoured in the breach than in the performance.[115] As has already been noted, plunder had always been proffered as an inducement for enlistment. But both Meneval and Petit were clearly under the impression that the terms of capitulation would protect the personal property of the inhabitants. Instead, Phips oversaw the looting and the *Journal* reported the search for hidden goods, even "underground in their gardens."[116] Goods taken included not only per-sonal belongings but also goods acquired for trade and the furs gained in trade though not yet sold for profit. The inventory of the plunder, which was made on the expedition's return to Boston, includes a wide variety of items.[117] First, there were the military and naval supplies, everything from 2 halberds and 103 swords to "15 great gunnes, 4 little guns," barrels of powder, shot, two ketches, a brigantine, and two compasses. Next, there were what might be called commercial goods: brandy, molasses, furs – both otter and beaver – bales of red and black cloth, fish hooks, boxes of can-dles, French salt. Then there were obviously domestic goods: among other items, linens, clothing, bolsters, bedding, boots and shoes, blankets and pillows, wine glasses, pots and pans, a firkin of butter, and a number of books. There were miscellaneous items, such as the blacksmith's tools and wafers from the church. Finally, there were a number of bags of coinage, adding up to the sum of £740. But, while the plunder taken meant a sig-nificant loss for the inhabitants of Port Royal, as a business proposition the expedition was not particularly successful for Massachusetts. Rawlyk cites a Boston merchant, James Lloyd, who "maintained that the enterprise had cost "£3,000 more than the value of the plunder."[118]

The long-term consequences of the attack on Port Royal went far beyond the impact of the immediate economic damage. To begin with, it resulted in the removal of the French governors to the St John River valley for the next decade, first at Jemseg, later at Nashwaak (Naxouet), and finally at the mouth of the river. This exposed Port Royal to attacks by privateers, which meant cattle killed, one or more houses burnt, and, more bitter, often the murder of one or more of the settlers before the ship left.[119] Officials from France did not play an essential role in the daily life of the largest settlement in the colony for the next ten years.

Phips's expedition also involved an attack on Chedabouctou. As he set sail for Boston, Phips dispatched Captain Cyprian Southack and the *Porcupine* to harass the Compagnie de la Pêche Sédentaire. Even after the raid of 1688, that body had continued to operate a fishing station at Chedabouctou. At some point in 1689, Meneval had stationed twelve soldiers there. They proved to be a gallant but totally inadequate force.[120] Southack landed eighty men and the defenders "fought them for Six houres" but fireballs and arrows were used by the attackers and the fort was set on fire. Southack wrote to his parents that "then the Govr struck the Flag, and he with his soldiers and Priests came out, and the Fort in one half houres time blew up with the Powder that was in it."[121] The loss to the company has been estimated at 50,000 crowns, an enormous amount of money.[122] While this raid did not destroy the Compagnie de la Pêche Sédentaire itself, there were no more attempts made by its shareholders to establish a fishing station at Chedabouctou. Salem had achieved at least part of its aims for the Acadian fishing banks. After 1690, French and Acadian control over the coast and the onshore fishery between La Hève and Cape Breton was non-existent.

At much the same time as Captain Southack left for Chedabouctou, Phips dispatched Captain John Alden and the sloop *Mary* to patrol the coast to the south. The Minas Basin and the Chignecto settlements came under his purview but neither seemed to suffer anything comparable to the damage done to Port Royal and Chedabouctou. In fact, the growth in the Minas Basin area between 1686 and 1693 was considerable: the population increased from 57 to 305; the number of cattle from 90 to 458; and the number of sheep from 21 to 320.[123] As for Beaubassin, in 1689 there were 83 people recorded there and in 1693 some twenty families, for a total of 119 people.[124] There is no data for the flocks and herds of the Chignecto isthmus in 1693.

Lastly, Phips attempted to establish some kind of English authority over the colony. To achieve this goal he imposed, on as many Acadians as possible, an oath of allegiance to King William and Queen Mary. In the late seventeenth century, oaths of allegiance were both important and commonplace in the legal and political life of France and England. Monarchs themselves swore them at their coronation: French monarchs took an oath seven times during their ceremonies[125] and, after 1689, English monarchs swore a most explicit oath to govern "according to the statues in parliament agreed upon and the law and customs of the same."[126] In both countries oaths of allegiance were a routine requirement for officers of justice, members of representative institutions, those with military commands, and those teaching in universities, as well as those holding positions in guilds. In New France, all those in the service of Louis XIV, whether church officials, members of the nobility, or appointed officials, swore some form of oath to do their duty in the service of the king.[127] Further, France had also used oaths to confirm the relationship of individuals, as subjects, to the crown of France. This was the case of the oath that La Vallière administered to the inhabitants of Port Royal in 1679.[128]

Similarly, oaths were equally commonplace in the British colonies in North America. In 1636 New Plymouth required "freemen" to swear that "you shall be truly loyall to our Sov Lord King Charles, his heires and successors ..."[129] By 1652, Massachusetts required a "Strangers Oath," which read: "You A.B. Do acknowledge your self subject to the Lawes of this Jurisdiction during your Residence under this Government and do here Swear, by the Great Name of the Ever Living GOD, and engage yourself to be true and faithfull to the same, and not to plot, contrive or conceal any thing that is to the hurt or detriment thereof."[130] Oaths of allegiance on the transference of a colony from one empire to another were an accepted practice of international law.[131] But, while oaths of allegiance were commonplace, generally accepted, and taken seriously at this time, the extent to which they were considered permanently binding is a matter of discussion. It was possible to renounce and forswear past loyalties with new oaths, a necessity when all armies had large numbers of mercenary troops. The question of duress and coercion were factors that were taken into account in judging the extent to which loyalty had been transferred or betrayed. It was, moreover, acknowledged that oaths signed were a greater matter than those to which assent was given only verbally.

Thus, Phips had a considerable number of precedents for his actions in compelling the Acadians to take an oath. From its form, it clearly was taken as a group by those to whom it was administered. It read as follows: "You and everyone of you do swear by the dreadful Name of the Ever Living God, that you will bear true Faith & Allegiance to Their most excellent Majesties William and Mary of England, Scotland & Ireland King and Queen: so help you God in our Lord Jesus Christ.[132] On Wednesday, 14 May, this oath was given to the inhabitants of Port Royal and it was reported that it was accepted with "great Acclamations and Rejoicings." Given the fact that those taking the oath were gathered together in the church and had had ample demonstration of the strength of soldiers surrounding them, it is not surprising that they assented to the oath without obvious reluctance. The next day a "Post was sent to Menus [Minas] and the places adjacent, to come to Port Royal and take the oath."[133] On Monday, 19 May, it is recorded that the "the Oathes of Allegiance [were] administered to them, which they accepted with great Joy."[134]

Phips also established an "elected" council to administer the colony. We know nothing of the form of the elections, neither the process of nomination nor who voted nor how. We do know the result. Villebon, who arrived at Port Royal within two weeks of Phips's departure, reported that the men in question had been "selected" by Phips.[135] The *Journal* recorded that the members of the council chosen by the inhabitants were "Mathieu De Goutine, Mr. Alexande l'Borgne, Sr. De Beliske, Mr. Price du Breuil, Mr. Rene Laudria, Mr. Daniel Leblanc."[136] They were, the form of the oath noted, "to be of the Council for the conservation of peace" and they were asked to swear "by the dread Name of the Ever Living God that you will bear true Faith & Allegiance to their Majesties of Great Britain King William and Queen Mary, and that you will administer Justice to all persons impartially, and keep the peace until further order from the Crown of England. So help you God in our Lord Jesus Christ." Finally, yet one more oath was administered to "Charles, Chevalieer St. de Latourasie, Signiour de Chatillon," who was chosen "by the Inhabitants of Port Royal, L'Accadie and Nova Scotia to the Place of President of the Council for the Conservation of Peace among the said Inhabitants."[137] Phips left instructions which emphasized the fact that the Acadians had sworn "Allegiance to the Crown of England"; that the inhabitants should not be coerced to follow "the way of Worship you have been brought up in, we hope that you will all ere long learn better than hitherto you have been taught"; that the property of Saint-Castin should be confiscated; that neither shot nor powder should be sold to the Indians; that Perrot, if found, should be seized; and that, from time to time, a report should be made on "how matters are with you" and sent to Boston.[138] Satisfied with his actions, Phips left Port Royal on Thursday, 22 May, taking with him Meneval, Louis Petit, and Petit's assistant, Father Claude Trouvé, as well as most of the French garrison.[139]

A week after Phips's departure, the complex and tangled nature of Acadian political and economic life became more than usually apparent. Both Perrot, the former governor, and Villebon, who would replace Meneval as governor of the colony within the year, arrived at Port Royal.[140] There was general rejoicing and considerable anxiety among the inhabitants at their appearance. The joy came from the arrival of supplies and the presence of French authority, the anxiety came from the matter of the oath that had been recently sworn. Perrot was the first to arrive, bringing foodstuffs and a general collection of merchandise. Villebon sailed into port three days later on board the *Union,* owned by the Compagnie de la Pêche Sédentaire. He was accompanied by Vincent Saccardy, the engineer-general for Louis XIV, and a small amount of military supplies. Further, since he had recently acted as Meneval's assistant, he had considerable official standing. To both Perrot and Villebon, it was soon made clear that, far from being assented to with great joy, the oath of allegiance had been a matter of coercion, sworn under duress.[141] The inhabitants asked that Perrot immediately send a report, both to France and to Frontenac, attesting to this. They wished to implore Louis XIV not to abandon them, stating that they were ready to die for their country and had no wish to repudiate their faith and convert to Anglicanism.[142] Considering that Acadia had no effective militia at this point, the expression of Acadian willingness to perish in battle can be taken with as much credence as the earlier assertion that the settlers had sworn loyalty to King William joyfully.[143] What the next years would amply demonstrate is that the people of Port Royal wanted to keep strong cultural links with France as well as the trade with Massachusetts, and that they had a clear sense of their own right to pursue both objectives at once and of the policies that would enable them to do so.

In the meantime, Villebon's attitude was, above all, pragmatic. Much of his life had been spent in the army. He had been born in Quebec on 22 August 1655, the second of seven sons of René Robinau de Bécancour, then surveyor general of New France, and Marie-Anne Leneuf, one of the children of the then governor of Trois-Rivières, Jacques Leneuf de La Poterie. Having been educated in France, Villebon served ten years in the army there before returning to Canada, probably in 1681. In 1684 he was a member of La Barre's expedition against the Iroquois and in 1685 he was briefly in Acadia, before returning to France in 1689.[144] Villebon considered himself the ranking official in the colony but consulted Perrot, Saccardy, and de Goutin as to the course he should follow.[145] It was decided that Villebon would gather together anything useful from the ruins of the fort and depart for Jemseg, accompanied by the five soldiers whom he had brought from France and the ten or so who had escaped being carried off to Boston by Phips.[146] Villebon intended to repair and occupy the fort that had been first established there by Thomas Temple in 1650 and further developed by Joybert in 1675.[147] Jemseg was thought to be sufficiently far inland that no large vessel could sail up the Saint John to attack it. On his way to Jemseg, Villebon would alert the Mi'kmaq as to the situation and attempt to incite them to attack the English.[148] Finally, before Villebon left, according to the *Journal*, de Goutin drew up a statement of protest against the oath that the inhabitants had sworn to William of Orange, and Villebon undertook to ensure that copies of this document would reach both Frontenac and Louis XIV.[149] Villebon, however, made no mention of this incident in his own writings.

On 17 June 1690, accompanied by de Saccardy, Perrot, and de Goutin, Villebon set out for Jemseg. He and de Goutin arrived there without mishap, having left the *Union* at the mouth of the Saint John in charge of Perrot and Saccardy and going on by ketch to the fort. Before the latter could also travel to Jemseg, however, the *Union* was attacked and captured by two privateers. Perrot and Saccardy were taken prisoner. Villebon estimated that there were about one hundred and sixty men on board the ships and considered he had no alternative but to retreat. He was later informed that these same pirates had arrived by way of Port Royal, where they had burnt some of the houses and hanged two of the inhabitants.[150]

At this point, Villebon decided to go overland to Quebec and ask Frontenac for both aid and instructions. From there, he went on to France where he received his commission as commander of Acadia, as of 7 April 1691.[151] He returned to Jemseg by way of Quebec, on board the *Sol d'Afrique*, in October of that year.

In the meantime. the Acadians, particularly those at Port Royal, took stock of their situation. They faced a much more hazardous situation than they had known for a generation. Since 1664 there had been skirmishes around Port Royal, difficulty with supplies, and problems with fishing fleets. But most conflict had been both temporary and limited. Now the settlement had endured capture, its inhabitants had been treated as conquered subjects, and most of the men had sworn an oath under duress. This had been followed by the arrival of a ship from France, with the governor's second-in-command on board, who had been unable to offer Port Royal more than sympathy and a bare minimum of supplies. Next had come a vicious attack by English privateers, who took no notice of the claim that Port Royal had surrendered to Phips. As summer gave to place to fall, it was "our friends, the enemy," in the words of Jean Daigle,[152] who arrived with supplies, in the person of John Alden. Alden had traded with Port Royal for the last two years and had captained the *Mary*, a sloop, in the recent attack.[153] In November 1690 he received a commission from the General Court of Massachusetts to "visett Port Royall to inquire into the state of the people ... and to carry some provisions for their supply."[154] He interpreted this commission to mean that he, and he alone, could trade with Port Royal. Thus, in April 1691, he found a small vessel belonging to Jean Serreau de Saint-Aubin, the *Speedwell*, at Port Royal and promptly confiscated it. [155]

Matters became even more complicated for the Acadians during the summer of 1691. By the fall of the year, it was difficult for them to know where the authority for the governance of the region was to be found. For example, in early April two of the inhabitants of Port Royal, Abraham Boudrot and Jean Martel, had gone to Boston. There they petitioned the Massachusetts council for freedom to trade because Acadia was under "the present Subjection of those parts to the Crowne of England" and Massachusetts "ought to be their protectors."[156] They then negotiated, with Pierre Faneuil and David Basset, the latter a Huguenot in-law of the Melanson family,[157] for textiles and linens.[158] On their way back to Port Royal, however, they were captured by Saint-Aubin and lost goods and ship. This violence between settlers, while not unknown in the past, reached new levels as the community struggled to accommodate itself to life in wartime. Over the next six years, the Acadians faced English privateers, as well as pressure from Massachusetts and France for demonstrations of allegiance.

The internal politics of New England in general, and Massachusetts in particular, continued to be a major influence on the course of events in Acadia. But Massachusetts politics were no more simple than those of any other colony of the time. The struggle between Phips and Nelson, for example, was also a struggle about the way in which the colony should confront the French presence on the frontier of the colony, with Phips recommending an aggressive policy against Quebec as well as against Acadia, and John Nelson advising a less controversial path. Phips had followed the attack he mounted against Port Royal with a disastrous campaign in the autumn of the same year, 1690, against Quebec.[159] Nelson, however, had begun to organize his affairs in order to trade with the Acadians. In the early summer of 1691, as the inhabitants of Port Royal worried about who could carry on trade with them, Nelson saw a possibility of rebuilding the prestige he had lost the previous year. Phips, by this time, had left for London, and, in his absence, Nelson and six other merchants offered to rebuild the fort at Port Royal, in return for a monopoly over the entire Nova Scotia trade. This scheme was accepted by the council.[160] Jean Martel, in order to recoup his own losses, agreed to captain one of Nelson's ketches and carry goods to Minas.[161] Nelson hoped to persuade Saint-Castin to become, once more, a trading partner but the latter politely refused and forwarded the correspondence to Quebec.[162] In spite of this rebuff, in late August 1691, Nelson and a number of colleagues set out for Port Royal and the enterprise began successfully enough. They soon collected a good cargo of elk, otter, and other skins, to the value of some 4,751 *livres*. However, when they left to go farther into the Bay of Fundy, they were captured by the *Soleil d'Afrique,* at that point carrying Villebon back to the Saint John.

While this foray of John Nelson ended with his capture and removal from the Acadian scene for nearly seven years, the interest and impact of Massachusetts on the colony continued as strongly as ever. At the time that Nelson was attempting to open trade with Port Royal, Phips was engaged in London in two related endeavours. First, he set out to make clear to the Lords of Trade and Planatations that Massachusetts interests embraced a broad territory which included Acadia, and, secondly, he sought to secure his appointment as governor of Massachusetts.[163] He was successful in achieving both of these goals. On 7 October 1691 the Charter of Massachusetts Bay defined the province as encompassing the entire area from the Pistaqua River up to and including "the Country or Territory Commonly Called Accadia or Nova Scotia," and on 27 November 1691 his appointment as governor of Massachusetts was approved by the Privy Council.[164] When Phips arrived in Boston on 14 May 1692, he was prepared to ensure that the Acadians understood their place within the boundary of his authority.

But the situation had, inevitably, evolved during Phips's absence from Boston. Villebon's instructions had been clear: he was to retrieve the situation in the colony by reasserting French authority over Port Royal, letting the inhabitants of Minas know of his presence, and encouraging the Abenaki to fight the English. His headquarters were to be on the Saint

John River. He carried out these instructions with considerable subtlety. On his arrival in the fall of 1691, Villebon saw that Port Royal had little or no means of defence against Massachusetts, and he had brought them none, neither soldiers nor supplies. The goods he had with him were designed for his own support and to cement the alliance of Abenaki, the Malecite, and Mi'kmaq with the French. So he limited his actions at Port Royal to such political advice as would not make the life of the inhabitants more precarious than it already was. The man whom Phips had left in charge, Charles La Tourasse, had served Meneval as a sergeant. Now he acted as much an agent for Villebon as the representative of Phips. The former in fact asserted that La Tourasse had accepted his appointment by Phips only because Villebon gave him permission to do so.[165] Villebon made no attempt to substitute a French flag for the English one that Phips had left to be hoisted when ships came into view, and he gave La Tourasse permission to continue as commander. Reporting these actions to the Comte de Pontchartrain,[166] who had succeeded Seignelay as minister for both the navy and the colonies, Villebon wrote that "without these compromises it would be impossible to exist in this country, where I am without troops, and these unfortunate people, living so far from help, are exposed to every attack."[167] What this meant is that since France had not sent force enough to reoccupy, in any official sense, Port Royal, or to reprovision the inhabitants with guns, shot, and other necessities, Acadian accommodation to the *force majeur* of Massachusetts would not be considered as disloyalty to Louis XIV. In fact, the following year, Villebon instructed the inhabitants of Port Royal "to obtain all the assistance possible from the English until they received other orders."[168]

One of the major reasons for this policy was Villebon's need to secure not only the Abenaki but also the Mi'kmaq and Malecite as committed allies to the French. To do this it was clear that gifts and subsidies were needed.[169] French officials were reluctant at this time to increase the monies spent in the colonies, and, consequently, colonial administrators had always to juggle the budget between what must be supplied to settlers and what should be spent upon ensuring good relationships with the neighbouring Amerindians. Nor was it just a matter of money. The space available for goods on board official French vessels was often scarce and always expensive. Thus, the possibility that Massachusetts could be brought to answer the Acadian demand for certain textiles, guns, shot, iron goods in general, sugar, salt, wines, and brandies (this last of particular importance in an age without anaesthetics and analgesics) was welcomed by Villebon. As George Rawlyk points out, between 1690 and 1697, "Yankee merchants supplied the growing Acadian population with badly needed merchandise, while French authorities, much relieved because of the unexpected Massachusetts benevolence, were able to channel most of their goods to the Indians who were encouraged to attack Massachusetts."[170]

The decision to court the Mi'kmaq with the rituals of major gifts, feasts,

and subsidies was, if not new in Acadia, at least new on the scale that Villebon carried out the practice during the winter of 1691–92. He provided a
feast for thirteen canoes of "Indians of the Micmac nation" on 24 October
1691.[171] In the spring and early summer of 1692, it was intended that
Abenaki attacks would increase from Pentagöuet southwards and that the
Mi'kmaq would rendezvous with them at Pentagöuet. Villebon recorded
that, on 25 May 1692, sixty-four Mi'kmaq arrived from Cape Breton, La
Hève, and Cap Sable, to whom he "provided a feast and afterwards supplied them with powder and balls and a little tobacco."[172] On 2 June 1692
yet another party of Mi'kmaq arrived from Beaubassin and Minas, according to Villebon, under the leadership of a missionary priest, Jean Baudoin,
and they were similarly gifted. From the viewpoint of the French, the campaign was not a great success, but the participation of the Mi'kmaq had
considerable significance. Henceforth, the military support of the Mi'k-
maq would, most frequently, be given to the French. As well, the Acadians
were now made fully aware of the fighting abilities of the Mi'kmaq.

This realization shaped Port Royal's reception of the *Nonsuch*, a forty-six-
gun frigate that Phips sent, along with an eight-gun brigantine, to emphasize his control of the area. The ships arrived in port at the end of June
1692, with, in Villebon's estimation, some two hundred men aboard. Captain Short, who was in charge of the ships, attempted to persuade the Acadians "to take up arms against all Frenchmen who might come from
Europe."[173] Villebon's account of these events stressed that the Acadians
refused to agree to this demand, or to "interfere" with French privateers.
Indeed, the Acadians asserted that, should Shortt use violence, "it could
only cost them their [Acadian] lives."[174] Villebon wrote that the Acadians
then said that "they were willing to promise they would not interpose and
would welcome the English unless they came with the intention of doing
damage; if they wished to establish a garrison, as they had long since
promised to do, they might take any action they chose about the French
vessels, but they themselves would remain neutral."[175] "The English," Villebon went on, "tried to make them sign a guarantee for their people against
the Indians in case a garrison should be sent there. But the settlers replied,
as I had told them to do, that, far from being able to answer for them, they
would be the first victims if the Indians came to regard them as friends of
the English."[176]

In this response are to be found almost all the elements of the various
Acadian replies to the demands of English authorities over the next two
generations: a point-blank refusal to take up arms against the French; an
equally clear policy of neutrality towards whatever military plans the English might themselves wish to carry out in Acadia; and a statement that the
Mi'kmaq would take action against them should they display a more positive friendship towards the English. This response should not be seen as
the implementation of a widely debated and clearly thought-out Acadian
policy at this time: it was the reaction of the leadership of the Port Royal

Acadians to the immediate circumstances of the summer of 1692. But it was a reaction that would be repeated in various ways, at various times and by various groups of Acadians, until it evolved into a policy during the first thirty years of the eighteenth century. In 1692 it did not imply much in the way of emotional commitment, except insofar as it revealed an obvious aversion to breaking ties with France. Nor did it amount to more than a fragile consensus among the leading inhabitants of Port Royal. The settlers of Port Royal were not a collection of unthinking puppets, all in agreement with one another and harbouring neither doubts nor hesitation about the best way to cope with the circumstances of life on a border during wartime. Indeed, in August 1692, Pierre Dubreuil, at that point the king's attorney in Port Royal, spoke to Villebon about the stance taken by the settlers and said that there was some who worried that he might not approve their actions. Villebon reassured him that he was not displeased and he suggested that in future they should "keep the best of their effects hidden in the woods lest they be taken by surprise."[177]

Port Royal, of course, did not encapsulate the experience of all the Acadian settlements. Nor did it weigh as greatly in the policy of either France or New France as did the question of the borders of the colony, particularly the conduct of the war in the area from Pentagöuet to Pemaquid. For both Massachusetts and Villebon, Minas and Beaubassin also demanded attention, as did the activities of French and English privateers along the coasts as well as in the Bay of Fundy itself. As with Port Royal, the importance of Minas and Beaubassin centred upon matters of trade and supply and information about the contacts the settlements had with both sides. At the same time, in very different ways, the governance of the settlements as well as the political and religious affiliations of the settlers was also the business of both those governing Massachusetts and the French officials in Port Royal. The former were concerned with the extent to which the Acadians accepted their regulation of trade and hoped to use them as a bulwark against the Mi'kmaq. Villebon was concerned about issues of supply, for himself as well as the Mi'kmaq, and the extent to which the Acadians would accept his authority in matters both secular and religious.[178] All of these matters were played out against constant interaction between the Acadian settlements and Massachusetts, some of which was hostile but a large amount of which consisted of peaceful trade.

This state of affairs was due in large part to the long-term trading relationship that had existed between Massachusetts and Acadia since the 1640s. Boston merchants were unwilling to forego the profits they made from selling the Acadians the goods they needed, above all guns, certain textiles, sugars, and spices. The Acadians were equally unwilling to do without these goods. France made no effort to supply them and the Acadians had furs and agricultural produce to sell and exchange. As well, there existed people, both in Boston and in the Acadian settlements, who had been involved in such trade for a number of years and were anxious to find ways of continuing it. In Boston the associates of Alden and others were quite willing to facilitate, for a profit, the exchange of goods. After all, Massachusetts claimed that Acadia was part of its territory and, from this point of view, trade between the two colonies was legal. In fact, Phips defended such trade against the custom officials in Boston.[179] In Acadia, members of the Boudrot and Melanson families were quite willing to take risks to carry on commercial ventures.[180] Those who traded in goods often also trafficked in information. Not infrequently, both sides considered a particular individual their sole agent; witness the comments on Abraham Boudrot and Charles Melanson by Villebon and Phips.[181]

Finally, the conflict between Massachusetts and Acadia, as opposed to the fighting between New England and New France, was a war less for the acquisition and settlement of territory than for the right to exploit and control the fisheries. It was a war primarily about not ideologies but resources. While the rhetoric of authorities on both sides sometimes reflected religious intolerance, it was not a crusading war. In fact, warfare struck the Acadian settlements only as an extension of battles fought elsewhere. This is not to say that the settlements did not suffer attack and losses but they were not a major battleground, as was northern New England. No Acadian settlement suffered the destruction of property and loss of life that was involved in the massacre at York, where, on Candlemas day, 1692, the priest Louis-Pierre Thury was one of the leaders of some two hundred Abenaki who "Killd and carried Captive 140 – 48 of which are killed."[182] While the Acadian settlements endured the attacks of regular military forces as well as privateering raids, the death toll among the population during these years was barely a score or so, not the hundreds that New England counted.

It was not so much that the Acadians lived apart from the war as that its impact upon them was uneven. No settlement escaped without a visit from the Phips expedition in 1690 and no settlement escaped without at least two destructive visits from privateers over the next five years. But the colony, as a whole, did not know the same degree of brutality and devastation that New England endured in this decade and New France had known in the 1680s. Minas, especially, was able to develop its dyked and cultivated land in the 1690s. Between 1686 and 1693, the population grew from 57 to 305, a number of whom were migrants from Port Royal. The number of farms, both at Minas and the adjacent settlement of Pisiquid (present-day Windsor), increased from 8 to 50, the acreage cultivated from 83 arpents to 360, and the number of cattle from 90 to 456.[183] Wheat was both grown and milled.[184] Villebon's journal recorded the extent to which he relied on Minas for flour, beginning in July 1692.[185] In one of his last reports on the colony, he noted that Minas had eight grist mills running.[186] His needs, however, were only one outlet for the surplus agricultural produce of the region. He also records the extent to which the English traded with the settlement as well as the provisions Minas supplied to the French privateer Pierre Maisonnat, known as Baptiste.[187]

Privateers, both French and English, were a major influence on the course of both King William's War and the war that followed, known as the War of the Spanish Succession in Europe and as Queen Anne's War in North America, which was fought between 1702 and 1713. Privateers were, as the name suggests, privately owned vessels with a government commission, letters of marque, licensing them to capture enemy shipping in time of war. Crews were usually unpaid, except by a share in the booty. They were gradually abandoned over the eighteenth century because it became more and more difficult to distinguish between privateers and outright pirates. During the war years, both English and French licensed such ships. English ones raided the Acadian settlements repeatedly, ignoring any Acadian protest that they were not to be considered enemies since they had taken an oath of allegiance in 1690 to King William.[188] Simultaneously, Maisonnat and François Guion attacked New England shipping and fishing vessels as often as they were able and then sold some of their booty to Port Royal and Minas, buying or bartering for provisions in exchange.[189] Both men were allied to Acadian settler families and both men were extraordinarily successful in their chosen profession. Baptiste, indeed, took nine vessels in six months in the late summer and autumn of 1692 alone.[190] The extent to which a small number of Acadian youths formed part of the crews of these men is difficult to determine. At any rate, William Stoughton, who had control over the government of Massachusetts in his capacity as deputy governor when Phips was recalled to London in 1694, was particularly incensed when Guion captured nine Yankee fishing vessels off Cap Sable in early September 1695.[191] As a result, Cyprian Southack made plans to attack Villebon, considering that, until his garrison was "removed," the privateers would not otherwise be defeated, "having the advantage of so many harbours and Islands Eastwards to shelter themselves."[192]

However, during these same months, the winter and early spring of 1695–96, France made the Acadian border with New England of major importance in its Canadian policy. The reasons behind this decision included the success of Frontenac's Iroquois policy,[193] the glut of furs on the French market despite the war, and the determination of Louis XIV and Pontchartrain to retain the Abenaki as allies of France. This last matter, the question of Abenaki loyalty, had been a major theme in the correspondence between Villebon and both Versailles and Quebec since 1691.[194] The steady flow of presents, not only to the Abenaki but also to the Mi'kmaq, during these same years is evidence of the extent to which these peoples were seen as crucial to French activity in the area.[195] Similarly, the support provided for the raids undertaken by Claude-Sébastien de Villieu and others underlines the amount of French support for the military activities that were carried out from Villebon's headquarters on the Saint John River.[196] Plans to capture Pemaquid were a logical outcome of French concern both for Acadia and for Abenaki loyalty. Thus, a successful expedition would, at one and the same time, define one of the boundaries of Acadian territory and give the Abenaki a demonstration of the strength of French arms.

Therefore, while Stoughton sought to assemble an expedition, under Benjamin Church, that would bring end to French privateers off the coast of Massachusetts and reassert Massachusetts control over Acadia, a much larger French enterprise was assembled to seize Pemaquid. Pierre Le Moyne d'Iberville was selected as its commander. Born in Montreal in 1661 to Charles Le Moyne de Longueuil et de Châteauguay and Catherine Thierry, he was one of a family of fourteen, the third of the twelve sons. Soldier and seaman, he had an adventurous and successful career and by the autumn of 1695 was acknowledged as a brilliant military commander.[197] By mid-July 1696, d'Iberville and his ships, the *Envieux* and the *Profond*, were off the Bay of Fundy and within the month they were off Pemaquid. Saint-Castin and over two hundred Abenaki were already there, as was Villieu and a score of French soldiers. The fort was an easy capture, although it had sixteen guns and twelve-foot walls.[198] D'Iberville razed the fort, then left for Plaisance.

By the end of August 1696, news of the fall of Pemaquid had reached Boston where Benjamin Church was assembling his expedition, supposedly to attack Villebon on the Saint John. Church was in his late fifties, having been born in Plymouth, Massachusetts, in 1639. He was a veteran of frontier warfare, having fought in King Philip's War in 1676 and been part of a number of skirmishes against the Wabanaki since 1692. He now gathered together some four or five hundred men, through his own vigorous recruiting in both Massachusetts and Connecticut.[199] He sailed from Boston with a collection of small vessels, arriving off Beaubassin on 20th September.[200] There are a number accounts of what then followed but there is agreement that Church acted with considerable duplicity. At first he seemed inclined to accept the testimony of the inhabitants that they had sworn loyalty to William III, but once he and his men had landed they "treated the place as if it was an enemy's country."[201] They stayed nine days and in his own account Church admitted that the settlers' "cattle, sheep, hogs and dogs" were left "lying dead about their houses, chopped and hacked with hatchets."[202] It is possible that some of the havoc was the result of frustration, because, in Villebon's account of the raid, it is said that, once the English ships were seen, "every one [of the inhabitants of Beaubassin] had taken to flight carrying with them their more valuable possessions."[203] The church and some of the houses were also burnt. Church claimed that his actions were designed to give the Acadians an idea of what New England villages had suffered from French and Amerindian raids. He said that he had gathered the inhabitants of Beaubassin together and told them that, should there be further raids on "the poor English," he (Church) "would come with some hundreds of savages and let them loose amongst them, who would kill, scalp, and carry away every French person in those parts; for they were the root from whence all the branches came, that hurt us."[204] Church then went on to the Saint John, where he discovered various supplies, including cannon, hidden there, in preparation for the establishment of a new fort at the mouth of the river.[205] With this booty, Church decided to return to Boston but met, in the vicinity of Passamaquoddy Bay, three Massachusetts ships under the command of Colonel John Hathorn. The two men joined forces, with no very great enthusiasm, and returned to attack Villebon at Nashwaak. They had no success in this endeavour, and, after a fruitless siege lasting some thirty-six hours, returned to Boston.[206]

Thus, at the end of six years of war, the relationship of Massachusetts and Acadia was, if anything, more uncertain than it had been at the outbreak of hostilities. The French never organized opposition to an attack out of Massachusetts that was aimed at the Acadian settlements. No New England force was able to put an end to Abenaki and Mi'kmaq raids on the settlements of northern Maine and Massachusetts, raids that, while instigated in some measure by the French, were grounded in the quarrels of the native people with the English settlers. The French authorities in Acadia could harass and raid Massachusetts, with the support of privateers and their Amerindian allies. Massachusetts could enforce a demonstration of Acadian submission to its authority, as and when there was Massachusetts strength actually present at Port Royal or elsewhere in the colony. The French had not halted Massachusetts exploitation of the Acadian fisheries and Massachusetts had not halted trade with the Acadian settlements.

This inconclusive state of affairs had much in common with what had been happening in the war in Europe since 1694. In the first years of the struggle there, France had seemed as strong as her opponents had feared. But after 1693, warfare on too many fronts, in Italy, along the Rhine, in Ireland, and at sea, prevented France from gaining any overwhelming victory. Louis XIV's generals won the great "pitched" battles but at considerable financial cost and France had no central banking institutions that could allow the crown to borrow money cheaply and efficiently. At the same time, weather conditions in Europe were everywhere appalling in 1693. In France, a late cold spring was followed by a short wet summer and harvest failures, particularly in the grain provinces.[207] All Europe suffered but, as John Wolf writes, Louis's opponents had control of the seas and this gave them the possibility of bringing in grain from the Baltic, where harvests had been much better.[208] This was not an option for France, which came close to famine, and, as always, severe food shortages were followed by higher than usual death tolls from smallpox and pneumonia. In 1694 the campaigns went badly and by the end of that year Louis XIV began to search for some mechanism that would allow him to disengage his forces without too great a humiliation. Above all, he wished to preserve French claims of inheritance to the Spanish throne and to avoid recognizing William III's accession to the English throne. The first of these goals he

achieved, the second proved impossible to attain. However much Louis
XIV wished to make his support for James II unequivocal, the English were
determined that their choice of monarch be acknowledged. The clause
that Louis XIV accepted stated that William was "King of Great Britain by
the Grace of God." The fighting was finally ended in 1697. Both sides
needed peace, partly because of the enormous casualties that the pitched
battles had cost both sides: that of Steenkerke had resulted in 20,000
dead.[209] The Treaty of Ryswick was a compromise between the armies of
Louis XIV and the growing force of the English navy. Problems and disagreements between the opponents remained, however, and war would
break out again in five years' time.

Peace in Europe meant, for the moment, peace in North America.
There was no real attempt to consider whether anything had changed in
the balance of power there. The Treaty of Ryswick restored, in international law, the status quo ante. Acadia was once more recognized as a
French colony. No specific action was taken to regulate any of the problems that existed between Massachusetts and Acadia. Even more than in
Europe, the years between the end of King William's War and the outbreak
of the War of the Spanish Succession were seen as years of truce, not of
peace, time to be spent preparing for the next war.

As the Acadians awaited the arrival of new officials from France, their situation was considerably better than might have been expected. The colony
had, in spite of six years of military action in the region, experienced both
an increase in population and economic growth. While the Acadian settlements had been spared major and continuous warfare, being subject
only to raids and skirmishes and having no army of occupation in their villages, there had been considerable disruption. Nevertheless, the Acadians
had managed to maintain a reasonable standard of living during this period, producing enough food for themselves and, in some years, a surplus.
The existence of a certain amount of trade meant that durable goods were,
if scarce, occasionally available. The trade goods Acadians needed for
themselves were products that meant comfort and relative ease rather than
commodities that were necessary for sheer survival.

The Acadians had also managed to tread a delicate line, during these six
years, between acceding to the demands of Massachusetts and repudiating
their connection with France. Their reaction to the actions of Phips and
Church was, to a large extent, pragmatic rather than the thoughtful implementation of a political stance. It expressed, however, the Acadians' belief
that they had a right to have political views, even if *force majeur* meant that
their expression of them would be tailored to the immediate circumstances. In these years Acadians faced the dilemma that would become
more and more acute as the decades passed: How should they establish
their right to be considered as something more than the subjects of a European power, as having a particular social and cultural identity, linked to the
land on which they lived, which should be recognized by whatever empire

sought to govern them? In the years between 1690 and 1697, there was only a semi-articulated desire, among a small group of first- and second-generation migrants, for recognition of their particular identity, but this would develop over the next two generations into an explicit demand that Acadians be recognized as a distinct people, separate from those of both France and New France.

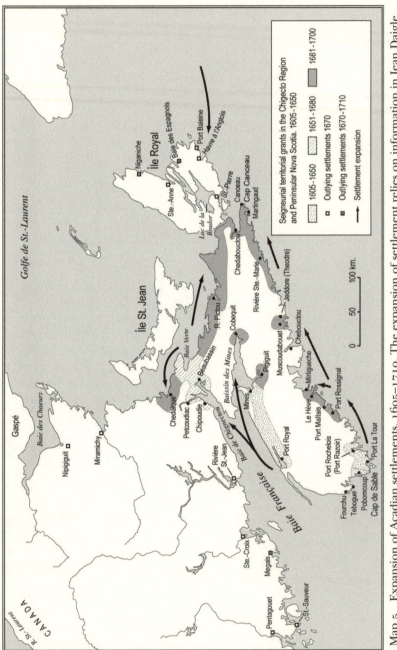

Map 5 Expansion of Acadian settlements, 1605–1710. The expansion of settlement relies on information in Jean Daigle and Robert LeBlanc, *Historical atlas of Canada*, vol. 1, edited by Cole Harris.

The map includes the following labels:

Golfe de St.-Laurent

CANADA
R. St.-Laurent

Gaspé
Baie des Chaleurs
Nipigiguit
Miramichy
Rivière St.-Jean
Ste.-Croix
Megais
Pentagouet
St.-Sauveur

Baie Française

Baie de Chignecto
Bassin des Mines
Basin des Mines

île St. Jean

Baie Verte
Beaubassin
Chedaique
Petcoudiac
Chipoudie
Port Royal

Cobequit
R. Pictou
Rivière Ste.-Marie
Jeddore (Theodre)
Chebouctou
Miriguiche
Muscoudabouet
Pigiguit
Mines
Le Hève
Port Maltais
Port Rossignal
Port Rochelois (Port Razoir)
Port La Tour
Pobomcoup
Cap de Sable
Fourchu
Teboque

île Royal
Niganiche
Baie des Espagnols
Ste.-Anne
Lac de la Brador
Port Baleine
Havre à l'Anglois
St.-Pierre
Canceau
Cap Canceau
Maringaud
Chedabouctou

Seigneurial territorial grants in the Chigecto Region and Peninsular Nova Scotia. 1605-1650.

1605-1650
1651-1680
1681-1700
□ Outlying settlements 1670
■ Outlying settlements 1670-1710
→ Settlement expansion

0   50   100 km.

CHAPTER SEVEN

Acadian Resilience

The Treaty of Ryswick did not eradicate the tensions between England and France on either side of the Atlantic. While it had brought the fighting to an end, it had neither solved the major European diplomatic problem of French links with Spain nor regulated the relationship between French and English colonies in North America. The first problem was rooted in the fear felt by the rest of Western Europe, especially by England, of French influence and power. Despite the impact of disease, famine, and war, the population of France hovered around twenty million throughout the seventeenth century.[1] By 1700, that of England and Wales was still below six million.[2] Furthermore, Louis XIV had backed James II with men and money and had tried to avoid recognizing William III as the rightful king of England. For the next half-century, the deposed Stuart line continued to find shelter in France and to plot their return at the head of an army. The possibility that France might, through the inheritance that could be claimed by a grandson of Louis XIV, gain control of Spain along with that country's extensive American possessions was a matter of much concern to England and to Austria. Similarly, the agreement by London and Paris to accept the status quo ante between England and France in North America did not do much more than halt officially sanctioned attacks.[3] All parties were well aware of the need for greater precision over boundaries and fishing rights, as well as the hostile implications of alliances made between Amerindian and European. Article 8 of the treaty established a commission to discuss, among other issues, the "the settlement of the limits and confines of ceded or restored countries by both parties."[4] This resulted in nothing more than an exchange of vaguely worded letters between the monarchs which contained the unrealistic order that the "Indians were to be disarmed," evidence, as Dale Miquelon has pointed out, "of a total ignorance of Indian life and the relative strength of Europeans and Indians on the frontier."[5]

As far as Acadian-Massachusetts relations were concerned, the commission failed signally to regulate either the question of the Acadian-New

England border or fishing rights on the Acadian banks.[6] This was due, in equal measure, to the attitudes of France and Massachusetts. Both seemed to believe that the status quo ante meant continued uncertainty as to the boundaries of Acadia and disputed claims over the Acadian fishing banks. The letter that Seignelay sent to Villebon on 26 March 1698 contained a copy of the treaty and instructions for future action. These instructions were a virtual repetition of those dispatched to Meneval eight years earlier: the Kennebec was to be considered the boundary between Acadia and New England, and "les Anglois" were to be prevented from trading with the Acadians and from fishing in Acadian waters.[7] But there was an important new element: in future, French concern for the Mi'kmaq and the Abenaki was to be exercised through Acadian commanders. Villebon wrote to the lieutenant governor of Massachusetts, William Stoughton, on 15 September 1698 to inform him of the French position. The Acadian commandant stated that he had been told to consider the Kennebec the boundary between Acadia and the English settlements and remarked that he expected Stoughton to "forbear in future to treat the Indians settled there as your subjects, in order to avoid regrettable consequences."[8] Throughout the negotiations Massachusetts had claimed the St George River, about halfway between Pentagöuet and the Kennebec, as the boundary, and so France's position showed a determination to withstand pressure from New England.[9]

While the policy on the fisheries was a repetition of past instructions, it was intended that these be enforced with a renewed vigour by the French, to counter what many New England fishermen considered "their ancient and indubitable priviledge of Fishing in the seas off the Coast of Accadie or Nova Scotia."[10] By the time Villebon's dispatch had arrived in Boston, boats out of Salem and Marblehead had spent the summer on the Acadian banks.[11] When the French seized a number of these vessels off Chibouctou (Halifax) that autumn, there were, as one would expect, vociferous complaints.[12] Even before the fishermen had delivered their petition to the authorities, the Massachusetts General Court had sent a dispatch to London complaining of "ye insults of the French in their ungrounded and unreasonable pretensions."[13] As George Rawlyk observes, Massachusetts leadership had come to the realization that diplomatic pressure from London on Versailles was necessary if Villebon's activities were to be curbed.[14]

Along with much more official activity in Acadia and Massachusetts, the 1690s also witnessed a significant increase in the Acadian population and a development and elaboration of Acadian political and social life. These factors are closely interrelated because the population expanded not only numerically but also spatially. Families from Port Royal, as well as migrants from France and Quebec, had settled in Beaubassin and Minas by 1689. It was during the next eight years that the development of these settlements, in spite of the war, changed Acadia from a colony with a single major settlement and a number of small outposts to one with three centres of pop-

ulation and several important fishing and trading outposts. The growth in
the total Acadian population is significant enough: it had grown by roughly a third, from about 800 to at least 1,200.[15] But it is the rapid expansion
of Minas and the slower, but continued, development of Beaubassin that
demands analysis: Minas is recorded as having a population of about 164
in 1689 and nearly 400 in 1697; Beaubassin grew more slowly from a population of roughly a hundred to 174 in 1698.[16] The increase in Minas was
due in part, but only in part, to continued migration from Port Royal: that
settlement also grew from 461 people in 1689 to 575 in 1698. In sum, the
years between 1690 and 1710 were the years when Acadian settlement
reaches a critical mass, the population being close to 2,000 by 1710, certainly a strong enough base to be demographically self-generating, had
that been necessary.[17] It is at this point, too, that the particular characteristics of specifically Acadian traditions begin to emerge. Commentators
from France, whether officials or visitors, write from the standpoint of outsiders, as people observing a society not their own. Dièreville, for example,
who spent a year in the colony as the representative of certain French commercial interests, granted the Acadians an identity of their own, separate
from that of France.[18]

The overall growth of Acadia and the development of particular settlements illustrate two fundamental demographic realities about the Acadian
population: the continued arrival of new migrants, albeit sometimes in
small numbers, and the fecundity of those who settled. The first factor has
sometimes been overlooked. There has been a tendency, among some
scholars, to present both Acadia and Quebec as some form of restricted
gene pool which was established before 1763.[19] But in fact the original
nucleus of settlers, in both regions, was constantly augmented with
migrants. In Acadia this influx was particularly important, given that a population of eighty families is generally considered the minimum to ensure
that inbreeding does not produce deleterious effects.[20] A fairly large pool
of unrelated prospective mating partners is also a necessity if the regulations concerning marriage among Catholics, dealing with the legality of
marriage between those with some form of kin relationship, affirmed by
the Council of Trent (1545–63), are to be respected. Marriage was forbidden between those related through four degrees, either by any form of
common ancestry or through a marriage, stemming from a common
grandparent, great-grandparent, or great-great-grandparent. In a recent
study, Jacques Vanderlinden has suggested that the first two generations of
settlers rarely needed episcopal dispensations from these regulations.[21]

Given the scattershot arrival both of families and of individuals in Acadia, both before and after 1670, this is not surprising. Kin links between
the migrants, before arrival in the colony, were relatively few and, to a large
extent, found mostly among those who came before 1670.[22] Nevertheless,
with the arrival of the third generation of settlers, new members of the
community became of particular importance, as the kin links among the

families already established multiplied. That the large families of the early settlers in Acadia led neither to the contravention of ecclesiastical strictures nor to inbreeding is testament to the disparate origins of those who first came from Europe, as well as evidence of the tiny colony's capacity to recruit and absorb newcomers. Even a cursory analysis of the thirty-seven families whose genealogies have been studied by Stephen White reveals the rich diversity of heritage that settlers in Acadia possessed, as well as their arrival at many different times.[23] During the early decades of settlement, these factors were of major importance for the health of the colony, but, even later, the arrival of people from different places enriched Acadian demography and broadened Acadian knowledge of the world outside the colony. Gysa Hynes discovered, from her study of Port Royal registers, that in "32 percent of all marriages [there] between 1705 and 1709 the husband came from France."[24] In fact, as A.H. Clark demonstrated, as far as marriage is concerned, Grand Pré in the 1730s and 1740s was "the precise opposite of bucolic isolation."[25] Finally, in terms of the genetic heritage of the Acadians, there is the question of marriage, according to Catholic rite, with the Mi'kmaq. As was mentioned in chapter 2, there is evidence that, during the 1730s and 1740s, members of the Lejeune, Thibodeau, and Martin families had Mi'kmaq spouses.[26] By 1671, Port Royal, then a community of some seventy households, had at least five homes where the wife was Mi'kmaq. The importance of these connections has been questioned by Vanderlinden.[27] However, their existence seems to be worth remembering, since such kinship relations meant not only an important source of biodiversity but also a channel of contact between the two peoples. Acadians acquired and used Mi'kmaq knowledge: of hunting and fishing techniques, of canoe building, of the value of local plants. *Passe-pierre*, or samphire greens, and *titine de souris* – a marsh plant that is still sold under that name in Moncton – remain Acadian spring delicacies to this day, as do the more well-known *fougères*, or fiddleheads.

Turning to the matter of sheer population growth, we need to consider a number of factors. First, as has been remarked earlier, in the late seventeenth century, in England and France as well as in North America, people were even less inclined to cooperate with official enquiries than the citizenry of the early twenty-first century. Further, the mechanics of gathering and reporting census data resulted in what must be viewed as statistics of approximate, rather than complete, accuracy. Populations were usually underestimated.[28] Secondly, census data can usually be checked against parish records but relatively few of the parish registers for the Acadian settlements, for any single period before 1800, have survived.[29] We have more for Port Royal than for elsewhere but even these registers have their deficiencies.[30] Thirdly, and perhaps most important, the Acadians remained, until well into the eighteenth century, such a small population that only a few questions can be answered by statistical analysis, since the database is often not sufficiently large to yield meaningful results. All this being said, however, there is still a considerable amount of evidence about the development of the Acadian population.

As was seen at the close of chapter 4, the Europeans who came to Acadia established large and flourishing families. This was, of course, a common experience of those European migrants to North America who survived beyond the first two or three years after their arrival. In New England during the seventeenth century, "a demographically completed family, that is one in which the wife survived to age forty-five, averaged about eight children."[31] In New France at this time, women marrying between the ages of twenty and twenty-four averaged eight children and those marrying between twenty-five and twenty-nine gave birth to six.[32] In Acadia, women marrying before age twenty had on the average ten children, those marrying between twenty and twenty-four had nine, and those marrying between twenty-five and twenty-nine had seven.[33] In all locations, women married earlier than their European counterparts, and thus there was the possibility of a longer period of fertility before menopause. But far more important than the number of births was, in all three locales, the survival rate of the children to maturity. The "905 pioneers (men and women) who were born in France, migrated to Canada before 1660, and both married and died in Canada produced on an average 4.2 *married* off-spring, a level of fertility which corresponds to a doubling of the population within a single generation."[34]

Among the Acadians, one of the earliest families to be established was that of Jacques Bourgeois, who married Jeanne Trahan in Port Royal in 1643.[35] They had ten children by 1671 and thirty grandchildren by 1686. The children and grandchildren of another marriage that took place early on in Port Royal, that of Daniel Leblanc and Françoise Gaudet, were even more numerous. It was the second marriage for Françoise, and she brought to it a daughter from her first. This was Marie Mercier, who married Anthoine Babin and herself had eleven children. Françoise Gaudet had six sons and a daughter with Daniel Leblanc.[36] The daughter, Françoise, was born in 1653 and married Martin Blanchard in 1670. She had three children before she died in 1681.[37] One son, Pierre, left Acadia. The remaining five sired fifty-two children among them.[38] Thus, Daniel Leblanc had fifty-seven grandchildren and his wife had a further six from her first marriage. In sum, the majority of children lived to become parents themselves. The contrast with the survival rate of contemporary Europe is remarkable; as we have seen, according to Pierre Goubert, 50 per cent of children born in seventeenth-century France died before the age of twenty and a further 25 per cent died before the age of forty-five.[39] In her study of Port Royal between 1671 and 1730, Hynes found that three-quarters of the children born there over these forty years reached adulthood.[40] Thus, one of the most striking aspects of Acadia, at the close of the seventeenth century, was the omnipresence of children. The partial census drawn up in 1698 recorded 98 families in

Port Royal, with 391 children among them, and in Beaubassin 30 families with a total of 117 children.[41]

Such statistics, however, are only the bare scaffolding for an understanding of Acadian life. First, it is clear from a comparison of the Beaubassin and Port Royal figures that family size was variable. An average of six children a couple, when some families had ten or eleven offspring, obviously meant that some families had no more than two or three. Secondly, the nutrition level in Acadia must have been generally excellent since inadequate diet has an impact on the fertility rates of men and women and on the survival rates of children. Similarly, the impact of infectious diseases, especially smallpox, must have been limited or the increase in population would have been less. Thirdly, the successful raising of children, in a society where food was produced locally and where domestic and agricultural technology was labour-intensive, demanded continual hard work from both men and women. The place of trade in Acadia has sometimes been over-emphasized and eclipsed the essential fact of life for the settlers: the successful production *within* the colony of the basic food supply, most of the wood for houses and barns, and the bulk of clothing, whether textiles or furs. The Acadian economy prospered through the mutual efforts of both men and women. It was neither as dependent as that of Quebec upon imports nor as harassed as that colony was by warfare.[42] Further, differences in soil and climate were of major importance for the relative ease with which basic necessities could be obtained in the smaller colony. But the family was the building block for Europeans in seventeenth-century North America and the contribution of men and women was equally important if the family was to flourish.[43] This was as true for Acadia as it was for New England and New France.

At the same time, whereas there is only general information about what was actually produced by the Acadians in the 1670s and 1680s, the comments, almost a generation later, by Dièreville, as well as the final reports of Villebon in the two years before his death in 1700, provide concrete evidence about what was grown, raised, and made in the colony. As in most agricultural societies of European heritage at the close of the seventeenth century, the partnership of men and women was accepted in the countryside and even in a majority of occupations in the small towns.[44] In rural life it was patently obvious that humanity needed both male and female to survive, let alone to produce the next generation. Usually, men ploughed, sowed and harvested the crops, and took care of flocks and herds as well as housing and barn construction, which meant lumbering and sawing. Some of the labour of animal husbandry was mitigated, at the opening of the eighteenth century, by the use of common pasturage, a practice that the then governor, Jacques-François de Monbeton de Brouillan, deplored because it made for difficulties in establishing property boundaries.[45] Dièreville commented on the extent to which the Acadians cultivated fields of good round cabbages and sweet turnips, preserving both through the winter months by various forms of cold storage. Potatoes, of course, became generally acceptable by those of European descent only in the eighteenth century. Cabbages were kept in the fields, by upending them and covering them lightly with soil, to be gathered through the snow as necessary. Turnips were stored in basements.[46] While comments on the prices of foodstuffs and labour by both Dièreville and Villebon make it clear that the colony was a monied society,[47] it is probable that such fields were jointly farmed and the produce shared, rather than sold. Dièreville remarked that the dyked fields were sometimes jointly owned, sometimes the property of a single farmer, but always jointly worked. Payment for labour might be in kind, the owner working in his turn for those who gave him labour, or in coin.[48] While the Acadians kept sheep and cattle, it was pigs that, along with game and fish, most often provided the protein in their diet. Both pork and beef were salted for the winter and Dièreville commented on how good the beef was, remarking that a whole animal cost about fifty francs.[49] Cows were kept for their milk, and Dièreville thought that this was the reason the Acadians had little taste for veal, preferring to keep the cow with calf and prolong the milking period. Sheep were valued, above all, for their wool, which the women spun for cloth. Villebon is more enthusiastic than Dièreville about the Acadian orchards in Port Royal, calling that region a "little Normandy" for its six or seven varieties of apple, which, Dièreville attested, kept very well over the winter.[50] As well, there were pear and cherry trees in the orchards.[51] Villebon also listed a great variety of vegetables grown: beets, onions, carrots, shallots, parsnips, green peas, and all sorts of salad greens. Nor did he overlook the production of corn, wheat rye, and oats at Port Royal. All in all, Acadian food resources provided a rich and varied diet throughout the year.

Dièreville praised Acadian industry and the ability of the men to turn their hands to many tasks, carpentry and iron work as well as husbandry, which is significant given his more general criticism of how easily the Acadians lived their lives, refusing either to make cider or cultivate the uplands.[52] It seems as if visitors from Europe were unable to accept the pace of the seasons and begrudged the abundant harvest that hard work produced. Acadians imported wine and brandy but also made a spruce beer, which Dièreville considered a strong drink.[53] Men mostly saw to the provision of fuel and to hunting and fishing. Game – partridge and hare – was shot and salted in the fall, fish were caught in the spring and summer. Dièreville reported that he had seen some thirty thousand fish, salted but not dried, in the spring.[54] Villebon listed cod, gaspereau, shad, sardines, and plaice as the most common varieties taken. He also spoke of the Acadian habit, learnt from the Mi'kmaq, of stringing nets across the small rivers to catch them.[55] Finally, the men worked with the tools available, almost all of which, ploughs, hoes, axes, knives, hammers, and sickles, demanded both physical strength and stamina for their employment.

The care of animals – feeding, breeding, and butchering – was some-times a joint effort and the care of hens, ducks, and geese was usually left to women. Their tasks also included the provision of three meals a day, with no running water and open fires rather than stoves. Unlike Quebec, Acadian villages did not have community bakehouses but had their own ovens attached to the outside of houses.[56]Apart from the provision of meals (the Acadians were particularly fond of a thick soup, based on turnips, cabbage, and onions and flavoured with pork[57]), and the imme-diate care of the very young, one of the most important daily tasks for women was the maintenance of a healthy environment for the family. A great deal of work was involved in keeping clothing and household linens clean, with soap, sometimes imported but more often made at home from lye, dredged from wood ash, and animal fat. There was the seasonal labour in the garden and kitchens: harvesting fruits and vegetables, preserving food for the winter. As well, weaving, spinning and knitting, and sewing and mending had to be done at a time when the daylight hours were stretched only by candles and oil lamps.

It is clear that, by the end of the 1690s, the Acadians were more than able to produce the basic necessities of food, clothing, and shelter within the colony. But metal goods for the house, such as iron saucepans, pewter plates, and brass and copper kettles, as well as scissors, pins and needles, thread and buttons, the latter usually of pewter, and combs, were import-ed.[58] Also, both Acadian and New England merchants provided tools for the farm, including guns and ammunition as well as fish-hooks and hoes. Acadian shippers, such as Charles Melanson and Abraham Boudrot, car-ried furs, coal, and flour as well as coinage to pay for their purchases in Boston.[59] In return, as well as the goods listed above, they carried tobacco and pipes, wine, fine linens, wax candles (as opposed to tallow candles made at home from animal fat), glassware, and pottery. Some shoes were imported, although the Acadians also made their own moccasins from sealskin, another skill acquired from the Mi'kmaq.[60] In terms of comestibles, brandy, molasses, oil, pepper, rum, sugar (although the Aca-dians used maple syrup[61]), and vinegar were imported. Vermilion dye and red serge appear on the list of goods shipped by Charles de Saint-Étienne de La Tour in 1696.[62] In sum, through their own efforts in agriculture and in the acquisition of furs, the Acadians enjoyed a much higher standard of living than was the lot of their contemporaries in Europe, but this reward demanded constant effort.

For both men and women, the parenting of children was a given. Women, inevitably, were primarily responsible for the early years of child raising. The birthrate would often mean that an individual woman had four children under six to look after, while she carried out the daily house-hold routine. Both parents, however, were closely involved in preparing the young for adult life. As was normal in rural society until recently, even young children were soon given chores to do and the idle adolescent would be rare indeed. Dièreville commented that children helped their parents from a young age, thus allowing them to save the daily wages that otherwise would have been paid to casual labour.[63] Particular skills – weaving, woodworking, food preservation, and animal husbandry – were handed down through the generations. Perhaps the most vital discipline that would be inculcated was the knowledge that one was at the beck-and-call of forces beyond one's control. Sheep have their own timetable, cows need milking twice a day, and the weather dictates rhythms of sowing and harvesting. No family, however successful in establishing itself, could survive without community support. Interdependence was the crux of Acadian life, not only because of the demands of the dykes but also for the host of tasks that needed doing, from barn building to ploughing and harvesting.

Acadians valued children and the community gave considerable support to young parents. As John Demos pointed out in a perceptive essay published nearly a generation ago on the New England experience,[64] small houses place a premium on civil behaviour among those who live in them. Acadian houses, like those of New England, were mostly a storey or a storey and a half, log-built, almost always with a basement, and the ground floor was rarely subdivided.[65] While more definite description must await further archeological research, it would be a mistake to imagine Acadian houses as all the same. Dièreville rented one that he said was the largest in Port Royal, with three rooms on the ground floor, a basement, and a loft.[66] Further, many farming families would have outbuildings near or attached to the living quarters. However, for much of the year, the ground floor of the house would be a crossroads of activity. There would be little chance of solitude within the home. If continual bickering and quarrelling was not to be the norm, a conscious effort had to be made to establish an affectionate relationship. The spacing of children roughly two years apart meant that, for the first year or so, a child had a relatively secure and tranquil time, breast-fed and frequently nursed, although the pattern of babe-in-arms, toddler, and small child must have left many a woman physically exhausted. Several lullabies, some traceable to France, others seemingly of Acadian origin, show adult pleasure in the new life.[67] Even if the infant was one of the younger siblings, there would still be a sense of intimacy in the household and, once the eldest sibling was seven or eight, an increase in the number of people ready to comfort the baby. Further, words for toys and for group play, such as hide-and-seek and catch-as-catch-can, are part of Acadian vocabulary and argue for a tradition that accepted the right of children to amusements.[68]

But, of course, Acadian family life was not uniformly pleasant for all. Even in a generally healthy community like Acadia, illness occurred and could produce great stress for the family. Not only that, but in-laws could be oppressive as well as supportive; closeness could be suffocating as well as nurturing; and sibling relationships could result in bitter rivalries as easily as they could give rise to life-long affection. While family size would mean that aging parents had greater possibilities for support when health failed and strength diminished, such support might come, often enough, with the loss of personal control.[69] My point, then, is not that the Acadians built an exceptionally loving community on the strength of their family connections, but that such connections did exist and were a crucial *two-way* conduit between choices made within the home and the level of support for those choices which was to be found in the community.

Family connections meant strong intergenerational links, which also helped strengthen the community. The household of a couple in their mid-forties might well contain a child about to marry and move to another dwelling, an infant still being breast-fed, and as many as eight children between the first and the last born. Nor was the family important only during childhood years. Young newlyweds might well build a house close to their parents. In the region of Port Royal, for example, Charles Melanson and his wife, Marie Dugas, established themselves in 1644 on the banks of the Rivière-du-Dauphin, some six miles north of the main settlement. They had fourteen children, eight of whom built houses within the immediate neighbourhood of their parent's lodging.[70] At least a minimum of positive family feeling must have been present for this to have occurred.

But the immediate nuclear family, composed of parents and their children, and their extensive kin links are only part of the story: almost as important are the relationships formed through marriage. The meticulous genealogical research that has been carried out by the Centre d'Études Acadienne at the Université de Moncton has allowed scholars to trace a number of patterns of alliances between the various families, albeit with the qualification that, as Vanderlinden has acknowledged, only tentative conclusions can be drawn from evidence generated by such a small and recently established society as Acadia.[71] Vanderlinden argues that, in the evidence available, one can discern the emergence of social hierarchy and, therefore, the importance of particular families in Port Royal before 1710. Having studied the records of 435 marriages, involving 65 families, which took place in Port Royal before 1710, he calculates that members of twenty-three families accounted for 240 of the marriages. Of these, one-third were marriages that linked two families for the second or third time. On further examination of the record, Vanderlinden concludes that marriages patterns among the families studied falls into four categories. The first category consists of four families who were allied in a complex web of repeated marriages, while the second is made up of thirteen families whose links with each other and with the four central families were less dense. These seventeen families Vanderlinden considers as the core of Port Royal society. Of the others, he says that ten of them had a peripheral relationship with the families of the core and that forty-two others had no marital alliances whatsoever with the core.[72] The four families that, for Vanderlinden, make up the kernel of Port Royal society during these decades are the Boudrots, the Bourgs, the Dugas, and the Melansons. All four families were neighbours of one another on either side of the Rivière-du-Dauphin, close to its mouth.[73] As Vanderlinden himself remarks, it is difficult to decide whether the strong links between the Bourdrot-Bourg-Dugas-Melanson families came about because of a definite strategy or was the result of chance and necessity: "the hasard of migration, chance meetings, the lottery of fertility, whether of the number of children born or of their sex."[74] After all, each of these families also had children who married outside the group. Two of Michel Boudrot's children married children of Pierre Theriot and Claude Landry. Jehan Bourg's children were allied with the families of Jean Dubois, Charles Robichaud, Jean Gaudet, and Pierre Leblanc, among others. Those of Abraham Dugas were linked with the Bourgeois and Leblanc families, and, finally, Charles Melanson's children married, among others, members of the Granger, Petitot, and Babineau families.[75]

Whatever the cause of the dense interrelationships among many Acadian families – and my own opinion is that propinquity and the relative scarcity of marriage partners had a lot to do with who married whom – this web of alliances structured the Acadian community in a number of ways. First, Vanderlinden's claim that intermarriage between four neighbouring families created a social elite in Port Royal society is probably more than the evidence can bear. The broader network of family interconnections that his work illustrates reveals a foundation of kin connection not only within Port Royal but also in the other major Acadian settlements. This kin network was one of the reasons why Acadians assimilated newcomers after 1685 with a minimum of hostility. Family connections were expected to provide help and support to the kin group. Once married to an Acadian, a person quickly assumed the obligations and benefits of the partner's kin. The situation of de Goutin, the French official who arrived as chief magistrate for the colony in 1688, is a good illustration of this. His marriage, in the eyes of Brouillan, who became governor of the colony in 1701, meant that de Goutin was "hardly in a position to make good judgments," since he had married into the Thibodeau family and, in consequence, "a third of the settlers are relatives of his wife."[76] The Acadians, of course, were not uniformly welcoming: the trial, on charges of witchcraft, of Jean Campagnard in 1685 bears all the marks of distrust of an outsider by a closed community.[77] He was accused of causing the death of both men and animals by the evil eye, but it appears that he was a good workman who was owed money by a number of the inhabitants. Campagnard was acquitted and the case can be considered almost as the exception that proves the rule.

As important as kin connections were to marriage within a particular settlement, it was the kinship lines between settlements that were a major binding force for the development of a distinctive Acadian culture. As has already been noted, Acadia, in common with New France and New England, often established new communities through migration from the older neighbourhoods. As the seventeenth century ended, these connections were primarily from Port Royal to either Beaubassin or the Minas settlements. Direct family links between Beaubassin and the Minas Basin and to the settlements being established along the valleys of the Shepody, the Memramcook, and the Petitcodiac would develop only in the third and fourth generations, a case in point being the marriage of Louis Allain of Grand Pré and Anne Leger of Beaubassin in the 1720s.[78] Until then, the majority of the connections between the separate communities within Acadia ran through the hub of Port Royal. Of course, not all those born and raised in Acadia during these years remained there. Those who migrated are difficult to trace but it would be highly unlikely that the daughter of Pierre Melanson was the only person to have married out of her community.[79] Nor should one forget that a number of the offspring of Port Royal settlers married partners from along the Saint John River or from the settlements along the coast. In the 1686 census, for example, Madeleine Melanson is recorded as married to Louis-Simon Saint-Aubin of Passamaquoddy.[80] Both inward and outward migration shaped Acadian customs and militated against Acadia becoming, in any sense, a closed society.

The most important lines of communication between all these settlements, throughout the seventeenth and early eighteenth centuries, were by water, whether by sea or river. This was due partly to the physical geography of a colony that was centred upon a peninsula and shaped by sea and river, and partly to the development of the marshlands, which meant, as A.H. Clark points out, that rivers became the main avenues of communication "by canoe for most of the year, and by snow-shoe when it was frozen over and snow-covered."[81] Again, canoes and snowshoes were tools that the settlers acquired from the Mi'kmaq. Observers were astonished at the Acadian skill with canoes. Antoine Laumet, *dit* de Lamothe Cadillac, who visited the colony in 1692, wrote that the Acadians, both men and women, travelled by birch-bark canoes and were quite fearless on the water.[82] Horses, and paths cleared sufficiently for these animals to be used for travel, were latecomers to Acadia. In the 1686 census there were only fifteen horses recorded in the colony, nine at Port Royal and six at Beaubassin.[83] Reports of coastal travel, by small fishing craft and by the boats used by those who traded with New England, argue for a considerable acquaintance among Acadians with sail. There is little primary evidence about how or where such vessels were built; however, it is clear that the physical connections between Port Royal, Minas, and Beaubassin were most often by water until late in the seventeenth century. By 1699, Villebon reported that the overland route between Port Royal and Minas took a day to traverse. It involved some travel by water, at least as far as the tide head of the Rivière-du-Dauphin and then a fair distance on a good level road to the outlying homesteads of Minas. He considered that the settlers could now drive their herds and flocks from one settlement to the other with considerable ease.[84] Villebon's report is that of a "best-possible" case: no bad weather making the route muddy or icy, neither too much sun and too many mosquitos nor too severe cold. Yet his optimistic estimate does reveal that the Acadians were developing an interconnected community, not just a number of independent settlements.

For much of this period, 1690 to 1710, as well as in later decades, even though the new settlements of Minas and Beaubassin were developing apace, Port Royal remained the centre of official life, of political and religious activity, and of commerce. What was happening there would always be of interest elsewhere in Acadia. And what had happened in Port Royal, both before and after 1671, was responsible, to a greater extent than any other single factor, for the formation of Acadian traditions in major areas of institutional life. It was the accommodations worked out there that laid the groundwork for the cooperation between local authorities and government officials sent from France. It was the economic success of Port Royal, both in terms of local agriculture and of trade with Boston, based, in its turn, upon the fur trade with the Mi'kmaq, that allowed for the successful foundation of Minas. It was the adherence of the settlers at Port Royal to the French language and Catholic beliefs that made Acadian society both French speaking and Catholic. But, while Port Royal was a necessary ingredient for the development of Acadian traditions, it was not, on its own, sufficient for the evolution of an Acadian identity. Without the emergence of local leadership among the Port Royal settlers, the colony as a whole could not have developed an indigenous social and political culture. Without the trading and fishing outposts of the Atlantic seaboard from the Baie des Chaleurs to Pentagöuet, as well as the settlements on the Saint John River, Port Royal would not have been able to evolve. The establishments of Minas and Beaubassin, and the later communities along the Shepody, the Petitcodiac, and the Memramcook, altered the character of Port Royal as they themselves developed with their own particular characteristics.

The pre-eminence of Port Royal arose, in the first place, simply because it was one of the oldest, continuous settlements in the colony and, after 1636, most often the centre of agriculture and trade. After 1654 it was also most often the seat for what civil and religious authority existed in the colony. In all three areas Port Royal produced successful men. Men like Jacques Bourgeois farmed well enough to be able to support the establishment of their children at the new settlement of Beaubassin, providing them with cattle and equipment for the enterprise. Others, like the Melanson brothers, mixed successful farming with trading, in particular as middlemen in the fur trade, and members of their families moved on, also with parental support, to build the Minas communities. In politics, the existence of leaders among the settlers themselves becomes clearly visible at this time. For example, Michel Boudrot was reported as a farm labourer in the 1671 census, having come to Acadia in the 1630s. In 1639, at the baptism of d'Aulnay's daughter, Marie, Boudrot was recorded as a syndic,[85] a post to which another migrant, Guillaume Trahan, would be appointed in 1654. Boudrot, like Trahan, would have been chosen by his fellow settlers to fill this position, which meant that he had the responsibility of representing them on matters of general concern to the leaders of the colony, men such as d'Aulnay and La Tour. By 1686, Boudrot had been appointed to the position of magistrate in Port Royal.[86] He was also one of the most successful farmers there.[87] What is important about the pattern of lives such as those of Boudrot and Trahan is that they illustrate the achievement of positions of influence by men *after* their arrival in the colony. Unlike the d'Aulnays and La Tours, the Le Borgnes and the Menevals, these individuals were migrants who arrived without the support of official status or grants of land obtained in France. Their achievements might have to be ratified by France but it was, above all, their accomplishments in the colony which gained them economic, social, and political standing among their peers.

While these decades saw the emergence of Acadian leaders, this did not mean the advent of hard-and-fast social stratification. The small population base and the relative uniformity of lifestyle worked against the development of social barriers. Even in 1701 there were only sixty-six married couples in Port Royal and no more than thirty-two in Beaubassin. The Minas Basin area, with a total population close to that of Port Royal, had eighty-one married couples, but this number included those who had settled in Pisiquid and Cobequid.[88] For any social activity to occur, Acadians had to accept one another without making any great distinctions in social status. As in early New England, this created "dense kinship and friendship ties"[89] and questions of status and rank were relatively unimportant.[90]

Another crucial influence on the way in which Acadian society developed was the fact that seigneurial grants in the colony did not result in the emergence of a distinct landowning class. The grants, from a very early period, had become deeply enmeshed in litigation, partly because of the interruptions to French control of the colony but also because appeals over disputed claims could be carried to France either directly or via New France.[91] Land ownership did not, of itself, confer status, although clear title to land was important. As a result, seigneurial rank was only one attribute among others for the colonists. At the same time, as has been mentioned before, much of Acadian agriculture demanded a high level of cooperation, primarily because of the demands of dykeland technology, thus encouraging reliance between neighbours and a mitigation of social division. In this period there were few landless families from which hired labour could have been drawn: in Beaubassin, for example, there were only three landless families reported in 1686 and two such families in 1698, and even these families had their own livestock to look after.[92] The standing of those who claimed some form of seigneurial rank among the settlers, at any given time before 1710, does not seem to have led to enduring status within the colony.[93] Dièrevillle, in an oft-quoted passage, remarked that the Acadians seemed to place little emphasis on rank in their marriage practices, regardless of the age of those being wed.[94] Further, the practice of co-ownership, usually by relatives, which, it has recently been suggested, came to Acadia from the Loudonais region, would have also worked against hard-and-fast social divisions in a small community. This custom becomes of particular interest in later years, when hamlets, collections of four or five houses inhabited by several generations of an interrelated family, developed throughout Acadia, particularly in the Minas Basin.[95] Finally, significant stratification emerges in small-scale societies only as economic life diversifies. At the close of the seventeenth century, the Acadian economy in all three major settlements was primarily agricultural, with an admixture of commerce, fishing, and hunting.

The argument for a relatively unstratified Acadian society at the turn of the century does not imply a society without conflict. There were disputes over land rights, particularly among the settlers along the Saint John River and in the Beaubassin region.[96] There were fierce debates over whether those appointed as magistrates were impartial. Acadians recognized both secular and religious authority and prestige but were not particularly enamoured of either. French officials found the Acadians less biddable than they expected, as witness the reaction to Meneval's appointment in the 1680s. This was much the same reaction to external control as that of the colonists along the St Lawrence. In 1674 Frontenac had written to Colbert that "it is necessary for the inhabitants to become less accustomed to licence, that one obtains greater authority and has more means to punish them."[97] In neither colony were the settlers inclined to accept official directives without question. Neither colony attempted to replicate the social divisions of seventeenth-century France, which, in any case, were far less rigid than popular myth has let on.[98] This was particularly true for Acadia, where not only were seigneurial rights honoured more in the breach than in the performance but the militia hardly existed.

The periods of English control had made little or no difference to the internal legal structure of the colony. This remained fundamentally French, built upon the customary law of the Parlement of Paris.[99] Consequently, as Vanderlinden has demonstrated, Acadians had a legal framework that structured landholding and marriage customs, as well as criminal matters.[100] Unfortunately, few legal records of the period before 1710 have survived, but there are enough to confirm that Acadian practice broadly reflected French traditions. The debate after 1697 between the colony and the metropolis revolved around the issue of local Acadian autonomy in matters of commerce and supplies for the commanders and garrison, rather than the Acadians' legal and political links to France. It is certain, however, that the Acadians recognized a certain of French authority. In January 1691 Villebon recorded a request of the inhabitants of Minas, made through their parish priest, that Villebon confirm the selection that had been made of "three of their number to settle the differences

which arise daily among them concerning their lands, and other disputes."[101] Further, after the Phips expedition, the inhabitants of Port Royal
sought Villebon's approval for their actions during the English attack,
showing at least some desire for French approval.[102]

Additional confirmation of the Acadian independence of spirit is to be
found in their attitude to ecclesiastical authority at this time. The presence
of priests in their settlements was important to Acadians. Port Royal, Minas,
and Beaubassin had all built churches, even though Dièreville considered
the one in Port Royal less than fitting for its purpose; he considered it indis-
tinguishable from the surrounding buildings and at first had taken it for a
barn.[103] The Acadians seem to have paid their tithes without argument.
These amounted to 1,500 *livres* yearly for the parishes of Port Royal and
Minas and 300 *livres* for that of Beaubassin.[104] In the fall of 1699, however,
Beaubassin had been without a priest for some time. This was due, in part,
to the settlers' refusal to put up with the behaviour of the former incumbent. Villebon had his own problems with the priests in the colony and it is
not surprising that he reported extensively on the dissatisfaction of
Beaubassin with Father Jean Baudoin. In common with a number of clergy
in both Acadia and New France, Baudoin had been a soldier before he
became a priest and was a man with a love of adventure and a short temper.
Assigned to Beaubassin, he treated the inhabitants with contempt, on occasion using physical force against those he considered malefactors. In
return, his parishioners accused him of spending all his time with the Mi'k-
maq and neglecting the needs of his parishioners.[105] Above all, both Villebon and the inhabitants complained of the lack of regular hours for mass-
es and public prayers, most particularly on Sundays.[106] Some sort of
timetable was of crucial importance, since the Acadian homes were scattered over a considerable amount of territory. Few Acadians had horses and
many lived some thirty or forty minutes' walk from the church. These complaints resulted in Baudoin's recall first to Quebec and later to France.[107]

On the larger stage, dominated as ever by international rivalry, the Acadians had become used to the demands of a life on the border between
warring empires, whose main interests were elsewhere but who, nevertheless, brought their military forces through Acadian lands. Acadians had to
cope with raids from Massachusetts without any immediate aid for the Acadian settlements from the garrison on the Saint John. For the colonists, it
was never clear, throughout King William's War, whether France or England would eventually control their region. This had resulted in the first
steps by Acadian men of influence towards a specifically Acadian political
stance vis-à-vis both powers. The first years of the eighteenth century would
show that Acadians had no intention either of ending their commercial
relationship with Massachusetts or of cutting their political and cultural
links with France.

The emergence of Acadian identity at the opening of the eighteenth
century was, of course, parallelled by the development of other European

colonies in North America at the time. By 1700, in Massachusetts, New France, and Acadia itself, more than three generations had passed since the first settlers arrived. Grandchildren and, in some cases, great-grand-children of the early migrants now lived in communities that were capable of sustaining themselves, economically, demographically, and culturally. But, at every step of the way, such colonial development was profoundly affected by three major factors, each of which was significantly different for each particular colony. First, there was the necessity of adaption by the migrants to their new circumstances, the need to learn how to produce food and shelter in a new environment, whose climate and landscape were radically different from that which they had previously known. Secondly, since the growing communities always maintained communications with Europe, this helped the preservation of many of the European customs and values which the migrants possessed. It was not solely a matter of commerce, an ongoing trade in specifically European commodities. Ideas and customs also spread across the Atlantic and local procedures were always tempered by official demands from those who claimed the migrants as their subjects. But each colony developed a different relationship with its metropolitan centre. Neither France nor England had consistent colonial policies in place when transatlantic migrations began and, as each colony came into being, its relationship with its European centre developed its own specific characteristics. Even such practices as did exist were haphazardly applied, subject to the urgency of the domestic issues of the moment that the European governments faced. Finally, from the outset, there was interaction between the migrants and the original inhabitants of the land, as well as connections among the colonies themselves. As well, the particular peoples already in the territory now claimed by the newcomers reacted in different ways to the intrusion. The relationship of European and the Six Nations peoples was not the same as that between European and Mi'kmaq. The end result of the combination of these factors, given the great variation produced by the circumstances of each locality, was the development of distinctive social patterns within each colony.[108]

Particular patterns of political action had also developed within each colony by the end of seventeenth century. Again, these patterns had a common root: the control sought by European governments over colonial development and the way in which European constitutional and legal institutions were adapted to the wants and needs of the new communities.[109] Acadians had already begun to evolve patterns of political action during the last decades of the seventeenth century. It was in the years after 1690, however, when the colony moved from being on the periphery of one European empire to being an outpost of another, that the Acadian community developed *distinctive* patterns of political action. As will be seen, from the arrival of Brouillan in the summer of 1701 until the arrival of the third governor appointed by the English, Richard Philipps, in Port Royal, now named Annapolis Royal, in April 1720, the Acadians responded anything but passively to the course of events.

The final months of Villebon's tenure – he died on 5 July 1700, aged only forty-five – reflected the energy of those who lived in Acadia. As might be expected, the ending of hostilities allowed the emergence of quarrels among civil officials, quarrels that had been present but kept in the background during the war years. Many of these disputes were what one might expect in a small frontier society, where lines of authority between civil and military officials were unclear and the officials themselves not necessarily compatible. Villebon's troubles arose as much from his character and his family connections as from any proven incompetence. He was clever, intelligent, quick-tempered, and impatient with those who challenged his authority. This led to bitter arguments with men such as the Damours brothers, who had settled on the Saint John River in the mid-1680s. Villebon complained to Pontchartrain that they had become so used to living without any external control over the past decade that they had become ungovernable.[110] The governor disliked the influence these men had on the Malecite. He believed that they traded too much and farmed too little, but there is little or no evidence to substantiate these charges.[111] Two of Villebon's brothers also served with him in Acadia, Daniel and René.[112] They were, and remained, bachelors, courageous, quarrelsome, and inclined to live more happily with the Malecite and the Abenaki than in the Acadian settlements. Their conduct reflected on Villebon, who himself was reputed to have an illegitimate daughter[113] and who quarrelled not only with Father Baudoin at Beaubassin but also with Father Abel Maudoux at Minas.[114] It is not surprising that charges of nepotism and loose morals were brought against the governor. The most formal indictment against Villebon was written in 1698 by de Goutin, who accused Villebon, among other matters, of profiting illegally from trade and not distributing the presents sent to the Mi'kmaq and Malecites justly. Further, de Goutin wrote, he "caused to be used up 112 pounds of gun-powder in a bonfire to celebrate the peace, while drinking healths to his mistresses, he and the Sieur Martel, became drunk while so doing."[115] It seems clear enough that Villebon did engage in trade, something not permitted to governors. Tibierge, an agent of the Compagnie de la Pêche Sédentaire (which was still struggling on despite the raid upon its Canso headquarters in 1690), reported in 1699 that Villebon sent beaver pelts to Boston.[116] The governor's stipend was not particularly generous and, as one of twelve children, he had no financial support from his parents. These charges were not brought to trial, however, before Villebon died.

Quarrels between appointed officials were not the only internal problems to emerge with peace. More significant were the debates about landholdings. These were not just the wrangles between the heirs of the Le Borgne and La Tour-d'Aulnay families, with counter-claims by Duret de Chevry, wrangles that had been before the courts since 1688.[117] Questions had been brewing for some time about who, precisely, had granted what to whom. Such queries were one more sign of the change in the colony from the era of minimal settlement to that of established communities. It was not only that the growing density of population in the Port Royal, Minas, and Beaubassin regions raised questions about property limits. After 1698, there were also arguments about rights of settlement in the Shepody Bay region, along the river valleys of the Memramcook and the Petitcodiac.[118] As well, as has been already mentioned, Villebon had reported complaints about the partiality of judgments made by de Goutin, the chief magistrate of the colony.

In the spring of 1699, French authorities decided that a general review of the situation should be undertaken. The Sieur de Fontenu, then a commissioner in the Admiralty, was being sent to the colony anyway, to report on the availability there of lumber for shipbuilding.[119] The instructions he received for this purpose, dated 8 April 1699, were followed within a week with another set outlining the situation in Acadia.[120] It was pointed out to Fontenu that Acadia had been divided in the past into a number of grants to individuals, some of whom were still in the colony, others having left. As a result, there had been a number of disputes over the different grants. The king had been informed that a number of these disputes were still continuing, which hindered the proper development of Acadia. He had also been informed that some of those who had been the very first to be granted land there now traded with the English and gave them permission to come for that purpose to Acadia. His Majesty, it was stated, wished to end this disorder and to restrict landowners within the limits of their grants. Fontenu was to publish far and wide the attached ordinance.[121] This was an explicit document which charged not only that some of the proprietors had not fulfilled the conditions of their grants but also that they had traded with the English of Boston. All, therefore, who claimed land in Acadia, whether by direct grant, inheritance, sale, or any other means, were directed to send proof of their titles to France within the year, either by presenting the original documents or through witnessed copies of same, under pain of having their rights revoked.[122]

The immediate result of this highly sensible enquiry was what one might expect. Within the year, the deadline for the presentation of documents had to be extended, because proprietors alleged that the deeds establishing proof of their claims were held in Quebec and it was impossible to retrieve them in the time allowed.[123] In 1701 the king appointed Henri-François Daguesseau to head a committee to resolve the whole question of Acadian land claims, including those brought forward by the La Tour family.[124] The order establishing this committee was more sharply worded. In it Acadia was described as being fertile, happily circumstanced, and capable of producing a considerable trade for the French and of becoming as strong as the neighbouring English settlements. But at present, it was claimed, the colony was almost a desert and incapable of supporting even one trading ship a year. The reason for this sad state of affairs, it was stated, stemmed from the haphazard and unjust way in which land had been granted, frightening away those who might have established themselves on the concessions.[125] The judgment that this committee published two years later, on 20 March 1703, provided a framework for the claims of landowners in Acadia.[126] Its influence was, as will be seen, more important in the long term than in the short term, since by then war had once more broken out.

The estimation of Acadian prosperity, in the preamble to the ordinance of 1701, illustrates one of the colony's major difficulties: confusion in France about what life in Acadia was really like. While official correspondence bewailed the trade between Boston and Port Royal, its true value was never properly assessed in France. Nor was the extent of the Acadian fur trade with the Mi'kmaq and Malecite ever recognized in Versailles. Even the fact that France supplied the Mi'kmaq, Malecite, and Abenaki throughout King William's War, leaving the Acadians very much to their own devices and encouraging them to continue trading with New England, did not make any real impression on officials in France. There seems to have been no understanding that the Acadians must have paid for their supplies in kind or in coin, generated within the colony. It is as if the Acadian population was seen as so negligible that their trading patterns were important solely in terms of what such activity might signify for the broader relationship between New England and New France. Yet, for the French officials living in Acadia, the trading relationship of the colony with New England was of crucial importance. No matter what was decided elsewhere and whether or not it would be considered as smuggling by one side or the other, there would be trade between Acadia and New England. By 1697, it was not merely a matter of this trade being profitable for New England merchants; it was also of major significance to Acadian families. As far as the general Acadian populace was concerned, France had consistently failed to provide adequately for Acadian needs since 1670, either in defence or in supplies. This had not, in any way, diminished Acadian attachment to many French cultural traditions but it had weakened Acadian links to French state politics.

As has been noted, trade between Acadian and Massachusetts had been carried on throughout the war, but after the Treaty of Ryswick it was pursued with even greater vigour. Tibierge, the agent for the French fishing company, wrote in October 1797 that Abraham Boudrot and Pierre Dubreuil made five voyages to Boston within the year, carrying shipments of grain.[127] He noted that there was little trade between Port Royal and Minas and the Saint John River because the journey itself was demanding and the Acadians feared to run into difficulties with the English.[128] But Acadians went enthusiastically to Boston to trade and New Englanders came to the Acadian settlements for furs. John Alden and Saint-Castin were trading partners once more at Pentagöuet in 1698, the former supplying a great deal of general merchandise and receiving, in exchange, all the furs that were available there.[129] The fact is that the Acadian economy was not a simple matter. The relative closeness of the major settlements of Port Royal, Minas, and Beaubassin has overshadowed the fact that the colony itself stretched from the Baie des Chaleurs in the northeast to Pentagöuet in the southwest. Further, the decision to develop forts on the Saint John River, and to transfer the governor's residence there, while perhaps strategically inevitable after Phips's raid, cut off both civil and military officials from the major centres of Acadian settlement for almost a decade.

Tibierge noted in this same report the extent to which the economy of the colony was fragmented, so that it was possible to have a surplus of food in one area and a dearth in another. He reported that the Saint John settlers had been short of food the previous winter since "they have no mill in which to grind the wheat they harvest, [and] they are in danger of faring badly again this winter, unless they have recourse to Minas or Port Royal."[130] Tibierge also reported that "the Indians have been starving this winter, and have been compelled to eat the skins of the moose they had killed."[131] He makes plain that it was to supply the Saint John area of the colony that help was requested from Boston by Villebon and de Goutin in May 1699. A letter was sent to John Nelson, the latter once more in Boston, asking him to send supplies to the Saint John River, in particular "800 bushels of Indian Corne 12 barrills of flower and six barills of molasses." In exchange, Nelson was promised payment "in good peltry and besides which I [Villebon] will give a permitte for fishing on our coasts to ye Master of the vessell."[132]

That these supplies were for the garrison and the local Malecite population rather than for the general Acadian population on the isthmus is clear, first of all, from the context of the letter that Villebon sent to the minister of the Marine on 27 April 1699, pointing out that supplies had been sent to Acadia only for six months and that it was indeed the supply of the garrison that was in question.[133] Secondly, the amount requested would supply the 80–100 soldiers then serving in Acadia but would have meant little for a civilian population of well over 1,000. It is an exercise in guesswork to find equivalents of weights and measures among North American colonies at the close of the seventeenth century, let alone between colonies. However, taking the "barrique" as being a rough approximation of a "barrel," there is a list of supplies to be sent in 1696 for the Acadian garrison, estimated to be a hundred strong, which includes the provision of seventy-five "barriques" of flour.[134] Whatever one might surmise about the quantity actually supplied, the amount requested from Boston was relatively small. Finally, the existence of a severe food shortage among the general population is certainly not apparent from the statistics of population growth. While the census data for 1698 and 1701 are incomplete, the total population for the latter year is around 1,500, an increase of roughly a third in nine years.[135]

Acadia would suffer more severely after the resumption of war between England and France, which occurred in the spring of 1702. Even then, however, the hardship experienced was not enough to affect population growth.

Matters of trade between New England and Acadia and internal arguments about political corruption and land ownership were two of the issues before Villebon. There was also the continuing problem of the boundary with northern New England and the annual dilemma of the fisheries. The question of the boundary was primarily a matter for diplomats in Europe, arguing before the international commission in London. However, Pontchartrain demanded, with growing impatience, that Villebon send him whatever records could be found on the issue at Port Royal. "There must be," Pontchartrain wrote, "in the record office at Port Royal papers which could shed some light on the matter, and a number of people there who have seen, or learnt from their fathers, the beginnings of English settlement. You could have taken their statements."[136] Six months later, Villebon replied categorically that "there is not a single act in the record office of Port Royal which mentions boundaries; the English took the precaution of taking everything with them when they were masters of Port Royal in the past."[137] In truth, the question of the boundary between Acadia and New England was, in times of peace, more an irritant than a serious problem for officials in Acadia. The continued presence of Saint-Castin in the Pentagöuet area meant that French claims were visible there. Any more vigorous action would demand aid and agreement from Quebec, if not from France.

The fisheries were another matter entirely. If trade between Acadia and Massachusetts was a given, no matter how unwelcome to authorities in France, so, too, was the presence of a New England fishing fleet off the Acadian banks every spring and summer. Villebon wrote a lengthy analysis of the coastal fisheries of Acadia in the fall of 1699, an analysis that contained not only an appraisal of that activity but also a shrewd commentary on New England's attitude to Acadia, as well as upon Acadian attitudes to commercial fishing. Villebon began by pointing out that whereas cod fishing in Newfoundland lasted for only the four months of late spring and summer – May, June, July, and August – off the coast of Acadia the fish began to run in March and continued until Christmas.[138] He emphasized the extent to which fishermen from New England exploited the fishery, often making more than one voyage, and considered that a small ship, no more than twenty to thirty tons with a crew of five men, could fish close to a hundredweight of fish in a summer. Almost as an aside, he went on to state that the Acadians were too shiftless to undertake such arduous work. A better comment would have been that the level of population in the colony, and the demands of agriculture and the fur trade, meant that there was no pool of labour available for such an enterprise. At any rate, berating the Acadians was not the main point of Villebon's memoir. What he was attempting to do was to propose a scheme whereby France would control the fishery. He had become convinced that it was not possible to exclude the English completely from Acadia and that, in any case, no attempt should be made to do this until the colony was properly garrisoned and could withstand attack. He was fully aware of New England's interest in the fishery off the Acadian coast and feared retaliatory raids should France attempt to enforce a strict ban against the New England fishing fleet. Instead of such action, Villebon argued, since the New England vessels had the right to continue deep-sea fishing, Boston's recent offer that each ship pay fifty francs for the privilege of getting wood and water from the Acadian shore should be accepted. He also recommended that New England ships be granted the right to establish curing stations for which they should pay extra. He thought that these licences would produce four or five thousand *livres* annually, which could then be spent on fortifications in Acadia. In many ways, this suggestion was an attempt to revive the policy that Meneval had sought to establish almost two decades earlier. Pontchartrain refused to countenance the scheme but this news reached Port Royal only after Villebon's death.[139]

Claude-Sébastien de Villieu took over temporary command of the colony on the death of Villebon. Villieu was then sixty-seven and had been in Acadia since 1693.[140] He remained the ranking official in the colony until the arrival in July 1701 of Monbeton de Brouillan, who had been appointed commander of the colony on 28 March of that year.[141] Short as his tenure was, it brought Villieu a problem of major proportions: the dissension that arose as Acadian settlement moved, decisively, into the region of the Shepody, Petitcodiac, and Memramcook rivers. He himself was personally involved in the questions of seigneurial rights and settlers' privileges that this movement involved. In many ways, the movement itself was similar to that which had resulted in the settlement of the Minas Basin and of the Beaubassin area, both in the way in which the new settlements were supported by prosperous families of the older communities and in the dispute over land rights. Both migrations were a testament to the healthy demographic and economic life of the colony as a whole.

The new settlements had begun in 1698 when one of the more prosperous inhabitants of Port Royal, Pierre Thibodeau, decided, much as Jacques Bourgeois had done a generation earlier, to establish a new community. In the same way as it is believed that Bourgeois first saw Beaubassin, as a result of coastal trading with the Mi'kmaq,[142] Pierre Thibodeau is reported as having visited the estuaries of the Shepody and Petitcodiac because of like activity.[143] There are other similarities between the two men: Bourgeois came to Port Royal as a surgeon and Thibodeau also arrived with an established trade, that of miller.[144] Readers in the early twenty-first century might find the status of surgeon and miller disparate, but in seventeenth-century Western society the social importance of the two occupations was quite similar. If not quite as successful a farmer as

Bourgeois, Thibodeau was prosperous enough. In 1671 he and his wife, Jeanne Teriot, had six children, seven acres of cleared land, a herd of twelve cattle, and a flock of eleven sheep.[145] Fifteen years later, the couple had fourteen children and ten acres of cleared land. While the number of cattle had increased slightly, to fourteen, they now had only five sheep. After this census, a number of the Thibodeau children married and moved elsewhere, to La Hève and Minas. In 1690 the seventh child, Jeanne, married de Goutin, thus linking the family to the closest official that Acadia ever had to an intendant.[146] In the summer of 1698 Pierre Thibodeau went to Fort Saint-Joseph at Nashwaak, where Villebon still lived, and requested permission to establish a settlement along the Shepody. A few days later a number of other well-established Port Royal men, led by Guillaume Blanchard, made similar requests.[147] Blanchard was a second-generation settler, having been born in Port Royal in 1654, one of six children of comfortably circumstanced parents, Jehan Blanchard and Radegonde Lambert. In 1671 the family had owned fifteen cattle, fourteen sheep, and fourteen acres of cleared land. By 1686, Guillaume Blanchard had married Huguette Goujon, and that year the couple already had five children (two boys and three girls), a herd of sixteen cattle, and a flock of twenty sheep.[148] The number of children had increased to twelve by 1698.[149] Villebon gave the men his approval for their plans, apparently overlooking that fact that his uncle, Michel Leneuf de La Vallière, had been granted a seigneury, with broad but vague boundaries, in the Beaubassin area.

Armed with Villebon's endorsement, Thibodeau and Blanchard began the arduous task of gathering and transporting food supplies and materials for buildings, including planks for grist and saw mills as well as seeds and stock. They were joined by adult members of their families, as well as others. Guillaume Blanchard decided to exploit the Petitcodiac, while Thibodeau remained enchanted with the Shepody estuary. As winter arrived, the buildings were secured and most returned to Port Royal.[150] The following spring, the work was begun again but at this point legal complications arose. Villieu, who had been on leave in France until the spring of 1699, returned to take up the command of his company in Acadia.[151] At some time before 1693, he had married Judith Leneuf, the daughter of Michel Leneuf de La Vallière, and he now tried to protect what he saw as his father-in-law's seigneurial rights, which Villieu considered included the north shore of the Bay of Fundy. Specifically, he attempted to establish the size of the holdings that could be developed and to exact dues from the settlers. Thibodeau and Blanchard led the challenge to these demands and the case was sent to Paris for adjudication. The first verdict was rendered in the general judgment of Acadian titles in 1703. It was in favour of the settlers but it contained the phrase that their rights were granted "without prejudice" to the seigneury of La Vallière.[152] Such a judgment merely exasperated everybody involved and further complicated the situation. What the French authorities were attempting to achieve becomes a little clearer with yet another judgment given in 1705. This stated that "Michel Leneuf, sieur de la Vallière" held an extensive estate centred on Beaubassin, for which he owed "foy et hommage" to the officials in Port Royal. However, it was expressly charged that La Vallière could not dis-posses settlers who were found in possession of lands and inheritances within this territory which they had cleared, lived on, and improved. Nev-ertheless, such settlers must pay dues to La Vallière for the territory in question.[153] What was being sought was the reinforcement of the legal base of seigneurial land ownership but also protection of the practical rights of those engaged in settling the land. In other words, the French crown held to the tradition that grants of seigneuries would not be allowed to inhibit the settlement of the lands in question, even if the settlers moved in first and sought to regularize their relationship with the seigneur later. As R.C. Harris writes, "that the seigneurial system was not a way of life in Canada during the French regime is certain beyond reasonable doubt, but that much of it remained as a legal system is equally definite."[154] The prop-erty rights inherent in the seigneurial system were not completely rejected and land transfers took them into consideration but such rights became more and more attenuated in Acadia as the French regime came to an end.

During these same years (1698–1705) Acadian settlement in the Minas Basin expanded successfully towards Pisiquid, the area at the very eastern limits of the region, and also took root at Cobequid (near present-day Truro). Records of formal grants of land in the Pisiquid area have not yet been recovered, but the 1701 census reported 30 families there, compris-ing 188 people.[155] Some of the records relating to Cobequid have sur-vived. In 1689 Mathieu Martin, one the first children born in Acadia, both of whose parents were European, was accorded a seigneury in the region of "oue[sic:ouest]-Cobequid."[156] The early years of settlement were trou-bled with disputes over ownership with de Goutin. However, by 1701 three families had been established there and by 1707 the number had grown to seventeen families and eighty-two people.[157]

Overall, the years of King William's War in no way stunted Acadian demographic growth and the few years of peace that followed the Treaty of Ryswick were a time of expansion for the colony. During these years, Acadia had a strong economy based on agriculture but leavened with trade, a nascent political and economic elite, and established social and cultural traditions. In 1701 it seemed set for further growth and develop-ment, but then, in 1702, war broke out yet again between England and France.

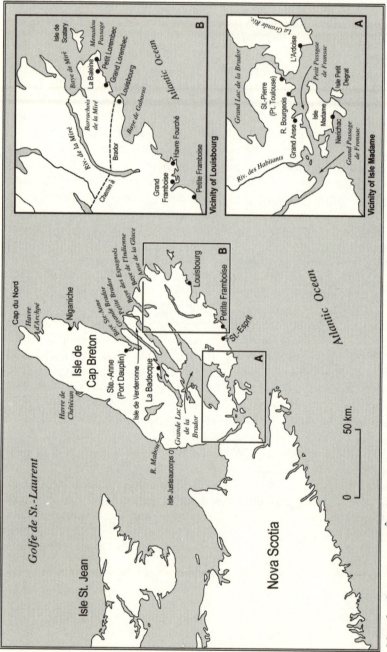

Map 6   Cape Breton (Île Royale) to 1758. Clark, *Acadia: The geography of Nova Scotia to 1776.*

CHAPTER EIGHT

The Last Years of French Rule

At the opening of the eighteenth century, North America was profoundly affected by the European politics of the time. This should go without saying, but, because the early 1700s are flanked by much more dramatic periods of European political life – previous decades of religious wars and succeeding years of revolutionary and nationalistic struggles – developments in early-eighteenth-century Europe are often taken for granted. European states in 1700 still were overwhelmingly monarchical and the rights and prestige of monarchies were reasons for war. In international affairs, it was the power of kingdoms, not of peoples, that was at stake. The claims of these kingdoms, however, were as much issues of international boundaries, of strategic advantages, of imperial aggrandizement as were the later wars fought by nation-states. Questions of religious belief and economic advancement affected both the conduct of war and the settlements of peace. But the actual conduct of war was rarely fuelled by bitter national enmity. Armies, until the latter of the part of the century, were armies of the monarch, the soldiers were subjects not citizens, and the impact of national sentiment was, inevitably, of much less importance than it would be later on. The employment of mercenaries, both individually and even as entire regiments, was common throughout the eighteenth century. Armies, as M.S. Anderson has written, were "thought of as state or dynastic instruments rather than repositories of national pride."[1]

The predominance of France among European powers was obvious, even when disliked and opposed. French culture, material and intellectual, was copied. French architecture was almost slavishly imitated: the Germans built the palace at Mannheim as a copy of Versailles. From Gobelin tapestries to cooking, France was, by the 1680s, the established leader of taste and, almost as important, of comfort.[2] In the world of the arts, the works of Pascal, Molière, and Racine were read, Lully's music played, and Lebrun's paintings admired throughout Europe. In the realm of power politics, the negotiations leading to the Treaty of Ryswick in 1697 demonstrated that France was the most powerful country in Western Europe. Its population equalled that of the British Isles, the Hapsburg empire, Prussia, and the United Provinces (Netherlands) combined.[3] The French monarchy had held off, for nearly a decade, the combined forces of Holland, England, and the major German states. While France's ambitions for expansion had been blunted on both land and sea, it had kept some of its conquests, including Strasbourg. The worst that could be said, from the point of view of Louis XIV, was that Ryswick represented a return to the status quo of 1689. Nor would the War of the Spanish Succession, also known as Queen Anne's War, which began in 1702, mean anywhere near a total defeat for France, although during its course that country suffered an unprecedented series of military defeats.

Finally, Europe in 1700 was still primarily rural, agriculture remained the mainstay of the economy, and industry and trade were only beginning to expand.[4] External trade for France was concentrated mainly within Europe, 74 per cent in 1726.[5] England was in a similar position, with some 70 per cent of its exports going to Europe and 61 per cent of its imports coming from there.[6] Trade with the world outside was still a matter for major exploration. As far as the Americas were concerned, it was largely a matter of profitable exports from Europe and the import from the Caribbean of items that might add significantly to the comfort of life of the well-to-do, with no effect yet on the living conditions of the majority. The fur trade with North America is a major example of an activity that, while involving venture capital and many subsidiary occupations, such as boat building and the making of goods for trade with the Amerindians, produced as an end result something of a luxury product rather than a vital necessity.

Here, the differing experiences of England and France need close attention for the particular choices each country made had a major impact on the development of their colonies in North America. Jeremy Black has recently argued that there was no fundamental difference in the political life of the two countries during this period. He makes the point that there was a general European "movement towards a reconciliation between Crowns and elites" and that the English "Parliament and the government, both central and local, secular and ecclesiastical, were dominated by the nobility and their relatives and dependents."[7] Yet the general similarity of political circumstance was no more than just that. The particular traditions of institutional change, as well as the vastly disparate geographical situation of each country, meant that the paths chosen by the two countries to deal with the need for political evolution were not the same. There are three major areas of variance which would affect the evolution of colonial policy. First, while social mobility in France was not, at this time, as impossible as has often been supposed, it was easier in England and the incorporation of the merchant venturer into the gentry was much more frequent in English aristocratic circles than in France.[8] This meant a more vigorous prosecution of colonial trade by a greater percentage of the pop-

ulation in England than in France. Secondly, partly because of the size of
the country, partly because of the way in which the regions were linked to
the central government, the power to influence the decisions of the crown
was more widespread in England than in France. The House of Lords
functioned, as did the House of Commons, as places where regional concerns were brought to the notice of the crown. There were no comparable
institutions in France, where the link between government and governed
was above all the intendant, an appointed royal official. The English system favoured the growth of informed ministerial action on particular
problems, the French encouraged the growth of an efficient bureaucracy.
All these differences, it can be argued, are a matter of degree rather than
of category. Together, however, they add up to a significant divergence in
the political cultures of the countries.

Finally, the English and French policy towards dissidents, especially religious dissidents, was utterly different. From the opening of the seventeenth century, the English had considered colonial settlement a means of
coping with what the authorities considered undesirable elements, in particular religious and political dissidents. As a result, English transatlantic
migration in the seventeenth century was an allowable path for those seeking better circumstances, whether this meant greater religious freedom,
economic advancement, or social mobility. The French government, on
the other hand, considered that there was a pressing need for men in both
the army and the navy. Migration outside the country, as opposed to within it, was only sporadically encouraged. Such migration as did take place
to North America, officials believed, should consist of those who would
build a society reflecting the best characteristics of contemporary France.
This desire to make France's North American settlements a different kind
of society, one free of the elements that disrupted the harmony of France
itself, slowed migration.

Both countries, of course, considered North America a territory open
for their exploration and exploitation and both claimed extensive rights
over the land. However, the European population of the English colonial
settlements grew much more swiftly than that of the French. In 1700 the
English colonies had a population of 250,000 between them, from a metropolitan base of between seven and eight million, if Scotland and Wales
are included.[9] The population of New France in 1713 was just over 18,000
inhabitants and that of Acadia no more than 3,000, and this from a
country of at least twenty-two million.[10] As Leslie Choquette has pointed
out, by the middle of the eighteenth century, the French colonies "could
boast about the same number of inhabitants as Nantes or Bordeaux, and
fewer than Marseille or Lyon."[11] There were a number of consequences
that stemmed from this disparity, two of particular importance. For New
France, the fur trade and its attendant emphasis on exploration encouraged France to emphasize territorial expansion rather than the needs of
the established settlements. Together with Louis XIV's policy on Spain,

this attitude was an important reason for the policy of the encirclement which France established in 1701. That year, Louis XIV wrote to the officials in New France, Governor Louis-Hector de Callière and Intendant Jean Bochart de Champigny, that he had decided to found a colony at the mouth of the Mississippi.[12] This, as W.J. Eccles points out, meant that "the French were now committed to occupying the entire western section of North America, from Hudson Bay to the Gulf of Mexico and to holding the English colonials on the eastern side of the Alleghany mountain range."[13] It was a policy based squarely upon a European view of North America, a policy rooted in European assumptions of North American realities. In practical terms, it meant that the settlers along the St Lawrence and in Acadia were now to have their needs considered as part of a broad scheme of French aggrandizement that emphasized the establishment of new frontier positions rather than the growth and development of the established communities. But at this time France had only one major colonial settlement in North America, which was both overextended and underpopulated, faced with English colonies whose population seemed to be growing without limit. Louis XIV's policy could succeed only if considerable military force was dispatched to reinforce the colonial militia.[14]

As far as England was concerned, the actual experience of the English settlers had a major effect on the formation of its policy towards its North American colonies. London was better informed not only about the New England and the southern colonies but also about what the colonists themselves wanted. North American interests were much more important in London than in Paris. English migration to North America was a continuous process throughout the colonial period and a process that meant the expansion and development of communications between the colonial and imperial societies. As well, although the North Atlantic was a one-way street for many migrants, a significant minority found it a two-way bridge to be travelled frequently.[15] Colonial leaders, especially merchants, worked to ensure that, when necessary, they would be able to speak to those influential in the political life of London. The interests of all the colonies but in particular those of Massachusetts and New York were, on occasion, a matter of consequence not only for the Board of Trade but also for the government as a whole. For France, in contrast, the circumstances of Acadia and Canada were rarely, if ever, a concern of those who had positions of influence in government. Thus, when war broke out in 1702, Acadia was of only minimal consequence for France but, largely because of Massachusetts, of considerably greater interest for England.

The roots of this war are to be found in the impact upon the European balance of power of dynastic claims. On 1 November 1700 Charles II of Spain had died, leaving Philip, Duc d'Anjou, grandson of Louis XIV, as his heir. Thereafter, the European rulers took a slow route to open conflict, attempting to come to some diplomatic agreement that would limit Bourbon power, which now ruled two great empires, that of France and Spain.

As James Collins writes: "Philip took over a vast empire, one whose extent we easily forget: Spain, the Southern Netherlands, the Kingdom of the Two Sicilies, several small states in Italy, and the massive empire in the New World." Further, "Louis XIV and his grandson controlled the European coast from Antwerp to Palermo, save for Portugal and a few isolated pockets in Italy."[16] Within the year, however, a Triple Alliance consisting of the Austrian emperor, England, and the United Provinces, the last led, of course, by William III, king of England, had come into being. The parties agreed to oppose any closer unification of the French and Spanish thrones. The accord might well have been a dead letter, for the English elites were uncertain that war was necessary. However, on 16 September 1701 James II died. Louis XIV immediately proclaimed the son as James III, the rightful monarch of Great Britain and Ireland, thus giving the English a dynastic reason for their involvement. War between France and England was now inevitable and it came in the spring. On 15 May 1702 the Triple Alliance declared war on France and Spain. The most bloody battles of the eleven years of war that followed were again in Europe. At the battle of Blenheim, in 1704, "the first great French defeat in battle since Louis XIV was king,"[17] saw the Franco-Bavarian forces lose 30,000 of 54,000 men.[18] The Austrian and English lost 12,000 out of 52,000.[19]

When the news of the outbreak of war reached North America in the early summer of 1702, Acadia was in reasonable shape. Brouillan, an experienced military administrator who had come to Canada at the age of thirty-six, as captain of a company of marines, had just taken up his post as commander in Acadia. Born into a Protestant family, he had become a Catholic in Quebec, and, from 1689 until his arrival in Acadia, he had served as governor of Plaisance. During these years, he showed himself courageous – a family trait, seven of his brothers having died in battle – an efficient administrator, and a good tactician. However, his irritability and short temper embittered relationships with most of those who met him. Brouillan played a leading role in the attack on St John's in 1696, during which he quarrelled with d'Iberville. Whatever the final appointment of honours may be for the success of that campaign, it is clear that Brouillan was an effective military leader.[20] Thus, when he arrived in Acadia, he had a good reputation both as a civil administrator and as a military commander. Over the next five years, he would need all his talents. As had been the custom since 1671, his instructions from the minister of the Marine required that he bring to an end the exploitation of the Acadian fisheries by New England, halt the fur trade with Boston, and protect the Acadians from raids originating there.[21]

Brouillan took ship for Port Royal out of La Rochelle in late May 1701. He had spent the last four years in France, attending to the affairs of Plaisance *in absentia*. Accompanied by an additional forty soldiers for the garrison, and provisioned with munitions and general supplies, he landed, unexpectedly, at Chibouctou, the future site of Halifax, because of contrary winds. He found the harbour very fine but considered that it would cost a considerable amount to make it defensible because its mouth was so wide and easy of access.[22] Brouillan decided to profit by this forced landfall to journey overland to Port Royal via the Minas settlements, leaving the ship, commanded by Simon-Pierre Denys de Bonaventure, to make its way around the coast. The journey through the forest from Chibouctou to the shores of the Minas Basin at Pisiquid was about thirty-five miles. To the major settlement at Grand Pré, it was another fifteen miles. His decision to undertake the trek is a measure of the man: despite suffering from gout and an unhealed wound on his cheekbone, Brouillan started his term as commander with a fair amount of travelling, thereby gaining first-hand experience of Acadian geography. This journey alone gave him the inestimable advantage of knowing, when he arrived in Port Royal, that there was more to the colony than this shabby-looking settlement with a dilapidated fort and a church with a thatched roof and paper window panes.[23]

Brouillan was impressed by the prosperity of the Minas settlements, reporting in his first major letter to France that the people there had a great number of cattle and were able to export seven or eight hundred hogsheads of wheat a year.[24] He was impressed in a slightly different way by the inhabitants themselves, considering them, in an oft-quoted phrase, "a demi des republicains" – practically republicans – and "most independent in character and accustomed to decide all matters themselves."[25] Short-tempered, perhaps, but by no means stupid, he set about asserting his authority with considerable intelligence and tact, suggesting to the settlers that a road be built between Minas and Port Royal and that its construction be a joint project, with the people of Minas beginning work from their side after the harvest was in. Villebon might have thought that a road already existed, but Brouillan considered that this rough track, covering some sixty-five miles and interrupted by a number of portages, was hardly adequate.

Brouillan then left for Port Royal, again choosing an inland route and arriving there on 20 June 1701. His reception by the inhabitants of Port Royal was ambivalent. He was, after all, the first French official since 1690 to establish his headquarters there. From his own account, it seems that the settlers thought his arrival was a prelude to new burdens and the possible return of a trading company. He was informed that the inhabitants would rather live under English control than accept such an imposition, and that they would do nothing to help improve the defences of the town if a French trading company were to be the beneficiaries of their work.[26] Brouillan managed to persuade the inhabitants that he was the representative of the king, not the agent of a company, and they agreed to start cutting and trimming wood for new palisades. Having reached this understanding, Brouillan set off for the Saint John River to view the fortification that Villebon, in 1699, had begun building at the mouth of that river. The new commander was appalled at what he found, considering that, while the fort was in good condition, it was too small and really of little use since, on one side, it was vulnerable to a battery situated on a nearby island, and, on the other, was overlooked from a cliff. Furthermore, since the Saint John River was still tidal at this point, its water was salt well beyond the site of the fort.[27] Brouillan had the forty or so officers and men that made up the garrison transported to Port Royal. He then organized the dismantling of the fort and surrounding buildings and shipped the timbers there. At one stroke, he had considerably strengthened the French military presence in Port Royal and provided some of the materials necessary to rebuild that fort.

On his return to Port Royal, Brouillan began the work needed to bring its fort into a state of repair. He obviously had some acquaintance with the ideas of his contemporary, Sébastien Le Prestre de Vauban, the chief engineer to Louis XIV and generally considered to be the "greatest of fortress builders."[28] In lengthy reports to the minister, Brouillan emphasized that he had used the natural advantages of the site by trenching the surrounding marshy ground and building up the banks, so that the actual fort itself was thirty-five feet above the rivers at its foot.[29] But he did not believe that this work was enough for the defence of Port Royal: he pleaded that the fort be rebuilt in masonry and outlined what this would cost, a matter of 66,635 *livres*, in terms of labour and materials. He was also unhappy with the manpower he had at his command. In October 1701 he had under one hundred men, organized into two companies, and he asked for reinforcements. In this particular report, he also commented upon the militia in the colony.

This seems to be the first recorded reference, by any French official, that considers the matter of an Acadian militia, though there are scattered mentions, in Villebon's correspondence, of men appointed as captains of the militia. In 1693 Villenon appointed Pierre Melanson of Minas as "captain of the coast."[30] Three years later, in 1696, Pierre's brother Charles, who had remained at Port Royal, asked for, and obtained, a similar appointment as captain of the militia in Port Royal from Governor Stoughton of Massachusetts.[31] We have no evidence at all, from Acadian sources, as to what these appointments really implied. Throughout King William's War, the main support that the Acadians had provided, both to Villebon and to Boston, had been supplies not soldiers. While some young Acadians joined French corsairs, there seems to have been no significant Acadian manpower involved in actual fighting during these years.[32] In Brouillan's view, whatever the militia represented, it was unlikely to be much help. He considered that there were six companies in the colony, numbering 328 men in all, but they were badly armed and lacked sufficient ammunition.[33]

The militia tradition in France itself was of recent origin, not having been established there until 1688.[34] Brouillan was apparently working on the assumption that Acadia had a militia organization similar to that of New France. Along the St Lawrence, the principle had been instituted, soon after the establishment of royal government in 1663 and the arrival of the Carignan-Salières regiment, that, in all settlements of a certain size, officers of the regular forces should organize and drill a militia company. These companies were to be made up of all men aged between sixteen and sixty, each one providing his own gun, powder, and shot. The comparative absence of regular troops in Acadia, as well as the periods of English rule, had meant that this practice had not taken root there. Brouillan seems to have arrived at his figures simply by estimating the number of adult males living in Port Royal, Minas, and Beaubassin. The partial census returns available for the years 1698, 1701, and 1703 provide evidence that the male population over the age of twenty-one, in these three settlement areas, amounted to about 350, out of a general population of roughly 1,500. (It should be remembered that, throughout the French period, and during a considerable number of years during the later English rule of Acadia, about half the population was usually under fifteen.)

Brouillan's initial instructions had ordered him to explore the possibilities of a better relationship with Massachusetts, possibly through a version of the Treaty of Neutrality signed two decades earlier.[35] It was not proposed that the clauses of that particular agreement be fully resurrected. What was suggested was that Massachusetts and Acadia should delay attacking one another for a year, if war broke out in Europe. Brouillan was to propose a treaty of "union and good faith" which would recognize the status quo and require that a year's warning be given before either side attacked.[36] He wrote in these terms to the Massachusetts government in August 1701.[37] Lord Bellamont, who had arrived in Boston as governor in May 1699, a year after he had received his commission, had died in March 1701 and his successor, Joseph Dudley, did not arrive in the colony until 11 June 1702.[38] The reply, made by the Massachusetts Council, was cautious, saying that it did not wish to make any binding agreement before the arrival of the new governor. Nevertheless, the Council stated that, "whilst on your side all acts of hostility shall be forborn, we shall not be forward to the Aggressors, or to enterprize anything to interrupt our mutual quiet and repose."[39] After receiving this letter, Brouillan reported to the minister that he was pessimistic about the possibilities of any special treaty with Boston but that he would endeavour to keep peace over the fisheries since he did not have sufficient force to repulse a major attack.[40] Versailles obviously approved of his actions, for on 1 February 1702 he was commissioned as governor of Acadia.[41] By this time, war had been declared by both England and France.

Thus, Brouillan's emphasis on the defence of the colony was proven eminently reasonable. While not on such a scale as Europe would experience, the fighting between England and France in North America would be bitter enough. It was slow to begin, except at sea. The news of the commencement of hostilities reached Boston on 19 June 1702 and the Council, encouraged by the new governor, immediately announced intentions of persuading the "merchants to equip some of their ships on H.M. Service, for the annoying of H.M. enemies."[42] This resolution translated into successful forays against ships off the Acadian coast as well as in the Gulf of St Lawrence and off Newfoundland. By 17 September 1702, fourteen French vessels had been captured.[43] Of these, nine had been taken off the Acadian coasts, effectively bringing to an end the French exploitation of the Acadian fisheries.[44] There was no immediate naval response by the French to this action and the Acadian-Massachusetts frontier remained relatively quiet during the winter months of 1702–03. The most important action for Acadia was taken in France where, as part of the general settlement of land disputes in the colony (discussed in chapter 7), it was decreed that, in legal matters there was to be a "a reunion of the province of Acadia with the dominion of His Majesty."[45] This attempt to bring the Acadian legal system completely under the control of New France, to end the Acadian habit of bypassing Quebec and taking disputes directly to France, meant little for Acadian daily life over the next eight years. It did mean, however, that Acadian officials were able to plead, in the strongest terms, for help from Quebec as the war continued.

In the meantime, 1703 was a year of relatively calm for Acadia. There was some desultory action by French corsairs, in particular by a man named Juin, who had come from Bordeaux to ply this trade. He captured three ships that summer and two were brought as prizes to Port Royal. The crew of the third, however, retook the ship and killed him.[46] Brouillan's reports of this time show him, first, as planning to carry further the war against Massachusetts and to maintain good relations with the Mi'kmaq. His second preoccupation was with the daily life of Port Royal, where he had undertaken the building of a new church. The charges and counter-charges that were rife among the chief men of that settlement also involved him, both as someone trying to make the small society united in face of external pressures and also because he was personally entangled in the bickering. Finally, Brouillan was concerned with the rest of the colony, particularly with the situation in the Pentagöuet area and the loyalty of Minas to the French cause. The governor sent plans for an attack on Boston to the minister in the autumn of 1702 but he was given no support to implement them.[47] As had been the case during the time of Villebon, gifts to the Mi'kmaq and the Malecite had a greater priority among supplies shipped than did provisions for the garrison.[48] Brouillan reported that the distribution of gifts to the former had been well received.[49] He paid considerable attention, too, to work on the fort and hoped to have it completed by 1704, despite difficulties with Labat, the engineer sent out to oversee its rebuilding.[50]

In terms of the settlement itself, consensus about the building of a new church in Port Royal was the sole issue of community agreement that

Brouillan reported in 1703. The inhabitants contributed willingly to the project and Louis XIV sent a grant in aid for the work. However, the daily round of life in Port Royal gave rise to enough backbiting and scandal to make the place anything but harmonious for the leaders of its small society. First and foremost, of course, Villieu, de Goutin, and Brouillan were at loggerheads, and all wrote bitterly, and lengthily, to France to complain about the other.[51] Brouillan requested, and was refused, permission to replace de Goutin. Most of the complaints about de Goutin were about nepotism, suspected rather than proven. Those concerning Brouillan involved charges of corruption and cruelty. The governor was charged with employing workmen from the fort on his own business, of having seized cleared land without compensation to its original settler, of trading on his own account (whether with the settlers, Boston, or the Mi'kmaq is unclear), and of melting silver sent out to the colony for paying the soldiers into plate for his own use. More seriously, he was accused in the fall of 1703 of having tortured soldiers, charged with theft, by placing lighted matches between their fingers.[52] The evidence was clear enough to persuade Louis XIV to sentence Brouillan to allot half his pay to one of the soldiers. This man had travelled to France to show his mutilated hands.[53]

At the same time as these charges were laid, both Brouillan and his protégé and second-in command, Denys de Bonaventure, managed to entangle themselves in love affairs. Port Royal in 1703 was home to two strong-minded, attractive women, one temporarily separated from her husband, the other a widow. Madame Barrat, who captured the governor's eye, was the wife of Claude Barrat, who had been clerk of the court and notary in Plaisance during Brouillan's time as governor there. Barrat became involved in the fisheries but lost money and turned to embezzlement. As a result, he lost his court appointment. At about this time, Brouillan was appointed to Acadia and Madame Barrat left Plaisance with her young son for Port Royal, where she kept a tavern and lived in the governor's house.[54] Madame Damours de Freneuse was the widow of Mathieu Damours de Freneuse, who had settled on the Saint John River near Nashwaak in 1686. In 1696 he died, leaving her with five children. In 1702 she moved to Port Royal where she soon formed a close friendship with Denys de Bonaventure, in whose house she and her two younger children stayed. Her three oldest children were young lads, between the ages of ten and fifteen. They were taken into the garrison. In November 1703 she bore Bonaventure a son, Antoine, whose baptism is recorded in the Port Royal registers.[55] All parties were roundly condemned by the bishop of Quebec, who requested that the women be removed from the colony.[56] These scandals did not help Brouillan to maintain order and discipline among the soldiery and divided the settlers. As well, they further diminished his influence with officials both in France and in Quebec. It is a moot point whether his lax sexual morality or his sadistic disciplinary practices was the most harmful to his career.

Another of the governor's preoccupations, the temper of the outlying settlements, was, in many ways, the most serious of his problems. Ever since 1697, New England had been attempting to reach an accommodation with the Abenaki, something that, if concluded, would make even Saint-Castin's position in the Pentagöuet area difficult to maintain. Villebon had feared that cheap goods from Boston might persuade the Abenaki to abandon their cautious alliance with the French.[57] Brouillan was sufficiently concerned that he requested that Saint-Castin, a man he neither liked nor respected, be urged to return as quickly as possible from his temporary sojourn in La Rochelle.[58] Doubts about the policies of the Abenaki were dissolved in August 1703 with the eruption of attacks on English settlements from Maine to Connecticut. These were carried out, essentially, by the Abenaki, urged on by both French civil and religious authorities. Such attacks resulted in death and destruction at a number of places. In New England in 1703, two communities were badly hit: Wells, where twenty-nine were killed or carried off, and Saco, where eleven were killed and twenty-four taken captive.[59] Some help had been provided in the organization and planning of these raids by Philippe Rigaud de Vaudreuil, who had become governor of New France in July 1703. The total manpower involved was perhaps five hundred men, of whom approximately fifty were Canadian. To what extent either Mi'kmaq or Acadian men were involved is impossible to determine, but one member of the expedition against Wells was Michel Leneuf de la Vallière et de Beaubassin, the fourth son of the former governor. The son had spent a fair amount of his life in Acadia and been attached to the garrison in Port Royal since 1701.[60] While the success of these actions might have provided Brouillan with some brief sense of security, the raids were cited in Massachusetts that autumn as a reason for mounting a concerted attack, as soon as possible, on Port Royal.[61]

Doubts about the attitude of the people of Minas were a more complex matter, although they were answered, to some extent, in 1704. It is clear from the documentation that exists, including Brouillan's report in 1701, that the settlers there were independently minded. Acadians in general, as Dièreville had pointed out, knew little of taxes. "Nobody talks to them," he wrote, "about either income or property taxes, they pay nothing at all."[62] Even the seigneurial dues at Port Royal were minimal and those of Minas were less onerous still. External authority, whether clerical or secular, was always something to be questioned and debated. The irritations of the *corvée*, labour to be given on public works when so required by those acting in the king's name, had not been demanded in recent memory. It seems clear that Brouillan's regime, from the time of his visit to Minas in 1701, aroused a deep suspicion among the Minas settlers that new obligations might be imposed. Brouillan reported in November 1703 that he had dispatched a small detachment to Minas because he had heard it rumoured that the inhabitants had declared that they would support the English, should they arrive.[63] He then noted, in the same letter, that after the visit from Sieur de la Boularderie with a small company of soldiers, Minas did, in the end, contribute a working party for the repair of the fort. In the context of French and English colonies at the opening of the eighteenth century, the unwillingness of the Minas settlers to obey, without argument, demands by officials, either military or civil, for labour and supplies is not unusual.[64] The temper of people in Minas, in the autumn of 1703, was no more disaffected towards those who claimed the right to order them about than the attitude of their contemporaries in New England and New France towards similar official requests.

But in the late winter of 1704 the lines between English and French hardened and in the summer of 1704 the settlers of Minas fought the English. The immediate cause was an attack against Deerfield, a small settlement on the northern frontier of Massachusetts, on 28 February (O.S.).[65] Its population at the time was about three hundred. The raid was carried out by a mixed force of some fifty Frenchmen, dispatched from Montreal by Vaudreuil, with perhaps two hundred Abenaki. It was a savage affair. Houses and barns were burnt, and forty-seven people were killed, including women and children. One hundred and eleven were taken into captivity, many of whom died on the journey north to Quebec. When news of the affray reached Boston, the General Court set about planning an attack to "Insult the Eastern Coast of Nova Scotia, and Port Royal."[66] To lead the expedition, Governor Joseph Dudley chose Major Benjamin Church. Now sixty-five years old, Church had spent much of his life fighting on the borders of Massachusetts and, as we have seen, in 1696 had raided Beaubassin and made an abortive attack on Villebon's fort at the mouth of the Saint John.[67] In 1704 Church managed to raise some "500 English and Indian volunteers from Plymouth, Barnstable, and Bristol counties."[68] On 15 May (O.S.) he sailed from Boston, his troops embarked in fourteen small transports and accompanied by three warships. Church carried detailed instructions from Dudley which enjoined him to search for booty in the Pentagöuet-Passamaquoddy area, then to continue to Minas and Chignecto and "use all possible methods for the burning and destroying of the enemies houses, and breaking the dams of their corn grounds in the said several places, and make what other spoils you can upon them, and bring away prisoners."[69] The prisoners were sought for exchange with those taken to New France after the winter raids on New England, including that against Deerfield.

The fact that Port Royal was not included as one of the main objectives allowed Dudley's enemies in Massachusetts to argue that the governor had some discreditable reason for sparing the fort. Cotton Mather criticized Dudley with biting sarcasm, saying that he himself was incapable of understanding the "mysteries" of the governor's plan.[70] Whatever the reasons behind the strategy, Church obeyed Dudley's commands. The transports and warships sailed together until they reached Passamaquoddy, attacking Saint-Castin's establishment at Pentagöuet on the way and capturing his daughter. This skirmish yielded the information that Michel Chartier was establishing a fort at Passamaquoddy. Chartier had been born on the Île d'Orléans but had moved to Acadia in 1694 and in 1695 been granted land on the site of present-day St Stephen.[71] Church and a small force took Chartier by surprise and the family fled into the woods. Church reported that "Madam *Sharkee* had left her Silk Clothes and fine linen behind her," which delighted the soldiers.[72] Church also attacked a Maliseet encampment nearby, killing one native and looting beaver skins and a quantity of dried fish. He and his men then set fire to what they could not carry away.

At this point, the ships divided. It is clear from the account left by Church that two of the three warships which accompanied him from Boston were Royal Navy vessels. Their orders were to go to what is now known as Digby Gut and lie in wait for ships, expected soon, carrying supplies for Port Royal.[73] Church sent the third warship, the Massachusetts vessel *Province Galley,* with them. On 2 July (N.S.) the warships were in the bay outside Port Royal.[74] Church, meanwhile, had sailed for Minas aboard the frigate *Adventure,* arriving there on 3 July (N.S.). He then launched the most serious attack that the settlement had had to endure. In all, he and his force remained about three days in the area, two nights burning and looting the settlement of Minas itself and another twenty-four hours at Pisiquid.

Matters did not go smoothly for the invading force. Those who had settled the area had done so in much the same way as had those who had settled Port Royal: a cluster of houses had been established close to the shore, along the banks of an inlet. Other dwellings had been built at intervals and at some distance from the main settlement. The configuration of the ground, however, is different from that of Port Royal. That settlement was sheltered by the narrow gut at the entrance to the bay that lies directly in front of the fort and the main cluster of its buildings. At Minas, the coast is dominated by the great cape, Blomidon, but the basin itself is broad and the settlements were developed along the shore, on the banks of a number of small streams running through the broad flat meadows to the sea. These streams fill and empty with the tides. A proclamation was sent on shore, about the middle of the day, asking the inhabitants of the village of Minas itself to surrender within the hour. But Church found his demands thwarted by the flow of the sea, which first made the narrow brooks impassable and then raised the transports high enough to be targets for the Acadians and Mi'kmaq on shore.[75] This allowed some of the Acadians to take to the woods, with "the best of their goods," before Church arrived next morning. At that point the pillaging began, followed by a skirmish in which two of Church's men were killed. That night, the town was set on fire and the next morning Church ordered his "Men to dig down their Dams, and let the Tide in to destroy all their Corn."[76] He then re-embarked his force but, during the following night, sent a number of men to ensure that the

Acadians could not immediately repair the breaches in the dykes. Next morning, however, the force left for Pisiquid, where prisoners were taken. Two men, whom Brouillan had sent from Port Royal to ask for aid from Minas, were also captured but were released. They were told to take back to Brouillan the message that this raid was but a foretaste of what would happen should hostilities such as those at Deerfield be repeated.

Church then left for Port Royal, where the naval forces had been marking time. He arrived there on 14 July (N.S.). There was an immediate council of war in which it was decided not to attack Port Royal but "quit it wholly and go on about our other business we have to do." It was considered that the combined English force was "inferiour to the strength of the enemy; and, therefore, the danger and risk we run is greater than the advantage we can, or are likely to obtain."[77] The warships began their voyage back to Boston via Passamaquoddy and Mount Desert. Church and his troops decided to raid Beaubassin before returning to Boston. When they arrived at that settlement, the Acadians were in arms and an indecisive skirmish ensued. After the Acadians retreated into the woods, Church and his men found that the inhabitants had removed as much of their household and farm goods as possible. Church set the buildings on fire and killed about one hundred cattle before leaving to return to Boston.[78] He had been away not much more than six weeks, during which he had gathered a moderate amount of booty, about which there was much wrangling,[79] and a number of Acadians as prisoners for exchange purposes. Six Massachusetts volunteers had been killed and the Acadians and Mi'kmaq had lost about the same number of men.[80] There were also wounded on both sides but the number is unknown.

What was the impact of this expedition on the Acadians? The statistics given in the report of the engineer, Labat, are those most often cited. He wrote that Church had taken forty-five prisoners from the Minas settlements, mostly women and children but including a number of young men, pillaged and burnt the church, killed one settler, and wounded another. All the homes except one had been burnt, seven of the dykes had been broken, and two hundred hogshead of wheat had been spoilt. His figures for Beaubassin were the same as those given by Church: twenty houses burnt and one hundred cattle slain.[81] Port Royal suffered minimal loss. At Minas, the loss to flocks and herds seems to have been recouped with no great difficulty. In 1701 the area of Minas and the Pisiquid settlement were reported as having 730 cattle, 706 sheep, and 410 swine; in 1707 the cattle herd numbered 766, the flock of sheep 718, and the swine 639.[82] Similarly, the growth of Beaubassin does not seem to have been seriously affected. In 1698 that settlement had 352 cattle, 178 sheep, and 160 swine; in 1707 the cattle numbered 510, the sheep 476, and the swine 334.[83] The seriousness of the material damage is more difficult to estimate. The firing of the buildings did not result in any of the settlements being burnt to the ground and, apparently, houses and barns were repaired or rebuilt reasonably quickly. The damage to the dykes, as opposed to the damage to the drained land, must have been fairly easily repaired. While breaches in their walls could be made quickly enough, the dykes themselves were huge earthworks, built upon complex foundations.[84] Their destruction, the breaking of their internal scaffolding of planks and logs, would have required considerable time and Church's men spent no more than a day at their work of destruction. The tides would have been able to inundate the lands behind the dykes through even small gaps, but it seems that the settlers were able to rebuild these barricades before the end of summer and the winter precipitation would have cleansed the land of the salt water sufficiently to make spring sowing possible in 1705. Certainly, by the harvest of 1706, the land was restored to its former productivity; de Goutin wrote in December of that year that the harvest was abundant.[85] Nevertheless, the damage inflicted meant the loss of most of the wheat harvest in Minas for 1704. This was also the case at Beaubassin, although that settlement raised cattle rather than wheat. Given that the harvest of 1703 had been severely affected by drought,[86] the loss of the 1704 wheat crop and the two hundred hogshead of stored grain at Minas meant a shortage of flour in the colony during the winter of 1704–05. Such scarcity did not mean anything approaching famine among the settlers, though the winter would have been less comfortable than usual, for both officials and settlers.

At the end of the year, Brouillan sailed for France, leaving Bonaventure in command. Intending to answer the charges against him and to plead for increased support for Acadia, he was moderately successful in both endeavours, although for his second purpose he arrived at a bad time. France was in the midst of a series of major setbacks to its forces in Europe. The disaster of Blenheim had struck in 1704 and Louis XIV, in his own words, had been forced "to recross the Rhine and abandon Bavaria."[87] Matters were no better in 1705, especially in Flanders, and that year Louis XIV instructed the general commanding that front to take particular care, pointing out to him "the smallness of the advantages if you should win, and the terrible results of losing."[88] France was not approaching defeat in 1705, but it was hard-pressed, served by incompetent generals and facing the rare military genius of Marlborough.[89] Louis XIV was now sixty-six, an advanced age for the period, and by no means sanguine about the outcome of the war. With France fighting on three fronts in Europe, events in North America, as ever, took second place. In these circumstances, after having been thoroughly rebuked for his errors as commander and administrator of Acadia, Brouillan was allowed to continue as governor and granted at least some of the supplies he requested. In August 1705 he left France for Acadia, bringing with him provisions and munitions but no additional troops.[90] He never reached Port Royal; he died at Chedabouctou on 22 September 1705, aged fifty-four.

Denys de Bonaventure continued to administer Acadia until the arrival of the new governor, Daniel d'Auger de Subercase, in October 1706. Bonaventure was liked well enough by the inhabitants and had hoped to be given the governorship, but his relationship with Madame de Freneuse and quarrels with the Recollet priests in the colony cost him the appointment. As a commander, he was solicitous of the health of his men. In a report to the minister on 30 November 1705, he wrote that he had only 185 men, nearly a third of whom were sick and too weak to perform their duties.[91] These he billeted with the settlers, an arrangement that provided them with better living conditions than those of the barracks, and he also allowed them to work for pay within the colony.[92] In the early months of his command, Bonaventure even received praise from the local clergy. This harmony did not last,[93] but, on the whole, the thirteen months following the departure of Brouillan, between January 1705 and April 1706, were a time of relative tranquillity for the colony.

One of the more interesting characteristics of the relationship between Acadia and France during these years was the way in which those who held any kind of official position within the colony often wrote directly to the minister, rather than going through local channels or communicating via the officials in New France. Such correspondence usually contained information about the state of the colony which amplified that sent by the governor. De Goutin, for one, wrote almost as often as the governors and commanders. His letters were gossipy and shrewd; that of 4 December 1705, for example, reported on the arrival of supplies, relations between Acadia and Boston, and the launching of a frigate, *La Biche*, which Brouillan had commanded to be built at Port Royal.[94] Sometimes those who wrote took other measures as well. Jean-Chrysostome Loppinot, for instance, was a notary who had held an official position at Port Royal since 1699.[95] Not content with writing about matters that concerned him, he went to France to complain, on behalf of the settlers, of the high price of supplies from La Rochelle and the attitude of the Recollet missionaries to the inhabitants.[96] Partly as a result of Loppinot's visit, in early May 1706 the minister wrote to the house in Brittany which supplied the Recollet priests for Acadia; he asked the provincial to ensure that such priests understood that they owed some respect to the secular authorities and must refrain from performing marriage ceremonies for officers, without the express permission of their commander. The negative aspect of such correspondence and visits was that they encouraged officials in France to undercut Acadian officials by offering advice and commentary on day-to-day problems to the governor and asking for further information about minor matters. As a result, the governor either had to spend time defending his judgment on local affairs or risk trivial matters becoming issues that would affect his career adversely. The experience of Bonaventure is a classic example of such consequences: gossip about his private life, relayed to the minister, meant the end of his advancement in government service.[97]

The appointment of Subercase, first as commander, later as governor, was made at the tail-end of this interlude of relative tranquillity. Like Brouillan, Subercase had a Protestant heritage but there is no record that he ever became a Catholic. Born on 12 February 1661, the son of a wealthy merchant, he came from Bearn, one of the most independently minded provinces of France, neighbour to the Basque country.[98] By the age of twenty-three, Subercase was a captain in the Régiment de Bretagne, and in 1687 he arrived in Quebec as the captain of a company of fifty soldiers. He saw service against the Iroquois and in the fall of 1690 was one of those who defended Quebec against Phips. Three years later, Subercase was appointed as garrison adjutant for the city and earned both praise and criticism for the way in which he carried out his duties. In 1696 he accompanied Frontenac, as the latter's adjutant-general, on the expedition against the Onondaga. Both governor and intendant were, by now, impressed with the quality of the man and recommended that Subercase be given greater responsibility and an increase in pay. On 1 April 1702 he was appointed governor of Plaisance, where he proved himself to be a good military administrator and managed to bring peace to a mixed population of soldiers, fishermen, privateers, and Amerindians. On 10 April 1706, at the age of forty-three, he was appointed to succeed Brouillan as governor and commander of Acadia.[99]

Arriving in late October, Subercase took some time to learn about the colony in general and Port Royal in particular before writing, in late December, two lengthy reports to the minister.[100] The first dealt with the men with whom he had to work. He wrote positively about both de Goutin and Bonaventure, commending the former for his actions in hiding money during Phips's raid and ensuring that the sum was taken back to France, and agreeing with the opinion that had been expressed in his instructions that Bonaventure's only flaw was his weakness for women.[101] The governor was unhappy with the priest Maudoux, who was, apparently, still in the colony, because he meddled in temporal affairs; however, Subercase believed that the two Recollets priests attached to the garrison were honest men who concentrated upon their duties as spiritual counsellors. Turning to questions about the garrison, the state of the soldiery, and the temper of the populace, Subercase was much more critical. The fort was disintegrating, some of the masonry crumbling. The lead shot and powder, dispatched by the intendant of La Rochelle, were of poor quality and insufficient in quantity, thus leaving the garrison no alternative but to seek supplies from Boston. Subercase considered that he needed five hundred soldiers to defend the colony properly, as well as a number of naval vessels. He also requested that a fort be built at the entry to Port Royal basin, to hamper any further assault on Port Royal. As to the soldiers themselves, he reported that they were badly clothed and badly provisioned. Like the inhabitants, they delighted in legal wrangles. Subercase described the settlers as "lazy and incapable of undertaking projects on their own initiative; they are not at all French, although well made and handsome. They like only litigation, and this colony will never be properly established if a means is not found to rid them of their quarrelsome temper and establish peace and concord."[102]

Both de Goutin and Bonaventure sent letters to the minister at much the same time as Subercase wrote his first reports. De Goutin remarked on the abundant harvest that the colony had enjoyed that fall, and mentioned that the exchange of prisoners with Massachusetts had resulted in considerable English merchandise being brought to Port Royal.[103] He also commented on the fact that the governor was making every effort to stop the circulation of paper money within the colony but that this caused hardship for the settlers. The lack of coinage in Acadia and along the St Lawrence was a constant trial in both jurisdictions. The practice of using playing cards, inscribed with a value of fifty or forty *sous*, signed by the governor or intendant and stamped with his seal, had originated with de Meulles in 1685. An order dated 8 June of that year stated that such cards were to be considered legal currency and would be redeemed in the fall, when the ships arrived with coinage from France.[104] The practice was intensely disliked by Louis XIV and his ministers, because of the ease with which the cards could be counterfeited. However, both colonies had recourse to the expedient on a number of occasions. What is particularly interesting about this comment by de Goutin is the evidence it provides, supplementing various invoices and price lists that have survived, of the importance of money within the Acadian economy. Too often the Acadians are assumed to be a people, almost exclusively, of barter. This is clearly not true: the Acadians had as much acquaintance as other European colonists of the time with cash.[105] Bonaventure's communication is largely concerned with his disappointment at not being appointed governor and other related personal matters, including a request for a seigneurial grant at La Hève.[106] He also mentioned, however, the need to repair the fort and commented on the mood of the Mi'kmaq, which he considered to be one of considerable disgruntlement. Subercase had also remarked, in his reports, that it was crucial to ensure that the supplies sent for Mi'kmaq and Abenaki be sufficient to enable them to survive in the winter months, without recourse to the English.

Tensions between English and French in North America became greater in the spring of 1706, to some extent because of Massachusetts trade with Acadia's native peoples. Such activity was commonplace, although it had been strictly forbidden not only by Governor Dudley but also through acts passed in London, particularly that of March 1705, which forbade supplying the French as well.[107] In October 1705 Vaudreuil had written angrily to Governor Dudley: "Sir, you need not wonder, neither can you blame me, about the repeated murders committed upon your people by the Indians, when your own vessels come privately and trade instruments of war with the savages. It is impossible for me to keep them in, when you whet their swords yourselves."[108] What made this issue one of particular importance in Boston in the spring of 1706 was the noticeable increase not only in Massachusetts-Acadian commerce but also in Boston trade with the Abenaki and Mi'kmaq. The activities of six Boston merchants, Ebenezer Coffin, John Borland, Roger Lawson, William Rouse, John Phillips, Jr, and Samuel Vetch, as well as Governor John Dudley himself, came under scrutiny by the Council on the suspicion that what was being conducted was a trade that "put knives into the hands of those barbarous infidels to cut the throats of our wives and children."[109] There was, wrote John Winthrop, "a horrid combustion in the town about it."[110] What then ensued was highly unusual. Governor Dudley's son, Paul, was the attorney general at this time and the investigation was carried out by the legislature on the grounds that the acts had been committed outside the jurisdiction of the Massachusetts court.[111] Verdicts were rendered by resolution and vote. The governor was exonerated, although there was an invoice in his handwriting which referred to a shipment by Rouse of a number of items for Acadia, including shingle boards and nails as well as table knives, serge, wine, and rice.[112] All others were fined: Coffin, £60; Borland £1,100; Lawson, £300; Phillips, £100; and Vetch, £200. Rouse was not only fined £1,200 but also barred from holding office in future. While six separate acts were passed to enforce these judgments, all were set aside by the queen in council, the following year, as being an usurpation of the powers of the ordinary courts of justice.[113]

Thus, during the weeks that Subercase spent learning about his new command, Boston was coping with the aftermath of the proceedings against those charged with supplying ammunition and stores of war to the French, and perhaps to their native allies as well. The guilty verdicts were delivered in late summer and the fines were imposed in December 1706.[114] There was bitter suspicion in Massachusetts that Governor Dudley had been far more deeply implicated in trading with Acadia than was publicly admitted. Samuel Vetch, who had departed for London immediately after the verdicts were pronounced, to appeal against the judgment before the Board of Trade, swore that Dudley played no part in the illegal activities.[115] As far as Vetch was concerned, the whole affair was a matter of politics rather than a criminal case, the governor's rivals seeking any way to discredit him. However, because those charged with illegal trading were not subject to the usual court procedures, the issue of the links between men such as Jonathan Belcher and Dudley's son, Paul, and the Acadian fur trade were never fully examined and became a topic of rumour and innuendo in Boston.

Fuel was added to the fire by events surrounding a voyage from Port Royal, destination Boston, made by Louis Aubert Duforillon. A ship's captain, he had been born in France at La Rochelle in 1674.[116] His father, Charles Aubert de La Chesnaye, was one of the most powerful merchants of that city, being profitably involved in the Hudson Bay fur trade. The family may have had Huguenot sympathies, since Aubert de La Chesnaye's nephew was Louis-François Aubert, the Dutch fur trader, established in Amsterdam.[117] We have little concrete information about Duforillon's career but in early January 1707 (N.S.) he was selected to transport thirty-five prisoners, whom Subercase had brought with him from Plaisance, to Boston. The voyage went badly; the prisoners escaped when the ship put into Portsmouth and the ship itself was impounded and the cargo seized.[118] The merchandise on board included barrels of beaver and mink. Dudley involved himself directly in the matter, writing to Sampson Sheafe, the official responsible for the seizure, that his actions had been "a great mistake," requesting that Duforillon be released, and instructing him further to "send all the Goods taken out of ye said Vessell forthwith to Boston."[119]

Such activity on the part of the governor of Massachusetts brought him even more criticism and he shortly set out to make it plain that, as George Rawlyk writes, "he was as anti-French as any man in Massachusetts and that he had nothing to hide at Port Royal."[120] In February 1707 Dudley wrote to Governor Fitz-John Winthrop of Connecticut about the possibility of another attack on Port Royal with "a thousand men, with two or three ships of strength."[121] The enthusiasm for this proposal within Massachusetts was less than overwhelming. There were lengthy discussions within the government as to how the troops should be recruited, how they would be paid, and in what way the hoped-for loot would be distributed. It was agreed that should not enough men offer "themselves voluntarily what are wanting be equally Impressed."[122] One contemporary, John Marshall, wrote that "people were generally dissatisfyed ... about a descent on poor Port Royal."[123] This is scarcely surprising since Dudley's motivation was clearly founded on matters of internal policy rather than on any external economic or political challenge from Port Royal to New England. While Massachusetts attempted to raise the support of the neighbouring New England colonies, this was largely unsuccessful. New Hampshire sent some sixty men and Rhode Island sent eighty,[124] but Massachusetts supplied the majority of the thousand or so soldiers and some four hundred sailors who were brought together in Boston in early May 1707.[125] Twenty-three vessels assembled to transport the men, led by the twenty-four-gun *Province Galley,* captained by Cyprian Southack, who had been involved in two previous attacks on Port Royal. As well, the fifty-gun *Deptford,* captained by Captain Charles Stukeley, accompanied the convoy.[126] The expedition was commanded by Colonel John March, a man who had seen a fair amount of service on the frontiers of Maine and was much liked by those he led. This mission, however, would prove to be one beyond his abilities.[127]

The expedition sailed from Boston in the last week of May and arrived off Port Royal on 6 June 1707 (N.S.). What then followed was the first of the two attacks against the fort that year, attacks that Brebner has described as the "most amateurish and inglorious attempts with overwhelming numbers and resources," both of which "dismally failed."[128] The first seems to have failed partly because of the incompetent leadership of March and dissension among the English officers, who were a mixture of Massachusetts militia commanders and English regulars. It also failed because of the leadership of Subercase, who was helped by the presence of sixty Canadians, under the command of Louis Denys de La Ronde, Bonaventure's brother and an experienced army officer, as well as by eighteen-year-old Bernard-Anselme d'Abbadie de Saint-Castin, who had been born and brought up in the neighbourhood of Pentagöuet, and a number of Abenaki, his mother's people.[129] La Ronde was thirty-two and had seen service in Ireland with James II as well as eight campaigns in New France between 1692 and 1707.[130] The second attack also foundered because of poor leadership and the tactical superiority of the defenders.

We have a number of contemporary accounts of what happened, including official reports by Subercase and Bonaventure sent to France within a month of the first attack,[131] Massachusetts government records,[132] and a number of diaries left by the six Harvard graduates involved in the expedition.[133] While there is no argument about the length of the engagement – eleven days – there is considerable disagreement as to the details of what occurred.[134] In the contemporary accounts, both sides overestimate the strength of the opponent: Subercase reported that he faced 3,000 men rather than the 1,600 who actually attacked.[135] March believed that there were 500 soldiers within Port Royal.[136] This was a better estimate than that of Subercase, but in fact the latter had no more than 100 regular troops, perhaps sixty to seventy Acadian men under arms, and, fortuitously, sixty Canadians under the command of La Ronde, as well as fewer than 100 Abenaki with Saint-Castin. So Subercase did indeed have somewhere between three and four hundred men under his command but they were a motley crew.[137] La Ronde and his men were present because they had been sent to take over the frigate *La Biche,* which had been built the previous year in Port Royal.[138] There is much debate about the number killed and wounded, who inflicted what damage on Port Royal, and who emerged victorious from the daily clashes.

While the English had an obvious superiority in numbers, Subercase was not, by any means, in a hopeless position. The fort had some cannon, mortars, and a small body of trained officers and soldiers.[139] It also had a commander who conducted an active defence, making intelligent use of the forces at his disposal. The attackers landed in two groups, late in the evening of 6 June. Somewhere between five and seven hundred, led by Colonel March, disembarked on the harbour side of the fort but about three miles away from it. Another two to three hundred were landed on the other side of the fort, again at some distance, under the command of Colonel Samuel Appleton. Their objective was to entrench themselves in a semi-circle before the fort and then prepare the ground for the siege artillery that was still on board ship. Subercase had summoned the militia in the area to the fort. He sent a number of these with the Abenaki, led by

Saint-Castin, to harry the enemy and slow their advances. There was some sharp skirmishing over the next two days and, by 9 June, the attackers had made their way to within a mile and a half of the fort.[140] That night Subercase had a number of houses destroyed, in order to provide a clear field of fire, but in spite of this he was unable to prevent the enemy from making an entrenchment from which they expected to be able to attack the walls of the fort.[141] Subercase therefore sent out a party of some eighty men, settlers and Abenaki, to prepare to ambush those English soldiers who had been sent out to gather wood, pillage the gardens, and capture livestock. As a result of this raid, rumours sprang up that settlers were arriving from the Minas settlements, together with Mi'kmaq reinforcements.[142] Over the next few days, there was fighting around the fort but Subercase was able to mount sufficient firepower to repulse the assailants. At this point, the attackers began to consider their attempt hopeless. Colonel John Redknap of the Royal Engineers, who commanded the ordnance for the expedition, decided that "it was morally impossible to send the artillery ... which must pass within command of the fort."[143] Another pause in the fighting followed, during which there was a council of war among the attackers. They decided, after much argument between the English regular and the Massachusetts militia officers, that "the enemy's disciplined garrison in a strong fort, was more than a match for our raw undisciplined troops."[144] Subercase had mounted exactly the right defence to cause alarm and despondency among the forces of an enemy ill-prepared to carry out an operation as difficult and challenging as a seige. On 17 June the expedition sailed, not to Boston but to Casco Bay (present-day Portland, Me.). There were extravagant claims made as to casualties inflicted by both sides, which are not borne out in the official reports. The total killed and wounded were probably some twenty or so on the side of the attackers, and many fewer among the defenders.[145]

On arrival at Casco Bay, March dispatched a delegation to Governor Dudley, asking what he should do next. The governor faced "generall discontent and dissatisfaction thro ye whole Province,"[146] as knowledge of the reverse spread. A future governor, Thomas Hutchinson, writing a generation later, believed that Dudley had been determined on the "reduction of Port royal [sic] from the beginning." As a result, "he was loth to give over the design, and sent immediate orders for the forces to remain where they were, whilst he considered of further measures."[147] The governor next sent two companies of fifty men to March and ordered him to go back and attack Port Royal again. As one participant wrote, these new recruits "did not near make up the number of our deserters, since we lay at Casco."[148] By now, the troops, including the new arrivals, numbered no more than 850, if that. Colonel March soon resigned the command to Colonel Francis Wainwright. With sullen troops and a less than strong leadership, the fleet set out once more for Port Royal on 14 August, arriving there on Sunday the 20th.

In the intervening period, Subercase had received further unexpected aid. Pierre Morpain, captain of the *Intrepide*, licensed as a corsair by the French authorities in the Caribbean, had arrived at Port Royal about a week previously. He towed behind him two prizes, one of which was laden with flour, butter, hams, and lard, which he left with Surbercase.[149] Morpain also stayed to fight. Subercase acknowledged that, without Morpain's gift of seven hundred barrels of flour, the garrison would have been in dire straits.[150] Again, the fighting lasted less than a fortnight and ended with the withdrawal of the attackers on 1 September. Once more, it was a largely a matter of the defenders launching well-organized attacks against superior but ill-disciplined forces, who had to fight through terrain that was a mixture of marsh and woodland. Having disembarked on 21 August, the troops spent the next two days building a camp. On the 23rd, a large detachment of about three hundred men set out to prepare the way for moving cannon up to the fort. This enterprise was frustrated and, in a letter describing the incident, Wainwright wrote that his force was "surrounded with enemies and judging it unsafe to proceed on any service without a company of at least one hundred men." "The forces," he went on, "are in a distressed state, some in body and some in mind; the longer they are kept here on the cold ground, the longer it will grow upon them; and I fear the further we proceed, the worse the event. God Help us."[151] Indeed, matters did then proceed from bad to worse. The major engagement took place on 31 August. The most important sector of the French forces was again that of Saint-Castin and his Abenaki. It was a confused affair, with sorties and retreats making the outcome uncertain for some time, but concluded in great confusion among the English, who, at the end of the day, re-embarked and sailed back to Boston. The expedition had "drained the inhabitants of this province [Massachusetts] of 22,000 pounds and more of their money"[152] and accomplished nothing. Again, casualties on both sides had been light.

Subercase had been victorious during this summer's fighting, but at a cost: French authorities now thought him to be in a much stronger position than he actually was. It was neither his own regular troops nor the settlers, nor the state of the fort and its provisions, nor any significant reinforcement from France that was responsible for turning back the expeditions from Massachusetts. While there is no doubt that his own military skills were crucial, Subercase could not have withstood the attacks without La Ronde and his Canadians, Saint-Castin and his Abenaki, and Pierre Morpain. Yet, as far as Pontchartrain and Louis XIV were concerned, Acadia had proved capable of defending itself without help from elsewhere, even though Subercase's dispatches clearly outlined the crucial nature of the assistance he had received.[153] The success of his defence undermined the pleas that Subercase sent to France later that year, which outlined in considerable detail the need for ordinary supplies as well as for major military reinforcements.[154] The eighteenth-century historian

P.-F.-X. Charlevoix believed that, after the summer campaigns of 1707, Acadia was more neglected than it had ever been.[155] The inhabitants of Port Royal had had a fair proportion of their houses and barns burnt, a good number of their cattle slaughtered, and their gardens and orchards pillaged.[156] De Goutin reinforced the accounts sent by Subercase. Writing to Pontchartrain in late December 1707 on the general situation in Acadia, de Goutin considered there were enough cattle and sheep to supply basic needs of food and clothing. But there were severe shortages of some goods; above all, there was no appreciable amount of salt left in the colony. This would have a serious impact on the preservation of meat and fish and thus on the food supply for the winter. Minas had harvested no flax for the past two years. A variety of textiles were needed and there was also a want of iron goods, including pots and pans for domestic needs, scythes and rakes for the farms, and hatchets and knives for trade with the Mi'kmaq.[157] This state of affairs, however, was not considered severe enough by officials in France to warrant either an increase in aid or even the shipping of regular supplies. In fact, in a dispatch sent in the summer of 1708, the minister stated bluntly that the king was unable to send Subercase the additional company of soldiers he had requested. Further, Pontchartrain emphasized, it was not possible to indemnify the inhabitants for the losses caused by war. Indeed, the minister stated, the king "would abandon the country if it continues to be so heavy a charge."[158]

The gulf between the needs of Acadia, as seen by its governor and inhabitants, and what Louis XIV and his advisers considered the colony should receive in general support is an indication as much of the severity of the problems confronting Louis XIV in Europe as of Subercase's inability to persuade the king and French officials of the realities of the Acadian situation. The fall and winter of 1707–08 had not been as militarily disastrous as the previous twelve months for France, which had seen Marlborough drive the French from the Spanish Netherlands and Prince Eugene of Savoy force them to retreat from Turin. French generals had a number of successes in Flanders and in Alsace, as well as in Franconia and Swabia. In March 1708 Louis felt able to back an abortive landing of the "Old Pretender," James Francis Edward, in Scotland, with both troops and ships, more in the hopes of causing difficulties for Queen Anne and the recently achieved union of England and Scotland than in any real expectation of placing him on the throne. But the "Sun King" remained under great pressure. He was still fighting in North America, on three fronts in Europe, and on the high seas.[159] France was weary of war, as was Louis XIV, who would be seventy on 5 September 1708. All sides sought peace, but the English, the Dutch, and the Austrians believed that they were winning and demanded more than the French and Spanish, who did not consider themselves crushingly defeated, were willing to concede. Louis XIV had to ensure that France negotiated from a position of strength in Europe and, as the serious fighting began again in the spring of 1708, his priority was the French commands in Europe, not those in North America. From this angle of perception, his policies are both intelligent and intelligible. The summer of 1708 brought the bitter defeat of French forces at Oudenarde on 11 July 1708 and the autumn saw the capture of Lille, the actual citadel falling on 9 December. For Subercase, however, the war in Europe was a war of tides, advantage now on one side, now on the other, with the French seemingly always recouping their losses, always managing to emerge, if not victorious, at least not defeated. If Louis XIV had nearly half a million men serving in his armed forces,[160] surely he could send a couple of frigates and five hundred soldiers to Acadia in order to counter the next expedition out of Massachusetts?[161]

Apparently not. From September 1707 until October 1710, when Port Royal fell decisively to English and Massachusetts forces, French supplies sent to the colony, whether military or commercial, were minimal. As far as military aid went, the frigate *Venus* arrived in April 1708, captained by La Ronde, but brought no supplies for the inhabitants nor any armaments other than those needed for the frigate itself.[162] In the fall of 1708, the *Loire* arrived with about a hundred new recruits. In a lengthy dispatch, which he sent to the minister on 20 December 1708, Subercase wrote that the majority of these were no more than boys, only six being over sixteen years old.[163] In fact, after 1707 Subercase was left to survive almost entirely on what he already had and what he was able to obtain locally: goods brought in by corsairs and the agricultural produce of the colony itself. In January 1710 he complained bitterly that he had received no supplies from France for three years.[164] This was in great part due to the terrible winter of 1709, which struck France even more severely than other parts of the continent. Voltaire called it the "cruel winter" and believed that it plunged the nation into despair,[165] while modern-day French historians have seen it as the last manifestation of "the little ice-age" which had brought that country its many agricultural crises of the seventeenth century.[166] It was this winter that was responsible for the last major famine that France knew, freezing the ground, the lakes and rivers, fruit trees and grain, and killing crops and seeds, from Normandy to Provence, Champagne to the Pyrenees. This in a country where, except in the mountainous regions, the inhabitants are used to relatively short and comparatively mild winter months, where snow, for the most part, melts within a week of its arrival. Brittany alone was left relatively untouched, protected by the moderating effect of its surrounding seas. The cold killed. Starvation and the resultant weakness of the population in the face of epidemics of smallpox and other diseases resulted in deserted hamlets and villages. Skilled labour was at a premium. At least one historian has estimated that the disaster killed more people than were lost in the war.[167] While the harvest of 1710 was good, France did not know either solid economic or demographic gains until after 1714. The rest of Europe suffered too; in England, the price of wheat in 1709 was nearly double that of the previous year.[168] But grain supplies for France were particularly difficult to obtain, while both England and the Austrian empire managed to buy flour from northern Europe.

At the same time as ships from France arrived without provisions for the Acadians, supplies shipped out of Boston to the colony virtually came to an end. This was only partly due to the prohibition that France placed on such trade. The minister had sent a dispatch to de Goutin on 6 July 1708, strictly forbidding the settlers to buy munitions or any other goods from Boston.[169] But French officials had been fulminating against Acadian-Massachusetts trade for decades; what made the difference now were highly successful corsair raids. Attacks on shipping that carried provisions to New England not only cut into any surplus available for re-export but made the whole idea of supplying goods to the Acadians much less attractive for Massachusetts merchants. Pierre Morpain was just one of a number of men who were engaged in harassing New England vessels and who regularly brought their prizes to Port Royal until its surrender in the autumn of 1710. Another was Bernard-Anselme d'Abbadie de Saint-Castin, who had turned to the sea for his fortunes when he married Marie-Charlotte, the daughter of Louis Damours de Chauffours, on 31 October of that year. Settling with his wife in the port, he combined, for the next three years, the life of a corsair with his activities among the Abenaki.[170] Pierre Maisonnat, who had been so successful as a corsair in the 1690s, returned to the fray. As Jean Daigle has pointed out, however, the goods obtained through the capture of shipping by the corsairs were not a perfect substitute for the former Acadian trade with Massachusetts. The goods gained from prizes were no replacement for regular commercial orders. Further, Acadians who had been the middlemen in Acadian-Massachusetts trade now lost a good part of their livelihood.

Subercase spent 1708 repairing the fort. The arrival of the *Venus* that year, even though it brought no supplies, did mean a form of aid. Subercase was able to order its captain, La Ronde, to take up his command as an infantry captain, which he had been awarded the previous year.[171] This did not particularly please the crew because it meant that, from April until late August, La Ronde and his men worked on strengthening the fort instead of cruising for ships to capture and acquiring a share in prize money. However, in exchange for their keep, Subercase was able to construct a proper magazine, capable of holding 60,000 pounds of gunpowder and strong enough to withstand a direct hit. He also had a building eighty feet long and thirty-three feet wide constructed, which was intended to house a chapel and lodgings for the surgeon and one or two others. His final work that summer was the completion of the barracks.[172] Once released from their unexpected labour, La Ronde and those of the crew who had not deserted, plus some men recently arrived from the West Indies, resumed activities as corsairs. They promptly captured two prizes worth more than

115,000 *livres*.[173] After this success, the *Venus* did not return to Port Royal but put in at Plaisance and thereafter worked from that port, much to the annoyance of Subercase.[174] Some of the prize money found its way to Port Royal, however, because Subercase mentioned in a subsequent dispatch that he had used part of it to provide presents for the Mi'kmaq.[175]

The governor wrote at length to Pontchartrain at the end of 1708, his tone that of an energetic, optimistic commander. It was not until January 1710 that he began to write in the voice of an exasperated and resigned subordinate. Through December 1708 and January 1709, the governor was still convinced not only of the immediate value of Acadia to France but also of its potential. In his dispatch of 20 December 1708, Subercase wrote that he considered the fisheries of the Acadian banks of more value than those of Newfoundland, reporting that some three hundred vessels from New England had fished off the Acadian shores that summer.[176] He went on to praise the fertility of the land, remarking that everything except olive trees flourished. The farms produced an abundance of grain, the forests had every type of lumber one could wish, and the coast boasted a variety of harbours. He was of the opinion that La Hève should be properly exploited and that it ought to become the chief port of the colony. Surprisingly, given the low opinion he expressed in his first reports about the settlers, Subercase wrote, at some length, on the virtues of the Acadians themselves, praising their ability as lumbermen and carpenters. He noted that those employed in rebuilding the fort had worked with enthusiasm and diligence.[177] In a further dispatch, completed on 30 January, Subercase reported that he had recruited a corsair to spend the winter at Port Royal, and he intended to use this ship to gather information about Boston.[178] Writing at much the same time, de Goutin considered that, in the fourteen months since the attacks by the English, the population had more or less recovered its losses. He warned the minister, however, that the settlers were as much at odds with one another as they had ever been and that tension between the Acadians and Massachusetts was considerable.[179] Yet, on the whole, 1708 had passed without any major crisis for the colony, despite the disappointing level of reinforcements sent from France.

These dispatches would have been reached France in the late winter of 1709, when the whole country was suffering from cold and hunger and its government struggling to negotiate a reasonable peace. To a startling extent, criticism of the king now circulated at court, including a parody of the Lord's Prayer: "Our father who art at Versailles, whose name is no longer hallowed, whose kingdom is no longer large, give us our daily bread which is lacking everywhere! Pardon our enemies who defeat us and not our generals who allow it to happen ..."[180] The attention of Louis XIV and his advisers was concentrated on the negotiation of peace and European power politics; the interests of those beyond the continental boundaries of the realm were not so much overlooked or forgotten as relegated to the edges of the French government's consciousness. With the country virtually broke – the state of its finances had brought Michel Chamillart, then finance minister, to resign in 1707 and matters had since grown worse – Louis XIV sought peace at almost any price. His foreign minister, the Comte de Torcy, wrote in his memoirs in early 1709 that "the King ... had taken the ultimate resolution. Sensibly affected by the distress of his people, he thought that he could not purchase peace for them too dearly."[181]

But France, it should be remembered, faced the demands not only of the United Kingdom of England and Scotland but also those of the Austrians, the German allies, the Savoyards, and the Portuguese, not to mention the Dutch. Torcy himself led his country's delegation to the peace talks. He was presented with the demand that Louis abandon the claims of his grandson to the throne of Spain and all the Spanish possessions in the Americas, expel the Stuart pretender to the British throne, demolish the port of Dunkirk, and relinquish Strasbourg and Newfoundland. Further, compliance with these terms would purchase no more than a truce of two months, during which the final peace treaties would be negotiated, treaties that would obviously mean even more French concessions. Should his grandson not renounce his Spanish claims, Louis XIV was to pledge himself to take arms against him.[182] More than anything else, it was this last request, that he take up arms against his grandchild, that caused Louis XIV to reject the terms and end the negotiations. He refused, it is said, "to make war on his children."[183]

At seventy-one, Louis XIV gathered his realm together and set about the seemingly impossible, the successful renewal of battle. If France was to gain more favourable terms, then a demonstration that France was not defeated, either militarily or economically, was vital. And against all odds, Louis XIV succeeded. As will be seen, the terms agreed on four years later at Utrecht saved the Spanish throne for Louis's grandson and preserved a great deal of French power and influence. This recovery was made possible by two major factors: the enlistment of the destitute, both the urban poor and the peasantry, in the army, and the work of the finance minister, Jean Desmarets de Saint-Sorlin, who produced sufficient taxes to equip and supply the troops.[184] It was also made possible not so much by French victories as by the pyrrhic success of Marlborough at Malplaquet, on 11 September 1709. This battle cost the British and Dutch forces 20,000 men, a total that represented a quarter of their forces and was twice the number of French casualties.[185]

Meanwhile, in Acadia, Subercase was managing well enough without the reinforcements he had requested. But it was management of the immediate circumstances only, with minimal preparation for a renewal of attacks from New England. From the middle of July 1709, Subercase sent dispatches to Vaudreuil and Pontchartrain that reported preparations being made in Boston and New York for an attack on Port Royal and, almost certainly, on Quebec as well.[186] At the same time, however, the governor also wrote about the success of corsair raids out of Port Royal. His dispatch of 23 July 1709 noted the capture of seven small vessels, laden with corn, flour, and bacon, among other supplies. Jean Daigle calculates that at least thirty-five vessels were captured in 1709 and brought to Port Royal.[187] In fact, the dispatch Subercase wrote on 19 October 1709 indicates that the colony was in a much better position than it had been for some years. The situation of the fort was reasonable; supplies of goods in general and food-stuffs in particular were more than adequate. Still, the amassing of forces in Boston was disquieting. It was hoped that a supply ship would arrive soon from France.[188] By January, however, the ship had not arrived. With a noticeable sense of urgency, Subercase warned that an attack would undoubtedly come that year, and he urged that troops be brought from Plaisance before April.

It would have been difficult for Subercase to overlook the preparations then under way in Boston. They were the end result of a strong lobby by Massachusetts of the British government, which had begun immediately after the defeat of the 1708 expeditions against Port Royal. The reverses of that year had left many in Massachusetts angry and bitter, both with the members of the expedition and with Governor Dudley, and there was a strong demand for a major investigation. Dudley refused to act on that sug-gestion, probably from fear that any such investigation would inevitably mean that he himself would be questioned.[189] Instead, he began an imme-diate campaign to persuade the authorities in London to undertake the conquest of Acadia. In October 1707 he wrote to the Lords of Trade, ask-ing for two thousand English regulars supported by five or six frigates to be sent to Massachusetts for the task.[190] At much the same time that Pontchartrain was writing to warn Subercase that France would not rein-force Acadia, the proposal for a "Glorious enterprise," aimed at the con-quest not only of Acadia but also of Canada, was being favourably received in London.[191] The origin and consequences of these developments are the subject of the next chapter.

CHAPTER NINE

Conquest and Reaction

In a perceptive overview of the historiography of the conquest of Acadia in 1710, John Reid remarks that, "when Canadian historians write about 'The Conquest,' it is not usually the conquest of Acadia they have in mind." He goes on to say that "the phrase is routinely applied to the events of 1759–60 in the St. Lawrence valley. And the normal absence of any qualifying words – such as 'The conquest of Canada' – carries the clear implication that this is the only eighteenth century conquest worthy of the name."[1] However, as Reid points out, in 1710 the "seizure of Port Royal by British and New England forces" was considered a matter of considerable importance, both in North America and in Europe. The British decision to support Massachusetts in a "great enterprise" against the French in North America in 1709, an enterprise that was aimed at the capture both of Port Royal and of Quebec, and the way in which it was carried out, reveals a great deal about British politics and the texture of Britain's relationship with its settlement colonies in North America at the opening of the eighteenth century.

The British government's actions in 1710 are rooted in the complex history of British political life at the time. The early eighteenth century saw Britain move from being a monarchy tempered by its aristocracy to a monarchy guided by its gentry. The settlement reached between June 1688 and December 1689, between the birth of a son to James II and the presentation of a Bill of Rights to Parliament, had brought an end to three generations of civil strife and established the principle that the constitution of England rested upon the authority of "the King in Parliament," making it clear that the monarch must rule through Parliament. It is also settled much of the religious debate, with both houses of Parliament passing a resolution in January 1689, later to be given statutory form, "that it hath been found by experience to be inconsistent with the safety and welfare of this Protestant kingdom to be governed by a Popish Prince."[2] The "Glorious Revolution," however, left the details of these principles' implementation to the actual process of government. Many of the crown's prerogatives, including the right to select the men who would serve as ministers of state, the creation of peers of the realm, and summoning and proroguing Parliament, had been left intact. The limits of religious toleration excluded, in general, Catholics and dissenters from overt political power, although they were not barred from membership in the polity in the same way as Huguenots had been in France after the revocation of the Edict of Nantes in 1685.

Thus, what dominated England in the years after 1689 was complex and, often enough, bitterly acrimonious political debates as the adherents of two profoundly differing views of the rights of monarchs and the duties of kings continued to clash. These debates were the inevitable background to all government decisions, domestic, foreign, and colonial, and had their echoes across the Atlantic in the British colonies in North America. On the one hand, there were those who argued for an explicit limitation to the rights of sovereigns; on the other were those who considered the monarchy the essential foundation of the political life of the country. As David Jarrett has written, the first, often labelled Whigs, "saw the presence of kings as potential tyranny, but [the second, generally known as] Tories was sure that the absence of kings was potential anarchy."[3] The power of the crown, how it would be exercised, how it would be contained, was the essence of British politics throughout the eighteenth century. Whigs and Tories were, as the eighteenth century opened, no more than loose alliances between men who frequently differed on every question save one: Where did the final arbiter of political authority rest? As the decades passed, however, more and more politicians came to accept the necessity of such alliances, and of more structured coalitions, in order to form ministries that could secure a majority in the House of Commons. The great aristocratic families of England fought among themselves to gain the favour of the monarch and the right to play a major role in the formation and execution of government decisions. Thus, during the decades immediately after 1689, government action tended to be pragmatic rather than theoretical. Decisions were most often the result of the immediate concerns of those who had the monarch's favour at that moment. As D.C. Coleman observes, legislation came about through a "bargaining process, as, so to speak, a series of games involving Crown, Parliament and sets of interest groups."[4] Over time, government action did show some consistency, if only because those who held power, whether Whig or Tory, had similar backgrounds. Great landowners were almost as likely to be Whig as Tory and those involved in the chartered companies and in finance were nearly as equally divided.[5]

This fundamental change in the institutions and processes of Britain's political life had a number of consequences for its colonies in North America. First and foremost, of course, the turmoil in England was echoed in the colonies. The debate about the extent to which colonial upheavals were the consequence of events across the Atlantic, or were sparked by purely local events, is not the issue I wish to address here.[6] What I wish to stress is, first, that there was considerable unrest in the colonies at the time that demanded a response from London, and, secondly, that transatlantic communication between London and the colonies was good enough for both sides to have a fair knowledge of the situation across the ocean. As W.F. Craven notes, "by the end of 1690, uprisings had occurred in no less than five of the North American colonies since the accessions of William and Mary," even if "only in the cases of Massachusetts, New York and Maryland can it be said that the explosions were unmistakably triggered by the news of developments in England."[7] Craven further points out that the Carolinas were waiting decisions from London on the fate of their governments while five additional colonies also had governments resting on "an uncertain and irregular basis." As a result, the 1690s were bound to see some action taken by the crown and, after 1689, in colonial as in domestic matters, the crown sought, successfully, to enhance the power of its permanent officials and to extend the areas in which it could exercise its prerogatives.[8]

From the time of the Tudors, England's political organization of colonial activity was grounded in the belief that colonial governments drew their authority from the crown and that the authority of a colony's political and legal system depended upon that relationship.[9] Assertion of these rights had produced various advisory committees to the crown during the seventeenth century. In 1696 the Board of Trade was established to advise the Privy Council on appointments of colonial personnel, to ensure that colonial legislation was compatible with the interests of the crown, and, in particular, to make certain that the Navigation Acts were respected.[10] These laws represented another important conviction behind much of England's imperial activities at this time: the belief that the commerce of any colony should be carried out for the benefit of the parent state. Laws to control colonial trade, which basically restricted the shipment of goods to and from the colonies to British or colonial ships, excepting the transport of goods directly from the European country of origin, had first been passed in 1651. Further regulations and legislation were enacted between 1660 and 1673 and in the latter year the English customs service was extended to North America to oversee their enforcement.[11] At the time of the establishment of the Board of Trade, a further Navigation Act was passed which sanctioned the use of Admiralty courts in the colonies.

By the end of the seventeenth century, the various English colonies in North America had developed at an extraordinary pace, demographically, politically, and socially, and, inevitably, their relationship with London authorities had become increasingly complex. The demographic growth of the colonies as a whole, from zero to a quarter of a million within three generations, with migration accounting for less than half,[12] was enough to ensure that the relationship changed radically. The colonies had become settlements for development as well as places for risk and adventure. They had developed into places of self-sustaining agriculture and in need of trade, in terms of venture capital as much as in terms of commerce. Meanwhile, English migration to North America was a continuous process throughout the colonial period and a process that meant the expansion of communication between the colonial and imperial societies. By the time of the Glorious Revolution, crossing the Atlantic had become relatively routine, both for government packets and for trade vessels. Routes included not only the direct London or Bristol voyage to Boston or New York but also sailings via the West Indies. In any case, slow communication has never meant no communication at all and knowledge as well as trade continuously travelled the ocean.[13] On average, news of events in London reached Boston within ten weeks.[14] In many ways, Massachusetts was no farther from London, in travel time, than the distant villages and hamlets of Wales and Scotland. Finally, colonial trade came to involve a considerable number of people in the financial and industrial world, as well as the labourers to provide the actual goods.[15]

In these circumstances, it is not surprising that colonial elites understood clearly enough the rules of patronage politics that developed in England after 1689.[16] Essentially, it was through patronage that Parliament was managed and, if nothing else had been achieved, the Glorious Revolution had made the managment of Parliament crucial. The House of Commons, composed of some 489 members, elected by no more than 300,000 men, was becoming the focus of political power at the end of the seventeenth century, and members of the House of Lords, approximately 220 peers, were of major importance in determining policies.[17] But the power of the crown remained considerable and the court at Whitehall was the centre of politics. As Ian Steele has written, "monarchy was at the legal core of the empire."[18] And so "ministers and courtiers lived, intrigued, competed and actually carried on administrative duties in a court environment," since "the first essential was to guide and influence kings and queens."[19]

The levers of power were to be found, at this time, in the personal relationships among a small group of people, those who were politically engaged. Intelligent lobbying was of crucial importance in achieving any political action. In fact, the leading men in the colonies had never been unaware of the need to lobby for their views in London. Almost from the outset, well-connected individuals had been sent to London from the various colonies on particular missions. The establishment of agents in London to look after the particular affairs of a colony developed apace after 1689, and after 1696 "the Board of Trade found colonial agents so important as sources of information and also as faciltators within the government that they actively and successfully urged that authorized agents be appointed from all the colonies to be available for consultation regularly."[20] As well as this intricate web of unofficial and semi-official communication across the Atlantic, there were also, of course, the official channels of correspondence between colonial governors and the Lords of Trade and, later, the Board of Trade. By 1702, the governors of most colonies had received explicit instructions to correspond regularly with the appropriate secretary of state and with the Board of Trade, and, as a result, "governors wrote Whitehall on the average about once every three and a half months and received an average of a letter a year in return."[21] Such patterns of communication meant that the interests of all the colonies were a matter of consequence not only for the Board of Trade but also, on occasion, for the government as a whole.

Nevertheless, the importance of the North American colonies, even Massachusetts, whose governor sent letters every two months to London and received a letter in return twice a year,[22] always ranked lower than European considerations. Imperial expansion was not the most urgent question for British government during the War of the Spanish Succession, and it has been suggested that "imperial policy" at this time "consisted of pragmatic responses to immediate problems and opportunities."[23] However, lack of emphasis upon colonial matters did not mean complete ignorance of colonial concerns. When, in the autumn of 1707, Governor Dudley wrote to the Board of Trade to request "2000 British regulars supported by five or six frigates" to drive the French from North America,[24] he was writing to officials and politicians who had an idea both of his circumstances and of those of Massachusetts. While some of Dudley's most important connections in London were out of office at this time, those who were in government were reasonably acquainted with the situation of the Massachusetts Commonwealth and were willing to listen to the argument for action.[25] Dudley had learnt from his defeat in the summer of that year, when "a ramshackle fort with crumbling walls, defended by only a few hundred men, most of whom were inexperienced soldiers," had avoided capture "by an invading force of almost 1,500 men."[26] He remained convinced that the subjection of Port Royal was necessary for the future not only of Massachusetts but of Britain's other North American colonies as well. His plans were considerably helped by Samuel Vetch, who was in London at this time, having left Massachusetts the previous year, 1706, to appeal the verdict of the Council against him on the matter of "unlawful trading with the Enemy."

Vetch had had a varied career before he became involved in Acadian affairs. His background was one of education and some social standing but of little financial stability. He had been born in 1667, the second of a family of eight children. His father, William Veitch, who always spelt his name with an "i," was a leading member of the Scottish covenanting clergy, people strongly opposed to any form of religious worship that seemed to be linked with Catholic traditions of ritual and episcopal control. Both he and his wife, Marion Fairly, belonged to established families of some social consequence. At the time of his son's birth, William Veitch had a price on his head. He had taken part in the uprising against Charles II at Pentland Hills in 1666. Throughout Samuel's childhood and early adolescence, the family would be almost continually on the run, moving to escape not only the persecution of the authorities but also the hostility of the general populace. William Veitch followed the only profession he knew and preached in the various small villages on the western border between England and Scotland until, in 1683, he prudently fled to Holland. His wife and children remained in England but, within the year, the two eldest sons joined their father abroad. Samuel Vetch was now sixteen, and he and his brother spent their days in study before joining the forces of William of Orange, sailing on the "Protestant breeze" to Torbay in November 1688.[27]

For the next nine years, until the Treaty of Ryswick in 1697, Samuel Vetch was a soldier, fighting mainly on the continent. By the time peace was negotiated, he was twenty-nine years old and had risen to the rank of captain in the Royal Regiment of the Dragoons of Scotland, soon to be known as the Scots Greys. He went back to Scotland where, thanks to the influence that his father had gained by his work as a minister in Edinburgh during the last decade, he was quickly accepted as a member of an expedition to found a Scottish colony in Darien (Central America). This was an ill-fated venture, ending disastrously. Three great ships, the *Caledonia,* the *Unicorn,* and the *St. Andrew,* sailed from the Firth of Forth Vetch in the summer of 1698. No more than a year later, two of the three arrived in New York, the third, the *St. Andrew,* in Jamaica. Their passengers, numbering less than half of those who had left Scotland, were more dead than alive. Dissension among its leaders, insufficient supplies, and poor communications with those who backed the enterprise in Scotland were among the major factors that contributed to the expedition's failure.[28]

Vetch was on board the *Caledonia* and it was in New York that he began his North American career. The way in which he established himself there owed much to his successful courtship of Margaret Livingston, the daughter of an important Scottish merchant in that city, Robert Livingston. The Veitch and Livingston families were distantly related. Samuel Vetch was married on 20 December 1700, and his wife's family provided him with connections to people of influence in New York, in particular, and New England in general. During the next six years, Vetch established a lucrative trade with New France. This was ended in 1706 with his conviction on charges of illegally trading with the enemy, but, as has been related previously, this conviction was soon overturned. His victory was important, not only at a personal level but also in terms of his role as a spokesman for Massachusetts interests and his ability to influence the British government to back yet one more expedition against French power in North America, particularly in Acadia.

On his arrival in London, Vetch found people ready to listen to his ideas about North American matters. In his detailed argument for an expedition aimed at conquering Acadia as well as Canada, Vetch emphasized two points: the obvious richness of Canada and the threat its control in French hands represented to the English colonies. He underlined the second point by presenting in detail the current losses suffered by the colonies through the action of French privateers and arguing that the disruption of trade was a matter not only for the American colonies but also for the West Indies. In particular, he pointed out that Port Royal was as much a nest of privateers as was Dunkirk, then a notorious port for ships preying on Anglo-Dutch vessels.[29] Vetch attached a plan for carrying out his ideas and concluded by saying that "he was certain only lack of information had prevented the government from seeing the necessity of such an expedition before this time."[30]

The members of the Board of Trade were impressed. They considered it a proposal that could be "of great benefit to this Kingdom in relation to trade and to the security of the Plantations."[31] Over the next months, the proposal received serious consideration and support both from Massachusetts and from New Hampshire, and on 29 November 1708 the board gave its approval to the enterprise.[32] Vetch had gained his success partly because of his own qualities. He had an organized and imaginative mind and was able to present his ideas clearly; he had a good reputation as an experienced soldier and someone who was familiar with North American colonial matters; and he was an excellent politician and used his connections in London well. It helped that his heritage was Lowland Scot and his ideas offered the possibility of another Scottish colony. Further, the recent union of England and Scotland had sharpened Scottish interest in overseas expansion, while, at the same time, making powerful representatives of Scottish interests in London well disposed to the idea of resurrecting Nova Scotia. Of help, too, was the international situation: Britain might not have been as tired of war as France but there was strong support for bringing it to a conclusion. Success in North America might provide the possibility for effective pressure on France to negotiate once more and, at this stage, the plan envisioned the capture of Quebec and Montreal as well as Port Royal. Finally, Vetch was helped by the constant stream of dispatches from both Massachusetts and New York over the past two years, on the lines of the petition of the Massachusetts General Court, which asked for "Royal Armes to reduce that Country and take it by force out of of the French hands."[33] In February 1709 Vetch was commissioned as a colonel, provided with the requisite order, and ordered to return to North America to oversee the preparations for the enterprise.

Colonel Francis Nicholson, who was also to have a major impact on Acadian life immediately after the conquest, accompanied Vetch, enlisting in the expeditionary force as a volunteer. He was to prove both a major support for the expedition and a bane for Vetch. While the idea for the expedition, the work for its acceptance in London, and much of the detailed planning were all done by the latter, Nicholson managed to outmanoeuvre him when it came time for the rewards of promotion that followed. Nicholson was fifty-four in 1709 and had had a long career as a colonial administrator. He was senior to Vetch, not only in age but in the army lists and in effective government service. As well, he had a powerful patron, the Duke of Bolton, who, it was rumoured, was his father.[34] Vetch could count only on much more generalized support, and little personal patronage. Nicholson had begun his army career in 1677/78, as Vetch had done, in Holland and then went on to join the Earl of Plymouth's regiment in 1680 and to serve in Tangiers. Six years later, at the age of thirty-one, he sailed for North America, as assistant to Edmund Andros, when the latter was appointed the governor-in chief of the short-lived Dominion of New England. In 1687 Andros sent Nicholson to Port Royal to negotiate the restoration of a fishing ketch. He was unsuccessful in this enterprise, but he did learn something about the geography of Acadia.[35] Over the next two decades, Nicholson's career included appointment as the lieutenant governor of New York, in 1688–89, followed by the lieutenant governorship of Virginia between 1689 and 1692. He then went to Maryland as lieutenant governor and in 1694 was appointed that colony's governor. In 1698 he returned to Virginia as its governor general, a position he held until 1704.[36] His recall to London that year was an issue of much debate in Virginia, but the opposition to him was founded more on the need to satisfy the demand of patronage posts for Marlborough's colleagues than anything else.[37] The expedition planned by Vetch would provide him with a chance to overcome this setback.

In his orders Vetch was told to "communicate your instructions to Colonel Francis ... [and] ... out of our regard, to his known abilities and zeal for our service, we do require that should admit him into your private consultations."[38] This partnership between Nicolson and Vetch was of crucial importance in the conquest of Acadia but, while it began with enthusiasm on both sides, it ended in bitterness. The probabilities of such a partnership lasting were slight: Vetch was an educated man, with Protestant beliefs grounded in opposition as much to the rituals and sacraments of Roman Catholocism as to the theological traditions of that creed. While a Royalist, he had a strong belief in the supremacy of Parliament.[39] Nicholson held equally strong Protestant beliefs, but he was a staunch adherent of the established Church of England, which accepted a fair amount of Roman Catholic rituals and traditions while being firmly opposed to the hierachical claims of the bishop of Rome. In addition, as will be discussed more fully in the next chapter, Nicholson considered that government in the colonies was best carried out through royal prerogative and that any other power must be strictly limited. What united Vetch and Nicholson at first was a common attitude, based on the belief that French power in North America was dangerous to the interests of the English colonies. Within two years, this would prove insufficient to prevent the emergence of serious differences between them. But without the alliance between these two men, however tentative, however short-lived, it might have proved impossible to coordinate the colonies' military contribution with the forces that came, after a year's delay, from Britain.

Vetch and Nicholson were well received when they arrived in Boston aboard the *Dragon* on 28 April 1709. At this time, the plan was still to mount an attack, first and foremost, on Montreal, with men from Connecticut, New York, New Jersey, and Pennsylvania marching overland from Albany while British troops, supported with men from Massachusetts, New Hampshire, and Rhode Island, sailed to attack Quebec. After much discussion, Nicholson was appointed the military leader of the proposed expedition, with Vetch retaining the position of adjutant-general and senior colonel of the forces.[40] During the summer of 1709, Nicholson and Vetch were encouraged by the general support to be found for the enterprise, not only in Massachusetts but also in New York, Connecticut, and Rhode Island.[41] However, as the summer months wore on and neither ships nor troops arrived from England, morale began to waiver. On 11 October 1709 Dudley, Nicholson, and Vetch received news that "H.M. had thought fit to lay aside at this time the designed Expedition to attack Canada."[42] As to Port Royal, an attack could be mounted against that target if it was felt expedient to do so. The disappointment at this turn of the events was made the sharper because of the delay in informing the colonies that the naval squadron intended for the expedition had been diverted to Spanish waters early in June.[43]

The year's delay, accompanied, as it was, by a decision to reduce considerably the scope of the enterprise, is an indication of the limits of the influence of the North American colonies on British decisions. At the opening of the eighteenth century, European affairs were still of paramount importance for the British government, however much attention colonial matters could occasionally command, however much knowledge some members of the British government circles had about colonial needs. The cruel winter of 1709 had, as has been related in the previous chapter, pushed Louis XIV to seek for peace. The breakdown of these negotiations during the following summer meant a renewed war effort on the part of Britian and its allies. The queen and her advisers were in no doubt that the need to shore up British efforts in the Mediterranean took precedence over North American matters.[44] In the face of this, it took a considerable effort for Dudley, Vetch, and Nicholson to ensure that postponement did not mean the complete abandonment of the decision to send military aid across the Atlantic. All three men had much to lose unless the venture was, in some measure, continued. Vetch faced loss of credibility and the possibilities of advancement; Nicholson, the end of his chance at another gubernatorial appointment in North America; and Dudley, the possibility of his recall from his position as governor of Massachusetts. At the very least, Dudley wanted Port Royal captured. During the summer of 1709, a minimum of thirteen vessels, destined for Boston, had been captured by privateers.[45] As Donald Chard has pointed out, whether or not the privateers had their base at Port Royal, New Englanders assumed that this was the case, "thereby reinforcing their desire to take the settlement."[46] Dudley also faced growing discontent within the Massachusetts General Court, which had found that some £31,000 had been spent on wages and subsistence for the 973 officers and men who had been gathered together in Boston over the past months in anticipation of the imminent departure of the expedition.[47] Even before the news of Britain's decision to "lay aside" plans for an attack on Canada had reached North America, Vetch had proposed a "congress" of colonial leaders to take place that autumn.[48] As a result, a meeting was held at Rehoboth, with representatives from Massachusetts, Rhode Island, Connecticut, and New Hampshire present but without anyone from New York, on Friday, 14 October. Few of the plans that were proposed there came to fruition. But what did become clear during these discussions was that a successful attack even on the limited objective of Port Royal required British aid.

Throughout the winter and early spring of 1710, considerable pressure was brought to bear on the Board of Trade to persuade the British government to undertake, at the very least, the expedition against Acadia. This pressure came in part from the "principal inhabitants and merchants" in Boston, who wrote in late October claiming that the French privateers threatened to destroy the economic foundation of the colony.[49] At the same time, Salem fishing interests, led by Colonial John Higginson, wrote, asking for the "free liberty of fishing on those coasts, harbours, etc." and expressing their wish to exploit the "sea-coale" and "mastes" of Acadia.[50] Finally, Dudley, Vetch, and Nicholson made every argument they could think of in letters to the Board of Trade, stressing the necessity of mounting a successful attack against Port Royal.[51] Nicholson himself went to London to lobby and, as a result of all these efforts, found himself with a royal commission as "General and Commander-in-Chief of all and sundry the Forces, to be employed in the expedition design'd for the reducing of Port Royal in Nova Scotia."[52]

Nicholson arrived in Boston on 15 July 1710 and was met with an enthusiastic welcome by the General Court. It immediately sent a memorial to the queen expressing gratitude for "the obtaining sea and land forces from Great Britain for the reducing of Port Royal ... and thereby to rescue us from the insults of our ill neighbours on that side."[53] Despite this reception, however, it took until mid-September before the expedition was ready to set out. Nicholson explained in a letter to Lord Dartmouth that "the vast expence and disappointment of last year made it a business of some time [for the colonial authorities] to get their troops, transports and provisions ready, the last being very scarce and dear."[54] When the fleet sailed from Boston on 18 September 1710 (O.S.), it was made up of five ships of the regular navy, the *Falmouth* and the *Dragon,* based at New York, and the *Chester,* the *Faversham,* and the *Lowestoft,* out of Boston.[55] In addition, Massachusetts furnished the *Province Galley* and there were also some thirty auxiliary transports. On board, as well as the over four hundred marines, brought out from Great Britain, there were some 900 troops from Boston,

180 from Rhode Island, 300 from Connecticut, and 100 from New Hampshire.[56] The fleet arrived at the entrance of Passamaquoddy Bay on 21 September (O.S.). Three days later, about noon on Sunday, 24 September (O.S.; N.S., 5 Oct.), the ships arrived in the vicinity of Goat Island, within the waters of the Port Royal basin.[57]

Since the outcome of the expedition was the surrender of Port Royal, Subercase has been criticised for his reaction, especially by Charlevoix.[58] However, his defenders, among them Yvon Cazaux, have considered that Subercase might well have surrendered immediately without blame.[59] He had received no supplies from France for three years, no material for repairing the fort nor for the refreshment of his forces, either in terms of personnel or equipment, guns or ammunition. He had less than three hundred men at his disposal, and, whatever the actual number of the enemy in front him, it was vastly greater than that of his own force. Further, whereas three years earlier he had had the additional support of Saint-Castin and the Abenaki, as well as a number of Canadian soldiery, this time he was bereft of both. Nevertheless, Subercase mounted such a vigorous defence that Nicholson was unable to bring about his surrender until 2 October (O.S.; N.S., 13 Oct.). Any idea that Subercase gave up his command without a struggle is contradicted both by the report he himself wrote and by Nicholson's journal. The first letter that Subercase wrote about the attack was to the minister, to inform him that the English were in control of the harbour. At this time, immediately after the appearance of the fleet, Subercase thought that its plan was to starve the garrison into surrender, something that he considered entirely possible if help did not arrive immediately. He also commented in this letter that morale was bad, both among the garrison and among the inhabitants, because of the lack of supplies. There had already been several desertions.[60] But a lengthy siege was not Nicholson's plan, and the next day troops took up positions on both sides of the fort. Charlevoix suggests that Subercase did not send a party out to skirmish "because he could not depend on either soldiers or settlers and was convinced that not a man whom he might send forth would ever return."[61] It is the more likely that Subercase had decided to conserve his small force. At any rate, Nicholson recounted that, as the English began to march towards the fort itself, its defenders "began a hot skirmish, the French firing upon our men from the Fort with their cannon."[62] As well, he continued, his men were fired on "from their Houses, Fences and Gardens with their small Arms, in our march for about three quarters of a mile, in which our men shewed a great deal of bravery and undaunted courage, wherin none were hurt, only two Marines and a Connecticut Soldier kill'd by a great shot." Despite this defence, however, a mixed party of grenadiers and marines came within four hundred paces of the fort and set about entrenching themselves, so that mortars might be brought up.

Over the next two days, Nicholson tried to establish his men, with

"Stores of War," on shore while Subercase "shot violently ... from the Fort."[63] But the superior strength of the attackers became increasingly clear. At nights, the fort was attacked by bomb ketches, which fired "forty two shells of two hundred pounds weight."[64] By 10 October (N.S.; O.S., 30 September), the morale of both settlers and the garrison was in tatters. Subercase had already written to the minister, reporting that people from both groups urged him to recognize "the pitiable state to which everything had been reduced," which, he wrote, "was only too true and [caused] several among them to desert."[65] It took almost another three days for terms of capitulation to be negotiated, to a large extent because Nicholson demanded that Subercase adhere to every convention of the "Rules of War" for capitulation.[66] It was not until 13 October (N.S.; O.S., 2 Oct.) that the terms of surrender were agreed upon. There are a number of versions of the articles of capitulation but both sides agreed that the gallantry of the defence made by Subercase entitled the garrison to leave the fort with all the honours of war, their "Arms and Baggage, Drums beating, and Colours flying."[67] Other articles provided for the transport of the garrison to the port of La Rochelle; gave the officers the right to sell their effects if they did not wish to take them back across the Atlantic; and allowed the governor to retain six cannon and two mortars, which he promptly sold to pay the debts owed to the inhabitants of Port Royal. One of the most important articles provided "that the Inhabitants within Cannon shot of the Fort of Port Royal, shall remain upon their estates, with their Corn, Cattle and Furniture, During two years, in case they are not Desirous to go before, they taking the Oaths of Allegiance & Fidelity to Her Sacred Majesty of Great Britain."

At the same time as the formal terms of capitulation were being settled, arrangements were being made for the transfer of authority between the French and the English, for the conditions of trade with the Acadians that were to be observed, and for the transport of the defeated to France. On Friday, 16 October (N.S.; O.S., 6 Oct.), Port Royal changed hands. Two hundred marines commanded by Vetch took it over and Nicholson renamed the settlement and fort Annapolis Royal. The next day, two hundred and fifty of the volunteers from New England agreed to remain in the fort in addition to the marines.[68] Within the week, two proclamations had been issued which attempted to tighten the control over the Acadians throughout the colony by making Annapolis Royal the only place where trade was to be carried on. One was addressed to "all Her Majesty's Subjects to whom it may concern" and the other to "all the Inhabitants of the above said Territories of L'Accadie and Nova Scotia, or others whatsoever French or Indians that any way formally depended upon or were under the Jursidiction of the French Kings Governor at Port Royal."[69] It was stated in the proclamation addressed to "Her Majesty's Subjects" that "the season of the year will not allow the total reduction of this large country of Nova Scotia, nor allow the disposal of the Inhabitants herin, Until Her Majesty's

Royal Pleasure therin, be more particularly notify'd." Whatever might be said about the conquest in Boston and New York, both Nicholson and Vetch were well aware that the final disposition of the fort and its dependencies was in the hands of the imperial authorities. Posssession might be nine-tenths of the law but fortunes of war could change and nothing was certain until peace was concluded and treaties ratified. Thus, "Her Majesty's subjects" were told that "they shall receive all manner of Encouragment in coming to traffick, make Fish or any sort of Commerce or Manufactory that this Country is capable of " but the sole place for such activities was to be Annapolis Royal. At the same time, the proclamation addressed to "all the Inhabitants" repeated the prohibition on trade except via Annapolis Royal but also stressed that "Her Majesty's Subjects" were to be permitted to travel without let or hindrance. It concluded by saying that should "the said Inhabitants ... behave themselves civilly and peaceably they shall meet with all manner of good treatment Imaginable until Her Majesty's Royal pleasure shall be more particularly notifyed with regard to them and their Country." The tone of these proclamations, half peremptory, half conciliatory, was to be repeated throughout the months leading up to the Treaty of Utrecht.

Transportation to France for Subercase, his officers and men, and a certain number of civilians, including de Goutin, was quickly organized. In all, 258 people sailed from the colony on 24 October (N.S.) on board the *Frigot*, the *Four Friends*, and the *John and Anne* and arrived in Nantes at the beginning of December 1710.[70] At much the same time, Saint-Castin and John Livingston left for Quebec, with copies of the terms of capitulation and letters from both Subercase and Nicholson for Vaudreuil.[71] Livingston was as much a soldier as a merchant, and, with the rank of major, served as a Connecticut officer on the Massachusetts frontier. He had been in charge of a group of Mohawk during the recent engagement.[72] Saint-Castin had arrived at Port Royal after its surrender and his ship had been immediately captured. He himself escaped into the woods but word was brought to him that his advice and help was sought by Subercase. Saint-Castin came into Port Royal and agreed to make the trek to Quebec.[73] Nicholson departed for Boston on 24 October (O.S.), leaving Vetch and the Acadians to assess what had happened and what it meant, both for the immediate course of events and for the future.

The situation was much more complex than might at first appear. While Port Royal was now quite definitely Annapolis Royal and controlled by the English, even Vetch and Nicholson in their proclamations had recognized the extent to which the rest of the colony might not prove as easy to subdue. Admittedly, since Subercase had gambled everything on the defence of Port Royal, once he and his officers had left there were "neither governor, nor officers, nor troops, nor artillery, nor French administration"[74] in the colony. Any resistance to the conquest would have to come from the local residents, either Acadian, Mi'kmaq, or Abenaki, or from Quebec. On the other hand, Vetch's situation was not particularly enviable: the state of the fort, partly because of the shelling it had received and partly because of the neglect that it had suffered in recent years, was lamentable, supplies were short, and the temper of the general population was uncertain. The condition of the fort posed a major problem, not only in terms of its fortifications but also in terms of the living quarters it offered the major part of Vetch's force. In a report written by the chief engineer in the command, one A. Forbes, the things that needed repair are listed in detail. The barracks were found to be "in such miserable order" that it was necessary to "Employ some of the Inhabitants" both as "Carpenters Smiths and Bricklayers."[75] Even when rebuilt, the barracks proved insufficient to house all the troops and most of the chapel had to be converted into sleeping quarters, leaving not more than a third to serve as a "small Church for the Garison." Beds had to be constructed and windows and locks replaced, and all this was made the more difficult because the forge itself had to be rebuilt. Bricks without number were needed to provide for the fireplaces and chimneys, and more than fifty thousand were made over the winter. The supplies that had been brought from Boston proved totally inadequate and a number of tools, as well as "nails boards Planks Sparrs and Beams," had to be bought locally. All the major buildings within the compound needed work. Not only had the ovens and bakehouse been damaged, but the wells were clogged and the sewage system had become "very Noysom." At the same time, while the question of the living quarters was an urgent matter, as urgent was the state of the fort as a fort. Guardhouses and sentry boxes had been destroyed or had slipped from the ramparts into the ditch. The ramparts themselves were in such poor condition, said Forbes, that the men "were all winter in fear of a Surprize." Gateways, bridges over the surrounding ditches, and the pallisades were all in a parlous state, as was the magazine. Logs to shore up the earthworks were a prime necessity. The majority of the repairs could proceed only if the local populace cooperated and supplied the necessary timber, felling the trees and floating them downriver to the fort.

The extent of Acadian cooperation with the English garrison and officials before the Treaty of Utrecht has become a matter of debate among historians, partly because many of those writing on Acadian history have considered that Acadian behaviour should be judged in terms of a code of loyalty to French imperial interests.[76] Because of the obvious links of the Acadians with France – their use of French as the language of the community and their adherence to Catholicism, as well as the fact that much of their institutional life connected them to the French state for most of the seventeenth century – there has, until recently, been comparatively little analysis of Acadian political and cultural life. The idea that the political beliefs and attitudes of European colonies in North America reflected, with little change, the dominant beliefs of their particular imperial power has been effectively challenged by those writing about the experiences of Spanish and English transatlantic migrants.[77] Work is only now beginning to be published, however, on the issue of divergent political and cultural patterns in the French colonial empire.[78]

Yet the truth is that the events of their history and their political geography helped to create distinctive Acadian reactions to political developments. After all, as John Reid has remarked, "Acadia was ... an unorthodox colony. The roots of the unorthodoxy lay in the paradox by which European authorities ... wished to behave as if they controlled and could defend the territory, when in reality they did not control it and had only a limited ability to defend the spheres of influence they did enjoy."[79] Indeed, the colony bore two names, "Acadie or Nova Scotia," for almost its entire history and its most important settlement changed hands six times during the seventeenth century.[80] The Acadians lived the experience of a border people, their territory the boundary area claimed by two much stronger powers: New England and New France. Thus, their sense of political loyalty was both acute and finely attuned to the changing circumstances in which they found themselves. Their actions after 1710 can be seen as a logical consequence of their own appreciation of the immediate situation and of their own judgment of the impact on that situation of the actions of others, that appreciation and judgment being the fruit of more than three generations of life in the particular circumstances of their "unorthodox colony." Port Royal had not been captured without difficulty and the Acadians did not accept the imposition of military rule without argument either.

The foundation of Acadian political culture in 1710 was based upon the realities of the changing nature of the control exercised over their communities by the more powerful, upon a belief in their right to regulate much of their social and economic customs themselves, and upon a determination to continue to live with the French language and the Catholic religion. From this standpoint, the most sensible course of action was to wait and see what would transpire. The Acadians had never experienced a military occupation by British forces before, either as result of the colony's capture by Temple or of its later capture by Phips. But the presence of Vetch and his troops did not need to be seen by the Acadians as the end of French power in the region. War was still being waged and Vaudreuil might very well organize a counter-attack; moreover, when peace was negotiated, the colony might well be returned to France, as it had been on three previous occasions. Vetch, therefore, was faced with a population sceptical of the future of English control over the colony. At the same time, his attempt to govern the Acadians as a population under military control met with little success. As we have seen, in common with most English and French colonial populations, the Acadians were anything but completely passive recipients of government instructions. Vetch held Annapolis Royal after the conquest but there were times, particularly during the late spring and early summer of 1711, when it was a close-run thing. The first year of his administration is a tale of a garrison in need of a great many provisions and finding only minimal aid from the locals. Wood, for heating and cooking, could be bought from the Acadians at a reasonable cost but a large quantity was required for the thirty chimneys that heated the fort.[81] As will be seen, the question of grain was much more complex and resulted in outright clashes between garrison and settlers.

The major source of information that is available about the events of the year, from the point of view of the garrison, is a report that a young officer named Paul Mascarene wrote for General Nicholson in 1713, as part of the inquiry that was made into Vetch's administration at that time.[82] The importance of Mascarene in the life of the Acadians over the next four decades would be difficult to overestimate. He was born in Languedoc in late October 1685, the son of Jean Mascarene and Margaret Salevy. The Mascarenes were wealthy Huguenots and the year of Paul's birth was the year of the revocation of the Edict of Nantes, which marked a terrifying increase in Louis XIV's action against Protestants. The persecution that the Mascarene family suffered led to its break-up: Paul's father was imprisoned, had his property confiscated, and was sentenced to the galleys for life, a sentence changed to exile in 1686. Paul's mother remained in France, converted to Catholicism, and had much of her husband's possessions returned to her.[83]

Paul was brought up, to a large extent, by his Huguenot grandmother, who sent him to his father, then living in Utrecht, in April 1686. By the time Paul arrived there, some two years later, on 8 April 1688, he discovered that his father had died two days earlier. The eleven year old had travelled on his own from Lyons to Geneva and had stayed nearly a year and a half in that city with the Rapin family before he went on to Utrecht. The death of his father left Mascarene once more dependent on the Rapin family. It was with their help that, sometime before 1706, he went on to England, where two of his uncles had taken service with William III. In 1706, when he was in his early twenties, Mascarene became a naturalized British subject and, that same year, received a commission in the Regiment of French Foot, Lord Mountjoy's Regiment, which had been raised from Huguenot immigrants to England.[84] In 1709 he was detached from this regiment and dispatched with Nicholson and Vetch to Massachusetts. As a result of his actions during the siege of Port Royal, Mascarene was promoted to brevet-major. Intelligent, self-reliant, and "having," as he himself wrote, "the advantage of the French language,"[85] Mascarene would prove of immense value to British administration in Nova Scotia.

Vetch and Mascarene sailed on the same ship, the *Dragon*, from England to Massachusetts, and became friends. Both their childhoods had been affected by the intolerance of the state and both had had an adolescence among strangers. Vetch considered the younger man one of his most promising officers and used him in a number of difficult enterprises. When men from Minas arrived in Annapolis Royal in late autumn to discover the new governor's intentions, Vetch decided not to answer them but to dispatch Mascarene to Minas to explain to all the settlers in the region precisely what was required. This was because what Vetch wanted was money and he had devised what, in his mind, was a legitimate way of making the Acadians pay him. His instructions to Mascarene were detailed and explicit: he was, Vetch wrote,

in my name to acquaint them [the settlers] by the fate of war – they are become prisoners at discretion and that both their persons and Effects are absolutely at the Disposal of the Conquerors – and had I not Interposed to protect them the army would have plundered, ravaged, Carried awaye, destroyed all they now have hence. But as out of pitty – I have hitherto save [saved?] them – so that their fate is three times [better] than those under the Capitulation Who have lost most of what they had – while they have lost nothing at all. Upon all which considerations you are to acquaint them that I expect of right due to me, ever [a very?] good present to the Value at least of — of Beaver, or 6000 Livres – value in money or peltry – together with a Contribution of 20 pistols pr month – from amongst all of Minas and Chignecto, towards maintaining my Table to commence from the day the Fort was surrendered acquainting them withall that the people here that are without the "Basten" [fort and vicinity] are to pay as much as they.[86]

Vetch, of course, was restrained by the terms of capitulation and the conventions of the time: those who surrendered with "all the honours of war" were traditionally preserved from organized looting and pillage, even though the latter practices were accepted by all as the expected consequences of defeat. Phips had plundered Port Royal in 1690, Church, the Minas basin area in 1704. As M.S. Anderson writes, "every army demanded 'contributions' from the population of the areas through which it marched and in which it fought, payments in money and kin, in food, fodder, clothing etc., which were enforced by the threat of burning villages and seizing livestock."[87] What is interesting is the Acadian reaction to this demand. Mascarene arrived at Minas on 13 November 1710 on board the brigantine *Betty*, with a mixed detachment of some twenty-five marines and as many New Englander crew members.[88] He wrote that he was received with "demonstrations of joy" by about one hundred and fifty inhabitants. Mascarene felt sufficiently secure that he decided to accept the offer of lodgings for himself and his men, whom he quartered in four houses throughout the settlement. The next move that Mascarene made was one that was to have considerable consequences for the future. When he spoke to the people "concerning what I was sent to them for," Mascarene reported that "they desired of me to have the liberty to choose some particulr. numr. of men amongst them who should represent the whole by reason of most of the people living scattered far off and not being able to attend for a considerable time." He continued that he "easily consented to it and accordingly they chose Mr. Peter Melanzon and yees [sic] four formerly captains of their militia, with another man for Manis, one for Chicanecto and one for Cobequid being eight in all."[89] Mascarene issued commissions to "Peter Melanson, Alexander Bourg – Anthony Leblan – John and Peter Landry" granting them the power to gather monies "for a present to our Governour" and to collect such monies "proportionable according to Each's Capacity."[90]

Here is the moment at which the system of delegates representing the Acadian settlements to the British began, a system that would grow and develop over the next forty-five years. It would be a system that kept British officials, whether military or civil, out of most of the major Acadian settlements most of the time. It also encouraged the development of leadership within the settlements. Its roots are to be found not only in the militia organization that Brouillan had strengthened ten years previously but also in the position of syndic among the Acadians,[91] a position that had never been suppressed in Acadia as it had been along the St Lawrence. Pierre Melanson and the other delegates selected in 1710 showed themselves to be skilled negotiators, both with their neighbours and with Mascarene. The delegates managed to persuade the latter that he should reduce the sum demanded by half, since at least a third of community was in parlous straits, or, to use Mascarene's words, "actually beggars." Further, according to Mascarene, these same delegates "drew up a list of their inhabitants and taxed them and themselves proportionally in respect both of the sum they were to make up of their respective capacitys."[92] The colony may have been denuded of French officials but the Acadian communities obviously had their own leaders.

In this first confrontation of French, Catholic settler and British, Protestant officer, the attitude of the individual commander, the Huguenot and French-speaking Mascarene, counted for a great deal. In his negotiations with the Minas Acadians, Mascarene showed that he could, and would, negotiate rather than just command: not only did he cut the sum demanded in half but he accepted payment in furs and in the bills which Vetch had paid at an earlier date to Subercase.[93] Mascarene treated the settlers as possible future subjects of the imperial power he represented, not merely as a conquered people, although he made sure that they knew the possibility of "Military Execution" should they resist his requests.[94] He even paid, on his departure, for the lodging and food provided him and his men. One might argue that, since he was also imposing a levy on the settlers, this was of no consequence. Its significance, however, was that it marked him, among the Acadians, as a man of integrity. On his return to Annapolis Royal, Vetch accepted the arrangements Mascarene had made. The question of the legality of this levy came up during the hearing that Nicholson conducted into Vetch's governorship and Mascarene pleaded ignorance of the grounds on which the levy was based, remarking that "I shall not take upon me to mark or reflect on any of the acts as ill or unjust practises, since by my being entirely ignorant or unacquainted with Coll. Vetches Orders or instructions, whatever was done by him or his command may have then appeared to me as just and reasonable."[95] Mascarene's attitude about his orders may have been partly formed by his years as a soldier, but it perhaps may also have stemmed from his childhood experiences of watching the brutal pressure that Louis XIV's troops applied to those of their countrymen who refused to convert to Catholicism.

Major Forbes, the chief engineer of the garrison, was given the task of raising a similar levy from the outlying settlers around Annapolis Royal. Perhaps because he was less diplomatic than Mascarene, perhaps because he spoke French less well, Forbes seems to have had less success. Mascarene said that he had no knowledge of the amount the inhabitants of the Annapolis Royal neighbourhood actually paid.[96] What is known is that the Acadians of the area wrote a letter to Vaudreuil in early November 1710, complaining that Vetch treated them as blacks ("comme des negres").[97] The letter goes on to say that Vetch maintained that the inhabitants were "under a great obligation to him for not treating us much worse, being able, he says, to do so with justice, and without our having reason to complain of it." This letter was taken to Vaudreuil by the seigneur and fur trader René Damours de Clignancour, but he could hardly have reached Quebec much before the new year.[98]

The news of the fall of Port Royal reached French officials on both sides of the Atlantic at much the same time, Subercase arriving at Nantes in the first week of December 1710 and Saint-Castin and Livingston at Quebec about 16 December.[99] In neither place was the news received with equanimity but perhaps official opinion in France was the more appalled. Pontchartrain had written to Subercase in May 1710, in a letter whose main burden was to tell the latter that he must manage on his own, that the English would not renew attacks on Port Royal because of their previous failure to capture the fort in the past.[100] This judgment of Pontchartrain meant that he was the more shocked by the news. He wrote about his concern to François de Beauharnois de La Chaussaye, formerly intendant of New France but in 1710 the intendant of the marine at Rochefort. Pontchartrain maintained that he had always considered Acadia as the key to Canada. He continued: "Since I have learnt of the loss of Acadia, I have not ceased to ponder the means of recovering this important post before the English become more solidly entrenched." "The preservation of eastern America and the fishery," he continued, "both require this. These are goals which greatly affect me."[101] His concern, however, was of little account, since he himself could not send aid because of the continuing financial difficulties of France, as the war in Europe dragged on. Nor were Vaudreuil and Philippe Pastour de Costebelle, the governor of Plaisance, despite the minister's urging that every attempt be made by them to recapture Acadia, capable of mounting any large-scale attack against Vetch. Vaudreuil was well aware that the plans to capture Quebec, abrogated in 1709, were still alive in Massachusetts and that the defence of New France had to be his primary concern. Costebelle, who had been actively working to ferment dissension against Queen Anne in Boston, had his agent there captured in November 1710. As well, the following months saw Costebelle suffering much from naval skirmishes offshore, by ships based in St John's.[102]

Neither the news of the capture of Port Royal nor the reaction of Pontchartrain surprised the governor of Quebec. Vaudreuil had come to Canada in 1687, and, ever since he had been appointed governor general in 1703, he had been aware of the danger posed to his command by Massachusetts and New York.[103] He was also well acquainted with Pontchartrain's repeated declarations of his ambitions for the expansion of French activities in North America, declarations that were almost never accompanied by the actual dispatch of men and supplies. Vaudreuil therefore took the path of direction of, rather than participation in, Acadian affairs. He named Saint-Castin as "Commander of all Acadia" and send him back with instructions to keep the Abenaki allied with France and the Acadians loyal to the French crown.[104] It is clear, from these instructions, that Vaudreuil considered the alliances with the Abenaki and the Mi'kmaq of much greater importance than the loyalty of the Acadians. He directed Saint-Castin to ensure that supplies of all kinds should be found for the native peoples at all costs, even if this meant pillaging Acadians. Bloodshed should be avoided, if possible, but anyone attempting to trade with the Indians without a passport from the French authorities, whether Acadian or English, should be taken prisoner and sent as soon as possible to Quebec. Saint-Castin was to persuade the Indians to continue fighting the English, pointing out that they had "only invaded this continent to make slaves of them [the Indians], by denying them, if they [the English] conquered [the French], the aid [the French] brought, clothing, powder, shot and arms."[105] By the time that Saint-Castin arrived back in Acadia, in the late winter of 1711 (he had not received his commission and instructions until mid-January) to begin the harassment of Vetch, the relationship between Acadian and the garrison had become very tense. Winter had set in hard. Not only was the garrison cold but, as Mascarene wrote, it was "pincht by other wants – that of Bread being very Sensible." The garrison had "nothing but pease and Beefe and Little or no pork."[106] The first attempt to requisition food from the inhabitants resulted in a brief affray. The men sent out to the farms were captured by "three or four fellows" and had to be rescued by another Acadian, Pierre Leblanc, who came to be considered an Acadian leader by Vetch. Although a reward was offered, and Pierre Leblanc, with three others, kept in custody at the fort for some time, in order to persuade them to reveal the names of the culprits, those who had engineered the capture were never apprehended.[107] This was a minor incident but it was followed by a much more serious disputes over grain shipments from Minas.

Within a few days of the trouble encountered by the foraging party, a sloop arrived from Minas, "laden with Corn – part of which was on the

Govers. Accot from the Inhabitants – but yee greatest share for the Inhabitants of the Banlieue [outlying farms]." As Mascerene went on to explain, "the French of the Banlieue raise but very little corn and are for the most part supplyed from Manis to which Place – they send effects – to purchase."[108] Vetch attempted to seize the whole cargo but the inhabitants protested so strongly that he had to back down. However, on the next occasion, Vetch was more successful and seized the cargo of a second sloop "entirely." The situation was partially remedied with the arrival of John Alden in the first weeks of January 1711, on board his sloop out of Boston, which "brought everything to Rights."[109] But it was clear that the problems of supplies for the garrison were great and that its position was precarious. Vetch, therefore, decided to return to Boston with Alden, to seek supplies, reinforcements, and money to pay the New England volunteers who remained at Annapolis Royal. Vetch was also understandably anxious to see his wife and young child, who were in lodgings there.[110]

Before his departure, Vetch did what he could to ensure that his command would endure. The attitude of the Acadians was irritable and ambivalent but there was some evidence that the authority of the governor was, however grudgingly, accepted. Vetch had put in place, sometime in December, a justice system to, as Mascarene wrote, "ease himself of the perpetualle Complts. of the French agst. one another" in their "private Feuds and Quarrells." Vetch named four men from the garrison, including Mascarene and Forbes, as justices of the peace. With two "Frenchmen of the Inhabitants, Messrs. Chouet and St. Scene," these men met twice a week as a court to adjudicate the cases brought, both "those who complained [and those complained] agst."[111] The use of this court by the Acadians argues a certain acquiesence with English control. Further, about fifty-seven settlers at Annapolis Royal had taken a simple oath of allegiance, in conformity with the articles of capitulation, by mid-January 1711.[112] Before he left, Vetch appointed Sir Charles Hobby, a Boston merchant who owed much to the position of his family for his advancement, as commander-in-chief in his absence.[113]

But during the ten to twelve weeks that Vetch was away, affairs in the colony remained tense and uneasy. Mascarene summed up the situation: "The French, who like any new conquered people, were glad to flatter themselves with yee hopes of recovering what they had lost – saw with a great deal of Satisfaction our moat walls everyday tumbling down – our hospitals filling with sick soldiers – and almost General discouragement through all the garrison – and thought no doubt no less than to oblige us – to relinquish the Fort and to fall undr their national Governm't again."[114] Vetch had given Hobby a number of instructions, the most crucial of which was "to find some way – for repairing the Several Breaches already in our Ramparts and like to be more in number – before the end of the Spring."[115] This task was urgent: Mascarene wrote, "There was not a Curtain nor a Face of a Bastion without a Breach in it."[116] The work demanded new supplies of timber – good straight tree trunks that could be set against the walls to support them. And such wood could be obtained only with the help of the Acadians, help that was given reluctantly and after many delays. The reason most frequently offered by the inhabitants was threats made against them by "Indians," who promised the "murthering and burning of them if they offered to carry a Single tree towrds the repairing of yee Fort."[117] This was an argument that they would make on a number of occasions in the next forty years. Hobby's view of it was similar to that of the British officials who succeeded him: one of profound scepticism. He sent out a detachment of fifty men, commanded by Mascarene, "to tell the Inhabitants *'that we wont be fool'd'* any more by their false pretentions" and to give them four days to start sending wood down the river.[118] This measure resulted in the arrival of some timber at the fort, but by no means all that was required.[119] For now, the Acadian position was reinforced by reports of "Indians," which suggest that Saint-Castin was once more in the region.

Vetch returned to Annpolis Royal in late April 1711. His stay in Boston had given him almost as many problems as it solved, since the charges that he traded with the enemy were once more revived. His response to these charges was so intemperate that it hampered his attempts to procure supplies and money for Annapolis Royal.[120] Vetch was informed that the New England volunteers at the fort would be paid for the period of the actual expedition itself when they returned to claim the money. In the meantime, such volunteers were considered in the queen's service and should receive their pay from the British government. Vetch, however, managed to bring back food and clothing for the garrison, which had also received supplies from another small sloop out of Boston, something that had "rais'd again the drooping spirits of the Soldiers."[121] But, while the circumstances of Vetch and the garrison might be better in the late spring of 1711 than they had been in December 1710, the general situation of the British force was weak. Vetch wrote to Lord Dartmouth in mid-June that "the Inhabitants in generall as well French as Indians continue still in a great ferment and uneasiness." He continued: "those within the Banlieu (who are but few) that have taken the oath of allegiance to her Majesty are threatned and made unsafe by all the others who call them traitors and make them believe the french will soon recover the place and then they will be ruined the priests likewise who are numerous among them and whome I cannot catch (save one sent to Boston) threaten them with their ecclesiastical vengeance for their subjection to Hereticks."[122] Writing again the next day to the Lords of Trade, Vetch commented that the fort was "every day more and more Infested with the skulking Indians who have pillaged and Robbed several of the ffrench Inhabitants within the Banlieu because they were Employed in cutting trees and Other Necessary's for the ffortifications which none but the ffrench are Capable of Doing, not Daring to venture our men in the woods but in a considerable body."[123] The only way that the safety of the garrison could be ensured, Vetch went on, was to obtain "a party of Indians who are Equall to them in the Woods." To this end, he suggested that New York be approached to permit Major Livingston to bring, at British expense, one hundred Iroquois to Annapolis Royal.

Vetch had barely dispatched this letter when some of his worst fears were realized. The first military reaction of the French to the fall of Port Royal took place on or about 21 June (O.S.).[124] Saint-Castin had organized a raiding party, essentially composed of Abenaki, to prepare an ambush for any target of opportunity that emerged from Annapolis Royal. The force had barely arrived in the area when it was presented with precisely what its leader must have wanted. The need for timber to repair the breaches in the fortifications had once more become serious and so a party of seventy men, under the command of Captain Pidgeon and accompanied by Major Forbes, was sent out to expedite matters. Their instructions were to assure the "inhabitants that if they will bring it [timber] down conform to agreement they shall be punctually paid and all imaginable protection [provided them]."[125] However, should they balk at this, they were to be threatened "with severity." Vetch ordered Pidgeon to "let the soldiers make a show of killing their Hoggs" but not actually to kill any. They were, however, "to kill some fowls – but pay for them" before leaving.

Pidgeon never had to decide how to carry out these somewhat contradictory orders. His command was ambushed within a day's journey of the fort. He himself and at least fifteen of his men were killed outright; the rest of the company were captured and held for ransom.[126] The strength of the attackers is a matter of dispute. Vetch reported a "Body of One hundred and fifty Indians" but most other contemporary sources estimate a force of no more than fifty.[127] The extent to which Acadians were part of this ambush has been much debated, too. Mascarene was convinced that the sons of Madame Damours de Freneuse were part of the raiding party and she, at least, acted as a spy for the French.[128] But he admitted that the raiding party had hardly had time to recruit Acadians, since it had recently arrived in the area.[129] At any rate, the size of the raiding party – whatever estimate is accepted – does not argue for the participation of a large number of Acadians. That said, however, what T.C. Haliburton called the "Battle of Bloody Creek"[130] seriously weakened a garrison already made vulnerable by death and desertion during the previous six months. Vetch estimated that, after it had happened, he commanded not "above two hundred Effective men Officers Included."[131] He had recently calculated that the garrison should have four hundred and fifty men if it was to control the colony effectively.[132] Mascarene believed that there were now " two hundred and forty odd fighting men."[133]

Regardless of their level of participation in this skirmish, it certainly made the Acadian population much less friendly to the garrison. Mascarene wrote that the "French after this changed their countenance at once – and of humble and in appearance obedient – turned haughty and imperious – and threateen'd no less than to take us – by assault – and put every one of us "to the Edge of the Sword."[134] Matters looked threatening for the garrison during the next month. In his letter to Governor Dudley about the situation, in which he requested one hundred good men, Vetch wrote that he "should not wish to Survive the Loss of this place."[135] He thought that this would not happen, however, and events proved him right. In essence, the attack had been an example of French irregular warfare, an action capable of spreading alarm and despondency but needing the support of a regular contingent of the army to convert it into a permanent victory.

Much of what now happened was due to Father Antoine Gaulin, who had been born on Île d'Orléans in 1674. He had been appointed the chief missionary to the Abenaki in 1698 and, since 1702, had served as vicar general for Acadia.[136] While the Acadian population would be, at various times, one of his administrative responsibilities, his main pastoral preoccupation was the Mi'kmaq and the Abenaki. His attitude towards the Acadians was, throughout his life, consistent and clear: they were French and Catholic, and these characteristics meant that they would be loyal to French interests. With his encouragement, an immediate semi-siege of the fort itself, by a mixed force of Abenaki, Mi'kmaq, and Acadians, was begun. Again, it is difficult to be certain of the extent to which the general Acadian population, either of the Annapolis region or of Minas, was involved. In a report to the minister of the Marine that he wrote in September 1711, Gaulin emphasized the extent to which the Acadians wanted to remain connected to France.[137] But how far the Acadians actually joined in attacks on the garrison is difficult to estimate. Some clearly did and Mascarene reported attacks on small groups of men sent into the town for supplies. One such attack killed two of a party of five.[138] In his September dispatch, Gaulin reported that his forces (Mi'kmaq and Abenaki) were joined by a fair number of the inhabitants, who took turns in keeping the garrison, in Mascarene's words, "closely block'd up" and accessible only by sea. Gaulin also reported that many of the settlers withdrew out of cannon range of the fort, transporting themselves and their cattle to the head of the river. At the same time, he asserted that the Acadians had "informed the Governor that, he having contravened the articles of Capitulation they were released from their oath not take up arms."[139] Writings by Vetch, however, make it clear that while some Acadians definitely joined the French forces, a considerable number did not.[140]

It was obviously impossible for Gaulin and Saint-Castin, even if aided by the whole population of adult Acadian males, to take the fort without cannon.[141] Its defence had been as well organized as it might be, the trench in front of it dug deep enough to repel any casual attack and a state of readiness imposed on the men defending it that allowed "but half of the soldiers, and that in their Cloaths and with their arms by them ... to sleep at night."[142]

Further, the garrison had recently been reprovisioned with both food and clothing. Gaulin and Saint-Castin, therefore, asked Costebelle, at Plaisance, for aid, particularly for some form of artillery.[143] At this point, events elsewhere began to have a major effect on the situation of Annapolis Royal.[144] General Nicholson had arrived in Boston, with orders for the colonies to prepare to join in an undertaking to capture Quebec and with the news that Admiral Hovenden Walker's squadron was close on his heels with "seven crack English regiments" on board.[145] This news spread quickly through New England and New France. It cheered the garrison at Annapolis Royal as much as it depressed its attackers. Vetch was informed and requested to come to Boston to command the New England troops who were to take part in the expedition.[146] He left the garrison once more in the hands of Sir Charles Hobby and arrived in Boston around 14 July (O.S.).

News of the armament being readied in Boston, for an attack on Quebec, had spread throughout the Acadian settlements. By the middle of July (O.S.), the authorities in Boston were coping with the arrival of "six thousand British Regulars, and the sailors from over sixty ships, in addition to the thousand or more colonial troops gathering for the expedition."[147] It was far too big a project to be kept hidden, especially since, while hostilities continued, fishing vessels from New England continued to ply the waters off La Hève and Canso. As well, small trading vessels continued to voyage to Minas and Beaubassin from several New England ports.[148] Such news as the crews of these vessels carried, along with the knowledge that leaked out from garrison itself, seems to have resulted in a gradual "melting away" of the Mi'kmaq and Abenaki from Annapolis Royal. Father Gaulin now decided that he must go himself to Plaisance to urge upon Costebelle the need for support. As Walker sailed out of Boston harbour on 30 July (O.S.), on the flagship *Edgar*, at the head of sixty eight vessels carrying over six thousand troops, Gaulin was within three days of Plaisance.[149] Costebelle responded with some enthusiasm to Gaulin and decided to send guns, powder, balls of lead, and woolen blankets to be distributed to the Mi'kmaq and the Abenaki. These supplies were immediately dispatched with Morpain, the same corsair who had so aided Subercase in 1707.[150] Costebelle further intended to send Major Jacques L'Hermitte, his chief engineer, with two mortars and ammunition for the bombardment of the fort, but then news came that a relief force of two hundred men, raised in the New York, had reached Annapolis Royal.[151] Costebelle decided that he should wait upon events and within two weeks heard that Morpain had been captured at sea, his entire cargo impounded.[152] At this point, Costebelle decided that his main priority had, once more, to be Plaisance.

To a large extent, the relief of Annapolis Royal was due to the ignominious failure of the expedition against Quebec. By mid-August (O.S.), the fleet was "well within" the Gulf of St Lawrence but contrary weather soon forced the admiral to take precautionary measures. By 20 August, the fleet had finally reached the broad mouth of the St Lawrence itself. That night, disaster struck. At least seven transports were wrecked on the north shore, and 740 men, as well as 35 and 150 sailors, were drowned.[153] Despite the fact that the main force was still relatively unharmed, the decision was made to retreat. Vetch, along with General Nicholson and other New England officers, bitterly opposed the abandonment of the expedition, which culminated in a decision, taken by Walker and abetted by General John Hill, that "the British ships should return to England, while the New England transports and men-of-war should make their way to Boston."[154] Having been overruled, Vetch now tried to ensure that Annapolis Royal would be properly protected. He managed to make his case with General Hill and, at the end of the summer of 1711, returned to Annapolis Royal with two companies consisting of about two hundred men. As well, he was accompanied by George Vane, who would serve as the fort's engineer, and Thomas Caulfeild, who was to replace Sir Charles Hobby and serve as deputy governor.[155]

By mid-September 1711 (O.S.), the situation of the garrison was somewhat less precarious that it had been in May. Vetch himself went on to Boston in late October, leaving Caulfeild in charge and the fort both better manned and provisioned that it had been for a long time.[156] Vetch wanted to see his family and was hungry for Boston society, as well as being well aware that the failure of the expedition to Quebec would result in political turmoil in Massachusetts.[157] He immediately set to work to ensure that Annapolis Royal would be reasonably supplied and dispatched Captain John Rous and the *Saphire* with provisions and reinforcements to the garrison in early November.[158] Vetch was convinced that the garrison would be attacked again in the spring and he took up his earlier request for a contingent of "Indians" under the command of Major Livingston to be sent to Annapolis Royal.[159]

The situation of the Acadians was still one of doubt and uncertainty. Those of Annapolis Royal had apparently come to terms with the immediate reality of the British occupation by the beginning of September 1711. This produced a letter to them from Saint-Castin, who, saying that he had been informed that they had come to some sort of arrangement with the English, expressed his hope that this news would prove untrustworthy. He warned the Acadians that they stood in danger of attacks by Indians "who wanted no accommodation with these People."[160] Saint-Castin was quite explicit, writing that "just when you have decided that there are none [no Indians] at Port Royal, and you consider that it is quite safe for you to supply [the English] with the wood they have requested, you will find yourself captured by the Indians who will kill your cattle and take you prisoners as enemies of the King."[161] Since the letter is dated 3 September, this would mean that it would have been written on 24 August (in English reckoning), well before the knowledge of Walker's retreat from the St Lawrence could have reached the Acadian settlements and well before Vetch could have arrived with the reinforcements. The situation was much the same at Minas, although there the presence of British military was much less in evidence. A report on the Acadians in that region was sent by Father Félix Pain to the minister of the Marine on 8 September 1711. While he promised that he would keep alive their loyalty to France, he admitted that, on the whole, they were well enough treated by the English.[162] By December 1711, Caulfeild had strengthened the fortifications and was writing to the secretary of state that he was pleased with the improvements made, that the soldiers were in better health and spirits than the previous year, and that the inhabitants seemed "satisfied" enough with their circumstances.[163]

During this second year of occupation, clashes between French and English in North America were both few and limited.[164] By the end of September 1711, it was clear in Boston as much as at Quebec that negotiations for peace between England and France had reached a new understanding about the major problems which had to be resolved.[165] During the winter of 1712, death and the possibility of death shook the courts of both countries. The immediate heir to the throne, the Duke of Burgundy, as well as his wife and eldest son, died during a six-week period in February and early March 1712, leaving a frail two year old as heir and the only person between the throne of France and Philip V of Spain. Europe was faced with the possibility of a strong hereditary claim, by an adult, to the two thrones. Peace had to be negotiated as soon as possible if war was not, once more, to rage across Europe. The delegates who had opened their meetings in Utrecht on 29 January 1712 (N.S.) now began to work with determination for a settlement. Intense diplomatic action between London and Paris supplemented these efforts. By mid-summer 1712, a truce between England and France had been agreed upon. On 21 August 1712 an armistice was signed, to run in Europe from 22 August to 22 December and in America from 22 February to 22 June 1713, a lag in keeping with the transportation difficulties of the time. [166]

Throughout the period between the conquest of 1710 and the Treaty of Utrecht, relations between the British garrison and the Acadians had been anything but straightforward. Vetch himself treated the Acadians alternately as a conquered people and as prospective British subjects. As will be seen in the next chapter, he was deeply ambivalent about the possibility of their becoming loyal subjects of the British crown and equally ambivalent about the possibility of the colony surviving, let alone, flourishing, without them. During these months of negotiations, Vetch had strengthened the position of the garrison with the temporary addition of roughly one hundred Mohawk under the command of John Livingston (now a colonel). This reinforcement arrived in early April 1712.[167] Vetch himself returned to Annapolis Royal in early June 1712 and remained there until after peace was announced in the spring of 1713. Few new settlers arrived, either from New England or from Britain, and the British presence in the colony between 1710 and 1713 was centred upon a garrison that was hap-hazardly maintained. However, with Acadian-Massachusetts commercial relations now legitimate in the eyes of the colonial officials at Annapolis Royal, some of those who came to Acadia after 1710 were able to prosper. William Winniett, for example, who had served as a lieutenant in the gar-rison for some time, left the military life in 1711 and began a long and rel-atively successful career as a merchant in the town.[168] While some Massa-chusetts merchants, such as John Alden, seem to have rented warehouses and accommodation in Annapolis Royal but rarely established themselves or new representatives from Boston there,[169] others, such as Francis Capon, turned to trading directly with the Minas region for both wheat and furs.[170] This meant a change in role for some Acadians, men such as François Boudrot, who, once merchants in their own right, now became ships' captains working for others.[171]

All Acadian settlements were aware of, if not actually visited by, British troops at one time or another. And all settlements knew of the activities of Saint-Castin and the opinions of the Catholic priests in the colony, though there were far fewer of the latter in the colony than Vetch believed. The Minas Basin, as well as the Annapolis Royal area, suffered economic loss because of the occupation. Mascarene and Forbes had extracted some money and goods from the Acadians, although it is important to remem-ber that the garrison did, in general, pay for the lumber the Acadians sup-plied as well as for their labour on the fort. Vetch faced the same difficul-ty as his predecessor in obtaining specie for such transactions and issued his own bills of exchange, "payable in six months in New England bills or bills on Great Britain's Treasury," to meet the need for currency.[172] While some Acadians, mostly young men, joined the crews of privateers – Mor-pain was one of these – or went with Saint-Castin and other raiding parties in the months leading up to the Treaty of Utrecht, most waited upon events. There was no radical change in the daily round of much of Acadi-an life. Crops had to be sown and harvested, cattle attended to, dykes repaired, and wood supplied for heating and cooking. Too many men off fighting for too long would have meant near disaster for communities dependent upon themselves for their own subsistence. The colony had experienced intervals in French rule in the past and there was little in the immediate circumstances of Acadian life to suggest that this was anything but another temporary interlude.

CHAPTER TEN

Utrecht and the
Policy of Acadian Neutrality

In most works of Canadian history, Utrecht stands for one particular treaty, that between Britain and France, a copy of which was sent in circular form to all governors of Britain's North American colonies in May 1713.[1] But the peace settlement, which brought an end to the War of the Spanish Succession, was a complex arrangement that affected much more than just Anglo-French questions in North America. Utrecht produced a bundle of treaties between the various parties who had fought, among them Holland, Spain, Austria, and the Rhenish states.[2] Unless this is kept in mind, the arrangements made between England and France in North America make little sense, for these were, to a large extent, subsidiary to the settlements of disputes centred elsewhere. While the negotiations were complicated and many-sided, they were, nevertheless, dominated by the agreements reached between England and France. From the beginning, Louis XIV had advised his diplomats that "there was nothing more important than to try and detach this Crown [that of England]" from its allies.[3] The French negotiators were successful in this endeavour: Britain was indeed detached from its continental allies. The peace settlement, essentially determined by these two powers, lasted for more than thirty years. What France and Great Britain wanted was an end to the warfare, which had been going on for twenty-three years, and their terms were compatible. While Britain obviously had European concerns, especially because of Hanover's importance to the crown, British diplomats worked above all to obtain trade concessions, particularly in the New World but also in the Mediterranean, that would repay their country's outlay on the costly European campaigns masterminded by Marlborough.[4] The war had cost Britain approximately forty million pounds, "or something like 10% of the national income each year of fighting."[5] France, on the other hand, worked, equally successfully, to ensure that its own territory was only minimally reduced and that its empire in North America, including its trade, its fisheries, and its settlements, remained not only viable but capable of expansion. By the Treaty of Utrecht, France retained a considerable amount of its power in Europe at the price of a lessening, but by no means an ending, of its authority in North America.[6]

In the fall of 1711 the preliminaries to the final settlement between Britain and France had already been agreed upon, except for the matter of the French empire in North America. Even in this area, there was considerable agreement, the most serious point of contention being the British demand to retain "whatever colonial possession Great Britain might have in its possession at the time the ratification of a final peace was published in Canada," including, should the British have conquered Canada by then, that colony as well.[7] In the event, this last point proved moot: no such British conquest took place. Throughout the spring and summer of 1712, French diplomats fought hard to retain Acadia but finally had to accept the loss of this colony, while retaining control of the St Lawrence, Cape Breton Island (soon to be renamed Île Royale), and Île Saint-Jean (Prince Edward Island), as well as other islands in the Gulf of St Lawrence. France relinquished to Great Britain all claims to Hudson Bay and to Newfoundland but fought successfully to retain the right for "the subjects of France, to catch fish and to dry them on land, in that part ... of the said island of Newfoundland, which stretches from the place called Cape Bonavista ... as far as the place called Point Riche."[8] As to Acadia, the treaty stipulated that "all Nova Scotia or Acadie, comprehended within its ancient boundaries; as also the city of Port Royal now called Annapolis Royal, and all other things in these parts which depend on the said lands and islands, together with the dominion, property and possession of the said islands, lands and places, and all rights whatever by treaties, or any other way attained, which the most Christian king, the crown of France, or any the subjects thereof, have hitherto had to the said islands, lands and places, and to the inhabitants of the same, are yielded and made over to the queen of Great Britain, and to her crown for ever."[9]

The Acadians had certain rights embodied in further clauses in the treaty. They were granted the liberty "to remove themselves within a year to any other place, as they shall think fit, together with all their moveable effects." If any decided to remain, they were "to be subject to the Kingdom of Great Britain" and "to enjoy the free exercise of their religion, according to the usage of the Church of Rome, as far as the laws of Great Britain allow the same." These latter provisions were further amplified in a royal letter sent to Francis Nicholson on 23 June 1713.[10] Nicholson, who had been appointed governor of the colony the previous year,[11] was instructed to grant to those "Acadians who are willing to Continue our Subjects to retain and Enjoy their said lands and Tenements without any Lett or Molestation as fully and freely as other our Subjects do, or may possess their lands and Estates, or to sell the same if they shall rather Chuse to remove elsewhere." There were a great many elements in these provisions which would complicate the lives of all parties in the years to come. The treaty was inevitably Eurocentric. As K.G. Davies has written: "England's gains at the treaty of Utrecht are sometimes advanced to prove the emergence of America as a major concern of European diplomacy by 1713; they could just as well, perhaps better, be used to prove the opposite."[12] The treaty's North American provisions were shaped with some acknowledgment of the needs of New England and New France but the priorities of the diplomats were elsewhere. What looked like, to many a European diplomat at the time, fairly minor alterations in the agreed restructuring of Anglo-French spheres of influence in North America would later prove to have been decisive for the balance of power there. The example of Acadia is very much a case in point. From the viewpoint of Europe, the major difference that Utrecht brought for Acadia was to change its status from a not overly inhabited territory recognized as French, with disputed boundaries, into a similarly underpopulated territory, recognized as English, with disputed boundaries.

Yet, for the Acadians, the change would be much more than this. Their circumstances were indeed altered, from those of a people on the periphery of French power to those of a border people of the English empire. International agreement had made them, should they remain on the lands they had settled, the legitimate subjects of the British crown. But, because the peace treaty would lead to the French development of Cape Breton and thus to a continued, strong presence of their former political masters in the immediate neighbourhood, the Acadian situation was now much more complex than it had been previously. French power, after all, had only been lessened, not in any way eradicated. France was still a major force in North America, retaining "the control and possession of the two great rivers of North America [the St. Lawrence and the Mississippi] which in each case gave an entrance to the very heart of that continent."[13] Further, as Gustave Lanctot remarks, Canada "emerged from the war with her essential territory from the Gulf [of St. Lawrence] to the Great Lakes intact, with a reformed economy and an optimistic and confident spirit."[14]

As far as the Acadians were concerned, French power was legitimately ensconced close to their major settlements. By 1716, with the arrival on Île Royale of the French population from Plaisance, numbering about one hundred and eighty persons, together with some Acadian families who had moved to Baie Sainte-Anne (Port Dauphin), as well as officials and their dependants from France, there was a resident population there of five hundred, based mainly in the Louisbourg area and around Saint-Pierre (Port Toulouse) and Sainte-Anne.[15] This was augmented, during the spring and summer, by nearly a thousand "servants and domestics," many of whom worked in the fishing industry, as well as another thousand, who are named in the lists of the crews of the French fishing vessels which sailed off the shores of the island. All told, the population of Île Royale, during the fishing season, has been estimated at 2,619 people in 1716.[16] In many ways, the official presence of France in the region was much stronger after 1713 than it had been when France held the peninsula of

Nova Scotia. Yet, at the same time, there was no doubt that the British were now the governors of the colony, with the goal of making Nova Scotia a useful imperial outpost. Thus, Acadian reactions to the situation after Utrecht were conditioned by a clear and present rivalry between imperial powers, a rivalry than ran not only on their borders but through their settlements. Utrecht may have produced an uneasy peace, rather than outright war, between England and France for close to a generation, but it also gave the Acadians something much more complicated than a tranquil, bucolic existence.

There were several players in the lives of the Acadians between 1713 and 1755; they themselves; two empires with other colonies in North America, the English and the French; the Amerindians – Mi'kmaq, Malecite, and Abenaki; and New England and New France. The actions of all parties were greatly affected by a number of major issues that had been left unresolved by the peace settlement: Where exactly were the territorial boundaries of Acadia? Under what conditions, especially those relating to time, did the Acadians have the right to emigrate? Could they sell their farms and buildings as well as their moveable goods? There had been no agreement as to how far north or west the limits of Acadia lay. Who owned the islands around Canso was a matter of debate. With the French legitimately ensconced on Île Saint-Jean and Île Royale, and with the southern limits of New France as imprecise as the northern limits of New England, the stage was set for continual sniping. The English garrisoned Annapolis Royal, the French established Louisbourg, and, in between, Amerindian and Acadian lived. To both the English and the French, the Acadians seemed to be the key to the control of the area.

Vetch, at this point the governor of Nova Scotia but resident in London, wrote to the Board of Trade in February 1715 that "no Country is of value without Inhabitants so the removal of them [the Acadians] and their Cattle to Cape Brettoun would be a great addition to that New Colony so it would wholly ruine Nova Scotia."[17] For Joseph de Monbeton de Brouillan, *dit* Saint-Ovide, who was one of those in charge of establishing the new French colony on Île Royale, and who would be made governor of that colony in 1718, the Acadians were the best possible settlers. "These people are naturally handy and industrious, above the level one finds in Europe," he wrote in 1717. "They succeed in all they undertake," he went on, "understanding by native wit what they know of various arts. They are born smiths, joiners, barrel-makers and Carpenters."[18] But the French had many unanswered questions. Would the Acadians remain in British territory? Could they be persuaded to leave their homes and villages and begin again on land less fertile? Would they prove loyal to British interests if they stayed? Or could they be kept fundamentally loyal to the king of France while they remained under British rule? For years, there were many contemporary French officials, both secular and ecclesiastical, who cherished hopes that the peninsula of Nova Scotia would be regained. In their letters over the next decades, they referred to the king of France as the Acadians' "souverain légitime" (legitimate sovereign).[19]

Great Britain, meanwhile, was faced with the problems posed in governing a territory whose inhabitants spoke a language other than English and whose Christian beliefs were predominantly Catholic rather than Protestant. It was not a particularly novel challenge. While never exactly colonies, Wales and Scotland had already introduced the authorities in London to the problems of governing a diverse population. Further, there was the experience of Ireland: the first colonial settlement of both England and Scotland. England's control over Ireland's fortunes, although dating to a much earlier period, was confirmed by Cromwell in the seventeenth century. Major Scottish emigration to northern Ireland had begun in earnest in the early seventeenth century, and it was in the last decades of that century that a significant influx of Presbyterian Scots moved across the narrow straits. At the opening of the eighteenth century, England governed a poor, bitterly divided land where the majority of people were Roman Catholic and where many still spoke Erse.[20] Thus, by 1713, the question of religious beliefs and political rights, as well as the issue of differing nationalities within a single state, had already led to the establishment of particular government policies. The two most important planks of such policies were the Declaration of Rights, the document that accompanied the establishment of William of Orange and his wife, Mary Stuart, as joint monarchs in 1689, and the parliamentary Act of Union of 1707, which made England (with Wales) and Scotland into one United Kingdom of Great Britain. Together, these instruments outlined the "rights and liberties of subjects," what was expected of them by the state, and what was owed to them.[21]

There was little theoretical alteration in the civil status of the Acadians in the change from French to British subject. There had been no room for direct political representation of the Acadian communities, as a whole, to the authorities in France, although petitions had been sent on occasion to Louis XIV. The power of appointment to official positions – ecclesiastical, military, and secular – in Acadia had rested with the French crown, or with authorities in France. Nor was there much greater opportunity for direct political participation of the general population in England at this time. Of a total population of some six and a half million in England and Wales, perhaps 5 per cent of the adult males had the right to vote.[22] The greatest barrier, of course, for direct Acadian political action was that of religion, for only members of the Church of England could exercise the franchise in Great Britain. In general, non-Anglicans were excluded not only from Parliament but also from local government and the universities. Thus, the possibility of Acadian representation in the British political process was apparently precluded. Catholicism was not proscribed in England, however, as Protestant beliefs were in France after 1685. Further, the system of delegates from the Acadian communities to Annapolis Royal, begun in 1710, would prove to be a formidable channel of communication between governor and governed. As Britain faced the problem of governing its latest colony, of bringing its inhabitants, both Acadian and Amerindian, into a proper understanding of what their roles were as subjects of the British crown, its officials quickly found that the leaders of the continually expanding Acadian population were bent upon having considerable say in the way in which power would be exercised over their communities and that the leaders of the Amerindian population had substantial reservations about British control of their lives. In sum, as John Reid writes, both Britain and France were to discover that while the treaty of Utrecht had imposed "a new political and military framework on the entire region," such "imperial agreements ... were not necessarily a conclusive or determining force"[23] on events within the region. Quite as much as Britain, France attempted to ensure that the provisions of Utrecht would be carried out for its ultimate benefit.

Even before the terms of the Treaty of Utrecht were agreed upon, the French had decided to take full advantage of its possession of Cape Breton as a way of minimizing the damage that the loss of Newfoundland and Nova Scotia would cause their fishing interests. French fishing fleets did, of course, continue to fish off the coasts of Newfoundland, but the prohibition against the establishment of permanent quarters, with defensive garrisons, slowed the previous pace of their development there. Nor was the exploitation of Cape Breton an entirely new idea. In 1706 Antoine-Denis Raudot, at that time the intendant of New France, had produced a lengthy report on the possible development of the island.[24] He envisioned a major port on the island where goods could be trans-shipped between France, Canada, Newfoundland, Acadia, and the Caribbean. At the same time, such a port would serve as base for the fisheries and guard the entry to the St Lawrence. The most commonly used passage into the St Lawrence at this time was the one south of Newfoundland through the Cabot Straits.[25] Raudot's ideas were behind the establishment of what was virtually a new colony for France.

As early as June 1712, Pontchartrain had written to both the governor and intendant of Canada, warning them that Louis XIV might very well cede both Plaisance and Acadia, thus making Cape Breton of great importance.[26] In March 1713 he wrote more specifically to Vaudreuil about his plans for this enterprise.[27] Within the week, Pontchartrain had also written to Saint-Ovide, giving him instructions about establishing a settlement on Cape Breton.[28] The minister considered that it would be easy to attract the Acadians to the island and that it would be a good idea, too, to persuade the "Indians" to make Cape Breton a major gathering place.[29] In the first week of September 1713, the *Semslack*, a ship of some 270 tons out of La Rochelle, anchored off the shore of what would soon be called Louisbourg. On board were Saint-Ovide, as commander of the expedition, four other officers, two cadets, two servants, and fifteen soldiers. Saint-Ovide, the nephew of the former governor of Plaisance and Acadia,[30] had been born in France in 1676. His career was that of a military administrator, most of which he spent in North America, having come out to Plaisance as a midshipman at the age of thirteen. The *Semslack* had called in at Plaisance on her way and had picked up from there the engineer Jacques L'Hermitte, Louis Denys de La Ronde, and Michel Leneuf de La Vallière as well as "twenty-five soldiers, some officials, women and children [and] meagre stores ..."[31] All these men, like Saint-Ovide and Costebelle, who would be appointed governor of Île Royale on 1 January 1714, having lost his governorship at Plaisance, had made their careers in Canada, Newfoundland, or Acadia. Costebelle himself, born in Languedoc in 1661, had served in Newfoundland since 1692.[32] The others had equally long experience of the region. Jacques L'Hermitte, born about 1652, had begun his career as an army engineer, coming out to Plaisance in 1694. There he spent seventeen frustrating years trying to bring its fortifications into order. It was his ability to understand the types of buildings required in an Atlantic climate that resulted in his being sent, in his early sixties, to survey and map Île Royale.[33] La Ronde had been born in Quebec in 1675 and had a career as officer in the navy and in the colonial regular troops. He had been much involved in Acadian affairs between 1705 and 1713 as captain of *La Biche*.[34] Michel Leneuf de La Vallière et de Beaubassin, of all the company, had the strongest ties to the region, his father having been active in Acadia for much of his life. Born in 1677, Michel had served in Acadia between 1701 and 1704 and then at Plaisance. He would prove of considerable value in establishing settlement in the colony.[35] On arrival, Saint-Ovide reported that there was "on the said island but one French inhabitant and twenty or thirty families of Indians."[36] Within the year, almost all the settlers from Plaisance had been transferred to Île Royale. They were settled in the area around Louisbourg, nearby in Baleine, or on Scaterie Island.[37] By October 1714, there were some hundred and eighty people in the Louisbourg area alone.[38]

The development of Louisbourg, as an established fortified port, and of Île Royale, as a location for both a seasonal and residential fishery, had a considerable effect on the policies of the Mi'kmaq and the Acadians. The immediate impact, between 1713 and 1719–20, was the result of the attempt made by the French to recruit both peoples as inhabitants for the colony. The long-term consequences came from the influence exerted by both military and civil officials stationed at Louisbourg. In some ways, the relationship between the Mi'kmaq and the French, from 1713 to 1755, was less complicated than that between the French and the Acadians during the same period. There was no doubt in the minds of the French officials that the Mi'kmaq were their allies. At the same time, however, there was also a clear understanding, on the part of the French, that the Mi'kmaq were to be treated as a people whose alliance with French interests could not be taken for granted. This was due to number of reasons. The influence of Europeans, whether French or English, on the Mi'kmaq was never a simple matter and there were elements in the immediate situation which showed the extent to which the Mi'kmaq had retained a considerable cultural and political autonomy.[39] The Mi'kmaq had signed no treaty with either French or the British at the opening of the eighteenth century and believed that they still had independent power over their territory and community, power that could be exercised through significant military action.[40] Throughout the seventeenth and early eighteenth centuries, the Mi'kmaq had traded mostly with the Acadians but there had been some direct trade with New England, whose continuous efforts to secure an alliance with the Mi'kmaq had certainly not disappeared with the Treaty of Utrecht. While the Mi'kmaq had shown themselves to be allies of the French, Mi'kmaq policy sometimes led to independent action for their own ends and sometimes meant little support for a particular French action. Finally, the Mi'kmaq population was small and scattered and each particular band needed consultation before any concerted action could be undertaken. The figures are a matter of debate but it seems clear that, by 1713, the Mi'kmaq population was about 2,000.[41] This did not make them a negligible factor in the politics of the region, since their capacity for raiding parties on land and boarding parties at sea made them a people to respect. As for the French, the attempt to make Île Royale the principal location of Mi'kmaq residence had minimal success. Few actually took advantage of the offer, confirming the truth of L.F.S. Upton's aphorism that what "Versailles proposed, the Micmac disposed."[42] The majority of the Mi'kmaq remained on the mainland and continued their own self-directed politics. Antoine Gaulin, the missionary priest who lived and worked among them for most of his life, considered that they "were of little use as our allies but could become a considerable force if they became our enemies."[43]

If the Mi'kmaq were a variable factor in the policy of both the English and the French, they were a constant element in Acadian life. As has been already discussed, traditional Mi'kmaq gathering villages were located close to what became Acadian settlements. Further, while marriage, according to Catholic rites, between Mi'kmaq and Acadian had not been a common practice, it had been an accepted relationship, especially along the eastern shore.[44] Given the kin links between the Acadian settlements, such marriages made for effective communication between the two communities. But it was the trading relationship between Acadian and Mi'kmaq that had produced, and would continue to foster, an enduring connection between them. As Bill Wicken has pointed out, by 1710 "the expansion of Acadian communities from Port Royal to Chignecto and racially mixed villages along the eastern shore led to the creation of relationships between succeeding generations of individual trading families and neighbouring Mi'kmaq villages." Adding that "very little trade occurred directly between New Englanders and the Mikmaq," the Acadians fulfilling a vital role in the transmission of furs and goods from one to the other, Wicken concludes: "These patterns were continued during the eighteenth century."[45] In sum, the contacts between Acadian and Mi'kmaq had deep roots and were, more often than not, peaceful. Acadian political thinking had almost always included some estimation of Mi'kmaq intentions and this habit would be of considerable importance for the way in which Acadian policy developed after 1713.

At the time of the Treaty of Utrecht, however, neither the French nor the British considered that the Acadians were significant enough to have a policy. They were colonists, not even colonials. Every aspect of Acadian life, in the view of London and Paris, was dependent upon their European heritage, specifically upon their links with France through government institutions, language, and religion. Acadian interests, culture, economy, institutions, and social customs – every facet of Acadian existence – were, in the view of imperial officials, nothing more than a reflection of the heritage the colonists brought from Europe. Acadian society had no particular, distinct characteristics of its own and every action that Acadians took was viewed as reactive, to be explained by their attachment to a particular European characteristic. Were the Acadians not as enthusiastic for the cause of France as they ought to be? This resulted from the unfortunate link between Boston and Port Royal. Did the Acadians refuse to swear an unqualified oath of allegiance to the British, in spite of the clear provisions of the Treaty of Utrecht? This was the work of the French priests. A distinct Acadian identity was unimaginable to those, whether British or French, who ruled this people at the opening of the eighteenth century.

Yet a distinct Acadian identity had been developing ever since the mid-seventeenth century. It was rooted in the circumstances of their daily life and their network of kin relationships, in the way in which the settlers fashioned a relative independence from the seigneurial system, in their contacts with New England, and in the evolution of their own small elite of prosperous farmers and traders. From the 1670s, both French and English officials found that there were Acadian spokesmen for Port Royal, Minas, and Beaubassin, men who served as intermediaries between the population and the government, as syndics, and as attorneys. These were individuals who had established a reasonable standard of living and who had been instrumental in building new settlements. One such was Jacques Bourgeois, who paid a major role in the foundation of Beaubassin; others were Pierre Terriau and Pierre Melanson, who were largely responsible for opening up the Minas region and did not passively accept the orders of those who arrived for short periods as representatives of authority established in Quebec or Boston. The emergence of a pattern of responses that placed the Acadians' needs first evolved slowly from within their communities as a result of their historical experience and of debate and compromise throughout the late seventeenth century. The foundation of Acadian neutrality was the belief, which had developed from the days of first settlement and particularly between 1670 and 1710, that they were the rightful inhabitants of the lands on which they lived, not just negotiable assets to be moved about as pawns for the purposes of a distant empire. During the years 1713–30, particular responses to British and French actions led to the emergence of a policy of neutrality, something that was never fully accepted as a reality by either British or French. But Acadian neutrality was not something that Acadians articulated fully in 1714.

By the summer of 1714, the convolutions of colonial patronage in London had seen Samuel Vetch recalled to account for his actions. General Nicholson, for his part, had been named as governor of Placentia and Nova Scotia and he sailed for Massachusetts in the autumn of 1713, being in Boston in mid-December.[46] He arrived at Annapolis Royal in the summer of 1714, armed with less than clear instructions. There were two related questions that would cause both immediate and continuing trouble. The first was the lack of agreement between the provisions of the treaty, which had specified that the Acadians were to have the liberty "to remove themselves within a year to any other place, as they shall think fit, together with all their moveable effects," and the letter of Queen Anne, which set no limit to the time during which the Acadians were to be allowed to quit their lands and could be read as giving them the privilege of selling their lands and buildings. The second was linked to the question of an oath of allegiance. The possibility that the Acadians might work towards a particular political status, neither emigrating nor accepting British rule without qualification, did not enter into imperial considerations.

It might be assumed that officials at Annapolis Royal would have raised the issue of an oath of allegiance to the British crown immediately after the news of peace and the provisions of the Treaty of Utrecht arrived there, sometime in the late summer of 1713. However, Vetch made no attempt that year to require any general affirmation of Acadian intentions through an oath. This might very well have been due to the political disputes within the garrison. As Brebner writes, "when they could think of nothing else to report of each other [to the home authorities], they whispered 'Jacobite.'"[47] Even Nicholson, in Boston, was aware of the quarrels and had written to the Board of Trade in December 1713 that he was "very much concerned that there has been Such Differences at the Garrison of Annapolis Royal, between Coll Vetch, Mr Vane and Mr. Hutchinson."[48]

When he finally arrived in Nova Scotia, Nicholson would find that the French had taken the lead in the matter of Acadian loyalties. Saint-Ovide had dispatched two officers, Jacques d'Espiet de Pensens and Louis Denys de La Ronde, to Annapolis Royal to make certain that the French understanding of the Treaty of Utrecht was known by the settlers. The officers were in Annapolis Royal by mid-July 1714, and on the 23rd of that month they presented a letter to Nicholson outlining the issues they wished addressed. They requested that the Acadians be assembled in each of the settlements – Port Royal, Minas, and Cobequid – to meet with them so that the decision taken by the settlers to stay or leave could be recorded; that a

British officer be appointed to accompany them to record this decision; that the Acadians who decided to leave should have a year to do so from this time, during which they were to live without harassment from the British authorities; that, on leaving, the Acadians be allowed to carry away all personal property; that the Acadians be permitted to build vessels for this purpose, and that French rigging be freely imported for these ships; that Nicholson should let it be known that the Acadians had permission to sell their lands, and, should buyers not be found, that the Acadians be allowed to appoint persons to manage such lands until they were sold; and, finally, that those Acadians who had grievances against the British authorities for treatment received between 1710 and 1713 should receive justice.[49]

As J.S. McLennan has pointed out, what then followed was a lengthy enough process, carried out with considerable formality, certified documents being interchanged between the parties.[50] At least two of the requests made by de Pensens and La Ronde went beyond any of the arrangements agreed upon at Utrecht, or immediately afterwards. One of these was the matter of allowing the Acadians to build boats for the proposed emigration. Constructing the vessels necessary to transport three thousand or more men, women, and children, plus their flocks and herds and personal belongings, was not a task that could be done easily and therefore would not be undertaken quickly. Should there be any form of mass emigration by the Acadians, ships would have to be provided by France or the enterprise would take an unconscionable time to complete. The request regarding property, similarly, was of major importance, and complicated as well. In developing a response to the French, Nicholson consulted his senior military advisers, Christopher Aldridge, a captain with the garrison troops, Thomas Caulfeild, who had been commissioned as lieutenant governor of the garrison in 1712, and Paul Mascarene.[51] A copy of the minutes of this meeting was sent to de Pensens and La Ronde in reply to their proposals. It was agreed that the inhabitants would indeed be assembled and that Mascarene and Lieutenant Joseph Bennett would be witnesses for the British at all such assemblies. It was also agreed that the time for the departure, of those who wished to leave, should be fixed and that the means of their transport should be arranged. As to the matter of the length of time, when the year of grace for such departure should begin and end, as well as the question of the sale of land and buildings, it was reported that Nicholson would seek the opinion of London on these issues. Finally, it was decided that any complaints about the treatment the settlers had received between 1710 and 1713 should be brought to Nicholson's notice.[52] This response angered the French officials, who believed that the combined provisions of the Treaty of Utrecht and Queen Anne's letter permitted the Acadians "to sell their Habitations and leave letters of Attorney for that purpose."[53]

On 14 August 1714 (N.S.), the feast day of St. Louis, the Acadians of

Annapolis Royal and the surrounding neighbourhood were assembled and addressed. De Pensens was ill and could not attend. After Queen Anne's letter was read to the Acadians and a translation provided, La Ronde spoke. He opened by remarking on the continued concern that the king of France had for them. He then promised that vessels would be provided for their transport (to Île Royale); that they would be supplied with provisions for a year after their arrival, should this be necessary; that they would be guaranteed freedom from duties on their trade for a period of ten years; and that they would hold their lands, directly from the king, without the intervention of seigneurs. On concluding, he presented the people with a declaration for signature.[54] This was not, in any way, an oath of allegiance but it was intended to be a serious indication of Acadian plans. It read as follows: "On this day, the feast of St. Louis, we the undersigned, with all the joy and satisfaction of which we are capable, give by this action the eternal proof that we wish to live and die as faithful subjects of His Most Christian Majesty, and we bind ourselves to go to Île Royale or other lands under French control should we be unable to establish ourselves on the said Isle, ourselves and our children, in faith of which we hereby sign."[55] All but four of the heads of the 170 families at Annapolis Royal signed; the population was then over nine hundred, among which were 593 children, thirteen widows, and three single men.[56] At a similar meeting at Minas, on 27 August 1714 (N.S.), the heads of 145 families signed, representing a population of 874, among which were 695 children. On this occasion, according to Mascarene's report, some women signed for their husbands, who were elsewhere at the time of the meeting.[57] There is a handwritten note attached to the Minas declaration, signed by a Pierre Terriot, which reads: "I inform you that I sign for our good King, it being impossible to go there because of the grain which is lost."[58] The final assembly was that held at Cobequid, where there were some 21 families recorded, for a population of 136, with 96 children. Here seventeen heads of families signed the declaration. No visit was made to the Beaubassin area, nor to valleys of the Petitcodiac and the Memramcook. Nor was any attempt made to reach the settlers at La Hève or Cap Sable.

The visit of de Pensens and La Ronde made both the Acadians and the British consider Acadian emigration a distinct possibility, not merely a treaty provision. As Brebner remarks, the process of settling Nova Scotia within the British empire "would be distributed over about fifteen years."[59] During this time, it would be difficult to overemphasize the importance of the French attention to Île Royale and to the role that the Acadians could play in the region's development, not only for the evolution of Acadian policy but also for that of the British. Yet, as will be seen, the importance of this factor does not mean that it was the sole determinant either. The actual relationship between British official and Acadian settler was equally important and the influence of Massachusetts must also be taken into account. Nevertheless, during the last weeks of Nicholson's brief stay in Annapolis Royal (he was back in Boston in November 1714[60]), the impact of the French on the Acadians was obvious and considerable. There was an immediate interest in emigration by some, especially by those who had no major landholdings. On 18 August (O.S.), a group of fifteen sailed from Annapolis Royale on the sloop the *Marie Joseph*, together with their assorted luggage, "12 sheep, Three Young Bullocks, a Cow, a calf, and 4 Barrels of grain."[61] The men in the group were mainly sailors and carpenters, although one was definitely a farmer.[62] At the same time, a number of men accompanied de Pensens and La Ronde back to Île Royale to view for themselves what their situation there might be, if they went. Two brothers from the Annapolis region had already made a voyage of exploration in early May, coasting along the shore via Saint-Pierre and Île Madame to Louisbourg, coming back via Canso and Baie Verte.[63] Now, in September and October, some seventy men, including those who had accompanied de Pensens and La Ronde, visited Île Royale.[64] These visits produced a clearer understanding among the French officials of the situation of the Acadians, of what would be involved in the movement of the whole population, and of the ideas of the Acadians themselves about the areas on Île Royale that they considered most advantageous. Pontchartrain was quite emphatic that the Acadians would not come unless sent for, that the king's ships should be used for transport, and that, without help, the Acadians would be unable to migrate.[65]

For Britain, the late summer and autumn of 1714 was a period of controlled but intense domestic politics, as the monarchy passed, on the death of the Stuart Queen Anne, to the Hanoverian King George. George I's title was parliamentary rather than hereditary, and the almost inevitable challenge by those who favoured the Stuarts meant that the British government was preoccupied with the question of the succession to the throne. For the next two years, until the late winter of 1715/16, Britain's government had its attention concentrated upon the defeat of an armed Jacobite uprising and sedition and treason among various members of the nobility, especially the Scottish aristocracy.[66] However, the great government departments did continue to gather information, even if they were slow to produce policies based on what they learned. In the case of Nova Scotia, the Board of Trade requested, and received, a lengthy analysis of the colony from Samuel Vetch but did not issue any major new guidelines to the officials in Annapolis for several years. Vetch was in London in 1714, seeking reappointment as governor of Nova Scotia. His report is dated 24 November.[67] He believed there to be "about five hundred familys at the rule of five persons to a family which makes two thousand five hundred souls." "Their leaving," he wrote, would leave "that country intirely destitute of inhabitants: There being none but French and Indians (excepting the Garrison) settled in these parts." He considered that the Acadians "will carry along with them to Cape Breton both the Indians and their trade,

Which is very considerable." Vetch went on to point out that removal of such a number to Cape Breton would "make it at once a very Populous Colony (in which the strength of all Countrys Consist)." He emphasized that "one hundred of the ffrench who were born upon that Continent and are perfectly known in the Woods, can March upon snow shoes and understand the use of Birch Canow's, are of more value and Service than five times their Number of Raw Men newly come from Europe." Then he outlined the wealth of Acadian society, pointing out that "their skill in Fishery, as well as by cultivating the soil must inevitably make that island [Cape Breton] by such an accession of people, and French, at once the most powerful colony the French have in America." He believed that the Acadians would take with them "five thousand Black Cattle besides a great Number of Sheep and hoggs," adding, "to replenish which ... at a modest computation of freight only ... will cost above forty thousand pounds." Clark estimates that, in 1715, the herds of Acadian cattle numbered approximately 4,000 and that there were 4,000 sheep as well as 4,000 swine.[68]

Vetch's report on the Acadian situation is fair enough as far as it goes and it is supported by the reports of Thomas Caulfeild.[69] Caulfeild had been commissioned as lieutenant governor of Nova Scotia in 1712 and had once more been left in charge at Annapolis Royal when Nicholson left for Boston, sometime in late September or early October 1714. What both Vetch and Caulfeild only partly recognized, however, was that Acadian society was much more than a just a random population of farmers and fishermen. Vetch did remark on the woodcraft of the Acadians and in a dispatch to the Board of Trade, written in November 1715, Caulfeild mentioned the important trade relationship with "the Indians of Penobscot, St. Johns [the river] and Cape Sables."[70] But neither man really viewed the Acadians as anything except farmers, with a seasonal interest in fishing. References to the trading done, whether with Massachusetts or with Île Royale, received scant attention. Nor did either man really analyse what Acadian farming involved. On the vexed question of whether the Acadians would leave for Île Royale, neither Vetch nor Caulfeild took any account of whether the Acadians continued to prepare the ground, sow crops, and care for the extensive dyke system in any given year, let alone what fishing vessels the Acadians actually possessed and whether such vessels could have moved a significant proportion of the population. Vetch and Caulfeild obviously based their estimation of the Acadians on their experience as officers in charge of a garrison who essentially lived apart from the community they oversaw. Their comments were also those of men who had spent their lives, primarily, as soldiers, used to military quarters and urban as opposed to rural life. They had no first-hand knowledge of the discipline imposed by the seasons upon those whose main source of necessities was the immediate terrain. Both men were essentially migrants, whose lives were lived in a number of different communities. Neither had personal knowledge of two characteristics of Acadian society that had a major influence on the formation of Acadian policy: the necessity for concerted joint action to maintain the dyke system, and the network of family relationships that aided communication not only within each settlement but between the villages.

On the issue of trade, the conquest certainly had an impact on the Acadians' relations with New England, with the garrison, now British, and with the Mi'kmaq, but it did not end Acadian commerce. For some Acadians, as has been noted, the conquest meant a change of role from that of an independent trader to that of a middleman between Boston merchant and Acadian settlement. Those who brought goods, now legally, from Boston to Annapolis Royal and the Minas Basin captained vessels that were owned by men from Massachusetts rather than by the Acadians themselves. For others, such as Prudent Robichaud, trade meant the supply of the garrison with firewood, lumber, grain, and other agricultural products, just as it had under the French regime.[71] For another group, trade was with the new settlement of Île Royale. Mascarene was convinced that such trade was carried on via Baie Verte. After his journeys with de Pensens and La Ronde, Mascarene wrote that "it is certain the french Inhabitants have had their little Shallops in that Bay and no doubt they have supply'd Cape Bretton's settlement by the way of Chicannecto, which is three leagues from Baie Verte as they may have done by Chiboucto, by way of Cobequid.[72] A later report confirms this trade, commenting on the arrival of French vessels in Minas "bringing Wine Brandy and Linens ... and take from thence nothing but Wheat and Cattle."[73] In this dispatch it is also reported that the cattle are driven over to "Bay Vert" and shipped from there.

While such trade was obviously against the mercantile practices of both France and Great Britain, it was not, once peace was signed, in any way a matter of "giving aid and comfort to the enemy." It was also of only minor importance in terms of the supply of Île Royale: New England, in particular Massachusetts, played a much more important role from an early stage in the provisioning of Louisbourg. At the very outset, in 1714, Boston merchants came to the rescue of the new settlers there when the French ships were delayed by ice conditions and contrary winds.[74] Despite continuous complaints from officials in Nova Scotia, Massachusetts, and France, the practice flourished. Essential supplies did arrive for Île Royale from France but New England sent a wide variety of goods, often via Canso: "cattle, sheep, beef, pork, eggs, poultry, wheat, flour, corn, potatoes, turnips, onion, apples, cider, and building materials of all kinds (shingles, planks, bricks etc.), in addition to the schooners and sloops often sold with their own cargoes."[75] By 1725, merchants from Quebec were complaining that prices in Louisbourg were kept low because of goods imported from Massachusetts.[76] But, for the Acadians, trading with Île Royale was important not only for the role it played in their own economy, providing specie for trade with New England,[77] but for the access it provided for news from France, including rumours that the war between England and France was about to recommence.[78] John Reid was one of the first historians to underline the fact that the Acadians, far from being a community of landlocked peasantry, living in a rural backwater with little or no contact with a wider world, lived at a crossroads in North America, a meeting place of English, French, and Amerindian.[79] When the Acadians were faced with the question of the oath of allegiance, therefore, they considered the matter in terms of their needs and priorities, their knowledge of the politics of the region, and their understanding of international politics.

It was Caulfeild who received the news at Annapolis Royal of the death of Queen Anne and who was faced with the question of obtaining oaths of allegiance to the monarch, both from the garrison and from the settlers. As has been suggested earlier, the actual requirement of an oath of allegiance was nothing out of the ordinary for the subjects of either France or England.[80] It was also a common enough procedure both in New France and in Britain's North American colonies. Admittedly, in the latter, the issue was a little more complex. Since there was considerable variation of belief among the various settlements – in principle Virginia was Anglican, Massachusetts was founded to foster a particular form of Protestant belief, and Pennsylvania was committed to allowing all variations of Protestant doctrine – the linking of an oath of allegiance and oaths involving a more specific religious creed was to be avoided. But, that said, oaths of allegiance on the transference of a colony from one empire to another was an accepted practice of international law, in North America and Europe alike.

With respect to the Acadians, there were two highly unusual aspects surrounding the matter of the oath of allegiance in 1714. In the first place, they were contemplating the choice of remaining on their lands or removing to Île Royale, a choice that had been clearly presented to them by de Pensens and La Ronde. Secondly, the process of having delegates from the Acadian villages represent the settlers in their relations with the British, which had been initiated by Mascarene in 1710, had become a much more formal arrangement by 1714. By that year, any request from the British officials was transmitted to the generality of the inhabitants through men who had been approved by the British; of these, some had also been selected by the British, but most were chosen by their villages.[81] Thus, when the question of an oath of allegiance arose, it became a subject of debate between the Acadians and the British, rather than a matter of immediate compliance. All the responses that the Acadians gave reaffirmed their conviction that they had a group existence and the right to debate the political conditions of their lives. Indeed, the very fact that they were represented by deputies meant that their response to the demand for the oath was more than the expression of the opinions of a number of separate individuals: it was an expression of group opinion. And the oath of allegiance demanded of the Acadians was at the centre of their political relationship with the British.

The instructions that were sent to Nova Scotia as to the manner in which the accession of George I should be proclaimed were not dispatched from London until the beginning of January 1714/15. By then, Caulfeild had already announced the death of Queen Anne and had attempted to have both garrison and settlers swear allegiance to the new monarch.[82] Their lordships instructed him to "tender the oaths of Allegiance to ye french inhabitants, with such English as you shall find, and administer the same to them in ye form prescribed."[83] The wording of the oath for the garrison amounted to a simple affirmation of loyalty, while that presented to the Acadians required an admission of the provisions of the Treaty of Utrecht. It read as follows:

Wee the french Inhabitants whose names are underwritten now dwelling in Annapolis Royal and the adjacent parts of Nova Scotia or Lacadie formerly subjects to the late french King who by the peace concluded att Utrecht did by articles therein deliver up the whole country of Nova Scotia and Lacadie to the late Queen of Great Britain, wee doe hereby for the aforesaid reason and for the protection of us and our Familys that shall reside in Annapolis Royall or the adjacent parts of Nova Scotia or Lacadie, now in the possession of his most sacred Majesty George, by the Grace of God King of Great Britain, and doe declare that we acknowledge him to be the Sole king of the said country and of Nova Scotia and Lacadie and all the islands depending thereon and we likewise doe declare and most solemnly swear before God to own him as our Sovereign King and to obey him as his true and Lawfull subjects in Witness whereof we sett our hands ...[84]

The Acadians of Annapolis Royal were the first to be presented with the demand for an oath in the winter of 1714.[85] As has already been noted, many of those who lived within the port itself, as opposed to those who lived along the river banks, had already sworn an oath to the British in 1710. Now, of the approximately one hundred and sixty-seven adult males living in the region, thirty-five signed a conditional oath which bound them to a "true allegiance to the King George as long as I stay in Acadie or Nova Scotia and it is permitted that I shall go there where I judge proper with all my moveable goods and effects when I judge it right without being hindered by anyone."[86] We do not know who composed the oath taken, although it may very well have been one of the three Robichaud brothers, perhaps Prudent, known for his ability to read and write. His signature is the first.[87] The Acadians in the Minas region, however, sent a lengthy reply without any signatures. They started by apologizing for the time it had taken them to answer; however, since not all of them could read, those who were literate had had to travel the region to translate the oath and to explain its terms to others. Having reached an understanding of the situation, the Acadians then noted that they were extremely cognizant of the "kindnesses of King George, whom we acknowledge as the legitimate soveriegn of Great Britain towards them."[88] The language then becomes flowery. The Acadians explained that they "would be most joyful to remain" under King George's "rulership" – "since he is such a good Prince" – were it not for the fact that they had "taken ... last summer ...[a resolution] to return to the rulership of the Prince King of France." The response concluded: "We undertake with pleasure and through gratitude [that] while we remain here, in Acadia, to do nothing against His British Majesty King George."[89]

During the next five years, the Acadian settlements would give the same response repeatedly, while adding various embellishments. In 1715 Caulfeild and his officers spent much time considering the best way to handle the situation. At this time, Caulfeild was convinced that the Acadians "if they continue in this country, will be of great consequence for ye better improvement thereof." He wrote this in a report to the Board of Trade in November of the year, and commented that while the present generation might not be of great value, "yet their children in process of time may be brought to our constitution." Unfortunately, it would be another five years before the beginnings of a civil constitution would be instituted in the province and, even then, it was a constitution that minimized the involvement of settlers in the government of the colony as a whole, whether they were of Acadian or British origin. Caulfeild thought that "there are several well-meaning people among them [the Acadians]" and remarked that he had "always observed since ... my coming here their forwardness to serve us when occasion offered."[90] From 1715 to 1716, only ten or eleven families went to Île Royale, mostly from Annapolis Royal but one or two from Minas and Cobequid.[91] As time went on, however, Caulfeild would become much less optimistic about bringing the majority of the Acadians to an acknowledge of British authority.

Within a year of Utrecht, a fair number of Acadian men, from Minas and Beaubassin as well as Annapolis Royal, had been to Île Royale, seen for themselves what conditions there were like, and returned to their homes to ponder the matter. As early as January 1715, Costebelle wrote to the minister of the Marine that the king risked losing his former subjects unless a ship was sent to help in their evacuation, bearing with it a year's provisions for the Acadians.[92] As Robert Le Blant has pointed out, the difficulties of such a large-scale movement of people, over half of whom were children, have consistently been underestimated by historians.[93] At the same time, the weak garrison at Annapolis Royal would have had great difficulty in stopping an exodus, should the Acadians have been determined to leave. To quote D.C. Harvey: "All that the Acadians had to do was to pick up their movables and drive their cattle to Bay Verte, Tatamagouche or Chibouctou, and with assistance from Ile Royale they would have reached their destination unmolested."[94] But to do this required a strong emotional commitment, based upon a rational assessment of the situation. It meant leaving houses and estblished farms. The trek to any coastal gathering point would not have been easy: families from the Minas area would have had to go to the Beaubassin area by boat, then to Bay Verte on foot or by frequent portages. Moreover, the necessity for large ships would still have to be met. At a minimum, the emigration of the total Acadian population at this time would have involved not only three thousand men, women, and children but a considerable quantity of livestock. Caulfeild had estimated that the settlers in the Minas region had at least 3,000 oxen and cows, 4,000 sheep, and 2,000 pigs.[95]

The majority of the Acadians spent the period between January 1715 and November 1717 biding their time and resisting the pressure of both French and English to take definite action. French officials on Île Royale wrote about Acadian wishes to move to Île Saint-Jean.[96] But the handful of Acadians who had settled at Port Toulouse were, in the eyes of La Ronde, in "a wretched state"[97] that year and this did not encourage others to follow their example. Caulfeild wrote to the secretary of war in October 1716 that he now believed one could place "but little dependence on their friendship," though, he went on, "at the same time I am persuaded it will be with reluctancy they leave the Country, most of those who had formerly gone being again returned."[98] At around this point, too, Costebelle wrote to his superiors that the Acadians showed little eagerness to come to Île Royale.[99]

In sum, during the four years following the settlements reached at Utrecht, the Acadians neither accepted the pressures from the French to emigrate nor acceded to British requests for an unequivocal oath of allegiance. In March 1716/17 Caulfeild died, a relatively young man in his thirties, and Captain John Doucett was sent to replace him as the colony's lieutenant governor, a post he was to hold until his own death in 1726.[100] He decided that the two questions of most immediate concern were the condition of the fort and its garrison and the oath of allegiance. In his first dispatch, written within a week of his arrival, Doucett linked these issues. He considered that the appalling state of the fort was one reason why the Acadians did not take the requests of the British seriously. He believed that the "Priests" had observed "the missery that I and our poor Soldiers have been reduced to for want of money and all sorts of necessary's ... and have taken it as a means to incalcate a notion among the french inhabitants, that the Pretender will soon be settled in England and that this country will again fall into the hands of the french King."[101] Problems with both the "Indians" and the Acadians, he stated, were due to the fact that "the country about us ... has been neglected (ever since the reduction of this Place)." His dispatch also announced his intention to ban the Acadians from the fisheries unless they signed the oath.

Early in December 1717 Doucett began his campaign to obtain an oath from the Acadians, those in the immediate neighbourhood of Annapolis Royal as well as those throughout the colony. The Acadians' response to this campaign was conditioned in part by their perception of the politics of the region as a whole, particularly the attitude of Massachusetts to Nova

Scotia. Massachusetts had been moderately pleased with the results of Utrecht but not overjoyed. Peace had brought the end of the depredations of corsairs on New England trade. As well, after 1713 the needs of the garrison at Annapolis Royal for many provisions – clothing, armaments and iron goods, candles, salt, sugar, and wine – were supplied by Boston merchants, although payment for goods was erratic.[102] Trade with Île Royale was significant, too, as we have seen. Nor was the trade between New England and the Acadians negligible: in 1720 it was estimated that such trade was worth £10,000 a year.[103] But New England's most important interest in the region – and this was especially true of Massachusetts – was the fishing, especially that around Canso. And it was from this activity that major trouble arose, since the uncertain nature of the boundaries between Nova Scotia and Île Royale allowed both France and Great Britain to claim the islands in the bay. At first, there was little antagonism among those who actually fished in the area. However, by 1717, relations between the authorities at Île Royale and the New England fishermen had become tense.[104] As they considered Doucett's demand, the Acadians were aware not only of the activity of all parties on the fishing banks but also of the variety of political views these parties represented.

The Acadians were equally alert to the position of the Mi'kmaq. As has been suggested earlier, the Mi'kmaq were a part of the Acadian environment and a crucial element in the Acadian trade with New England. In 1716 and 1717 twelve vessels left Boston for Annapolis Royal. Having docked there first, most proceeded to Minas, Pisiquid, Cobequid, and the Beaubassin region. On their return voyage, nearly all carried furs and skins.[105] The Acadians also sent other products to Boston, including beef, grain, peas, fish, sea coal, and lumber products of all kinds.[106] But it was the furs and skins that were vital if Acadian traders were to turn a major profit and the Acadians obtained these primarily through the Mi'kmaq. Boston merchants put an exorbitant price on the goods *they* sold.[107] Any disaffection of the Mi'kmaq with the British, therefore, which might spill over into Acadian-Mi'kmaq relations, was to be avoided at all costs. Nor were the Mi'kmaq the only Amerindians whom the Acadians had to consider. The settlers in the Beaubassin as well as those who had moved to the valleys of the Petitcodiac and the Meramcook were in contact with the Malecite of the Saint John. The settlers of the Annapolis Royal region also had to take into account the possibility of Abenaki retaliation, which Saint-Castin had warned about seven years earlier, if they were overly friendly with the British.

It is not surprising, then, that all the communities took as long as possible in replying to Doucett's request, then sent responses that temporized further, and, later still, offered excuses which made it seem as if they might leave for Île Royale. All the responses affirmed the Acadian conviction that they had a group existence and the right to debate the political conditions of their lives. The Acadians living within the immediate neighbourhood of

Annapolis Royal framed their response in terms of their connection to the population as whole. They began by requesting that the lieutenant governor assemble deputies from Minas, Beaubassin, and Cobequid so that a general response might be made. They went on to say that, until they could be protected from Indian attacks, they could not take the oath. The response concluded with the first statement of the idea of Acadian neutrality. "In case other means cannot be found, we are ready to take an oath, that we will take up arms neither against his Britannic Majesty, nor against France, nor against any other subjects or allies."[108] That same year a reply from Minas characterized the request for the oath as an *offer*, not as a demand. The settlers wrote that they were honoured by being presented with "the offers and the advantages that have been made by the King George King of great Britain [to them]."[109] The reply went on to apologize for the tardiness of the reply but pointed out that it was necessary for the Acadians to assemble from the surrounding neighbourhood in order to decide on a proper response and that the roads and the weather had made this impossible. To the extent that a reply could be formulated, however, the communication noted that they were "in despair at not being able to respond as you would wish."[110] Three reasons were offered for their refusal to take such an oath: first, freedom of religion was not fully guaranteed; secondly, they would be subject to attacks from the Indians if they allied themselves more closely with the British; and thirdly, when "our ancestors had been under English domination no one had demanded any comparable oath."[111] This last comment was probably a reference to the brief episode of Massachusetts's rule in the early 1690s or perhaps to the even earlier experience of the 1654–70 period.

The reasons for the Acadian refusal to take the oath in these years, and throughout the 1720s, has been a matter of considerable debate among historians. In particular, among anglophone historians, the influence of Roman Catholic priests has been seen as the main determinant in the development of Acadian policy. This interpretation continues a tradition traceable to nineteenth-century historians, such as Parkman, as well as to even earlier accounts, such as that of Haliburton.[112] It seems to be based on a number of assumptions, some clustered around the idea that Catholics are never anti-clerical, others based upon the particular nature of the Acadian relationship with their clergy, and yet others centred on the particular character of the priests who served in the colony. The unity of the Catholic Church has almost always been more apparent to those outside its realm than to those within, yet the Gallican debate in seventeenth-century France was almost as intense as the division between Protestant and Catholic within that state. As for the Acadians, the strength of Catholic belief among them is both a matter of fact and a matter of debate. On the one hand, there is no doubt that the Acadians valued their Catholic traditions. They built churches, with occasional aid from the French crown, and they paid, through tithes, some of the expenses of the priests and missionaries who came to the region. La Ronde believed that Acadians would leave their lands should an attack be made upon their religious beliefs.[113] On the other hand, the Acadians certainly did not consider the priests as people who could not be contradicted. In this connection, it is well to bear in mind that the Recollet Justinien Durand, who had served in the colony since 1704, failed in his attempts to persuade the Acadians to emigrate.[114] There were other, equally unsuccessful, efforts by other priests. The Recollet Dominque de La Marche, who was stationed on Île Royale, had visited Minas early in 1716. There he preached to the settlers about the danger to their faith if they remained under British control.[115] There was no positive response to this appeal. It should also be remembered that the priests in Acadia were not numerous. While the parishes of Annapolis Royal and Minas usually had a resident incumbent, Cobequid, Beaubassin, and the newer villages in the Chignecto area were usually cared for by itinerant clergy.[116]

Roman Catholic priests may have had an effect upon Acadian policy, but other influences were as, if not more, important. In the first place, whereas the priests were few in number, all settlements had a number of men in positions of public importance, men who played leadership roles in the community.[117] Not only were there the delegates who acted as intermediaries with the British officials, but there were also those who acted within the communities as overseers of the communal work that was necessary to build and maintain dykes and to coordinate the use of common pastures.[118] Certain historians, muddling education and intelligence, have considered that because many Acadians were illiterate, they were a relatively unsophisticated people.[119] But what the Acadian community was in 1717 was a small, highly successful North American colony, with its own elite and its own sense of identity.

For this society, the decision to remain in Nova Scotia was unsurprising. The majority of the population had been born in the colony and most of them in the settlements where they now lived. A large proportion of them had experienced English rule in the past thirty years, a rule that had not had a great impact on their daily lives. There were no particular signs that, this time, the British would remain. The garrison was poorly housed, poorly equipped, and poorly supplied. There was no maltreatment by the soldiery: looting, shootings, expropriations, and imprisonments did not take place. Payment was made for goods supplied. The sole obvious inconvenience was the demand for an oath. On the other hand, emigration meant the abandonment of a well-established way of life, based upon an agricultural economy that was supplemented with other activities: fur trading, lumbering, and fishing. While the years leading up to the conquest of 1710 and the months that followed had seen the Acadians exposed to war, there had been neither widespread slaughter of the population during the hostilities nor widespread death from famine and disease in its wake. There was no doubt that the British now held title to the colony but they did not occupy it. A policy that allowed the Acadians to continue on lands they, their parents and grandparents, and their siblings and their children had brought into fruitfulness had obvious attractions.

Doucett received the Acadian responses towards the end of 1717 and early 1718. He took no action but left the next step to the new governor, Richard Philipps, who arrived in the spring of 1720. Philipps was nearly sixty at the time and had been in the army since he was seventeen. Though without important court connections, he had supported the claims of William of Orange from the outset, had served competently in Spain and Flanders, and was able to purchase his colonelcy in 1712.[120] Philipps would remain governor of Nova Scotia until 1749, a year before his death at the age of ninety, but he spent the majority of his term in London. He had the good sense to demand not only a formal commission before accepting his posting but also instructions as to the form of government that he should institute.[121] He received both. The Board of Trade had decided against allowing Massachusetts to absorb Nova Scotia. Instead, the latter would be governed in the same way as Virginia. There was to be a governor, appointed by the crown, and a council appointed by the governor, with twelve members serving and a further twelve named as alternates. Philipps was instructed to act in all things according to orders from London "and according to such reasonable laws and statutes as hereafter shall be made and assented to by you with the advice and Consent of our Council and Assembley of our said Province hereafter to be appointed."[122] As Brebner points out, neither Philipps nor any subsequent official was able to appoint twelve men to the Council and it usually had no more than eight members, with an attendance that often only met the quorum of five.[123] The task became more complex when Philipps discovered that the governor and council of Virginia by law formed the Supreme Court there. Within two years, the Nova Scotia Council ordered that a court should sit at Annapolis "which court to have the same Style and Cognizance of all matters and pleas brought before them and power to give Judgment and award execution thereupon, by the same manner of proceedings as the General Court so called of governor and council has in Virginia, and practices at this time."[124]

As well as making certain that his appointment was as formally correct as possible, Philipps had taken other measures to prepare his way. In 1717 he had managed to have the independent companies serving at Annapolis Royal and those at Placentia, which was also part of his jurisdiction, formed into Philipps's Regiment of Foot – later the 40th.[125] It was at this time that he met Mascarene, whom he appointed as a captain in the regiment.[126] He sent him immediately to Placentia to bring the fort there into some sort of repair, an experience that would help prepare Mascarene for what would face him on his return to Nova Scotia in 1720.[127] Philipps also carried on considerable correspondance with Doucett before leaving London for Boston. He had already written to the Board of Trade in 1718, pointing out that it was of the utmost importance to have the boundaries between Nova Scotia and Cape Breton settled and a man-of-war on the scene to prevent French encroachments.[128] Even before he arrived in Annapolis Royal, Philipps had felt able to send an overview of Nova Scotian affairs to the Board of Trade. On 3 January 1720 he wrote to the board that the best argument for British authority within the colony would be a reinforcement of troops under his command. This was probably, in part, the common demand of all military commanders of the time for reinforcements. But it was also a reflection, as will be seen, of Philipps's understanding that he had to keep law and order not only at Annapolis Royal but throughout the colony, at Canso and Beaubassin as well as Annapolis Royal and Minas. This letter emphasized his concerns for Canso, which he believed by "all accounts the best and most convenient fishery in any part of the King's dominions." He believed that the influence of the priests on Mi'kmaq and Acadian alike to be much against British interests. As to the Acadians, he judged that "they will neither swear allegiance nor leave the country."[129]

Philipps arrived in Annapolis Royal in late April 1720 and remained there for more than two years. Whether by good judgment or good fortune, his appointment was a wise move, for Philipps proved to be a vigorous and talented administrator, one with both intellect and courage. In this he was like one of his French predecessors, Subercase. Both had made their way in the military service of their respective countries more by merit than by patronage and both were capable of action after careful analysis of the situations with which they had to cope. Their letters and dispatches show great capacity for cogent reasoning and solid command of the language in which they are written. Both men learned as much as they could about their jurisdictions and both could, and did, make effective decisions. Further, both provided the settlers in their charge with some idea of what colonial rule might really mean, while they worked with insufficient resources supplied by the home authorities. But the major difference in their situation was crucial: Subercase governed in the middle of a war and Philipps tried to establish his rule in a time of peace. For Subercase, the settlers were a basically civilian population, who, if not actively engaged in battle, were unlikely to give aid and comfort to the enemy, except by desultory trade. For Philipps, the settlers were a foreign population whose temper was doubtful, whose loyalties were uncertain, and whose trading links with his former enemy were considerable. Subercase could not persuade his superiors that the warfare in his jurisdiction had become truly dangerous; Philipps found it equally hard to persuade the Board of Trade that peace in the same region was less than stable.

On his arrival, Philipps had to assess the needs of the fort and its garrison, institute civil government, regularize the relationship of the Acadians with that government, and work towards a better understanding with, and of, the Mi'kmaq. He began by attempting to ensure that the situation of the garrison and fort was reasonable.[130] Philipps wrote to James Cragg, the secretary of state, that the garrison's complement of two hundred men, excluding the officers, was not in bad shape. This was optimistic. Doucett had written two years earlier that "the men [are] so disgusted that they cannot get their account for 'Subsistance' settled with their officers" and that "wee doe not trust them with theirs arms but when they mount guard."[131] It is probable that the garrison put on its best appearance to meet the new commander. On the condition of the fort, Philipps and Doucett agreed. It was in "as bad a state as possible to describe, both within and without, with several practical breaches, so wide that ten men might enter abreast."[132] However, the immediate military position of the British was by no means hazardous. It was a time of peace, which was firmly established between France and Great Britain in Europe even if it was less firmly rooted in North America. There was no attempt by the Acadians to mount guerilla attacks upon Annapolis Royal. Mi'kmaq raids were no more than sporadic forays against New England fishermen and traders. Fear lay in apprehension of future events, especially in the consequences of the French development of Île Royale, not in the current situation. Philipps did his best to provision the garrison more effectively and to see that the soldiers were better clad and paid more regularly, that the fortifications were rebuilt, and that the home government was made fully aware of French activities in the neighbourhood.[133]

If firmly establishing the British military presence in the colony was important, the establishment of civil government there was equally crucial.[134] Major Caulfeild had seen the necessity for some judicial system for the colony and had written to the Board of Trade in 1716 to this effect.[135] Vetch brought the matter up with the board at the very moment that Philipps was attempting to frame civil government within the colony. Vetch wrote in June 1720, lamenting the fact that no one had "established any civil government [in Nova Scotia] since its reduction."[136] However, within a month of his arrival, Philipps had set up the Council and appointed various administrative officials. On 25 April 1720 (O.S.) he named Doucett, Lawrence Armstrong, Paul Mascarene, the Reverend John Harrison, Cyprian Southack, Arthur Savage, Hibbert Newton, William Skene, William Shirreff, and Peter Boudre to the Council. In addition, three days later, John Adams was also sworn in. Arthur Savage was further appointed as public secretary for the province and its naval officer.[137] Thomas Barnes has summarized the provenance of these men, pointing out that "three were regimental officers (Doucett, Armstrong and Mascarene); one was the chaplain (John Harrison); one was the surgeon (William Skene); two were civilian officials (William Shirreff, commisioner of musters, and Hibbert Newton, collector of customs) and five were merchants (Cyrpian Southack, Arthur Savage, John Adams, Peter Boudre, and Guilliam Philipps)."[138]

The establishment of the Council was only the first step in the work that Philipps undertook to build a judicial and political system for the colony.

The next was his attempt to obtain an oath of allegiance from the Acadians and to do this using the system of deputies first established by Mascarene. The governor had been given explicit enough instructions on how he should treat the Acadians. He was to invite them "in the most friendly manner by Proclamation otherways, as you shall think fit, to submit to your government and Swear Allegiance to His Majesty, within the space of four months from the Date of Such Your Proclamation, upon which condition they shall enjoy the free exercise of their Religion, and be protected in all their Civil & Religious & Liberties so long as they shall behave themselves as becomes good subjects."[139] Should they reject the oath and decide to emigrate, however, they were not to be allowed to take their effects with them, nor destroy what they left behind. Those who refused the oath and remained in Nova Scotia were to face punishment, specifically, the loss of fishing rights and other civil privileges. It is difficult to imagine what exactly the Board of Trade had in mind when it instructed Philipps to invite the Acadians "in the most friendly manner" to take the oath. At any rate, in attempting to carry out these instructions, the governor acted with both firmness and determination, and little discernable hostility, if some exasperation, towards the settlers.

His first contact with the Acadians in the Annapolis Royal area occurred when, three days after he arrived, a hundred and fifty young men, headed by the Recollet Justinien Durand, visited the fort.[140] Durand had served as parish priest in the area as well as the vicar general for the region as a whole since 1704. He had been considered a troublesome character by Samuel Vetch, who had sent him as a prisoner of war to Boston in 1711.[141] Once more in the colony, Durand sought to impress upon Philipps his view of the Acadian situation and the extent to which it was supported by his parishioners. Philipps reacted by assuring his unexpected visitors of "his Majesty's favour and Protection" and requested Durand to read a copy of the general proclamation, which he would send out to all the settlements within the week. It was to be read at Mass on Sunday and affixed to the doors of the churches. It summarized the instructions Philipps had been given and promised the Acadians the civil rights of British subjects in return for the oath of allegiance.[142] Philipps asked Durand if he did not think that this was more than just but the latter replied that the terms were unacceptable. His first point was one that would fairly quickly fall by the wayside, although it would be argued in a desultory fashion for a year or so. Durand asserted that "the people were not at liberty to swear Allegiance because that in General Nicholson's time they had sett their hands unanimously to an Obligation of continuing Subjects of France and retireing to Cape Breton." This attempt to turn a declaration of intent into something akin to an oath of obligation was brought to an end when France, having sought the opinion of its own jurists, admitted that the Acadians had to take an oath of allegiance if they remained in British territory.[143] The political theory of the state in France during the seventeenth century would not accept the toleration of subjects who refused an oath of allegiance to the monarch.[144] Obviously, there was no direct communication of this judgment to the Acadians, but it would reach the priests working among them within six months. Further, it would be reiterated in official correspondence with Île Royale in later years.[145]

Durand's second point proved more durable. According to Philipps, the priest said that the Acadians "were sure of haveing their throats cut by the Indians whenever they became Englishmen." This immediately raised the question for Philipps of the relationship not only between the Acadians and the "Indians" but also between the French and the "Indians." Before his arrival in Annapolis Royal, the governor was convinced that the Acadians conspired with the Mi'kmaq, writing to Lord Carteret from Boston that the former "daily in secret, [were] inciting the Indians to robbery and murder to the destruction of trade and hinderance of settling the country."[146] During his sojourn in the colony, Philipps modified his views somewhat; however, he, in common with most of the senior British officials who followed him, worked on the premise that the relationship between the French at Île Royale and the Mi'kmaq was close. Philipps wrote in September 1720 that, while he had "taken particular care to treat them [the Indians] in the civillest manner ... I am convinced that a hundred thousand [pounds] will not buy them from the ffrench interest."[147] He was also convinced, again in company with most of his successors, that there was a considerable friendship between the Mi'kmaq and the Acadians, and that the latter were quite strong enough to withstand any Mi'kmaq attack and were also capable of influencing Mi'kmaq policy towards the British. As will be seen, these convictions influenced British policy both towards the Mi'kmaq and towards the Acadians. Philipps considered that he had countered Durand's arguments well, but he went on to point out to the Board of Trade that "arguments prevaile little without a power of inforcing." For Philipps, and again for his successors, Britain's military strength in Acadia was insufficient for the task it faced. Yet an argument can be made that, until the outbreak of Anglo-French hostilities twenty-five later, in 1744, the British garrison was adequate for keeping the peace in the colony and preventing French expansion on the Nova Scotian peninsula. Philipps was on much firmer ground when he wrote, in the same dispatch, that "[the Acadians] find themselves for several years the only Inhabitants of a large Country, except the small Garrison of this place, which having been so much neglected they make no acct. of, and began to think they had as much right here as any other: they were indeed very much surprised at the arrival of a Chief Gov'r which they never expected, often saying that the person was not borne."[148] It was not so much the strength of the military force at Annapolis Royal that made the Acadians consider the British merely a temporary phenomenon: it was the absence of any major British migration into the colony.

As a result, the Acadian responses were once more ambiguous. Nine more families left for Île Royale. Seven of them had been residents of Annapolis Royal, one came from Beaubassin, and one from Cap Sable. Two from Port Royal are to be found in the 1707 census as having a small amount of land: Maurice Vignau had half an acre and Gabriel Sanson two acres.[149] But emigration was not the option chosen by most of the Acadian population in 1720. The reply of those in the Annapolis Royal region was complicated by arguments over who was qualified to act as a deputy for the community[150]; the reply from Minas, by their consultation with Saint-Ovide as to whether, indeed, Philipps had the right to demand that they take the oath on pain of compulsory emigration with a minimum of their property.[151] Interestingly enough, when the Minas settlers asked Philipps's permission to consult Saint-Ovide, he agreed. Philipps then wrote a clever and diplomatic letter to the latter, in which he pointed out that he "the more readily condisened [to grant their request], as not in the least doubting that you are perfectly acquainted with the intentions of the most Christian King, to preserve inviolably the strict alliance offensive and defensive between the two Crownes." Having placed the relationship between the two colonial governments in the context of contemporary European international politics, Philipps then continued by expressing his confidence in Saint-Ovide's reasoned acceptance of this state of affairs and his hope that the governor of Île Royale would "therefore ... make no other use of the power and influence you have with these people, than to persuade them to take such measures as may tend to their own good, and at the same time to preserve the peace and tranquillity of these Countrys." He concluded with a comment that underlined the reality that both governors had others to whom they must report and that the affairs of the region were of interest to a broad audience. "I cannot help thinking, " he wrote, "that whatever happens in this affair, whither good or evil, will naturally be construed the effect and consequence of your Council."[152] Sainte-Ovide replied within the month to Philipps, denying that he taken any action as the regards the Acadians that would disturb the peace between the two crowns.[153]

Whatever advice Sainte-Ovide might have provided, it did not change Acadian policy. By the end of May 1720, the settlers of the Annapolis region had responded by saying that "they will Oblige themselves to be good subjects in every respect excepting that of taking up arms against the King of France."[154] The inhabitants of Minas replied in much the same way, at much the same time, writing that "we promise you we shall be equally as faithful as we have hitherto been and that we shall not commit any act of hostility against any right of his Britannic Majesty, so long as we shall continue to remain within the limits of his dominions."[155] The Acadians had thus laid out their position for Philipps: they would not take the oath as presented; they would not make war on the British while remaining in British territory; and, by implication, they retained the right to emigrate on their own terms, removing with their belongings along with their families. Throughout the summer months, Philipps sought to understand fully what the Acadian policy meant and what a reasoned response to it should be. Even at this early stage, after barely a month in the colony, he was considering some modification of the oath and, in his dispatch reporting the Acadian replies, Philipps commented:

I would humbly propose that if an Oath were formed for them [the Acadians] to take whereby they should oblige themselves to take up arms against the Indians if required, to live quietly and peaceably in their houses, not to harbour, or give any manner of assistance to any of the King's Enemys, to acknowledge his Majesty's rights to these countrys, to pay obedience to his Government, and to hold their lands of the King by a new Tenure, instead of holding them (as at present) from Lords of Mannors who are now at Cape Breton where at this day they pay their rent, how farr this may be thought sufficient to bind them.[156]

Around this time, Philipps asked Mascarene to prepare an account for him of his own view of the situation. As Barry Moody has pointed out, Mascarene's report is that of a man in his mid-thirties, impatient to make his way and support his wife and two daughters in Boston.[157] Sharply written, the judgment of a hard-working, sophisticated Huguenot about rural Catholics, it has often been taken as a dispassionate account of the Acadian population at this time, but its political analysis is rooted in the experience of someone who knew, first hand, the French government's actions in the years following the revocation of the Edict of Nantes, when at least 165,000 Protestants were forced to emigrate.[158] Mascarene wrote it, to a large extent, drawing on memories of the period before 1715, when he had left the province for Boston. He would come to a different judgment of the Acadians later on in his life, but in 1720 he saw them controlled by "missionaries of the Romish persuasion." In Mascarene's opinion, such missionaries "have that ascendance over that ignorant people ... as to render themselves masters of all their actions, and to guide and direct them as they please in temporal as well as in spiritual affairs." He believed further that the Acadians were "forever inciting the Salvages [sic] to some mischief, to hinder their corresponding with the English" and that "were the French Inhabitants (who are able to appear a thousand men under arms) hearty for the British government, they could drive away, or utterly destroy the Salvages in a very little time." In his conclusion to this paragraph, Mascarene wrote: "The French Inhabitants besides are for the generality very little industrious, their lands not improved as might be expected, they living in a manner from hand to mouth, provided they have a good field of Cabbages and Bread enough for their families with what fodder is sufficient for their cattle they seldom look for further improvement."[159]

Mascarene's advice for his readers, Philipps, and the Board of Trade on the way to handle the new colony was twofold: to dispatch "six hundred men to be divided into the several parts already inhabited by the French

inhabitants," and to encourage new "British Inhabitants" with "free transportation, free grants of land, and some stock of Cattle out of what such of
the French who would rather choose to with draw, than take the oaths,
might be hindered to destroy or carry away."[160] These conclusions were
reported in a joint dispatch, sent to the Board of Trade by Governor
Philipps and the Council on 27 September 1720, in which Mascarene's
report was an enclosure. The body of the dispatch was, to a large extent, a
précis of the report that focused as much on the military situation as on the
civil state of the colony. It began in point form, noting that the "the french
inhabitants ... look upon themselves as the Indispensable liege subjects of
France." It went on to remark that "that by continuing to plow and till their
lands, to build new houses, and other improvments [sic]: they seem to have
no thoughts of quitting this Country, which we have reason to believe pro-
ceeds from a contempt of this Garrison and a dependance on their own
numbers, with a reliance upon the assistance of the Indians, who are their
firm allies and dependants, by the tyes of long acquaintance, consanguini-
ty and religion." The governor and Council stated their conviction that the
policy of "these Inhabitants and the Indians, are intirely influenced and
guided by the government of Cape Breton, and the Missionary Priests resid-
ing among them, by which they privately or publickly obstruct everything
that may turn to the advantage of the Brittish Trade or security of his
Majesty's Government here." Finally, governor and Council said that they
were "sensible by dayly experience that there is in general an intire repug-
nance amongst them [the Acadians] to obey the Orders which in anyway
tend to the good of his Majesty's service, and that they pay little regard to
the King's authority beyond the reach of the gunns of this fort." Having
summarized the situation, the dispatch then requested that 600 men, with
provisions for a twelve-month period and the stores and tools necessary to
establish garrisons at Minas, the Chignecto isthmus, and Canso, be provided. This, then, was the situation as seen by the British at Annapolis Royal in
the autumn of 1720: the Acadians could not be made to take the oath nor
could they be prevented from emigrating if they so desired.

While the question of the oath of allegiance was of central concern to
Philipps and his administration at this time, and was the background for
all other issues in the colony, it was not the sole problem which they had
to face during the summer of 1720. There was also trouble at Canso and
difficulties with the Mi'kmaq, and both of these not only brought to bear
the interests and opinions of Massachusetts upon the Nova Scotia government but also entailed direct action by Boston in Nova Scotian affairs. To
complicate matters further, there were bitter squabbles between the officers of the garrison and its suppliers as well as feuds among the officers
themselves.[161] If Acadian policy was the product of a wide variety of considerations, so, too, was the response of the British administration. In both
cases, relatively trivial matters of everyday life jostled against estimations of
international circumstances, the end result of which was anything but a
knee-jerk reaction to policies fashioned in Europe.

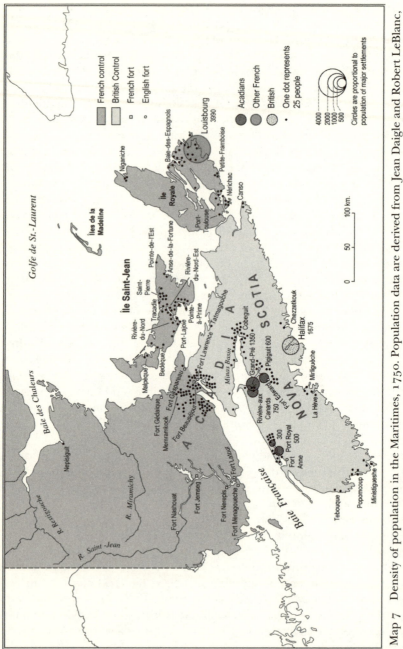

Map 7   Density of population in the Maritimes, 1750. Population data are derived from Jean Daigle and Robert LeBlanc, Plate 30, *Historical atlas of Canada*, vol. 1, edited by Cole Harris.

CHAPTER ELEVEN

Accommodations

Many of the debates about Acadian identity turn not so much on what it involves but on whether or not it exists at all. If it does not, can there can be such a thing as an "Acadian policy"? Is Acadian life, in all its aspects, simply a set of variations on ideas and values rooted elsewhere? That point of view is a common one, and, according to it, not only every major event in the region in which the Acadians live but also every reaction of the Acadians to the changing conditions of their lives are the result of overwhelming outside pressures.[1] As a result, little attention is paid to Acadian historical development; the actions of greater powers upon Acadian society, rather than the experiences of the Acadians themselves, is the central concern of those who write from this perspective. Their attitude – that Acadian history is not important in itself but only as a minor detail in a larger picture – has been summed up and criticized in an article by Jacques Paul Couturier.[2] In some sense, of course, Acadian history is, indeed, a relatively minor part of world history, but, that said, a close examination of its intricacies may be an aid to understanding the larger problems of the relationship between national identity and the state. In particular, the era before the deportation of 1755 repays close scrutiny because it was a time both when Acadian life was exposed to many outside influences and when the texture of the society exhibited its own special characteristics, quite distinct from communities on Île Royale or others along the St Lawrence as well as from those of France.

In 1720 the Acadians were part of a small human population living throughout a large area. In that year, Acadian settlement had reached the north shore of the Bay of Fundy, along the river valleys of the Shepody, the Memramcook, and the Petitcodiac. It was well established on the marshes of the Beaubassin-Chignecto isthmus and had populated the Minas Basin area, including the Cobequid Bay inlet. Throughout the Annapolis basin, Acadians could trace many of their dwellings back to foundations laid in the 1640s and 1650s. Around the coast towards La Hève, site of Razilly's settlement in 1632, one or two families of European descent still gardened, fished, and hunted. While there were few, if any, settlers between La Hève and Canso, Acadian fishermen were as familiar with that shoreline as they were both with the tip of Île Royale and with Île Madame and Port Toulouse. Finally, of course, Acadians were knowledgeable about the coastline bordering the Northumberland Strait and reaching north as far as the Baie des Chaleurs, although settlement along these shores was, between 1720 and 1740, minimal. The majority of the Acadians were to found in four areas: Beaubassin, the three river valleys of the Petitcodiac, the Memramcook, and the Shepody, the Minas Basin, and the Annapolis Royal settlements. However, the whole peninsula and the neighbouring territory on all its borders, northeast and northwest along the Saint John River valley, was well known to them. By 1720, the Acadian population in these areas was somewhere in the region of 3,000. In much the same region, 838 Mi'kmaq lived.[3] Their population centres were in the regions of Annapolis Royal, where there were 43 people; Cap Sable (94); La Hève (157); Chebenacadie (115); Minas (44); Sainte-Marie River (50); Île Royale (107); and modern-day Antigonish (93), Pictou (45), and Chignecto (86).[4]

It is important to bear in mind how extensive an area this was. To drive through it or fly over it flattens out the uplands and smooths away their importance as barriers to travel. Yet such barriers are significant enough, especially when combined with winter snowfalls, that ground travel must often be by roundabout routes. These routes often depended, in the seventeenth and eighteenth centuries, on canoe travel as much as passage over land. This was one of the reasons why a major road along the valleys of the Cornwallis and Annapolis rivers was a matter of debate until well into the 1740s. Most travel between settlements, for both the Mi'kmaq and the Acadians, was along the coast, mostly in small boats and subject to the vagaries of the winds and fog. The seagoing skills of the Mi'kmaq would become more than usually apparent after 1720 as they attacked New England fishermen off the Nova Scotian coast. In winter, of course, the sea is always particularly risky but at other times of the year, too, coastal voyages can be treacherous. A journey between Minas and Annapolis Royal, or Minas and Beaubassin, that in good weather would be made in well under a week might take, even in summer, three times as long, or end in shipwreck. The majority of Acadian travel, except when a new settlement was being established, was linked to the fisheries and to trade and was a matter for men. Mi'kmaq women voyaged much more often than their Acadian counterparts.

The landscapes of the various settled regions were dramatically different, emphasizing the distance between them. At Minas the massive presence of Cape Blomidon provided a dramatic background to the tidal farmlands of the Acadians. People in the Beaubassin area looked across grasslands, where unfenced flocks and herds roamed. At Annapolis Royal, the tail end of the North Mountain, curving to shelter the basin in front of the settlements, also protected the farms established along the shore of the basin and the river. In environmental terms, what bound the Acadian settlements together, and the families that had moved to the river valleys on the north side of the Bay of Fundy, were the agricultural practices that depended upon the building and maintenance of the dykes.[5] There were marked differences between the various districts, however, as subtle variations in the weather and in soil conditions favoured the production of different foodstuffs. While no area was without a particular crop or stock, by the 1720s it was clear that Minas had become the grain-growing centre of the colony, that Beaubassin specialized in livestock, and that the orchards and vegetable gardens of Annapolis Royal were widely envied. As to the weather, the most significant factor for all settlements was "that no place in Nova Scotia or in the south-eastern parts of New Brunswick settled by the Acadians, is more than thirty-five miles from tide-water, and 95% of the population and of productive agriculture is within ten or fifteen miles of the coast."[6] This meant weather conditioned by the sea, with fog in summer and gales in spring and fall. While the seasons were relatively uniform throughout the Acadian settlements, there was enough variation between Beaubassin and Annapolis Royal for the distance between the two to be reflected in some difference in the length of the seasons and in precipitation rates.

During the years between 1720 and 1744, the Acadian population more than doubled, giving it a critical mass sufficient to develop and preserve its own unique community identity. The kin relationships between the various Acadian villages was, of course, the most important connective element of the society. But aiding the evolution of Acadian identity at this time were three closely related factors: first, the absence of war from the region as a whole, and in particular from Acadian population centres; secondly, the impact on the settlements of the British colonial rule; and thirdly, the ability of the Acadians to act on the belief that the pattern of their lives was their own to weave. The first of these elements has often been overlooked, as historians have focused upon what skirmishes did take place. Yet, after Utrecht, hostilities in the region had almost entirely ceased by the mid-1720s, not to break out again in strength until the 1740s. Except for the clash between Massachusetts and French fishermen at Canso in 1718, the skirmishes were largely between the British and the Mi'kmaq. Occasionally, some of the young Acadian men would join in as allies of the latter, and very occasionally there were brawls between French and New England fishermen. But the actual scale of the fighting was limited. There were rarely more than fifty participants involved and the clashes were of short duration.

It is hardly surprising that Canso proved to be a major point of dissension. The area had always been a place of brawls and skirmishes between competing fishing interests, often enough between companies from the same lands, if not the same ports. After Utrecht, that tension escalated.

This was in large measure due to the arrival, in force, of the French on Île Royale and the re-emergence of New England fishermen, in strength, off the coasts of Nova Scotia.[7] But it was caused by the vagueness of the provisions of the peace treaties over Canso, since, at the opening of the eighteenth century, the chief watering place for the fishing vessels and the main fishing sheds and other buildings were established on the offshore islands.[8] Great Britain and France debated fiercely whether such offshore islands, along with others, such as Île Madame and its neighbours, were British, under the provisions of Article XII of the Treaty of Utrecht, or French, under the provisions of Article XIII, which had allotted Cape Breton and all other islands in the mouth of the St Lawrence river and the Gulf of St Lawrence to France. As well, after 1720 the violence there was not solely a matter of British and French. It also included the Mi'kmaq.

Saint-Ovide was aware, from the outset of his command at Lousibourg, of the importance of the area and the possibility of trouble. In November 1717 he had La Ronde examine the situation and the latter reported that there were some six Frenchmen at Canso and a few Englishmen.[9] The "six Frenchmen" were obviously engaged in small fishing businesses and had established some kind of year-round dwellings. At first, relations between them and the English in the region were wary though not overtly hostile, but this soon changed. The New England fishing interest in the Canso region at this time was predominantly a schooner fishery on the various offshore banks and there was almost no shore-based boat fishery;[10] however, buildings on shore to store gear and supplies, as well as flakes for drying fish, became more and more common after 1713. By 1718, New Englanders were increasingly concerned over what they saw as possible French claims of jurisdiction over Canso itself. In June of that year a memorial was presented to Governor Samuel Shute of Massachusetts by a number of fishing captains, complaining that the French had "seized the best places to make their fish and threaten the English with a removal pretending what they act is by the advice and direction of the Governor of Cape Britton."[11] Cyprian Southack, whom Philipps would name to the Council of Nova Scotia in 1720, supported the memorialists and added that two of his men had been captured by Mi'kmaq off La Hève and he had paid £20 for their ransom.[12] Governor Shute reacted strongly to these complaints, ordering Captain Thomas Smart, the commander of the British frigate *Squirrel*, then stationed at Boston, to set sail for Canso, accompanied by Southack, in late August 1718. The expedition included a visit to Louisbourg to discuss the boundary issue with Saint-Ovide and concluded with the seizure of "a brig, a sloop, and a quantity of fish and goods" from the French at Canso.[13] The plunder was valued by the French at 200,000 *livres*.[14]

The expedition was much in the nature of a pre-emptive strike. It did not bring peace but it made clear to all concerned that New England claimed "a base for their trading and fishing operations in the area."[15] Indeed, the New England exploitation of the Canso fisheries was, for a time, considerable. It reached its peak in 1729, when 223 schooners were reported there, and had declined, to no more than forty-six such ships, seven years later.[16] The reaction of Saint-Ovide to the Smart-Southack challenge was hesitant and he made no direct military response. Instead, he reported the matter to his superiors in October 1718.[17] They brought it up as part of the boundary negotiations then going on between London and Paris.[18] Three-way diplomacy between Louisbourg, Boston, and London, with some pressure from Paris, led to an order to Captain Smart to pay a measure of compensation to the French.[19] It was clear that, whatever disputes might arise between French and English in North America in the first ten years after Utrecht, diplomats in London and Paris were in no mood to brook renewed warfare between their countries.

By the end of 1718, it was obvious that, while the Smart-Southack episode might have signalled New England intentions, the French were not about to stop coming to the region. In December 1718 two New England vessels were seized.[20] During 1719 and the early part of 1720, Canso was relatively calm but on 8 August 1720 there was a major raid on the English there, primarily by the Mi'kmaq but with some French participation.[21] In the mêlée, two fishermen were shot and one drowned as he tried to get away. The plunder taken, "fish, goods, clothes, bedding,"[22] was estimated at between £14,000 and £18,000 pounds. The Mi'kmaq claimed that they had "Orders to robb ... from the Governor of Cape Britton."[23] In response to a delegation that arrived from Canso within twenty-four hours to complain of the raid, Saint-Ovide stated that "any Fr. taken in the act sh'd make satisfaction, but was not responsible for the Indians."[24]

This raid had a number of important consequences, all of which would have an impact on the relationship of the Acadians with the British. One of the first and most important was that Governor Philipps assumed primary responsibility for the governance of the Canso fisheries. His reaction to the affray meant that after 1720, while Massachusetts authorities would occasionally provide support for Nova Scotian efforts, it was to Annapolis Royal that Canso fishermen looked for protection against attacks. Nova Scotia was regarded, from 1713 onwards, by New England in general and by Massachusetts in particular, as a colony that should be a strong supporter of their interests.

Philipps had been brought the news of the clash by Henshaw, a trader from Boston, rather than by one of the fishermen out of Annapolis.[25] The governor immediately responded by providing Henshaw with "arms, ammunition and provisions."[26] He then sent Lawrence Armstrong to Louisbourg to discuss the matter with Saint-Ovide. Their meeting resulted in an agreement to refer the matter to Paris.[27] In October, Philipps sent Armstrong with provisions and a small command to Canso. This was the beginning of a British military presence there that would continue for more than a decade. Philipps himself spent the winter of 1721–22 at Canso, and other senior officials would do likewise later in the decade.

The orders that Philipps gave to Armstrong in 1720 were to establish himself in the fort which was being built there and to organize the distribution of the beaches (for drying the cod) and the allotment of gardens among the crews when they arrived in the spring.[28]

Meanwhile, an incident had occurred at Minas on 22 August, roughly two weeks after the Canso raid. This was the plundering, "to the value of Two hundred and Sixty pounds at least," of the sloop of Captain John Alden by a band of "Eleven Indians."[29] Alden reported that they first accosted him and asked for "fifty livers for liberty to trade, saying this Countrey was theires, and every English Trader should pay Tribute to them." This, Alden felt, he was in no position to refuse but, in spite of his payment, five days later the Indians "& two more from Cobequet came on board in a Hostile manner and drove him & his crew on shoare." What enraged Philipps the more was the report that "the Inhabitants ... lookt on without restraineing those wretches under the sham pretence of being afraid of provoking them."[30] Philipps had thus received the news that there was trouble in two widely separated places in the colony during the same week. Clearly, he and his successors would have to cope as much with pressures from outside Nova Scotia as with internal matters.

In many ways, Philipps faced the same obstacle in assessing the Mi'kmaq that he did with the Acadians: an inability to believe that such people could have their own political agenda. Further, he, like his fellow administrators at Annapolis Royal and his counterparts at Louisbourg, Quebec, and Boston, believed that the Treaty of Utrecht was to be observed, even if certain provisions might need elucidation. There also seems to have been no doubt in the minds of British officials that the treaty gave Great Britain clear title to "Acadia or Nova Scotia." In any case, the British appear to have considered that Mi'kmaq sovereignty over the territory of the region was never more than minimal because of their semi-nomadic life.[31] But, for the Mi'kmaq, the provisions of Utrecht, as an agreement binding upon their future conduct and determining their relationship to the British, had no meaning.[32] Such was the view expressed to Philipps by the Mi'kmaq who pillaged John Alden's ship. They informed the governor that "this present land which God has given us of which we are counted as early a part as the very trees seeded here cannot be claimed from us by anyone ... We are Masters independent of all and want to have our country free."[33]

When he reported to Secretary of State Cragg in September, Philipps expressed his general views on the situation that he faced. The Acadian population had shown itself as independently minded as ever and, after five months at Annapolis Royal, Philipps was not particularly optimistic about the possibilities of making the colony a flourishing British settlement unless considerable expense was authorized to reinforce the garrison and to encourage immigrants who would be loyal to Great Britain. "What has hapned at Cansoe," he wrote, "and the damage done there to the ffishery, by way of reprisall (as the Savages give out) for what was taken from the ffrench by Capt Smart, is an unhappy confirmation that I have not been mistaken, for nothing is so evident, as that our ffrench Inhabitants and the neighbouring ffrench Govermts are Equally secrett Enemys to the Brittish interest in this Province & consult together how they may disturb and obstruct it being settled; especially at this juncture they are more busy than ordinary, seeing their hopes of this Country's falling into their hands again is like to be at an end. And that the Savages are the tooles in their hands with which they worke the mischiefs which themselves dare not appear in."[34] The belief implicit in this letter, that the Acadian and the Mi'kmaq are fundamentally allies of France and are themselves close allies, was common among the British administrators of the colony before 1755. It coloured the way in which Acadian actions were viewed, and those officials, such as Mascarene, who considered the Acadians differently had to argue vigorously to have their ideas considered.

But Philipps had grounds for his belief that both Mi'kmaq and Acadians were under pressure from the French, both those at Louisbourg and those at Quebec. While the British and French monarchies found it mutually profitable to cooperate during the first two decades after the treaties of 1714,[35] the political elites in their North American colonies were much less convinced that such harmony should be pursued. At home, both countries faced major domestic problems and Nova Scotia was of small importance in their affairs. France had to work through first the Regency and then the early years of a young monarch. Great Britain was by no means certain of the succession of the Hanoverians, especially given the assassination attempt against George I in 1722. Both needed to recover from the cost of the previous wars. At the same time, especially in North America, the possibility of renewed conflict between the states was taken as a matter of course. Rumours that "the peace between the two Crownes [was] on the point of dissolving" were common.[36] The correspondence of those responsible for colonial matters, whether French or British, constantly spoke of strategic and tactical concerns should hostilities break out again. Pontchartrain, for example, in requesting funds for Louisbourg, remarked that in time of war the post would be crucial for French interests.[37] In these circumstances, it made sense for the officials at Louisbourg and Quebec to do everything possible to retain the Mi'kmaq as allies and to persuade the Acadians to consider French rulership as their proper political destiny.

French pressure on the Mi'kmaq and Acadians to support French policies in the region was often intense. But such pressure was always met, on the part of the Mi'kmaq and the Acadians, with their own sense of what was in their best interests. French demands were considered in the broader context of the social and cultural aims of the group to whom the request for alliance and loyalty was being made. Thus, the Mi'kmaq, while often carrying out raids at the behest of the French, would also raid on their own account, in spite of French requests to stop.[38] Further, the Mi'kmaq and the Malecite would cheerfully accept presents from the English and, as will be seen, in 1726 the Mi'kmaq signed a treaty with the British officials at Annapolis Royal. In writing of the Mi'kmaq, Olive Dickason has concluded that, "while there is no question that the French manipulated the Indians for their own ends, it is equally true that the Indians were engaged in the same game. However, the goals were different: the French were building and maintaining an empire, while the Indians were seeking self-survival."[39] Much the same judgment can be applied to the Acadians, who, by 1730, had managed to work out a compromise with the British as to the terms upon which they would accept the latter's rule.

But the accommodation that was reached by that year between the Acadians and the British officials at Annapolis Royal was an intricate matter, involving as it did not only the differing politics of the various Acadian communities vis-à-vis the British officials but also the way in which the internal politics among these same officials affected the Acadian community. As well, the development of the relationship between the administration at Annapolis Royal and its superiors in London was important for the Acadians. The impact of the quarrels among the British officials at Annapolis Royal was no help to Philipps, as he tried to administer Nova Scotia in 1720. Infighting among those serving in small garrisons, whether English or French, was commonplace but what erupted in Annapolis Royal in 1720 was a bitter rivalry that would continue for almost twenty years, all but destroy Paul Mascarene's career, and be a contributing factor in the suicide of one of Nova Scotia's lieutenant governors, Lawrence Armstrong. As Barry Moody has pointed out, the feuding was not just a matter of quarrels over professional status and advancement but "an intensifying struggle for control of the trade of the colony."[40] In particular, this meant a struggle over the government's commercial business in the colony, something that inevitably caused ripples among those Acadians who were also engaged in trade. On the surface, the disputes were almost farcical, but they continually distracted the attention of the small band of administrators at Annapolis Royal, demanding time and attention from other, more serious matters, and blocked at least one possible channel of communication between British and Acadian, that of the Winniett-Maisonnat clan.

The arguments centred upon the supply of the garrison through Boston, a lucrative commercial venture. This had been handled in the years before Philipps's arrival by William Winniett, a merchant-trader, and Lieutenant John Washington, a master gunner who was expected to keep the accounts for the garrison. Winniett may have been a Huguenot, born about the time of the revocation of the Edict of Nantes. He was certainly bilingual. Having come to the region as part of Walton's New Hampshire Regiment in 1710, he resigned his military commission in 1711 and established himself as a merchant-trader operating out of Annapolis Royal.[41] That same year he married fifteen-year-old Marie-Madeleine Maisonnat and together they had thirteen children. The family was to link the British and Acadian communities through the marriage of three of their six daughters to members of the Nova Scotia Council. Before this happened, however, Winniett played a major role in organizing provisions for the garrison and, as a member of the Council, in determining official policy towards the Acadians. John Washington, for his part, had been sent to the colony early in 1719 by the Board of Ordnance, the body responsible for providing sterling to the colony and honouring the appropriations made by Parliament for the support of the garrison at Annapolis Royal.[42] This meant that he could, and did, write directly to the paymasters about the expenses not only of the garrison but also of the civil administration of the colony. Until 1749, the public revenues of Nova Scotia were pitiful: a report to the Board to Trade in 1740 stated that "quit rents amounted to £12 to £15 a year; the secretary of the province received no allowance for office expenses; the executive councillors received no remuneration; the local government had no power to tax; and there was no fund to meet contingencies such as postage on letters."[43] From all accounts, Washington was a violent and intemperate man, paranoid to the brink of insanity. In particular, he believed that evil influences from New England would ruin Nova Scotia, writing to his superiors in London that "the taint of New England vizt Hypocrisy, Dissimulation, Malice and Overreaching has all ready made passage over Fundy Bay."[44]

Washington reacted violently against Philipps and Mascarene and refused to deal with any other merchant except Winniett. Philipps and Mascarene would have preferred to do business through Arthur Savage, another trader from Boston who had moved to Annapolis Royal in 1720 and whom Philipps had appointed that year as secretary to the Council.[45] Until 1724, Washington used every means in his power to avoid giving any account of his transactions to either Philipps or Mascarene. He wrote frequently to London, accusing the governor and Mascarene, and others as well, of graft, corruption, and peculation of all kinds. While it seems clear that Washington was unbalanced, it is also clear that, at best, patronage for particular friends was a mark of the official dealings of Philipps and Mascarene. At any rate, the charges and counter-charges were sent across the Atlantic and the whole affair became a matter of public controversy at Annapolis Royal and a matter of debate by the Board of Ordnance. Both Mascarene and Philipps defended themselves at length.[46] But, even after Washington's recall in 1724, the affair continued to shadow relationships among the British officials in Annapolis Royal, various Acadian merchants, and the partisans of different Boston merchants.

Despite these troubles, Philipps managed, during these same months, to lay the foundation for three important elements of the future British administration of Nova Scotia: the reorganization of the system of deputies sent by the Acadian settlements; the establishment of a court system for the colony; and the creation of a policy to be followed with the Mi'kmaq and the Malecite. None of these initiatives meant that the colony was brought into a highly bureaucratized, efficiently organized imperial system, in the main because, as will be demonstrated shortly, the British empire was not such an entity at this time. Nor did the governor's actions entail any immediate alterations in the day-to-day living conditions of the Mi'kmaq and the Acadians. But all underlined the reality of a British presence in the region, a presence that was much greater than any earlier British activity had produced. The use of the system of representation by deputy meant that there was a recognized form for political communication between the British administrators and the Acadian communities, and changes to it were an indication that the British intended to remain in control of the colony. If the Acadians wished to have any form of discussion with British officials about political matters, they had to employ the new system. While contact with both Mi'kmaq and Malecite was minimal over the summer of 1720, Philipps met with leaders from both these communities and attempted to assure them that British would allow their trading patterns to continue and permit them priests to minister to their religious needs.[47] This was an effort, at least, to work with the Mi'kmaq and Malecite in the way that the French had found to be successful. Finally, the appointment of the Council allowed the organization of a judicial structure for the colony. At a meeting of this body on 19 April 1721, it was agreed that the governor and Council should constitute a Court of Judicature, to act in the manner of the General Court of Virginia, for Nova Scotia.[48]

The role of the delegates both vis-à-vis the British officials and within the Acadian communities was of major importance in the development of an Acadian political identity. It was a role that evolved considerably over the next several decades. Mascarene, and other British officials, had left the selection process in the hands of the Acadian communities and, to a large extent, Philipps did so as well. But when the names of the first deputies chosen by the Acadians of Annapolis Royal were brought to the governor and Council, almost immediately after the Council's creation, two were rejected. One of them, Joseph-Nicolas Gautier, *dit* Bellair, was turned down because he was "not a freeholder of this Province; only a transient person."[49] In the case of the other, Prudent Robichaud, the Council stated specifically that he had "but a slender propriety in ye said Province." Philipps informed the settlers of Annapolis Royal in writing that Gautier and Robichaud did not have the necessary qualifications for the role of deputy, "as ancientist and most considerable in Lands and possessions."[50] The stipulation that property and standing within the community were qualifications for the role of deputy is scarcely surprising in a British jurisdiction at the opening of the eighteenth century. Property qualification of some sort was almost a uniform criterion for any formal political role in the European states of the time.[51] Nor is it surprising that, throughout the next decades, the British at Annapolis Royal wanted those who were elected deputies to be men of some standing within their community. Since one of the major issues between 1720 and 1730 was the matter of an oath of allegiance, it would be important to have community leaders acting as liaison with the community at large. As well, the development of judicial responsibilities for the deputies took place fairly rapidly. As will be seen, this meant that the deputies acquired functions similar to those of a justice of the peace and, in fact, in spite of the provisions of the Test Act, Lieutenant Governor Armstrong appointed Prudent Robichaud to this office on 5 April 1727.[52] From the outset, the British clearly hoped that the deputies would serve not only as a channel of communication between them and the Acadian communities but as interpreters within that community, as individuals who would bridge the gap between settler and administrator.

The action taken by the governor and Council in 1720 was merely the first step to making the position of deputy something more than just that of a spokesperson for the community. Soon the number of deputies expanded from the six, elected in the Annapolis Royal region in 1720, to twenty-four by the end of the decade: four each for Minas, Pisiquid, Cobequid, and the Chignecto region and eight for Annapolis Royal.[53] The increase was, in at least one case, in response to a specific request from the region for more.[54] The number varied, and often, while three or four deputies were elected, only one was required to come to meetings with the governor. According to Beamish Murdoch, it was decided as early as the summer of 1721 that the deputies were to be chosen annually.[55] This may well have been the case, although there is no record to that effect either in the Council minutes or in the official correspondence. By 1733, however, Armstrong, then lieutenant governor, wrote that "the inhabitants are free to choose their own deputies; that elections are annual (in order that each in turn may share in the fatigue or honor of the office)."[56]

There was one important matter on which Philipps made no progress at all: this was the question of migration *to* the colony. As early as 1711, Vetch had proposed that the authorities support the migration of British and Irish Protestants to the colony. In a long dispatch that year, he urged that the queen afford such migrants "free transportation, tools and a twelve month subsistence as she was pleased to do with the Palatines in New York."[57] The advice came to naught, as did the later plans put forward in 1718.[58] After the appointment of Philipps, the Admiralty asked the Board of Trade in 1719 that no lands be granted in Nova Scotia for settlement until "a total of 200,000 acres of woodland most suitable and most conveniently located as a source of mast timber for the navy" had been "marked out by His Majesty's Surveyor General of the Woods in America in one or more parcels."[59] The request was granted. As a result, the ability of the governor and Council in Nova Scotia to make any significant grants of land of land was severely curtailed and hopes for the settlement of large groups of new immigrants to Nova Scotia never came to fruition.[60]

Philipps's early months in office demonstrated the kind of difficulties that he, and other colonial administrators, faced in dealing with authorities in London. Philipps and his successors wrote lengthy dispatches to the Lords of Trade detailing the problems they confronted, but, partly because of the hazards of transatlantic voyages, replies from London often contained instructions that were no longer relevant. Further, the instructions that did arrive were often vague, unclear, and imprecise. This was due in part to the London authorities' ignorance of the realities of the situation in Nova Scotia but also to the system of governance then in place. The debate over when it is reasonable to place the beginning of the British empire – that is, the point at which there was a sufficiently strong set of political institutions to allow the development of consistent policies that could be carried out over a number of years – has become a matter of growing interest since the publication of the first two volumes of the *Oxford History of the British Empire*.[61] As Bernard Bailyn has written in his review of these volumes, however, the basic conceptual problem is that Britain's overseas colonial activities hardly constituted anything approaching an empire much before the mid-eighteenth century and it is difficult to describe precisely what they did constitute.[62] Part of the problem lies in the fact that, until the late eighteenth century, power still resided in the crown and the relationship of individual ministers to the crown. The ability to initiate and carry out a policy changed as men fell in and out of favour with the monarch.[63] The absence of any real sense of cabinet solidarity at this time meant that there were no generally accepted norms of order, regularity, and consistency for the implementation of long-term policies. The changing views of the monarch and his current favourites had great importance. Further, until at least 1780, the bureaucracy was not, in any sense, a civil service. Both in the lower ranks and at the more rarefied levels, the process of appointment was as much a matter of patronage as anything else. As E.P. Turner points out, "in the offices of the secretaries of State, the officials were not even servants of the Crown, but were employed by the head of the office and remunerated by fees."[64] Nor were the means to organize and maintain policy, even over the medium term, present; this was still the time of pens cut from the pin-feathers of poultry, of ink made from soot and oak gall, and of files organized idiosyncratically. Grand schemes had a small chance of being implemented, although ideas that were broached in reports often lingered, to be brought forward by other hands at other times.

Finally, what Winthrop Bell stigmatizes as the "sluggish" attitude of the authorities in London[65] also stemmed from the intricate rivalries between the Board of Trade and other emerging government departments, especially the Secretary of State, the Treasury, and the Royal Navy, which considered that they had an interest in Nova Scotian matters. By 1720, the influence of the Board of Trade was waning and the necessity of consulting the more powerful, when all written communications, originals and copies, were the work of a small group of clerks, inevitably resulted in decisions being made slowly and infrequently. This was another reason, in conjunction with the policy of timber reserves, why every proposal to encourage Protestant emigration to Nova Scotia, between 1711 and 1749, came to nothing. There was no clear path for any proposal of that kind to obtain strong government approval and support. When one such proposal did reach the Board of Trade, forwarded by British administrators in Boston or Annapolis Royal, it would be sent out for commentary to "the Lords Justices, the Solicitor General, and the Committee of the Privy Council for Hearing Appeals from the Plantations."[66] As Bell has noted, even should the Privy Council finally grant the petitioners' request, the various bodies that had been consulted would have attached such conditions to the land grant as to make it impossible for the petitioners to carry out their plans.[67]

When one tries to outline British policy towards Nova Scotia in 1720, there seems to be only one incontrovertible point that can be made: Britain was determined to retain the colony. How this was to be achieved and the ways in which the colony would be developed were unclear.

It is in this context that the first mention of the possibility of deporting the Acadians, as opposed to facilitating a voluntary emigration, occurred. The possibility was put forward in a dispatch from London to Philipps, dated 28 December 1720, in the following words:

As the French Inhabitants of Nova Scotia, who appear so wavering in their inclinations we are apprehensive they will never become good subjects to His Majesty whilst the French Governors and their Priests retain so great an influence over them, for which reason we are of the opinion they ought to be removed as soon as the forces which we have proposed to be sent to you shall arrive in Nova Scotia for the protection and better settlement of Your province, but as you are not to attempt their removal without His Majesty's positive order, for that purpose you will do well in the meanwhile to continue the same prudent and cautious conduct towards them, to endeavour to undeceive them according to the exercise of their religion which will doubtless be allowed them if it be thought proper to let them stay where they are.[68]

Ever since the conquest of 1710, the possibility of the Acadians leaving the colony had been discussed by the British officials at Annapolis Royal, but the consensus reached had been that they should be persuaded to remain. Mascarene summed up the arguments for this conclusion, pointing out that there were but "two reasons for keeping those French Inhabitants in this country": "1st," he wrote, "the depriving the french of the addition of such strength, which might render them too powerful neighbours ... and secondly, the use that may be made of them [the Acadians] in providing necessaries."[69] The dispatch of December 1720 was written before Mascarene's report arrived in London.

The idea was brought up again the following year in the general report on "the state and condition of His Majesty's Colonies on the continent of America, with their [the Board Trade's] opinion of what methods may be taken for the better government and security of the said colonies."[70] In common with many such general surveys, the importance of the report is to be found in its administrative suggestions rather than in its ideas for immediate executive action. Its plea that the Board of Trade be given the exclusive responsibility for colonial matters signalled the beginning of a lengthy public debate among ministers of the crown, each one defending the particular interests of the Admiralty, the Treasury, and the Foreign Office. But its prescriptions for immediate action were of much less consequence, often being widely at variance with what colonists might find acceptable or the British government be willing to finance. The authors, for example, considered that relations with Amerindians could be improved by offering bounties to those who entered into marriage with them. As for Nova Scotia, it was recommended that the military complement there should be increased to four regiments, the English settlers of Newfoundland should be moved to the colony, and the Acadians should be evicted. As far as the British government was concerned, the matter of the Acadian eviction was the only one of many such recommendations that would be taken seriously, but then only after thirty years had passed.[71] The idea of the removal of the Acadians would be put forward by British administrators in Annapolis Royal with some frequency before 1729 and much more often after 1748. For the moment, however, the British policy towards the Acadians was still one of accommodation, particularly on the part of Philipps, whose attention was taken up by the Mi'kmaq and the Malecite.

The steps that the governor took towards stabilizing relationships with the Amerindians were by no means as innovative as his decision to institutionalize the selection of Acadian deputies. Nevertheless, they were the beginning of a process that led to treaties between Nova Scotia and certain leaders of these communities. The problem was at least as complex as those posed by British-Acadian relations and, indeed, British relations with the Acadians were greatly influenced by the ideas of the former about Acadian-Mi'kmaq relations. As Bill Wicken has pointed out, the tendency to generalize about all the various societies that made up the human demography of Nova Scotia has not helped our understanding of what was happening there in the eighteenth century. The indigenous peoples are depicted as all having the same political objectives and almost no attention is paid to differences within the various Amerindian groups, for instance, to "the clear distinctions between the numerous Mi'kmaq villages."[72] As well, British and French colonial administrators are seen as all cut from the same cloth. So, Wicken continues, "'English' people [are portrayed] as irreconcilable enemies of the Mi'kmaq while the 'French' have been viewed as their allies and friends." It is also often the case that differences between the policies followed by Massachusetts and Nova Scotia in dealing with "Indians" have not often been examined. This is particularly true of the 1720s, when the difficulties between New England and the Abenaki became linked with those faced by Annapolis Royal with the Mi'kmaq and Malecite. Further, almost all accounts of the relationship between European and Amerindian, whether sent from Louisbourg or Annapolis Royal, were written to persuade European authorities to provide additional support to the colonial authorities, whether such support was to be in the form of presents for the Amerindians or a naval vessel to ply the coastal vessels. Both French and English saw the Amerindian as a major factor in their own rivalries, and both recounted events in a way that would substantiate their particular view of the Amerindian situation. English accounts inevitably placed the blame for Mi'kmaq raids on the French, while French accounts always emphasized English brutalities against the Mi'kmaq.[73] Both accounts tended to refer to the Acadians as less than innocent bystanders in the affrays that occurred and as quite willing to aid the Mi'kmaq.

The latter presented Philipps with three problems: the raids upon fishing and trading vessels, at Canso as well as along the whole shore between Canso and Cap Sable and, on occasion, deep into the Bay of Fundy; the occasional attacks upon English traders, such as the one at Minas; and the possibility of an alliance of the Mi'kmaq and Malecite with the Abenaki, such as one that resulted in an attack on Annapolis Royal in 1724. The Mi'kmaq population base for these attacks was under a thousand, including women and children, and, as McLennan points out, it is interesting that so small a number of raiders "could have caused such widespread dismay."[74] The crews of the sailing vessels were often as numerous as those of the sea canoes attacking.[75] As has been noted, too, Philipps responded to the attack of 1720 by stationing one company on Canso for the winter of 1720–21. He increased that to two companies over the next year and himself went to Canso in September 1721. There, he wrote to the Lords of Trade that he was agreeably surprised that it was in a flourishing state and considered that "my good neighbors at cape Breton seem to give up their pretention of right and talk only of its being a place neutral."[76] He considered that this was due to the realization in Louisbourg that his administration saw the fishing station as important to British interests. To emphasize this, Philipps decided to spend the winter there and to seek for help from the traders in the area to provide better housing for the soldiers he intended to station at Canso in the future.[77] However, while this sojourn might have reaffirmed, in the eyes of the French, Britain's determination to control Canso, it did little to persuade the Mi'kmaq to end their raids.

In fact, the summer of 1722 saw such raids reach their peak. British accounts report that "18 tradeing vessells in the Bay of Fundy" and a further eighteen fishing schooners between Cape Sable and Canso were captured.[78] French sources record that between twenty and twenty-five ships were taken in the Bay of Fundy alone.[79] The reaction at Canso among the fishing crews, many of whom were from Massachusetts, was one of considerable concern and irritation. Philipps later wrote that at the time "we were in the middle of the fishery and the harbour full of ships wayteing their loading ... fresh advices came that the Indians were cruising upon the

Banks with the sloopes they had taken assisted by the prisoners whom they compell'd to serve as marriners, and gave out that they were to attack this place with all their strength, which alarm'd the people to that degree, bringing to mind theire sufferings two yeares ago."[80] Philipps also received news from Governor Shute of the Abenaki raid in June on the Kennebec and the subsequent declaration of war by Massachusetts against "the Indians." He responded to these events by outfitting two sloops, and shortly afterwards he informed London that within "three weekes time I retooke all the vessells and prisoners, except four which the New England people poorly ransom'd." What he did not mention in this dispatch was that all this had taken some fierce fighting and, on occasion, the outcome was in doubt.[81]

At some point during this summer, probably in late August or even early September, Philipps received a dispatch from the Lords of Trade, dated 6 June 1722, acknowledging his reports of September and November 1720 and of 1 October 1721.[82] It is a prime example of how generally unhelpful such dispatches were to the administrators actually in a colony. As Murdoch comments, "the measures of improvement and defence [Philipps] urged on the governmentt are civilly alluded to; but the delay of reply, and the cool answers, must have tended to check the zeal he had evinced for the prosperity of the province."[83] There was no promise of new supplies or provisions for the defence of Canso, nor immediate redress for the lack of a contingency fund. The governor was merely informed that he should have written to the Treasury on that matter. As to the lack of a surveyor, to advise on what lands should be reserved for His Majesty's needs, in particular woodland for furnishing the navy, their Lordships told Philipps that he had the power to set out these lands and that he could permit himself to grant lands to settlers, providing such lands were surveyed. In considering what he had done in allotting beaches for fishery needs and small gardens for those engaged in this occupation at Canso, he was to remember his instructions and ensure that "the coast is left free for the fishery to all H.M.subjects." About the Acadians, their lordships wrote never a word. Such tepid advice must have reinforced the decision that Philipps had taken to "wait upon ... [their] Lordships in person this fall" to explain in person the situation of the colony.[84] The governor left for London sometime in early September 1722, not to return to Annapolis Royal until December 1728. John Doucett served as president of the Council and senior official until the appointment of Lawrence Armstrong as lieutenant governor in May 1725. In spite of the tension that existed between the two men, they served together reasonably well until Doucett's death in November 1726.

During Philipps's absence, there were significant alterations in the politics of the region which resulted in strained relations between the Acadians and the officials at Annanpolis Royal. The war declared by Massachusetts, against the Abenaki and their allies, continued until late December

1725, and, while no such formal step was taken by Nova Scotia against the Mi'kmaq and Malecites, Amerindian shipping raids occurred off Canso in 1723 and 1724. These, however, were more of nuisance than a threat and had no appreciable impact on the development of the Canso fishery. In 1723, 33,000 quintals of fish were sent to market from that fishery, and by July 1724, a third of the way into the fishery season, 8,000 quintals had been dispatched.[85] But there was also one skirmish on land, against Annapolis Royal in 1724, and this raid hardened the garrison's attitude towards both the Amerindians and the Acadians. The skirmish involved a mixed group of Mi'kmaq and Malecite, perhaps thirty of the former and twenty-six of the latter, who attacked the fort. Murdoch shrewdly remarks that "[the Indians] made what they called war, but which the English described as robberies and murder."[86] In the minutes of the Council, which was held on 8 July 1724, the event was recorded as one where "[Indians] Barbarously Murthered a Sergt. Of this Garrison and then Openly attack'd our Partys and the Garrison itself and were the means of Another Man's being Killed and An officer and three private Men Dangerously Wounded & the fireing Fireing [sic] of two English Houses & the takeing of two men of this Garrison with a woman and two children who have been Since Releas'd out of their hands by the french Inhabitants."[87]

Doucett and the members of Council who attended the July meetings not only reacted quickly but with brutality obviously inspired by fear.[88] They began by deciding to "make Reprisalls by the Death of one of the Salvage [sic] prisoners in custody"; a Mi'kmaq, who had been held prisoner in the fort for the past two years, was shot.[89] Murdoch considers that, while "this action may be palliated, I can see no grounds on which it can be in any way justified."[90] A series of inquiries was then begun to discover why no warning of the attack had been brought to the garrison. Witnesses interviewed by the Council, presided over by Doucett, included the Massachusetts traders John Alden and James Blin, several settlers from the Minas area, and the then parish priest of Annapolis Royal, Charlemagne Cuvier.[91] All agreed that there had been a gathering of "Indians" in the Minas area before the attack but there was conflicting testimony about who then knew what was planned, and whether or not those who considered an attack on Annapolis Royal imminent had made every effort to warn the garrison. The conclusion reached by Doucett and the Council was that Cuvier and Félix Pain, the parish priest at Minas, could easily have warned them of what was afoot. Both were to be expelled from the colony. As to the settlers, though Doucett and the Council obviously believed that they might also have found some effective means to bring news to Annapolis Royal, it was decided not to impose any major penalty. This judgment was reached on the grounds of "the present Unsettled State of Affairs" and the fear "that by pursuing Matters to ye Extremity might Occasion the Inhabitants to Rebell and Joyn perhaps with the Indians as formerly." It was also stated in the minutes that the officials believed that they did not have "force enough to keep [the settlers] under Due subjection" and that they had been punished "in Some Measure" by Father Pain having been sent away.[92]

The apprehension and fear of the garrison in the face of what were, compared to the contemporary experiences of New England, minor affrays is a measure not only of the extent to which New England attitudes affected the ideas and beliefs of the British officials in Nova Scotia at this time but also of the general sense of insecurity felt by the small garrison of that colony. There was a continuous exchange of letters and information between the officials of the two colonies.[93] While it would be wrong to think that the Nova Scotian administration was little more than an extension of that in Boston, it is clear that the policies of Massachusetts towards the Abenaki had an impact on those of Annapolis Royal towards the Mi'k-maq. As well, the general opinion in Boston about the proper place of the French in North America helped to form the attitude of the merchants and garrison of Nova Scotia towards Acadians and Amerindians alike. But there was also another, more determinative, factor. What primarily inclined the Nova Scotian administration to develop a harsh policy towards the Acadians and, at the same time, to work towards a more positive accommodation with them was the weakness of the garrison. Between 1713 and 1748, no British governor of Nova Scotia had more than 500 men at his command in the colony, and rarely more than 300, of whom about a third would often be stationed at Canso.[94] Philipps had written to London in 1720 that the defence of the colony required constant support by the navy and "at least two regiments to defend a province as large as New England and New York put together."[95] As will be seen, the main fort of the colony was always in ill-repair and the ordnance available inadequate. Furthermore, the garrison was dependent upon the Acadians, to a great degree, for supplies of firewood for cooking and heating as well as for fresh meat, vegetables, and a considerable proportion of the flour needed. Finally, while the officials might view the Acadians with distrust if not active dislike, the provisions of the Treaty of Utrecht made them, in the view of the Lords of Trade, British subjects who were to be accorded a measure of civility. London might ponder the question of their deportation but, in the meantime, the Acadians were to be shown the benefits of British government.

The officials at Annapolis Royal also made a determined effort to come to terms with the various groups of Amerindians in the region. This endeavour was helped by a similar peace effort on the part of Massachusetts. Agreements were reached in late December 1725, by both Boston and Annapolis Royal, with the Abenaki, the Mi'kmaq, and the Malecite. Mascarene had been appointed as the negotiator for Nova Scotia in August 1725 and left for Boston to take up his duties with alacrity.[96] What the treaties meant to those who signed them has been a matter of considerable debate in recent years and, as Dickason has pointed out, "each side had a different understanding of what a treaty meant."97 At the time there was clearly confusion, since the varying groups of Mi'kmaq and Malecite had their own interpretation of what British suzerainty implied and there was argument among the varying bands as to whether all the Mi'kmaq peoples were bound by the actions of any particular one of their leaders. Subsequent actions indicate that, to British officials in Nova Scotia, the agreements had a simple meaning: the Mi'kmaq and the Malecite populations recognized that the Treaty of Utrecht had granted Nova Scotia to the British and that, in consequence, the "Indians" were now subject to British rule. In return, the British agreed that they would respect the latter's hunting and fishing rights, though, obviously, they had no intention of granting the natives exclusive rights to any particular area for these pursuits.98 The special relationship which, according to officials at Île Royale, existed between the French and the Mi'kmaq had been, if not ended, at least much diminished. Saint-Ovide tried hard to blur the importance of the agreements,99 and he encouraged the Mi'kmaq to continue to harass fishing vessels out of Massachusetts.100 In the immediate future, however, should Anglo-French warfare once more break out, the Mi'kmaq could be no longer be considered as, automatically, allied with France. As it happened, the agreements of 1725 were successful enough that aboriginal raids were not to occur again in Nova Scotia for a considerable time.

Partly as a result of these peace treaties, the matter of the oath of loyalty once more surfaced. The colony now had a new lieutenant governor, Lawrence Armstrong, a man approaching sixty. Of Irish-Protestant extraction, Armstrong had been a soldier since his mid-twenties, seeing service with Marlborough before coming to North America. He was part of Hovenden Walker's ill-fated expedition and had arrived in Annapolis Royal in 1711. From then on, his career had been that of a garrison officer, with debts he struggled to clear, colleagues with whom he quarrelled, and superiors who did not favour his abilities. He has generally been considered an irritable, quick-tempered person with a talent for an exaggerated turn of phrase and a deep suspicion of Catholics, whether lay or clerical. He spent the first year after his appointment as lieutenant governor at Canso, carrying on an acerbic correspondence with Saint-Ovide, whom he suspected of plotting continuously against the British regime in Nova Scotia.101 Armstrong proposed to make Canso "the chief place for population" in the colony and hoped to bring the Council to sit there.102 Arriving in Annapolis Royal in the late summer of 1726, he decided to settle the question of the oath of allegiance. He was convinced that, as he had written to the Lords of Trade the previous year, the British would never "be safe or secure" in the colony "so long as [the Acadians] are permitted to be Snakes in our Bosoms that would Cutt our throats on all occasions."103

Armstrong began by calling the Annapolis Royal deputies to a Council meeting on 25 September 1726 and asked them to swear an oath of his own wording, which referred to "his Sovereign Majesty George of Great Britain France and Ireland." The Acadians, after having heard the oath read in French, requested that a clause be inserted into it "whereby they might not be Obliged to Carry Arms."[104] Armstrong responded by saying that "they had no Reason to fear Any Such thing as yt it being Contrary to the Laws of Great Britain yt a Roman Catholic Should Serve in the Army." However, the minutes report that Armstrong, with the advice of the Council, "Granted the Same" – the right not to bear arms "to be writt upon ye Margent of the french Translation in order to gett them over by Degrees." The minutes also report that the meeting ended with everyone drinking "His Majestys ye Royal family & severall Other Loyal healths ..."

Two matters here are particularly worthy of note. First, Armstrong's actions embody, to some extent, the idea that Philipps had put forward six years earlier, when he suggested that the Acadians should be offered an oath which bound them to keep the king's peace and to give no assistance to his enemies, leaving aside any matter of active support for British military efforts. This position was built upon the continued assertion of the Acadians that, while they remained in the colony, they would do nothing against the interests of George I but did not wish to bear arms against the French. Secondly, while the Council minutes report the verbal and written assurances given to the Acadians, exempting them from military service, Armstrong remained silent about these assurances when he reported to London. In this case, the minutes, which sometimes formed part of his dispatches, were omitted. In the letter he sent to the secretary of state in November, Armstrong wrote of the ratification of peace with the Mi'kmaq and the needs of the garrison and referred to the fact that "oaths had been administered to the inhabitants of the river Annapolis, who could never be persuaded to take them before."[105] This was misleading: Armstrong had not only failed to mention the inducement he had offered but also overlooked the oath taken by these particular Acadians in 1715.[106] Over the next three years, other British officials in the colony would send equally misleading reports back to the Lords of Trade, preventing those in London from forming any clear idea of what the Acadian attitude to British rule was.

Armstrong's belief that he could gradually entice the settlers to take an unqualified oath of allegiance was contradicted by events in the spring of 1727. The response of Beaubassin and Minas to his request for an affirmation of allegiance to the British demonstrated, in the view of the lieutenant governor and Council, "Rebellious Behaviour."[107] Beaubassin had refused the request by arguing that the Mi'kmaq would attack them if they took such an oath; Minas prevaricated in much the same manner. Both settlements, however, promised not to commit any hostile acts against the British regime.[108] Armstrong and the Council responded by attempting to restrict all direct trade between the Minas and Beaubassin regions and Boston, an attempt that proved unsuccessful.[109] Over the summer, tension between the garrison and the settlers increased, with arguments taking place over the prices that the settlers wanted for wood and other supplies they sold to the garrison.[110] In September, news of the death of George I reached Annapolis Royal and, as was customary, the lieutenant governor and members of Council themselves swore "the Oaths appointed by Law to be taken" on 9 September.[111] This provided the occasion for Armstrong to make yet another effort to obtain the oath from the settlers.

Ensign Robert Wroth was given the commission of proclaiming the new king in the villages and procuring oaths of allegiance from the inhabitants. He reported to the Council on 13 November 1727 that he had obtained oaths of allegiance from the villagers of Beaubassin, Minas, and Pisiquid. He had, he acknowledged, succeeded by giving the following written assurances: that they would have the free exercise of their religion and missionaries to instruct them in the beliefs of Roman Catholicism; that they would never be required to bear arms under any circumstances; that their rights and those of their heirs to their lands were recognized; and that they were at liberty to leave the province as and when they so wished.[112] The Council was not pleased and informed him that the "Concessions are unwarrantable & dishonourable to His Majestys authority and Government & Consequently Null & Void."[113] At the very same meeting, however, the Council also resolved that the inhabitants who had taken the oath for Ensign Wroth "shall have the Libertys & Privileges of English Subjects." Brebner asserts that the trade embargo was then lifted "forthwith,"[114] but, in the account that Armstrong sent to Newcastle on 17 November, the former wrote that he had decided to punish Minas by "a withdrawal of traders who purchase their grain, the only trade they have."[115]

In this dispatch, and a similar communication sent on the same day to the Lords of Trade,[116] Armstrong reported his dissatisfaction with the state of the colony, starting with the dissension within the garrison, outlining the quarrels with the traders from Boston, and concluding with his displeasure with what he considered the obduracy of the Acadians. He described the actions he said he had taken, including the temporary imprisonment of two deputies for what he considered their intolerable behaviour. The deputies were released on bail, however, "till his Majesty's pleasure therin shall be known." These dispatches show a man caught between strong beliefs about what the Acadians, as subjects of Great Britain, owed their sovereign, Armstrong's understanding of the wishes of his superiors that the Acadians should remain in the colony, and his bewildered outrage at not seeing a clear path of action. His exasperation was given full rein in a dispatch he sent in the summer of 1728. Armstrong wrote that he considered the Acadians as having an "Insuperable aversion to the English nation both Church and State" and hoped that the Lords of Trade would act "speedily to curb their Insolence and reduce them to their duty before the Task becomes much harder." He himself, he went on, had "no Warrant nor Authority ... to proceed further against them."[117] He also mentioned in this letter his ongoing disputes with Alexander Cosby, Philipps's brother-in law, who had come out to Nova Scotia in 1722 and had been at odds with Armstrong ever since.[118] Cosby had been appointed the lieutenant governor of the fort and town of Annapolis Royal in 1727 and the quarrel between the two men had intensified over the winter.

While the Lords of Trade did not answer Armstrong as he might have wished, when his letters of November 1727 arrived in London in the spring of 1728, the secretary of state, Newcastle, immediately asked the Lords of Trade to prepare new instructions for Philipps as governor of Placentia and Nova Scotia, taking into account Philipps's own view of what measures "were most necessary for the better settlement of Nova Scotia."[119] The instructions that were issued, on 16 July 1728, however, were little more than a repetition of past orders to Nova Scotian officials.[120] Little notice had been taken of the points that Philipps had reiterated in his various reports since 1722: the need for British-backed settlement and for additional military strength. On 29 June 1728 orders-in-council were issued to Philipps commanding him to leave immediately for Nova Scotia.[121] It took him not quite a year to comply with these orders. During the intervening months, there was considerable discussion about the possibility of settling Irish Protestants and some five hundred Palatinate families in the colony.[122] As has already been mentioned, these proposals were never acted upon.

Philipps arrived in Canso at the end of June 1729 and spent the next four months there. He was much pleased with "the great growth of this Harbour in the fishing trade," reporting to London that there were "not less than two hundred and fifty Vessells and fifteen hundred or two thousand Hands imploy'd in Catching, Cureing and Loading of Ffish for severall Markets ..."[123] He left Canso in late October and had a rough passage to Annapolis: the voyage took five weeks, a particularly severe passage. On arrival there, Philipps wrote to London that he had great hopes for the submission of the French inhabitants because of the "Joyfull reception" he had been given by them.[124] He intended to have the oath of taken "in the most solemn Manner" at Annapolis Royal and thought that, once this had taken place, "the French Inhabitants ... of Minas and the other settlements at the Head of the great Bay of Fundi" would follow suit.

Philipps's dispatches to London, between 3 January 1729/30 and 2 September 1730, read as if the governor had no difficulty in persuading the Acadians, one and all, to take a simple and unconditional oath of allegiance. To explain this surprising achievement, he pointed in part to the "joy and satisfaction" that appeared "in every countenance among the people" when he arrived at Annapolis Royal.[125] That good humour resulted, to some extent, from Philipps's attitude towards Catholicism and his confirmation of René-Charles de Breslay as an acceptable parish priest for the port. Unlike Armstrong, with his northern Irish Protestant childhood, Philipps was born into a rural Anglican family with strong commercial connections. Whereas Armstrong considered Catholics fundamentally politically untrustworthy, Philipps saw Catholicism as merely one indication of a person's political nature. By Christmas 1729, Philipps had administered an oath, witnessed by Breslay, to 194 men over sixteen then living in the Annapolis Royal region.

It was a simple oath, administered in French and transmitted in that language to the Lords of Trade. It read as follows: "Je Promet et Jure sincèrement en Foi de Chrétien que je serai entièrement Fidelle, et Obeirais Vrayment sa Majesté Le Roy George le Second, que je Reconnois pour le Souverain Seigneur de la nouvelle Ecosse et de L'Acadie. Ainsi Dieu Me Soit en aide."[126] A generally accepted translation reads: "I promise and Swear on the faith of a Christian that I will be truly faithful and will submit myself to His Majesty King George the Second, whom I acknowledge as the Lord and Sovereign of Nova Scotia or Acadia."[127] On receipt of the text, Secretary of State Sir William Popple wrote indignantly that, while the oath "seems to have been a Translation of the English Oath of Allegiance ... the different Idiom of the two languages has given it another turn."[128] The Lords of Trade accepted Popple's idea that there was some material difference between the English and French versions and that "French Jesuits may explain this ambiguity so as to convince the people ... that they are not under any obligation to be faithful to his Majesty."[129] Philipps, however, did not receive these quibbles until he had administered a similar oath to the majority of the other adult males in the colony. In writing to the Lords of Trade, in November of the year, Philipps asserted that he thought he "had made it [the oath] stronger than the original English."[130] By that time, he had reported, in a dispatch sent to the Duke of Newcastle from Canso on 2 Septmber 1730, that he had, personally, obtained "the entire submission of all those so long obstinate people."[131] Philipps emphasized in this letter that the oath was the more necessary because of "the great increase of those people, who are at this day a formidable body and like Noah's progeny spreading themselves over the face of the Province." He considered that his success was due to his personal intervention and to the "good temper" of "the Indians" that had resulted from the presents made to them.[132]

While there is no official document that confirms the contention of the Acadians, at the time and later on, that this oath was sworn on the understanding that they had been granted the right not to be bear arms, there is considerable evidence that this was so. The records of the Council during Armstrong's tenure points to the probability of such an exception being made. Moreover, there are accounts, drawn up by the priests in Grand Pré and Pisiquid immediately after the signing of the oath, indicating that the settlers had indeed been exempted from bearing arms and fighting for either French or English.[133] As well, there are statements, contained in petitions written by the Acadians when in exile, to this effect.[134] Finally, as Brebner points out, there clearly was a common acceptance that

Acadians had gained this provision since, after 1730, "most English men spoke of them as 'the Neutrals' or 'the Neutral French.'"[135]

While oaths of allegiance had been an accepted part of European politics for centuries, they had become a much more complex matter by the opening of the eighteenth century. With the acceptance of the possibility of religious diversity within the state, there arose questions about the extent to which a particular oath would bind the actions of the person swearing it.[136] The very fact that, after 1688, England, and later Great Britain, accepted as loyal subjects those of diverse Protestant beliefs, as well as those who were Catholic or Jewish, had led to the oath of allegiance gaining in importance as a means of testing a man's political loyalties. The actual wording became less critical than the willingness to make a public declaration of loyalty to the authority of the particular state. The French government never argued over whether the British had the right to demand an oath of allegiance from the Acadians. The writings of French political thinkers of the time were quite clear: oaths were required if subjects were to enjoy rights of property ownership of any kind.[137] Indeed, in 1731 the president of the Ministry of the Marine wrote to the officials at Louisbourg that Philipps was right "in causing the Acadians to take the oath of allegiance."[138] Some of this enthusiasm might have arisen because a small number of Acadian families moved at this time to Île Saint-Jean, where Jean de Pierre was in charge of yet one more attempt to establish a French colony there.[139] The Acadians themselves obviously considered the oath something of consequence, or they would never have put so much energy into their quest for a particular wording.

This being said, it becomes necessary to consider what the oath taking of 1729–30 implied for the parties directly involved. Why did Philipps accept an oath that was sworn with reservations? And why did the Acadians swear an oath, even with conditions attached, which recognized British rights over Nova Scotia? The answer, in the first case, revolves around Britain's determination to remain a strong force in the region, and, in the second, around the Acadians' estimation of the immediate situation and of the probabilities of the consequences of their actions. There is no doubt that the British officials sent to govern the colony saw their charge as a permanent acquisition for British rule. At the same time, however, it was equally clear to those actually present in Nova Scotia that major financial investment in the region by the British government was unlikely to happen in the near future. This bolstered the Acadians' position, for, while they had displayed no enthusiasm for British rule over the past twenty years, neither had they shown any sustained hostility towards the British presence. In fact, while Acadian behaviour had been argumentative, there had been considerable trade between garrison and settlers. The British relied on the Acadians for most of their food supplies. Further, there was at least a minimal political cooperation between settler and garrison through the work of the deputies. Finally, though the arrival of Protestant settlers, whether Irish or Palatinate, had yet to occur, there was a constant discussion of such a possibility. For the officials at Annapolis Royal, the settlement of the colony by English-speaking Protestants and the integration of the Acadians into the resulting polity was a distinct possibility, if not an immediate probability. An oath that had the Acadians recognizing British claims in the region, even if it carried no military obligation, was a step in the right direction. Nor was such a modified allegiance unknown in British legal history: the Channel Islanders had achieved a similar non-combatant status much earlier.[140]

The Acadian position was equally firmly rooted. Since 1710 they had carried on their lives without any major, sustained emigration. They had attended to the demands of their rapidly expanding families for housing, clothing, and food by continuing their traditional pursuits of fishing, farming, hunting, and trading. Though there is some dispute over the rate of population growth, there is a general consensus that it was remarkable.[141] I have suggested a figure of 3,000 for 1714, a number that includes the population of the outlying Acadian settlements in the Chignecto-Memramcook area as well around Cap Sable, and, on that basis, and accepting the figures used by Clark, I estimate that by 1730 the population of Annapolis Royal, Pisiquid, Minas, and the entire Beaubassin area together was at least 5,000.[142] Whatever the actual figure chosen is, however, there can be little debate about one of its consequences: Acadian communities were settlements of the young, where the demands of child rearing, in terms of food and clothing, not to mention energy, were considerable. The taking of an oath, with the understanding that they would not be called upon to fight either French or "Indian," showed a determination by the greater part of the Acadian population to remain where their ancestors had settled. In their view, the Acadians remained in Nova Scotia very much on their own terms.

Yet the swearing of the oath and the Acadian acceptance of the role of their deputies, as well as the Acadian resort to the Council for the settlement of certain disputes, meant that the Acadians accepted that the English officials at Annapolis Royal had a considerable jurisdiction over a broad area of Acadian life. Since 1710, the role of the delegates had moved from being primarily concerned with the oath of allegiance to a much broader field of responsibilities, including everything from the execution of Council orders after 1720 to discovering facts in property disputes.[143] As Thomas Barnes has pointed out, "because of the absence of a sheriff and bailiffs, [the deputies] executed council orders and judgments, summoning parties, enforcing appearances, putting parties in possession, attending surveys to show lines and bearings, receiving road assessments paid on council order and even arresting fugitives."[144] By 1732, it was acknowledged that the delegates had power to decide disputes about land in their villages, even if, on occasion, their decisions were appealed to the council in Annapolis Royal.[145] While Brebner recognizes that the delegates were "in effect the local government bodies of the Acadian population,"[146] he is convinced that they were "not politically minded"[147] and so does not view the delegate system as the political framework of the Acadian community. But in many ways the deputies were much like justices of the peace and, like the justices of the peace, drew much of their authority from the willingness of the community to accept that authority. The consent of the Acadians for the exercise of this role was a clear acknowledgment that, in civil matters, there was an alternative to the judgment of the clergy.

Thus, one of the crucial aspects of Acadian political life after 1710 was the part played in the lives of the villages by the deputies. This meant that a tacit recognition of British authority was reinforced by the development of the role of the Council as the judicial arbiter of the colony. There was, quite clearly, a legal process among the Acadians that was overseen by officials at Annapolis Royal. It was something that developed slowly; during the 1720s, roughly three cases were decided annually.[148] One such involved the payment of tithes to a Father Ignace by the inhabitants of Beaubassin. In this case, brought to a Council meeting in late April 1726, the Council found for the priest and against the villagers.[149] The same Council meeting also gave judgment in a paternity suit, ordering the reluctant father to pay "three Shillings and Ninepence every Week Until the Child Arrive to the Age of Eight."[150] During the 1730s, the hearings of civil litigation, involving Acadians alone, increased considerably: fourteen cases being heard in 1731, twenty-one in 1732, thirteen in 1733, six in 1734, seven in 1735, and ten in 1736.[151] After twenty years of British control of Nova Scotia, a significant sector of the Acadian population had accepted a certain British authority in their lives and, at the same time, the local British officials had accorded the Acadians a voice in the direction of their own lives.

This accommodation did much more than merely establish a modus vivendi between Acadian settler and British official. It provided the framework for the emergence of an Acadian political leadership, a crucial step in the continued evolution of a distinct Acadian identity. The selection and role of deputies meant political activity and negotiation within the village communities. Those who accepted this position learned not only how to persuade their fellow villagers but also how to argue with officials. Mascarene wrote of his vision of their activities in 1740. He wanted the deputies to be "men of good sense, upright, men of property, and having the good of the community at heart and sensible of the duty to which they are bound by their oath of allegiance ... [who] having fixed times for meeting and consultation should act together in the execution of the orders, etc., of the Govt. in the interests of justice and of the good of the community."[152] While this was an ideal that was rarely attained, those men who served managed to combine the wishes of their village with the necessity of accepting official requests. Prudent Robichaud, on many occasions a deputy for Annapolis Royal, had a career that included rent collecting from the Acadians, interpreting between the British officials and the Mi'k-maq, and performing a quasi-legal role in the judicial work of the Council.[153] In sum, both the judicial role of the Council and the political role of the deputies provided a framework for the evolution of the Acadians' social and economic traditions during the 1730s.

Acadian society flourished during this decade. The population continued to increase and kin links between long-established families were reinforced. Many marriages were between people of close kin, between individuals whose brothers and sisters, aunts and uncles, had already chosen partners from the same lineage. Trahants very often married Grangers; Blanchards, Leblancs, and Landrys intermarried.[154] There is also some documentary evidence that can be interpreted to suggest that marriage between second cousins, a marriage that required a religious dispensation, was relatively common.[155] At the same time, however, the parish registers show that a number of marriage partners, mostly male, came into the Acadian settlements at Pisiquid and Grand Pré from Canada and France as well as from Île Royale and the Saint John River.[156] Further, there were marriages between members of the Acadian elite and members of "English" Annapolis society, such as that of William Winniett.[157] These meant, at the very least, an access to ideas and information of some importance for Acadian politics. Scholarly works such as William Godfrey's study of John Bradstreet,[158] one of the children of Agathe de Saint-Étienne de La Tour and an Anglo-Irish officer serving in Annapolis Royal, illustrate the existence of social relationships between Acadians and the garrison government. While arguments will undoubtedly continue over the rate of growth of the Acadian population, and the extent to which newcomers were assimilated before 1748, what is undeniable is that not only were most Acadians members of large extended families but that all major settlements had kinship links with one another.

By 1730, most of the Acadian communities were established settlements of well-built and well-furnished houses. In 1731 Robert Hale, a young New England doctor, journeyed from New Hampshire to Annapolis Royal and Beaubassin on a sailing ship engaged in transporting coal from present-day Joggins to Charlestown Ferry. He kept a diary of his voyage, commenting on the scenery, the people he met, and the customs that impressed him.[159] He described the entrance of the Annapolis Basin as being surrounded by "low shrubby Trees" which look "as tho' not one had ever been cut down here since the Creation." He was informed that "French pple. [sic] are settled for 30 miles up ye river" and their settlements were small villages "of about 4, 5, or 6 Houses" set apart from one another by "Small Intervals." His description of the buildings in the Beaubassin area, buildings that included barns and wharves, chapels, and even an inn, paints a picture of an expanding community. Like most of the population of Great Britain and France at this time, most people lived in hamlets, the *clachan* or the

bourg, nouns that describe small collections of dwellings with few additional outbuildings, whether for agricultural or fishing use or for religious or
other community needs.[160] Where the present-day Sackville now stands, at
places such as Westcock and Shepody, the houses were recognizably a
group, even if their placement was by chance rather than planned.

Hale recorded that he visited the three or four "French houses called
Worfcock and the French entertain'd us with much Civility and
Coutesy."[161] He was fascinated by both their architecture and their furnishings. Describing the houses around Beaubassin as all built low "with
large Timber and sharp Roof (not one house being 10 feet to the Eves),"
he noted that the insides of the houses that he visited "have but one Room
... besides a Cockloft, Cellar and sometimes a Closet." It is a little confusing to decide quite what Hale was talking about, for he goes on to say that
"their Bedrooms are made something after the Manner of a Sailor's Cab-
bin, but boarded all round about ye bigness of ye Bed except one little
hole on the Foreside, just big eno' to get into it."[162] But the archaeological work being done on the upper Belleisle marsh in Annapolis County,
Nova Scotia, has already shown that at least some Acadians lived in
dwellings of proportions that would be considered comfortable today, with
expensive furnishings.[163] Once again, uniformity is not the norm. For
those near Annapolis Royal and on the Grand Pré marshes, present opinion holds that houses would have been built *en colombage*, "a sturdy framework of hewn timbers, mortised, tenoned and pinned with tree-nails."[164]
On the marshes around Beausejour, it has been suggested that sturdy
houses were built with a variation of this technique, a combination of
straight pine or spruce trunks, cross timbers of birch and willow, the whole
packed tight with clay, itself bound with salt-marsh hay.[165] At the mouths
of rivers, building materials available included clay and shells ready to be
crushed into chalk, allowing further adaption of the housing styles originally developed around Annapolis Royal and along the Minas Basin.

The common experience of the political situation of the colony, both
internal and within the region as a whole, the strong kin relationships
both within and between the settlements, the general high standard of living: all these factors helped the development of a sense of collective Acadian identity. During the 1730s and 1740s, the Acadian settlers in Nova
Scotia were part of what one can call an emergent ethnicity. The elements
of such a community, in the view of Anthony Smith, are "a collective
name, a myth of ancestry, historical memories, shared cultural elements,
association with a homeland, and (partial) collective sentiments."[166] All
these were present in the Acadian communities during these decades. Of
great importance in the growth of this sense of Acadian identity was the
impact of the communal work needed to build and repair the dykes, the
observance of common religious practices, and the development of a unifying cultural life.

Dyke building had, since its origins in the 1630s, always been a labour-intensive enterprise. By the middle decades of the eighteenth century, however, the scope of Acadian dyking in the Grand Pré and Beaubassin areas was of major importance for the entire population of the local farming communities. In the Minas Basin, for example, great earthworks were needed for the farming of that immense thousand-acre marsh. They demanded engineering skill and hard labour as well as a considerable amount of organization for their building. We have an account of the construction of a major dyke in the region of Memramcook in 1775 which gives some idea of the scale of the enterprise.[167] The workforce included almost the entire adult male population then settled along the banks of the Memramcook and the Peticodiac, to the number of fifty-eight. They worked twelve days straight, days of something between twelve and seventeen hours, before what was constructed was in a shape to withstand the immediate impact of tide and weather. Many of the workers brought their own teams of horse or oxen. The final dyke measured 13.5 metres wide at its base, 7.2 metres high, and 59 metres long.[168] Such an enterprise would bind the villages together, not only during the actual months of its construction but in the demands for repair and maintenance. The Acadian historian Gabriel Bertrand considers that the building and maintenance of the dykes was much more than a crucial factor in the formation of Acadian sense of community. He maintains that the dyke system was also the basis of the Acadian agricultural exports and, by providing the people with economic freedom, made it possible for them to argue with the British garrison.[169]

The common bonds of religious belief also brought the Acadians together. There is no doubt that the Acadians were Catholic and wanted to have Catholic priests within their communities. But the immense political importance given to the priests by the officials at Annapolis Royal, and by a number of later historians, has obscured the reality of Acadian Catholic life.[170] As is generally the case, there was a difference between those who gave little credence to the commonly held religious creed and those who attempted to practise its precepts. A report sent to the archbishop of Quebec in 1742 gives a picture of rural congregations that can be found again and again in many diocesan archives over the years.[171] Drunkenness, even on Sundays and holidays, even during Mass, was a major complaint, it being alleged that the local bars (*cabarets*) were kept open throughout the services. Such behaviour, the commentator went on, led to quarrels and dissension among family members. He was also appalled at the fact that some communities not only allowed men and women to dance together after sunset but even permitted the singing of "des chansons lascives." One would like to know whether the alcohol was spruce beer or rum? Were the *cabarets* just someone's front parlour or did the settlements all have something like the taverns mentioned by Hale? Was the dancing anything more than square dancing of some sort? It is clear that the Acadian interpretation of Catholicism owed little to Jansenism. Further, if one takes into account the letters of the missionaries, to both their secular and their religious superiors, it is also clear that Acadian acceptance of priestly dictates was rarely without argument.[172]

Nevertheless, in spite of arguments with their priests and a tendency to interpret the regulations of the church in a broad rather than a narrow sense, Catholicism was a fundamental element in Acadian lives. All the major settlement areas – Annapolis Royal, Minas, and Beaubassin – had small wooden churches dating from the late seventeenth century. Hale recorded "2 Mass Houses or Churches" in the Beaubassin area.[173] Enough parish registers have survived the turmoil of the deportation years, 1755–64, to provide evidence that the recording of the milestones of human life – birth, marriage, and death – was a matter for the parish priest.[174] The Acadians might not have been as fervent Catholics as their priests wished, but Catholic observances were woven into the texture of their lives. Hale noted that there was a cross on the small beach "where the French dry ye fish" at the entrance to "the Annapolis Gut."[175] He also recorded the ease with which an Acadian household incorporated matters of faith into its daily life. As a guest in an Acadian family, Hale observed that "just about Bed time wee were surprize'd to see some of ye family on their Knees paying yr Devotions to ye Almighty, & others near them talking and Smoking &c. This they do all of them (mentally not orally) every night and Morning, not altogether, but now one and then another, & sometimes 2 or 3 together, but not in Conjunction one with the other."[176]

While Catholicism was of importance in Acadian society during these years, there were other elements that made up Acadian cultural identity. The idea that the Acadians possessed a strong cultural life before the deportation was not taken seriously until the 1970s. Even then, Acadian culture was seen as essentially a limited folk culture, its major attributes being crafts, folk songs, and legends.[177] There is no doubt, of course, that this description holds a great deal of truth. Acadians had to turn to what their environment provided for the materials to house, clothe, and feed themselves and had, inevitably, developed their own particular styles of building and construction, weaving and sowing, and cooking and baking.[178] It is also true that there was a strong oral tradition in Acadian society and, as Antonine Maillet's doctoral work shows, these traditions drew strength from the regional diversities of seventeenth-century France.[179] But, if the words "folk culture" are taken as implying an uneducated and inward-looking society, they are an inadequate description of Acadian culture in the 1730s and 1740s.

Indeed, the Acadians lived at a major crossroads that in many ways were a meeting point of French and British colonial activity in North America. Often overlooked is the fact that Acadian communities were, *as communities*, bilingual. Not all inhabitants spoke both French and English but the trading links with Boston, not to mention the presence of an English-speaking administration, meant that a number of people throughout the colony knew both languages. The connections with New England, almost as old as the colony itself, had made the Acadians familiar with European migrants of another language and other traditions. At the same time, the emergence of Louisbourg after 1719 meant the continuance of a strong source of French influence in the region.[180] Lastly, the Acadians' agriculture was strong enough to enable them to export both meat and grain and made commercial activities a much more important element in their lives than has generally been recognized. As Darrett Rutman points out in a thought-provoking article, the connections that join small communities to other places are of crucial importance in the way in which these communities develop.[181] Acadian merchants brought news of two very different worlds back home: that of Massachusetts and that of Louisbourg. Whatever else the Acadian communities may have been, they were not isolated from a wider world.

The question of the level of Acadian literacy is difficult to resolve. The time-honoured method of using the signatures of couples in the parish registers on the occasion of their marriage has been applied to the Acadians. The result of such work provides a picture of the Acadians as, on the whole, less able to read and write than their contemporaries in Quebec and New England after 1720.[182] However, the evidence is based upon parish registers that are incomplete. After 1720, while no Acadian parish was entirely without the benefit of visiting priests at some point during the year, certain parishes went without a resident priest for extended periods of time.[183] At the same time, the loss of parish registers during the 1755–63 period means that, except for Annapolis Royal, the data is fragmentary. The best that can be said, using the parish registers as evidence, is that, as a whole, the Acadian community had people within the settlements who could read and write. But there is no doubt, given the papers relating to landholdings, such as the agreement concerning the sale of a meadow in 1738, that the Acadians were accustomed to using written documents. This particular agreement recorded the conditions of ownership of land in common between three families and the way in which it would be managed.[184] It was drawn up by Prudent Robichaud, the same man who served as a deputy for the Acadians of Annapolis Royal. Further evidence of written records, relating to wills and to the payment of quit rents, can be found in the Council minutes, especially of the meetings of that body which were held to deal with judicial matters.[185]

In sum, the history of Nova Scotia between 1720 and 1740 was not one of static confrontation between British and Acadian. Both communities developed, the Acadians becoming more sure of themselves, more accustomed to having government officials as an ongoing part of their lives, the British searching for a policy that would prevent the Acadians from turning to the French, whose ambitions for Île Royale and Île Saint-Jean were growing more and more clear-cut. The accommodations that took place between settler and garrison in the 1720s allowed the Acadians to develop a strong sense of themselves, something that would be invaluable during the years of turmoil that began in the 1740s.

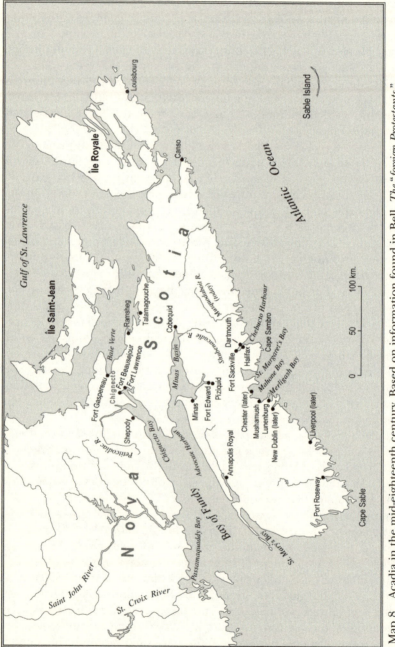

Map 8   Acadia in the mid-eighteenth century. Based on information found in Bell, *The "foreign Protestants."*

CHAPTER TWELVE

British Administration, Acadian Settler

For twenty years after the conquest of Port Royal in 1710, one of the most important questions for the British administrators of Nova Scotia was whether the Acadians would remain or leave. In 1731 this question was put aside for fifteen years, not to be raised again until Massachusetts broached the subject during the War of the Austrian Succession. But Philipps's acceptance of a non-combatant status for Acadians did not make the colony an easy posting for the British garrison and officials. After swearing the oath, the Acadians gained a sense of security for the conduct of their daily lives and believed that they had achieved a recognition of their rights as inhabitants of the colony. The British, however, were still deeply suspicious of Acadian loyalties and were puzzled over questions of land ownership, in particular those arising from the expansion of Acadian settlements. The situation was all the more uncomfortable for the officials because of almost continual dissension among themselves, their quarrels made the more bitter because of the actions of Philipps before he left the colony in the late summer of 1731. What became more and more clear over the next fourteen years was that the British government of the colony was a matter of day-to day improvisation which led, inevitably, to clashes between officials and settlers, since what was viewed as a temporary concession by the former was seen as a precedent for the future by the latter.

The governor had been recalled to answer questions about the non-payment of the officers of his regiment.[1] The orders for his return, and the instructions for Armstrong to leave for Nova Scotia as the colony's lieutenant governor, were issued on the same day, 15 March 1730/31. Philipps was appraised of the news when the latter arrived at Annapolis Royal on 22 July 1731.[2]

Philipps greatly resented his recall. He wrote to the Duke of Newcastle that "it imports me much to be very careful of delivering up the government to lieut. governor Armstrong with the greatest exactness, who is turning up every stone, and raking into every kennel, to find some dirt to bespatter me with, in hopes that some may stick."[3] In order to ensure that

what he saw as Armstrong's ingratitude would be checked, Philipps, before
he left, appointed his brother-in law, Major Alexander Cosby, as president
of the Council, over the heads of the other senior administrators, John
Adams, Paul Mascarene, William Skene, and William Shirreff. A general
petition of these men to London objected that Cosby's appointment had
been made by executive fiat and contradicted the principle of advancement by length of service.[4] As Barry Moody has remarked, at first sight one
might not consider preferment in early-eighteenth-century Nova Scotia
worth a squabble but advancement in the colony's administration was the
only avenue open to most of those stationed in the colony.[5] To see someone promoted "out of step" might deny the rest an opportunity in the
future for a higher rank. It took the Lords of Trade over a year to answer
but their reply upheld the petitioners. They ruled, in a directive sent to
Philipps as governor, that "no Governor has a right to alter the Rank of
any Councillor and you are to take notice that the eldest Councillor
upon the List of Councillors ... is always to act as President of the Council
and to take upon Him the Government in the Absence of the Governor
and Lieutenant-governor."[6]

The squabbling among his subordinates was the least of the problems
facing Armstrong, and one that he left for the authorities in London to
solve. His difficulties ranged from the pressing need to buy the food supplies for the garrison to the obvious problems of the upkeep of the fort.
There were also questions to be answered about the payment of quit-rents
by the Acadians and the need to have lands surveyed, both to settle disputes among present landholders and to be able to make future land
grants. Overriding these concerns were the larger problems of the lack of
new settlers for the colony, Armstrong's unease with the Acadian attitude
towards his administration, and, after 1734, growing international tension
between the European powers.

The matter of the food and fuel supplies for the garrison was a peren-
nial headache, not so much because of scarcity but because the greater
part was bought from the Acadians. Delivery of the goods was often slow
because of transportation problems and there were disputes between garrison and settler over the price of foodstuffs and firewood.[7] Immediately
after Philipps had left Annapolis Royal, Armstrong wrote to the deputies at
Grand Pré and Beaubassin to announce that His Majesty had appointed
him to the post of governor. Armstrong then requested that he be sold
"two hundred Quinteals of Biskett and Sixty Hogsheads of pease" as well as
"Sheep and Black Cattle." He concluded his letter by hoping that there
would be no difficulty over a matter "what may prove of so Great advantage
to Yourselves."[8] The British military presence, like the earlier French one,
was an economic asset for the Acadian farmers.

Armstrong, of course, faced not only the question of the day-to day provisioning of the garrison but also that of the long-term needs of the soldiers and the fort. On his return to London, Philipps escaped censure in

the matter of his regiment's victualling debts but his care for the troops under his command was mean-minded. It is recorded that he ordered the issue of men's clothing to be restricted to twenty-six outfits for companies whose strength was thirty-one.[9] As Maxwell Sutherland remarks, Philipps can "at best be charged with miserliness ... and he falls under a suspicion of building a personal fortune at the expense of his troops and council."[10] If the actual supplies for the troops were barely adequate, the possibility of more men being sent to the colony was non-existent. Armstrong, until his death in 1739, never had more than five companies of men at Annapolis Royal and four at Canso, for total of some 278 men, 155 stationed at Annapolis Royal and 123 at Canso.[11] At much the same time, the French garrison at Louisbourg consisted of six companies of sixty men each for approximately 336 in all, as well as a Swiss company of 120 men, for a total of around 460.[12] In 1741 reinforcements brought the military strength at Louisbourg to some 710 men.[13] The dilapidated state of the fort itself at Annapolis Royal, and of the military buildings at Canso, was somewhat mitigated by supplies and workmen sent out to repair these establishments by the Board of Ordnance in the fall of 1733. Armstrong recorded the arrival of a ship "with cannon, carriages, shot and other ordnance stores, with bedding and clothes for the poor men."[14] He went on to emphasize how much the consignments had meant for morale, "they having also sent some artificers, with directions to their storekeeper to put the garrison and outworks in repair, which at present wants it much."

Meanwhile, the détente between England and France, which had come into being in the 1720s with the arrival of Cardinal Fleury as the major political force in France and of Robert Walpole to a similar position in Great Britain, held until the end of the decade. Relations between the states did become frayed once France became embroiled in the War of the Polish Succession in 1734.[15] Nevertheless, there was no major military clash between France and Great Britain in North America or elsewhere until 1744. The British garrisons at Annapolis Royal, Canso, and Placentia served, above all, as agencies of government, dealing with matters of trade, order in the settlements, and other questions usually regulated by other institutional structures.

This absence in Nova Scotia of any form of an elected assembly, what the Massachusetts governor of the time, Jonathan Belcher, called an " an easy civil government," has been cited as a major reason for the failure to attract Protestant emigrants to the colony. Belcher believed that "the government of the paultry Province of Nova Scotia has been but one constant source of tyranny ... God deliver me and mine from the government of soldiers."[16] While this may have been a determining factor in the decision of some New Englanders not to move to Nova Scotia, it is unlikely that it would have been a factor of similar importance among those brought from Europe under various auspices – universal manhood suffrage was not a feature of any European jurisdiction at this time. It is more likely that, as has

been already mentioned in a previous chapter, the major stumbling block
was the appalling bureaucracy of the authorities in London in dealing with
migration initiatives for Nova Scotia. But there is no doubt that the attitude of Massachusetts towards Annapolis Royal was less than helpful in
this, and also in other matters, even if that attitude was rarely a matter of
officially backed policy. As George Rawlyk points out, "from 1718 until the
early months of 1744, the policies adopted by the Massachusetts General
Court, as well as matters publicly discussed in debate, clearly reflected the
widespread indifference in the colony towards Nova Scotia, especially that
part of the colony excluding Canso ... the only mention of the Annapolis
Royal region during these years in the Journals of the House of Representatives was on November 11th, 1724."[17] On that day, the House refused a
request from the lieutenant governor of Nova Scotia for thirty men to aid
in the defence of Annapolis Royal.[18]

The idea, put forward so eloquently by Brebner in his first major work,
that Massachusetts was always the crucial influence in Nova Scotia affairs –
that the latter was New England's outpost, in the sense of being attached
to British interests as conveyed through and by Massachusetts – arose from
his vision of the development of British activities in North America. The
very fact that *New England's Outpost* still serves as a useful introduction to
the history of Nova Scotia and to Acadian history seventy-five years after it
was written is a testimony to the meticulousness nature of Brebner's
research and the care with which he argued his case. However, Brebner's
interpretation of events was written without the benefit of later research,
not only into the intricacies of intercolonial relationships but also into the
imperial priorities of British government policies in the eighteenth century. The questions Brebner brought to the past were shaped by the circumstances of his life and times. The impact of the First World War, of patterns
of international relations, and, above all, of relationships between nation-
states informed his writing. He was interested in the politics of power in
the light of nineteenth- and early-twentieth-century European experience.
Brebner's context for his study was his perception of the ways in which
European international relations affected Nova Scotian politics and he
considered that the relationship between the New England colonies and
the government in London was the linchpin of British policy in North
America.[19] In essence, Brebner wrote about the impact of the Acadian situation on the policies of others, rather than considering the impact of
external events on the Acadians. As a result, understandably, he paid only
brief attention to the continued impact of New England fishermen on the
development of Canso and the considerable trade that Massachusetts
developed with Louisbourg. Nor did he spend much time on Acadian-
British relations within Nova Scotia during the 1730s.

The very excellence of Brebner's work had the unfortunate effect of discouraging other scholars from considering Acadian-Nova Scotian affairs.
There seemed little to add to his clearly told account, and so questions

about the eighteenth-century experience of the Acadians, which Brebner did not see as relevant to matters he wished to investigate, were, for many years, neglected. But, while the development of British policy within Nova Scotia and the Acadians' adaptation to being British subjects during this decade had little impact on Anglo-French affairs, they did shape profoundly the response of both the British Nova Scotian administrators and the Acadians to the years of war that followed.

The decade and a half between Philipps's final visit to Nova Scotia and the outbreak of war in 1744 saw an extraordinary gap develop between the lifestyle of the British in Nova Scotia and that of the Acadians, a gap that also led to a considerable difference of attitude, between British official and Acadian settler, as to what the Acadian response to being sworn subjects of the British crown involved. Murdoch writes eloquently of the situation of the British in the 1720s and 1730s. He describes "a government without citizens or subjects to whom it could look for support, – a fortress whose ramparts and lodgings were tumbling down or washed away by autumn rains, – a province without any revenue and but little commerce, and a garrison whose supplies of clothing, pay or provisions, were scanty and precarious, – a small military, perched upon a strip of land, environed by races hostile in many respects and themselves not too friendly or confiding in one another ..."[20] He goes on to detail a litany of troubles: "the decay of the barracks and storehouses, the embezzlement of regimental funds, the wrecked condition of the provincial vessel the William August, the jealousies that kept Armstrong unhappy, and made him angry with Cosby and Winniett, the grievance attending the collecting seigneurial dues and the ever recurring discord with the missionaries ..." Those serving in Annapolis Royal were well aware of the lack of an English-speaking population, the failure of one immigration scheme after another, and the relative stagnation of British trade with the colony. Their frustration was increased with the obvious development of the Acadian settlements, which flourished demographically, economically, and socially.

The growth in the Acadian population was plain. Unfortunately, the end of the French regime in the colony meant the virtual end of the nominal census, which had been compiled for the population since 1671. After 1714, the data available comes from documents compiled for purposes other than demographic information, such as letters on general topics between administrators, lists of the men who signed an oath, and estimations based upon studies of fertility. As we have seen, between 1714 and 1748, even the most conservative historians estimate the population to have grown from 2,528 to 10,500,[21] while I have suggested a figure of between 7,000 and 8,000 by the end of the 1730s[22] and well over 11,000 by 1748.[23]

For the British, and particularly for Armstrong and the Council, the expansion of the population raised questions about the future of the province and particularly about land tenure. The issue of land tenure, as was the case with most matters that Armstrong would raise with the Board of Trade, had been an issue for all his predecessors. For more than twenty years, those sent to govern Nova Scotia colony had sent missive after missive to the Lords of Trade, to the Admiralty, and to the secretary of state asking for directions about the matter. Only the most unhelpful responses came. The question was complicated by the matter of timber reserves for the Royal Navy and the lack of a proper survey of the colony, both major factors in the failure of immigration schemes, both matters insoluble without directives from London. Meanwhile, the expansion of established Acadian settlements continued, as did the creation of new Acadian hamlets along the Saint John, in the Memramcook/Petitcodiac area, and along the coastline between Baie Verte and Tatamagouche.[24] Given the means at their disposal, there was little that the officials at Annapolis Royal could do to exercise control over this expansion.

Armstrong might have been opinionated, prejudiced, cantankerous, capricious, and a constant trial to his companions at Annapolis Royal, but he had an original mind and a considerable, if undisciplined, intelligence. As his biographer has written, his reports to London were "a mixture of shrewd assessment and administrative myopia, of objectivity and gross exaggeration."[25] On the question of land tenure, Armstrong outlined his view of the difficulties it raised in one of his first dispatches to the Lords of Trade, on 5 October 1731. In a marvellously breathless sentence, the lieutenant governor brought together questions of Acadian land rights, problems of colonization, the links he perceived between Acadians and Louisbourg, and the penury of his administration. He began by acknowledging that, since the Acadians "have taken the Oath of Fidelity," they were "thereby admitted to the privileges and liberty of subjects."[26] But, he continued, "I beg Your Lordships to inform me how far they or their Seigniors are entitled to lands abandoned ever since the reduction of this place, and other waste and uncultivated lands to which especially since taking the oath they lay claim, and plead the treaty of Utrecht, tho' for these many Years noways cultivated or improven, which if they are to enjoy without a limitation of certain conditions, the Country will in a great measure remain a wilderness." Armstrong then mentioned what was obviously a major consideration: "and there will be scarce one acre left, especially in this place, to be granted to Protestant subjects, who are much desired, and for whom room might be found here, if these Seigniors did not thus pretend a right to the greatest part, if not the whole Province." At this point, clearly, it was not only the claims of Acadian landowners that bothered Armstrong but also their relationship with the British government, for he went on (still as part of the same sentence) to point out that such Acadian claims were made "without complying with such conditions as may be naturally conjectured, that first moved his most Christian Majesty to make such concessions." This state of affairs, Armstrong believed, "if not remedied, will render this part of the Province a continual expence, and of no advantage to his Majesty, for whose use, there is not an inhabitant that pays a farthing rent towards the defraying of necessary charges [for administration] that attends all governments, as to which the gentlemen of the Council, who are daily employed and harassed with their affairs (there being no other Court of Judicature) do and not without reason complain, in whose behalf I humbly recommend to Your Lordships, to send us a table of fees, both in that respect, and the giving of grants, for wax and other kinds of stationary ware here, is very dear and expensive, and its hoped than an annual supply thereof may be ordered us from Britain."

In the rest of the dispatch, in sentences as convoluted but mercifully shorter, Armstrong elaborated on the issues that he raised, and, as he did so, it became evident that his attitude to the Acadians was one of exasperation rather than contemptuous dislike. He considered them "a very ungovernable people and growing very numerous," but he accepted that the best, if not the only, "method of treating with them upon any subject, is by deputies," through men with some standing in their own settlements. Because of this nascent political activity, Armstrong went on to propose a radical step: he asked "if their [sic] might be a small Assembly constituted [so that] they [the Acadians] in time may be perhaps brought through their own free and voluntary acts to pay a greater obedience to the Government, and contribute to its supports." The sentence continues with a further discussion of the idea of bringing the Acadians directly into the institutions of the government of the colony, suggesting that "as Civil Magistrates are much wanted, I entreat Your Lordships directions for appointing at some justices of the Peace, and other inferior Officers amongst them, to act in things especially that may relate to themselves, with such decorum as may oblige them still further to depend upon the Government by giving us information of the behaviour and clandestine proceedings of the rest."[27] The Lords of Trade took until 2 November 1732 to answer, and their reply did not reach Armstrong until well into 1733. In it they made no comment on the suggestion that an assembly might be established. Their Lordships' response to the suggestion of appointing Acadians as justices of the peace was to sidestep the barrier of religious confession, expressing the wish that "an English gentleman lived near, as no one can be a Justice of the Peace without taking the regular oaths."[28]

At the conclusion of his dispatch, Armstrong dealt with an issue that was much more immediate for him than the disposition of waste land and the payment of judicial fees. Before he received any direction from the Lords of Trade, he was forced to act on the confusing matter of requests for land, a question that had not been helped by grants that Governor Philipps had recommended to the Council but had not yet made. These particular requests were mainly from Acadians "for small plots in and adjacent to this Town for Houses and Gardens, and others for Tracts fit for Farms, at Mines, but especially by several Young people who have settled themselves, some years before, at ... Chippody ..."Armstrong was in favour of making these grants because he thought that it would help him to disentangle the rights claimed by those Acadians who had left the colony for brief periods of time since 1710, some of whom, he believed, paid quit-rents to absentee landlords in "Dominions of France" (probably Louisbourg). There was also at least one petition at this time from an English inhabitant, James O'Neale, for land at "Shickanetau" (Chignecto).[29] In a second dispatch, dated only two weeks later, Armstrong referred to something that even further complicated land tenure in the colony. The Acadians were, in his view, "a litigious sort of people, and so ill-natured to one another, as daily to encroach upon their neighbours properties, which occasions continual complaints ...."[30] In sum, the problems that Armstrong outlined, in his order of priority, were Acadian financial support for judicial services, quit-rents, the granting of new lands, and the settlement of disputes over property boundaries.

Armstrong relied on institutions of government that had been developed for Virginia, a very different society in a very different political and geographical environment. As Thomas Barnes has remarked, Virginia was to prove "a fungible model, a convenient device, and a security blanket for the governor and council in ambiguous and contentious situations."[31] Thus, Armstrong and his councillors solved the question of a quorum for the Council, often a problem because of the workload of its members, by adapting "the 7th Article of the Instructions for the Governance of Virginia where three Councillors upon Extraordinary Emergencys make a Quorum."[32] Armstrong worked not only with minimal direction from his superiors but with limited personal and material resources. He was never able to appoint as many civilians to the Council as he wished, because of the small number of British settlers in the colony. The officers he appointed were also carrying out a full complement of military duties running the garrison. Armstrong had some precedents to guide him, particularly the work of Doucett, who, as lieutenant governor during the years 1724 to 1726, had presided over a fair amount of judicial action brought before Council. In the early summer of 1725 there were six consecutive meetings which dealt only with litigation, nine cases in all.[33] After 1731, however, the judicial work increased considerably. As for the issue of the oath of allegiance, no matter how confused both British administrator and Acadian settler might be over what had been achieved by Philipps on this question, one thing is clear: the matter was removed, at least for the time being, from its dominant position as the major political issue within the colony. Time and energy could now be given to matters that had been neglected over the past decade. What faced Armstrong and the Council was the task of establishing due process in both criminal matters and in civil cases and seeing that judgments reached in both areas were carried out. At the same time, since there was no assembly, they also had the task of legislating by general orders when the situation so required.

The extent to which this work demanded the cooperation of the Acadian settlers, not only through their deputies but also from the settler population as a whole, has not been much emphasized. The political importance of the oath of allegiance has encouraged the idea that the relations between the deputies and the British officials were ones of continuous argument. It has obscured the degree to which Acadian-British collaboration in other areas not only existed but was crucial both for the everyday functioning of the Acadian communities and for the British administration of the colony. As the minutes of the Council meetings and the letter-books of governors and lieutenant governors show, there was a general acceptance by the Acadians of the framework for civil life brought into being by the British officials. The position of considerable influence and authority held by the deputies was a major reason why this was so. They were elected by the villagers, even if finally selected by the British, with remuneration (intermittently) provided by the villages and payment for attendance at Council hearings (intermittently) provided by the British. They were the only police force that was available to impose the authority of the Council in criminal matters. It was the deputies who took the necessary steps to ensure public order in cases of assault and robbery and it was they who took action against those who refused to appear before Council when called, or disobeyed orders issued by that body, such as the general regulations governing the branding of sheep pastured in common.[34] Their work could not have been carried out had they not had support from within the Acadian villages. It was perhaps fortunate that criminal cases were few and the Council never had to face a murder charge in the Acadian community.[35]

Armstrong tried hard to ensure that the deputies chosen had some backing from the settlements they represented. In the summer of 1738, Armstrong responded to complaints that some deputies had concerning the "expense and loss of time in the fulfilment of their duties and also that they were chosen by Govr. Philipps and not by the inhabitants."[36] He immediately ordered an interim selection to be made, asking the present deputies to bring together the inhabitants and separate them into "eight equal divisions," so that each division might choose "an honest discreet person" to represent them until the annual election of deputies, held always on 11 October, Sundays excepted.[37] The choice had to be reported in writing and signed "by at least a majority of the inhabitants." As to the expenses that the deputies incurred, Armstrong suggested that each division should "provide for the deputy's expenses before they proceed to such election." Armstrong always emphasized that the deputies served only with the approval and consent of the governor and Council but he was well aware that he could not govern without the assistance of the deputies. He understood that the deputies would not be able to provide the services he required unless they had the support and confidence of the settlers.

As a result, the deputies formed the sinews of the civil administration of the colony. First and foremost, they were the channel of communication for Council orders and proclamations. They were the disseminators of official information, whether it be about the regulation of the size of the half-bushel for measuring grain[38] or the matter of marking property boundaries.[39] At the same time, the deputies were those who oversaw compliance with Council regulations and orders. They acted in many ways as constables, being given orders, for example, to settle a dispute over hay between Alexandre Le Borgne de Belle-Isle and Charles Richards at Minas by actually returning cut hay from Richards to Le Borgne and summoning Richards to appear before the Council.[40] Further, the deputies were given administrative duties, such as overseeing the maintenance of roads. In 1740 Mascarene ordered the deputies of Annapolis Royal to make every *habitant* contribute to repairing the public highway along the Annapolis River, pointing out that it was used by everyone and thus everyone "must, according to custom, contribute in proportion, material, labor, or carriage, or else make a payment."[41] The deputies also undertook tasks usually given to local magistrates, such as finding facts in property disputes[42] and settling suits referred to them by the Council.[43]

Another matter that sometimes fell to a deputy was that of collecting quit-rents. The payment of quit-rents was important not because of the amount of money it involved but because such payment was a material acknowledgment that one held the land "of" the person to whom the sum was paid.[44] Mascarene, indeed, wrote in the 1740s that "the trouble of gathering the same was scarcely answered by what was received, and it was claimed of the inhabitants more to show their dependence on the Crown than for any profit that accrued from the sum gathered."[45] Difficulties had arisen because of confusion between the quit-rent, as it was instituted by the British in Nova Scotia, and the seigneurial dues that had been paid over the years by some of the settlers to those to whom the French crown had granted extensive estates. Neither payment was particularly onerous, seigneurial dues usually being no more than a couple of bushels of wheat and two capons for a considerable holding.[46] In the instructions of the Lords of Trade to Governor Philipps in 1719, the quit-rent for new grants of land was to be one shilling for every fifty acres granted.[47] Eleven years later, Philipps bundled together all payments that he believed the Acadians owed and ordered that "all the quitt rents, homages, and other services, formerly paid by the inhabitants at Mines and other places up the bay of Fundy, should then be paid to his sacred Britannick Majesty, as their own lord Paramount and sole and only seignior of the province."[48] There was an immediate reaction on the part of the great-granddaughter of Charles de Saint-Étienne de La Tour, Agathe Campbell, the widow of a British officer then living in Annapolis Royal. That same year, 1730, she presented a petition to the Board of Trade claiming that she was the sole heir to rights granted to her family by the terms of the decree granted by Louis XIV in 1703. She requested compensation for the abrogation of her seigneurial rights.[49] Despite Philipps's considerable misgivings about her claims, her petition was granted. Secretary Popple had argued that Campbell's rights should be purchased in order for the British to be able to grant land without encumbrances in the colony.[50] In 1734 the Board of Trade paid her £2,000 for her "Right of seignory" but gave her liberty to collect rents that were owed to her from previous years.[51] What Philipps had achieved with his order, and the subsequent purchase of Campbell's rights by the Board of Trade, was an affirmation of the British crown as the sole source of property rights in the colony.

The collection of the quit-rents thus became a matter of importance, despite the small sums involved. The rents for the Annapolis district for 1732 and 1733 amounted to just over £11.[52] In the 1730s the majority of settlers paid in kind, bushels of wheat at fifty pence the quarter-bushel, chickens and pullets at eighteen pence a piece, and partridges at sixpence each. Philipps had appointed only one individual for this task as a rent collector, Alexandre Bourg, *dit* Belle-Humeur, who, as notary, or *procureur du roi*, was commissioned to collect all monies due to His Majesty from "Mines and Piziquid, Cobequid and Chignecto." He was to report twice a year and to be paid for his labours; his compensation was to be three shillings per pound sterling collected.[53] Bourg does not appear to have been a deputy. Nor does Jean Duon, whom Armstrong appointed as the rent collector for the town of Annapolis Royal. But Prudent Robichaud, one of the deputies for the Annapolis River region, was appointed by Armstrong as the rent collector for that area.[54] All were ordered to "keep an exact rent roll and a just account." By the end of the decade, there was a considerable increase in the number of those who paid the small sums in coinage.[55] This trend continued and the quit-rents paid in the 1750s, up to and including the spring of 1755, were almost all paid in coin.[56]

That the Acadians accepted in principle the authority of the British over the disposition of land is further evidenced by their use of the judicial services provided by the Council, where receipts given for the payment of quit-rent were cited as evidence of ownership.[57] Between 1731 and 1736, the Council heard ninety-nine cases of civil litigation, dealing mostly with questions of property limits and wills. Of these, seventy-one were cases between Acadians and four were between the Acadians and the British. The Council minutes provide short accounts of the disputes, the names of the plaintiffs as well as those the names of who represented the plaintiffs, and the action decided upon.[58] None of those who gave judgment was a lawyer, although the garrison surgeon, Skene, a Scotsman, was said to have "read in Civil Law."[59] The conduct of the Council, when acting as a judicial body in civil suits, was informal but not summary. The parties were given time to appear and hearings delayed if one or other was absent. The Council allowed those who appeared to have help in presenting their cases or defending their actions. It heard oral testimony and accepted written evidence. The councillors also used the deputies to seek out more information, which could involve either the discovery of further witnesses to sales of property[60] or general knowledge of "the Ancient Inhabitants"[61] of the village about the pretensions of the plaintiffs.

One of the questions that members of Council had to solve was what particular rule of law should be followed. Barnes has pointed out that "it was clear in English jurisprudence, following the law of nations, that the king might impose upon a conquered people what law he chose, subject only to the condition that until he did so, if the conquered were Christian, their existing law would obtain."[62] The constitution of Virginia, of course, had established a legal system and its laws were an amalgam of English common law, some acts of the English Parliament, and acts passed by the Virginia assembly.[63] Nova Scotia councillors did not reach that far for grounds on which to base their decisions: their judgments rested upon a mixture of French customary law and English common law. They acknowledged title rights based upon French documents issued more than fifty years earlier.[64] Further, the Council sought to understand what the French custom was in matters such as the right for relatives to have the first refusal of family property sold on someone's death. This was the course taken in the settlement of a dispute over the conditions of sale of land, at Port Royal, among the Robichaud and Hebert families in 1732.[65] There is no doubt that, once established in the role, the Council gained the trust of the Acadians in the settlement of disputes over land ownership.[66]

This picture of administrative reasonableness, however, is not the whole story of Acadian-British relationships between 1731 and 1744. There were also the inevitable clashes between the Council and deputies when the latter did not act with dispatch on the orders they were given.[67] More serious than disagreements of this type, which occur among any such group of judicial figures and those responsible for carrying out their orders, was the issue of land grants held in the more distant regions of the colony. This issue first emerged over lands settled by the Acadians in the Memramcook-Shepody area. A dispute between the Landry and Leblanc families over property in these river valleys came before Council in March 1732.[68] The Council decided then that there was no proof of any right of settlement previously established and refused to acknowledge the claims of either family. It appears that the 1703 decrees of Louis XIV for the settlement of this region were not brought forward. This is a rare occasion of carelessness on the part of the Acadians, who had a habit of bringing faded legal documents to court to prove their claims. The Council took the position that, until some sort of survey had been made of the area, work done by the settlers "is to be at their Risque," in other words, the land so settled could be claimed as crown land and the settlers dispossessed.

But this judgment was based on something more than just opposition to settling Acadian claims for land settled but not surveyed. There is no doubt that the British officials were concerned with the future of the colony and the extent to which there would be land available for a large influx of Protestant settlers, if and when such appeared. Thus, in the fall of the same year, an appeal from settlers on the Saint John River to be given title to their lands was met by procrastination.[69] The Council accepted oaths of allegiance from the settlers but granted no title to the lands claimed. Four years later, in the summer of 1736, representatives of the fifteen families were berated for a general lack of respect for the British authorities.[70] In 1738 Armstrong ordered a report on the Shepody, Memramcook, and Petitcodiac area because persons "have taken possession of and improved large portions of the crown lands, disobeyed repeated orders and defied the government, to the prejudice of one another and causing 'great Confusion and Disorder among the Inhabitants.'"[71] Mascarene, in a dispatch written immediately after he had assumed control of the administration in 1740, stated the grounds on which he thought Armstrong had acted. Mascarene pointed out that Armstrong's administration refused to give new grants to the Acadians because it had been believed that such grants "of unappropriated lands should be given to Protestant subjects only."[72] But "the increase of the French inhabitants" has resulted in their settling themselves "on the skirts of this Province ... notwithstanding proclamations and orders to the contrary ..." This analysis, however, brushed over the rights of Acadians whose settlements were made quite legally under the French regime in the early years of the eighteenth century.

Fundamentally, the issue turned on the rights of the Acadians as colonists, as settlers who were rooted in the area, and whether they had an unlimited right to expand their settlements into the neighbouring countryside unless such land had been specifically granted to others. The British believed that they held the same authority over Nova Scotian territory that they did over that of any other British colony in North America, including the right to oversee and approve settlement. As well, the British considered the Acadians as subjects who owed duties to the British crown and who were notoriously unwilling to assume those duties. The Acadians, on the other hand, believed that while the British had acquired the territory of Nova Scotia in 1713, this did not mean that the Acadians had become subjects without rights. On the contrary, the Acadians were convinced that their relationship to the British was based on legal agreements, agreements that granted them not only religious rights but freedom of migration and property rights as well. The British regarded these agreements as privileges accorded and expected the Acadians to be properly grateful for the magnanimity shown them.

By 1740, a generation after the conquest of 1710, the majority of the Acadian population had been born British subjects and had experienced only British administration. But this meant little in terms of any emotional attachment to British interests in the area. Outside the Annapolis Royal region, there was little social contact between Acadian and British during these years. Even around the fort, social relationships between garrison and settler seem to have been minimal. There is no body of evidence, either from British sources or from the French ecclesiastical records, which suggests anything more than business and government interchanges between the two populations. The Council minutes record disputes, such as that between René Leblanc and a certain widow Johnson, over the possession of a house in town,[73] but there are few references to meetings between Acadian settlers and the British, apart from those concerning the provisioning of the garrison. The marriages between Acadians and the newcomers that are known to us were those of the elite, for example, Agathe de Saint-Étienne de La Tour with Edward Bradstreet and Marie-Madeleine Maisonnat with William Winniett. Three of the Winniett-Maisonnat daughters married men of British background who served on the Council.[74] There may have been other marriages but the lack of any sort of written record suggests that they were few in number. There was no major socialization of the Acadians to ways and customs other than their own. Further, there was no influx of new ways of farming or fishing into Acadian life, no new products for the Acadian home. What new commercial opportunities there were came from the French presence at Louisbourg. And, of course, the difference in religious practices served to reinforce the gulf between the two societies.

The British administration at Annapolis Royal had always been somewhat sceptical of the extent to which the Acadians would become fully reconciled to British rule. During the late 1720s and 1730s, when relationships between Great Britain and France, both in North America and Europe, were tranquil, this attitude resulted in little more than wariness in relying upon the Acadians to obey Council orders. After 1734, as the war over the succession to the Polish throne spread, the years of peace, managed by Walpole on one side of the Channel and Cardinal Fleury on the other, gave place to growing tensions between the two countries. At this point, what the Nova Scotian officials reported as "disaffection to His Majesty's government" on the part of the Acadians became a common complaint and dispatches sent to the Lords of Trade began to emphasize how troublesome the Acadians were. Philipps now described them as being "rather a pest and incumbrance than of advantage to the country, being a proud, lazy, obstinate and untractable people, unskilful in the methods of agriculture, nor will [they] be led into a better way of thinking and (what is worse) greatly disaffected to the government."[75] On the face of it, Philipps, now resident in London, in common with Armstrong and the Council, wanted the Acadians to be a docile and obedient populace, who would accept with respect, and promptly fulfil, all requests from the British officials. Since this subservience was not forthcoming, the Acadians' actions, which were very much the reaction of colonial populations in general to those in authority over them, were seen as disloyalty. The complaints of the officials of New France about "the spirit of independence" of the French Canadians are similar to those written about the Acadians in Annapolis Royal.[76] What gave an added edge to the Annapolis complaints, however, was the growing apprehension of renewed fighting in the region. A detailed request for a report on the situation of Nova Scotia in 1734 emphasized military matters and the reply the Lords of Trade received was uniformly gloomy. The colony's administrators were asked about the strength of the militia, to which the response was: "No militia established, the french Inhabitants being all Papists."77 The question concerning the Mi'kmaq was answered with the report that those tribes within the colony were for "the most part inclin'd to ye French Interest & may when joyn'd together make about five hundred fighting men." In the answers given to queries about the "Strength of your neighbouring Europeans, French or Spanish" and the effect such people had on the population of Nova Scotia, there is a sense of being encircled by powerful enemies. The officials in Nova Scotia estimated that French forces in Canada amounted to ten thousand men, that the fortress at Louisbourg was "almost impregnable," and that the regular troops on Île Royale consisted of "of Six hundred Men & their Militia a thousand at least ..." As to the extent of French influence on the Acadians, there was nothing but bad news. It was believed that the "Inhabitants being of ye same Nation and Religion with them," little reliance could be placed on "their Oath of Allegiance taken to Ye Crown of Great Brittain." Thus, "in Case of a rupture at any time between ye two Crowns [the French] may easily make themselves Masters of that Province in a few Hours."

The French officials in Louisbourg were equally nervous about the onset of war but much less sanguine about the chances of a swift French victory. Saint-Ovide, still governor of Île Royale, believed that the Acadians could not be relied upon as allies, "as uncertainty of success would keep them wavering."78 While he thought that both Canso and Annapolis Royal would be taken easily enough, Saint-Ovide had a shrewd appreciation that Massachusetts would be a determinant in any outbreak of hostilities, something that the Nova Scotian officials did not mention. Anglo-French tensions, both in Europe and in North America, subsided for a while in 1735, and, on the surface, relations between Louisbourg and Annapolis Royal returned to polite bickering. But in both places, the question of how the Acadians would act if war came to the region was a matter of concern and debate. On the whole, the British were more doubtful of the Acadians' non-combatant status than the French. The latter felt that the Acadians must have a sense of community with the interests of France.

The British considered that it was, above all, the influence of the priests that kept the settlers emotionally distant from their rule. There were a number of reasons for this view, one of them being the place that Protestant and Catholic belief played in state politics. By the 1730s, religious intolerance was waning among the different Christian confessions in Europe but it still played a role in both domestic and international politics. This was particularly true in Anglo-French relationships. The French government was not pleased by the shelter that Great Britain provided for

Huguenot refugees, such as the Mascarene family. Great Britain was even more unhappy with the support that France gave to the Stuart line and its repeated attempts to overturn the Hanoverian succession. In Annapolis Royal, this general atmosphere of wariness was increased by the way in which priests were recruited to serve in Nova Scotia and by the fact that they were the spiritual advisers not only to the Acadians but also to the Mi'kmaq. French ecclesiastical authorities in France selected those sent to the colony, both those who were primarily responsible for work among the Mi'kmaq and those chosen to live as parish priests in Annapolis Royal, Minas, and the Beaubassin area. The larger part of their expenses were paid by the French and ecclesiastical jurisdiction was exercised over them sometimes through Louisbourg and sometimes via Quebec. Further, all priests were subjects of France, thus foreign visitors in Nova Scotia. Any priest who came to Nova Scotia was expected to appear before the authorities at Annapolis Royal and receive formal permission to minister solely to the spiritual needs of their flock.[79] On more than one occasion, however, priests were expelled for refusing to acknowledge British authority throughout the colony.[80] It was agreed, in principle, by the French secular authorities that the priests were not to concern themselves with temporal matters. In fact, in 1743 the minister of the Marine, the Comte de Maurepas, wrote Bishop Pontbriand of Quebec to point out that, for the welfare of the Acadians' religious life, the missionaries must conduct themselves "fittingly towards the English governor and other officers of the colony."[81] However, as the politics of the region grew more fraught, the line between temporal and spiritual matters tended to become blurred and the instructions of Maurepas were, if not totally ignored, certainly not followed with enthusiasm.

Already in 1729, Armstrong had described the difficulties he saw at first hand in Annapolis Royal. He wrote to London about the local incumbent, Breslay, "the Popish priest ... assuming to himself the authority of a judge in civil affairs, and employing his spiritual censures to force [the Acadians] to a submission."[82] Partly because of such actions on the part of some of the clergy, Armstrong gave considerable support to the judicial functions of Council. However, it is clear that at least some temporal matters were judged by the parish priests. Just over a decade later, Mascarene exchanged letters with a Sulpician priest, Jean-Baptiste Desenclaves, at that time serving the congregation of Minas, about the problem of "the Missionaries" who make "themselves the Sovereign judges & arbitrators of all causes amongst the People ..."[83] Mascarene reiterated the fear, common among Protestants, that the priests would use the "the Power to grant or withhold of pardon of his sins" to persuade the Acadians to accept ecclesiastical judgment of temporal matters.[84] While anti-clericalism and fear of the abuse by the clergy of their spiritual powers was widespread within British North America at this time, these attitudes were also to be found among the French. For the authorities of Île Royale and Quebec, the priests were a mixed blessing, certainly sympathetic to the French cause but by no means under the control of the French colonial administration. De Pensens, stationed at Louisbourg at this time but overseeing the attempt to establish French settlement on Île Saint-Jean, wrote that many of those sent as missionary priests were better suited to a seminary. "These gentlemen," he remarked, "when they are left alone imagine they have a tiara upon their head and desire to be out and out little bishops, they wish to be supreme in spiritual as well as temporal matters, and if any one resists them it is a crime of treason against the Divine Being."[85]

In assessing the extent to which Acadian opinion was moulded by their clergy, it is well to bear in mind that the priests were few in number and not all of one mind, and that, during their sojourn in the colony, they sometimes changed their attitude to the British and/or French authorities, depending on the circumstances of the moment. There were never more than five priests, at any one time, working within the colony and usually only three or four.[86] All, even those attached to Annapolis Royal, had extensive parishes, difficult to oversee and demanding a great deal of physical stamina to serve. Several were criticized by their superiors, both secular and religious, for being far too friendly with the British. Maurepas, writing to the bishop of Quebec after François Du Pont Duvivier's attack on Annapolis Royal in 1744, complained that Desenclaves had "informed the English governor exactly of all that he could learn of the proceedings of the French and exhorted his parishioners to be loyal to the king of England."[87] Others, such as Jean-Louis Le Loutre, who arrived in Louisbourg in 1738 and was appointed missionary to the Mi'kmaq that year, wholeheartedly supported France. Before the outbreak of war in 1744, Le Loutre remained on cordial enough terms with Annapolis Royal; however, once hostilities began, he became, without question, an agent of the French government.[88]

The last years of Armstrong's administration were filled with rumours of war. The War of the Polish Succession was essentially a dynastic quarrel between Bourbon and Hapsburg, a continuance of the rivalries of earlier decades. On a number of occasions between 1731 and the conclusion of peace in 1738, it seemed as if Great Britain would be involved, but Walpole, and his supporters, managed to resist the pressure for direct intervention. As the decade ended, however, dissension between Great Britain and Spain arose over British trade with Spanish colonies in the Caribbean, especially over the activities of the South Sea Company. War was declared between Great Britain and Spain in October 1739.[89] Given the recent alliance between France and Spain, there seemed every likelihood of war between France and Great Britain. By the time the news reached Annapolis Royal of the Anglo-Hispanic conflict in early June 1740, Armstrong had committed suicide.[90] He had been found in his room, on the morning of 17 December 1739, with five wounds in his chest. A nineteenth-century account, that of Murdoch, reported that his sword was "lying carelessly by him." Murdoch also reported that his fellow officers held a "jury of inquest, and [that] they brought in a verdict of lunacy."[91] The possibility of murder is not discussed in the surviving official reports.[92]

Mascarene took over control of the colony in early April 1740; he was now fifty-five. While he had been associated with the British government of Nova Scotia since 1710, he had spent a fair proportion of the past thirty years in Massachusetts. He had established his family home in Boston and, since 1720, had spent more than half his time there.[93] Partly as a result of this, he was challenged for the position of lieutenant governor by John Adams, who had also been present at the capture of Port Royal in 1710 and had remained in Nova Scotia ever since. Now "in his sixty-eight year," Adams sought the presidency of the Council and the post of lieutenant governor. Mascarene, however, was unanimously selected for the former position by the Council members – with the exception of Adams himself.[94] Mascarene received his appointment as lieutenant governor in August 1740, but this was not the end of his troubles, both with his fellow members of Council and with officers of the garrison.[95] Cosby was the senior military officer in the colony and, it might be recalled, also Philipps's brother-in-law. Mascarene, however, by virtue of his appointment as the lieutenant governor, was commander of His Majesty's forces in Nova Scotia and thus superior to Cosby, although his junior on the military rolls. Until Cosby's death on 7 January 1743, the two men continuously niggled at one another, punctiliously exchanging letters that attempted to make each other accept that the writer had the superior rank of command.[96] Philipps, safe in England, refused to issue more than vague orders, expressing the hope that Cosby would not be so foolish as to clash "with the Civil power, a Rock more Dangerous than Scylla or Charibdis to make a ship wreck on."[97] Throughout his administration, Mascarene would have to cope with those who were less than content with his leadership. After 1742, however, the infighting lessened a little.

The first four years of Mascarene's administration were the last years of peace that the region would experience until 1763. But rumours of war not only infected European policies and international relations; they also increased the anxieties of those living where war, if and when it came, would probably be fought. The strong possibility of an Anglo-French conflict was a subject that was almost always mentioned in the correspondence between London and Annapolis Royal, Versailles and Louisbourg, during these years. In early June 1740, Mascarene sent Newcastle an overview of the situation in the colony. He did not think that the Acadians "could be depended upon in the event of a war with France, it is as much as can be expected if they can be kept from acting against the government." He went on to say: "The Government of Cape Breton, by means of emissaries may stir them up, and to this their bigotry to the Romish religion may contribute." Mascarene pointed out that "there are not above half a dozen English families in the Province, except those belonging to the garrison here and at Canso, so that there are at least thirty French to one British subject, including officers and soldiers in both garrisons."[98] The slow pace of communication added to apprehensions of the lieutenant governor and he wrote to Newcastle in March 1741 that "we have no news from Europe later than July last, nor from our neighbouring government of New England since last October, so that we are entirely ignorant of any transactions in relation to war or peace."[99]

Mascarene had sketched his ambition for his administration in a dispatch he sent to Newcastle on 15 November 1740. "Since I have had the honour to preside here," he wrote, "my study has been to make the French inhabitants sensible of the difference there is between the British and french governments, by administering impartial justice to them, and in all other respects treating them with leniety and humanity, without yielding anything wherein His majesty's honor or interest were concerned."[100] Behind this policy was a strong belief that the Acadians were, indeed, British subjects, however imperfect their behaviour might be, and that the matter of the oath of allegiance had been settled ten years before. In one of his earliest letters to the deputies at Minas, written in May 1740, Mascarene urged them not to take any action that might then "become Suspected [by] the Government under whose Subjection they are and to which they have Taken an Oath of fidelity."[101] When all was said and done, the Acadians were no more rebellious than the populace of New York and Boston, who were given to much more serious rioting against government authority. Nor were the Acadians any more recalcitrant than their contemporaries in Wales and the Scottish Highlands when it came to resisting cultural assimilation by the English.[102] Mascarene governed in an era when the majority of men and women were barred from direct participation in the constitutional political processes of the state and when the law bore heavily upon those without social status. As ever, successful civil administrators were those who tempered the assumptions of the age with an awareness of the need to govern with the general support of the governed, however this last was demonstrated.

Mascarene showed, throughout his administration, a clear appreciation of what he could not afford to yield in terms of control over the colony and what was unrealistic to require from the colonists. He was never in doubt of the right of Great Britain to govern Nova Scotia, as a result of the settlement of Utrecht, and he never hesitated to emphasize this right in his correspondence both with the priests and with the deputies. From the outset of his administration, Mascarene insisted that all priests recognize that they were in the colony as foreigners, on sufferance from His Majesty's government.[103] In 1741 he emphasized in a letter written to Father Charles de La Goudalie, then serving in the Minas Basin, that all "Missionarys Comeing to this Province" must "have the approbation of this government before They enter on the Function of their office." He continued: "It is a Prerogative I shall maintain to the utmost of my power As it is of absolute Necessity for the support of His Majesty's authority."[104] As he pointed out to the priests their civil status within the colony, Mascarene also continuously emphasized to the deputies the position of the Acadians as subjects of the king of England, living in a colony that "was transferred to him by the King of France."[105] His acceptance of the value of the oath of allegiance implied his acceptance of the non-combatant status of the Acadians but also his belief that they were, indeed, British subjects. He wrote to the deputies of Chignecto, on the eve of the outbreak of war: "I must inform you, that in the petition which you have presented to me, you make use of terms which require explanation: for thereon you say 'that you will adhere to the promises you have made to take up arms neither for nor against the King of Great Britain' ... In consequence of your oath you owe every obedience and every assistance to the King your Soverien; and you ought to take it a great favour that he does not compel you to take up arms."[106] Mascarene believed strongly that he would be able to bring the Acadians to a state of contentment with British rule, "to wean them from their old masters," although he admitted that "to do this effectually a considerable time will be required."[107]

Mascarene's attitude was a result, primarily, of his wide experience of life in France, Great Britain, and Massachusetts. This helped to form his judgment as to what he could expect from the Acadian population in terms of emotional attachment to the British government. It was significant, too, that he lived at a time when the serpentine coils of state nationalism were only in their infancy.[108] Further, he had served in a military that quite happily used mercenary troops, a practice that inevitably softened expressions of unbridled patriotic fervour. Finally, having experienced a policy of active religious intolerance on the part of Louis XIV's government, he was inclined to see diversity of opinion as something that must be accommodated. In 1739, on the eve of the Great Awakening in New England, he wrote to Abbé Claude de La Vernède de Saint-Poncy, then the parish priest of Minas, that "as long as there are men, there will be different opinions and sentiments on certain points. It is enough that the Churches, which are all members of the Universal church can agree on the fundamental points of the doctrine of Jesus Christ and do not impose on each other the terms of communion as being articles of faith."[109]

Above all, Mascarene worked with what he found in Nova Scotia and with his knowledge both of what aid could be expected from London and of the internal politics of Boston. Within two years of his appointment as lieutenant governor, Mascarene was confident enough of his control over the colony to write to Newcastle that "the frequent rumours we have had of War on the point of being declared against France, have not as yet made any alteration in the temper of the Inhabitants of this province, who appear in a good disposition of keeping to their oaths of fidelity and of submitting to the orders and regulations of this government for maintaining peace, except in the matter of settling themselves on unappropriated lands, which irregularly arises from the great increase of their Families."[110] This judgment as to the temper of the Acadians was Mascarene's sole reason for optimism. The military situation was deplorable, whether one considers the fortifications in place, the soldiers stationed there, or their armaments. Armstrong's dispatches requesting supplies and additional manpower had had no result. Murdoch wrote, a century later, that at this time "the officials in England seem to have slept over their American interests, and to have partially wakened up about once a year to remember the names of their colonial possessions – to look or rather yawn over the governor's despatches and sketch some answer, deciding nothing and doing next to nothing."[111] This view might be a little overstated – but not much.

Philipps himself, still resident in England, wrote to the Lords of Trade in the summer of 1740, deploring the defenceless state of the colony and urging the necessity of repairing the fortifications and finding out the precise level of ordnance in the colony.[112] One James Wibault, in a report sent to the War Office that same year, noted that the palisade set on the covered way "was of no use in the world but to keep the Cattle out of the Ditch." He went on to point out that, since there were no "casements or shelters, the men off Duty will when in their Bedds be exposed almost to as much danger as the men actually on duty."[113] In 1743 the Lords of Trade sent a circular to all British North American colonies, warning them to be on their guard against an outbreak of hostilities with France. In his answer, Mascarene described the parlous condition of the fortifications at Annapolis Royal and Canso. He pointed out that, because the fort and its buildings at Annapolis Royal were built mostly out of "earth of a sandy nature," it was "apt to tumble down in heavy rains or in thaws after frosty weather."[114] While some work had been done to the fortifications over the years, this had been mainly by "revestment of Timbers," which remedied "the evil but for a short space of time." Nothing of any significance had been done to the fortifications since its capture in 1710. Further, while Mascarene acknowledged that the Board of Ordnance had recently sent "Engineers and Artificers in order to build the Fort with Brick and Stone," no progress had been made with this project, for one reason or another, over the past two years. As for Canso, there was nothing there save "a Block house built of Timber by the Contribution of the fishermen who resort there and a few inhabitants settled in that place ... It cannot be expected that that place can make any considerable resistance against the force the people of Cape Breton may bring against it."

The condition of the soldiers was no better than that of the buildings. There were supposed to be four companies of thirty men at Canso: in fact there were no more than eighty-seven soldiers under the command of Captain Patrick Heron, of whom "one third was sick or lame."[115] At Annapolis Royal there ought to have been five hundred men in the garrison; there were no more than 150.[116] Writing to the regimental agent, King Gould, in 1744, Mascarene remarked pessimistically that "our prospect is indeed dismal ... our men by age and fatigue are so worn out and the place to be defended so large that without some assistance of a sea force, an augmentation of the Garrison or a good healthy and lively recruit, it cannot be expected that this place when attacked can hold out long."[117] Eight years later, in a letter to an old army friend, Mascarene recalled his situation on the eve of war: "I was then in a fort," he wrote, "capacious enough but whose works neglected in time of peace were all in ruins and instead of five hundred men requisite at least to mann it I had but one hundred, twenty or thirty of which were utter Invalides, of ten or a dozen Officers not above two or three had ever seen a gunn fir'd in anger, and who were for the most part tainted by Republican principles."[118] Buildings in poor repair, the soldiery dispirited, it almost goes without saying that supplies of clothing and armaments were also problematic. In these circumstances, convinced that there would be an attempt by France to retake the colony, Mascarene naturally concentrated his attention upon keeping the French inhabitants in "their fidelity to his Majesty." This, Mascarene wrote in a dispatch to the Board of Trade early in 1744, was possible since the Acadians seem to have given proof of their loyalty by providing "us their assistance in the works going on to the repairs of this Fort."[119]

If Mascarene feared a French attack but hoped that the Acadians would remain neutral, the authorities in Louisbourg planned such an event and hoped that the Acadians would support them. In 1740 Isaac-Louis de Forant, who had been governor of Île Royale for barely a year, died.[120] He was succeeded by Jean-Baptiste-Louis Le Prévost Duquesnel, who was appointed commandant on 1 September 1740.[121] His instructions from Maurepas informed him that, once war had broken out, it was the king's intention that he should consider an expedition against Acadia.[122] The plan for this expedition had been sent by Forant to Maurepas in November 1739 and called for two frigates and a force of two hundred regular troops from the Île Royale garrison, reinforced by two hundred sappers and engineers brought out especially from France.[123] There is also a later plan, dated August 1741, for retaking Nova Scotia. Its anonymous author began by remarking that the cession of Acadia and Newfoundland had always been looked upon as "infinitely prejudiceable" because of the impact on the French cod fisheries. The settlements on Île Royale, "of which the English were extremely jealous," had somewhat compensated for the losses but "it had always been envisaged that advantage would be taken of the first opportunity to retake Acadie."[124] It is probable that this memorandum was written by François Du Pont Duvivier, who would lead the raid on Annapolis Royal in the late summer and fall of 1744. He was of part-Acadian extraction, being the second son of François Du Pont Duvivier, a sublieutenant in the French navy who had served in Acadia and had married Marie Mius d'Entremont de Pobomcoup in 1705 at Port Royal.[125] The family had moved to Île Royale in 1714 and by 1717 François, then ten years old, had joined the garrison as a cadet.[126] He and his brothers became important members of the Louisbourg community, trading both with the Acadians and with merchants from Boston. François was promoted to a captaincy in 1732 and had a fair influence on then governor, Sainte-Ovide. In a memorandum written sometime in the 1730s, he pointed out that he was the great-grandson of "the Sieur de La Tour, the founder of the colony [Acadie]" and had "in the country his grandfather and his grandmother, three of his uncles and many other of his relatives."[127] He expressed the opinion that "the inhabitants who remained there [when the colony was ceded to Great Britain] ... preserved the hope of returning to their allegiance to the king [of France] ... One may reckon on the zeal of the inhabitants and the greater part of the savages ..." The early French attack on Annapolis Royal, which Duvivier led, was planned with this belief in mind.

There was a belligerent mood, in the 1740s, among the French officials and some of the officers at Louisbourg, but the state of preparedness for war there was not that much better than it was at Annapolis Royal. The reports of both Forant and Duquesnel on the situation of the fortress had much in common with the complaints that Mascarene brought forward about Annapolis Royal. The fort itself needed repairs, especially the barracks.[128] The soldiers were in poor condition, many old and sick, and the garrison generally needed supplies and reinforcements.[129] What particularly worried Duquesnel and his advisers was the food supply, which was always precarious and depended a great deal on imports from Massachusetts and Nova Scotia. In 1743 seventy-eight vessels from New England and Acadia traded with Louisbourg, a number not only greater than the fifty-eight ships from France but also greater than the number of ships from France, New France (seven), and the French West Indies (thirty-two) combined.[130] The division between New England and Acadian trade with Louisbourg was overwhelmingly in favour of the former but contemporaries at Canso estimated that the Acadians shipped annually a minimum of "6 or 700 Head of Cattle, and about 2000 sheep" to Louisbourg.[131] In sum, as McLennan writes, "the condition of Louisbourg" on the eve of the outbreak of war in the region "was in the highest degree unsatisfactory ... it was inadequately supplied with provisions and munitions of war; its garrison was not only inadequate but of poor quality; [and] its artillery required an increase of seventy-seven guns to make all its fortifications effective."[132] Nevertheless, as soon as the news that France had declared war on Great Britain reached Duquesnel, on 3 May 1744,[133] the governor set about fulfilling the instructions he had received from the minister to embark upon an aggressive campaign.

As was expected, Duquesnel chose Canso as his first objective. It was known to be poorly defended but there was another reason for wanting its capture. The year before, Duquesnel had reported that the small garrison there and the lone guard vessel had been a noticeable harassment to the Acadian trade with Louisbourg,[134] and, in the spring of 1744, food was once more scarce for the garrison, the fishing fleet, and the civilian population.[135] With supplies from New England likely to be scarce, if not completely stopped, and shipping from France unreliable, the need to secure the Acadian supply lines was obvious. The taking of Canso was the necessary first step to an attack upon Nova Scotia, because, with the outbreak of war, the British would obviously make every effort to bring the Louisbourg-Acadian trade to an end. So, on 23 May 1744, a small flotilla sailed out of Louisbourg, under the command of Duvivier. It was made up of two privateering vessels, a supply sloop, and fourteen fishing boats carrying twenty Swiss and French officers, eighty French soldiers, thirty-seven Swiss soldiers, and 212 sailors.[136] Within a day, the force was off Canso and the defenders capitulated immediately. The terms were reasonable: the women and children were to be sent to Boston as soon as possible, and the troops were to remain prisoners of war for a year.[137]

Duquesnel, encouraged by this easy success, gained without loss of life and with a minimal expenditure of stores and ammunition, now set about organizing the expedition to capture Annapolis Royal, with Duvivier again in charge. This had become the more urgent because Mascarene had indeed attempted, with some success, to halt Acadian trade with Louisbourg.[138] Duquesnel had tried to prevent this by writing to Le Loutre at the same time as Duvivier was dispatched to Canso. Duquesnel encouraged Le Loutre to send war parties into Nova Scotia and "to accompany them as chaplain in all their expeditions."[139] Le Loutre took a while to gather the Mi'kmaq warriors together and it was not until 12 July that three hundred or so Mi'kmaq began their assault on Annapolis Royal. It was a desultory affair, and when on 16 July the *Prince of Orange,* out of Boston, arrived with seventy soldiers on board, it ended.[140] Mascarene wrote to Shirley, on 28 July, that the Mi'kmaq had departed for "Minas, where they have been living on the cattle and poultry of the inhabitants."[141] He went on to say that, as soon as "the Indians withdrew, the inhabitants brought provisions and testified their intention to keep to their fidelity as long as the fort is kept." Duquesnel wrote in his instructions to Duvivier, at the end of the month, that the Mi'kmaq were molesting the Acadian farmers in the Beaubassin area, killing cattle and looting instead of harassing the English.[142]

Duvivier did not leave Louisbourg until 29 July. Duquesnel planned a combined land-and-sea assault on Annapolis Royal and he waited upon ships from France. When *Le Caribou,* one of the two he expected, finally arrived in the last week of July, he gave orders for Duvivier to leave. Duvivier was thirty-nine years old, and his sole experience of battle had been the expedition against Canso. Forant's plan for the capture of the peninsula had envisaged a force made up of two frigates and two hundred regular troops.[143] Duvivier had to make do with a smaller and more diverse detachment. He commanded only fifty regular troops, a hundred or so Mi'kmaq from Île Royale, accompanied by Abbé Pierre Maillard, and seventy or so Malecite from the Saint John River.[144] Only about thirty Mi'k-

maq from Nova Scotia bands joined the expedition, their enthusiasm having been tempered by their earlier defeat and Le Loutre did not accompany them.[145] It is clear that the success of the enterprise depended upon
the naval support it would receive at Annapolis Royal as well as considerable cooperation from the Acadians.

From the outset, Duvivier acted as if the enterprise was the return of a
native son to liberate his people from a foreign yoke. Four of his six officers were related to him in one way or another, one of them was his brother, and all, of course, had relatives among the Acadians.[146] Duvivier's journal shows his intense belief that the Acadians were not only a people of
French heritage but a people whose natural inclination was to consider
themselves French, that is, allied by emotional ties to the policies of contemporary France. Such ties were founded upon a present commonality of
interest and cherished memories of the past. Duvivier made a number of
speeches to assembled villagers as he crossed from Baie Verte to Annapolis Royal, telling those who heard him that they "knew he was an Acadian"
and that "everything in the country gave him pleasure."[147] At Beaubassin
he informed the populace that the young men should join him in order to
defend "their liberty and the tranquillity of their religion." He went on to
state that "the declaration of war deprived them of the continuation of
their rights which Louis the Fourteenth of happy memory had preserved
for them when deeding the country to the King of England." Duvivier then
remarked that they should always consider the English as their cruel
enemy, "flattering only to deceive [Acadians of] good faith because the
laws of England were not compatible with the Roman religion."[148] He concluded these remarks by pointing out that the only choice for the Acadians was to join with the French, "their old friends and the only people with
whom they would be able enjoy their possessions and their religious beliefs
in peace."[149] Duvivier stayed in the Beaubassin region for four days, and
after Mass on Sunday, 16 August, he called for a show of support from the
congregation, saying he was confident that "the old French heart would be
found among our Acadians."[150] He added that all were free to express
their own opinions and he considered that about three-quarters of those
present responded with enthusiasm. Given that Duvivier was at the head of
some two hundred armed men, the enthusiastic reaction is scarcely surprising; what is surprising, however, is the level of abstentions. Duvivier
noted in his diary that those who thought they could remain unnoticed in
the crowd would find themselves mistaken.[151]

A much more significant indication of Acadian sentiment in the
Beaubassin region is the actual support, in terms of armed men, that
Duvivier obtained. It is difficult to be precise about the number of adult
Acadian males in the area who were capable of bearing arms and so it is
equally difficult to form an estimate of how many men Duvivier might have
expected to rally to his side. An approximate number of possible recruits
would be around two hundred and fifty, but, given the fact that this was a

labour-intensive farming region, the number who would be available to join the army, let alone want to "go for a soldier," would not be large.[152] Further, though there is no report on the number of men at Mass that morning, the scattered nature of the congregation at Beaubassin meant that there were probably no more than a hundred adult males present. Taking all these factors into account, and without regard to Duvivier's own report that a quarter of the population showed no apparent enthusiasm for his cause, it is still surprising that when he left for the Minas Basin, Duvivier took with him only ten new recruits. Those who remained behind promised him that they would hold the region tranquil in the ensuing weeks. Duvivier explained the small number of recruits by remarking, correctly, that the harvest was in urgent need of labour.[153] He wrote that he did not wish to take men from this task, which, given that he was deeply involved in the Acadian trade in foodstuffs with Louisbourg, is understandable. Duvivier's concern with the supply of Louisbourg was also in the forefront of his mind when he reached the Minas Basin, and within a day or so of his arrival there he had arranged for cattle to be sent back to the fortress.[154]

At Minas, too, there was certainly no universal support for the campaign, or even for sending supplies to Louisbourg.[155] The priest, Jean-Pierre de Miniac, irritated Duvivier by challenging his view that the laws of England were fundamentally anti-Catholic. Duvivier dismissed him as someone who was supremely comfortable in his situation, where he behaved as a little pope.[156] Miniac's attitude might have been one of the reasons that caused Duvivier to act much more imperiously in the Minas region than he had in Beaubassin. He demanded that the deputies attend him, on pain of death, to hear his commands. In his diary, he wrote that he never had any intention of coercing the Acadians but had taken this step in case, by chance, they did not accept his invitation. As well, he considered that his action would shelter them from any later reprisals by the English.[157] At least one of Duvivier's written orders, demanding horses and powder from Grand Pré, Pisiquid, and Rivière-aux-Canards, has survived. He concluded it by threatening that disobedience would be treated as rebellion and those who did not obey would be given up for punishment to the Indians ("livres dans les mains des Sauvages").[158] At the same time, he required a pledge of fidelity to the French from the general populace, threatening them as well with reprisals from the Indians, if they did not comply. No matter how much Duvivier might consider these threats merely a ploy, they would not be seen as such in a settlement occupied by armed men. In the event, Duvivier's belligerent attitude did not result in any significant recruitment. The population of the Minas area was in the region of two thousand, that of Pisiquid about another thousand, and Cobequid had around eight hundred people.[159] Such a population would have about a seven hundred adult males capable of carrying arms. Once more, the actual number who joined with Duvivier was minimal, two dozen at the most.[160] But there is no doubt that, if Duvivier did not attract men to join his troops, he did receive some supplies and aid, in terms of couriers and the servicing of weaponry.

This was due, above all, to the enterprise of one man, Joseph Leblanc, known as Le Maigre. There is little known about his early life, except that he was born at Minas in 1697, the seventh of the eleven children of Antoine Leblanc and Marie Bourgeois.[161] He wholeheartedly supported Duvivier and acted as a kind of commissary for him. Leblanc presented an account for 518 *livres* to Duvivier for monies he paid out.[162] Much of the outlay went to the purchase of 104 knives from the two blacksmiths, four axes from separate individuals, and the repair of guns by the gunsmith. Duvivier had been joined at Minas by seventy Malecite, and it is probable that the knives were hunting knives. There was a significant amount of money paid to men who acted as carters between Minas and Annapolis Royal and some small sums were given to those who provided lodging, care for two sick men, and five barrels of flour. There are no accounts for major purchases of meat or bread. While Duquesnel had provided Duvivier with guns for the Malecite, the knives must have been a valuable and useful acquisition. However, the work of the eleven men who drove wagons loaded with general supplies, including munitions, to Annapolis Royal was probably the most important help Duvivier received.

On 30 August, Duvivier left for Annapolis Royal, arriving there eight days later. During the weeks after the departure of Le Loutre in mid-July, Mascarene had received further aid from Boston, in the form of some supplies and fifty-three additional soldiers.[163] John Henry Bastide, who had been appointed the chief engineer for the fort in 1740, had managed to repair the ramparts and to place huge logs on them, to be rolled down on any who tried to use ladders to scale the walls.[164] Mascarene had over two hundred and fifty men, well enough supplied with weapons. In military terms, Mascarene was in the better position, as long as no French ships arrived with reinforcements of regular soldiers and guns capable of shelling the fort. Duvivier had few regular troops and his Mi'kmaq and Malecite allies were better at night raids and daring skirmishes than keeping the fort under close siege. On 15 September, after roughly a week of desultory attacks, Duvivier demanded the capitulation of the fort, saying that he expected shortly the arrival of three ships, carrying on board a total of a hundred and seventy guns and bringing "two hundred and fifty men more of regular Troops with Cannon, mortars and other implements of warr ..."[165] The two sides parleyed for about a week, each keeping watch for the arrival of warships. By 23 September, hostilities had once more begun, and, three days later, two ships did arrive. They were from Boston, not Louisbourg, and caused much rejoicing in the fort. Duvivier retreated, having besieged the fort for less than two weeks. His withdrawal was hastened by the arrival from Louisbourg of Michel de Gannes de Falaise, with orders for Duvivier to return to Louisbourg.

Duquesnel's decision was based on instructions he had received, after Duvivier's departure, to deploy the two ships that arrived from France for the protection of the fisheries and commercial shipping.[166] François Bigot, who was then serving as Île Royale's financial commissary, urged Duvivier to comply with this directive because the New England privateers were making considerable inroads on French trade. Duvivier was reluctant to accept Duquesnel's orders, especially since they were conveyed by de Gannes, who barely outranked him. The latter, born in 1702, was also the son of an Acadian mother, Marguerite Leneuf de La Vallière et de Beaubassin, and a French officer, Louis de Gannes de Falaise.[167] Michel's childhood had been spent partly in Acadia, after 1710 in France, and then for some years in Quebec. He was made an ensign at Louisbourg in 1719, a lieutenant in 1725, and a major in 1730. Unlike Duvivier, de Gannes does not appear to have had any links to the commercial life of Île Royale. Events would show that, at best, the relationship between the two men was strained. De Gannes's orders were to establish himself at Minas, with his detachment of fifty-four regular soldiers and some eighty Mi'kmaq, and avoid upsetting the settlers.[168] He arrived at Annapolis Royal on 2 October, assumed overall command, and by the 5th had ordered, and organized, the retreat of the French force.

Throughout Duvivier's assault on the fort and occupation of the town, the Acadian community of Annapolis Royal and its surroundings had behaved very much as one might expect. The bulk of the population waited on events, attempting to survive the presence of the military in the streets and responding to the demands for food, lodging, and general support, requests that were backed with the authority of force. Among the elite, some openly supported the British. Louis Robichaud, whose father had almost continuously worked with British officials since 1715, did what was possible, in terms of supplying information to the garrison, during these weeks.[169] Kin connections with the Winniett family, four of whom had married British officers, might have had some weight in the opinions of Louis Robichaud. But, as is generally the case, political loyalties split families. Other relatives, including the brother of the Winniett daughters and one of Louis Robichaud's first cousins, actively supported the French.[170] The most important support for the latter, however, was provided by Joseph-Nicolas Gautier, known as Bellair. Gautier had been born in France in Rochefort in 1689 and had come to Nova Scotia in his mid-twenties, sometime before 1715. That year he married the daughter of Louis Allain, a blacksmith and considerable landowner. During the early years of the British regime, Gautier was not accepted as a deputy, on the grounds that he was only a transient in the colony, but by 1732 he had become not only an important landowner but also the proprietor of two flour mills and a grist mill. The lack of property as a qualification had obviously been overcome. Moreover, he had two small trading vessels, which sailed to the Caribbean as well as to Île Royale.[171] Clark calculates that his total worth by the 1740s was in the region of 80,000 *livres*, making him one of the richest men in the colony, if not the richest.[172] One of his daughters was married to one of Duvivier's brothers. Gautier would be a consistent supporter of French activities, which would bring him imprisonment and financial ruin.[173] He died in Port Lajoie (Charlottetown) in the spring of 1752.

As soon as the retreat from Annapolis Royal began, whatever support there had been for Duvivier among the generality of the population faded away. His officers reported that they left Annapolis Royal, having with difficulty commandeered only thirty loaves of bread and three head of cattle as supplies. On arrival at Minas, they were forced to send out foraging parties to discover the bread which the inhabitants had hidden.[174] However, Joseph Leblanc *dit* Le Maigre proved, once more, his value and helped obtain not only bread and beef but also boats and payment to speed the Malecites on their way to the Saint John valley. In the accounts that were later presented, monies were recorded as owing not only to Le Maigre but also to nine others. There was a small sum owed for two carcasses of beef to Jean Landry, another for eight pounds of butter to Pierre Leblanc. The largest sums were payable to those who were engaged in seeing the Malecite depart.[175] This second presence of the French at Minas turned out to be the last stage in the fortunes of the expedition. Duvivier was back at Louisbourg late in the evening of 23 October; de Gannes arrived there three weeks later.

As might be expected, both men faced an inquiry as to whether their actions had been appropriate. Duquesnel had died during Duvivier's absence and Louis Du Pont Duchambon, Duvivier's uncle, was now in charge. Duvivier, having arrived in Louisbourg before de Gannes, received a sympathetic hearing when he placed the responsibility for his failure squarely on the shoulders of de Gannes.[176] This would mean that no blame could be laid at the feet of those who dispatched Duvivier with a much smaller force than Forant had deemed necessary for the enterprise. Nor could France be condemned for not providing effective naval support. De Gannes's defence was presented nearly a month later, and was based, in part, on a letter he had in his possession, signed by a number of the leading men, including deputy Alexandre Bourg, *dit* Belle-Humeur, of the Minas region. The letter argued that, because the harvest had been much less prolific than expected, providing the French with the grain and beef requested would force the settlers to kill all their cattle and use up their seed grains for next year's crops.[177] The letter went on to express the hope that de Gannes could not wish to plunge them and their families into the misery of complete destitution and that, as a result, he would withdraw both the Indians and his troops from the settlements. "We are," the text continued, "under an easy and peaceful regime and we have every reason to be content with it."[178] On the manuscript itself, there is a note in the margin to the effect de Gannes prodded the Acadians to write the letter.[179]

If this comment is accepted, the Acadians could still be considered as covert Frenchmen, quite ready to give aid and comfort to future expeditions. In any event, if de Gannes was the scapegoat, all the other major players in the affair were absolved from any responsibility for the outcome of events.

At much the same time as Duvivier and de Gannes were defending their actions in Louisbourg, Mascarene was giving an account of his defence of Nova Scotia to the Lords of Trade and to Governor William Shirley of Massachusetts. Mascarene's dispatch to London, dated 20 September (O.S.; N.S., 30 Sept.), referred to Duvivier's expedition as a "flying party."[180] Mascarene's fear was that the provisions in the fort would run out before help arrived. Writing again, five days later, Mascarene mentioned the arrival of the brigantine from Boston and said that recent skirmishes had shown "how much the preservation of this place is owing to the Reinforcements we have received from the Province of Massachusetts."[181] Mascarene's most lengthy account of the events of the summer was written in two letters in December, the first to Governor Shirley and the second to an unnamed correspondent.[182] It is in the second of these that Mascarene wrote, bluntly, that "to the Breaking the French measures; the timely succour receiv'd from the Governor of Massachusetts, and our French Inhabitants refusing to take up arms against us, we owe our preservation." He stated that the French "had prepar'd such a Force as in the opinion of all, considering the ill condition of this Fort, we should not have been able to resist," but, thanks to the Acadians' conduct, "our men were eas'd in the constant Duty the many ruinous places in our Ramparts requir'd to attend; and if the Inhabitants had taken up arms they might have brought three or four thousand men against us who would have kept us still on harder Duty, and be keeping the enemy for a longer time about us, made it impracticable to repair our Breaches or to gett our firewood and other things of absolute necessity."

During the late winter and spring of 1744–45, Mascarene and the Council interrogated the Acadians closely about their actions during the Duvivier expedition. Not surprisingly, the settlers spoke unanimously of the dread that Duvivier had inspired in them. In the report of the Council meeting of 11 December 1744, for example, it was recorded that the deputies from Cobequid said that "none of their inhabitants [had] joined the enemy nor given them any assistance but as force obliged them to it."[183] The deputies continued by acknowledging their "submission and fidelity to His Majesty the King of Great Britain their lawful Sovereign." Mascerene then questioned them about cattle "conveyed to Lewisbourg by way of Chiconecto and Tadmigouch." The deputies answered that there had been two droves of black cattle and sheep from Minas, herded by Joseph Leblanc *dit* Le Maigre and Joseph Dugas.

As the winter months passed, the picture of the Acadian behaviour that emerged was of a people caught, unexpectedly, in a situation where political beliefs had immediate and uncomfortable consequences. The colony had been without major strife for thirty-four years, and any settler younger than thirty-four had been born under the British regime. But the influence of France was a part of their lives, intertwined with the religious practices of the majority. During 1744, the existence within the villages of a minority who felt passionately about the political situation of the colony, whether those who had made terms with the British administration or those who cherished the links that remained with Louisbourg, raised the level of political consciousness of all Acadians.[184] Nothing was as certain or as simple in the fall of 1744 for the settlers as it had been earlier in the spring and summer. Then, the public actions of particular individuals were very much their own affair and had only an economic or social, rather than a political, impact on the community; now, actions such as a trading trip to Louisbourg or supplying wood for the repair of the fort at Annapolis Royal were liable to be seen as representative of the political views of a much greater part of the community. Reports of the situation at Minas, given at the same Council meeting in December, were that the "situation was in such disorder, there being no new Deputies chosen."

Attitudes towards the Acadians gradually became harsher, especially on the part of people from Massachusetts. Mascarene, however, never wavered in his belief that it was the support of Governor Shirley for Nova Scotia, coupled with Acadian neutrality, that preserved the colony. The reasons for Mascarene's confidence in Shirley will be discussed in the next chapter. As for Mascarene's belief in Acadian neutrality, this was based not only on the actions of the majority of the Acadians in 1744 but also on a clear idea of how these people could be expected to act when their villages were occupied by an army. Mascarene had known what it was like to be a member of a family that was ideologically split. He had experienced living in a neighbourhood controlled by troops, whose presence was supported by some of the inhabitants and not by others. He could appreciate the extent to which Duvivier's expedition was, for some of the Acadians, as much a civil conflict as a war between competing states.

The adoption of neutrality as a course of action by a community is as complex a decision as the adoption of any other policy. One of the major reasons for the choice of neutrality is the belief that, no matter who emerges victorious, the life of the community will not be substantially altered. Another is the presence of pockets of strong support, within the community, for both sides but a general unwillingness on the part of the majority to become involved in the struggle. Finally, neutrality also means a belief that the antagonists will respect that position. There is no doubt that the Acadian experience of alternating French and British rule inclined the community to believe that, regardless of who administered the colony, their lives would continue relatively unchanged. By 1740, Nova Scotia was part of a much larger region and the Acadians were commercially linked with both the French and English interests in the area. There might be proscriptions on trade with the neighbouring settlements of a different empire but neither French nor British really controlled Acadian commerce, any more than they controlled the trade of Île Royale and Massachusetts. The question of the emotional attachment of the Acadians to the French monarchy is a more difficult matter to estimate. As Anthony Smith has pointed out, the failure to recognize the importance of sentiment in political life is as serious a mistake as the failure to recognize the extent to which other factors, such as economic self-interest and the wish for political stability, play a role in political choices.[185] That the Acadian community harboured more than one viewpoint on the choices that it confronted is hardly surprising. Nor is it surprising that, for some, the oath that had been taken in 1729–30, fifteen years earlier, would be a serious matter and, for others, something of minor importance.

While Mascarene and the Acadians believed that the Acadians had indeed maintained a neutral position during the summer and fall of 1744, neither Louisbourg nor Boston was convinced that this was so. As the war went on, and as the balance of power in the region shifted from Annapolis Royal to Boston and from Louisbourg to Versailles and Quebec, the situation of the Acadians would become more and more fraught. The Acadians believed, as they asserted at a Council meeting held on 4 January 1745, that they had been granted "a Dispensation from everything that related to War."[186] Those who contended for the military control of the region over the following years would show themselves unwilling to accept this proposition.

CHAPTER THIRTEEN

Years of War, 1745–48

The retreat of Duvivier and de Gannes in the fall of 1744 did not, of course, end military activity in and around Nova Scotia. Over the next three years, Great Britain and France, as well as their officials in New England and New France, continued to consider the colony as both strategically and politically important. Throughout the region, from Île Royale to Massachusetts, and from Annapolis Royal to the Saint John valley, as well as along the Atlantic coast from Canso to the Baie des Chaleurs, forays and skirmishes, attacks and counter-attacks by both French and British were commonplace. Both powers believed that they had a legitimate right to rule Nova Scotia and both regarded the population as a potential resource, one that could prove to be of major importance for the outcome of the war in that area. And both became more and more exasperated with the unwillingness of the majority of the Acadian population to commit themselves, without reserve, to the party that, obviously, would most benefit them. The French believed that ties of language and religion, as well as links to a common experience in the not too distant past, should sway the Acadians to a wholehearted support of their cause; the British considered that the Acadians ought to recognize the benefits of their rule and show themselves obedient British subjects. Neither power, however, was fully confident that its views about the proper Acadian response would prevail in the community itself. As a result, both regarded the use of intimidation as a proper measure to coerce the right response from the Acadians. With one or two notable exceptions, such as Mascarene, few gave credence to the possibility of Acadian neutrality and even fewer believed that neutrality was an acceptable moral choice. As the war continued, these attitudes hardened and pressure on the Acadians, by both the British and the French, to abandon any attempt to remain non-combatants became much stronger.

The change in attitudes that the war brought to Nova Scotia was reflected in the meetings of the Council at Annapolis Royal. Within a month of Duvivier's retreat, that body decided to place controls on the trade carried

on at Minas, forbidding ships to carry there "all kind of clothing peculiar
to Indians such as blanketing" and to restrict their cargoes to "what is for
the consumption of the inhabitants themselves."[1] During the next four
months, the Council considered the behaviour of the Acadians both during the recent French occupation of the settlements and in the days since
then, particularly in connection with demands for pilots and guides for a
New England expedition that intended to distress "the Indian Enemy."[2]
On the latter point, the expedition at issue had been proposed by Captain
John Gorham, an officer in the 7th Massachusetts Regiment, whose arrival
at Annapolis Royal, in late September, had been partially responsible for
Duvivier's retreat. He was accompanied by some fifty Mohawk and now
wanted to "pursue the Indians" in the Saint John River area.[3] In the end,
Gorham returned to Boston without undertaking this enterprise. His
request for guides and pilots, however, had raised the question, for both
the Council and the Acadians, of precisely what services, during wartime,
would be required of the settlers by the British authorities.

It is clear, from Mascarene's correspondence with the Lords of Trade
even before war broke out, that there was no expectation that the Acadians would take up arms for the British. But this did not mean that no support for the British was expected or that obvious aid for the French would
be tolerated. The questions and answers, given in December and January
1744–45 during the Council's examination of leading men from the Minas
area, demonstrate what this meant in practice.[4] Deputies were expected to
publish orders sent to them by Annapolis Royal, which declared war
against France and prohibited "trade & Commerce with the Subjects of yt
Crown & with their Allies."[5] They were expected to stop overt trade with
the enemy and to aid those who actively wished to "hinder the "Conveying
of Cattle and other Provisions" to the French. At the same time, the
deputies were required to inform the British of French activities and, con-
versely, not to inform the latter of British plans. Finally, as became clear in
the argument over the provision of guides and pilots for Captain Gorham,
the Acadians must understand that, whatever the actual terms of the dispensation granted them, the dispensation itself was a matter of grace and
favour. There was no doubt in the minds of the councillors, or in Mascarene's, that the Acadians were British subjects who, even though they
were to be considered as non-combatants in any war with France, nonetheless owed a measure of obligation to the British crown.[6]

Mascarene always made a clear distinction between the actions of the
pro-French Acadians and those of the rest of the community, which included those, such as members of the Robichaud and Leblanc families, who
were actively pro-British. Throughout the years of war, he maintained the
attitude he had in the early spring of 1745, when he wrote to one of his
correspondents that he considered that "the French Inhabitants have in
general behav'd well ..."[7] As the war was brought to a conclusion in the
spring of 1748, Mascarene still believed, as he wrote to the secretary of

state, Newcastle, that "the French had been able to entice into open rebellion only a few of the inhabitants."[8] However, while Mascarene always hoped that it would be possible "with time and good care to bring these French inhabitants to be good subjects ...,"[9] as the fortunes of war swung back and forth, there was a hardening of opinion among the Council members against the Acadians. At times, even Mascarene wondered whether eviction might not be considered. On 8 November 1745 a joint representation was sent to the Lords of Trade, from Mascarene and the Council, suggesting that the Acadians "cannot be accounted less than unprofitable Inhabitants" and therefore "it is most humbly submitted whether the said French Inhabitants may not be transported out of the Province of NOVA SCOTIA and be replac'd by good Protestant Subjects."[10] It is important to remember that, as has been shown earlier, the British crown considered transportation of recalcitrant or rebellious populations, whether Scots, Cornish, or English, an acceptable procedure.

Mascarene signed his name to this representation, probably because, as will be seen, it was clear that Governor Shirley of Massachusetts was much in favour of the idea. However, at the same time as Mascarene forwarded this to London, he sent a lengthy letter to Shirley presenting strong arguments against such a course.[11] Mascarene pointed out that, given the ties of common language and religion between the Acadians and the French, "it is less to be wonder'd att, that the Enemy has had so much influence on this People lately as that he has not had much more." While he considered that populating Nova Scotia with good English-speaking Protestants "would be very advantageous," he noted that there were a number of both legal and practical difficulties with achieving this end through deporting the Acadians, not least of which was the fact that the Treaty of Utrecht might well be taken to make such an action illegal. At the same time, Mascarene questioned where the Acadians could be sent and how they would be transported. He believed that the Acadian population was "above butt not certainly under, twenty thousand souls." Removal would not be easy and, unless it was firmly decided upon, it should not be talked about, since rumours of such an undertaking would throw "the Inhabitants into despair" and, inevitably, drive them into the arms of the French.

The emergence of Governor Shirley as the major player in military and political affairs of the region brought into the picture someone with strong personal ambitions that were linked with a particular vision of British expansion in North America, a vision that would obviously provide major career opportunities for people such as himself. From the moment that he decided to dispatch troops and provisions to Annapolis Royal in June 1744, the governor of Massachusetts played a crucial role in Nova Scotian affairs. It was his leadership that was primarily responsible for the attack on Louisbourg in 1744, and it was the success of this enterprise that gave him a great deal of influence on future British activities in the region. But no matter who had been in charge in Massachusetts during these years, the interests of the Commonwealth would have had a strong influence on the British administration at Annapolis Royal. Geographical propinquity obviously played a role, as did the fact that at this point, 1744, the administrations of both colonies were part of the same empire and thus close allies in any war against France. The disparities of population size and of general political experience meant that the relationship was bound to be difficult. Massachusetts had, in 1740, some 1,616,130 white settlers, of whom more than 90 per cent were of British descent.[12] Nova Scotia, including the garrison, had well under five hundred residents with such a background. The Commonwealth had been a colony of the British empire since its inception whereas Nova Scotia had known French suzerainty for the greater part of its existence. But, despite the more powerful position of Massachusetts, which meant that the activities of that colonial government had a particularly strong impact on the smaller colony, the Nova Scotian officials retained and exercised a certain independence.

This was particularly obvious in the matter of relations with the Mi'kmaq. In October 1744 Massachusetts declared war on the Mi'kmaq and offered bounties for Mi'kmaq scalps, £100 for that of an adult male, £50 for that of a woman or child.[13] Nova Scotian relations with the Mi'kmaq, while usually tense, had never been as hostile as those of Massachusetts. The Acadians had, however, continuously emphasized Mi'kmaq hostility to the British and had always maintained that Mi'kmaq threats prevented greater Acadian cooperation with Annapolis Royal. That the Mi'kmaq had their own political agenda, independent of either British or French policies, is now generally accepted. Yet, while this makes Acadian-Mi'kmaq relationships more complex, it does not diminish their importance. By January 1745–46, rumours were rife in the Minas Basin and the settlers sent letters to the Council concerning their fears. They had heard that "several armed Vessells were arrived from New Engld ... to go against the Indians" and "that they were coming up the bay ... to destroy all the Inhabitants that had any Indian blood in them & Scalp them ..."[14] The letter went on to say that "as there were a great number of Mulattoes among them who had the Oath & who were allied to the greatest familys [this news] had Caused a terrible Alarm ..." Mascarene attempted to reassure the Acadians by repeating "his resolution to give the Inhabitants his protection," provided "they continued steadfast in ye Promises they had made not to do anything against His Majestys Interest." As for "the Notion the inhabitants had amongst them that all who had any Indian blood in them would be treated as Enemys," Mascarene added that this "was a very great Mistake since if that had been the design of the New Engld armed Vessells it might very well be supposed that the Inhabitants of this river [Annapolis Royal] many of who have Indian blood in them ... would not be sufferd to live peaceably as they do ..."

The reaction of the Mi'kmaq was considerably stronger than that of the Acadians and, from this point on, they allied themselves almost exclusively with the French. In May 1745 the Mi'kmaq joined an unsuccessful foray against Annapolis Royal. This venture, led by Paul Marin de La Malgue, had been ordered by the governor, Charles de Beauharnois de La Boische, and the intendant, Gilles Hocquart, of New France in answer to a request from Louisbourg. Marin had left Quebec on 19 January 1744/45.[15] He was in command of about two hundred men, half of whom were Canadian volunteers and the rest a mixture of Abenaki, Algonquin, and Huron. They went to the Chignecto area by way of Rivière-du-Loup, Lake Temiscouata, and the Saint John River and arrived at their destination within a month. There they were expected to await orders from Île Royale in order to be part of a combined land-and-sea attack on Annapolis Royal.[16] At the beginning of April, Marin moved to the Minas area and in early May was encamped at Annapolis Royal.[17] Intelligence about this force reached Mascarene only a day or so before it actually appeared in the Annapolis region.[18] The records we have about the force's size are contradictory: William Pote, a ship's captain whose merchant's vessel was captured during the affray, believed that Marin had about seven hundred men with him.[19] If this figure is even approximately accurate, it would mean that Marin had been joined by a significant number of Mi'kmaq, since the maximum number of men he is reported to have had with him, when he left Quebec, was two hundred. Marin's offensive came to an abrupt halt almost immediately, partly because the expected naval support never arrived and partly because the expedition that Governor Shirley had coordinated had arrived at Louisbourg. Marin had barely encamped in front of the fort at Annapolis Royal before he received orders from the commandant of Île Royale, Louis Du Pont Duchambon, to proceed immediately to Louisbourg, where Duchambon had finally realized that he was under attack.

The capture of Louisbourg marked Nova Scotian affairs, and the relationship between the Acadians and the British administration, as significantly and as deeply as did the return of the fortress to French hands by the Treaty of Aix-la-Chapelle in 1748. The conquest of the fortress made Shirley's personal ambitions and dreams of imperial expansion a determinant of British action in Nova Scotia. Its return to French control anchored the idea of Nova Scotia as an essential element of Massachusetts security in the minds of that colony's elite. As has been suggested, even without Shirley, once war had broken out, Massachusetts would have focused its attention on Nova Scotia. The question of privateering action alone would have ensured this. From the outset, New England had some success with its own ships; Captain Joseph Beal, for example, took twelve to fourteen small vessels with his small schooner.[20] But, during the summer and early fall of 1744, "some thirty New England ships of from twenty to 180 tons were carried into Louisbourg along with six shallops and 1350 quintals of cod."[21] The value of the vessels was estimated at 114,409 *livres*.[22] It was the war at sea that roused public opinion in New England, where the depredations of privateers sailing out of Port Royal a generation earlier were still remembered.[23] It was Shirley, however, who directed this opinion into backing an expedition against Louisbourg and it was the success of this enterprise that was the background to later Massachusetts public opinion against any manifestation of French power in the region.

In 1744 William Shirley was fifty years old and had been a resident of Massachusetts for thirteen years and governor of the colony since 1741.[24] He had come to Boston, with his wife and children, to improve his fortunes. Before he left London, he had taken care to obtain a letter of recommendation from the Duke of Newcastle to the then governor of Massachusetts, Jonathan Belcher, as well as a promise from the duke of a further patronage appointment when possible. Shirley was soon admitted to the bar and swiftly built an important legal practice, at the same time as he began to shape his political future in the colony. He was appointed advocate general of the Admiralty Court in 1733, a position that allowed him to learn a great deal, very quickly, about trade between New England and Great Britain.[25] It also allowed him to keep in touch with his friends in London and to expedite their affairs. His duties, which were primarily judicial, included "the welfare of seamen, partnership disputes, smuggling and trade regulations, supervision of port business and ... the presentation of cases before civil and admiralty judges."[26] When he was appointed governor, Shirley was well versed in the business affairs of Massachusetts as well as conversant with the bureaucratic thickets of communications between the colony and Great Britain. From the moment that war broke out in the region, he not only set about the organization of support for Mascarene but also attempted to direct the latter in the way in which this support should be deployed.[27] Further, Shirley made sure, in his correspondence with the Duke of Newcastle, that his successful efforts to defend the neighbouring colony were properly recorded. In this Shirley was much helped by Mascarene, who after October 1744 often left it "to Governor Shirley who has acted in so generous and Vigorous a manner for our support to explain [the situation] to you."[28] In sum, Mascarene "reported to Shirley, and Shirley, embellishing and expanding, reported to London."[29] But, while Mascarene both sought and accepted Shirley's leadership on many occasions, he was also able to influence the ideas of the younger, better placed, and more important governor.

Shirley had began in earnest to consider what would be involved in the capture of Louisbourg and "the great consequences of the acquisition of Cape Breton" soon after Duvivier had left Nova Scotia.[30] He rightly considered that the reinforcements sent to that colony had preserved Annapolis Royal but had not resolved the situation. It was not until 5 February 1744/45 that specific plans for the expedition took shape; the delay arose to a large extent because, at first, Shirley saw the venture as an operation in which imperial military forces would play the larger part. In the event, however, imperial support was restricted to the vital area of naval activities. The expedition became, above all, a New England enterprise, and, while it would not have occurred without Shirley's leadership, it received valuable support from William Vaughan and William Pepperell. Vaughan, an important lumber merchant in Maine who had ambitions for political office, helped raise public awareness of the enterprise not only in Massachusetts but throughout New England.[31] Pepperell, another wealthy merchant and also a member of the Massachusetts General Court, accepted appointment as commander-in chief.

Even with their aid, the first Massachusetts contingent did not set out until the end of the first week in April. But, finally, the "largest New England force recruited to fight a foreign war in the seventeenth and eighteenth centuries" was assembled.[32] As well as ten eighteen-pound cannons and other siege equipment, Connecticut, New Hampshire, New York, and Rhode Island contributed over 2,000 men, while Massachusetts recruited 1,000 sailors and 3,000 troops.[33] British naval support, four warships, joined the New Englanders at Canso in the first week of May, thanks in large measure to a broad interpretation of his orders by Commodore Peter Warren.[34] By the final stages of the attack, Warren had eleven ships under his command, carrying 550 guns. Louisbourg was an imposing fortress, but its commander had barely 1,300 troops at his command, less than a third of whom were regular troops, and no immediate naval support in the area.[35]

By 11 May, the first wave of attackers had landed at Gabarus Bay. On 28 June 1745 (O.S.), Duchambon surrendered. During the intervening weeks, both French and British became inflamed at the way the other fought, each considering their opponents' tactics, at one and the same time, dishonourable and inept.[36] The French waited for relief by sea and encouraged Mi'kmaq attacks on the enemy. On the British side, the relationship between Warren and Pepperell became embittered, leading to immediate quarrels between them as to who was the overall commander and considerable dissension later on between the New Englanders and British naval personnel.[37] By the time the terms of capitulation were signed, the morale among the besiegers and defenders alike was low. As might be expected, neither side felt properly served either by the process of the negotiations or by the way in which the agreements reached were implemented. Indeed, the actual surrender had resulted in a major split between Pepperell and Warren, both claiming the lion's share of the credit for the victory.[38] The occupation of Louisbourg and the treatment of its inhabitants was, in the opinion of the French, deplorable. Pillaging and insult was the lot of those who withstood the siege, while they waited to be transported back to France.[39]

Imperial policy in both countries was affected by the capture of this great fortress, both in short-term military deployments and in the later negotiations for the Treaty of Aix-la-Chapelle. The news of the fall of Louisbourg meant rejoicing in Boston and London and equivalent discouragement in France and Quebec. In New England, the victory was seen by many as an affirmation that they were much favoured of God, since the support of the Almighty "has been so conspicuous in every circumstance of this expedition."[40] The success of the New England troops produced a mood of self-confidence, especially in Massachusetts, which showed itself both in future military expeditions and in the political temper of the Commonwealth. In London, rejoicing at the victory was the greater because of the crushing defeat of Great Britain and its allies at Fontenoy/Fantan in early May. At the same time, this enthusiasm was less than universal among the members of the government searching for a way to bring the war to an end. The Earl of Chesterfield wrote to the British minister in Holland that "one, almost insurmountable, difficulty I foresee in any negotiations with France, is our new acquisition of Cape Breton, which is become the darling object of the whole nation ..."[41] Among the populace in London, the enthusiasm for this North American acquisition was further strengthened when the second Jacobite rebellion broke out in July 1745. But the British government faced the problem of defraying the cost of the venture. Massachusetts had been driven close to bankruptcy by the heavy commitment of ships and men, and the financial circumstances of New Hampshire, Connecticut, and Rhode Island were not much better.[42] In sum, the immediate reaction in London and Boston was satisfaction, followed by a reckoning of the cost.

As Britain reacted to news of an unforeseen victory in 1745, France responded to an unexpected defeat. There is no doubt that Maurepas had been aware of the need to dispatch ships to Louisbourg at the beginning of the war but he was frustrated in his attempts to send effective aid by the unprepared state of the French navy and by those who opposed him at court, believing that French interests in the Mediterranean and the Caribbean were more important than North Atlantic ventures.[43] When the confirmation of the surrender of Louisbourg arrived at Versailles, in mid-August, Maurepas's plans to recapture the fortress received strong, if not universal, support.[44] The reaction at Quebec was similar. A dispatch written by Beauharnois and Hocquart in early September 1745 emphasized the need for a strong French response, pointing out that "the English being now masters of Isle Royale, will become more jealous, and more careful than ever to secure Acadia to themselves. That beautiful and fertile province is essential to the maintenance of their new conquest ..."[45]

Maurepas began the task of coordinating French and Canadian efforts by instructing Beauharnois to send a force to the Chignecto area, prepared to attack Annapolis Royal once a massive fleet had arrived in the region. This fleet left France on 22 June 1746. It was made up of "45 troop transports, storeships, and merchantmen, escorted by ten ships of the line, a hospital, three frigates, and two corvettes [and] ... set sail with 3,500 infantrymen and an artillery train on a mission to defend French possessions in America. In all, nearly 11,000 men embarked in over 25,000 tons of shipping." Its goals, for its commander, the Duc d'Anville, were ambitious but clear: Maurepas hoped that through its actions "Canada would be secured, Louisbourg recaptured, Acadia retaken, and the coast of New England ravaged as far south as Boston, perhaps further."[46] Five months later, the remnants of this huge expedition regained the coast of France, having achieved nothing for all the expenditure of men's lives and money. Somewhere between a half and two-thirds of the eleven thousand men who had set sail had been lost.[47] The fleet had been defeated by storms and disease as much as by any failure of leadership. The crossing took the best part of three months. Storms drove the convoy in separate ways and a quarter of the ships never reached Nova Scotia. D'Anville himself finally anchored in Chebucto Bay on 14 September. Almost immediately, the appalling state of health of the men, sailors and soldiers alike, became apparent. The expedition fleet suffered from an epidemic of different illnesses: scurvy and pulmonary, venereal, and various infectious diseases, above all typhus and smallpox.[48] While the number of dead was significant, the number of those seriously ill had as great an impact on the viability of the force owing to the labour-intensive nature of seamanship in the eighteenth century. An officer on board the *L'Alcide* reported that, during the final stages of the voyage, "all were obliged to lend a hand on the ropes, to help the wretches who no longer had the strength to do anything."[49] D'Anville himself died on 27 September; he had turned thirty-seven three weeks earlier.[50]

By this time it was clear that there was no possibility of attacking Louisbourg and secondary plans for the conquest of Annapolis Royal soon proved unsuccessful. In terms of French policy, it was the negotiation of the Treaty of Aix-la-Chapelle that addressed the loss of the fortress, not the organization of this force. But in terms of the Acadians themselves, the fall of Louisbourg and the failure of this expedition shaped their lives as much, if not more than, the policies of the British and French governments and the negotiations of imperial diplomats. Even rumours of the existence of the fleet had an impact on Massachusetts's perception of the strength of French forces. The news of the imminent arrival of the armada off Nova Scotia roused the general population in the Commonwealth to anxious prayers and the Council to see to the strengthening of coastal defences. The retreat of the ships reinforced the belief of many that God was the power that had guaranteed the survival of New England.[51]

For New England and New France, the war in North America was not merely one theatre of war among others of equal, or greater, importance. It was an immediate experience for many and a continuing priority for most. In Boston and in Quebec, the fall of Louisbourg was seen as anything but a conclusion to the hostilities. Shirley and his advisers sought to exploit their victory to the fullest, Beauharnois and Hocquart to minimize the impact of the French defeat. The Acadians and the Mi'kmaq continued to be viewed as possible allies or probable opponents, depending on who was contemplating their strength, and Nova Scotia was, inevitably, territory open to attack and counter-attack.

The months, stretching into years, between Duvivier's raid and the conclusion of the war have often been considered a fairly tranquil period for the majority of the Acadians, with what strife there was being intermittent and, when it did happen, more or less restricted to those unfortunate enough to live in areas of fairly concentrated population. Since the Acadians built their houses throughout a broad area of the lands they inhabited, it has been assumed that warfare would not have intruded to any great extent on many of the homesteads, especially since the number of Acadian men who were killed in these years was small. The actual number can only be a matter of conjecture but there is no evidence, in either French or English documents, of large numbers of Acadians taking up arms and being directly involved in combat. Nor do the genealogical records of this period reveal an unusual number of deaths of young Acadian men. Morever, the prosperity of the Acadians at the end of the decade argues that the presence of soldiers did not lead to the destruction of a significant amount of property, deplete harvests to the point of famine, or produce widespread mortality among the general population.

Still, the view of a relatively tranquil existence for the Acadians during these years needs to be modified. From the time of Duvivier's retreat in 1744 until the signing of the Treaty of Aix-la-Chapelle in 1748, each year most Acadians saw either or both British and French forces, with their Amerindian allies, in their neighbourhoods. Both British and French expected the Acadians to provide supplies, and the French demands strained Acadians resources. These demands, of course, were made when French forces were in the immediate neighbourhood and able to bring pressure upon the Acadian farmers to comply with their requests for meat and grain. Further, especially after the capitulation of Île Saint-Jean in August 1745, almost all the settled regions within the Nova Scotian peninsula, except Annapolis Royal, sheltered some number of refugees. The majority of the civilian population of Île Royale had been transported back to France, via Boston, within the year.[52] Some of the men, however, managed to arrive at Beaubassin. After Île Saint-Jean capitulated in early August 1745, Peter Warren wanted to transport that population too but was frustrated because of a lack of ships.[53] Some of the inhabitants who had arrived on the island only in the last two or three years returned to their former villages on the mainland.[54]

Thus, war and its consequences were a constant reality for the Acadians during these years. And, in the midst of everything, rumours of impending disaster were rife. The possibility that the Acadians would be forcibly removed from their lands by the British had been a cloud "no bigger than a man's hand" ever since 1710, an option considered and rejected by one set of British politicians and administrators after another since that date. However, in 1745 it became a matter of serious discussion among those who had been engaged in the capture of Louisbourg. It was this debate that had led to the joint letter of Mascarene and the Council to Newcastle, mentioned earlier, in the first week of December 1745. But reports about the possibility of deportation were common in the region well before November. In September, Beauharnois and Hocquart had thought the possibility serious enough to warrant an explicit dismissal of it, informing the minister that they could not imagine that the English really intended removing the Acadians in order to bring in English settlers.[55] Yet that was precisely what was being discussed by Shirley and Peter Warren, the latter at this time being governor of Île Royale. Warren wrote to the secretary of state in October 1745, arguing that "while such a number of French are suffer'd to remain in [Nova Scotia] with a very little admixture of English ... it will ever be a thorn in our side ..." He went on to note that "Governor Shirley, who is better acquainted with the State of that Colony, tells me, he has represented this to the Ministry, and proposed to repeat it again. If an equivalent could be found for these French by intermixing them in some of the remotest of our Colonys, from the French, a great advantage would thereby accrue to our Country ..."[56] From this time forward, the possibility of such an exile was part of the political discourse in the region, particularly in Boston, while the authorities in London showed themselves willing to consider deportation as a possibility but repeatedly refused official sanction for such an enterprise.

As some of the British leaders were working on the assumption that the Acadians would never become loyal subjects of the crown, an attitude sharpened by the events of the Stuart uprising in 1745, the French authorities in Quebec were working on the parallel assumption that the Acadians were deeply attached to the French monarchy. The orders given to the expedition that Beauharnois and Hocquart dispatched to the Baie Verte region in early June 1746 were drawn up in the belief that the Acadians were only waiting for the right circumstances to declare their wholehearted support for France. The governor and intendant of New France had written, in the long letter sent to the minister the previous autumn, that they had been assured by Marin and all the officers involved in his failed attacked on Annapolis Royal, as well as by the missionaries, that almost all the Acadians hoped that France would once more govern them. The dispatch emphasized that the Acadians would unhesitatingly take up arms for the French once the latter were installed at Port Royal or had supplied powder and munitions to the Acadians and had established troops in the colony.[57]

In an attempt to produce these necessary conditions for ensuring Acadian support in the re-conquest of Nova Scotia, Beauharnois and Hocquart sent Jean-Baptiste-Nicolas-Roch de Ramezay to Baie Verte with a significant force. Ramezay left Quebec on 5 June, accompanied by some seven hundred men, aboard seven ships. According to Lieutenant Daniel-Hyacinthe-Marie Liénard de Beaujeu, who kept a journal during the expedition, they were a mixed group of marines raised for the occasion and some Abena-ki.[58] Ramezay had orders to bolster the French position within the region and to coordinate with the force expected from France in an attack on Annapolis Royal. His ships ships arrived off Baie Verte on 10 July, over two months before d'Anville would find shelter at Chebucto. On 15 July, Ramezay sent one of his officers, Louis de La Corne, with two hundred men to Minas. Their instructions were to stop any further contact between the Minas settlements and Annapolis Royal. The next day, Ramezay received letters from Abbé Le Loutre, who was then at Chebucto, suggesting that he join with two frigates cruising in the area, the *Aurore* and the *Castor,* in an immediate attack on Annapolis Royal. After discussing the matter with his officers, Ramezay decided against the project. Instead, he mounted, with some difficulty, a small expedition against Port Lajoie, on Île Saint-Jean. His plans had to take into account difficulties between the local Mi'kmaq warriors, who had arrived to support him, and the Abenaki, who had sailed with him from Quebec.[59] The raid was a success and the men returned with some forty prisoners. These would prove as much a bother as a prize, for they had to be guarded and fed and, finally, transported, under guard, to Quebec.

Over the next three to four weeks, that is, from 20 July 1746 to the last week of August 1746, Ramezay managed to distribute his forces effectively from the Minas settlements to Baie Verte. However, his circumstances became increasingly difficult. Illnesses of various kinds began to strike not only his own troops but also the Mi'kmaq. At the same time, the delayed arrival of the French armada began to be worrisome. The number of English prisoners under guard increased and the Acadians of the Minas region became less and less enthusiastic about the presence of the French force. On 24 August, the Minas deputies confronted Ramezay with the news that it would be impossible for them to feed the detachment of soldiers that were supposed to remain there for the foreseeable future.[60] The deputies explained that the only cattle that now remained for slaughter were the oxen and, should they be killed, farming would have to be abandoned. The presence of the soldiers, the deputies continued, "decided nothing, embroiled them to an ever greater degree with the English and they much hoped that their justified representations would result in their leaving."[61] Ramezay responded by saying that he had to follow the orders of his superior officer, whom, however, he would inform of their concerns.

The question of supplies bedevilled the French forces over the next months. Ramezay left for Beaubassin on 1 September with a small group of soldiers and prisoners. But it proved no easier to buy food there. Beaujeu's journal records that the settlers provided a number of cattle and sheep "but much fewer than we needed."[62] Acadian farms were prosperous but the grain, cattle, and sheep produced were not inexhaustible and the summer of 1746 had seen drought conditions in the area. Yet, at the same time, the wavering nature of the Acadian enthusiasm for French expeditions in the area was also in play. This was commented on in the report written about the Acadian response to the arrival of the French fleet in Chebucto Bay. On its arrival, letters had been dispatched to Le Loutre requesting that he immediately ensure that at least fifty cattle be brought from Beaubassin, for which the settlers would be immediately paid the going price.[63] The Quebec report remarked that the immediate Acadian reaction was one of rejoicing, since they had given up any idea of any French force arriving from Europe. But the account continues with the remark that the Acadians had refused the most necessary aid to the troops expected to winter in the region because of fears of delayed payment.[64] Joseph Leblanc, *dit* Le Maigre, who had strongly supported the Duvivier expedition two years earlier, was one of those who organized supplies for the ships at Chebucto. He later acknowledged that he was paid for the cattle he delivered there.[65] But he also testified that he was never paid for the eighty cattle and fifty sheep delivered later on in October to the Annapolis Royal area. Thus, the increasing difficulty of obtaining provisions from the Acadians can be attributed, in part at least, to uncertainty of payment. But the Acadian reaction is an indication that their support for the French was neither uncritical nor unlimited.[66]

The order, given by François Bigot, to herd animals to the Annapolis Royal region was made in anticipation of the joint assault on that port, which would be carried out by Ramezay and a number of the ships presently anchored at Chebucto Bay. As has already been remarked, this enterprise failed. Whether or not Annapolis Royal could have sustained a joint assault by both land and sea forces in the autumn of 1746 is open to question but such an attack never took place and Ramezay's force alone was insufficient to defeat Mascarene. This was partly due to the reinforcements in supplies and manpower that Annapolis Royal had received over the past year but also, in large measure, to the state of Ramezay's command. The seven hundred men who had disembarked at Baie Verte in July had become, by 10 October, no more than three hundred, with "a very small number of Indians, illness having almost completely winnowed them."[67] It quickly became clear that Mascarene commanded a much greater number of men, was ensconced in a recently repaired and reprovisioned fort, and was content to allow the attackers to wear themselves out in a hopeless siege. There were a number of forays and skirmishes and, by the first week of November, Ramezay was in obvious difficulty. Food was scarce, illness was widespread, the cold had come early, the men were badly clad, and no French ships had appeared.[68] On 3 November, Ramezay received a letter from Jacques-Pierre de Taffanel de La Jonquière, who had been appointed governor of New France on 19 March 17476 and was now in charge of the remnants of d'Anville's fleet. In the letter were orders for Ramezay to retreat.

On 4 and 5 November, Ramezay began his withdrawal, first to Minas, which was reached on the 8th of the month. From there, about two weeks later, the majority of the detachment was taken by ship to Beaubassin and then marched the fifteen or so miles to Baie Verte. The remainder made the trek overland directly from Minas to Baie Verte. Strong winds and early snow had prevented an earlier departure from the Minas area. Throughout this period, rumours had swirled around that "les anglois" were in hot pursuit and were coming, by boat, to crush them at Minas. Beaujeu wrote a bitter entry in his journal on 14 November, accusing the Acadians of informing the English about the miserable circumstances of the expedition. There were now fewer than two hundred men, eaten up by lice, beaten down by misery, clothed miserably, and utterly unable to defend themselves. This state of affairs, Beaujeu wrote, was reported "to the English by the same Acadians who had seemed us the most friendly."[69] He continued, somewhat more philosophically, that, more often than not, "one opted for the stronger party" and concluded that "in any case, the English were determined to chase us out of Minas and would spare only those inhabitants who had kept the most strict neutrality."[70]

Once Ramezay had begun his retreat from Annapolis Royal, Mascarene and the Council immediately began to plan the re-establishment of their authority throughout the colony, particularly in the Minas area. Such plans depended upon troops and officers provided by Massachusetts, and, given the views previously expressed by Shirley, and others, such as Charles Knowles, the then governor of Cape Breton, about the Acadians, it might have been expected that a highly punitive operation would be devised. However, over the intervening months, Shirley had changed his mind about the desirability of evicting the Acadians. It is possible that Mascarene's argument that rumours of possible deportation would push the Acadians into outright alliance with the French weighed with the governor of Massachusetts. At any rate, on 12 September, while d'Anville's fleet was still expected, Shirley wrote to Mascarene on the issue, enclosing "printed Lettes [sic] in Ffrench to be disposed of among the French Inhabitants."[71] In these letters, Shirley wrote that he had heard "that the French Inhabitants of Nova Scotia were uneasy least the English should remove them from their Estates and transport them and their Familys to France or Elsewhere." He went on to say that he had never heard that "his Majesty had any Such Intentions ... and [he] is therefore of opinion that their Fears are without Foundation." He concluded by saying that he would use all his influence "in favour of those who behave themselves Peaceably and Quietly as his Good subjects ..." But he also warned that "those who shall do otherwise and join the Enemy, Especially those from Canada ... they may expect to be treated as his Majesty's English subjects are treated in the like provoking cases." Shirley was correct in asserting that he knew of no intention on the part of the British ministers in London to deport the Acadians. In fact, in the spring of 1747, Newcastle urged that the Acadians be informed that it was "the King's resolution to protect all who remain in their duty and in the free exercise of their religion."[72] Shirley's letter was distributed throughout the region of Annapolis Royal and, as widely as Mascarene could manage, elsewhere in the colony. This proclamation by the most powerful British administrator in the region signalled clearly that the Acadians were to be treated as British subjects, not as undeclared aliens. While this helped to allay fears of immediate expulsion of the whole Acadian community from the colony, it did not provide much comfort to those villages who had been occupied by French military forces, since it promised retribution for those proved guilty of enthusiastic aid to the French.

The communication of 12 September 1746 was important, not only because of its impact among the Acadians, but also because it meant that British orders for the expedition to Minas were drawn up with some belief in the possibility of the neutrality of the majority of the Acadians. By the second week of December 1746, a New England force was in the Grand Pré region. Though definitely under the direction of Mascarene, it was led by Arthur Noble, a lieutenant-colonel in the 2nd Massachusetts Regiment who had taken part in the capture of Louisbourg. Noble had come to Maine from Ulster in the 1720s and settled on the Kennebec, prospering over the years as a tanner and shoe manufacturer.[73] He had about four hundred men under his command and his orders were to ensure the departure of the French from the area and to find out as much as possible about whether there was still a French force at Chignecto.[74] Serving as commissary officer was Edward How, who had come to Nova Scotia in 1720 and was not only a member of the Nova Scotia Council but also a justice of the peace.[75] He had married into the Winniett-Maisonnnat family and thus had extended kin connections among the Acadian elite. Another member of the Nova Scotia Council, Erasmus James Philipps, was also with the force.[76] The tenor of the expedition's instructions made it clear that the lieutenant governor had re-established a moderating influence over the Council. How and Philipps were to "examine the conduct of the Inhabitants and Show some difference between those have been Inclind towards Serving the Enemy and have showed themselves active in it," an instruction that was obviously based on the belief that there were measurable differences of opinion among the Acadians. Indeed, in a private letter to the two men, Mascarene emphasized that they were to make such a "distinction [that] those of ye French Inhabitants who have a mind to keep in their fidelity to His Majesty and live peaceably may be encouraged and others deterr'd from acting contrary to their Oaths of Fidelity."[77] How and Philipps were also instructed to purchase grain and "a Number of sheep and Black Cattle" for which the Acadians were to be paid" at the usual rate.[78] But perhaps the most important civil function of the expedition was to "make them [the settlers] chuse New Deputys and Return them here as soon as possible."

Deputies from Grand Pré and Pisiquid arrived to attend a meeting of Council at the end of November, bringing with them a letter that gave an "account of their Miserable state during the war with Acknowledgmts of Obligations to govr Shirley for his Letter and Promises strictly to observe and adhere to their Oath of neutrality."[79] The deputies asserted that Ramezay "had at one time 1650 Men Canadian Militia Fishermen Volunteers Indians" under his command. On being questioned about their behaviour "whilst the Enemy was amongst them," the deputies replied that "none of their Inhabitants had Offer'd to take up arms in conjunction with the Enemy ..." However, they agreed that they had been "oblig'd to furnish them Provisions and Horses in former times." They went on to say that the French depredations had been somewhat less than previously because they had brought a great deal of flour and pease with them. At the conclusion of their testimony, the deputies were asked whether, "now that the Enemy was with drawn ... they would not undertake in Behalf of the People of Menis to take up those who were suspected by the Government to have been Willingly active for the Enemy and bring them here [to Annapolis Royal] ..." The deputies replied bluntly this was an impossible undertaking, since "the Inhabitants could not be brought to a Resolution of laying hands on their Brethren in Order to bring them to Punishment." Given that the families within all Acadian settlements were closely linked with one another, as immediate kin and through intermarriage, "brethren" is a particularly appropriate word to emphasize the conflict of loyalties that such an undertaking would mean. The Acadian sense of neutrality clearly encompassed a belief that individuals were not obliged to offer information, to either party, about the activities of others within their communities. Family arguments about information given to either side, and about the amount of aid that would be offered to those faced with an armed force, were arguments within families and among the villagers. To outsiders, whether French or British, Acadians proffered little about the activities of their kin.

As 1746 drew to a close, the detachment at Minas settled in for the winter months. Officers and men were billeted in the village of Grand Pré itself.[80] How had made a survey of the grain and herds throughout the Minas area and concluded that the Acadians had been less than accurate about their reserves. He was present at a Council meeting in late December, when the Acadian deputies were told that the settlers could well spare one in twelve of their cattle, which would provide enough beef for "a thousand men for three months."[81] As to the grain, any shortfall would be in the grain kept for sowing and that could be replaced in the "Spring either in Specie or in Indian Corn." The Council believed that the deputies "were fully Satisfied" with these arrangements. From the point of view of Mascarene and his officers, it looked as if matters were now settled until the spring, since it seemed obvious that the French would not venture another attack in the Minas area until then. There were, admittedly, a number of warnings by various Acadians that a winter attack was a possibility[82]; however, Noble and his officers deferred the organization of defensive measures until the arrival of better weather, leaving the shot for the cannon on boats in the river rather than with the gun emplacements in the village of Grand Pré.[83]

The French, now encamped at Beaubassin, had learnt, within a week of their arrival, of the presence of the British force at Minas.[84] Determined to oust the British before they could entrench themselves, and to reinforce the idea of French authority over the Grand Pré region, Ramezay and his officers set about preparing for an overland trek in winter. Ramezay himself would prove too sick to lead the expedition and so the command fell to Joseph Coulon de Villiers de Jumonville, a captain in the regular troops. He was thirty-three, the eldest son of a "typical Canadian military family."[85] His father and two of his brothers all had military careers and he himself served in the army from the age of seventeen, participating in an expedition against the Fox nation in 1733 in which his father, a brother, and a brother-in-law were killed and his other brother wounded. In sum, he was a seasoned soldier, well acquainted with the tactics of European fighting in North America. Among the officers he had with him was the equally experienced La Corne. It took almost two weeks to organize men and supplies, since the French had been camped partly on the Beaubassin side of the isthmus and partly at Baie Verte. Sleighs had to be made and snowshoes provided for the company. Finally, some three hundred men, mostly regular French troops but with approximately sixty Mi'kmaq and Malecite, were brought together at Baie Verte.

The extraordinary feat that this body of men then accomplished has been recounted a number of times, first and foremost in the diary of the campaign written by Beaujeu, who participated in it.[86] In brief, on 21 January the men left the Baie Verte region and, on 10 February, arrived at Grand Pré. They had snowshoed about 120 miles in appalling weather, bringing with them, in backpacks or on the sleighs they pulled themselves, all necessary military supplies and equipment as well as a considerable amount of food.[87] They had to negotiate the moving ice over tidal rivers and streams and deep snow. Tree trunks brought down by the winds made the carrying of supplies particularly difficult. Now and again, at the small settlement at Tatamegouche and at Cobequid, they found settlers who provided, willingly or unwillingly, food and shelter. As they journeyed, about a score of young men joined their ranks and acted, above all, as guides and as informants about the organization of the British force.

On 9 February, in the midst of a snowstorm, Coulon's force had arrived at Pisiquid, where they were sheltered and fed by the settlers. The force stayed overnight before setting out, despite the continuing snow, at midday on the 10th for Grand Pré. Coulon had organized his men into ten companies. Beaujeu wrote that the Acadians, who accompanied them, had enrolled as ordinary soldiers but served as guides, being much needed in that role.[88] They halted in the late afternoon on the Gaspereau River and waited until early evening before taking over the dwellings in the area. At this point, Coulon and his men were about two miles from Grand Pré itself. At three o'clock in the morning of 11 February, the attack was launched. Captain Noble had billeted his officers and men among the twenty-four houses that were strung out along the slopes of the ridge that bordered the reclaimed marshlands. Coulon's tactics were similar to those that had characterized French actions against Massachusetts for decades but that had not been seen before in Nova Scotia. The defenders were taken completely by surprise, having posted no sentries, and the attackers were able to come to within musket range of the houses before any alarm was sounded. Captain Noble was killed early in the engagement. By the afternoon of the next day, Noble's successor, Benjamin Goldthwait, had capitulated.

It had been a one-sided affair. The New England force lost not only its commander but five other officers and seventy men, according to their own records. As well, thirty-eight others had been wounded and between forty and sixty had been taken prisoner. According to Beaujeu, however, who helped bury the dead and made his calculations with How, 140 of the New England force had been killed, thirty-eight wounded. and fifty-four taken prisoner.[89] La Corne reported much the same totals for dead, wounded, and captured. The French had lost fewer than ten killed and under twenty wounded, one of the latter being Coulon, who handed over his command to La Corne.[90] The differences in the totals of dead, wounded, and captured in the British and French records do not alter either the overall picture of the engagement being the bloodiest fighting ever to take place in the colony or the fact of the French victory. The visible carnage in the area was the worst that the Acadian settlers would have seen in their lives. Furthermore, the massacre took place in and around the Acadian houses. The aftermath of the conflict – the work of caring for the wounded with few resources and of burying the dead, mostly in a common grave in frozen ground – would provide further evidence of the costs of war.

The articles of capitulation were simple. First, the New England troops were to leave the Grand Pré area within two days, "with the honours of war, six days of provisions, their knapsacks, a pound of shot and one of powder." It was also agreed that those previously taken prisoner were to remain captive, and that the boat and schooner that had been seized, as well as what the Indians had pillaged, would not be restored. As to the sick and wounded on the British side, they were to be allowed to rest in the settlement at Rivière-aux-Canards – the other side of the expanse of drained marshland – until they had recovered, the expenses for this being later paid by the British crown. Finally, no one who had fought the French at Grand Pré was to serve in that region, or in or around Pisiquid, Cobequid, or Beaubassin, for six months.[91] As Benjamin Goldthwait prepared to return to Annapolis Royal, he issued an invitation to the French officers to dine with him and his men, so that they all might become better acquainted over a bowl of punch.[92] The invitation was accepted. The next day, on 14 February, the New Englanders left for Annapolis Royal.

The Acadian leaders met with La Corne on 19 February and made it clear that feeding the various French and English soldiers who had been billeted among them over the past years had reduced them to a pitiable state.[93] The deputies went on to say that, since they were overjoyed to have the French among them, they obviously could not refuse to provision them, yet it was difficult to do so.[94] Beaujeu wrote that food was short and, further, many of the soldiers were ill. In the light of this, La Corne decided to return to the Baie Verte-Beaubassin area and his command marched away from Grand Pré on 23 February. By 7 March, most had reached Baie Verte. There they discovered that Ramezay had received orders to send the majority of officers and men back to Quebec. Ramezay himself remained at Beaubassin, with a small number of men, until late June.[95] Led by La Corne, those who had fought at Grand Pré made one more exhausting journey. This last trek, Beaujeu wrote, was particularly hard, accomplished on snowshoes and with the men pulling sleds, and the only food available being flour and candle-fat made into an unappetizing paste.[96] They reached Quebec on the 27th of the month.

The impact of this bloody clash on the politics of the region was considerable but it lay more in the confirmation of the present policies than in any dramatic change of either the tactics or strategy of the parties involved. This was because the French victory proved indecisive, their forces incapable of holding what had been captured. It was a punishing raid whose effect on the opposing force was not consolidated. In writing about it to Newcastle, Governor Shirley spoke of the extent to which the defeat of the Massachusetts force was due to the "want of a proper Security for the Men" and the lack of support provided Noble.[97] Shirley was more than ever convinced that only the establishment of garrisons throughout the peninsula would provide "an effectual Security to the Province against the enemy and oblige the Inhabitants in a little time to contribute towards the protection & Expence of the Government ..."[98] He wrote in this same dispatch of the unreliability of the "Inhabitants of Minas," who, he believed, had given the French "very certain Intelligence." However, he admitted that the Acadians had been courteous to Noble's force, supplied "the King's Troops with Provisions," and professed sorrow for what Shirley himself described as "the late Accident there." The French believed that their expedition had boosted Acadian morale, something that would be of considerable help when another effort at re-conquest was made.[99] Mascarene remained equally convinced that the majority of the Acadians had been neutral during the conflict. In a dispatch to the Lords of Trade on 12 May 1747, he wrote that those who helped the French at Minas "were chiefly outlaws; those of any figure were from the Island of St. John and from St. Peter's on Cape Breton."[100]

Strengthened by victories in Europe and in the Far East, France now had the will, the men, and the money to attempt, once more, to retake Louisbourg and Annapolis Royal and to reprovision New France. But, while sending supplies to Quebec posed no particular problems, the task of retaking Louisbourg and Annapolis Royal involved the difficulty of, once more, bringing French troops to the Atlantic coast. That matter was made more complex by the administrative situation at Quebec at the time. Beauharnois had been appointed governor in 1726 and in the spring of 1747 he was approaching his seventy-sixth birthday. His successor, La Jonquière, had been appointed the previous year but had not yet arrived at Quebec. Thus, the convoy of thirty-nine merchant ships, three frigates, and two ships of the line that set out from Île d'Aix on 10 May 1747, under the command of La Jonquière, was as important for the people it carried as for its cargoes. It fell victim, however, to weather and a British force under the command of Vice-Admiral George Anson and Rear-Admiral Peter Warren.[101] As a result of this setback, Roland-Michel Barrin de La Galissonière, a man whose service experience was navy not army, whose expertise was the sea not land, governed New France until La Jonquière arrived in Quebec in August 1749. La Galissonière was more than competent and had a passionate belief in the future of New France, writing to Maurepas on 6 November 1747 that any idea of abandoning the colony should be unthinkable.[102] But, not unnaturally, La Galissonière concentrated his attention on defence rather than offence, and establishing the best possible alliances with the Iroquois rather than supporting another foray into Nova Scotia.[103] Much as he wished to extend the French empire in North America, he could do little until he received the ever-promised but always elusive supplies from France. Plans for the recapture of Louisbourg and Annapolis Royal were postponed. During the months leading up to the Treaty of Aix-la-Chapelle, the main articles of which were agreed upon in late April 1748, the French presence among the Acadians was mostly a matter of particular individuals, acting as agents and informants.

This was enough, however, to make certain that the Acadians, especially in the Minas and Beaubassin regions, were kept constantly aware of the French claims to Nova Scotia and their demand for Acadian loyalty. In fact, Ramezay issued two proclamations before he himself left for Quebec in the early summer of 1747, stating that the victory at Grand Pré had made the Acadians once more subjects of France.[104] But there was no military action to reinforce this claim: Ramezay's announcement was in the nature of a warning to the Acadians that their loyalty should be to France, something that Abbé Le Loutre would emphasize when he returned to the region in 1749. The uncomfortable situation of the Acadians after 1747 became particularly clear with the arrival of Captain John Rous, a member of the Nova Scotia Council, a naval officer, and a privateer, at Minas, with a twenty-gun brig and two smaller vessels,[105] on 12 April, less than a fortnight after Ramezy had issued his first proclamation. Mascarene intended the force to be primarily a matter of civil administration not military action, with the purpose of making "the French Inhabitants of [Minas] sensible of their being still under the Dominion of the King of Great Britain ..."[106] In fact, Mascarene explicitly told Charles Morris, one of military officers who accompanied Rous, "to treat the Inhabitants with mildness and to prevent your Party from doing them any Damage in their Persons or Effects and Properties ..."[107] Morris, who would become increasingly important in the administration of Nova Scotia over the next eight years, was Massachusetts born and bred and had been at Grand Pré with Noble in February.[108]

During the final months of the peace negotiations, Mascarene steadfastly held to his beliefs that the majority of the Acadians had remained non-combatants throughout the war, despite the pressure brought on them by the "Canadians." In a letter he wrote to Shirley in April 1748, Mascarene articulated, with great clarity, what he saw as the position of those who wished to treat the Acadians as inveterate enemies. He remarked that

there are here [Annapolis Royal] Persons prejudic'd against the French Inhabitants three different ways. The first is by an inbibed notion that all who bear the name of French must be natrual Ennemies of great Brittain; the Second from views of Interest and other Relations, and those so affected tho' in public they runn down these Inhabitants yet underhand favour them and are partial towards those By whom they find their Interest promoted; the third deem this People by their being originary from another nation, differeing in language, manners, relation and Religion, no better than in a continual State of Rebellion and are ever talking of ousting them, transplanting or destroying them, without considering the Circumstances this Province has lately been and still is in, and the fatal consequences that might have insued from any Violent measures.[109]

This analysis of the state of Nova Scotia, and the attitudes of those he governed, was the basis of Mascarene's policy for the last months of his service. In addition to the dispatch of troops to the Minas area, he attempted to re-establish his authority there by encouraging trade between the settlers and Boston merchants, by organizing reparations for a number of those whose houses had been damaged in the recent affray, and by presenting a reasoned argument to the Acadians on the realities of their position. The first trading vessel quickly followed on the Rous expedition.[110] Mascarene saw commerce primarily as the fulfilment of an obligation, something that "those Inhabitants who whilst they behave as their oath of Fidelity obliges them to have a right to claim their being supply'd by us with their Necessarys."[111] But he also saw the purchase of surplus grain from the inhabitants, which was a crucial part of such commerce, as a "means to prevent the Canadians in their descents upon this Country from finding any Subsistance ..."[112] The reports that Mascarene received that "the Inhabitants were very glade of their [the traders] coming" are hardly surprising. A considerable amount of money and goods exchanged hands, partly because of the normal buying and selling of agricultural products for condiments, cloth, and tools. The traders brought molasses, salt, linen, sugar, wood axes, and scythes. The largest component of trade was for payment to the

Acadians for goods already supplied in 1746 and for repairs to two of the houses in the village of Grand Pré.[113] The extent to which the Acadians did have, in the spring of 1747, surplus grain and cattle to sell is an interesting question, given the representations of the deputies to La Corne in February that they would have difficulty providing him with supplies.

The help provided by Mascarene to René Leblanc and a certain Baptist Babin for the repair of their dwellings is some indication of the extent to which men known to be friendly to the British were rewarded. Leblanc had been appointed as notary for the Grand Pré area in 1744.[114] He obviously supported the British claims as firmly as one of his relatives, Joseph Leblanc, supported the French. In a letter to the captain of a trading vessel that left Annapolis Royal for Minas at the end of April 1748, Mascarene had asked that he "advance to old Rene La Blanc to the value of fourty pounds old Tenor such necessarys as he may want but let none know of it but himself." Mascarene went on to advise the trader to show little confidence in Leblanc in public but remarked that "in private if he can do it without being observed he may give you Information tending to the good of the Public service whereof I will be glad ..."[115] One thousand *livres* was awarded to Leblanc and 600 *livres* to Babin (It is unclear whether the payment was in specie or in goods.) These payments were something of a counterweight to the proscription of twelve men as guilty of treason, men such as Louis Gautier and his two sons, Joseph and Pierre, as well as Joseph Leblanc.[116] Rewards of £50 were offered for help in apprehending these men.

While commerce and the payment for goods and services rendered were important elements in Mascarene's government of the Acadians, he also spent time and energy on attempts to persuade the Acadians, through argument, of what their right conduct should be. The last lengthy communication that Mascarene addressed to the deputies of Minas shows both his respect for the Acadians and his exasperation with their actions. He opened his letter with a complaint. He was pained to discover, he wrote, that the Acadians' promises of "Strict Obedience to his Britannic Majesty" had not been borne out by their actions. The result, he went on, will "undoubtedly Cause the sincerity of your Promises to be much suspected and consequently render all my Endeavours to promote your happiness to be aborted ..."[117] He acknowledged the deep divisions within the settlement but this, in his view, did not excuse their attempt "to live as an Independt. State ..." Specifically, he charged them with not "strengthening the Hands of this Govmt." so that "those Turbulent and unruly Disturbers of the peace, Especially such as are prescribed" could be brought to book. The unwillingness of the community to expel "the Rebellious faction," those "Banditti who are surely seeking your ruin as well as their own by involving you thus Insensibly in their guilt," meant that the whole community could possibly be charged "with perjury as well as with Contempt of his Majesty's Bounty." Mascarene also objected to the settlers' support of Alexandre Bourg as notary instead of "the proper person René Le Blanc" and demanded that this matter be regularized immediately. Finally, he mentioned that "the Community in General" had provided a far too "kind reception & Entertainment ... [to our Deserters]."

Mascarene's opening complaint, that there was a difference between Acadian promises and their actions, was more in the nature of a general comment than anything else. Mascarene knew only too well of the impact of the French on the Acadian communities, although whether or not he knew of Ramezay's proclamation ordering the Acadians to have no further dealings with Annapolis Royal is not clear. But Mascarene also realized that others took a much less charitable view of the Acadians' temporising, viewing their actions with a jaundiced eye. In the letter, already cited, that Mascarene had sent Shirley in April 1748, he had acknowledged that no consideration of Acadian circumstances, no understanding of the nature of life on the border between two empires, entered such minds. He was well aware of the readiness with which any Acadian actions helpful to France were judged treasonous by some, including what may well have been merely humanitarian aid to a bewildered Irish Catholic lad who no longer wanted to serve at Annapolis Royal.

But the next issues raised by Mascarene are more serious, for they are matters of self-determination if not self-government. The refusal of the Minas settlers to turn over those who allied themselves with the French and Canadian forces arose, as Mascarene suggested, from the divisions within the settlement. But it also amounted, obviously, to non-cooperation with the British authorities. Indeed, the settlers in the Minas had not merely remained uncooperative when asked to hand over those proscribed but had prevented a copy of the proclamation being taken to the Chignecto area by burning it.[118] Such actions were to some extent no more than the Acadian equivalent of the impressment riots in Boston.[119] But, while these riots were the reaction of a part of a community against the demands of its government, the actions of the Acadians were part of a struggle to limit acknowledgment by that community of the ways in which those who claimed them as subjects could exercise authority within their settlements. This refusal by the Acadians to cooperate with any attempt to bring to trial those who had undeniably supported the French may have had roots in the strong kinship ties among the Acadians, but it was also a denial of the supremacy of British law within the colony. In addition, Acadian support for the continued service of Bourg as a notary, rather than for the man named by the Annapolis authorities, René Leblanc, was a defiance of the British right to appoint civic officials for the Acadians. Together, these actions raised questions about Acadian acceptance of the right of the British to govern the colony, according to the norms of eighteenth-century European constitutional practice.

That this was not articulated in such words, either by the Acadians or by Mascarene, does not alter the fact that what was in debate between Mascarene and the Acadians was a basic issue of governance. Acadians presented the British with the challenge of subjects who would be citizens. That is to say, instead of accepting the generally held view that their relationship with the British monarchy was simply one of subjects and rulers, the Acadians acted as if they had rights of citizenship. Subjects have, as Anne Dummett and Andrew Nicol point out, "a personal link ... [it is] ... a vertical relationship between monarch and individual, not a horizontal one between members of a nation or citizens of a body politic."[120] Consciously or unconsciously, the Acadian stance represented two beliefs. The first was that they were indeed a people, distinct from both the French of France and French Canadians. The second was that, despite the actions of empires and the decisions of princes, the Acadians had every right to debate and present ideas about how and where they should live. The Acadian experience of life on a border that was the meeting place between two empires, each interested in expanding into territory claimed by the other, had sharpened the Acadian sense of their political needs. Ever since 1710, the Acadians had continuously and explicitly expressed their desire to remain on the lands they had settled, to have the services of Catholic priests within their villages, and not to bear arms. Broader questions, involving the final authority of a particular power over their lands, were secondary to these desires. This attitude is understandable, given the freedom from central control that their farms and villages enjoyed, no matter what power considered the Acadians to be their subjects. However, with the War of the Austrian Succession, imperial affairs intruded directly into the Acadians' lives, and these affairs required the Acadians explicitly to declare an interest in the outcome of great-power rivalries.

Since 1710, clearly, the possibility that the Acadians would be compelled to recognize that they lived in an era when the governed were considered subjects had increased. For nearly four decades, however, they had avoided confronting this reality of eighteenth-century European politics. In the 1740s this was due to Mascarene, a man who, while he gave his allegiance to the established monarchical structure of government, worked hard to make that government as flexible as possible. He was in his mid-sixties in 1748. Now at the end of his career, he was a shrewd pragmatist, not an idealist, and his view of the Acadians was based upon more than thirty years' acquaintance with their society and those chosen by them as representatives. Further, Mascarene was at home in the transatlantic world of the mid-eighteenth century, a world where political power was in the hands of those favoured by birth or the patronage of the well-born. He was fully cognizant of the power of the hereditary landowners and the growing influence of the newly wealthy who had obtained the approval of such men.[121] Accordingly, Mascarene was not someone who worked for a major change in the structure of politics and society; rather, he strove to make the situation he inherited function as effectively as possible. He sought to accommodate the Acadians not by changing the system of governance he knew but by opening their eyes to the benefits of that system and thus making them, as he wrote on more than one occasion, "good subjects" of the British crown.[122]

The outbreak of war in 1744 had made Mascarene's ambitions almost impossible to realize, although he himself never lost faith. The region was now in contention between empires and all those with an interest in Nova Scotia brought pressure to bear on its inhabitants, whether members of the British administration and garrison, the Acadians, or the Mi'kmaq. Massachusetts's influence on Nova Scotian affairs meant that Mascarene had to oppose the Draconian plans of Shirley and Warren while countering the efforts of the French to bring the Acadians wholeheartedly to their support. The conclusion of hostilities did not usher in tranquillity and, in 1748, the Treaty of Aix-la-Chapelle merely increased tensions in the area. Within less than a year, Mascarene had retired to finish his days in Boston, "reading, playing chess, and cutting the modest figure of a comfortably retired officer ..."[123] Over the next six years, the difficulties of the Acadians would increase as the aftermath of one war proved to be nothing more than the preparation for the next.

CHAPTER FOURTEEN

The Splintered Truce

The War of the Austrian Succession (known later in the United States as King George's War), and the Treaty of Aix-la-Chapelle, which brought it an end in 1748, have been most often studied as a prelude to the more dramatic Seven Years' War of 1756–63 and the subsequent Peace of Paris. This has come about partly because the latter is not only more eventful but has always been considered more particularly important to American history.[1] It has also happened because, even for many of those who were part of the negotiations, the agreement reached in 1748 was seen more as a truce than a lasting settlement.[2] By 1747, both Great Britain and France were appalled by the heavy cost of war and neither could see any way to defeat the other in their particular area of strength. France seemed as obviously superior on the European continent as her opponent did at sea and in the colonies. Both sides had won major victories, the French at Fontenoy/Fanton and in India, the British at Louisbourg and in the Caribbean. Overall military honours were not uneven, and thus it is not surprising that one of the main agreements reached was the mutual restitution of conquests, including the return of Louisbourg to France. However, not only the governments of the two powers but also many of the elite in both countries were convinced that the treaties neither accorded them their due nor gave them proper compensation for the cost of the war.

In France, the public mood was expressed by the Comte d'Argenson, who wrote that "the French wanted peace ... but they also wanted glory and honour ... they were filled with consternation at the poor conditions which France had obtained ... 'What!' they asked, 'have we really surrendered all our conquests?'"[3] A contemporary report in the *Caledonian Mercury* expressed much the same opinions but from the point of view of Great Britain, emphasizing the loss of men, the increase of the national debt by some thirty million pounds, and above all the restoration of "*Cape Breton* to the Crown of *France* ..."[4] The renewal of conflict was almost inevitable. When it came it was a conflict that had a very different temper from previous wars between the two powers, where the pretexts for hostilities had been rooted in the confrontation of monarchies, centred above all on their European interests and possessions. After 1748, Britain and France fought for rights to imperial expansion in the Caribbean and in North America as much, if not more, than for dynastic rights. Commercial matters became of far greater importance than in the previous war, as did military action to defend the demands of expanding trade.[5] At the same time, ideological concerns about cultural superiority entered the political arena to a far greater extent than they had in the past.

The years from 1744 to 1755 were, in many ways, the years in which national pride became not merely one issue among many in Franco-British affairs but one of the most important. The mid-eighteenth century in Europe continued to see the development of a cosmopolitan culture at the level of the elite. Great Britain's links to Hanover were only part of a network of connections between European aristocracy which supported a continental culture, not only in music, art, philosophy, and literature but also in porcelain and household furnishings.[6] In 1740, 49 per cent of the fellows of the British Royal Society were foreigners and Laurence Sterne was immensely popular in Paris.[7] But there was a growing support for a much more parochial cultural nationalism among the developing urban middle classes. French actors were booed in London throughout the 1740s[8] and, in the same period, a leading French essayist wrote that "the English are a rational and trading people, who seek only to enrich themselves and have not that powerful motive ... to make them act for the public good preferably to their own."[9] It was beliefs of this type that promoted an ever stronger sense of national identity as something that should have political expression. National identity was now becoming something much more complex than common social behavioural patterns among a monarch's subjects. The idea that nations existed, which in one sense has been current since Tacitus wrote, began to be linked to political principles. By the mid-eighteenth century, nationalism was not merely the belief that each nation had "an explicit and peculiar character" but the conviction that "the interests and values of this nation [should] take priority over all other interests and values."[10] That was the background to the New Englanders' enthusiasm over the defeat of the French at Louisbourg in 1745. It was also the root of La Galissonière's argument in 1748 for the preservation of French possessions in North America. "Motives of honour, glory and religion forbid the abandonment of an established Colony," he wrote, "the surrender [of it] ... to a nation inimical by taste, education and religious principle to the French who have emigrated thither ... in fine, the giving up of so salutary a work as that of the conversion of the heathen who inhabit that vast continent."[11] Thus, while Aix-la-Chapelle brought an official end to war between Great Britain and France in 1748, it also, as George Stanley wrote in 1968, began a "cold war on the Atlantic coast."[12]

Of course, the eighteenth-century "cold war" was not fuelled solely by emerging national ideologies: the competition for empire also involved acquisition of territory for strategic reasons and of markets for commercial advantages. In this situation, the region that was the northeastern flank of the British empire in North America and, simultaneously, the southeastern border of the French empire became a crucial area of the rivalry of the two powers. And so in 1749 Great Britain and France immediately set about strengthening their forces there. For France, this meant the repossession and rebuilding of Louisbourg and the repeopling of Île Royale and Île Saint-Jean. For Great Britain, it meant the establishment of a military counterbalance to Louisbourg in Nova Scotia. Both tasks required men and money and their accomplishment would be subject to the vagaries of government politics.

Charles Des Herbiers de La Ralière was appointed governor of Île Royale. He arrived there with five hundred soldiers on 29 June and the transfer of control took place on 23 July 1749 (N.S.).[13] Eight days before he reached Louisbourg, on 2 June 1749, Colonel Edward Cornwallis, newly appointed captain-general and governor of Nova Scotia, arrived in Chebucto Bay on board the *Sphinx,* a sloop of war. Within the month, a fleet of thirteen transports from London also arrived there, carrying some 2,576 people, 500 of whom were the crews of the vessels.[14] Des Herbiers was forty-nine, a naval officer in a family of naval officers, his uncle a rear-admiral. Edward Cornwallis was the sixth son of the well-connected Charles, 4th Baron Cornwallis.[15] Both Des Herbiers and Cornwallis had seen action at Fontenoy and Cornwallis had been part of the forces sent to control Scotland after the 1745 Stuart rebellion. The instructions given to each were, in sum, to defend and extend, by all possible means including limited military action, the territorial claims of their own government throughout the region. As a consequence, each man's life was immeasurably complicated by the actions of his counterpart.

Neither man faced an easy assignment. In more than one respect, their situations were similar. Both men had neighbours with a vital interest in their affairs and the tacit, if not direct, right to proffer advice which could not be cavalierly dismissed. Des Herbiers's freedom of action was clearly limited by the projects undertaken by the governor of New France and by the fact that François Bigot, the current intendant of New France, had served at Louisbourg. Cornwallis had more freedom, especially since Governor Shirley of Massachusetts had departed Boston for four years in London just before Cornwallis arrived at Chebucto Bay. Nevertheless, Shirley's ideas had been a significant part of the instructions that Cornwallis received and his successors would find Shirley as dominant an influence as he had been for Mascarene. Des Herbiers's immediate problems were marginally the less difficult, perhaps, since he had to rebuild and repair a fortress and a town, while Cornwallis had to establish and build both new fortifications and a new city. Des Herbiers had to resettle old colonists, some of whom he brought with him, and, if possible, attract Acadians, people already familiar with the region, to his territory. Cornwallis, on the other hand, had not only to plan the new city that would be the major garrison for his colony but also to settle somewhere between three and five thousand inexperienced new colonists, mostly within that same city, although his instructions had called for their distribution throughout the colony.[16] At the same time, he had to prevent the Acadians, at the very least, from becoming a major population resource for the French by emigrating to French-held territory. While Des Herbiers had to deal with the independence of the Mi'kmaq as temperamental allies, Cornwallis had to ward off attacks from these same Mi'kmaq as well as the Malecite.

The most crucial difference between the situations faced by Cornwallis and Des Herbiers, however, was in the level of support given to the two men. While there is no doubt that Great Britain intended to strengthen Nova Scotia, and would spend a great deal of money to achieve this end, the colony did not have the same importance for the British that Louisbourg had for the French. Massachusetts, and the other British North American colonies, obviously had a much greater weight in the evolution of colonial policy in London than did Nova Scotia. In 1749 London was not at all clear on what its military policy ought to be in North America, or how Nova Scotia should be integrated into that policy. The French, on the other hand, had a much more centralized imperial strategy for their North American possessions; they knew clearly how they wished to establish their military supremacy on that continent, what part Louisbourg, Île Royale, and Île Saint-Jean should play in their endeavours, and what steps should be taken to counter British actions in Nova Scotia. The French minister, Maurepas, outlined his thinking in a lengthy memorandum that was read to the king on 29 August 1749.[17] The minister opened his exposition with an overview of the British settlements in Nova Scotia, which he represented as stretching from Chebucto Bay to La Hève, Minas, and Baie Verte. He believed that these communities would be supported by a garrison of two thousand soldiers. This was a far rosier picture than the reality of what the British had achieved at that time, or would achieve in the next six years. But Maurepas was convinced of the accuracy of his analysis and he believed that the inevitable result would be that "the old settlers who had always kept the wish and hope to return to French control, would have to renounce both and submit formally and for ever to English domination."[18] As well, the memorandum continued, there would be other, perhaps more serious, consequences: the Acadians would be prevented from supplying meat and other food to Île Royale and, should war break out, English warships would be able to wreak havoc with French shipping and supply lines. The minister then went on to say that it was impossible to oppose the British openly, "since they had the right to make whatever settlements they deemed appropriate in Acadia."[19] The sole recourse left to France, therefore, was "to place, indirectly, as many obstacles in their way, without [self-] incrimination."[20] The impediments that were proposed were two and of equal importance. The first was to persuade the Mi'kmaq to harass the British openly, and then to persuade the Acadians to encourage such harassment. The missionaries, both those ministering to the Acadians and those with the care of the Mi'kmaq, had been given their orders to support this enterprise and had intimated that they were willing to do so.[21] Secondly, every effort was to be made to draw off the Acadian families to Île Saint-Jean and Île Royale, something that was considered to be easy enough, given the supposed Acadian discontent with the British.

The policy having been decided, the French set about re-establishing Louisbourg as one of the bases for the development of these ideas, the other base being Quebec. A fair number of the settlers who had been deported to France from Louisbourg, or left on their own for Acadia and Quebec in 1745, now returned. For the first two years, they were supplied with rations from the king's stores[22] and by 1752 the population of Louisbourg itself approached two thousand and that of the outports about fifteen hundred.[23] At the same time, the garrison had been augmented with twenty-four companies of fifty men each and a further company of artillery, making a garrison of well over a thousand men.[24] Over the next five years, this garrison was maintained at nearly the same strength as the regular garrison at Quebec, an indication of precisely how important Île Royale was considered by the minister. Maurepas was convinced that French control not only of Île Royale and Canada but also Louisbourg and the West Indies depended on Louisbourg.[25] Further evidence of this view is found in a dispatch of Louis Franquet, one of the most renowned military engineers of the time, who had been sent to oversee the restoration of the fortress and draft the plans for whatever military works were considered to be necessary elsewhere on Île Royale and Île Saint-Jean.[26]

Partly as a result of Maurepas's activities, Cornwallis faced immediate security problems on two fronts: the integrity of the boundaries claimed for the colony itself, particularly in the Chignecto isthmus area, and Mi'kmaq attacks on the new settlements. The difficulties of the Chignecto boundary were exacerbated by actions taken by both the British and the French in late 1748 and 1749. It had become clear, during the negotiations for the peace, that the question of the limits of Nova Scotia was one "of the most important [points] to be Determin'd for settling the same Tranquillity in America as had been so happily established in Europe."[27] There were two major reasons for this: one arose from the wording of the treaty itself and the other from the fact that much of disputed area had been actually fought over between 1744 and 1748. The relevant clause in the Treaty of Utrecht had stipulated that Great Britain should receive "all Nova Scotia or Acadie, comprehended within its antient boundaries."[28] Did the territory include, as the most extreme demands of Great Britain maintained, everything north and east from the Bay of Fundy to the St Lawrence? Or, as the French argued, was the territory they ceded in 1713 merely a thin sliver of land surrounding Annapolis Royal?[29] The less absurd claims of the two powers were no less contentious. France demanded the north shore of the Bay of Fundy, the isthmus of Chignecto, and connecting territory from that isthmus along the Atlantic coast to Canso. Great Britain, on the other hand, claimed the whole of present-day Nova Scotia to the Missaguash River and much of the north shore of the Bay of Fundy. It was agreed that an international joint commission would be established to settle the issue. This body met for the first time in September 1749 and continued to assemble, sporadically, until 1753. It accomplished almost nothing, and its lack of progress helped to confirm William Shirley, who was one of the commissioners,[30] in his belief that force of arms was the only way to safeguard British interests in North America.[31]

The immediate source of trouble for Cornwallis, however, was less the inadequacy of the commission than the determination of both sides to control as much territory as possible in order to establish the widest possible bounds for their claims by fait accompli. The cessation of formal hostilities in the autumn of 1748 meant that both sides began informal testing of the other's resolve to protect territory and, at the same time, to bolster their own claims by pre-emptive definition of where the boundary ran. Thus, even before Cornwallis arrived, trouble was brewing. In January 1749 La Galissonière had written to Mascarene complaining, not only of the expedition that had been sent to the Saint John but also of the latter's attempt to enforce British control over the Minas region.[32] At the same time, he himself had dispatched Charles Deschamps de Boishébert et de Raffetot to the mouth of the Saint John to hold that area for France.[33] So, if there was no fighting between British and French forces in Europe at this time, in North America there was a definite atmosphere of challenge and response throughout the Chignecto area and along the north shore of the Bay of Fundy. If he was to ensure that Nova Scotia became, in fact, a strong British colony, Cornwallis was faced, on his arrival, with the need to make certain that the Minas area recognized British authority and that the Chignecto area was, at the very least, aware of his strength. But, until sometime in 1750, Cornwallis lacked the necessary force to achieve these aims.

Such military weakness is surprising, given that one of the major reasons for his appointment as governor and his instructions to establish new settlements in the province was to provide a counterbalance to the French strength in the region. As well as the disappointment in England over the return of Louisbourg to France, there had been thunderous criticism from Boston over this provision.[34] Massachusetts not only felt that the expenditure of its men was undervalued but also that it was once more militarily weakened in the face of French power. It had been partly in response to these criticisms that plans had been drawn up in London to make Nova Scotia a colony that would be a reliable outpost of the British empire instead of a region of doubtful security, inhabited mostly by Amerindians and people of French descent, neither community seeming to have a proper attachment to His Britannic Majesty. The plans included not only money for an enlarged garrison, a new fortified settlement on the Atlantic coast, and the appointment of an influential and well connected soldier, Edward Cornwallis, as governor but also assistance for Protestant migration to the colony. In the early months of the new regime, plans for sending Protestant settlers to Nova Scotia took precedence over matters of military organization, which helps to explain Cornwallis's lack of sufficient resources to deal with the French threat.

Yet, in the immigration scheme itself, there was a marked disparity between vision and execution, one that was at least partly due to the inexperience both of the British government and of Cornwallis. No other British colony in North America had, as Winthrop Bell has pointed out, been established "under the direct authority and immediate auspices of the British government itself."[35] Bell notes that, in the case of all the other colonies, the "chartered company" or "proprietorship" model had been used, with an intermediary between the British government and the immigrants who arranged the necessary financial backing for the enterprise, recruited the settlers, and organized their transportation. There was no past experience to draw upon in British government circles, even if some individuals, such as Shirley, offered considerable advice about how the settlement venture should be carried out. As has been mentioned, many of Shirley's dispatches on the matter to Lord Bedford, who from 1748 to 1751 was the person in charge of the Northern Plantations for the Lords of Trade, were given to Cornwallis, along with his official instructions.[36] Cornwallis himself had no colonial experience. The comment of one emigrant, after a year in the colony, was that even "their Lordships of Trade and Plantations" admit that "they were mistaken in their Knowledge of this Country."[37] In later years, Cornwallis reflected that the nature of the undertaking had "proved to be quite different from could be thought of at first setting out."[38]

The plans for this new effort in Nova Scotia had been brought together with extraordinary speed. According to the minutes of the Board of Trade, Lord Halifax had presented the plans to its members only two days before advertisements were published for colonists.[39] Nor had much time been spent on drawing up the design, it being brought before Halifax himself only in the fall of 1748.[40] The first advertisement for settlers appeared in the London *Gazette* on 7 March 1749.[41] The ships sailed in mid-May.[42] They were loaded with an immense variety of provisions, from bricks to blankets, fishing gear to stores of meat, flour, and seeds. There were medical supplies on board, as well as an apothecary and a midwife. There were surveyors with the instruments of their trade. There were field guns and swivel guns, muskets, powder, and shot.[43] Cornwallis was also provided with nearly £4,000 in gold and silver for the needs of government, a sum that would make the new settlement the most attractive public pork barrel yet opened in British North America.[44]

But both design and subsequent provisioning had been based upon a poor understanding of the tasks that Cornwallis faced, with minimal logistical support, on land that had never been permanently settled by Europeans before. He would find himself trying to do far too much with far too few resources. As soon as the transports arrived, he was confronted with the challenge of organizing unruly migrants into building the town. He had to ensure that those unloading the transports, which were urgently needed to fetch the garrison and stores from Louisbourg, piled the supplies in the most appropriate sites for future use. A quantity of building materials had to be brought from Boston, especially pre-cut lumber for building. Local sawmills needed to be established. Law and order had to be imposed on the new colonists, many of whom were in a pitiable state, without "shoes, stockings or shirts," and a number of whom, Cornwallis wrote, were "most troublesome and mutinous."[45] The new governor had also to reorganize the Council, which meant the appointment of new members, and to make an immediate impression on the Acadians as an effective British governor for the colony, which meant, among other matters, organizing the building of a road between Chebucto Bay and the Minas Basin. Finally, some sort of barricade against Mi'kmaq attacks was needed. While the Mi'kmaq had been remarkably tolerant of British activity thus far, that activity had been concentrated in the Annapolis Royal area. The establishment of settlement in the Chebucto area was a much different matter.

Des Herbiers could, and did, complain of the state of Louisbourg when he took it over but at least he had buildings that could be repaired and that provided some shelter from the elements.[46] Cornwallis faced the problem of building Halifax within the three months left before winter arrived. Housing had to be provided for more than two thousand people, not only the settlers but also the military forces that finally arrived from Louisbourg and Annapolis Royal during July and August. Des Herbiers had a civilian population that, in the main, was accustomed to North American life and, to a large extent, had chosen Île Royale as their destination, with some idea of what conditions there would be like. Within a short space of time, there was a relatively stable core population in Louisbourg. But Cornwallis had to care, in the first place, for a population of migrants, the majority of whom had little idea of pioneer living. As well, he had to come to terms with a much larger population of settlers, the Acadians, in the colony, about whom he knew little and whose political reliability he doubted.

The problems of the immigrants were the most immediately pressing. The impact of a significant mortality rate, the common experience of newly arrived migrant populations in North America, had to be weathered during the winter of 1749–50.[47] At the same time, the ebb and flow of people exacerbated the attempts made to develop a sense of community among the newcomers. There was an onward exodus to Massachusetts of many of the more able migrants, such migration assisted by Boston merchants.[48] There was immigration from New England, some of these people looking for a place to build a new life and some looking for a new career of embezzlement and thievery. It is difficult to determine exact figures for this influx. Cornwallis believed that "a thousand settlers had been attracted from other colonies."[49] Given the casual attitude to statistics in the eighteenth century, it as well to bear in mind that, unless the basis is a nominal register of some kind, most population numbers are only approximate and usually to be discounted by 20 to 25 per cent. Bell estimates that the nucleus of the population of Halifax during the governorship of Cornwallis was under three thousand.[50] Probably the best that can be said of Halifax was that, between 1749 and 1752, the size of its population was highly volatile, dependent on a large number of variables, and never more than the three thousand that Bell proposes.

One of the variables was the number of soldiers in the nascent town. Cornwallis did not arrive with any major reinforcement of manpower for the military needs of the colony. There were roughly a hundred former soldiers among the migrants.[51] The only others with military experience among those who accompanied Cornwallis were his personal aides and those who manned the *Sphinx*. His immediate forces were slender indeed: on 23 July 1749 Cornwallis reported to Lord Bedford that he had only two companies at his disposal and sixty members of Gorham's rangers.[52] The latter, and their commander, John Gorham, were the most formidable of the troops within the colony that the British commanded. Gorham had been born in Massachusetts in 1709, and his great-grandfather had been one of the first Europeans to be married in the new Plymouth colony, in 1643.[53] His men were a mixture of full-blooded Mohawk and colonial volunteers, and by 1748 his company numbered a hundred or so. There was also the remnants of Richard Philipps's regiment commanded by Mascarene at Annapolis Royal, somewhere between three and five hundred men. Cornwallis considered this regiment to be in an appalling state, writing that its management "has been so shameful that 'tis almost incredible."[54] The two companies that Cornwallis had at his immediate disposal were those of Colonel Warburton's regiment, formerly stationed at Louisbourg. By the end of July, it seems that four companies, perhaps 120 men, had arrived from there.[55] No further reinforcements came to Halifax until 1750, when, on 30 July of that year, the Lascelles regiment arrived from Ireland. It is reported as being made up of ten companies of twenty-nine men each.[56] This brought the number of troops available to Cornwallis in the late summer of 1749 to under a thousand and probably no more than seven hundred. With these companies, of course, came women and children, the number with the Lascelle regiment being reported as 130 women and fifty children, all of whom would have to be fed and lodged.[57]

It is while he was in the midst of this jumble of responsibilities and attendant problems that Cornwallis first met with the Acadian deputies, through whom he was to endeavour to "induce" the Acadian population as a whole "to become good subjects" and assist "the New Settlers with Provisions and other necessaries."[58] His command might be stretched horribly thin, with insufficient military support and stationed in a yet to be built city, but Cornwallis was expected to "prosecute vigorously" a new policy for the colony, one radically different from the old. Halifax was no more than a disorganized building yard when, on the deck of the *Beaufort* in Chebucto Bay on 12 July 1749, Cornwalllis first met with Paul Mascarene. In spite of appearances, the occasion really did represent the opening of a new era for Nova Scotia.[59] The financial support alone was greatly superior to anything those who preceded Cornwallis had known. The supplies voted by the British Parliament were, in the view of Cornwallis and his successors, always insufficient. However, the sum granted for supplies in 1749 was £40,000. It was increased to £61,000 in 1751 and to £94,616 in 1753. It fell back in 1754 to just under £58,500 and in 1755 the sum voted was £49,418.[60]

On 14 July 1749 Cornwallis held the first Council meeting of his administration on board the *Beaufort*.[61] The constitutional provisions laid down for the colony in 1719, those of Virginia, had not been significantly altered and Cornwallis was to govern by his own authority, with the advice of a Council of twelve "fitting and discreet persons" appointed by himself.[62] The Council would develop, over the next years, into a much more formidable body than it had been during Mascarene's time but it would still be very much a moveable feast. Its membership varied, according to those the governor selected from men present in Halifax. Further, those appointed attended its meetings irregularly. For this meeting, Cornwallis had gathered together eight men. Six of these – Colonel Mascarene, Captain John Gorham, Captain Edward How, and Benjamin Green, a Harvard graduate – had been in the region since 1745,[63] while the other two, Hugh Davidson and John Salisbury, had sailed from London with Cornwallis.[64] The governor had no intention of allowing Mascarene to continue to hold any great authority in the colony and the latter would quickly return to Annapolis Royal. Cornwallis opened the proceedings of this meeting by reading his commission and instructions. These stated that the new governor must issue a proclamation to the Acadians, reminding them of their position as British subjects. They were to take the regular oaths of allegiance, without any reservation whatsoever. They were to be allowed their priests but every provision was to be made to encourage them to become Protestants. Every possible communication between old and new settlers was to be encouraged as well, in the hope that the Acadians would be influenced to display a greater loyalty to the British. At this time, both France and Great Britain considered that proximity to the good and faithful would influence the rebellious and disloyal.[65]

The Council members having been informed of the general outlines of what the home government expected, the oath that the Acadians had accepted in the past was read out: "Je ... promets and Jure sincerèment en foi de Chrétien que Je serai entièrement fidele et obéirai vraiment Sa Majesté Le Roi George le Second que je reconnais pour le Souverain Seigneur de l'Accadie ou nouvelle Ecosse. Ainsi Dieu me soit en Aide."[66] Mascarene then explained that "the French pretended that when they took this Oath it was upon condition that it should be understood that they should always be exempted from bearing Arms." There was some debate as to whether, therefore, the words "ce serment Je prens sans reserve" be added but the general opinion was that the oath, in its present form, was "as strong as any Oath of Allegiance can be." It was decided that "it would only be necessary to let the French know that they must take the Oath without any reservation whatever."

At this point, three Acadian deputies, Jean Melanson from Rivière-aux-Canards, Claude LeBlanc from Grand Pré, and Phillippe Melanson from Pisiquid, were called in. Cornwallis assured them of "all Protection and Encouragement" but informed them that he expected that "the Inhabitants would take the Oath of Allegiance to his Majesty in the same manner as all" England's subjects did. He asked them whether they had any comment and received the reply that they had come solely "to pay their respects to His Excellency & to know what was their Condition henceforth, & particularly whether they should still be allowed their Priests." Cornwallis stated that, provided the priests obtained a licence from the Council first, there would be no difficulty with this matter. The meeting ended with the deputies being given copies of a general declaration for the information of the Acadian population and copies of the oath.[67] The deputies left with instructions to return within a fortnight with the "Resolutions of their several Departments" and to inform the other settlements that His Excellency wished to meet with their deputies as soon as possible.

The declaration in question was consistent with the attitude shown by Cornwallis and the Council during the meeting. Its underlying assumption was that the Acadians had yet to become good British subjects but that this transformation was perfectly possible. Its tone was one of reasonable command. It opened with the announcement that a number of British subjects were to be settled in Nova Scotia for the improvement and extension of its trade and fisheries. It went on to state that in the past the Acadians had been treated with great indulgence, being allowed "the entirely free exercise of their Religion and the quiet and reasonable possession of their Lands." However, it was remarked that this treatment had not been met with appropriate loyalty and that, in future, they could not expect similar leniency unless "the said Inhabitants do within Three months from the date of the Declaration take the Oaths of Allegiance." In the meantime, it was emphasized, the Acadians were to extend all possible aid and comfort to the new immigrants that "his Majesty shall think proper to settle in this province."

There is no doubt that the three Acadian deputies who attended the meeting of 14 July, and the other seven who came, as bidden, to a further meeting on the 31st of the month, were deeply concerned with making a true estimate of their situation. For France and Great Britain, Louisbourg and Quebec, Halifax and Boston, the centres of political power whose policies determined, in large part, the course of events within the region, the issue was the control of territory and of its resources. For the Acadians, it was the rulership of the lands on which they lived, lands settled and farmed by their ancestors. This point of view, of course, was one held equally, if not more strongly, by the Mi'kmaq, whose ancestors had lived in and controlled the region for numberless generations. Neither Acadian nor Mi'kmaq had accepted the viewpoint that other powers should determine political life of the region without reference to those already living there. The Mi'kmaq continued to challenge the right of Europeans to exercise any overall sovereignty over them, believing that they were the equals of the newcomers and not a subject people. In the case of the Acadians, their political culture acknowledged that the final authority of France or England was the basis of their legal practices. The question that faced them, however, was the extent of the authority that could be so exercised by either Great Britain or France. As these two powers struggled for control of the region between 1749 and 1755, both French and British demands for Acadian obedience to their commands increased.

During the summer of 1749, Acadian resistance to their assigned role as passive subjects of Great Britain became clear. At the Council meeting of 31 July 1749, there were deputies from all the major Acadian communities present, and in the Council minutes their names and communities are listed as follows: "Alexander Hebert and Joseph Dugad from Annapolis, Claude Le Blanc from Grand Pre, Jean Melancon from Riviere de Canard, Baptiste Gailliard and Pierre Landry from Piziquid, Pierre Gotrau from Cobequid, Pierre Doucet and Francois Bourg from Chinecto and Alexr. Brossart from Chippodie."[68] Phillippe Melanson had not returned. The attendance of a deputy from Shepody is of particular interest, since this community on the north shore of the Bay of Fundy was at the extreme northwestern limit of Acadian colonization. Its past relationship with both French and British administrations had been not only quarrelsome but tenuous and, on occasion, almost non-existent. The deputies presented a joint written response, which asked for a clarification of their right to have priests among them and for the exemption from bearing arms in time of war. The Council decided to confirm the Acadian right to priests but unanimously rejected the second request.[69] Those who came to this decision included a number of newly arrived officers from Louisbourg, among them Peregrine Hopson, who would succeed Cornwallis as the governor of the colony, and Charles Lawrence, who in turn would succeed Hopson. The deputies were told of the decisions reached by this body the next day. Their response was to ask whether "if they had a mind to evacuate their Lands, they would have leave to sell their Lands and Effects."[70] They were informed that "those that should chuse to retire rather than be true Subjects to the King could not be allowed to sell or carry off anything." Further, they were told that those who did not take the oath of allegiance before the middle of October would "forfeit all their possessions and rights in this Province." The deputies then asked for "leave to go to the French Governors & see what Conditions might be offerd them." To this, Cornwallis replied that anybody who left the province without having taken the oath of allegiance would "immediately forfeit all their Rights." Cornwallis issued another declaration immediately after this meeting, which was distributed throughout the Acadian settlements and emphasized the need for the Acadians to take an unqualified oath before 16 October.[71]

Just over a month after this meeting, on 6 September 1749, the Acadians presented the governor and his Council with their answer. Mascarene was not one of the councillors present at this meeting but the group did include John Horsemen and Charles Lawrence. The Acadian response was in the form of a letter, signed by a thousand persons. It represented a unanimity of opinion among a significant proportion of the Acadians, although the extent of support for it among the Acadian population as a whole is debatable. A thousand signatures would, if all were authentic, amount to, at maximum, less than half the adult male population.[72] But it must have taken a considerable effort to generate such a response and the support the document received is the more significant because it came from all the major centres of Acadian settlement and represented the dominant, if not the majority, opinion in the communities. The letter opened with a lengthy reference to the oath that Philipps had administered. Philipps had assured the Acadian population, it was stated, that this oath "secured to us the full enjoyment of our property, and the free exercise of our religion, in giving us as many priests as we required."[73] Further, it went on, "two years ago His Majesty was pleased to grant us letters, in which he grants us the enjoyment of our property." The response continued by stating that, if His Majesty knew the truth of the Acadian situation, "he would not propose to us an oath which, if taken, would at any moment expose our lives to great peril from the savage nations, who have reproached us in a strange manner, as to the oath we have [already] taken ..." The Acadians then made their stand: "If Your Excellency will grant us our old oath which was given at Mines to Mr. Richard Phillips with an exemption for ourselves and for our heirs from taking up arms, we will accept it." "But," the letter continued, "if Your Excellency is not disposed to grant us what we take the liberty of asking, we are resolved, everyone of us, to leave the country."[74] They admitted that they were apprehensive about the possibility of having English living among them.[75] In conclusion, the letter asked whether His Majesty had annulled the oath given by Governor Philipps.

Later that same day, Cornwallis delivered an answer to the deputies, one that was a mixture of outrage and reason. It was built upon three arguments, arguments that would be the foundation of the British policy towards the Acadians in the coming years. The first dealt with the matter of whether the Acadians were subjects of the king of Great Britain; the second, with what that implied; and the third argued for the Acadian need to demonstrate that they understood their situation. Cornwallis opened his discourse by commenting that this was the third time that a meeting had taken place and the Acadians "did nothing but repeat the same story without the least change." This time they had presented a letter "signed by a thousand persons, in which you declare openly that you will be subjects of His Britannic Majesty only on such and such conditions." He continued: "It appears to me that you think yourself independent of any government; and you wish to treat with the King as if you were so."[76]

This, of course, was the crux of the situation: What right did the Acadians have to argue with the British authorities? In the eighteenth-century European political world, after all, monarchical power was limited by tradition rather than by constitution. Even in Great Britain, the rights of the sovereign were curtailed, and only to a limited extent, by institutions that represented the beliefs and wishes of only a small part of the overall population. (Out of a total population of some six and a half million in England and Wales, perhaps 5 per cent had the right to vote.[77]) Cornwallis, therefore, was well within the political norms of his time when he asserted that the Acadians were deceiving themselves if they considered that they were at liberty to choose whether they would be "subject to the King or no."[78] He declared firmly that "from the year 1714, that no longer depended on you. From that moment you became subject to the laws of Great Britain and were placed precisely upon the same footing as the other Catholic subjects of His Majesty."[79] In this perspective, no reservation as to the limits of loyalty was admissible. The oath administered by Philipps, whether or not it granted the right not to bear arms, had not fundamentally "in the slightest degree lessened [the Acadians'] obligations to act always, and in all circumstances, as a subject ought to act, according to the laws of God and King." The governor further stated that "it is not the oath which a King administers to his subjects that make them subjects. The oath supposes that they are so already. The oath is but a very sacred bond of the fidelity of those who take it."

Cornwallis did not offer any reminder about the need to take the oath of allegiance, without reservation, by mid-October. Instead, he suggested that Acadians would have better served their cause if, instead of frequent consultations among themselves, messages to the French government, and a letter signed by a thousand persons, they had sent to Halifax "a hundred

... to work in the service of his majesty ..." Speaking in particular to the deputies from Minas, Cornwallis told them that, on their return, they would find a detachment of "his Britannic majesty's" troops there. They had been sent for the protection of the settlers and Cornwallis expressed the hope that he would hear that the Acadians had "aided and assisted them as much as you could." To encourage such help, Cornwallis told them that "I have ordered [this force] to pay for everything in ready money, or in certificates which I shall cash immediately." His final words were: "Manage to let me have here in two days, fifty of your inhabitants whom I shall employ in assisting the poor to build their houses, to shelter them from the bad weather. They shall be paid in ready money, and fed on the king's provisions."

The meetings between Cornwallis and the Acadians during the summer months of 1749 ended with both sides restating positions that they had held since 1730. The Acadians clung to their wish for non-combatant status and their bargaining power remained their threat to quit the colony. Cornwallis, on the other hand, was as exasperated as previous British administrators had been with the Acadian conviction that they had the right to decide their own future. At the same time, he hesitated to make any real move to force the Acadians to a crisis without explicit instructions from London. On 11 September he sent a dispatch to the Lords of Trade in which he gave his opinion that there was no danger of an immediate Acadian emigration. This being the case, Cornwallis wrote that "my view is to make them as useful as possible to His Majesty while they do stay. If afterwards, they are still obstinate and refuse the Oath, I shall receive in the Spring further Instructions from your Lordships."[80] The October deadline came and went. On the 22nd of that month, the Council met and decided to accept the submission and approve the names of those who had been elected deputies for the coming year. Apparently, as Brebner writes, "the relations between governor and habitants had fallen into the old ruts and were wearing them deeper."[81]

But these "old ruts" were on a new road and, over the next months, the difference between the time of Cornwallis and the period when Governor Philipps had visited the colony almost twenty years earlier became more and more obvious. The 1730s had been an era of relative calm in the region, as Fleury in France and Walpole in Great Britain worked to preserve peaceful relations between their countries. The settlement of 1748, however, had brought no more than an uneasy truce between imperial rivals, a truce that was destined to be frequently broken. The borders of Nova Scotia had been no less vague during the 1730s than in 1749 but they had been far less subject to military trials of strength. Also, until 1749, it had seemed obvious that the Acadians would determine the demographic development of the colony. They had been the clear majority of the population within Nova Scotia since sometime in the 1720s, when their numbers surpassed those of the Mi'kmaq. But, with the arrival of new migrants in the colony, it no longer seemed certain that the Acadians would retain their majority status. Finally, the total military forces of France and Britain within the area were significantly larger after 1748 than before and it was clear that both powers now considered that a military struggle for its future was likely.

How serious was the Acadian threat to leave their lands should Cornwallis not accede to their request for the provision of Catholic priests and the granting of non-combatant status? This is not an easy question to answer. Cornwallis himself thought that there was no danger of them "leaving their Habitations this Season."[82] In this he was right, since no mass migration would be undertaken without a consultation with the authorities at Louisbourg and considerable debate within the settlements. The Acadians needed to determine, in the first place, the extent to which the policies Cornwallis proposed were abhorrent to them. They then needed to consider what Cornwallis would do if they continued to refuse the oath. Given Shirley's proclamation, less than two years earlier, that the British government had no intention of sending them into exile,[83] the Acadians would have to decide what alternative measures, other than deportation, Cornwallis might be able to use against them. Lastly, there was the matter of what conditions the Acadians might find on Île Royale and Île Saint-Jean and the extent to which migration there would be helped by France.

The provision of Catholic priests was more of an irritant than a major issue. While it was clear that the British administrators would have much preferred the Acadians to be Protestant, the matter of their Catholicism was far less crucial than the issue of military service in time of need. While anti-Catholicism certainly played a major role in British politics in the mid-eighteenth century, Catholic belief was not proscribed in Great Britain to the same extent that Protestant belief was in France. There had been no migration of Catholics from Great Britain in the eighteenth century comparable to the departure of Huguenots from France after 1685. There were too many Catholics in England, as well as in Scotland and Ireland, for that interpretation of Christianity to be fully proscribed by the British government. As well, the existence of Catholic members of the aristocracy served to ensure some measure of tolerance of Catholics during this era. The correspondence of the London authorities with the various British administrators in the region, including Governor Shirley, had continually emphasized that the Acadians were to be allowed priests, provided that these men obtained the authorization of the local authorities to exercise their ministry. To be sure, anti-Catholic sentiment was strong in New England at this time, but, nevertheless, Cornwallis insisted that there would be no difficulty over the provision of priests. He did attempt, in his first meetings with the Acadians, to add a new condition to the granting of licences: he tried to impose upon the priests, sent by France and French subjects, the obligation to "take an oath of Allegiance to His Majesty."[84] This initiative proved stillborn.

What did limit the number of priests was the availability of men wanting to undertake parish work among the Acadians. In 1748, excluding Le Loutre, whose activities were above all peripatetic and centred upon the Mi'kmaq, and Abbé Maillard, who was based on Île Royale, there were five priests reported in Acadian parishes. There was Miniac, "half-blind"; La Goudalie, "quite old and a little deaf"; and Desenclaves, who suffered "from a weak chest." This left Charles-Jean-Baptiste Chauvreulx and Jacques Girard, who were apparently hale and hearty.[85] In 1754 there were just three priests working within the Acadian settlements. Brook Watson, who was in the colony in 1750, commented some time later that the priests "were few in number and moderate in their views."[86] Missionary work among the Mi'kmaq was seen as a more attractive option by members of the Catholic clergy and it was those who undertook this work, such as Le Loutre and Maillard, who combined zeal for Catholicism with anti-British activities. In Watson's view, it was "la Loutre [sic] ... who laid the foundation for the miseries [the Acadians] experienced in 1755."

The question of non-combatant status was a much more complex issue. There is no doubt that the majority of Acadians wanted to live where they had settled, with as little interference as possible from outside administrators. Yet it is also clear that the events of 1744 to 1748 had forced the Acadian community to understand, at the very least, that war would be fought in their villages, even if the hope still lingered, for many of them, that their participation in the armed conflict could remain minimal and restricted to questions of supply. These years had also brought home to the Acadians the deep divisions among them, with some much more willing to support actively one side or the other. It would not have been easy for the Acadians to judge the relative military strength of France and Great Britain in the area and make a decision on a purely practical ground to support the probable victor. The capture and return of Louisbourg made that centre of French power questionable but by no means negligible, while the French force at the mouth of the Saint John, commanded by La Corne, emphasized the continuing interest of Quebec in the area. On the other hand, the arrival of immigrants with military reinforcements over the summer made Britain's growing strength in the region impossible to ignore.

A number of Acadians left for Île Saint-Jean and Île Royale even before the talks between Cornwallis and the deputies had run their course. By the middle of August, some seven or eight Acadian families had arrived at Port Lajoie, a total of between fifty and sixty people. These included men such as Joseph-Nicolas Gautier, formerly of Annapolis Royal, who, because of his proven support for the French during the recent war, had been specifically excluded from amnesty when peace was concluded.[87] By the end of the year, over a hundred and fifty had arrived from the mainland; some of these people were new to Île Saint-Jean but others had left the island for Beaubassin and Minas after its capture by the English in 1745.[88] There were also a few Acadians who moved to Île Royale in 1749 but these seem to have been a handful of single men. The greatest emigration of Acadians from Nova Scotia, between 1749 and 1755, took place in 1750 as a direct result of warfare in the Chignecto region.

As already noted, the boundaries of the Chignecto area, like those of the Minas Basin, were indeterminate. Its name could cover everything between the rivers Maccan, Nappan, and Hebert to the east of the Cumberland Basin and the Shepody River on the northwestern shore. It could include in its sweep the estuaries of the Petitcodiac and the Memramcook as well as the Chignecto isthmus, including Baie Verte.[89] On the other hand, the name might be used to refer only to the original Beaubassin settlement along the Missaguash. But, however its boundaries were drawn, the region as a whole was a strategic centre of trade and communication, and of particular importance to France. The portage from Baie Verte to Beaubassin was the shortest route from the Northumberland Strait to the Bay of Fundy and had been used in this fashion for generations by the Mi'kmaq. It linked the land route from Quebec, via the Saint John River valley, to Île Saint-Jean and Île Royale. Further, it contained some of the richest agricultural land in the colony. The farms, in the Beaubassin area particularly, were of long standing and produced not just cattle and sheep but grain. Charles Morris, who produced a geographical survey of the colony in 1749 for Governor Shirley, wrote that when one looked across its lands there "may be seen Rivers turning and winding among the Marshes then Cloath'd with all variety of grain."[90] Clark estimates that in 1748 the Chignecto area had 7,000 black catttle, 8,000 sheep, 4,000 pigs, 500 horses, and 3,000 acres of dyked land.[91]

Settlement in this area had grown considerably since the opening of the eighteenth century. Beaubassin was the largest village, having been well established by the end of the 1680s and possessing a church and the greatest concentration of farms and hamlets. By the end of the 1740s, there were not only solidly rooted farming communities in the valleys of the Petitcodiac, the Memramcook, and the Shepody rivers but a good number of small hamlets stretching along the seashore on both sides of Baie Verte. Population figures are even more difficult to estimate for this region than for the Minas Basin and the Annapolis valley. Clark suggests that in 1749 the Beaubassin area had approximately 1,200 people; the Memramcook, Petitcodiac, and Shepody valleys, 1,200; and the other outlying settlements accounted for perhaps 500 more.[92] Given the lack of any official count at this time, and the movement of families to and from Île Royale and Île Saint-Jean after 1744, any estimate is liable to be seriously wrong. Certainly, there is at least one contemporary source that places the Acadian population in Nova Scotia in 1755 at 18,000, a figure that would require the Chignecto population to be closer to five or six thousand than the three thousand suggested by Clark.[93] Whatever the actual population figure, however, the area held a rich and complex assortment of villages and hamlets which would bear the brunt of the first serious clash between the contending forces in the region.

The origin of the fighting was the wish of both the French and the British to retain as much territory as possible in the area and to persuade, by whatever means, the Acadians to support their claims. For the French, as has been suggested, this meant the employment of the Mi'kmaq and Des Herbiers had moved before the beginning of August 1749 to organize them.[94] Abbé Le Loutre had returned to Louisbourg with Des Herbiers and had written to Maurepas to say that he would do his best to assemble "my Savages and since one cannot openly oppose the English, I think one cannot do better than agitate the Savages to continue to war with the English, my plans are to persuade the Savages to tell the English that they will not permit them to make new settlements in Acadia, that they believe the English should remain where they were before the war." He would also urge the Mi'kmaq to state that, should the English persist, the Mi'kmaq would never be at peace with them and would "declare eternal enmity."[95] Bigot, at this time intendant of New France, provided Le Loutre with additional cloth, powder, and shot in order to encourage the Mi'kmaq raids and to ensure attacks on Halifax in particular.[96]

For their own reasons, the Mi'kmaq responded favourably to the proposals of the French. Although they were encouraged in their hostility to the British by the French, it was the British intrusion into land that the Mi'kmaq considered their own territory, particularly in the region of Halifax, that was the real basis for the disputes between them and Cornwallis. As has been indicated, throughout the years of the European exploration and settlement of Acadia, the Mi'kmaq never ceased to consider themselves the rightful tenants of the land. Further, the Mi'kmaq were not so much allies of the French in the 1750s as they were a people convinced of their own autonomy, who were taking all means within their power to ensure their continued independence. Their use of land might not have given them the same type of territorial imperative that European politics had inculcated in the inhabitants of that continent, but the very importance that the Europeans attached to land ownership had taught the Mi'kmaq a great deal.[97] The Mi'kmaq had long-established gathering places, some of which were inhabited the year-round, on the sites on which the British were now attempting to build. After 1748, British settlement seemed to pose a much greater threat to Mi'kmaq control over their lives than possible French expansion. On 24 September 1749 the Mi'kmaq formally declared their hostility to the British plans for settlement without more formal negotiations.

The document containing this declaration was written by Pierre Maillard, the missionary priest who worked among the Mi'kmaq based on Île Royale. However, the tone of the document is that of the previous Mi'kmaq communications in defence of their rights. It reflects the words of a Mi'kmaq who had been captured raiding a British ship in 1720: "This land here that God has given us of which we can be accounted a part as much as the trees are born here," he said, "cannot be disputed by anyone." He continued: "We are masters independent of everyone and wish to have our country free."[98] The declaration of 1749 used much of the same rhetoric. This document exists in two versions, Mi'kmaq and French. The connection of the Mi'kmaq to the land itself is presented in the preamble: "The place where you are, where you are building dwellings, where you are now building a fort, where you want, as it were to enthrone yourself, this land of which you wish to make yourself now absolute master, this land belongs to me, I have come from it as certainly as the grass, it is the very place of my birth and of my dwelling ..."[99] The text then goes on to argue that the Mi'kmaq have already been driven from the larger part of their lands and that, if Chebucto is now settled, there will nowhere left for them to take refuge. This final "great theft," the text states, is the immediate cause of the present Mi'kmaq unrest.

There has, of course, been considerable debate as to whether this declaration expressed French policy to a greater extent than it did Mi'kmaq resolve.[100] Neither French nor British administrators of the time considered the Mi'kmaq as being fully capable of expressing an independent collective political will.[101] Both powers tended to regard the Mi'kmaq essentially as pawns to be manipulated, while ascribing to them bouts of rebellion against European civilizing influences and outbreaks of ungovernable behaviour. For Cornwallis, the Mi'kmaq on this occasion had been swayed by French missionaries, in particular Le Loutre, "to begin hostilities."[102] The governor's response to the Mi'kmaq challenge was to issue a proclamation on 2 October commanding all good subjects "to Annoy, distress, take or destroy the Savages commonly called Micmacks, wherever they are found."[103] In addition, as was customary in British North America, he offered ten guineas for any Mi'kmaq scalp. Meanwhile, he set about distributing some of his forces throughout the colony. Mascarene, now back at Annapolis Royal, received orders to send a strong detachment of a hundred men to Grand Pré. As well, he was to remove one of the old blockhouses and have it rebuilt near present-day Horton.[104] The men were to be quartered in houses which were close to one another and which were rented for the purpose. The blockhouse was to be positioned in the centre of such houses and the whole to be palisaded against attack.[105] At the same time, Cornwallis pressed ahead with ensuring that a "road" was cut to the Grand Pré area from Halifax, running along the trail that the Acadians had used to move cattle from Pisiquid to Chibouctou.[106]

The Mi'kmaq challenges to British settlement in Nova Scotia became one of the focal points for the fighting between the British and French and the resulting skirmishes inevitably entangled the Acadians. Sometimes a handful of young Acadian men were directly involved in the fighting. This was the case of the assault on the Grand Pré blockhouse in December

1749. That month, villagers in the Minas and Pisiquid regions had been told by the Mi'kmaq that it was their duty to help in the expulsion of the English and, unless they did so, the Acadians themselves would be attacked.[107] Acadian reaction was much as one might expect: a negligible few turned out with the Mi'kmaq; others reported the state of affairs to the British. Eleven names, out of an adult male population of between one and two thousand, appear on a list as having been part of the December attack on the British force in the Grand Pré area. This list was attested to by Honoré Gautrot, an Acadian living at Annapolis Royal.[108] Even such a derisory number, however, was enough to increase suspicion about Acadian intentions among the members of Cornwallis's staff. Much more serious, from every point of view, was the confrontation over where the boundary should run in the Chignecto area. It was this bitter and continuing dispute that led to the burning of Beaubassin in the early summer of 1750, when over a hundred homes were set on fire and close to a thousand people forced to flee. The fires were set by the Mi'kmaq but the responsibility for this action lay with La Corne, the senior French officer in the region, and Abbé Le Loutre.

During the winter of 1749–50, it had become clear to Cornwallis and to La Corne that control of the Chignecto isthmus was a crucial military necessity. Both men took steps in the spring to strengthen their position in the area. Cornwallis dispatched Major Lawrence and Captain Rous with a force of four hundred men and instructions to establish themselves at "Chinecto."[109] They were to "erase" any French fort which had been established in the area. Cornwallis wrote in an additional instruction that, should Major Lawrence meet with La Corne, he was to inform him that it was Cornwallis's express order that he should "leave this Province directly and return to Canada, otherwise that no orders whatever that he may produce shall protect him from being treated as an Incendiary."[110] When Lawrence arrived off Beaubassin on 21 April 1750, it was to find the lower part of that town in flames. Lawrence met with La Corne and asked him by "whose orders he was there within his Majesty's undoubted limits ...?"[111] La Corne told Lawrence that he was acting on the orders of the governor of Canada, La Jonquière, who had directed him "to take possession of Chipoudie St. John's River Memre Cook, Petcodiak, and all that country lying on our right as being the property of the French King or at least that he was to keep it & must defend it until the boundaries between the two Crowns should be settled by Commissioners appointed for that purpose." The inhabitants, La Corne responded when Lawrence pressed him further, had been dispersed about the [French] territories, there were no deputies among them, and it was "the Indians" who had burnt Beaubassin, since they claimed the territory as their own. At this point, Lawrence lost his temper and asked to see La Corne's orders, which the latter quite properly refused to show him. Lawrence was very much at a disadvantage. As he himself wrote, La Corne's situation in military terms was "properly chosen." "He had everything," Lawrence continued, "so much under his command on that side of the river that divided the ground he claimed and Beaubassin which he allowed to be ours, that I too much feared we had no pretensions to dispute that part of the country with him."[112] Lawrence retreated to Minas but this incident confirmed the Missiguash River as the dividing line between the British and French territories for the next five years. The major powers had drawn a "line in the sand" right through the Acadian settlements of Chignecto.

There is no doubt that the idea of withdrawing the Acadians to French-held territory was official French policy after 1748. Nor is there much doubt that the use of extreme measures by Le Loutre and the Mi'kmaq had, if not outright approbation, tacit approval from La Jonquière and Bigot; there is no condemnation whatsoever of these tactics in the secular correspondence of the French authorities.[113] In fact, a few months after the burning of Beaubassin, when the British returned to establish, successfully, Fort Lawrence on the southeastern shore of the Missaguash, the French organized an evacuation of settlers in the Acadian villages of Maccan, Nappan, Hebert, and Minoudy, burning their homes and barns in the process. These barns had contained that year's harvest, and their destruction caused a considerable shortage of food among the Acadians in the region during the coming months. The loss of forage meant that there was nothing to feed the cattle and, the Acadians having no stores of salt, the meat was lost as well.

The French made considerable efforts to transport the refugees to Île Saint-Jean and by early October six or seven hundred had arrived there in pitiable condition.[114] They were in dire need of all kinds of provisions and La Jonquière sent "pickaxes, [smaller] axes, ploughshares, and some clothing ..."[115] It was admitted that the settlers had been forced to flee with few of their possessions.[116] The migration from the Chignecto isthmus to Île Saint-Jean took months but by 1752 the population in that colony was 2,200, some 368 families; 1,188 people had arrived from mainland Acadian villages in 1750 and 1751.[117] Government subsidies of flour and grain, tools and textiles were vital. Some of the more elderly refugees, such as Jean Bourg, a ploughman, aged sixty-nine, and his wife, Françoise Aucoin, who was five years younger, were obviously helped by having adult children living with them. This couple, who had been settled at Rivière-du-Ouest (Eliot River), near Port Lajoie, for fifteen months in 1752, had three daughters, aged twenty-three to twenty-eight, and one son, aged twenty, living with them. The family had four cows, a calf, a sow, and four pigs as well as eight chickens. They also had cleared land on which they had sown three bushels of grain.[118] Not by any means a wealthy household, this family would, however, be able to attain a tolerable standard of living when in receipt of aid from the government. On the other hand, a much younger family, that of Baptiste Olivier, also a ploughman, aged twenty-four, and his wife, Suzanne Pitre, who was twenty-two, would find life much more difficult. They, too, had been on Île Saint-Jean for fifteen months in 1752. When Joseph de La Roque recorded them in his census, they had three children, daughters, under three: Marie, who was thirty-one months old; Marguerite, aged eighteen months; and Magdelaine, a newborn of just fifteen days. They had more livestock than Jean Bourg and Françoise Aucoin: two oxen, a cow, a bull, four heifers, one ewe, a sow, two pigs, and a horse. They had managed to establish a garden but not to clear any land. Both husband and wife would have to be in good health and strong enough to work long hours everyday to obtain a reasonable living. Again, government supplies, especially of grain and flour, would make the difference between poverty and reasonable subsistence. But, between 1750 and 1755, the food and clothing supplied by the French authorities often arrived late and was never quite enough.[119]

Those who migrated to Île Saint-Jean between 1750 and 1753 had left farms tilled for three generations and long-established patterns of life on known and cultivated lands. They were now faced with all the difficulties of establishing themselves anew on what was uncleared land, having seen their homes burnt and many of their personal possessions destroyed. It is not surprising that they adapted to their new circumstances slowly. Jacques Prevost de La Croix, however, in charge of the supplies for the island, wrote to France complaining about Acadian indolence.[120] Both those who went almost immediately from Beaubassin to Île Saint-Jean and those who remained in the region of their former homes were subjected to almost continual stress and, often, repeated migration. Some eighty families remained on the land around what would soon be Fort Beauséjour; others moved to the valley of the Memramcook.[121] All voiced their discontent with their situation and some spoke of returning to their former lands, now controlled by Britain. This roused Le Loutre to a passionate denunciation of those he considered the ringleaders, threatening them with excommunication in this world and damnation in the next.[122] The use of hellfire as a tactic of persuasion has most often been attributed to him, and it is unlikely that the Mi'kmaq would have burnt the Acadian settlements without his approval since they did not resort to this expedient elsewhere in their attacks. Until his departure for France in December 1752, Le Loutre continued to threaten Mi'kmaq attacks upon Acadians unwilling to declare themselves wholeheartedly in support of French policies.

Events throughout the colony between 1749 and 1752 underlined the fact that the peace of Aix-la-Chapelle was no more than a shaky truce. The preparations of both the British and the French for the settlement – by "cannon," as Des Herbiers put it[123] – of the boundaries between their territories in the area were obvious. France and Britain set about building new fortifications in the region, not merely entrenching themselves in positions established earlier but erecting, staffing, and provisioning new forts. Both sides had to cope with skirmishes while they undertook this work, the British with Mi'kmaq raids and the French with naval action both in the Bay of Fundy and in the Northumberland Strait. Cornwallis and his staff had been infuriated with the rebuff which Lawrence had met at Beaubassin in the spring of 1750 and in September another attempt was made to establish a British stronghold in the area.[124] In the middle of that month, Lawrence arrived once more at the head of Cumberland Basin with seventeen ships and between six and seven hundred regular troops, including Gorham's rangers. While La Corne did not attempt a major sortie against this expedition, there were a number of other incidents. At least one party of some thirty Acadians, with Mi'kmaq support, made forays against the landing parties.[125] As the fort was being built that fall, there were frequent parlays along the Missaguash between the French and British. It was during one of these that Edward How was shot in early October, most probably by Mi'kmaq, while carrying a flag of truce.[126] The French officers indignantly denied any complicity in the affair but it became a continual matter of reproach by the British to the French. The building of what would be known as Fort Lawrence went on over the winter and by the springtime it was well established. It would not be completed for another two years but it was already impressive. When it was finished, it contained a house for "the Commandant, officers' guardroom, soldiers' guard room, officers and soldiers' barracks, and a store."[127] In the spring of 1751, the French began the construction of a major fort at Beauséjour as well as one where the Gasperau River flowed into Baie Verte. Both were completed by the fall of that year.[128] Beauséjour was well situated on a rise that sloped gently almost a hundred feet on all four sides. It was a pallisaded structure, shaped as a pentagon, with five strong bastions capable of bearing cannon, and also had a ditch beneath the walls. Gaspereau was much smaller, a square palisade enclosing six buildings but not built to withstand much more than musket fire.[129] By the fall of 1751, as John Reid has written, "separated only by the low lying marsh and the tiny Missaguash river, the representatives of the world's two most expansionist empires looked warily at one another, and waited."[130]

Over the next months, the pressures on the Acadians increased. Both the French and British had clear ideas as to what the proper conduct of the Acadians should be. The French firmly believed that the Acadians wanted to be governed by France. This was in part due to the reliance placed on the judgments of Le Loutre by French authorities at Quebec and at Versailles. Le Loutre's opinion of the Acadians, that fundamentally all wanted nothing better than to live under French rule, was precisely what French officials wished to hear. The conviction of men such as La Galissonière and La Corne that the British should and would be driven out of Nova Scotia was part and parcel of the ambitions of mid-eighteenth-century France for its empire in North America, ambitions comparable to the British desire to preserve and extend their own empire on that continent. To the French, the view of Le Loutre that the Acadians were quite ready to abandon their lands in order to live happily under French rule and that, in case of outright war between Britain and France, there would be a thousand men "to march against the English and fight with courage against the enemies of the state"[131] was perfectly reasonable. Le Loutre was convinced, as was his administrative superior, Pierre de La Rue, Abbé de L'Isle-Dieu, that the spiritual welfare of both Acadian and Mi'kmaq depended on the defeat of the British. In a letter to Bishop Pontbriand of Quebec, in 1750, L'Isle Dieu wrote that the domination of Nova Scotia by the English meant not only a considerable population loss to the state but also incredible danger to the immortal souls of the Acadian people.[132]

La Corne and other French officials made every attempt possible to bring the Acadians to declare themselves unequivocally for France. In the spring of 1751, for example, La Jonquière reported to his superiors in France that he had issued a proclamation to those Acadians who lived within French jurisdiction, either on Île Royale or Île Saint-Jean or in the Beauséjour region. It informed the Acadians that those who did not take an oath of fidelity to "the King our Master" (Louis XV) and become members of a militia company within eight days of the publication of the proclamation "will be declared rebels to the orders of the King and as such expelled from the lands which they hold."[133] At the same time, the British were also making every effort to extract a similar declaration of loyalty from the Acadians to their monarch, George II. The authorities in London were optimistic about the success of the policy, outlined in their letter to Cornwallis of February 1750.[134] Then, their lordships had been hopeful that by "proper measures," which would protect Acadian lives and property, they "would no longer stand out against the government."[135] Now they wrote that the recent decision by Cornwallis not to allow the "French Inhabitants of the district of Menis and Annapolis" to depart had been right. The dispatch went on to say that their lordships were "extremely glad to hear, that so few of the better sort of those Inhabitants have withdrawn themselves." They did not doubt in the slightest that, if such emigration could be prevented, "when the ffrench are particularly industrious to draw them off from their Allegiance to the Crown of Great Britain ...," Cornwallis would be able to remove Acadian "Prejudices and firmly unite them to the British Interest."[136]

But British policy for Nova Scotia at this time depended less upon any interpretation of Acadian attitudes than on the assisted immigration of upwards of two thousand "foreign Protestants" to the colony and their settlement at Lunenburg and the immediately surrounding area. Nova Scotia would become a solid British colony, it was thought, once people whose loyalty to the British crown was without question were settled there. The influence of such subjects on the Acadians would persuade the latter to fulfil their duties to the British government. Some of these immigrants began to appear in Halifax, as a distinct category or group, with the arrival of the *Alderney* and the *Ann* in August 1750.[137] But the majority did not arrive until the following year. They came mostly from a number of the small German states that existed at the time and in some few cases from Switzerland and the Netherlands.[138] While Governor Shirley had counselled that mingling these migrants in settlements among the Acadian villages "as contiguous to theirs as may be" would enhance Acadian loyalty to Great Britain, this vision was no more than advice and advice not followed.[139] It became quickly clear by early 1750 that the Nova Scotian officials concerned with these migrants envisaged them as being settled in townships of their own. The newcomers were established in the region known to the Acadians as Merligash and La Hève. Again, as with Halifax, the actual settling of new migrants proved much more difficult than had been anticipated. Further, the foreign Protestants proved to be far less tractable than had been hoped and some deserted to the French.[140] The actual founding of Lunenburg, which was not begun until 1753, when Peregrine Hopson had taken over as governor of Nova Scotia, was beset with difficulties. But by 1754 the new town was in existence, built, without compromise, on a gridiron pattern across the steep hillside with relatively horizontal streets running parallel to a narrow waterfront and cross streets running at right angles straight up the hill.[141] That year, sawmills were in operation, houses had been built and some farms established, and the settlers were beginning to adapt to a new life.

By that time, Cornwallis had sailed from Halifax. Ill health and disagreements over what supplies were necessary to establish Nova Scotia as an effective British colony had led to his resignation in the spring of 1752. Cornwallis had quickly realized that he needed a greater force than he had been granted to establish British military strength throughout the region. The Board of Trade, however, had become increasingly aware of the cost of supporting a settlement which had no immediate economic resources of its own. Taking stock of his situation in the autumn of 1749, Cornwallis wrote to the board, on 17 October of that year, asking for two additional regiments with which he would be able "to make Nova Scotia in four years His Majesty's [and] to all intents and purposes a great [colony] and more flourishing than any part of North America."[142] In answer, he received a lecture on the necessity of frugality and the need not to waste His Majesty's funds. The dispatch listed several suggestions for economies, including being more careful over expenditures on boards and shingles and properly controlling the purchases of rum and molasses.[143] By March 1751, the correspondence between London and Halifax was carried on, by both sides, in tones of increasing asperity. Simultaneously, Cornwallis was discovering that his work demanded constant effort and produced few rewards, in terms either of career advancement or of personal satisfaction.[144]

Whatever personal disappointment Cornwallis might have felt about his time in the colony, however, there is no doubt that the years of his governorship saw the groundwork laid for the future development of Nova Scotia within the British empire. First and foremost, he oversaw the arrival of a significant number of settlers, supported by British government funding, who were clearly subjects of the British crown, however unruly they might be. Next, while his military resources were not great, Cornwallis deployed them effectively. With the exception of the burning of Beaubassin, he was able to counter most of the skirmishes mounted by the Mi'kmaq and the French. Though raids by the former spread terror among the new settlers at Dartmouth and Lunenburg, they were relatively minor affrays and the death toll they inflicted amounted to well under a hundred. Halifax was never the subject of a major attack, although fear of such an event was a factor in slowing the development of British settlement outside the city. Cornwallis shored up the garrison at Annapolis Royal, established a military outpost in the Grand Pré area, and built a solid fort on the Missaguash. There were, however, two major areas in which he achieved little or no change. One was the issue of control over seagoing traffic, whether this was a matter of communication networks, migration, or trade.[145] Cornwallis's administration was land-centred and even the supply of the garrisons at Annapolis Royal, in the Minas area, and at Beaubassin was too often a matter of chance. Cornwallis was, of course, helped by the ships of the Royal Navy, which made a number of successful forays against the French positions at the mouth of the Saint John River and captured French ships in the region of Canso and Baie Verte.[146] But, on the whole, the control of the coasts was no more effective under Cornwallis than it had been under Mascarene. What British authority existed was maintained, to a large extent, less by the ships of the Royal Navy than by traders out of New England, and their conduct was dominated by commercial gain rather than a militant desire to control French activity. Merchants from Massachusetts and other New England colonies did make some distinction between supplying Louisbourg and supplying Halifax but not very much.[147]

The other matter that Cornwallis was unable to resolve was, of course, that of the Acadian relationship with British rule. Like his predecessors, he could not obtain a response from the Acadians which he felt adequately demonstrated an essential loyalty to British interests and a clear recognition of their being subjects of the British crown. Nor, on the other hand, could he persuade the Lords of Trade to issue him clear instructions as to what his reaction to Acadian obduracy should be. Their lordships temporized, expressing the hope that the matter would sort itself out now that there were other colonists in the region. This hope was informed with the belief that the Acadians would, *must*, sooner or later, understand the benefits of British rule. Until then, no steps should be taken that would cause the Acadians to desert en masse and reinforce the French. This the Acadians showed no sign of doing. On the other hand, it became increasingly clear to Cornwallis that few among them were content with the strengthening of the British administration of the colony.

The Acadian position was, at it had been for decades, a complex mix of political, economic, and social considerations. It seems clear that the majority had no wish to leave the lands on which they were settled. At the same time, there were obvious divisions between and within the various settlements as to how they should respond to the immediate situation. As Colonel Michel Le Courtois de Surlaville and the lawyer Louis-Léonard Aumasson de Courville wrote, it was a time of rumours manufactured and spread by deserters from both French and British garrisons. It was reported that the boundary commission would rule quickly, restricting the British to the territory around Annapolis Royal. It was also reported that the Acadians, as reliable foes of the British and therefore a defence against British encroachments on French territory, were to be resettled along whatever final boundaries were decided upon. Further, it was rumoured that those who had migrated from Nova Scotia would never be allowed back.[148] The founding of Halifax had severed the influence that some of the Acadians had upon the British officials at Annapolis Royal and it also greatly reduced the amount of solid information about British plans that had previously been available to the Acadian leadership. The relationship between the Acadian deputies and Cornwallis and his Council in Halifax was a much more rigid and formal affair that the relationship that had existed between Mascarene and his Council and the deputies. In this atmosphere of unease and hearsay, most of the Acadians – between 75 and 80 per cent of them – remained on their lands and pursued their lives as best they might, tending their flocks and herds, working their fields, and repairing their dykes as they had always done. But the existence of new fortifications, both British and French, meant an increased wariness as to the future throughout the Acadian villages. The minority who migrated to French-held territory did so either under duress or because of a conviction that such a move would be for the best. The Acadians who were reported as being part of the Mi'kmaq raids on the British would come mainly from this group.

Throughout the 1740s, the Acadians resisted pressure from both British and French to become unequivocally committed to either. Wherever they lived within the region, from the settlements along the river valleys of the Memramcook and the Petitcodiac to the fishing villages on Île Royale, from the outskirts of Annapolis Royal to the farms of Grand Pré and Beaubassin, they had experienced the repercussions of the Franco-British struggle for domination of the region. At the same time, it was apparent that there was no clear victor in the war. Louisbourg had been captured by the British but returned. Annapolis Royal had been besieged and Grand Pré had seen a massacre, but French military strength had been insufficient to consolidate whatever success had been attained. Cornwallis had founded Halifax but Mi'kmaq raids had hindered the expansion of British settlement. The only conclusion that it was possible to draw from these events was that, without an unambiguous agreement between the imperial authorities in Europe, neither France nor Great Britain would give up its attempt to control the region. The most common Acadian reaction to this reality – of temporizing wherever possible, of providing support for one side or the other only when compelled to – is understandable, as is the fact that some individuals clearly favoured either France or Great Britain. In the context of 1754–55, the latter strategy was hazardous, but, as will be seen, the majority's calculated decision to adhere to a policy of neutrality would not prevent the cataclysm of the deportation.

CHAPTER FIFTEEN

The Final Months
of Accommodation

As has been related in previous chapters, the possibility of a massive Acadian migration from Nova Scotia, either voluntary or forced, had been a matter of discussion ever since 1713. By 1730, however, it had become clear that the majority of the Acadian population within the colony did not wish to leave their farms and villages and begin their lives anew elsewhere. Most of the settlers believed that an accommodation had been reached with the British, who had gained Nova Scotia as a colony through the provisions of the Treaty of Utrecht. This accommodation, as far as the leaders of the Acadian communities were concerned, involved a recognition by the British of non-combatant status for the Acadians if war broke out between the French and British, or between the British and Mi'kmaq. While there was relative calm within the region, this accommodation held. When war broke out in 1744 and Franco-British battles for control of the region became intense, however, the position of the Acadians as bystanders become more and more difficult to maintain. It was obvious after 1748 that the British resolve to retain Nova Scotia was quite as strong as the French determination to recapture it. When Cornwallis was replaced by Peregrine Hopson as governor of the colony in August 1752, both empires had strengthened their armed forces within the region and were clearly expecting that, sooner or later, there would be military action there.

Hopson, who took the oaths of office as governor of Nova Scotia on 3 August 1752, was a career officer. He came to his new position with a fair experience of the region, where he had served for most of the previous six years.[1] He had taken part in the capture of Louisbourg and had been appointed governor of Cape Breton in 1747. After the peace of Aix-la-Chapelle, he oversaw the return of that colony to the French and supervised the transfer of the British garrison, with their supplies, to Halifax. He had considerable skills, among them a reasonable acquaintance with the French language, and the fifteen months of his administration were remarkable for their tranquillity – something that could not be said of

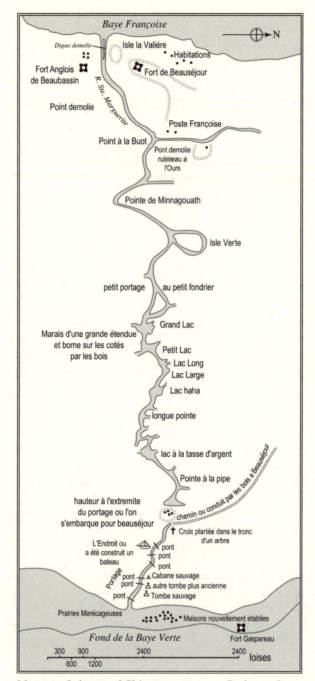

Map 9a   Isthmus of Chignecto, c. 1750. Redrawn from a map by Franquet (1752), reproduced in Ganong, *Historic sites of New Brunswick*.

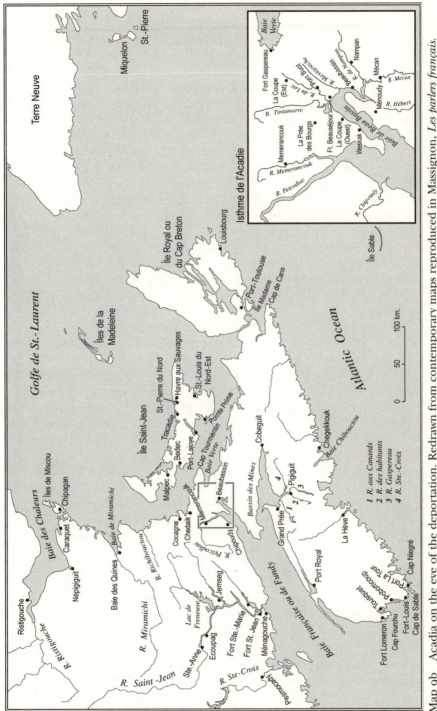

Map 9b Acadia on the eve of the deportation. Redrawn from contemporary maps reproduced in Massignon, *Les parlers français*.

conditions on the other side of the British-France divide in Acadia. Des Herbiers had resigned from the governorship of Île Royale at much the same time as Cornwallis concluded his administration. Jean-Louis de Raymond arrived in Louisbourg as the new governor in August 1751, a man of fifty, and also a career army officer.[2] As personalities, Hopson and Raymond had little in common. By all accounts, Hopson was a man of shrewd intelligence, a conciliator par excellence, in Brebner's words, "a man of moderation and personal charm who looked about him enquiringly and used his own judgment when he felt he was sufficiently informed."[3] Raymond, on the other hand, has been called "the most flamboyant governor of a Canadian colony between Frontenac and Lord Durham."[4] Hopson's administration was remarkable for his ability to cope with a series of disputes among the different groups of migrants within the colony and for the steps he took to improve the relationship between the settlers who had arrived from Europe and those from New England, particularly Boston.[5] Raymond's governorship of Île Royale was marked by his ability to imagine expensive schemes for the improvement of life in the colony and to provoke the financial commissary, Jacques Prevost de La Croix, without whose cooperation none of Raymond's plans could be brought to fruition.

Both men remained only fourteen months in the region, Raymond leaving in the fall of 1753 and Hopson handing over the command of Nova Scotia to his lieutenant governor, Colonel Charles Lawrence, on 1 November 1753. Raymond's administration, despite his grandiose schemes for settling soldiers in agricultural communities and attempting to build a road from Port Toulouse to Louisbourg, made little impression on the colony as a whole, on the Mi'kmaq, or on the Acadians. Hopson's tenure in Nova Scotia, on the other hand, was much more a matter of continuous attention to everyday problems and, as a result, had both a greater immediate impact and, as far the continued British settlement of the colony was concerned, a greater long-term influence on life in the region, particularly in Nova Scotia. There continued to be a similarity in situation of the governors of Île Royale and Nova Scotia, however, even if it was not as great as had been in the case with Cornwallis and Des Herbiers. Both Raymond and Hopson benefited from the hard work of their immediate predecessor as the foundation for their own efforts. Both also benefited from a respite in the tension between the two colonies, which was due in large measure to the departure of Le Loutre for France via Quebec in August 1752. He was absent from the region until the early summer of 1753.

During his administration, Hopson's most pressing concern was the government of Halifax and the settlement of the new migrants at what would become Lunenburg, while coping with the Acadians, the French, and the Mi'kmaq. At least part of the growing harshness of attitude that developed among the British officials in Halifax towards the Acadians stemmed from the fact that the governor, or lieutenant governor, with the advice of the

Council, had to contend with considerable unrest among the newly arrived settlers, as well as what was seen as hostile intransigence among the Acadians. Exasperation with the former inevitably bred intolerance for the Acadian opposition to administration demands. The difficulties posed by discontent in Halifax would not be laid to rest until 1758, when the structure of government in the colony was changed and the first Nova Scotian assembly came into being. In 1752 the structure was that of a military regime, with little formal channel for civilian influence. The Council was appointed by the governor and until 1759 was weighted heavily in favour of the military. At the same time, the governor had the right to appoint the judiciary.[6] As a result, there was a constant series of complaints about favouritism in the appointment to minor administrative posts, the award of land grants and agreements to purchase supplies, and, above all, the way in which justice was administered. In December 1752 forty-six of the leading citizens of Halifax presented a petition asking for an inquiry into the behaviour of the justices of the Inferior Court of Common Pleas.[7] It was alleged in the petition that, not only had there been specific instances of improper conduct in some cases, including the refusal by the justices to allow cross-examination of crown witnesses, but there was a general tendency among the justices to overstep the boundaries of their commissions and to rely too greatly upon Massachusetts law and practice.[8] Hopson responded by calling daily sittings of Council between 9 January and 1 February 1753, which examined the charges brought and interviewed witnesses. As he wrote to the Board of Trade, he considered that an inquiry was preferable to a formal trial, since the latter would probably have "kept up a spirit of strife and contention in the Colony very detrimental to the public tranquillity."[9] The Council completely exonerated the judges.[10] At the same time, however, Hopson added two more judges to the bench and appealed to the Board of Trade to send out a trained lawyer to advise the administration on points of law.[11] This request resulted in the appointment of Jonathan Belcher as the first chief justice of Nova Scotia in October 1754. While Hopson's action brought an uneasy peace to the rancorous political life of Halifax, and laid the groundwork for a more permanent solution in the future, there continued to be a division between civilian and military authorities in the town until the death of Colonel Lawrence.

Hopson's reaction to the difficulties of settling the German Protestants in what would become Lunenburg both addressed the immediate problem and paved the way for later measures. These migrants had arrived at Halifax during the administration of Cornwallis but he had not managed to do more than provide them with temporary quarters there, leaving the question of where they were to be permanently established to his successor.[12] It was a matter of urgency because their situation was desperate: there were close to fifteen hundred men, women, and children, who had expected to be given supplies for a year, including the necessary implements they would need to make themselves self-sufficient.[13] The delay in organizing their permanent settlement meant that, in the eyes of the officials in London, much of this support should be brought to an end.[14] In his analysis of the situation, which was part of the dispatch he sent to London on 16 October 1752, Hopson wrote bluntly that "these foreign settlers are now become so very uneasy and discontented, that many of them have gone off from this place to the Island of St. John's, as we have great reason to believe and except some method can be fallen upon to prevent a further desertion, which will be very difficult to do, I apprehend that many more will follow."[15] Desertions of soldiers from both sides were sufficiently common that, in the early winter of 1752, Hopson concluded an agreement with the newly installed governor at Quebec, Ange Duquesne de Menneville, for the mutual return of these men.[16] The "desertion" of recently arrived migrants, however, especially to French territory rather than to New England, was much more disconcerting. Hopson requested the Board of Trade to halt the passage of assisted foreign Protestants until he had satisfactorily organized the "outsettling" of those then living in Halifax.[17]

The need to establish these new migrants effectively and without further turmoil was thus obviously a matter of great importance for the peace and security of Nova Scotia and also for the financial accounting demanded of its administrators by the British Parliament. But there was a considerable number of problems that had to be solved. These included the selection of a site and the transfer of a large body of people with their personal belongings, as well as provisions and building materials from Halifax, to the spot chosen. The men to oversee this operation had to be appointed. As has been suggested, fear of Mi'kmaq attacks had been partially responsible for the delay in deciding where to establish the new migrants. Within ten days of his arrival, Hopson asked the Council for suggestions for a site.[18] Some months passed before he decided upon the selection of the Merligash area. He was persuaded as much by the advantages of the site itself as by the disadvantages of other possibilities. Merligash was a short sea voyage from Halifax and there had been French settlement in the area in the seventeenth century. This had been continued in a desultory fashion until 1720 so that there was already some three or four hundred acres of cleared land there.[19] At the Council meeting of 10 May 1753, it was agreed that the new settlement should be "made at Merlagash [and] be called the township of Lunenburg."[20] The actual planning necessary for the enterprise took time; ships had to be hired out of Boston, the newcomers brought into a state of readiness for the move, and building materials and provisions collected together. Colonel Lawrence was appointed the officer in charge and he kept a journal of his experiences.[21] On 29 May 1753 the first of two small convoys set out from Halifax, heavily laden with luggage and supplies and carrying 692 settlers. The second left Halifax on 15 June, with approximately 800 settlers.

Lawrence found his work both exhausting and exasperating. The settlers argued with him about the way in which the town should be built, and were never as energetic and hard-working as he expected. Those who had been appointed as militia captains, and were responsible for seeing that the orders given by Lawrence were obeyed, reported to him that the settlers were "all differing in their ideas, they could not be brought to herd together, or to encamp otherwise than with every family separated by their baggage about them."[22] The aggressive reactions of the settlers to being told what to do is hardly surprising They had been subject to considerable delays and disappointments ever since their arrival in Halifax. Now, at last, on the land where they were to build their future, they found that they had to set about building their houses and planting gardens if they were to have their own shelter and necessary provisions any time in the foreseeable future. To be told to work on communal projects, for minimal or no wages, or to do their own work to a particular schedule was, to say the least, provoking. Lawrence faced argumentative and unruly men as he tried to organize defences for the town and put together at least some barracks to shelter the families while their own houses were being built. Discontent was increased by the way in which general supplies of food and clothing were distributed. By the end of June 1753, it was clear that it was not merely a matter of how these provisions were handed out but also of the amount given. The quantity of food provided, particularly bread, was inadequate.

Lawrence had a great deal of sympathy for the settlers' plight. The hard physical labour that the construction of houses and other buildings involved meant that, as he wrote, "the people being closely engaged on their lots and otherwise ... [have] consequently no time for fishing and helping out their allowance of provisions thro' their own means."[23] What faced Lawrence was the problem not merely of managing the supply of provisions so as to keep the settlers healthy over the summer but also of storing enough to feed them until harvest time the following year. He had also to minimize desertions of the young and the restless to the French at Beauséjour. As had been the case at Halifax, such desertions were not numerically significant but they added to the tensions between the settlers and the officers in charge. Lawrence managed to control the situation until his return to Halifax in September but, at this time, the establishment of the foreign Protestants at Lunenburg was no more than begun. Events in late autumn would show clearly enough that the new settlement in no way provided the administration of the colony with a community of unquestionably loyal citizenry.

At this time, Hopson was preparing to leave for London, having spent just over a year in Halifax. His months in the colony had seen a reasonable settlement of the political disputes in the city itself and the beginning of the settlement of the foreign Protestants. He had also worked to secure a better understanding with particular Mi'kmaq bands, something that Cornwallis had started to do just before he left.[24] Hopson had a small measure of success when, in September 1752, Jean-Baptisite Cope came to Halifax to negotiate on behalf of a small group of Mi'kmaq who lived in the Shubenacadie region. Cope informed the Council that he had "about 40 men under him,"[25] a number representing a community of about ninety. An agreement was soon reached. It was little more than a limited alliance that, after acknowledging previous disputes between British administration and Mi'kmaq in general, asserted that "all Transactions during the late War shall on both sides be buried in Oblivion." Further, the Shubenacadie band was asked to "use their outmost endeavours to bring in other Indians to Renew and Ratify this peace." In return, the British promised aid should there be hostility from other Mi'kmaq bands towards those of Shubenacadie because of this demonstration of friendship for the British. It was agreed that the "free liberty of Hunting and Fishing as usual" would be accorded to the band. Finally, this group of Mi'kmaq agreed that all future disputes with His Majesty's subjects would be resolved "in His Majesty's Court of Civil Judicature, where the Indians shall have the same benefit, advantage and Priviledges as any others of His Majesty's Subjects." Hopson was quite clear that this treaty was no more than a beginning of what he hoped would be the regularization of British-Mi'kmaq relations. He wrote to the Board of Trade that, even if the agreement was only with "a small tribe," he hoped that it might "have the good effect to bring over the Rest," though, he added, " this is more to be hoped for than trusted to."[26] To ensure that the treaty was known throughout the colony, Hopson and the Council had it proclaimed on 24 November 1752.[27] The impact of this treaty upon British-Mi'kmaq relations during the remaining months of Hopson's personal administration of the colony is difficult to gauge. There was, however, despite continual rumours of Mi'kmaq action, relative calm in the colony on this front until the summer of 1753.

While the politics of Halifax, the settlement at Lunenburg, and relationships with the Mi'kmaq engaged a considerable amount of Hopson's time during his sojourn in the colony, he also managed to pay a good deal of attention to the Acadians. From the outset of his administration, he considered them as part of the colony, as much a feature of its life as the Mi'kmaq and the newly arrived Protestant settlers, whether the latter were from New England or recently arrived from Europe. His views were no doubt shaped by his previous service at Louisbourg, where he would have gained an insight into the difference between French policies and Acadian attitudes. In his first lengthy overview of the situation of the colony, dated 16 October 1752, Hopson made it clear to the Board of Trade that he thought the "French inhabitants" had no intention of leaving the colony at this time nor did he wish them to do so.[28] In a further dispatch, sent two days later to the secretary of state, Hopson remarked that there was no possibility of obtaining any oath from the Acadians without a recognition of their neutrality. Nevertheless, he went on to say that "they appear to be much better disposed than they have been, and I hope will still amend and in a long course of time become less scrupulous ..."[29] He concluded by remarking that Cornwallis would undoubtedly confirm his opinion of the Acadians and agree as to "how useful and necessary these people are to us, how impossible it is to do without them, or to replace them even if we had other settlers to put in their places ..."

By December 1752, Hopson had clear ideas about how his administration was going to deal with the Acadians on a daily basis and on how he would cope with the vexed question of the oath of allegiance. Difficulties in the Minas region, where garrisons had been established by Cornwallis both in the basin itself and at Pisiquid, allowed Hopson to make perfectly clear how he considered the Acadians should be treated. A petition from the inhabitants of Pisiquid was discussed at a meeting of the Council on 12 December 1752, at which Hopson presided. Lawrence and William Cotterell were present along with Benjamin Green, William Steele, and John Collier. The petitioners complained of the conduct of the officers in the Minas area, in particular of a certain Captain Hamilton, who had allowed his troops to carry off "sheep, Fowls and other things," which "is absolutely contrary to the Laws and Priviledges of His Majesty's subjects."[30] Further, it was reported that the settlers were sent for on frivolous grounds and kept in the blockhouse at the whim of the soldiers, without any due process whatsoever. This behaviour was roundly condemned by Council. Orders were given that the deputies should make an inquiry as to damage suffered by the settlers and "put into writing an Account of what each Person ought, in reason, have to Indemnify him."[31] As well, Hopson dispatched a strongly worded order to the officers at Vieux Logis (the barracks at Minas) and Fort Edward (at Pisiquid) which left no room for misinterpretation. "You are to look on the French Inhabitants," he wrote, "in the same light with the rest of His Majesty's Subjects, as to the protection of the Laws and Government, for which reason nothing is to be taken from them by Force, or any Price set upon their goods but what they themselves agree to."[32] Hopson continued: "And if at any time the Inhabitants should Obstinately refuse to comply with what His Majesty's Service may require of them, You are not to redress yourself by Military Force, or in any unlawfull manner but to lay the case before the Governor & wait His Orders thereon." To ensure that the settlers were aware of his wishes, the governor ordered that notices be "stuck up in the Most Publick part of the Fort, both in English and in French," stating that provisions and other commodities that were brought to the fort for sale should be paid for "according to a free agreement made between them & the Purchasers" and further that "no Officer, non-Commissioned Officer, or soldier, shall presume to insult or otherwise abuse any of the Inhabitants of the Country who are upon all occasions to be treated as His Majesty's Subjects, & to whom the Laws of the Country are open, to Protect as well as Punish." In sum, at this time both Hopson and the members of Council treated the Acadians as subjects of the crown and with rights as well as duties.

Hopson's attitude towards the question of the oath was a logical extension of this view of the Acadians and was also in agreement with the ideas of Cornwallis as to their civil status. Cornwallis had asserted, on more than one occasion, that the Acadians were "the subjects of the king of Great Britain and not of France."[33] To both men, the oath was the recognition of the situation of the Acadians as subjects of the British crown, and, in taking it, the Acadians did not become British subjects but gave a formal recognition to this state of affairs. The matter of the oath, they believed, was one for the government of Great Britain to decide. The Treaty of Utrecht had transferred the Acadians to British rule and the Acadians were, therefore, in law, British subjects. This, for Cornwallis in particular, settled the matter: if there was anything that the Acadians wished to change in their circumstances, then the route for discussion was by appeal to the governor of the colony and thence to the British monarch. Cornwallis had, indeed, informed the Acadians that it was the business of the monarchs and their courts to interpret treaties, and not for others to "meddle with the politics and affairs of government."[34] It should be remembered, of course, that British subjects at this time, whether living in London or Edinburgh, Cardiff or Boston, were just that: subjects of the monarch, not citizens of the state. Accordingly, for Cornwallis and Hopson, all questions the Acadians wished to argue about their right to noncombatant status, to migrate freely after selling their lands and buildings, and to be provided with priests were to be decided by British law and precedent. Any such action would result from petition, not by negotiation.

It is with this conviction about the status of the Acadians that Hopson wrote to the Board of Trade on 10 December 1752 asking for advice on "the Oaths to tender to the French Inhabitants as directed by the 68th article of My Instructions."[35] He went on to point out that to demand the same oath which Cornwallis had proposed would be fruitless and suggested that the matter be left in abeyance for a while. Hopson did not present any argument for this course of action other than expediency. It was expediency, however, that envisaged positive future consequences. Like Mascarene, Hopson believed strongly that once "the French King is removed out of this Province ... the French Inhabitants will take the Oaths and, giving over all hopes of any change, enjoy the benefit of English laws and Liberty ..."[36] The oath was immaterial as a determinant of the right of the British crown to treat the Acadians in the same way as it would treat any other community of its subjects.

But a close analysis of the available records reveals that many Acadians did not fully subscribe to this belief that they were, with or without their formal taking of an oath of allegiance, unequivocally British subjects, with no recourse but to accept British jurisdiction. For a significant number of them, they were British subjects, not because of an international agreement, but because they subscribed to an oath of allegiance, either in 1727 or in 1730, with certain conditions explicitly granted to them at that time. Should these terms and conditions not be honoured, the Acadians' position was that they would then be, to a greater or lesser extent, relieved of their obligations to the British crown. For the Acadians, the oath, and the terms on which they had accepted it, was what determined their status as subjects of the crown. Just before Hopson left Halifax, he and the Council were presented with two petitions from Acadian leaders of various settlements which shed light on the Acadian sense of their political situation. The first petition, which was discussed at the Council meeting of 4 October 1753, concerned the matter of whether or not the priests, who were provided by France to serve the Acadian communities, should be required to take an oath of allegiance.[37] Such priests were, of course, subjects of the king of France. The forty-five Acadian men who signed this petition were from the Minas area, Grand Pré, and Pisiquid. They argued that when they "took the oath of allegiance to his Britannic Majesty, we took it only that we should be allowed the free exercise of our religion, and a sufficient number of ministers to perform the services."[38] It was contended that, should the missionaries sent to the settlements be forced to take the oath, they would not remain. The petitioners went on to say that this would mean that they would "see [themselves] deprived of the essence of what had been granted."[39] The argument made was essentially that the provision of priests was a contractual obligation of the British crown, without which the Acadians would not have agreed to become its subjects. Hopson and the Council decided to allow priests to continue to minister to the Acadians under the old arrangement of the grant of an express permission by the Council to each priest to do so. The reason given in the Council minutes for this resolution was that the whole issue was a ploy by the French "to prevent the Inhabitants from having any Priests ... and ... by this means to induce the Inhabitants to leave the Province on account of their being denied the free Exercise of their Religion ... to the great Detriment of this Province."[40] No credence was given to the Acadian argument that priests should be provided as result of the terms on which they had become British subjects. Governor and Council considered the issue solely in terms of the immediate politics of the region rather than as a matter of the long-term relationship between the Acadians and the British crown.

The petition presented to Hopson at the meeting of Council on 17 September 1753 contains a much stronger statement of the Acadian sense of their rights. It was unsigned and was brought to Halifax by two men, who said that they had authority to negotiate on behalf of some "fourscore" of those who had fled their lands in the Beaubassin area in 1751.[41] The tone of the document is one of a community convinced of the reasonableness of its position. It opened with the assertion that the sole reason that they had left their lands was that the demand made by Cornwallis for "the new oath which his Excellency Mr. Cornwallis wished to exact from us" would "break and revoke the one granted to us on the 11th of October 1727." However, it now appeared that, if they returned, they would "have the same favours that were granted ... formerly ..."[42] The document then went on to give the oath that they were prepared to take, with the explicit terms that must be granted before they bound themselves by it. This oath, offering a simple promise of fidelity to George II and his successors, read: "Je promets et jure sincèrement que je seraie fidèle à Sa Majestée le Roi George Second et a ses successeurs. Dieu me soit en aide." The oaths that had been sworn in the presence of Ensign Wroth and Governor Philipps, a generation before, had had additional refinements of intent and of the Acadian acceptance of the British control of Nova Scotia. Those who had sworn had promised that they would be "entirely faithful (entièrement fidèle) and that they would give "true obedience" (Obeirai Vraiment) to the orders of George II. Each of the earlier oaths had also included the affirmation that the person who took it recognized George II as the "Soverain Lord of Acadie or Nova Scotia" (le Souvrain Seigneur de l'Acadie ou Nouvelle Ecosse).[43] The petitioners now asserted that it was impossible for them to accept any stronger affirmation of allegiance than a vague promise of "fidelity" because of the attitude of the "savage nations" among whom they lived.[44]

Thus, the oath that these Acadians offered in 1753 was the irreducible minimum for an affirmation of the loyalty of a subject. The terms that these Acadians now wished to have granted, when the oath was sworn, were particularly solicitous of Acadian freedom of action. It might be argued that there was no fundamental difference between what was now requested and the rights Wroth had granted the settlers of the Minas area in 1727. However, the new wording for the provisions sought – religious freedom, the right to non-combatant status, the terms on which land and property were held, as well as the right of migration – were much more explicit. In fact, given the omission of any recognition of British suzerainty over the colony as a whole, what was asked for could be said to change the relationship between Acadian and crown to that of citizen rather than that of subject.[45] Subjects accept the commands of the monarch and modification of those commands comes about through institutions that proffer advice to the crown. Citizens, ruled by a monarch, debate the limits of monarchical power and are able to negotiate its boundaries. There is no doubt that the conditions asked for by the Acadians in 1753 would, if granted, have placed restrictions upon the power that the British monarch could exercise over their lives.

In these petitions, the question of religion played a less important role than that of neutrality. The right to remain Catholic was stressed as well as the right to have a sufficiency of priests. There was an additional demand on this matter to what had been accorded in 1727, the explicit recognition of the right of the priests not to take the oath of allegiance.[46] In general, however, the petitioners of 1753 were much more articulate about what they wished than their predecessors. In 1727 the Acadian right not to fight had been expressed simply enough, the article in question stating that "they would not in any manner be obliged to take up arms against any person, and having no duties in questions of war."[47] In 1753 the wording was considerably more emphatic: "we shall be exempt from taking up arms against anyone whatever, whether English, French, Savages, or people of any other nation: and that neither we nor any of our descendants shall be taken to pilot or go where we would not wish to go."[48] The second article proposed in 1753 dealt with the right of the Acadians and their descendants to leave Nova Scotia for wherever they wanted, "their heads high," as and when they wished, with all their moveable goods, "having sold what could not be carried."[49] This article then concluded by saying that their departure would free them from any obligation to Britain as soon as they had quit British territory.[50] In 1727 Ensign Wroth had accepted the Acadians' right to leave when they wished and to sell their houses and farms, providing the purchasers were "natural born subjects of Great Britain." The question of the right of future generations was not considered by Wroth but he did include the provision that, once the Acadians had left "His Majesty's territory," their obligations under the oath would be at an end.[51]

The last article proposed dealt with the Acadian rights to the land they had settled. In 1727 Wroth had recognized the status quo, and the terms accepted stated that the Acadians and their descendants were accorded the right to hold their lands to the same extent as had been hitherto granted, paying the customary dues.[52] The proposal put forward in 1753 was that the Acadians "shall have the entire enjoyment" of their property "without being disturbed by anyone in the world; and that the lands occupied by the English shall be restored to those to whom they formerly belonged."[53] The lands in question, it becomes clear in the context of the rest of the document, were those taken for the construction of Fort Lawrence, after these particular Acadians had left the area because of the destruction of Beaubassin. The petition continued with the hope that these articles would not only be granted by the governor but "even ratified by the court of England, so that those who may succeed your Excellency shall not make the pretext that His Excellency Cornwallis made in saying that Mr. Phillipps had no authority from the court of England for the oath he granted us."[54] It ended with a request for a speedy resolution of the matter, in order they could begin to bring back the value of their land, which had been almost ruined because of the neglect of the last three years.[55] Quite apart from what was actually requested, the tone of this petition shows the confidence of the Acadians in claiming what they considered to be politically theirs by right.

Six men discussed this petition, Governor Hopson presiding. Four of them would later take part in the fateful Council meeting of 28 July 1755 which would decide to deport the Acadians. Those who attended both meetings included Charles Lawrence, who, as lieutenant governor, presided over the later meeting; John Collier, a retired army officer who had been among the arrivals of 1749 and who was almost immediately appointed a justice of the peace[56]; William Cotterell, who seems also to have been a recently arrived settler from England; and Benjamin Green, the son of a Harvard graduate who was rector of Salem, with commercial interests linking Halifax and Boston. Green had seen action at Louisbourg and in 1753 was serving in Halifax as a naval officer.[57] At the meeting in 1753, Robert Monckton, the officer then in command of Fort Lawrence, and William Steele, about whom little is known, were also present. The Council minutes did not record the discussion, merely the decision reached. Those who wished to return, it was decided, should be tendered a simple version of the oath but one that included a specific pledge of "perfect loyalty" to His Majesty King George II.[58] The petitioners were given until 20 November to take this oath, some six weeks, and, if they did so, they were to be "admitted to Return to a peaceable and quiet possession of their Lands at Chignecto (reserving the Land on which the Fort Stands and such a further Quantity Round the same as shall be thought necessary for His Majesty's Use)." The Council further agreed that they would be allowed the "free Exercise of their Religion and a sufficient number of Priests ... and shall Enjoy all the privileges granted to them by the treaty of Utrecht." No comment was recorded in the minutes on the particular requests embodied in the petition.

As Hopson's administration drew to a close, the attitudes of the British and the Acadians towards one another were becoming more and more influenced by arguments on both sides as to the legal aspects of the British colonial administration. Cornwallis and Hopson had taken the position that the Treaty of Utrecht had settled the status of the Acadians as British subjects, and the matter of the oath was a reasonable affirmation of the loyalty that the Acadians owed to their monarch. The Acadians continued to challenge this, insisting that the transfer of Nova Scotia from French control to British had been accomplished with the granting of specific rights to them by the British. The Acadians claimed that they had sworn an oath, which had been accepted by the British, and that, at the time of that oath, British officials had recognized Acadian claims in the matter of religion, property, and non-combatant status. Hopson, as Mascarene had before him, believed that the Acadians would become satisfactory British subjects in time. His policy was not to enter into unproductive discussion with the Acadians over matters which he believed would eventually, and inevitably, be solved in favour of the British.

Hopson's patience was one of the factors that contributed to the relatively peaceful temper of his administration. But it was only one of the factors that made his stay in Halifax more tranquil than those of both his predecessor in office, Cornwallis, and his successor, Colonel Charles

Lawrence, and it was by no means the most important. The impact of events elsewhere, as well as the return of particular individuals to positions of strength within the region, was of much greater significance in the development of British-Acadian relations after the departure of Hopson than the particular personality of his successor. Throughout its existence, whether the government had been British or French, "Acadia or Nova Scotia" had been shaped, to a greater or lesser extent, by the impact of events provoked by policies that originated elsewhere and by the ambitions and conflicts of stronger neighbouring colonies. There had been fairly lengthy periods when such influences were relatively mild, even benign. But from 1753 onwards, international relations and colonial politics, as interpreted by powerful men within the region, were of overwhelming importance for the lives of the Acadians and these influences, this time, spelled tragedy. Even if the years after 1753 had been ones of tranquillity for the region, there is no way of knowing whether or not the passage of time would have vindicated Hopson's belief that the Acadians were destined to become satisfactory British subjects. But the reality was that tensions between the British and French, both in Europe and in North America, had been steadily increasing throughout 1753. Any hope of peaceful development in Nova Scotia was brought to a halt as relations between the two powers continued to deteriorate.

Whatever the ambitions of the other European states, it was the expanding commercial interests of Great Britain and France that, in the mid-1750s, dominated not only their own international policies but also those of the others. In 1753 France was an expanding world power, solidly established in trade with the Caribbean, with growing interests in India and Africa, and bolstered by a large home market for her emerging industrial products, above all textiles and metal goods.[59] Contemporary Great Britain was seen as a power of growing importance because of its navy, but there is no doubt that, at this time, France was the stronger. Both at home and abroad, however, the growing importance of the British mercantile lobby in London was undeniable.[60] Inevitably, the interests of British merchants in India and the Caribbean meant clashes with French activity in those regions, clashes that quickly involved British government action. It was in North America, where the colonies that the two powers had established had almost always been in open competition with one another, that Franco-British discord was the most bitter.

Whatever desultory attempts the two countries made elsewhere to prevent the outbreak of war after 1748, even the word "truce" is inaccurate to describe the state of affairs where their colonial patterns of trade and settlement came into contact in North America. The region encompassing Nova Scotia, Île Royale, Île Saint-Jean, and the Saint John River is a case in point. But it was only one of many locations between the St Lawrence and the Mississippi delta where, after 1748, skirmishes broke out and both sides readied themselves for more serious combat. Between the Atlantic on the one hand and Lake Erie and the Ohio valley on the other, there was continual skirmishing wherever British and French encountered one another. The Ohio valley had become a major area of contention by 1753. In 1749 Captain Jean-Baptiste Céleron de Blainville had buried a plaque at the confluence of the Ohio and Kanouagan rivers claiming the Ohio river "and ... all lands on both sides up to the source" for France.[61] But traders and settlers from New England, New York, Pennsylvania, and Virginia had already begun moving into this territory.[62] In the summer of 1753 the lieutenant governor of Virginia, Robert Dinwiddie, sent the young George Washington to reconnoitre the situation south of Lake Erie. He spent some time as the guest of the French officers at Fort Le Boeuf and he reported that they told him that "it was their absolute design to take possession of the Ohio, and by G—, they would do it ..."[63] By the end of 1753, both British and French colonists were primed for a major confrontation.

The historiography, concerned with the process by which the antagonism of Britain and France in Europe and the hostilities between their colonies in North America gathered strength between 1753 and 1756, is both wide-ranging and extensive. Almost all major accounts concentrate either upon developments in North America or the interaction between international relations and political influence in London and Paris. Was the pattern of events merely the inevitable collision of two inherently expansionist empires? Was it, above all, the result of the political ambitions of British ministers of the crown? Or of the ambitions of the advisers of Louis XV? Did they evolve in a particular fashion because of imperialist dreams of the governor of New France? Or from the unbridled greed of British colonists for land, more land, and yet more land? Or from a muddled combination of all these factors?[64] Whatever interpretation is chosen, one thing is clear: the events of these years, 1753–56, saw increasing talk of a Franco-British war in Paris and London, and increasing importance given to their American colonies by both countries. Both began to pay more attention, if not give greater consideration, to matters of colonial defences.[65] By the time Lawrence assumed control of Nova Scotia in November 1753, tension between the British and the French in North America was as great as it had been in 1744, and not merely in the Atlantic region. Both sides actively encouraged raiding parties and prepared for a full-scale war most considered to be inevitable.

The control of the "continental cornice," as Brebner names it, the region running northeast of Massachusetts and Maine and southeast of New France, embracing the lands and waters of present-day southern New Brunswick, Prince Edward Island, and Nova Scotia, including Cape Breton Island, had been a major area of contention between England and France since the arrival of migrants from these countries at the opening of the seventeenth century. Now, in the middle of the eighteenth century, the region was one of the most important areas in North America for the military strategists of both France and Great Britain.[66] For both sides, the loyalty of the Acadians was a matter of debate and concern because it was generally believed that they represented a possible military force of between three and five thousand. That the Acadian communities did not have a strong militia tradition and that neither British nor French had ever managed to recruit extensively among them does not seem to have entered into imperial calculations. The strategists' reasoning seems to have been based on the perception of a potential, one that war would bring into being. The French were convinced that the ties of religion and language would sway Acadian loyalties and the British were almost equally convinced that such links would prove decisive in a crisis. What was overlooked by both European powers was the fact that, in 1750, the overwhelming loyalty for the majority of the Acadians was to the lands where they lived and to their own communities.

At the heart of the Acadian political actions, whether these were concerned with internal issues of property ownership or external matters of state control, was the conviction that their ownership of the lands they had settled and farmed was incontestable, not to be alienated by any international treaty. As soon as the matter of mass migration was raised in 1713, the Acadians brought forward their right to sell and dispose not merely their moveable goods but also their farms and buildings. In Acadian eyes, the terms of the Treaty of Utrecht, as they related to Acadian matters, were a matter of continual negotiation and interpretation, not matters that had been clearly decided, once and for all, by a binding and clear, international agreement. As a corollary of this position, the Acadians saw themselves not as a subject population but as a people with legal rights, to be respected by both British and French. The Acadians were, in their own minds, the legitimate inhabitants of the lands they had settled, whoever might claim sovereignty over the territory as a whole. Emigration would be on their own terms, as a result of their own decisions, neither a right that could be denied nor a choice that could be imposed upon them. The Acadians considered that they had every right to debate and present ideas about how and where they should live to those who administered, or who wished to administer, the lands on which they lived.

This sense that they had an entitlement to the land on which they had settled, independent of the decisions of distant authorities, arose, in part, because the British had done little to challenge the Acadians' sense of ownership of their lands. Disputes about boundaries were either settled by the Acadian deputies or were adjudicated by the Council until 1748. The imposition of quit-rents by the British, and the payment of these by the Acadians until the spring of 1755, was a tangible recognition for the latter that they had certain rights to their farms.[67] Conviction of ownership was supported by emotional attachment to the lands on which they lived, an element of Acadian life that was consistently overlooked by most of their contemporaries, just as it has been by many later historians. Yet it was clearly recognized by La Galissonière, commandant-general of New France between 1747 and 1749, who wrote that such an emotion was "entirely natural" but, at the same time, the root of all the Acadians' problems.[68] The link between strong feelings for a broad community and the political and religious institutions of a modern state has led to a lack of appreciation for of local and regional loyalties.[69] But a strong sense of commonalty can be discerned in many societies even when, and perhaps particularly when, the lives of their inhabitants are not strongly linked to a political centre. In fact, strong European nations have emerged only by assimilating or crushing local identities.[70] In the case of Acadia, a strong sense of connection between the settlers and their villages had developed by 1755. The Acadians had known excellent agricultural productivity, minimal external political control, few epidemics, and, until the last fifteen years, few incursions of warfare into their villages. Life expectancy and fertility rates were such that a significant number of men and women would have the satisfaction of seeing not only their children but their children's children well established. New lands for cultivation and settlement were within reasonable travelling distance, at most no more than a week to ten days' voyage along the coast. In one of the few Acadian literary writings to survive from the pre-deportation era, a poet muses on the inevitability of death, comparing the life of meadows and fields to that of humanity, all caught by the turning of time.[71]

Before 1755, the Acadians did not live in an earthly paradise without humanity's usual problems, from sibling rivalries to the idiocies of the more powerful, but they did live in remarkably beautiful countryside with considerable political and social freedom, and, as La Galissonière remarked, it was indeed quite natural that they did not find calls to leave their homes compelling. In their own eyes, the Acadians were as firmly rooted on their lands as anyone else in their vicinity. After all, had not they received, in October 1747, a proclamation in the name of George II, dispatched by Governor Shirley in response to a letter from the Duke of Newcastle, explicitly stating that "there is not the least foundation for any Apprehensions of his Majesty's intention to remove the said Inhabitants of Nova Scotia from their Settlements and Habitations within his said province ..."[72]? At the same time, their experience of life on a border between two great powers, of having been for more than a hundred years the pawn of rival Anglo-French imperial designs, had led the Acadians to an unusually clear-sighted sense of the need for a particular policy: that of neutrality. From 1713 until 1755, the majority of the Acadian community supported the oath to which, by 1730, they were convinced they had subscribed: allegiance to Britain, with the proviso that they would not be asked to bear arms. But, unhappily, by the 1750s, both French and British saw the Acadians, above all, as a potential military resource. These powers assessed the Acadians not as community to be understood but as an obstinate peasantry to be brought to a proper sense of their obligations, obligations that naturally stemmed from the Acadian relationship with France and Great Britain rather than from the Acadians' sense of themselves.

As already noted, by the late summer of 1753, when Lawrence became the lieutenant governor of Nova Scotia and William Shirley returned to Boston as the governor of Massachusetts, war was clearly imminent. The year before, the Marquis Duquesne had arrived at Quebec as the new governor, with orders to ensure that the claims of France were to be properly upheld, whether these were centred on the Atlantic coast or along the Ohio River and the rivers that flow into it.[73] In Boston, people talked of the possibility of a French sweep through Nova Scotia from their forts at Beauséjour and Gaspereau, preparatory to driving the British from "all their other Colonies in North America."[74] In London, the Earl of Halifax, as president of the Board of Trade, informed the cabinet in 1753 that, should the French establish themselves in the Ohio region, they "will be in possession of near two thirds of the very best unsettled land on this side of the Mississippi and the St. Lawrence, while Great Britain will not only lose near one half of the territory, to which it is undisputably entitled, but in the case of a future Rupture will find it extremely difficult to keep the other half."[75] In these circumstances, whoever served in the Atlantic region in 1753, from Massachusetts to Louisbourg, from the mouth of the Saint John to Île Royale, whether French or British, military officer or civilian administrator, would have been foolish not to consider what would happen to his responsibilities in time of war. The correspondence of Jean-Louis de Raymond, governor at Louisbourg, with Quebec and France is mainly concerned with armaments and fortifications, a theme that also dominates the correspondence of Charles Lawrence with Boston and Great Britain.

But in considering the way in which the decision to deport the Acadians was made, the general circumstances of North American affairs in the mid-eighteenth century has often been seen of less importance than the career, personality, and character of Charles Lawrence. Since there is no doubt that Lawrence did, indeed, play a major part in the way in which the events culminated in the deportation, an understanding of his character is of considerable importance. There seems general agreement that he was above all "a military man," but what this phrase might signify is hotly argued. Does it imply someone with no interest in the human consequences of his actions? Does it suggest a person whose overriding concern was always the defeat of the enemy? Does it presuppose a person whose fundamental motivation was rooted in contempt for his opponents and a conviction that "the end justifies the means"? One view, expressed with vigour by the French historian Émile Lauvrière, sees in Lawrence "the hateful example of the English military caste which, in the eighteenth-century, showed itself destitute of any scruple or honour."[76] Lauvrière is convinced that

Lawrence, "like the greater part of his compatriots, detested the French and wanted at any cost the ruin of their power in North America."[77] He goes on to depict Lawrence as a "tyrant of low cunning and accomplished flattery" who "crushed anyone who did not hold his views."[78] For one Canadian, Arthur Doughty, Lawrence was man of rigid military principles. "He was," Doughty writes, "unaccustomed to compromise. He kept before him the letter of the law, and believed that any deviation from it was fraught with danger."[79] Both authors consider Lawrence a man of little imagination and a stickler for correct behaviour. But, for those who ascribe to the ideas of Lauvrière, Lawrence was not only a man of rules and regulations, he was also someone motivated by scorn for those who differed from him. Historians such as Brebner, who agree with Doughty's evaluation of Lawrence, see the lieutenant governor as someone moulded by his patriotism, his devotion to a vision of what was due to British rule, which implied a scorn for other peoples but not necessarily hatred. Brebner writes that Lawrence resolved the situation which he faced "with a soldier's cold and arbitrary logic into the mathematics of military terms. He knew allies and enemies, not 'neutrals,' and his calculations could not easily include elements he could not accurately and confidently estimate."[80]

One of the difficulties in forming an estimate of Lawrence is that information about his career before his arrival in Nova Scotia is unreliable.[81] He was probably forty when he arrived in Halifax, having served with the 11th Foot in the West Indies from 1733 to 1737. He then spent some time at the War Office, being promoted to lieutenant in 1731 and captain in 1745. He fought at Fontenoy and joined the Warburton regiment, the 45th, at Louisbourg, as a major in 1747. It appears that he enjoyed the patronage of the 2nd Lord Halifax, sometime president of the Board of Trade. He was obviously a competent officer, though also, as his confrontation with La Corne in 1750 showed, a man with a quick temper. As the commanding officer in charge of the establishment of Lunenburg, Lawrence handled that difficult situation with considerable skill. He judged that the exasperated and exasperating foreign Protestants in his charge were sturdy but had little common sense. "They are inconceivably turbulent," he wrote. "I might have sd mutinous, and are only to be managed like a great ship in a violent storm, wt infinite care, vigilance & attention."[82] In sum, what is known, as opposed to conjectured, about Lawrence before his appointment as lieutenant governor in 1753 attests to an efficient officer with a service record that had earned him fairly rapid promotion, a person of considerable administrative talent who was trusted by both Cornwallis and Hopson.

The debate about the character of Lawrence before his appointment as lieutenant governor is no more than a prelude to the much more wide-ranging arguments over the role he played once appointed as lieutenant governor of Nova Scotia. Once in power, did Lawrence immediately put into place a policy that was aimed at removing the Acadians from Nova

Scotia as soon as possible, or did he decide upon this action as a result of the events of the early spring of 1755?[83] Was such a policy, whenever it was decided upon, the fulfilment of a British "crusade" against the Acadians, which had been a goal of the British administration since 1713?[84] Or was it a matter of personal conviction and belief?[85] Was the deportation the result of a concatenation of immediate circumstances?[86] When did the authorities in London learn of Lawrence 's intentions? Did they approve of his decision?

Arguments about whether or not Lawrence was considering deportation of the Acadians from the moment he was confirmed as lieutenant governor are rooted in varying interpretations of his first major dispatch, which was sent from Halifax on 5 December 1753.[87] In it, Lawrence presented a wide-ranging analysis of the situation of the colony. On the whole, he was pleased with the state of affairs in his jurisdiction, opening his letter by telling their lordships that "hardly anything worth your notice has happened since Governor Hopson's departure." Halifax, he remarked, was quiet and "the spirit of mutiny and violence" at Lunenburg had diminished. The dispatch went on to note that the Acadians were also "tolerably quiet, as to Government matters, but exceeding litigious among themselves." Lawrence then raised the issue of how such disputes were to be settled unless the Acadians had taken an accepted oath of allegiance. This question of Acadian property rights was clearly a matter of considerable importance for Lawrence. The dispatch, after a number of comments on the situation at Minas and the possibility of a treaty with the Cape Sable Mi'kmaq, concluded with the matter of the "deserted inhabitants" of Chignecto. At issue was the petition, already mentioned, of those particular Acadians wishing to return to the Beaubassin area, which had been discussed at the Council meeting of 27 September 1753. Lawrence acknowledged that their return to British rule would have a good effect on the Acadian population as a whole, but he concluded that "your Lordships may be assured that they will never have my consent to return unless they comply with the demand for an unqualified oath without any reservation whatever."[88]

According to Brebner, this judgment showed that Lawrence was determined that the Acadians "must take the oath or suffer the consequences."[89] But Brebner also remarks that Lawrence offered, at this point, no specific idea of what the consequences should be. To interpret the sentences, which are clearly concerned with the action of a number of Acadians who wished to return to Nova Scotia, as indicating a policy of deportation for those within the colony seems to me to be stretching the evidence. A much more obvious, and more significant, misinterpretation has been attached to the part of the dispatch that dealt with the issue of the adjudication of Acadian disputes over land. It is clear, if the complete passage is read, that Lawrence, in noting how difficult it was to administer justice among the Acadians, was referring to the problem of Acadian settlements on land which had not been surveyed and which had not been authorized by the crown. He wrote: "To give them a hearing in our Courts of Law would be attended with insuperable difficulties; their not having taken the oath of allegiance an absolute bar in our Law, to their holding any landed possessions, and your Lordships may imagine how difficult it must be for the Courts to give judgement in cases where the proprietors' claims are far from being ascertained, and where the disputes commonly relate to the Bounds of Lands that have never yet been surveyed that we know of." In the next sentence, Lawrence made it clear that he was talking about the difficulty of regulation only in cases where no title of ownership had been granted by either France or Great Britain. The lieutenant governor wrote that "the Council, as your Lordships will see by the enclosed copy of their Minutes, have determined some few cases for them in which His Majesty's interest could possibly suffer no detriment, which is all we could do for the present." In other words, the problems that Lawrence is pointing out are those that had bothered British officials since the 1730s: the unauthorized settlement of crown lands by the Acadians. Rumilly, among other historians, however, has interpreted this dispatch as a new and vicious policy, one which meant that henceforth "the inhabitants who refused the oath without qualification had no right to property."[90] But, read in its entirety, the dispatch contains almost nothing that had not already been brought to the attention of London by either Cornwallis or Hopson. It is little more than the first overview of the colony by the new administrative head.

For the next six months, until June 1754, Lawrence had much of his time and attention taken up with troubles at Lunenburg. In his dispatch of 5 December, the lieutenant governor reported that "the inhabitants of Lunenburg are much reformed; that spirit of mutiny and violence which possessed them so strongly in the beginning is now in a manner subsided, the agreeable situation of their settlement and the hopes of the live stock that the Governor has desired your Lordships to grant them next Spring has produced in them more orderly behaviour." On 17 December, less than two weeks after he had written these words, Lawrence was informed that the settlement was in armed rebellion. Confrontation between the setters and the local garrison had broken out over a rumour of a letter being received by a settler, one Petrequin, suggesting that supplies sent out from London had been embezzled en route.[91] Within another week, Colonel Robert Monckton had arrived at Lunenburg, with some two hundred men, and had brought the situation under control. Its aftermath, however, the trial of those considered to have committed "high treason" and the general need to calm the town, demanded and received a great deal of attention, not only from Lawrence but also from the Council. Throughout the winter and early spring of 1754, Acadian matters are rarely mentioned in Council minutes, the problems of merchants and craftsmen at Halifax and of law and order at both Halifax and Lunenburg taking pride of place on the agenda of that body.[92]

The silence of the Council minutes on Acadian developments during these months did not mean that all was peaceful and quiet in the settlements and villages. Nor did lack of immediate action from Lawrence about the oath of allegiance mean that he had decided to ignore the matter. One clear source of unrest for the colony was the return of Le Loutre to the Beauséjour region sometime in the summer of 1753. He had immediately begun to plan work on a major dyke on the Aulac River, organizing for that purpose those Acadians who had lived as refugees in the region since the burning of Beaubassin. This was an immense undertaking, since the daily cycle of tides continuously interrupted the work. In his own account of the project, Le Loutre remarked that, at one time and another, he employed more "than 300 men working day and night."[93] Certainly he assembled a considerable workforce, a part of which was supplied, to the great annoyance of Lawrence, by Acadians from the Minas Basin area.[94] At the same time, the abbé once more preached vehemently against any contact between the Acadians and the British, fulminating against those who were known to have approached the authorities at Fort Lawrence about the possibilities of returning to their former lands.[95]

But the Chignecto isthmus was only one source of the increasing unrest throughout the region during the spring and early summer of 1754. The French government, while attempting to keep costs within bonds, insisted that particular attention be paid to the fortifications of Louisbourg.[96] In late March, Governor Shirley reported to the General Court that the French had advanced into the Kennebec region, and an expedition to dislodge them was planned for the early summer.[97] In the first week of June 1754, Lawrence wrote to the Board of Trade, reporting that the French had established a good road between Beauséjour and Baie Verte and were doing "all in their power to seduce the French Inhabitants to go over to them."[98] During the next weeks, Lawrence began to decide his policy towards the Acadians, a process that was made the more urgent because of the very tentative advice he received from the Board of Trade in their reply to the dispatch that he had sent them in the first week of December 1753.[99] Their lordships' missive, which had been written in the first week of April,[100] was of little help to the lieutenant governor as he considered how to counter the ways in which the French were strengthening their position in the Chignecto area and how to persuade the Acadians to demonstrate greater loyalty to the British.

In particular, while their lordships sympathized with the problem that Lawrence faced over the disputes among the Acadians about land which they had settled but to which they had been granted no formal title, their dispatch had no suggestions for its resolution. The acquisition of crown land by the Acadians was a question that every British administrator since 1730 had brought to their lordships' attention. No clear answer had ever been given. But, unless proof of ownership was established by means of legal documents demonstrating right of ownership, disputes over boundaries and other matters of property could not, in the nature of judicial matters, be settled. It is important to clarify that the question raised did not affect the tenure of land by those who could prove they held their lands by grants from the previous French rulers of the territory or from later British administrators. The Anglo-French tradition since medieval times had been that, unless there is specific reference to the ownership of lands acquired by conquest in the negotiated documents of the peace treaties, the implicit right of ownership remains with those who held legal possession under the previous regime.[101] The ultimate assertion of sovereign power, of course, always allows those governing to requisition property or, as in the case of the exile and deportation of many Scottish landowners after the rebellion of 1745, to declare land forfeit without compensation.

But the problem raised in 1753 by Lawrence was the regulation of land acquisition through settlement and usage. It had become of greater urgency as the Acadian settlements grew, and, after 1749, with the arrival of new colonists, it was crucially important for anyone engaged in the general settlement of the colony that an official survey of all of Nova Scotia be undertaken and that grants of land be registered. The difficulty arose with those Acadians who had occupied farmland under the British rule but had not secured any official title. The granting of crown land, whether by the British or the French monarch, required an unequivocal recognition of the crown's sovereignty. In this area, the governors and lieutenant governors had always worked for an unqualified oath of allegiance from the would-be freeholder. But formal registration of holdings in the region of Beaubassin and the Memramcook and Petiticodiac rivers had often been neglected and ownership through family had often been used to establish title rather than the outright formality of a new concession. The policy that Lawrence now wished to establish was in part the result of those Acadians wishing to return to lands on the British side of the Missaguash, around Fort Lawrence. He wanted to enforce the policy, which the last Council meetings under Governor Hopson had discussed in 1753, of requiring those who wished to return to take an unqualified oath of allegiance to the British crown. In considering the matter, the Lords of Trade wrote an opinion that deserves to be cited in full. It consisted of one long sentence, which read: "The more We consider this Point the more nice and difficult it appears to us; for, as on the one hand great Caution ought to be used to avoid giving any Alarm, and creating such a diffidence in their Minds as might induce them to quit the Province, and by their Numbers add Strength to the French settlements, so on the other hand We should be equally cautious of creating an improper and false Confidence in them, that by a Perseverance in refusing to take the Oath of Allegiance, they may gradually work out in their own ways a Right to their Lands and to the Benefit and Protection of the Laws which they are not entitled to but on that condition." Their lordships concluded this section of the dispatch by praising Lawrence for "refusing to admit the deserted French Inhabitants to return to their lands, Unless they take the Oath without any Reservation."[102]

In sum, their lordships dodged the issue and left to Lawrence the responsibility and the liberty, accorded most colonial governors at this time, of coping with the immediate problems of his colony as best he might. Such freedom was due in part to the slow pace of communication. The combination of the time it took for London authorities to attend to their overseas correspondence, coupled with time taken for letters to cross the Atlantic, approximately fifty days outward from London to Halifax and thirty days for the return journey from Halifax to London, meant that even the best advice from the Board of Trade or the secretaries of state would be of little help in a crisis. However, in this case, the continued refusal to establish firm guidelines for the enforcement of land-ownership regulations was doubly unfortunate. In the first place, it encouraged the Acadian belief that their right to the lands of the colony could not be disputed. At the same time, this dispatch gave Lawrence a particularly broad latitude to act as he saw fit.

Over the next six months, Lawrence began to establish his own policy towards the Acadians. His letters and dispatches during this time emphasize over and over again the security of the colony and the strength of the Acadian population, in comparison to that of the newly arrived settlers. His correspondence also reveals that, until January 1755, he was cautious about acting on his own initiative without clear instructions from London. Yet Lawrence did not hesitate to act on matters requiring immediate attention. During the last week of June 1754, he and the Council considered the petition of a number of Acadians to return to their former lands on the British side of the Missaguash, despite the continued preaching of Le Loutre against such a project. The group, some eighty in all, asked for the right to live again under British rule, providing they were assured that "they should remain neuter [sic] and be exempt from taking up Arms against any Person whatsoever ..."[103] This was refused. The dispatch of the Board of Trade, which Lawrence had received at the beginning of the month, provided him with all the guidance he needed to hew to a firm line and reinforce the policy laid down during the last Council meetings chaired by Governor Hopson. The general disposition of both Lawrence and his fellow councillors – on this occasion, Benjamin Green, William Steele, John Collier, William Cotterell, and Robert Monckton – had not been improved by the fact that, despite being forbidden to do so, "the French Inhabitants of Annapolis, Menis and Piziquid ... had presumed to go [to Beauséjour] to the number of three or four hundred." At this same meeting, the Council decided to issue a proclamation ordering those who had gone to Beauséjour to return forthwith to their homes and instructing the deputies to report their names.

A month later, at the beginning of August 1754, Lawrence wrote a long dispatch to the Board of Trade, very much a companion piece to the dispatch he had sent eight months earlier on the state of the colony and his views on how it should be governed. Its tone shows clearly that he was moving away from the position taken by Mascarene, Cornwallis, and Hopson, that the Acadians were, first and foremost, no matter how recalcitrant, British subjects. Further, while these governors had a certain admiration for what they saw as the Acadian character, Lawrence had little sympathy for those he referred to as "our French inhabitants."[104] Less than five years earlier, in the spring of 1750, Cornwallis had written a general address to the Acadians, pointing out to them that he and the Council were "well aware of your industry and your temperance."[105] "This province is your country," Cornwallis had continued, "you or your fathers have cultivated it; naturally you ought yourselves to enjoy the fruits of your labour." For Lawrence, however, the Acadians were the source of the "many inconveniences" under which the British had laboured, owing to their "obstinacy, treachery, partiality to their own Countrymen, and their ingratitude for the favor, indulgence and protection they have at all times so undeservedly received from His Majesty's Government." He was clearly convinced that their refusal to take an unqualified oath of allegiance was enough to deny the Acadians the status of British subject.

It is in the body of this dispatch that Lawrence first expressed, tentatively, the possibility of deportation. He opened the discussion by remarking that the Acadians "have always affected a neutrality, and it has been generally imagined here, that the mildness of an English Government would by degrees have fixed them in our Interest, no violent measures have ever been taken with them." He went on to observe that, in his view, "this lenity has not had the least good effect" and commented on the number who went to aid Le Loutre. Lawrence considered that the Acadians had always provided the French and Indians with "provisions, quarters and intelligence" and thought that there was no hope of their acting differently in the future. His next sentence has been often quoted. It reads: "As they possess the best and largest Tracts of Land in this Province, it cannot be settled with any effect while they remain in this situation, and tho' I would be very far from attempting such a step without your Lordships approbation, yet I cannot help being of the opinion that it would be much better, if they refuse the Oaths, that they were away."[106] What has been infrequently cited is the conclusion of the next sentence, which reads: "tho indeed I believe that a very large part of the inhabitants would submit to any terms rather than take up arms on either side; but that is only my conjecture and not singly to be depended upon in so critical a circumstance." Lawrence concluded his dispatch by turning to the problems of the Chignecto area. He proposed that a new fort be built on the banks of the Shubenacadie River, which would hinder Acadian trade with the French and the Mi'kmaq, impress the latter with British strength, and put a stop to the desertion of Lunenburg settlers to the Baie Verte area.

In general, analysis of this dispatch has been a matter of interpretation of particular sections taken in isolation from the rest.[107] With this technique, commentators have been able to present Lawrence as articulating a clear policy that he is fully confident he will be able to implement. The lieutenant governor's doubts and hesitation become obvious only when the dispatch is considered as a whole. Then, the juxtaposition of the idea of the deportation with the judgment of the general temper of the Acadians as a people attached above all to their lands reveals a mind as yet unclear as to how to proceed. Brebner considers this dispatch as very much that of "an aspiring military governor, who could see no good in the Acadians but who stated his case and deferred to the judgment of his superiors."[108] I think it is also a dispatch of someone trying to judge not only the immediate situation but what would be the solution that his superiors would consider the best for their long-term political ambitions. Unfortunately, we do not have much in the way of private diaries and letters written by Lawrence but we do know something of what he had experienced. His service in Europe and North America had given him a wide knowledge of eighteenth-century warfare. He had been wounded at Fontenoy and had been in London when the British government dealt with the aftermath of the Stuart rebellion, including the resulting deportation of many of the Highlanders to British colonies in North America.[109] Since 1747 he had been in the region and was thoroughly familiar with the settlements of Nova Scotia, from Annapolis Royal to the Chignecto area, Halifax to Lunenburg, the Minas Basin as well as Beaubassin. He had also visited Louisbourg. The basis for his actions, as shown by his official correspondence, was clearly his career as a military officer, which had made him, unquestioningly, a servant of the British crown. Throughout his life, he had a strong belief in the rightness of the way in which, as he understood it, the British government worked. He considered that British rule was a pattern of reasonable behaviour. For him, France was in an essential way a foreign country, its foreignness underlined by its Catholicism, a form of Christianity he distrusted. As with all European professional soldiers in the eighteenth century, his sense of what national allegiance meant was tempered by working with mercenaries, but he had no doubts of the legitimacy of the Hanoverian monarchy nor of the rightness of British foreign policy in general and British colonial development in North America in particular.

To the extent that one can tell, Lawrence had not previously been faced with as complex a situation as that which confronted him in the summer of 1754. It was not merely a question of military strategy, though that was difficult enough. Unlike his predecessors, who, in the last resort, had only Annapolis Royal as the focal point of the colony which it was imperative to defend, Lawrence had to protect that port as well as Halifax and Lunenburg. Further, the Acadian settlements of the Minas Basin, not to mention the Chignecto region, had become much more vulnerable to French attacks. As well, the population of the colony in 1754 presented him with an increasingly sharp challenge to his capacity for political action. He was faced with a mixed population, migrants from the slums of London, Germans, and New Englanders, along with Mi'kmaq and Acadians, few of whom could be counted on for significant aid in time of war. In the case of most of the recently arrived settlers, their loyalty to the British crown was either untried or unreliable, this being particularly worrisome in the case of Lunenburg. As far as the Acadians were concerned, their neutrality was, in Lawrence's judgment, unproven and they were by far the most numerous group within the colony. The Mi'kmaq, for their part, had shown themselves openly hostile to the British crown in the past. As the weeks went by, and news arrived, via Boston and New York, of what was happening elsewhere in North America, it is not surprising that Lawrence became more and more convinced both of the possibility of a direct attack upon Nova Scotia by the French and of the general vulnerability of his position.

This fear about the military state of the region, and in particular of the exposed position of Nova Scotia, was also a concern of Governor Shirley. In early April 1754, Shirley had persuaded the General Court to back an expedition to defend "His Majesty's Territories against the encroachments of the French and the Ravages and Incursions of the Indians" in the Kennebec region.[110] Shirley saw this action as the first step to making certain that French incursions into the region were brought to a halt. He outlined his plan in a letter to the secretary of state, Sir Thomas Robinson, on 8 May 1754. Once the Kennebec area had been made stable, a combined force of men was to be raised from Halifax and New England and would drive the French forces from the Saint John River and the Chignecto isthmus.[111] As spring gave way to summer, the news from the Ohio valley increased the apprehension of both Lawrence and Shirley about the possibility of a French attack on Nova Scotia. The report that Washington had made, in January 1754, to Governor Dinwiddie of Virginia, about the conditions in the Rivière-aux-Boeuf area, led that colony to attempt to establish control at the forks of the Ohio. The French reacted swiftly, establishing Fort Duquesne close to where the Virginians had hoped to build a fortification of their own. This provoked to a bitter little action in the area between Washington and a French force in late May, an action that the French regarded as treacherous, given that Great Britain and France were still formally at peace. The twenty-two-year-old Washington was the victor but the skirmish led, within a month, to a much more serious engagement, which he lost. This occurred at Great Meadows, where he met Louis Coulon de Villiers, aged forty-four, one of whose five brothers had been killed in the previous engagement.[112] Washington was soundly defeated in this encounter, losing almost a hundred men, 25 per cent of his force. The French, according to Stanley, had lost "two soldiers killed and one Indian."[113] Washington signed what would later prove to be a damaging document of capitulation on 4 July 1754, the wording of which was a confession that the death of Louis Coulon's brother had been murder.[114] War might not have been declared between the European monarchs, but their North American colonies were clearly engaged in organized combat and preparing for the outbreak of formal hostilities.

By the end of August, Lawrence and Shirley were in agreement that, since the Kennebec area was now reasonably secure, the French of the Chignecto isthmus and the Saint John River should be attended to. On the 20th of that month, Shirley wrote to Lord Halifax from Casco Bay on the success of the Kennebec expedition and mentioned that he had corresponded with Lawrence. He remarked that he was glad to find the latter "of sentiment with me, that the refusal of the revolted Inhabitants of Chignecto to comply with the terms, upon which they had permission given to come to their former possessions there, is happy for the country, and even thinks it would be fortunate, if a favorable opportunity should offer for ridding His Majesty's Government there of the French Inhabitants of the two districts of Minas and Annapolis River ..."[115] Lawrence himself wrote to Halifax three days later and presented a much longer, more carefully considered, plan of action in which there is no mention of the Minas area. The correspondence between Lawrence and Shirley, which Shirley's letter implies, does not seem to have survived, so one cannot tell whether the comment about Minas is an elaboration of Shirley's, a hangover from his ideas of 1745–46, when he proposed the wholesale deportation of the Acadians, or whether Lawrence was its originator. There is no hint of such an idea in Lawrence's letter of 23 August. This communication opens with the acknowledgment that the new settlements within the colony have been placed a great strain on his resources, since "our Troops are so much divided, and of consequence our military Strength so much impair'd that We are in no condition to assert His Majesty's just rights, in the manner I could wish, against those unwarrantable Encroachments the French have made on the North Side of the Bay of Fundy, where they are every day doing all in their power to inhance the difficulty of removing them, and from whence (particularly from Beau Sejour) they have made all their incursions upon us, and committed every kind of outrage." Having set the stage, Lawrence continued by proposing his solution. "As this is a growing Evil, and the greatest Obstacle that can be imagined to your Lordship's design of establishing this Province, I should esteem myself most happy in having the least hint from yr Ldship how far any attempt I should make to dispossess them would be well received at home: If such a Step should be approved of, I flatter myself I could with Mr. Shirley's assistance raise a Body of Men in New-England, which joined to the few troops we could muster on so good an occasion would I believe make a pretty successful Campaigne."

Lawrence then went on to discuss other problems of the defence of the colony, in particular those related to the safety of Halifax harbour. However, he returned once more to the matter of Chignecto at the end of the letter. He introduced this second reference by commenting on the general situation of British forces at the time, mentioning "the late Ill-Success of our Arms upon the Continent under Col Washington" and the failure of the recent Albany conference, which had been called together to see whether the British colonies might cooperate in their efforts against the French. The widely known position of the British, Lawrence wrote, would "do much to strengthen the French in their Encroachments to the Southward, that they will soon begin as heretofore to give us all the Trouble they are able." He continued: "While the Opportunity yet remains I would willingly endeavour to put it out of their power, and that effectually." It was, in his view, the complete "demolition and destruction of Beau Sejour" that must be undertaken and to achieve this "the French inhabitants on that side must either be removed to this or driven totally away by Fire and Sword." He concluded by warning that "if all the villages beyond Beau-Sejour are not destroyed, and some of the Dykes cut, the French (who will easily know that the Force we had collected was but occasional) would immediately return to take possession of their habitations, and rebuild their Forts." Lawrence asked for a response as quickly as possible, since such an expedition would take considerable preparation. "Not only as I must apply to Mr. Shirley, before I can begin but if it could be carried thro' before the Ships of War from France arrive at Louisbourg, we shall be in a better capacity to repell any attempt they may form to revenge or reinstate themselves."[116]

This dispatch is a clearly argued request, by the lieutenant governor of Nova Scotia to his superiors in London, for permission to undertake a limited action on the borders of his colony. No previous governor had proposed to initiate a military action in the Chignecto area, their attention having been concentrated either upon the Saint John River or upon Louisbourg. Lawrence clearly envisaged the colony very differently from his predecessors. His policy was the result of the wish to make Nova Scotia a secure and flourishing outpost of the British empire in North America, not merely to establish a strong presence on the periphery of an empire. He had two but, in his view, completely interdependent objectives: first, the preservation of the British possessions in North America; and second, the strengthening of Nova Scotia as a crucial and significant part of those possessions. The arrival of Protestant settlers with Cornwallis had made this vision possible. But Lawrence, when he was made lieutenant governor of the colony in 1753, after he had been some six years in the region, had come to the conclusion that the Acadians' refusal to take an unqualified oath of loyalty to the British crown made them a major stumbling block to fulfilling this ambition.[117] The eventual decision, taken by Lawrence and his advisers, to deport the majority of the inhabitants under his jurisdiction, without anything approaching express permission from those superiors so circumspectly consulted nine months earlier, arises directly from Lawrence's concept of what Nova Scotia ought to be and what he had the duty to ensure that it should be.

CHAPTER SIXTEEN

The Decision to Deport

One of the earliest historical accounts, as distinguished from the contemporary reports in newspapers, of the events of 1755 was published by Abbé Guillaume Raynal in 1766.[1] In his opinion, the Acadians had been deported because of the prevailing climate of the time, a period of "national jealousies, and of that greed of government which devours country and man."[2] But, Raynal concluded, the British had committed a great crime in removing an innocent pastoral people from their lands. Two years later, a work by a certain William Burck appeared in translation in Paris. He believed that, while the deportation was justifiable, in terms of the Franco-British conflict at the time, it involved actions that any "humaine and generous heart only takes with regret."[3] These differing opinions, one an explicit condemnation of a crime, the other a regretful verdict that what had taken place had been a cruel necessity, were only the first of many, increasingly bitter, disagreements over how the deportation of the Acadians should be judged.[4] By the middle of the twentieth century, more than two hundred articles, books, and pamphlets had been published on the subject and since then a great many more have seen the light of day.[5] As was the case with Raynal and Burck, a significant number of the authors have made their judgment of what happened in 1755 the pivotal question of their work, spending relatively little time on a close analysis of the way in which the decision was reached or the immediate situation in the region at the time when the actual decision was made. The emphasis has been placed less on what is usually the first step of historical inquiry – "How did this happen?" – than on a search to discover the guilty. This is hardly surprising, since, in the view of many, as Mason Wade wrote in 1942, the question of the deportation "was essentially a national and religious one, which accounts for the bitterness which its discussion evokes."[6]

In seeking to construct another and different narrative of the deportation, I have no intention of denigrating the importance of previous accounts, nor do I have any wish to deny that my account has its own bias. Living at the beginning of the twenty-first century, when communities

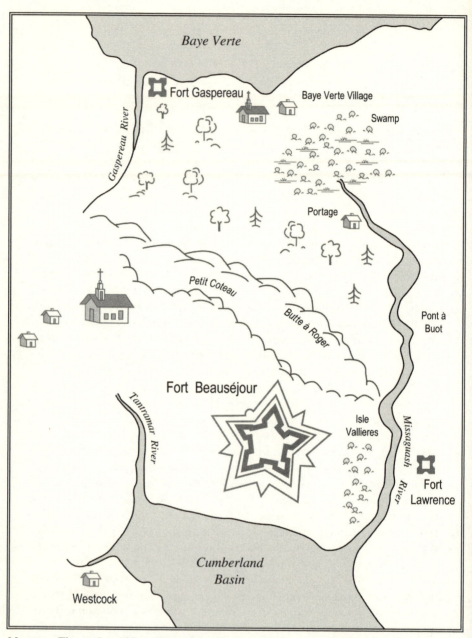

Map 10   The region of Beaséjour, 1755. Redrawn from a map by Louis de Courville (1755), reproduced in Stanley, *New France*.

ready to fight for beliefs about culture and identity are found around the world, I am unable to deny that emotional loyalties are a major factor in peoples' political lives. Nevertheless, an emphasis upon ideologies, whether of nascent nationalism or religious conviction, as the only important aspects of past human experience tends to give a higher importance to political and economic matters than to social and cultural concerns. My approach is different. The focus in what follows is upon the actual experiences of those who lived in Nova Scotia in 1755, whether British administrators, French officials, military officers, or the Acadians themselves. More than anything else, this analysis has sought to present the realities of everyday eighteenth-century life for people of the North Atlantic world. In many ways, the argument I have with a number of colleagues rests as much upon an interpretation of the norms of eighteenth-century life as it does upon questions of ideology. The crucial debate turns upon whether the deportation was the result of a planned policy flowing from ethnic hatred or something that occurred as a consequence of local military action at a time of intense rivalry between competing empires. My interpretation suggests that short-term decision making is central to what happened, the personal convictions of the individuals in question being the framework for their actions but of less immediate significance than the immediate problems that had to be solved.

Of major influence upon the course of events leading to the deportation was the way in which the relationship between Lawrence and the Acadians developed between the late summer of 1754 and the capture of Beauséjour on 16 June 1755. Throughout these months, whenever Lawrence considered the problem of Nova Scotia security, the reliability of the Acadians during an attack by the French was always a major concern for him. The information Lawrence received about the international situation, the knowledge he had of the balance of power between Massachusetts and Île Royale, Louisbourg and Boston, and his opinion of the reality of Acadian neutrality governed many of his reactions to Acadian matters. The Acadians' response to his internal administration of the colony, towards requests made by his forces for food and labour, as well as the intelligence he received about the strength of the forts at Beauséjour and Gaspereau were major considerations in his thinking. When the steps he took to bolster his command of the colony showed some success, Lawrence was encouraged to continue along the same lines. His organization of the forts, the cooperation of the Acadians with requests for wood for the local garrisons, tentative peace proposals from the Mi'kmaq, and some lessening of the trade between Acadian farmers and Louisbourg and Port Lajoie – all confirmed Lawrence's belief in the wisdom of his tactics. From August 1754 on, one can see Lawrence becoming more and more confident in his office. He began to take decisions without waiting for less than clear-cut directions to reach him from London. This penchant for independent action was strengthened by Governor Shirley's support of his plan to attack Beauséjour as well as by their common interpretation of the freedom of action accorded them by the imperial authorities.

In many ways, of course, Lawrence had no alternative but to act independently, decisively, and with dispatch on matters that were brought either directly to his attention or to his notice through meetings of the Council: as we have seen, it usually took five months, and often more, before Lawrence received an answer to his letters to London. But Nova Scotia was ruled by a governor and Council, which he appointed to advise him. Lawrence was charged with the day-to-day administration of a sparsely settled colony, with a minimum of troops and his few councillors. Together, they were responsible for the way in which the civil administration of the colony was carried out and for the security of its settlements. The questions confronting them involved not only the usual difficulties of colonial administrations with matters of local government but also the complex relationship of the British administration with the Mi'kmaq and the Acadians. As well, there was the constant problem of France's strength on the borders of the colony and its influence upon the Acadian population. While clashes with French land forces during the last months of 1754 were rare, two priests, Le Loutre at Beauséjour and Henri Daudin at Pisiquid, did everything in their power to stir up both the Mi'kmaq and the Acadians against the British.[7] Le Loutre, for example, saw himself as a spokesman for the Mi'kmaq and presented terms to Lawrence for a peace between them and the British. Their terms, according to Le Loutre, were generous: in return for a promise not to molest the British or to insult them on the highways, the British would relinquish all claims to the Chignecto isthmus, including Fort Lawrence, as well as all lands north and east of Cobequid as far as the entry to the Minas Basin.[8] At the Council meeting of 9 September, it was decided that the proposal was "too insolent and absurd" to warrant a direct reply to Le Loutre but that Captain Hussey, who was in command of the garrison of Fort Lawrence, should "acquaint the Indians that if they have any serious Thoughts of Peace, that they may, as they have been already informed, repair to Halifax, where they will be treated with on reasonable terms." Lawrence commented, in a letter he sent to Captain Hussey in early November, that he thought Le Loutre intended to inform the Mi'kmaq "that he has made such overtures of Peace for them to us, as we might well have granted, and by that means endeavour to make them believe they can never have peace with us."[9] Had Lawrence responded favourably to Le Loutre's proposal, it would have meant that the British accepted that the boundaries of their jurisdiction in Nova Scotia were confined to the southwestern section of the peninsula.

At the same time, a number of Acadians were also criticizing Le Loutre. Their complaints reached the ears of Bishop Pontbriand of Quebec, who told the abbé that while the French court thought it necessary to persuade the Acadians to leave their lands, this was not a matter about which the clergy should be concerned.[10] But Le Loutre was convinced that he had been given all the authority he needed from his spiritual superiors, especially Abbé de L'Isle Dieu, who, as has been mentioned, worried continuously about the spiritual life of the Acadians should they remain under British rule.[11] As far as the support of the civil authorities was concerned, since 1748 Le Loutre had steadily received supplies and encouragement both from Louisbourg and from France.[12] Le Loutre never admitted, either in his autobiography or in his private letters, that his actions were influenced by anything more than his desire to ensure that the Acadians and the Mi'kmaq remained under French government and so preserved their religious beliefs. To this end, he was prepared to act without any specific orders from either religious or secular French authority.[13] In doing so, he pursued every political avenue, including asserting his right to speak for the Mi'kmaq, haranguing the Acadians about their duty to support French interests, and using his influence to persuade other French priests to imitate his actions.

Among his supporters was Henri Daudin, who had arrived at Annapolis Royal in 1753 and was transferred to Pisiquid in 1754. He was a man in his early forties, much the same age as Le Loutre, with whom he had studied at the Séminaire du Saint-Ésprit in Paris. Le Loutre had recommended Daudin to Abbé de L'Isle-Dieu as a good candidate for work among the Acadians.[14] Daudin endeavoured to persuade the Acadians to seek their future with the French. He tried to persuade his parishioners to move to the valley of the Memramcook and, in the meantime, to support the work of Le Loutre at Beauséjour. Some young Acadian did men go and work on Le Loutre's proposed dyke, but there was no significant emigration from the Acadian settlements to French-held territory at this time and a few families even came back to their old villages, in spite of Le Loutre's fulminations. In October 1754 six families returned, twenty-eight people in all, who said they had been persuaded to leave the colony by the abbé. They took an unqualified oath of allegiance and it was hoped they would serve as a good example to their neighbours.[15] However, this small success for the British has to be considered against the considerable turmoil in Pisiquid at much the same time. On the surface, the trouble was minor, involving the Acadians' provision of wood for the fort. Though it was resolved within a month, the dispute was seen by Lawrence and his Council as an indication of the Acadians' unreliability and the extent to which they were, apparently, influenced by pro-French clerics.

On 22 September 1754 Captain Alexander Murray, who was in command of the garrison at Pisiquid, wrote to Lawrence, reporting difficulties with the settlers over the supplying of wood for the fort. He included a remonstrance, signed by eighty-six men, which stated that the deputies were of unanimous opinion that their oath did not bind them to supply the fort with wood but only to live in tranquillity on their lands.[16] In his covering letter, Murray wrote that he was convinced that Daudin had been "very busy," since, before his arrival, the "Inhabitants [had] brought in their wood fast ... and not one Stick since." Lawrence and the Council had Daudin and the deputies who had presented the remonstrance, Claude Brossart, Charles Le Blanc, Baptiste Galerne, and Joseph Hebert, brought to Halifax, under escort, to explain themselves. The Council spent the evening of 2 October questioning the inhabitants and the priest about their actions. The deputies denied any intent to disobey the commands of Captain Murray but said that not all of them had wood available for the garrison.[17] Daudin was asked in what capacity he thought he acted and replied that he served "only as a simple missionary to occupy himself in Spiritual affairs and not Temporal." Many of his answers were in flat contradiction to the written testimony of Captain Murray that the priest had informed him that there were three hundred armed Indians in the region and that "the Inhabitants to the number of three thousand had assembled together to consult mischief against the English and that tho' they had not all arms yet they had hatchetts."[18] Daudin insisted that he had never advised the Acadians on how they should respond to any orders given them by the British and that he was not the author of the remonstrance. At the Council meeting of 3 October, the deputies were "severely reprimanded and exhorted to return [to Pisiquid] and immediately bring in the Wood as had been ordered, which Duty if they neglected any longer to perform they would certainly suffer military Execution." Daudin was informed that he had behaved in "an unbecoming and insolent manner ..." and that his "behaviour amongst the Inhabitants has been such as has a Tendency to promote Seditious and undutiful behaviour towards his Majesty's Government ..."[19] He was therefore ordered to leave the colony. However, within three weeks, the Council received a petition from the settlers of Pisiquid and Grand Pré for his continuance as their priest. At their meeting on 21 October, the councillors agreed that he should remain since "the Inhabitants had returned to their Duty and Mr. Daudin had made the highest submissions, recanted his former behaviour and promised to comport himself dutifully to the Government ..."[20]

The influence of Le Loutre in the Chignecto isthmus on the French, the Acadians, and the Mi'kmaq was considerable, if not always the determining factor in their behaviour. The situation of the Acadians who lived on land controlled by France was mixed, whether they were settled in the valleys of the Petitcodiac, the Memramcook, and the Shepody, on the Chignecto isthmus from Beauséjour to Fort Gaspereau in the Baie Verte region, or on Île Sant-Jean. Around Beauséjour, there were farmlands that had been settled since the 1680s, while, similarly, the river valleys had farmlands that had been tilled since the early eighteenth century by members of families that were well established at Grand Pré and Beaubassin. A much greater number of holdings in these territories had been organized over the last twenty years[21] and a large percentage of the population, especially those living in the immediate area of Beauséjour, towards Gaspereau and on Île Saint-Jean, were refugees from Beaubassin. Their circumstances were difficult and much less favourable than those that they had enjoyed before 1750. This population, if one includes those settled on Île Saint-Jean, numbered about seven or eight hundred families, perhaps four thousand people in all. There was more than one political attitude to be found among them. Some, like Joseph Brossard, who had settled south of present-day Moncton in 1740, were actively and passionately pro-French.[22] Others, while not committed to the British, would have been happy to endure British rule if they could return to their old lands under the conditions which they had known there in the past. But, from what one can discern through the reports of Le Loutre and the French officials at Beauséjour and Louisbourg, the majority were waiting on events, committed fully to neither French nor British. This is hardly surprising, if one accepts that the most significant characteristic of the Acadians in the years after 1713 was their attachment to their homes and farms, not to whatever imperial power ruled over them.

The behaviour of the Acadians of the Pisiquid and Minas region at this time is more difficult to analyse. Their communities were undeniably under British control and there were British forces close to, and sometimes within, their settlements. Here, there was obviously an attempt made to exact some conformity to British policy, quite apart from the question of supplying the fuel needs of the garrison. Efforts were made to have the settlers comply with British restrictions on their export of agricultural products, in particular wheat, and this annoyed the farmers. Lawrence had issued a proclamation, on 17 September 1754, forbidding the export of corn.[23] This was followed, on 5 October, with a much more explicit "Act to regulate the shipping and Exportation of Grain," including "Wheat, Rye, Barley, Oats or any other kind of grain whatever," without a permit.[24] The lieutenant governor and Council were attempting to bring a halt to Acadian trade with Louisbourg, which had evidently been on the increase during the summer of 1754. It was an effort that had little hope of success.

The reality was that trade within the region, between Massachusetts and Maine on the one hand and Nova Scotia and Île Royale on the other, had been a norm of economic life in the area for more than a hundred years, despite denunciations of the practice by French and British officials. It was carried on because it was profitable for all those involved in it. Between 1750 and 1755, for example, there were, in the words of François Bigot, "always more than thirty ships" in the Louisbourg harbour in May.[25] But the total number of ships there from New England, in any given year, was much greater. In 1752 at least 156 ships from New England stopped at Louisbourg.[26] Their cargoes were made up of livestock, iron and copper goods, wood and wood products, furniture in general, foodstuffs, and a number of miscellaneous items.[27] Replying to a lament from Lawrence in the spring of 1754 about this trade, the Board of Trade informed him that it was "sensible of [its] pernicious consequence" but there was little that could be done to prevent it.[28] In fact, the board was not even sure that such trade was "contrary to the Law." Whether or not it was contrary to law, the real question was the lack of ability by any authority, imperial or colonial, to bring it to a halt. In particular, the strength of naval forces at the disposal of the colonial powers was inadequate to patrol the waters sufficiently to stop the majority of small craft flitting along the coast from one place to another with what, in the eyes of the local officials, was "contraband."

In many ways, the problems of Acadian trade was indicative of the broader problems that Lawrence and his Council faced in dealing with the population's general behaviour. The Acadians were spread throughout a considerable territory, a territory that was divided into zones ruled by two different and competing empires, both of which wanted to possess all of the land in question and considered the Acadians as no more than a people subject to their competing claims. The Acadians, however, considered themselves to have rights of settlement throughout the territory, no matter who governed a particular area. The majority of the population looked upon themselves as the rightful inhabitants of the lands they farmed, the woods they hunted, the seas they fished. While the Acadian population was small in 1754, numbering somewhere between fourteen and eighteen thousand people,[29] and widely dispersed, it was a population that had a considerable sense of community identity. Information, true or false, would be known from Annapolis Royal to the Chignecto isthmus, from Louisbourg to the Minas Basin, from Île Saint-Jean to Pisiquid, in a matter of weeks, if not days. Within all the Acadian villages that were in British-held territory, there were those who accepted that country's rule, such as the members of the Robichaud family in Annapolis Royal and the family of René Leblanc in the Minas Basin, and others who hoped and worked for the arrival of French government, such as members of the Theriault family in Pisiquid. By far the majority of the population, however, went about their lives, taking as little notice as possible of the officials, secular or religious, French or British, who attempted to regularize their conduct.

This did not mean that the Acadians were unaware of the tension between these two empires that fought both within and around their homes, or of the possible consequences of this for themselves. But it did mean that the leaders of the Acadian community tried, as much as possible, to remain on the edges of the struggle, concerned with the immediate problems of the region rather than with broader international matters. Beaubassin had been burnt five years previously, however, and while the attack did not have as the Acadians as its avowed target, they had been its victims. Now that the possibility of renewed fighting within Acadian lands was becoming clear, the Acadians were forced to consider how they should act. Should the population in British territory continue to remain neutral, to abide by their interpretation of the oath they had taken? Or should they decide upon a more vigorous policy of action? Their difficulty in agreeing on what should be done sprang partly from disagreement over how much they were bound by their oaths and, perhaps to a greater extent, from the fact that different circumstances faced their widespread yet connected families: what seemed an obvious choice for those who lived in the Annapolis region was less clear for those who lived at Pisiquid. At the same time, the choice for Lawrence and his Council was becoming much more plain.

Information about events in North America had arrived in London and Paris throughout the spring and summer of 1754. The reaction in London was both stronger and more immediate than that of France. The influence of Governor Dinwiddie of Virginia and Governor Shirley of Massachusetts was far greater upon the course of British politics than that of any French North American colonial official on French policies. As well, at this time, the French were more deeply concerned with European affairs than with matters across the Atlantic, whereas the British saw North American issues as of considerable moment. Between the summer of 1754 and the start of 1755, the French were bemused at the strength of British feeling about matters in North America. In mid-September 1754, Antoine-Louis Rouillé, Comte de Jouy, the French foreign minister, informed the British ambassador in Paris, William Kepple, the Earl of Albemarle, that he hoped "means wd soon be found, to put an end to these Jealousies and misunderstandings."[30] But the Duke of Newcastle, who had come to power in March 1754, had considerable sympathy with the colonists and had written in early June to Walpole that "our Rights and Possessions in North America must be maintain'd, and the French obliged to desist from their Hostile Attempts to dispossess us."[31] Newcastle had been forced to accept the support of Henry Fox and the Duke of Cumberland, both of whom he greatly disliked, in order to remain in power.[32] Both these men favoured a strong and belligerent stand against France in North America.[33] There is no doubt, however, that there was a general consensus among the political elite that British interests, whether in Europe or in North America, had to be defended. The debate between the different factions centred, of course, upon how, when, and where action should be taken.

Newcastle had chosen Sir Thomas Robinson as secretary of state and leader of the House of Commons.[34] On 5 July 1754 Robinson wrote to both William Shirley and Charles Lawrence. To the governor of Massachusetts, he wrote that the king approved of his actions on the Kennebec and hoped that he had "given immediate intelligence thereof, to Colonel Lawrence ... and will have concerted the properest measure with him for taking all possible advantage in Nova Scotia ... in case Mr Lawrence shall have force enough to attack the forts erected by the French in those parts, without exposing the English Settlements ..."[35] Robinson concluded this letter by saying that a copy had been sent to Lawrence and that it was His Majesty's wish that Shirley and Lawrence should act in concert. In his letter to the latter, Robinson wrote that Lawrence should cooperate with Shirley and act "with the greatest Prudence and zeal and that you will take such effectual measures as will frustrate the desires of the French and will procure an essential Benefit to your own Government."[36] It took four months for these letters to reach their destination, Shirley reporting that he received his in the first week of November.[37]

Lawrence received his in Halifax at roughly the same time but did not send a reply to London until 12 January 1755.[38] Much of the dispatch he then wrote was taken up with a defence of his preparations for action in the Chignecto region, without prior approval from London, and his relief at the support he now felt he had received from Robinson. Both Lawrence and Shirley considered that these letters gave them the liberty to mount a joint expedition against the French in the Saint John valley and in the Chignecto isthmus. For Lawrence, Massachusetts cooperation was crucial. Without Shirley's permission to raise volunteers from Massachusetts, without loans from Apthorp and Hancock, Boston merchants and bankers, Lawrence had neither the manpower nor the money to undertake any major military enterprise, let alone one that would require at least an additional two thousand men to serve in Nova Scotia. Shirley wrote to Robinson, on 11 November 1754, a lengthy dispatch in which he rehearsed in full his arguments for "driving the French of Canada out of Nova Scotia."[39] He was convinced that war was imminent and that "if an open Rupture should happen between the two Crowns before the French are dislodg'd, whoever considers the superior strength of their Fort on the Isthmus to those of the English, and the superior number of the inhabitants there who are in the French Interest to those whose attachment to the English Interest can be depended upon will not be at a loss to determine which nation would be most likely to stand their ground longest in the Province ..." Shirley believed that, should Nova Scotia be lost, "the Eastern parts of the Province of Massachusetts Bay, and the whole Province of New Hampshire ... together with the Rivers of St. John's, Pentagoet, and Kennebeck with the whole fishery to the Westward of Newfoundland" would soon be in French hands. It was this conviction that fuelled Shirley's support of Lawrence and ensured a sympathetic reception for the latter's request for assistance when it reached him in the first week of December.

Lawrence had sent his letter to Shirley with Lieutenant-Colonel Robert Monckton and Captain George Scott. Monckton was provided with "a letter of unlimited credit" for use with Apthorp and Hancock to obtain supplies and was to ask Shirley's aid in raising two thousand men "with the greatest privacy and despatch for the service of this Province who are early in the Spring to be employ'd under your command for the reduction of ... Beauséjour ... as well as to remove [the French] from any Encroachments they have made on his Majesty's dominions in the Province."[40] Monckton was also to purchase "12 Eighteen pound guns with Appurtenances and 100 rounds of Ammunition wch. will bee about 150 barrels of Powder, Tents, Small Arms, Ammunition Flints and other things necessary for the Troops, Harness for 50 horses, 200 Bill Hooks, 500 Pickaxes, 500 Iron

Shod Shovells, 50 Wheel barrows." Shirley took some time to make public his own support for the expedition and to ask for the help and approval of the General Court for the enterprise. When, in August, he had arrived back in Boston after his sojourn in London, he had found the colony as a whole less than enthusiastic about further adventures in Nova Scotia. A special committee of the General Court, chaired by William Pepperell, had met to discuss the French threat to Massachusetts in January 1754 and had been lukewarm about action in Nova Scotia, although its members remarked that they were "very sensible of the Necessity of his Majestys Colonys affrding [*sic*] each other mutual Assistance ..."[41] Bitterness over the return of Louisbourg still lingered. However, Shirley's speeches to the Court on 7 and 13 February produced the necessary agreement for the raising of a regiment for the purpose.[42]

Shirley's rhetoric on the opportunity for "ridding the Province of its dangerous Neighbours, with all the Mischiefs that threaten'd it from their remaining so near"[43] was not the sole argument in favour of Massachusetts endorsing the governor's proposal for raising two thousand volunteers. There was also the matter of the immediate financial benefits to Boston merchants, since it was they who would provide supplies and services for the men. There would also be further economic advantages to the Commonwealth, flowing from the terms under which the men would serve. They were promised "the King's Bounty Money, pay, uniform, Cloathing (the most that can be got here) and Arms, and have everything provided for them which is necessary for their comfortable Subsistence." The question of security and the possibility of financial gain proved useful arguments for John Winslow, who was given the rank of lieutenant-colonel and put in charge of recruiting for the new regiment.

Winslow had led the expedition that Shirley had sent to the Kennebec and had a considerable success in that endeavour.[44] Partly because of the reputation he had gained in the Kennebec, he was very successful at recruitment, raising just under two thousand troops for the expedition against Beauséjour.[45] His own personal appeal helped his efforts but he was aided also by the fear of French "Encroachments" and the possibility of a general war. General Edward Braddock had arrived in Virginia on 23 February. The two regiments of regulars sent for his command, the 44th and 48th Foot, arrived on 10 March. The purpose of his mission was generally known throughout the northern colonies within the month.[46] Braddock's instructions required him to put an end to French activity in the Ohio valley, dislodge them from various forts in the Niagara region, and then turn his attention to the problem of Beauséjour.[47] Winslow benefited from news of these events and also from the tide of war propaganda, based upon a bitter dislike of Catholics, preached in pulpits in the small towns of Massachusetts.[48] In spite of the fact that recruitment was also taking place for regiments to join Braddock, Winslow managed to present the attack upon Beauséjour as something of major importance to young men of the Commonwealth.[49]

Winslow was fifty-two in 1755, a member of one of the most prominent New England families, whose great-grandfather and grandfather had both been governors of the Plymouth Bay colony. However, the commander-in-chief of the expedition remained Lieutenant-Colonel Monckton, aged twenty-nine, a regular army officer who would end his career as a lieutenant-general, governor of Portsmouth, England, and an MP.[50] The two men were antipathetic to one another and the poor relationship between regular army and colonial militias, which had characterized the attack on Louisbourg in 1745, was started anew.[51] From the start, Winslow was convinced that the success of the expedition against Beauséjour depended on the troops he had raised. Monckton, after all, had no more than three hundred regulars under his direct command, some of whom were part of the garrison at Fort Lawrence, others taken from the garrison at Halifax.[52] Monckton remained in Boston until May, when he sailed aboard the schooner *Lawrence* for Annapolis Royal with some thirty-nine other ships, including three frigates. They anchored at Annapolis on 25 May.

During the months that Monckton had spent in Boston, overseeing the preparations for the expedition, Lawrence had been considering what would follow the capture of Beauséjour. The lieutenant governor had been aware that those Acadians who had lived in the area, some only since Beaubassin had been set on fire in 1750, would present political difficulties. Many of the Acadians had established farms on land which had previously been under British supervision but which had not yet been surveyed. As a result, the Nova Scotian administration considered their title to the land dubious at best. As far as Lawrence was concerned, the attitude of these Acadians could be expected to be the same as that of those who had asked to be readmitted to British-controlled territory: argumentative, disputatious, and motivated by a strong belief that they had political rights that the British must respect. But, as will be seen, Lawrence in January 1755 was still unclear as to what would be the appropriate measures to take once the fort was captured. When he had written to the Board of Trade at the beginning of August 1754, he had tentatively stated that, should these Acadians refuse the unmodified oath of allegiance, when the opportunity to take it was given to them, he was of the opinion that it would be "better if they were away."[53] The lieutenant governor had hedged this suggestion by remarking that he "would be very far from attempting such a step without your Lordships approbation." The Board of Trade did not compose a response to this letter until 29 October 1754.[54] Their dispatch arrived in Halifax at the beginning of January 1755.[55] It was not, in any way, a clear directive for decisive action. The major part of it was concerned with the Lunenburg settlers and the state of relations with the Mi'kmaq. Their lordships approved the idea of building a fort at Shubenacadie and then turned to the issue of the status of the Acadians as British subjects. They were as perplexed over this issue as they had been in the dispatch they had sent in March 1754. The best advice they could offer was that the matter should be referred to Chief Justice Jonathan Belcher, who had taken the oaths of office at the Council meeting of 21 October 1754.[56] Apart from a short dispatch dealing with the complaints of a surgeon, John Grant, about the way in which the Halifax hospital was run, dated 31 January 1755,[57] this was the last major communication from the Board of Trade to Lawrence until a dispatch sent on 7 May 1755. This last was not received until after the fall of Beauséjour, and, in any case, it contained no directions concerning the treatment to be accorded the Acadians, whether those living outside British territory or those within Nova Scotia.[58] In sum, in shaping his policy towards the Acadians, Lawrence was left to his own devices and to what guidance and recommendations members of the Council could offer.

Their lordships were aware, of course, of the parameters within which Lawrence would work. He was a successful regular army officer, whose career showed the extent to which he accepted the ideas of the politically and socially powerful of the time. Eighteenth-century society, French or British, Germanic or Hispanic, was hierarchical and brutal and paid considerable attention to hereditary rights.[59] Government measures taken to control dissidents differed from state to state but were, without exception, ruthless, without mercy. France chose to coerce rebellious subjects to more conformist behaviour within its frontiers or force them to leave; Britain transported them to its colonies. The most well-known example of the French policy of forced exile is that which occurred after the revocation of the Edict of Nantes in 1685, the repercussions of which lasted until 1789.[60] In Britain, transportation of the indigent, vagrants, and children without visible means of support had begun in the reign of James I. In 1617, for example, a hundred children were dispatched from London to Virginia, their passages paid for by collections from various parishes, where they were considered a burden.[61] Those transported were referred to as "the surcharge of necessitous people," whose circumstances in England seemed without hope. The majority of them were indentured on arrival, that is, bound as servants for a period of time, such time as would repay the cost of passage plus other charges contracted. The period it might take to discharge the obligations so contracted was usually between four and ten years. Even for those who freely entered into such an arrangement, bonded service was often a period of hard work for minimal return. For those transported as punishment, bonded service could be little better than slavery. The English Civil War provided the greatest impetus to the practice of removing difficult subjects from the care of the home government to the colonies. In 1648, when Cromwell's forces were unquestionably victorious, transportation for the defeated Stuart forces became commonplace.[62] From this time on, the English colonies in North America, as well as in the West Indies, received diverse groups of dissidents, Scottish covenanters, youngsters from Ireland, and Scottish military exiles. The return of the monarchy did not end the practice. In the aftermath of the

Monmouth rebellion, Judge George Jeffreys sentenced 890 rebels to life in the West Indies as bonded servants, although probably no more than 522 were actually embarked.[63] Similar treatment was accorded the defeated after the Jacobite risings of 1715 and 1745. Thus, by the middle of the eighteenth century, British authorities, civil and military, colonial and imperial, were accustomed to transporting a motley collection of subjects, under varying regulations, from one jurisdictional area of the realm to another.

Further, Lawrence would have been aware not only of the general use of transportation but of the deportation of some two thousand French and Acadian inhabitants of Île Royale to France in 1745 and of the forced French relocation of a minimum of fifteen hundred Acadians from the Beaubassin area to Île Saint-Jean after 1750. And so there was nothing original, in late 1754 and early 1755, in Lawrence considering deporting the Acadians in the Beauséjour region, and it is clear from his correspondence with Monckton that the lieutenant governor was, indeed, thinking seriously about such a possibility. In a letter to Monckton written on 30 January 1755, Lawrence told him that, once the fort had surrendered, he would not have the oaths of allegiance proposed to "the French Inhabitants" of the Chignecto area "as their taking them would tye our hands and disqualify us to extirpate them, should it be found (as I fancy it will) everafter necessary."[64] Lawrence, at this point, was in the process of making up his mind over the best way to secure Nova Scotia. He was hopeful of populating the Beaubassin area with English-speaking Protestants, concluding his letter to Monckton with the suggestion that, if any of the Massachusetts troops had the "least disposition" to settle in the lands that were already controlled by the British but had been deserted since the burning of Beaubassin, they should be told that they would receive "all the encouragement" he had the power to offer. He ended his dispatch by saying that "we must have an Eye to the security of this place; particularly after the Information we have received of the extraordinary Embarkation that went lately to Canada."

The mention of "an extraordinary Embarkation that went lately to Canada" needs some explanation, for the major reinforcement destined for Louisbourg and Quebec did not embark until 15 April 1755.[65] For Lawrence, however, the rumour was almost as important as reliable information would have been. Whether it reached him from Massachusetts or from elsewhere, it would have been readily accepted and stiffened his resolve to bring to an end, by all possible means, any further incursions into Nova Scotia from the Chignecto region. At the same time, his attitude towards the Acadians was reinforced by the appointment of the chief justice, Jonathan Belcher, as a Council member. It was Belcher who, on the day that Nova Scotia Council resolved to deport the Acadians, wrote the legal and political defence of the action.[66] Belcher had been born in 1710 to an established New England family, his mother's father having been lieutenant governor of New Hampshire. His other grandfather had been a successful Boston merchant and member of the Massachusetts Council. His own father was governor of Massachusetts and New Hampshire from 1730 to 1741 and governor of New Jersey from 1747 to 1757.[67] Jonathan Belcher's early education was at Harvard but he continued his studies in Great Britain, graduating from Cambridge University in 1733. He then went on to study law at the Middle Temple and was called to the English bar in 1734. He practised law in London with only moderate success until 1741, when he went to Dublin, where family connections helped him. It was there that he attracted the attention of Lord Hardwicke, at that time the chief justice of England, who organized his appointment as deputy secretary to the lord chancellor of Ireland in 1746. For the next eight years, Belcher was immersed in the study of Irish statute law. Therefore, until his appointment as the first chief justice of Nova Scotia, at the age of forty-four, Belcher had spent his working life outside North America but his childhood and early adulthood had been as a privileged member of the New England elite.

For the early months of 1755, the major collection of evidence about the influence of the new chief justice upon events in Nova Scotia is in the records of the Council meetings. The first two meetings in February, on the 12th and 13th of the month, were concerned with the possibility of a treaty with certain groups of the Mi'kmaq.[68] Of the twelve Council meetings that took place between the middle of February and the middle of June, only one, that of 29 April, mentioned anything that was directly linked to the Acadians and the proposed attack on Beauséjour. At that meeting, members of Council were informed that the plans that the lieutenant governor had "projected with Governor Shirley for raising sufficient troops to drive the French from their Encroachments on the north side of the Bay of Fundy ... were now ripe for Execution."[69] The other dozen or so meetings were chiefly concerned with matters relating to commerce, particularly the trade in spirits and foodstuffs. In fact, the Council minutes provide no indication that there was any major problem within the colony, save that of the continuing need to supply provisions for the settlers at Lunenberg.[70]

The absence of any major discussion about the Acadians during this period by the Council is no indication of the actual relationship that existed at the time between the Acadians within Nova Scotia and the British administration. The rancour of the previous autumn continued. News about the lives of relatives on the Chignecto isthmus and along the Memramcook, the Petitcodiac, and the Shepody, where Le Loutre was active, served to sharpen Acadian ambivalence. Le Loutre was engaged not only in overseeing the building the dyke on the Aulac River in the Beauséjour area but also in encouraging the construction of smaller dykes on the Memramcook and the Shepody.[71] His aim was to stabilize the Acadian settlements, within the territory controlled by the French, by strengthening the development of traditional Acadian farming practices. At the same time, he worked to persuade the Acadians to recognize his authority to confirm their rights to the lands they farmed. The Acadians were hesitant, especially those who had their lands granted to them before 1710. Many had no wish to accept greater regulation of their affairs from any source, whether from the military at Beauséjour or from Le Loutre personally.[72] As well, the abbé demanded that they swear loyalty to Louis XV, their "legitimate sovereign,"[73] a demand that the French government had made ever since 1751 with respect to the Acadians who came under their control.[74] J.C. Webster and Rumilly have both speculated that the demand for an oath to the French monarch greatly troubled many of those who had recently left lands controlled by Britain.[75] On the other hand, in a more recent interpretation, Stephen Patterson has argued that the one thousand Acadians of the "Memramcook-Petitcodiac-Shepody area" were "all of them claiming that this was the territory of the King of France."[76] But a considerable number of them had already sworn an oath to George II and many were well aware that the British claimed the territory now under French control. After all, just over five years earlier, deputies from the Shepody and Memramcook area had accepted an invitation to meet with Cornwallis. Now, they temporized and asked for reassurance from some higher French authority, either at Louisbourg or Quebec, but preferably from France, as to their proper course of action. But there was no immediate response. What the Acadians were witnessing, either directly or through information received, was the attempted French administrative organization of Acadian hamlets and villages, stretching from Shepody to Baie Verte, much of whose government, in the immediate future, looked as if it would be effectively determined by Abbé Le Loutre. All this activity seemed to presage French determination to remain an effective power in the region and perhaps the possibility of French reoccupation of Nova Scotia.

But the most important determinant of the attitude of many of the Acadians, in the spring of 1755, must have been the manner and policies of the French officials in the region. There were four administrators, the most senior being Augustin de Boschenry de Drucour, who had arrived to take charge at Louisbourg in 1754. That same year, Gabriel Rousseau de Villejouin had been appointed as major and commandant of Île Saint-Jean. Charles Deschamps de Boishébert et de Raffetot, who had played such an important role in the engagement at Grand Pré in 1747, was at the mouth of the Saint John River as commandant of Fort La Tour, and Louis Du Pont Duchambon de Vergor was the commandant of Beauséjour. Of the four men, Drucour was a naval officer and a good administrator but, until his arrival at Louisbourg, had no first-hand knowledge of the military and political situation of the region.[77] Villejouin had been born in Placentia in 1709 and was a career officer who had seen some service at Louisbourg. He was, however, a man with limited authority. Boishébert was very much, like the rest of his family, a professional military man, a Canadian in the service of France rather than part of the colonial administrative structure. Vergor was perhaps the most complex and the least competent of the four. According to many of his contemporaries, he owed his position solely to the patronage of Bigot, with whom he had served at Louisbourg in the 1740s.[78] Vergor was the son of Governor Duchambon, who had surrendered Louisbourg to an Anglo-American force in 1745, and an Acadian, Jeannne Mius d'Entremont de Pobomcoup. He had a moderately successful career when, at the age of forty-one, he was posted to Beauséjour, but it was a career marked by physical courage rather than any ability for military command. Whether or not he was without any education at all is debatable.[79] His reputation was that of man driven by greed, controlling the provision of liquor and firewood to the fort for a personal profit of 60,000 *livres* a year. Vergor was joined at Beauséjour by the appointment that same year, 1754, of Louis-Thomas Jacau de Fiedmont as the chief engineer for the fort, and Louis-Léonard Aumasson de Courville as notary for the Acadian settlements in the area. Jacau left an account, from a military perspective, of the fall of Beauséjour and Gaspereau which, as Webster points out, sought to place the blame everywhere except upon his own shortcomings as the man in charge of the defences of the fort for the two previous years.[80] The memoir of Aumasson de Courville is a much longer work and includes a wide variety of comments on Vergor and Le Loutre.[81] Together with the journal of Thomas Pichon (Tyrell), a British spy who had somehow attached himself as a commissary officer to Beauséjour, these works provide a vivid picture of the disorganization among the officers stationed there and the general state of disrepair of the fort in 1755.[82] Vergor himself was convinced until the day the British force arrived that there would be no major fighting in the region that year, so nothing had been done to prepare a defence against an attack.[83] There had been no concerted effort during the last weeks of winter and the first weeks of more clement weather to recruit Acadians to strengthen the fort or to assemble those who had been given militia responsibilities.

So, before the anchoring of the Boston fleet in Annapolis Bay, little had taken place that would have alerted the Acadians to the possibility of a major outbreak of warfare in their lands. Evidently, only the vaguest of rumours about the recruitment of volunteers in Massachusetts for an expedition against Beauséjour had reached the Acadian population. Certainly, the possibility of a major disruption of Acadian life throughout the Acadian villages of Nova Scotia would not have entered their minds. As Lawrence prepared to make Nova Scotia a completely secure outpost of the British empire in North America and to establish once and for all British control of the colony, the Acadian population, as a whole, still believed that British administrators of Nova Scotia continued to take Acadian reactions into account when making policy decisions. The existence of Halifax, of a Protestant population within the colony that was more than ten times what it had been a decade before, was not something that had made the Acadians consider any revision of their political stance. For the majority of the population, the need to alter their religious beliefs and linguistic heritage in order to remain on their lands would have been unimaginable. Even if the French never reclaimed Nova Scotia, the strong French presence in the region meant visible support for Acadian retention of their customs and traditions. French control of Île Royale and Île Saint-Jean did not appear to be weakening at this time, especially after the return of Louisbourg to France in 1748. Since then, the build-up of French forces in the Chignecto area had served to strengthen the conviction, among the British as well as among the Acadians, that France was prepared to defend its presence in the area and probably had plans to expand the territory under its control.

The rapid conquest of Beauséjour, followed by the fall of Fort Gaspereau, and the lack of any immediate French response fundamentally altered the military situation in the region. As a consequence, the political options for the British administration at Halifax were broadened and those of the Acadians narrowed. Vergor had received no warning of the presence of the strong force, gathered at Annapolis Royal as of 25 May, until eight days later, when, a few hours before the ships were sighted at Fort Beauséjour, he was told of their impending arrival. This is an interesting absence of information, since ships carrying two hundred British regulars had left Halifax to join Monckton's command during these days, something that would be easily observed by the settlers. While the journey from Annapolis Royal to Beauséjour by sea would have taken four or five days, news could have reached Vergor at least twenty-four hours before the British expedition. However, Jacau reported that Lawrence had taken every possible precaution to restrict the Acadians of the Minas Basin and Annapolis Royal to their villages, cutting all communication with the fort.[84] It appears that Vergor's judgment that "nothing unusual will take place in Acadia this year"[85] was based as much upon lack of intelligence about British plans as upon inadequate analysis of what information he did have. Indeed, the French do not seem to have had any organized network of informants among the Acadian settlers in British territory. Drucour at Louisbourg was quite as confident as Vergor that there would be no trouble on the border and had written to the minister, on the day that the Anglo-American fleet arrived off Beauséjour, that "all was quiet on the frontiers of Acadie."[86]

As soon as Vergor was told of the approaching fleet, he dispatched couriers to Louisbourg, the Saint John River, and Quebec asking for help. He also sent messages to the Acadian villages asking for men to come to the fort for its defence.[87] What he did not do was organize anything to oppose the landing of the Anglo-American force, which disembarked near the mouth of the Missaguash and, despite the marshy terrain, then marched to Fort Lawrence where it was quartered for the night.[88] To a certain extent, Vergor had no option but to resort to strictly defensive measures. He had no more than 160 regular soldiers, if that, in a fort that was in bad repair.[89] He had written a description of its state when he arrived there in the late summer of 1754, pointing out that everything was "poorly built, in bad condition, very damp and the rain comes in everywhere." He went on to note that, among other major disadvantages, "the wells are of no use. The water is thick and muddy and can never be made pure." Little had been changed in the intervening months, since most of the available labour in the area had been corralled by Le Loutre to build dykes.[90] In hindsight, there was never any doubt that the vastly superior Anglo-American force would prevail but it took not quite two weeks for this conclusion to be realized.

Monckton and Winslow spent 3 June organizing the landing of the tents and other equipment. On the 4th, field guns were moved to Pont à Buot, the best crossing place over the Missaguash for an advance on Beauséjour. The French, once it was clear that Fort Lawrence was to be built, had erected a redoubt on their side of the river at this point, but it was in bad condition by 1755.[91] Vergor organized a force, made up of a two junior officers, some twenty regular soldiers, and some two hundred Mi'kmaq and Acadians to hinder the building of a bridge over the Missaguash.[92] After exchanging fire for an hour, both sides retired, the Anglo-American force having suffered one sergeant killed and seven soldiers wounded.[93] But they had managed to construct a bridge over the steep banks of the tidal river. Before departing, the French set the redoubt on fire and burnt other adjacent buildings. They had lost one regular soldier and had two Acadians wounded in the action.[94] Winslow commented that, towards the end of the engagement, "the Indians had retreated beyond the range of the guns and most of the Acadians followed them, leaving only the officers and some soldiers at the retrenchment."

During the next few days, Monckton and Winslow began the placement of batteries within shelling range of Beauséjour and bringing up stores from the ships.[95] Vergor attempted to ready his command for a siege by ordering supplies to be brought into the fort and all buildings in the vicinity, including the church, destroyed.[96] He also made a great effort to recruit the local Acadians to come to his aid but few responded. One officer sent out on a recruiting mission returned with only two men, having been informed that "the rest had refused to come and had discarded their guns and ammunition, saying that they did not intend to run the risk of being hanged, as the English had announced that this would their fate if they took up arms."[97] Until 12 June, both sides attended to their particular tasks, paying little attention to one another: Monckton consolidated the placement of the batteries and Vergor tried to strengthen the defences of the fort.[98] On the 14th, Monckton was ready to attack. John Thomas, the surgeon's mate, wrote in his journal: "We dugg Trench All Night this day we threw Bumbs all Day with Eight and four Intch Morter."[99] The effect of this attack on the defenders' morale was predictable, as Jacau attested.[100] There was one death as a result of the bombardment. The next day, 14 June, John Thomas recorded the increased mortar fire and the delivery of "bombs of large calibre ... though with small results." Thomas wrote of the same action that "Major Goldthwait Commanded at the Trenches they Kept up a warm Fire all Day they Got our Large Mortar to Bair on ye Enemy's Foart and threw Several Shell of 13 Intch Diameter."[101] Two of the defenders were wounded and, though Jacau's courage might have remained high, others began to waver. But it was not Monckton's attack that brought, first, a request for a ceasefire and then, within hours of the truce being granted, Vergor's capitulation.

A reply had, at long last, reached Vergor from Drucour at Louisbourg, late on 14 June, that no assistance would be forthcoming from that great fortress. Vergor's courier had reached Drucour five days after he left Beauséjour, on 7 June, the governor writing to the minister that day that "Fort Beauséjour is threatened by the English."[102] Within a day, Drucour replied to Vergor, saying that the presence of English ships outside Louisbourg made it impossible to dispatch help.[103] Drucour went on to warn Vergor to keep this news from the Acadians but this proved impossible, and that same day, eighty immediately left the fort.[104] The next day, the 15th, the remaining Acadians chose a spokesman to inform Vergor that "as there was no hope of help, there was no possibility of further resistance to superior force, and they did not wish to remain and sacrifice themselves needlessly."[105] This opinion was met, at first, by the French officers with considerable anger and there was a discussion as to whether an "order should be issued prohibiting such statements being made by the Acadians under penalty of being shot or having their land and property confiscated."[106] However, calmer and wiser heads prevailed. It was clear to Vergor that the lack of reinforcements meant defeat and he sent an officer to Monckton asking for a forty-eight-hour truce. This led to terms of capitulation being signed by Vergor on 16 June. On the evening of the 18th, Colonel Winslow, at the head of a force of some five hundred men, received the surrender of Fort Gaspereau, which had been held by Benjamin Rouer de Villeray and a garrison of thirty regulars.[107]

There has been considerable criticism, both by contemporaries and later historians, about the conduct of Vergor and Villeray. They were, however, exonerated at the subsequent court martial held at Quebec in 1757. One wonders, given the strength of the attackers, what either man was supposed to do. Neither fort was in any condition to withstand a long siege and, indeed, as Villeray pointed out, Gaspereau was only a depot for stores in transit to Beauséjour, being no more than a palisade on four sides and blockhouses at the corners, which were partly rotted away.[108] While Vergor's position was a little better, Beauséjour was bound to be taken unless help arrived quickly, and the question that really faced the commandant was simple: At what price should it be defended? In their analysis of the conventions governing eighteenth-century siege warfare, a distinguished trio of military historians has written that "the attack was placed in the hands of engineers, who through the precise application of mathematics brought their trench network and batteries to such a position that the defending commander, caught in the toils of Euclid, could honorably yield up his fortress."[109]

The animus against Vergor is largely the result of the fact that the fall of Beauséjour was, at the time, a great shock to the French authorities, not only in North America but also in France. The president of the Ministry of the Marine wrote to Drucour on 5 September 1755, admitting that the present situation was "embarrassing" and that it was "vexatious that the English have captured the posts on the boundaries of Acadia."[110] But the fall of Beauséjour and Gaspereau was to prove to be much more than an irritating, minor counterbalance to the defeat of General Braddock at Fort Duquesne (Pittsburgh, Pa.), the news of which had reached the French court at the same time.[111] It would prove to be the end of any French, as opposed to Acadian, presence in what was still known, in European diplomatic circles, as "Acadia or Nova Scotia."

Militarily speaking, it was a stunning defeat, due, above all, to the lack of a French sense of the importance placed upon Nova Scotia by the British after 1748. France had difficulty appreciating the influence of Massachusetts on British government policy and, therefore, had little understanding of the extent to which the interests of that colony had a steering effect on British policy in the region. For France, the most important feature of the area was Louisbourg and its links to Quebec. Nova Scotia was "Acadia," whose population was made up of the Mi'kmaq, who were friendly to French interests, and a French-speaking Catholic people who were anxious to be returned to French rule in the next round of international treaties. The importance of the Mi'kmaq in the military affairs of the region has been a matter of considerable debate and it is clear that fear of Mi'kmaq attacks played a part in the development of British policies.[112] Certainly, the French considered them an important bulwark against the British. In short, France believed that no plans needed to be made for a major military expedition in this area after 1748, especially since the inland route between New France and Louisiana was of much more importance. Future events would unfold in good time and Nova Scotia would once more return to France. There was no suspicion that there would be an Anglo-American military attack on the French positions on the Chignecto isthmus and at the mouth of the Saint John River, even after the successful Massachusetts foray on the Kennebec. French military efforts in the region were concentrated upon Louisbourg and keeping open the land route, via the Saint John River and the Chignecto isthmus, from Quebec to Baie Verte. Acadian trade with Louisbourg was important, but less so than that of Boston. Since the British had never been able to put a stop to what Acadian trade did exist, it seemed unlikely that this would occur in the immediate future. The founding of Halifax, the establishment of a considerable immigrant population of close to five thousand in less than seven years, certainly worried the French administrators in the region but had no real impact on the development of French policy.

But these very same events, the establishment of Halifax and the founding of Lunenburg, had presaged a decision, on the part of London, to make Nova Scotia as much a British colony as the other British colonies in North America. From the moment he was appointed as lieutenant governor, Lawrence was eager to make this decision a reality. We have a great deal of information on how Lawrence saw his own policy. He wrote, at length, to Governor Shirley of Massachusetts, to other governors of British colonies in North America, and to the authorities in London. By the summer of 1754, Lawrence had decided that those Acadians who refused to take an unqualified oath of loyalty to the British crown were a major stumbling block to fulfilling his plans.[113] At the same time, he saw that the French control of the Chignecto isthmus was both a constant encouragement to those Acadians who were dissatisfied with the British government and a potential military threat to British control of Nova Scotia. While the attack on Beauséjour was taking place, his view of the unreliability of Acadian neutrality was strengthened. As has been previously mentioned, Lawrence had taken steps to prevent any major aid being sent to Beauséjour by the Acadians under his jurisdiction. He also had made an attempt to disarm the Acadians of the Minas Basin and Captain Murray had issued orders to this effect from Fort Edward in the first week of June.[114] As well, a number of Acadian canoes were confiscated. The extent to which the Acadians complied has been a matter of debate among historians but the evidence shows that the majority of them did surrender at least some of their guns. Judge Isaac Deschamps, who was in Pisiquid at the time, stated that just under three thousand guns had been brought in.[115] The strongest evidence for their compliance, however, is the petition of the Acadians for the return of their guns, which was presented to Captain Murray on 10 June and forwarded to Lawrence within the week. It is hardly likely that the Acadians would have taken time and effort to ask for their guns back had they not given up sufficient to make the request worthwhile.

This petition was sent and received *before* the outcome of the siege of Beauséjour was known. It had been written with all the asperity that Acadian deputies had been wont to use in the past when arguing for what they believed their due before their British administrators.[116] It opened by going to the heart of the matter, stating that the "Inhabitants of Minas, Pisiquid, and the river Canard" wished to testify to their "sense of the care which the government exercises towards us."[117] However, the petitioners continued, "it appears that Your Excellency doubts the sincerity with which we have promised to be faithful to his Britannic Majesty."[118] The petitioners then went on to state that, not only had they not violated the oath, they had "maintained it in its entirety, in spite of the solicitations and dreadful threats of another power."[119] At this point, the tone of the petitioners changed, for, while they averred that they intended to prove "their unshaken fidelity to his Majesty," they finished the sentence with the words, "provided that His Majesty shall allow us the same liberty that he has granted us."[120] The petitioners then listed their complaints. First and foremost, the confiscation of their canoes imposed great hardship on them, especially since they had never transported provisions to Beauséjour or the Saint John River nor traded in cattle. The loss of their canoes, it was emphasized, was particularly onerous for poor families who supported themselves by fishing. Secondly, the confiscation of their guns was equally burdensome, particularly because they "regarded their guns as personal property."[121] Guns were necessary to defend their animals against wild beasts and for protection against "the savages." After all, they argued, "it is not the gun which an inhabitant possesses, that will induce him to revolt, not then privation of the same gun that will make him more faithful; but his conscience alone which must induce him to maintain his oath."[122] Finally, the twenty-five men who signed this petition remarked that they "were grieved, Sir, at seeing ourselves declared guilty without being made aware [that their actions were against the law]." This, they said, was the case of Pierre Melanson, who was arrested and his canoe confiscated before he was informed by any government order that his actions were illegal.[123]

Captain Murray reported to Colonel Lawrence that, while the Acadians had been generally cooperative for some time before the delivery of this memorial, they had treated him with "great Indecency and Insolence" when they brought it to him.[124] Murray believed that the change in attitude came about because they had intelligence of a French fleet being in the area. On 24 June the Acadians arrived with another communication to the captain, this one much shorter and signed by forty-four of the settlers "in the name of them all."[125] Obviously, the news of Beauséjour's capitulation on 16 June had reached the Minas Basin for in this communication "the Inhabitants of Mines, Pisiquid and the river Canard" begged Lawrence to understand that "if there shall be found any error or want of respect towards the government" in their recent memorial this was "intirely contrary to their intention."[126]

It is unlikely that this memorial would have reached Lawrence until just before the Council meeting of 3 July. Certainly, he could not have received it before 25 June, on which day he sent a dispatch to Monckton about the treatment to be accorded to the Acadian settlers in the Chignecto area. In this communication, Lawrence showed his continued concern for the security of the colony, his exasperation with the settlers in the Chignecto isthmus, and the policy he wished to pursue towards them as well as the uncertainty he had about implementing that policy. He was convinced that "unless we remain in possession undoubtedly the French will return and re-establish and we can never expect a lasting peace with the Indians, without first totally extirpating the French who incite them to make war ..." He continued: "By the French, I mean both Acadiens and Canadiens for it is a question with me, whether the former in those parts are not more our inveterate Enemies than the latter." In a later paragraph in this letter, it becomes clear that Lawrence was still mulling over what arrangements should now be made to govern the Chignecto area. He wrote that he was "as yet far from being determined about the fate of your Rebellious Inhabitants; their pretending to have been forced to take up Arms is an insult upon Common sense." There is no doubt that Lawrence had a great wish to solve the Acadian problem, once and for all, but he hesitated over the imposition of truly Draconian measures. As well, he obviously considered that an unqualified oath of allegiance was something which would have to be taken into account. These views are the foundation for the passage in the letter in which he congratulated Monckton on avoiding anything in the articles of capitulation that might "entitle [the inhabitants] to the future enjoyment of their Lands and Habitations." "I am too well satisfied," Lawrence wrote, "that should they [the Acadians of Chignecto] be suffered to remain they will prove forever a sore Thorn in our Side; with their help the French may be able to do much against us; without them I think nothing of much importance." In concluding this section of this letter, the lieutenant governor stated: "Suffer them by no means to take the Oaths of Allegiance you may remember that I forbid that in my letter of the 29 of January least they should claim under that title ..."[127] Thus, on 3 July 1755, when Lawrence met with fifteen Acadian leaders from the Minas area who had been summoned to Halifax to explain their reasons for the petition of 10 June, the lieutenant governor was a man still unsure of the military security of his colony, wanting unequivocal proof that the Acadians had accepted the reality of British government of Nova Scotia and of their role as British subjects. He was also aware that, however inconvenient it might be, the Acadians had some civil rights under British law.

Nevertheless, Lawrence had written to the Board of Trade, four days before this Council meeting, about what he intended to do with the Acadians settled in the isthmus. His dispatch first reported the surrender of Beauséjour and Gaspereau and then went on to state that "the deserting French" were surrendering their arms, after which they were "to be driven out of the country," although they might very well be put to repairing Fort Beauséjour, now renamed Fort Cumberland, before they were sent into exile.[128] While there is no evidence that, at this point, Lawrence contemplated the wholesale deportation of the Acadian population, the possibility of the dispersal of a significant number of Acadians was definitely in his mind.

The attitude of the Acadians at the Council meeting of 3 July was in keeping with their past behaviour over close to a century. It did nothing to make Lawrence reconsider his position. It was the same attitude that had caused Perrot to call them "Republicans" in 1686 and suggest that they had been infected with the political beliefs of the people of Massachusetts, and that had caused more than one British administrator to name them "Rebellious." Whether French or English, those sent to administer "Acadia or Nova Scotia" in the name of a European empire had maintained that the orders that they gave should be accepted without argument. The Acadians had consistently taken the position that such orders were open to debate. During the decades when Port Royal/Annapolis Royal was the administrative centre of the colony, when there were marriages between the elite of the Acadian settlements and the tiny enclave of civil and military officials serving there, social channels of communication facilitated relationships between government and governed. With the founding of Halifax, these relationships ceased to develop. There was little appreciation by Cornwallis and his successors of the complex nature of Acadian political society. In fact, as the minutes of the Council meetings throughout the month of July 1755 show, Lawrence and his advisers considered the Acadians not only politically unreliable but also socially impertinent, lacking in proper deference to their betters.

It is not surprising, then, that the atmosphere at the Council meetings in the first week of July was one of mutual incomprehension.[129] Colonel Lawrence chaired this and all other Council meetings during July. There were four other Council members present on the meetings of the 3rd and 4th of the month: in the order given in the minutes, they were Benjamin Green, John Collier, William Cotterell, and Jonathan Belcher. All were recent arrivals in the colony and no one, including Lawrence, had yet been in Nova Scotia for a decade. Benjamin Green, as noted earlier, was Massachusetts-born, had served in Louisbourg after 1745, and had arrived in Halifax in 1749 at the same time as Lawrence, as did John Collier. The latter was a retired army office and had been appointed as a justice of the peace for the new settlement soon after he arrived. Little is known about William Cotterell but apparently he was also among those who came out with Lawrence. Jonathan Belcher, of course, was New England-born and raised but had arrived in Halifax only in 1754. None of them had any personal acquaintanceship with the Acadians, knowing them only as a French-speaking, Catholic people who claimed to be different from the French but whose behaviour in the face of French intrusions on the borders of the colony was, at best, unreliable.

It was clear from the outset that the councillors found the Acadians' rhetoric deeply offensive. Before the Acadians were called into the meeting, Council members had come to the unanimous conclusion that the memorial was "highly arrogant and insidious, an insult upon His Majesty's Authority and Government, and deserved the highest Resentment ..."[130] Once the Acadians were present, it became quickly apparent that the two parties were at complete odds. The Acadians had composed their petition in the belief that Lawrence and the Council regarded them as people to be accorded consideration. The inhabitants had tried to explain, in the second paragraph of their communication, their difficulties. "Permit us, if you please, Sir, to make known the annoying circumstances in which we are placed, to the prejudice of the tranquillity we ought to enjoy," words that showed that, in their own eyes, they had every right to complain to those governing them.[131] They went on to ask the Council to take their past conduct into consideration as proof of their loyalty to the British. To this, the councillors answered that "their past Conduct was considered, and that the Government were sorry to have occasion to say that their Conduct had been undutifull and very ungrateful for the Lenity shown to them." From that point on, the minutes show that the councillors were united in demonstrating to the Acadians that the latter had shown a "constant disposition to Assist His Majesty's Enemies, and to distress his subjects."

The issue of the guns was dismissed on two grounds, first, that as Roman Catholics they had no right to carry arms, and second, that there no real threat from wild animals, either to themselves or to their flocks and herds.[132] Towards the end of the meeting, the essence of the administration's position became clear: the Acadians were told that their loyalty and obedience could best be properly demonstrated by "their immediately taking the Oath of Allegiance in the Common form before the Council." Until this point, and including the request for the oath, the members of Council, while more abrasive than their predecessors, had acted much as former administrations had done. But when the Acadians responded, as they had done in the past, by saying that "they had not come prepared to resolve the Council on that Head," they were then informed that for "these Six Years past, the same thing had often been proposed" and that they must have "fully considered and determined this point with regard to themselves before now." The Acadians next asked to return and "consult the Body of the People ... as they were desirous of either refusing or accepting the Oath in a Body." The councillors rejected this reply as "extraordinary" and gave them an hour to consult among themselves. On their return, the Acadians were of the same mind but offered to take the oath "as they had done before." The councillors answered that "His Majesty had disapproved of the manner of their taking the Oath before" and that any such compromise was now unacceptable. At this point the meeting was adjoined until the next day at ten o'clock.

The next morning, the Acadians repeated their decision that they could not take the oath without consulting their communities. At this point, Lawrence and the Council, composed of the same people as the day before, informed the Acadians that they had now provided enough evidence to make the Council consider them "no longer as Subjects of His Britannick Majesty, but as Subjects of the King of France, and as such they must hereafter be Treated; and they were Ordered to Withdraw."[133] The minutes record that the Council members then decided among them-

selves that Captain Murray should order the "French Inhabitants forthwith
to Choose and send to Halifax new Deputies with the General Resolution
of the said Inhabitants in regard to taking the Oath, and that none of them
should for the future be admitted to Take it after having once refused to
do but that effectual Measures ought to be taken to remove all such Recu-
sants out of the Province." The fifteen Acadians were now required to
return to the meeting and were told of this decision. They then offered to
take the oath but were informed that "they would not be indulged with
such Permission, And they were thereupon ordered into Confinement."

It is striking that the Council decided, at this point, that refusal to take
the oath of allegiance as offered would deprive the Acadians of their status
as British subjects. In fact, it was a judgment that even Belcher and
Lawrence would not repeat. It went against the tradition of international
law, which had been accepted, particularly in the case of the Acadians after
Utrecht, by both France and Great Britain, that peoples whose territories
changed governments through treaties became unequivocally subjects of
their new rulers.[134] In also went against all previous arguments by British
administrators, including Cornwallis, on the status of Acadians. Finally, it
contradicted English legal tradition since before the Tudors, as it had
evolved with the linking of Wales and Ireland to England. By the time of
Henry VIII, those born on territory ruled at the moment of their birth by
England were considered as natural-born subjects.[135] The majority of the
Acadian population within peninsular Nova Scotia had by this time, forty-
two years after Utrecht, been born on British territory. Belcher's influence
on the matter is difficult to assess. His experience in Ireland ought to have
prevented him making a judgment that the Acadians' status as subjects
depended on an oath of allegiance. By the end of month, when he wrote
a defence of the decision to deport the Acadians en masse, he based his
opinions upon the question of their loyalty as subjects, rather than upon
their position as aliens. This is the argument that would be used in the
future to defend the deportation.

The legal argument over the link between the oath of allegiance and
the rights of the Acadians as British subjects had little import for the
immediate circumstances of the Acadians in July 1754. At that time, their
fate depended upon the designs of Lawrence and the Council, designs
that become clear when the complete records of the Council meetings for
4, 14, and 15 July are read. The brief minutes of the meeting of 4 July
alone leave some question in one's mind as to whether the decision to
remove out of the province those who refused the oath referred to just
certain individuals from the Minas area or to the Acadians as a whole.
However, appended to the minutes of that same meeting is a laudatory
address to Lawrence from the Council members and his reply. In the
address the Council members praise the "easily and Signal success of
those wisely concerted measures for chastening the Insolence of the
French Arms obtruded into this Province ... in which you have had the

first and principal concern." The address concludes with the assurance that the Council members will "embrace every Opportunity of Contributing our Assistance in all further measures your wisdom and zeal shall suggest for perfecting the Tranquillity of the Province ..." There was full support for the position that Lawrence wished to take towards Acadians who would not show themselves unequivocally dutiful British subjects. In his reply, the lieutenant governor thanked his colleagues for their "wise and timely counsels" and finished by saying that, with their assistance, he was ready "to effect every measure that has hitherto been planned to render this colony flourishing and Happy."[136] While this address and reply could, perhaps, be interpreted to mean that the deportation of only a few Acadians was envisaged at this time, the next Council meetings indicate clearly that something more fundamental was being considered. In preparation for this, the Acadian communities had been sent orders, on 12 July, that they elect deputies to report to Halifax as soon as possible, prepared to swear the unqualified oath of allegiance.[137]

Three days earlier, on 9 July, Admiral Edward Boscawen dropped anchor in Halifax harbour, and his second-in command, Rear-Admiral Savage Mostyn, arrived two days later. On 14 July, Lawrence called another Council meeting; it was attended by the same people who had attended the meetings of 4 and 5 July.[138] Lawrence informed the Council that he had received instructions, which had been sent from the secretary of state to all governors on 15 April, requesting them to cooperate with Admiral Boscawen and provide him with all obtainable intelligence.[139] Lawrence then said that both admirals would be invited to attend a Council meeting the next morning "to Consider what Steps it may be proper to Take for the Security of the Province against any Attempt that may be made to Annoy us from Canada or Louisbourg ..." In writing the day before, 13 July, to Monckton, Lawrence had remarked that "on the Subject of the French Inhabitants; they shall go as soon as you have made the use of them you proposed [to repair the fort at Beausejour] I am fully determined."[140] Now, at the meeting that took place on the 15 July, once more attended by those members who had been present at the meetings earlier in the month but with the addition of the two admirals, Lawrence laid out "the proceedings of the Council in regard to the French Inhabitants, and desired their opinion and advice thereon."[141] The admirals agreed that "it was now Time to oblige the said Inhabitants to Take the Oath of Allegiance to His Majesty, or to quit the Country." At this meeting, it was also decided that it was "absolutely necessary for the Good of His Majesty's Service and the Security of this His Province, to retain in pay the Two Thousand New England Troops ..."

The support of the admirals for Lawrence was precisely that: support. Obviously, they had not arrived in Nova Scotia with instructions to take over the administration of the colony, nor did they have either the requisite knowledge or the interest to do so. What they did provide was an agreement by senior British naval personnel that the policy being pursued by the administration of Nova Scotia seemed sensible, considering the overall military situation. Boscawen's presence at Halifax until October 1755, and the presence of the fleet in the region, obviously encouraged Lawrence.[142] But Lawrence remained the person in charge of the colony and ultimately the one responsible for its security. Fighting in the region was still continuing and a report from John Rous, on the Saint John River, was discussed at the 15 July meeting. Rous had been successful in capturing the French fort at the mouth of the Saint John, Fort La Tour, and now asked for instructions as to what he should do next "in order to prevent the French availing themselves any further of their late Possession thereof."[143]

Three days after this meeting, Lawrence wrote to the Board of Trade, presenting his view of the situation that confronted him. Neither in this dispatch nor in any other of his letters to London did Lawrence suggest that anyone else was responsible for the evolution of his policy towards the Acadians. Of course, he sought, and gained, the approval of the Council at each stage of its development; it was not a policy that the lieutenant governor had fashioned against the general beliefs and attitudes of his advisers. However, essentially, it was his policy and the administrations of Cornwallis and Hopson had shown that it would have been possible to pursue another course. One of its most important antecedents was Shirley's proposal after the capture of Louisbourg in 1745, but no dispatch from London, whether from the Board of Trade or from any of the secretaries of state, suggested anything similar. Ever since 1713 the policy of the British government was one of determined refusal to admit that there was any great necessity to resolve the issue, one way or another, of the oath of allegiance. Further, Britain had consistently argued against sending the Acadians out of the colony and these arguments were repeated again in a letter from the secretary of state, Robinson, to Lawrence on 13 August 1755.[144] In it Robinson wrote that "it cannot, therefore, be too much recommended to you, to use the greatest Caution and Prudence in your Conduct, towards these neutrals, and to assure such of Them, as may be trusted, especially upon their taking the Oaths to His Majesty and His Government, That they may remain in quiet Possession of their Settlements under proper Regulation ..." This dispatch was in reply to one sent by Lawrence on 28 June 1755, in which he had broached the possibility of deporting Acadians, primarily from the Beauséjour region. Unfortunately, Robinson's dispatch arrived in Halifax only in late October 1755. As has already been mentioned, Lawrence's dispatch of August 1754, in which he pleaded for guidance on the issue, had received no other answer than that the problem he raised was, indeed, interesting and he should seek the advice of Belcher, the newly appointed chief justice of the colony.

Now, on 18 July, Lawrence reported his actions to his superiors.[145] It is a highly intelligent dispatch and guilty less of direct lying than of suppressing evidence and suggesting misleading implications. In relating what had happened at the Council meetings of 4 and 5 July, he omitted to mention that he had not, in fact, informed the Acadians clearly, before the final request to take an unqualified oath of allegiance, that their refusal would see them imprisoned and deported to France at the first opportunity. Moreover, he concluded the dispatch by saying that he was "determined to bring the Inhabitants to compliance, or rid the province of such perfidious subjects." There is no evidence whatsoever to suggest that Lawrence was then determined to exile not only the fifteen men from the Minas Basin but also the Acadians who had settled in the Chignecto area, let alone all the Acadians settled elsewhere. Indeed, the information in his dispatch concerning the incarceration of the deputies on George's Island, until they could be sent to France, increases the impression that Lawrence was considering only a small group of the population for exile. It is possible, of course, that Lawrence was convinced that the Acadian population, especially those of the Annapolis region, would not prove obdurate.[146] The dispatch of 18 July, however, quite plainly ruled out any possibility of negotiation with those who did prove recalcitrant. Any softening of this position became less than likely when rumours of Braddock's defeat reached Halifax on 23 July.[147]

In the meantime, of course, from the moment the men from Minas had been detained at Halifax, the Acadian communities had been forced to consider their position on the oath. They responded to the demand for their presence at Halifax, thirty men from Annapolis Royal arriving there on 25 July and seventy from the Minas settlements on 28 July. The written response brought by the Annapolis group emphasized their past conduct, asserting that "several of us have risked our lives to give information to the government concerning the enemy; and have also, when necessary, laboured with all our heart on the repairs of Fort Annapolis."[148] The memorial stated that the deputies had been "charged strictly to contract no new oath."[149] It concluded: "We are resolved to adhere to that which we have taken ... the enemies of His Majesty have urged us to take up arms against the government but we have taken care not to do so."[150] It was signed by 270 of the inhabitants.[151] Polite, unafraid, sure of the righteousness of their position, of the rectitude of their past conduct, the Annapolis deputies stated their policy: they would abide by the oath they had sworn in the past, but they would take no new one. Their answer was discussed at the Council meeting of 25 July. Once more chaired by Lawrence, this meeting was attended not only by Green, Collier, Cotterell, and Belcher but also by John Rous. The two admirals, Boscawen and Mostyn, were also present. On this occasion, the Acadians were told clearly that "if they once refused the Oath, they would never after be permitted to Take it, but would infallibly lose their Possessions." They were then dismissed but required to attend another Council meeting on Monday, 28 July.

The same men were present at this meeting as had been in attendance three days earlier. Belcher presented to this meeting a memorial bringing together his ideas as to why the Acadians should be expelled. It was not sent to London until the spring of 1756.[152] It was a mean-minded document, full of historical inaccuracies and of specious arguments. In it the Acadians were accused of outright and continuous support of the French since 1713, and it was implied that all British administrators since 1713 had acted contrary to "the spirit and letter of His Majesty's Instructions." Belcher went on to assert that, to allow the Acadians to take the oath once they had refused to do so, would defeat "the Intention of the Expedition to *Beau Sejour*." He went on to say that the Acadian presence "may retard the Progress of Settlement ... since the French at Lunenburgh and the Lunenburghers themselves ... are more disposed to the French than to the English." In any case, Belcher wrote, even if the Acadians did take the oath, "it is well known, that they will not be influenced" by it "after a [papal] Dispensation."[153] He concluded by remarking that the presence of Massachusetts forces in the colony had provided an opportunity to remove the Acadians which, "once the armament is withdrawn," would be lost. At that point, the Acadians would "undoubtedly resume their Perfidy and Treacheries and with more arts and rancour than before." Belcher therefore advised that "all the French inhabitants may be removed from the Province" from "the highest necessity which is *lex temporis*, to the interests of His Majesty in the Province."

And so, when the Acadians were called before the Council on 28 July, their fate had already been decided. Those from the Fort Edward and Pisiquid area presented their views first. Their memorial was unequivocal. Its prose was unadorned with any nicety as to the good qualities of the king and stated bluntly that they had enjoyed "peaceably our rights according to the terms of our oath in all its tenor and reserve" and that the settlement was "resolved with one consent and voice, to take no other oath."[154] One hundred and three men of the Pisiquid area signed this response. The final reply from the settlers of the Minas Basin was the most polished of all the answers – the most argued and the most combative. The 203-man delegation began by saying that the oath which they had taken had been approved several times, most recently in 1746 and 1747 by Governor Shirley, and that they would "never prove so fickle as to take an oath which changes ever so little, the conditions and the privileges obtained for us by our sovereigns and our fathers in the past."[155] They acknowledged that it was because of the "the king, our master" that they enjoyed their property and the free and public exercise of the Roman Catholic religion and they wished to be allowed to continue so to do. They concluded by asking for the release of those detained in Halifax. After these memorials had been placed on record, the deputies from all three districts were presented with the oath.

There had been no attempt made, in any of the Council meetings, to persuade the Acadians that taking the oath would guarantee them the peaceful possession of their lands. From the beginning, Lawrence had treated the Acadian population as a liability and something to control by fear. His policy had been one of accusation and demand. He had a fundamental disbelief in the possibility of the Acadian population being of any value to Nova Scotia and thus his communications with the various settlements were always threatening: "this will happen if you do not conform to my orders." Such a policy was bound to be less than successful, given that the Acadians had heard threats of exile and eviction from British administrators before. For more than forty years, such threats had been no more than words. It was unlikely that the Acadians were disposed to take Lawrence seriously at this point, even with the presence of much greater military resources in the colony than they had ever known. As well, their forced exile would have seemed an almost unimaginable possibility – they could not conceive of a worse fate than transportation to France. Thus, the Acadian delegates unanimously refused the request to take the oath. They were sent into confinement and the minutes record that "as it had been before determined to send all the French Inhabitants out of the Province if they refused to Take the Oaths, nothing now remained to be considered but what measures should be taken to send them away, and where they should be sent to." The final paragraph of the minutes of this momentous meeting noted that, "after mature Consideration, it was unanimously Agreed That to prevent as much as possible their Attempting to return and molest the Settlers that may be set down on their lands it would be most proper to send them to be distributed amongst the several Colonies on the Continent, and that a sufficient Number of Vessels should be hired with all possible Expedition for that purpose."

An understanding of the sequence of events that led to the deportation leaves unanswered a great many questions. But it goes a long way to answering how such a catastrophe, the destruction of an established community of people, who had built a thriving society over more than a century and a half, occurred. It even goes some of the way to disentangling the complex of ideas and decisions that turned the possibility of the removal of Acadians from Nova Scotia, broached at the time of the Treaty of Utrecht, into the reality of exile. Insistence upon the context of eighteenth-century European life leads to a greater place being given to the contemporary realities of communication through time and across space. It provokes questions about how the belief and opinions of the elites affected the actions of those who lived on the periphery of the European empires in North America. Above all, the reconstruction of who actually did what and when brings to the fore the political and social conventions that were widespread at the time.

The Acadian deportation, as a government action, was of a pattern with other contemporary happenings, from the deportations after the 1745 rebellion in Scotland to actions on the European continent during the War of the Austrian Succession. It was, in many ways, quintessentially an act of a time when the state rested its authority upon the hereditary right of the monarch and when, as Dummett and Nicol have pointed out, there was "a vertical relationship between monarch and individual, not a horizontal one between the members of a nation or the citizens of a body politics."[156] But this conclusion, that the Acadian deportation was not *essentially* an extraordinary incident, does little more than scratch the surface of the questions posed. There are at least three ways in which the events of 1755 were significantly different from the other such occurrences. First, as we have seen, the possibility of removing the Acadians from the colony had been a matter of discussion by both French and English from the time of Treaty of Utrecht in 1713.[157] It had a long history as a proposition whereas the other deportations were the immediate consequence of particular actions, the solution to recent and immediate problems. Secondly, the actual pressure for the deportation came as much from a neighbouring territory as from within the jurisdiction itself. The Commonwealth of Massachusetts and its governor, Shirley, were as fully implicated in the event as were the officials in place in Nova Scotia. Further, as has already been mentioned but bears repeating, the final authority, London, had consistently argued against such action since 1713 and reiterated this argument once more in a letter sent from Whitehall on 13 August 1755. Thirdly, the enterprise itself was significantly different from the deportations that followed the Monmouth and Jacobite rebellions. Those were organized after battles had been fought against those sent into exile and were the result of judgments made in a law court about individuals. As well, the number deported was, in each case, only a fraction of the communities concerned. The Acadian deportation involved the removal of almost an entire society, which had been judged as a collectivity. People were dispatched to other communities with a letter of recommendation by the man in charge of the operation, suggesting that, since the deportation would divide Acadian strength, "they May be of some Use as Most of them are Healthy Strong People; And as they Cannot easily collect themselves together again, it be out of their Power to Do any Mischief And they May become Profitable and it is possible, in time Faithful subjects."[158]

Finally, of course, the greatest difference between the Acadian deportation and the other events is what happened afterwards: neither Jacobite nor Huguenot went into exile with the capacity to retain a coherent identity. The Acadians did. They had always been involved in shaping their own lives. In 1713, when "Acadia or Nova Scotia" was transferred to Great Britain, the Acadians themselves, as much as the French or the English, decided that they would remain as subjects of the British empire rather than move to Île Royale, territory that the French still held.[159] In fact, the Acadians' stance represented two political beliefs that confronted the principles of hereditary power. The first was their conviction that they were indeed a people, distinct from the French of France and therefore with different political ambitions. The second belief was that, despite the actions of empires and the decisions of princes, the Acadians had every right to debate and present ideas about how and where they should live to those who claimed them as subjects. However sceptical others have been about the existence of Acadian identity, the Acadians themselves never seem to have doubted it. In considering their history, one has to give this "obstinacy" its due, particularly when "what happened next," the aftermath of the deportation, is examined. The Acadians had not been a collection of uneducated, illiterate, and ignorant peasants – the goods and chattels of others – before July 1755.

What happened next – the actual logistics of the deportation, the way in which the decision was carried out, and, most important, its impact on the Acadians and upon the polity of Nova Scotia and the future colonial policies of Great Britain – form as intricate and as fascinating a story as what had gone before. Between 1604 and 1755, the Acadian community came into being and an Acadian identity developed. The history of that community after July 1755 shows Acadian society as one capable of surviving extraordinary travails. The Acadian sense of identity that had been brought into being by 1755 allowed a considerable number of those sent into exile to endure as a community. There was, inevitably, some disintegration of social bonds and some assimilation of individuals into the larger societies that surrounded them. But a significant segment of those deported retained a strong sense of their origins in Acadia. Theirs was an identity based upon impressive social and political skills. The history of the development of this identity after July 1755 is as complex as was its original creation.

Notes

ABBREVIATIONS

AAQ	Archives de l'archevêché de Québec
AC	Archives des Colonies
ADCM	Archives de la Charente-Maritime
AM	Archives de la Marine
AN	Archives Nationales
BL	British Library
BM	British Museum
BN	Bibliothèque Nationale
BRH	*Le Bulletin des recherches historiques*
BTNS	Board of Trade, Nova Scotia
Cal St. Papers	*Calendar of state papers, colonial series, America and West Indies, 1661–68*
CEA	Centre d'Études Acadiennes
CHR	*Canadian Historical Review*
Coll. Doc. Inédits	*Collection de documents inédits sur le Canada et l'Amérique*
Coll. Man. N.F.	*Collection de manuscrits contenant lettres, mémoires et autres documents historiques relatifs à la Nouvelle-France*
DCB	*Dictionary of Canadian Biography*
Doc. Hist. St. Maine	*Documentary History of the State of Maine*
DUA	Dalhousie University Archives
EO	*Édits, ordonnances royaux, déclarations et arrêts du Conseil d'État du roi concernant le Canada: revus et corrigés d'après les pièces originales déposées aux archives provinciales*
FCGAR	*French Canadian and Acadian Genealogical Review*
Journals B.T.	*Journals of the commissioners for trade and plantations*
LHSQ	Literary and Historical Society of Quebec
MA	Massachusetts Archives

Mass. Records	Records of the governor and company of the Massachusetts Bay in New England
Mém. des Com. du Roi	Mémoires des commissaires du roi et de ceux de sa majesté britannique
Mem. Eng. and Fr. Com.	Memoirs of the English and French commissaries concerning the limits of Nova Scotia or Acadia
MHS	Massachusetts Historical Society
Mon. N.F.	Monumenta Novæ Franciæ, vol 1, La première mission d'Acadie 1602–1616 (Lucien Campeau, ed.)
NAC	National Archives of Canada
NBHS	New Brunswick Historical Society
NBM	New Brunswick Museum
NSHA	Nova Scotia Historical Society
Nouv. acq. fr:	Nouvelles acquisitions françaises
PAC	Public Archives of Canada
PRO	Public Record Office
RAPQ	Rapport de l'archiviste de la province de Québec
RHAF	Revue d'histoire de l'Amérique française
RJ	Relations des Jésuites
SGCF	Société Genéalogique canadienne-française
SHA	Société Historique Acadienne
WMQ	William and Mary Quarterly

N.B. In order to avoid duplication of archival references, when copies of primary documents are held by the National Archives of Canada, that archive is the sole repository listed in the Notes. For full archival references, see the Bibliography.

PREFACE

1 Griffiths, "The golden age: Acadian life, 1713–1748."
2 The lectures were published as *The context of Acadian history 1686–1784*. A French translation, *L'Acadie de 1686 à 1784*, translated by Kathryn Hamer, was published in 1997.
3 Brockliss and Eastwood, *A union of multiple identities.*
4 McCrone, *Understanding Scotland.*
5 Horsman and Marshall, *After the nation-state.*
6 There have been a number of excellent bibliographies published by the Centre d'Études Acadiennes at the Université de Moncton on Acadian studies. Of particular use are: *Bibliographie acadienne: liste des volumes, brochures et thèses*; and Harbec and Lévesque, *Guide Bibliographique de l'Acadie, 1976–1987.*

CHAPTER ONE

1 The best introduction to the beginning of European maritime exploration is Parry, *The discovery of the sea.*

2 See Meinig, *The shaping of America*; and Canny, ed., *The origins of empire*.

3 "Commission du Roy au Sieur de Monts, pour l'habitation ès terre de la Cadie, Canada, & autres endroits en la Nouvelle-France," in Lescarbot, *The history of New France*, 2:211–16; French: 490–4 (hereafter *Lescarbot*). The origin of the name Acadia has caused as much debate as any other aspect of Acadian history. Does it have a link to the Greek word "Arcadia"? Are its roots Mi'kmaq or Malecite? Etymologists do not agree, although there seems to be a growing consensus that the word has an Amerindian origin. Geographically, the issue is less complicated. The word "Acadie" is found on many European maps of the sixteenth century, attached to the region that today includes part of northeastern Maine, southeastern Quebec, New Brunswick, Prince Edward Island, and Nova Scotia. Spelled in many different ways – including La Cadie, Lacadye, and Acadie – the name is printed consistently south of the St Lawrence River, but by no means consistently in one location. Most often it appears written across lands south of the Gaspé, including Nova Scotia. The geographer E.H. Wilkins writes, in an article entitled "Arcadia in America," that "on a map published in 1586 the name *Arcadie* is applied specifically to Nova Scotia; that the name *Arcadie* was used by Thevet in 1575 for the whole region ... that a map made by Levasseur in 1601 bears the regional name Coste de Cadie in association with, but to the left of, *Nouvelle France* ... "

4 "reconnu sur le rapport des Capitaines de navires, pilotes, marchans & autres qui de langue main ont hanté, fréquenté, & traffiqué": *Lescarbot*, 2:490.

5 NAC, AC, C11 A1, 76ff., patent, 8 Nov. 1603; ibid., 58ff., de Monts's commission as lieutenant general of Acadia, 29 Jan. 1605. The most accessible printed version of the various patents and commissions of de Monts is found in *Lescarbot*, 2:211–26.

6 "de la dite terre de la Cadie": *Lescarbot*, 2:218; French: 490.

7 "traiter & contracter à méme effet paix ... bonne amitié ...": *Lescarbot*, 2:491.

8 "Et outre ce ayant receu divers avis, qu'aucune étrangers designent d'aller dresser des peuplems & demeures vers lesdites contrées de la Cadie, si comme elles ont esté jusque icy, elles restent encore quelque temps desertes & abondonnées": *Lescarbot*, 2:218; French: 493.

9 George MacBeath, "Pierre Du Gua de Monts," *DCB*, 1:291–4. There is no doubt that de Monts was a Calvinist, nor that he remained loyal to Henry IV, even after the latter's conversion to Catholicism. Born about 1558, he died in 1628, having devoted much of the last thirty years of his life to New France.

10 Biggar, *The works of Samuel de Champlain*, 1:231 (hereinafter *Champlain*).

11 "dudit Sieur de Mons, qui les prenoit, & empeschoit de faire leur pesche, les priuans de l'usage des choses qui leur auoient tousiours esté libres: [bientôt] leurs femmes & enfans pauvres & miserables, [seraient] ... contraints à mendier leurs vies": *Champlain*, 3:323–4.

12 *Mém, des com. du roi*, 18 Dec. 1603, 1:147–8.

13 Huguet, *Jean de Poutrincourt*, 159.

14 Lettres missives de Henri IV, vol.8, 897, cited in Huguet, *Poutrincourt*, 159.

15 BN, Mss. française, 18,176, f.4.

16 Archives de la Seine-Maritime, Rouen: Tabellionage de Rouen, meubles, 2e, série, registre de janviers à mars 1604, "Association de Samuel Georges et Jean Macain à la compagnie de Pierre du Gua, sieur de Mons, 10 fev. 1604." Printed in full in Le Blant and Baudry, *Nouveaux documents*, 1:80–1.

17 Gosselin, ed., *Nouvelles glanes historiques normandes*, 18–19.

18 Making sense of the monetary terms of seventeenth-century France is difficult. The best guide is Braudel, *Capitalism and material life*. The point to remember is that the *livre* is an abstract noun and its worth, at any given point, has to be estimated from what it could buy in that locality, at that time.

19 *Champlain*, 1:231.

20 Oddly enough, the names of the ships are difficult to discover. Trudel, *Histoire de la Nouvelle-France* (hereinafter *HNF*), vol.2, *Le Comptoir, 1604–1627*, 22, is one of the few to provide even a single name.

21 We have a number of accounts of this expedition, those most often cited being by Champlain and Lescarbot.

22 "Il assembla nombre de Gentils-hommes & de toutes sortes d'artisans, soldats & autres, tant d'une que d'autre religion, Prestres & Ministres": *Champlain*, 3:321.

23 *Lescarbot*, 2:227.

24 Huguet, *Poutrincourt*, 4, 83.

25 "étoit desireux dés y avoit long temps, de voir ces terres de la Nouvelle-France, & y choisir quelque lieu propre pour s'y retirer, avec sa famille, femme & enfans ...": *Lescarbot*, 2:227; French: 499.

26 To avoid confusion, father and son will be known, respectively, as Poutrincourt and Biencourt. The former's full title was Jean de Biencourt de Poutrincourt et de Saint-Just; the latter's, Charles de Biencourt de Saint-Just.

27 The variation of names at this time in French history reminds one of a Dostoevsky novel. This man, like his son Robert, is also known as Dupont-Gravé, Gravé Le Pont, Pont-Gravé, Le Pont, and Gravé. See Marcel Trudel, "François Gravé Du Pont," *DCB*, 1:345–6.

28 William E.F. Morley, "Pierre de Chauvin de Tonnetuit," *DCB*, 1:209.

29 *Champlain*, 1:27; *Lescarbot*, 2:450.

30 Aubry was a young man of good family whose parents were much against him pursuing his vocation in Acadia: *Champlain*, 1:253ff.

31 *Champlain*, 3:327.

32 An analysis of the make-up of this expedition is found in Jones, *Gentlemen and Jesuits*, 6–11.

33 Handcock, *So longe as there comes noe women*, especially 31.

34 "Engagement, par Daniel Boyer, de François Rocques, et de Robert Lescuyer ... 9 mars 1605," Tabellionage de Honfleur, registre du 14 septembre 1604 au 1er mai, 1605, f.277. Printed in full in Le Blant and Baudry, *Nouveaux Documents*, 99–100. For an analysis of this material, see Choquette, *Frenchmen into peasants*, passim.

35 See Green and Dickason, *The law of nations*; and Williams, *The American Indian in western legal thought*.

36 Wicken, "Encounters with tall sails and tall tales," 2.

37 Norman Clermont, "L'adaptation maritime au pays Micmac," in Martijn, *Les Micmacs et la mer*, 22.

38 Philip K. Bock, "Micmac," in Bruce G. Trigger, ed., *Northeast*, vol.15 of W.C. Sturtevant, *Handbook of North American Indians*, 109.

39 Vincent O. Erikson, "Maliseet-Passamaquoddy," ibid., 123.

40 Ibid., 125.

41 Clark, *Acadia*, 57–8. See also the discussion of Mi'kmaq population in Martin, *Keepers of the game*, 43–55; and in Trigger, *Natives and newcomers*, 238–9.

42 For a general overview of Micmac life, see Philip K. Bock, "Micmac," in Trigger, ed., *Northeast*, 109–22. See also Snow and Lanphear, "European contact and Indian depopulation in the northeast"; Henige, "Primary source by primary source?"; Pastore, "Native history in the Atlantic region"; and Miller, "The decline of the Nova Scotia Micmac population."

43 There is conflicting evidence about whether the ships sailed on 7 March (Lescarbot) or 7 April (Champlain). Biggar considers the first date to be the most credible, especially since it is confirmed in *Le Mercure français, 1608* [1611], 294. See *Lescarbot*, 8:228; and *Champlain*, 1: 234.

44 "se ne sont que taillis & herbages que pasturent des bœufz & des vaches que les Portugais y portert il ya plus de 60. ans": *Champlain*, 1:235.

45 Ibid., 1:236.

46 The inlet where the incident took place is now called Liverpool Bay but the small river that flows into the sea there is still called the Rossignol. Champlain and Lescarbot do not give the same dates for these incidents but agree on the sequence: *Lescarbot*, 2:229; *Champlain*, 1:227.

47 *Lescarbot*, 2:229.

48 *Champlain*, 1:238.

49 "guidé d'aucuns sauvages, le long de la coste d'Accadie, chercher Pôt-gravé": ibid.

50 "Toute la Nouvelle-France en fin assemblée en deux vaisseaux": *Lescarbot*, 2:232; French: 502. There is a marvellous insouciance towards dates in the accounts of Lescarbot and Champlain: the month is usually noted, the week sometimes, and the actual day much less often. Further, as Biggar points out, Champlain was usually wrong. The expedition mentioned here probably set sail on this stage of their voyage on 16 June. *Champlain*, 1:253.

51 Throughout the time period covered by this volume, the French always used the term "Baie française" for these waters.

52 "un des beaux ports que i'eusse veu en toutes les costes, où il pourroit deux mille vaisseaux en seureté": *Champlain*, 1:256.

53 "Ce lieu estoit le plus propre & plaisant pour habiter que nous eussions veu": *Champlain*, 1:259.

54 AN, série E, vol.78a, 304; see also Huia Ryder [in collaboration with], "Jean de Biencourt de Poutrincourt et de Saint-Just," *DCB*, 1:96–9; Trudel, *HNF*, 2:29.

55 Bock, "Micmac," in Trigger, ed., *Northeast*, 110.

56 *Lescarbot*, 2:257.

57 *Champlain*, 1:270.

58 *Lescarbot*, 2:257.

59 *Champlain*, 3:349–51.

60 Ibid., 1:275.

61 "car il y eust plusieurs de nos gens qui eurent le visage si enflé par leur piqueure qu'ils ne pouvoient presque voir": ibid.

62 "que le cidre étoit glacé ds les tneaux, & falloit à chacun bailler sa mesure au poids": *Lescarbot*, 2:257; French: 515.

63 Ibid., 2:258.

64 "Il estoit mal-aisé de recognoistre ce pays sans y avoir yuerné ...": *Champlain*, 1:307.

65 Ibid., 1:310.

66 "N'ayant trouvé aucun port qui nous fut propre pour lors": ibid., 1:367.

67 *Lescarbot*, 2:280.

68 Bishop, *Champlain*, 74.

69 Sagard, *Histoire du Canada*, 1:26.

70 "L'hiver venu les Sauvages du païs s'assembloient de bien loin au Port Royal pour troquer de ce qu'ils avoient avec les Francois, les uns apportans des pelleteries de Castors, & de Loutres (qui sont celles dont on peur faire plus d'état en ce lieu là), & aussi d'Ellans, desquelles on peut faire de bons buffles: les autres apportans des chairs freches ...": *Lescarbot*, 2:281; French: 528.

71 "Ç'a esté le plus grand, renommé et redoubté sauvage qui ayt esté de mémoire d'homme. De riche taille et plus haut et membru que n'est l'ordinaire des autres, barbu comme un Françoys, estant ainsy que quasi pas un des autres n'a du poil de menton; discret et grave, ressentant bien son homme de commandement...": P. Pierre Biard to P. Cristophe Baltazar, Port Royal, 31 Jan. 1612. Printed in full in *Mon. N.F.*, 1:235.

72 The most succinct account of this is in Bishop, *Champlain*, 78–9, but see also *Champlain*, 1:377–80.

73 *Lescarbot*, 2:284.

74 The most detailed account of de Monts's troubles is to be found in Trudel, *HNF*, 2:65ff.

75 Ryder, "Jean de Biencourt de Poutrincourt."

76 MacBeath, "Robert Gravé Du Pont," *DCB*, 1:346–7.

77 Trudel bases this opinion on the contract documents between the recruits and de Monts; the average wage offered was 120 *livres* a year. Trudel, *HNF*, 2:55.

78 *Lescarbot*, 2:288. Bishop believes that recruitment was particularly difficult because the survivors of the winter on St Croix had spread "their tales of terror, cold and death" in every tavern on the Norman and Breton coasts, tales that "grew more dreadful with every round of drink." Bishop, *Champlain*, 81.

79 "liqueur Septēbrale"; "qui nous en pourveurēt tat honnétenēt": *Lescarbot*, 2:554.

80 *Lescarbot*, 2:320.

81 Bertrand, letter of 28 June 1610, *JR*, English, 1:101, French, 100; Trudel, *HNF*, 2:56.

82 Bailey, *The conflict of European and eastern Algonkian cultures*, 11.

83 *Lescarbot*, 2:319.

84 Morrison, *Samuel de Champlain*, 88; Bishop, *Champlain*, 84.

85 "estoit venu aussi beau qu'on eut sceu desirer, & quantité d'herbes potageres qui estoient venues belles & grdes": *Champlain*, 1:393.

86 Ibid., 1:415.

87 *Lescarbot*, 2:384–5.

88 "comme de forçats au moulin à bras & à couper des bois": *Lescarbot*, 2:338; French: 565.

89 Lescarbot published his masque on his return to France, with the title *Les Muses de la Nouvelle-France*. It was included by Biggar in *Lescarbot*, 3:461–513.

90 "quelques gaillardises": *Champlain*, 1:438.

91 "une chaine que nous mettions avec quelques petites ceremonies au col d'un de nos gens, luy donnant la charge pour ce iour d'aller chasser: le lendemain on la bailloit à un autre, & ainsi consecutiuement": ibid., 1:448

92 "(quand il en arrivoit quelqu'un), ils étoient à la table mangeans & buvans comme nous: & avions plaisir de les voir, comme au contraire leur absence nous étoit triste ...": *Lescarbot*, 2:342, 344; French: 569.

93 Bishop, *Champlain*, 101. See also Reid, *Acadia, Maine and New Scotland*, 18.

94 Quinn, *The English New England voyages*, series 2, vol.161, 46ff.

95 *Lescarbot*, 2:367–8; "Observations de Peiresc sur les curiositiés rapportée d'Acadie par Pierre du Gua, sieur de Mons": text first published, with commentary, by Gravit in *La Revue de l'université Laval*, 1946. It is also published in full in Le Blant and Baudry, *Nouveaux Documents*, 102–6.

96 While this would prove to be the case, it is also clear that the fur trade was an important part of the Acadian economy throughout the seventeenth century. See, besides the present work, Clark, *Acadia*, passim.

97 BN, Arrêt du 29 mars 1608, Ms 18,173:194.

98 *Champlain*, 3:325.

99 Ibid., 4:31; *Lescarbot*, 2:368ff.

100 See in particular Bailey, *The conflict of European and eastern Algonkian cultures*, 11.

101 The *Inventaire général des sources documentaires sur les Acadiens*, vol.1, V, 6:248–53, is the best introduction to these records. See also the accounts of such vessels in Bréard, *Documents relatifs à la marine Normande*.

102 MacBeath, "Robert Gravé Du Pont."

103 See Bréard, *Documents relatifs à la marine normande*; and Biggar, *The early trading companies of New France*.

104 See "Factum du procès entre Jean de Biencourt et les PP. Biard et Massé, 1614," printed in full in *Mon. N.F.*, 1:320–406, 433–7, 555–62.

105 *Lescarbot*, 3:320.

106 Their names were Du Jardin and Du Quesne: "Factum du procès entre Jean de Biencourt ... et ... Biard ..., in *Mon. N.F.*, 1:330. Campeau takes up the issue of where Poutrincourt raised this particular money, and his argument that it did not come from the Huguenots, in this case, is persuasive.

107 *JR*, 1:109–13.

108 Ibid., 1:76,108–12.

109 Ibid., 1:161.

110 Ibid., 1:163.

111 "Car, disent-ils, vous ne cessez de vous entrebattre et quereller l'un l'autre; nous vivons en paix. Vous estes envieux les uns des autres, et détractez les uns des autres ordinairement; vous estes larrons et trompeurs; vous estes convoiteux, sans liberalité et misericorde: quant à nous, si nous avons un morceau du pain, nous le partissons entre nous": ibid., 1:173; English:172.

112 Lescarbot, *Relation dernière dece qui s'est passé au voyage du Sieur de Poutrincourt* ... [Last relation of what took place on the voyage made by the sieur de Poutrincourt ...], *JR*, 2:168–9.

113 The best short biography of this woman is in Jones, *Gentlemen and Jesuits*, 131–4.

114 Biographical note given in *Mon. N.F.*, 1:679–80. She was born *c.*1570 and died 5 Jan. 1632.

115 "Contrat des Jésuites avec Charles de Biencourt, Dieppe," 20 Jan. 1611, *Mon. N.F.*, 1:109–16.

116 "Factum ...," in *Mon. N.F.*, 1:334.

117 *JR*, 3:173.

118 AN, Consentement de Nicolas Desnoyers au paiement des sommes dues à Jean Dujardin and Abraham Duquesne, 10 mai, 1613, Minutier central XIV, 13.

119 *JR*, 2:184.

120 There has been an erroneous tradition that European women did come to Acadia during these years. This arose because of a translation of the Latin phrase *sine femina* as the "women followed," instead of "without women."

121 "qu'en quelque habitation que ce soit on ne fera jamais fruit sans la compagnie des femmes": Lescarbot, *La conversion des sauvages* ...: *JR*, 1:100–2; English: 103. He linked his comments to the fact that no man knew how to cope with cows in calf, a point he had made six years earlier at the time of the de Monts expedition.

122 The complicated story of this contract is told in Trudel, *HNF*, 2:112–13.

123 The major documents in this case were gathered together in the "Factum du procès entre Jean de Biencourt et les PP. Biard et Massé."

124 Lucien Campeau, "Gilbert Du Thet," *DCB*, 1:299.

125 *JR*, 3:6.

126 Ibid., 2: 262–4.

127 *JR*, 3:62; 4:8–10.

128 See Purchas, *Hakluytus Posthumus*, vol.19; *JR*, 3:10; 4:34.

129 See Cell, *English enterprise in Newfoundland*; and Handcock, *So longe as there comes no women* ...

130 W. Austin Squires, "Sir Samuel Argall," *DCB*, 1:67.

131 Trudel, *HNF*, 2:137; Huguet, *Poutrincourt*, 424.

CHAPTER TWO

1 See David B. Quinn, "Colonies in the beginning: Examples from North America," in Palmer and Reinhartz, ed., *Essays on the history of North American discovery*, 10–34.

2 Sully's opposition to spending any money on the colonies, on principle, is well known, but see Barbiche, *Sully*, for a detailed examination of both his and Henry IV's colonial policy.

3 This commission is printed in full in Grant's introduction to *Lescarbot*, 2:211–26.

4 For a survey of such material, see Bréard, *Documents relatifs à la marine normande*; and Biggar, *The early trading companies of New France*.

5 Brenner, *Merchants and revolutions*, pt.1, passim.

6 See studies such as Dardel, *Navires et marchandises*; and Delumeau, *Le mouvement du port de Saint-Malo*.

7 Europe's need for protein in the sixteenth and seventeenth centuries, if its population was to grow, has become a commonplace of economic histories of Europe, but see in particular Rich and Wilson, ed., *The economy of expanding Europe*.

8 On the issue of technology, see La Morandière, *Histoire de la pêche française*, 1:35ff.; and Innis, *The cod fisheries*, 55ff. In the case of dry-fishery techniques, see especially Harris, ed., *Historical atlas of Canada*, vol.1, *From the beginning to 1800*. The relevant sections are those by Graeme Wynn, Ralph Pastore, and Bernard G. Hoffman ("The Atlantic realm") and by John J. Mannion and C. Grant Head ("The migratory fisheries").

9 Wynn, Pastore, and Hoffman, "The Atlantic realm."

10 This account is a modified version of a passage first published in Griffiths, "Fur, fish and folk," in Buckner and Reid, ed., *The Atlantic region to Confederation*, 47–8.

11 Innis, *The fur trade*, 16. His view is that "in the final analysis the pull of a relatively simple civilization on the resources of a complex civilization may be regarded as of paramount importance. No monopoly or organization could withstand the demands of the Indian civilization of North America for European goods ... As Cartier noted of the Mi'kmaq, 'the savages showed a marvelously great pleasure in possessing and obtaining these iron wares and other commodities, dancing and going through many ceremonies ...'"

12 See chapter 1 and Biggar, *The early trading companies of New France*, 63–4.

13 According to Innis, this was an unusual load: the average 100-ton ship most generally brought back 20,000 to 25,000 fish: Innis, *The cod fisheries*, 49, 84.

14 La Morandière, *Histoire de la pêche française*, 1:352.

15 The fullest account of the economics of this activity is that of La Morandière, *Histoire de la pêche française*, 1:35–212. There are excellent illustrations in that work of the ships and their tackle.

16 See Innis, *The cod fisheries*, 84–5. He cites Henry Harisse, *Découverte et évolution cartographique de Terre Neuve* (Paris, 1900), as noting that in 1612 there were

five companies founded to support fishing vessels from Rouen, Dieppe, and other ports.

17 Davies, *The North Atlantic world,* 49.

18 *Champlain,* 1:466; *Lescarbot,* 2:350.

19 Innis, *The cod fisheries,* 83–4n.93.

20 Ibid., 84.

21 *Lescarbot,* 3:52; Innis, *The cod fisheries,* 85.

22 George MacBeath, "Claude de Saint-Étienne de La Tour," *DCB,* 1:596–7; Clarence-Joseph d'Entremont, *Histoire du Cap-Sable,* 2:282–3.

23 MacBeath, "Claude de Saint-Étienne de La Tour." There is some debate over when Charles was born, and various authorities believe that he was no more than ten when he first came to Acadia.

24 Ibid. Claude de Saint-Étienne de La Tour's whereabouts between 1614 and 1627 are a matter of conjecture. While he seems to have been in Acadia for part of this time, there is documentary evidence to show that he was more often in France. See Couillard Després, *Charles de Saint-Étienne de La Tour,* 162ff.

25 Clark reports that in 1616 the Acadian fur trade produced 25,000 pelts but he gives no reference for this figure: Clark, *Acadia,* 82.

26 BN, Nouvelles acc. fr., Clairambault, 9281, f.25. The letter is printed in full in *Collection de documents,* 1:57–9.

27 "Cependant il peuple puisamment la Virginie et la Vermude [sic], où il envoye des colonies tous les ans, et naguerres est icy passé une flotte de cinq cens hommes avec nombre de femmes de la dite nation, laquelle s'est pourvue d'eau douce et de bois en mon voisinage": ibid. The numbers are almost certainly an exaggeration, and it is hard to say what English ships were doing so far off course.

28 "plusiers qui gémissent en secret et n'osent faire paroiste leur nécessité": ibid.

29 "abondance de cuirs, graisses, chairs et laitages, d'où vostre peuple aura de soulagements comme aussy les bois de deça vous fourniront de navires, de cendres et secours de bastimens que vous faictes venir de Suède, Danemarck ou Moscovie, avec une navigation plus longue et périlleuse que cell-cy": ibid.

30 *Doc. Hist. St. of Maine,* 7:25 . English ventures into this region were part of the Virginia company's area of operation and what would be Maine and Massachusetts were explored by Sir Fernando Gorges. See Preston, *Gorges of Plymouth Fort.*

31 De Monts's commission had granted him rights between 40° and 60°.

32 A short history of this momentous voyage is that of Dillon, *A place for habitation.*

33 Scotland, Privy Council, *The register of the Privy Council of Scotland* (hereafter *P.C. Register,* series 1, 12:774.

34 Ibid. 24.

35 For details of Alexander's endeavours, see Insh, *Scottish colonial schemes.*

36 "On raconte que les premiers émigrants qui furent envoyés par Sir Wm Alexander les [les Français] trouvèrent si nombreux, si bien armés, si préparés à une défense énergique qu'ils n'osèrent pas débarquer ...": Jules de

Menou (comte), *Mémoires historiques sur la colonisation de l'Acadie par Charles d'Aulnay de Menou et son administration*, 8–9, cited in d'Entremont, *Histoire du Cap-Sable*, 2:216. See also d'Entremont's discussion of Menou (1790–1863), a descendant of La Tour's major rival, d'Aulnay. Menou's papers are in the library of the MHS

37 This branch of the Franciscan order was suppressed in 1791. On the issue of early missionary activity in North America, see Jaenen, *The role of the church in New France*; Codignola, *Guide to documents*; and Dickason, *The myth of the savage*.

38 Le Clercq, *Premier établissement de la foy*, 1:239–41; Hugolin, *Les Récollets*, 12–14.

39 There is debate over when and where the Recollets arrived; see d'Entremont, *Histoire du Cap-Sable*, 2:388–91. Trudel lists the priests as: Sebastien or Bernadin, arrival in Acadia, 1620, died there 1623; Jacques de La Foyer, arrival in Acadia, 1620, left for Quebec in 1624; Louis Fontiner, arrival in Acadia, 1620, left for Quebec in 1624; Jacques Cardon, arrival in Acadia, 1620, left for Quebec in 1624: Trudel: *HNF*, 2:462. See also Le Clercq, *Premier établissement de la foy*, 1:242.

40 "la plupart se marièrent à des sauvagesses, et passèrent le reste de leurs jours avec les sauvages, adoptant leur manière de vie": Maurault, *Histoire des Abénakis*, 84.

41 De Nant, *Pages glorieuses*.

42 "se meslant avec les sauvages et vivant d'une vie libertine et infame comme bestes brutes sans aucun exercice de Religion nayant pas mesme le soin de faire baptisé les enfans procreez d'eux de ces pauvres miserables femmes au contraire les abandonnoit a leurs mères ...": BN, Fonds français, vol.15621, ff.265–71, "Mémoire de d'Aulnay contre La Tour."

43 "Les côtes de l'est de l'Acadie ont toujours été un centre demi-sauvage, demi-civilisé, où se réunissaient volontiers des familles métisses, dont la première origine remonte certainement jusqu'aux compagnons de Biencourt et de Latour [sic]": Rameau de Saint-Père, *Une colonie féodale*, 2:348.

44 For a lengthier discussion of this issue, see Griffiths, "Mating and marriage."

45 Registres de Baptêmes, 1629–1632, f.107, printed in d'Entremont, "Premier enfant né en Acadie, 1620," 352.

46 See Macdonald, *Fortune and La Tour*.

47 "Registre des concessions en Acadie," 17 Oct. 1672, in *Inventaire des concessions en fief et seigneurie*, 6:11. A full discussion of this is found in d'Entremont, *Histoire du Cap-Sable*, 2:404ff.

48 Couillard Després, *Charles de Saint-Étienne de La Tour*, 130–1.

49 Massignon, *Les parlers français*, 1:69; and Rameau de Saint-Père, *Une colonie féodale*, 2:348.

50 Bailey, *The conflict of European and eastern Algonkian cultures*, 111.

51 This paragraph is based upon Bock, "Micmac," in Sturtevant, ed., *Handbook of North American Indians*, vol. 15, Bruce G. Trigger, ed., *Northeast*, 114.

52 About which, perhaps, the thirteenth-century poem of Lady Horikara says it all: "How can one e're be sure/if true love will endure? My thoughts this

morning are/as tangled as my hair." Mark van Doren, ed., *Anthology of world poetry* (London: Literary Guild of America 1929), 29.

53 Van Kirk, *"Many tender ties,"* 6.

54 Ibid., 6, 28.

55 "Au Roy, Port Lomeron: xxv de juillet, 1627": BN, Nouv. acq. fr., Ms 5131, f.102, cited in full in Couillard Després, *Charles de Saint-Étienne de La Tour*, 149–50. See also the version in Bib. Institut de France, Portefeuille, 270.

56 "qu'ils ont charge et dessein de se saisir du pays de la nouvelle-France et s'approprier la pêche des morues sec et vert et la traite de la pelleterie": Couillard Després, *Charles de Saint-Étienne de La Tour*, 149–50.

57 "trois petits barque Contre lesfort des françoys qui vont a la grand riviere qui Jusques à pnt mont pousuivy jusques à la mort ...": BN, Charles de La Tour à Monseigneur le Cardinal Richelieu, du fort Lomeron en la Nouvelle-France, le XXVme juillet 1627, Nouv. acq. fr., no.5131, f.102, printed in full in Couillard Després, *Charles de Saint-Étienne de La Tour*, 151–2.

58 Trudel, *HNF*, 2:428–9.

59 Cited in Cell, *English enterprise in Newfoundland*.

60 Trudel, *HNF*, 2:431.

61 An account of these rights and privileges is to be found in Marcel Trudel, "Samuel de Champlain," *DCB*, 1:186–99.

62 Two members of this family, Ezechiel and Emery, were Catholic, and one, Guillaume, the most powerful, was Huguenot.

63 Biggar, *Early trading companies in New France*; Marcel Trudel: "Guillaume de Caën," *DCB*, 1:159–62 at 160.

64 Bréard, *Documents relatifs à la marine normande*, 128n.2.

65 *Champlain*, 5:128, 136.

66 "il y auoit sur la terre quatre pieds & demy de neiges, & à Miscou huict ... ils faillirent tous à mourir du mal de terre": ibid., 212–13.

67 NAC, C11, 1, f.71, "Édict du Roy, pour l'établissement du commerce en France par mer et par terre. Levant, Ponant, et voyages de Long cours," July 1626.

68 Born in 1587, Razilly was appointed to the order of St John of Jerusalem at the age of eighteen and immediately entered the navy. He saw service in the Mediterranean and lost an eye during the siege of La Rochelle in 1625. See George MacBeath, "Isaac de Razilly," *DCB*, 1:567–9; and Trudel, *HNF*, 3: *La Seigneurie des Cent-Associés*, I: *Les Événements*, 4–6.

69 Mémoire du chevalier de Razilly, 26 Nov. 1626, in *Revue de géographie*, 1886, 374–83.

70 Document du 29 avril 1627 ..., in *EO*, 1:5–11; document du 7 mai 1627, *EO*, 1:12–17.

71 Édit du 29 avril 1627, *EO*, 1:10.

72 Document du 7 mai 1627, *EO*, 1:13–17.

73 Édict du 29 avril, 1627, *EO*, 1:10.

74 See Goubert, *L'Ancien régime*, 133–8; Bitton, *The French nobility in crisis*; Collins, *Fiscal limits of absolutism*.

75 Trudel queries the extent to which this was observed in practice (*HNF*, 3:I), but see Choquette, "French and British emigration to the North American colonies." She estimates that fewer than one in ten of those who left for North America actually stayed there.

76 Acte pour l'établissement de la Compagnie des Cents Associés, 29 April 1627, *EO*: 1:5–11. At the same time, it was stated that any native who had converted to Catholicism would also have the right to French citizenship. Trudel remarks that there is no record of any such person making a claim, on this basis, for French citizenship: *HNF*, 3:I, 11n.38.

77 Acte pour l'établissement de la Compagnie des Cents Associés, *EO*, 1:7. As Trudel has pointed out, this particular provision has caused considerable historical debate. He himself does not believe that it made any significant difference to the development of New France: *HNF*, 3:II, 12n.44.

78 Cardinal Richelieu (Armand Jean Du Plessis), *Testament politique* (Paris: Louis Andre 1947).

79 "Lettres Patentes ... pour la ratification des articles de la Compagnie du Canada," *EO*, 1:19.

80 Letters of marque gave vessels the right to capture ships of what was considered to be an enemy nation, even if there was no declared state of war.

81 John S. Moir, "Sir David Kirke," *DCB*, 1:404–7.

82 James VI to Privy Council of Scotland, 18 Oct. 1624, *P.C. Register*, series 1, 13:616. The best account of these years is to be found in Reid, *Acadia, Maine and New Scotland*; see also his article "The Scots crown and the restitution of Port Royal." The charter granted to Alexander – entitled "Charter in Favour of Sir William Alexander, Knight, of the Lordship and Barony of New Scotland in America" and dated 10 Sept. 1621 – is found in Bourinot, "Builders of Nova Scotia."

83 Reid, *Acadia, Maine and New Scotland*, 24; proclamation, 30 Nov. 1624, *P.C. Register*, series 1, 13:649–51.

84 *Doc. Hist. St. Maine*, 7:76–80; proclamation, 30 Nov. 1624, *P.C. Register*, series 1, 13:649–51.

85 D.C. Harvey, "William Alexander," *DCB*, 1:50–4.

86 Griffiths and Reid, "New Evidence on New Scotland, 1629," 496.

87 Ibid., 502.

88 René Baudry, "Charles Daniel," *DCB*, 1:247–8.

89 The French view of this is given by one of Daniel's company: André Malapart, *La prise d'un seigneur escossois*. It is a longer account than that found in Félix, ed., *Voyage à la Nouvelle France*.

90 "J.L. Ochiltrie account," printed as an appendix to Félix, *Voyage à la Nouvelle France*, 5–13 at 7.

91 Ibid., 9, 10–11.

92 Griffiths and Reid, "New Evidence on New Scotland," 503.

93 *Champlain*, 6:176.

94 Ibid., 5:280.

95 There is much debate over this period in Claude de La Tour's life: Clarence

d'Entremont presents the arguments at length in *Histoire du Cap-Sable*, 3:440ff.

96   30 November 1629 and 12 May 1630: Laing, ed., *Royal letters, charters and tracts*, 122. Account of 6 Oct. 1629: BL, Egerton Mss., 2395, f.17: "bons et fideles sujets et Vasseaux dudit Roy, et luy rendre toute obeissance et assister vers les Peuples a la reduction dudit Pais et Coste d'Accadie."

97   Nicolas Denys reported in the history he wrote in his old age that the elder La Tour arrived with "deux navires de Guerre": *Description géographique et historique*, vol.1, chapter 3, 69. Denys's writings need to be used with caution but his imaginative reconstructions are usually based on some fact. That the ships were warships is unlikely; that there were two ships and that they carried arms is highly probable. The text of Denys's work was edited by Ganong for the Champlain Society as *The description and natural history of the coasts of North America (Acadia)* (hereafter Ganong, ed., *Description*). There is also a facsimile edition published by Clarence J. d'Entremont, entitled *Nicholas Denys, sa vie et son œuvre* (hereafter *Denys*), which has an interesting introductory essay and notes.

98   Ganong, ed., *Description*, chapter 3, 135–6.

99   *Champlain*, 6:173, 175.

100   "pour le remettre en s deuoir, comme pour sçauoir de luy l'estat des Anglois & leur dessein, pour en suitte se gouuerner selon qu'ils aduiseroient suyuant sa relation": ibid., 6:175.

101   Ganong, ed., *Description*, chapter 3, 136–7; George MacBeath, "Nicolas Denys," DCB, 1:256–9.

102   The most recent analysis of this effort is that of Le Blant, "La compagnie de la Nouvelle France."

103   George MacBeath, "Bernard Marot," DCB, 1:490.

104   *Champlain*, 1:173.

105   MacBeath, "Bernard Marot."

106   Charles de La Tour's commission as lieutenant general is printed in full in Couillard Després, *Charles de Saint-Étienne de La Tour*, 191–6.

107   Le Tac, *Histoire chronologique*, 160; Dragon, *L'Âcadie et ses 40 robes noires*, 80.

108   "s'y accommodoient touts les jours de mieux en mieux": Le Tac, *Histoire chronologique*, 160.

109   Andrews, *The colonial period of American history*, 3:373.

CHAPTER THREE

1   Mario Belada was one of the first scholars to use the term "founding migration" for "those immigrants who, for the most part, founded large families constituting what was to become the nucleus of the Quebecois population." See Belada's PhD thesis, "Les migrations au Canada sous le régime français."

2   Choquette, *Frenchmen into peasants*, 54. Her work has shown that 64.6 per cent of migrants came from towns.

3   Ibid., 21.

4 Lauvrière, *La tragédie d'un peuple*, 1:48ff.

5 NAC, C11D, 1, f.48, Convention du 27 mars 1632.

6 "prendre possession du Port-Royal": NAC, C11A, 1, f.49 and NAC, C11D, 1, f.52, printed in *Coll. Man. N.F.*, 1:110.

7 "gouverneur et Lieutenant-General de Sa Majestye, en la coste de l'Acadie et lieux qui en dependent": ADCM, 8 Feb. 1631, reported in *Gazette de Renaudot*, 6 March 1633, 103.

8 George MacBeath, "Nicolas Denys," *DCB*, 1:256–9; d'Entremont, *Denys*, 24.

9 "chargez de toutes choses necessaires et de trois cens hommes d'élite." D'Entremont considers 4 July the more likely date: *Histoire du Cap-Sable*, 2:469.

10 These include memoranda that were part of the legal disputes that took place in the 1640s: BN, Nouv. acq. fr., Ms 9281, f.104, "Extrait et mémoire de ce que le sieur d'Aulnay a fait dans la Nouvelle France."

11 DeGrâce, *Noms géographiques de l'Acadie*, 29.

12 "Memoire du chevalier de Razilly," 26 Nov. 1626, included, with a biography of Razilly, in Deschamps, "Un colonisateur du temps de Richelieu."

13 *Gazette de Renaudot*, 1634: published letter, dated 24 Nov. 1632, at Fort Sainte-Marie-de-Grace, Port de la Hève, asserting arrival there on 8 September, the Feast of the Virgin Mary's birthday. There is, however, debate about whether Razilly was in the region much earlier: see d'Entremont, "Le 350ième anniversaire de La Heve."

14 There is some confusion over what this fort is called. Most of those writing in English about the events of the 1640s refer to "Fort La Tour." However, this name should be reserved for La Tour's buildings on the Atlantic coast. Throughout this book, I use Fort Sainte-Marie for La Tour's Saint John headquarters.

15 ADCM, La Rochelle, B 5654, Report of Jean Daniel Chaline, 1 Nov. 1632; and see also George Macbeath, "Andrew Forrester," *DCB*, 1:310–11.

16 Report from La Rochelle, 11 Feb. 1633, *Gazette de Renaudot*, 39, 70, 71.

17 George MacBeath, "Isaac de Razilly," *DCB*, 1:567–9.

18 Letters patent of the king of Great Britain, in Latin, 4 July 1631, under the seal of Scotland: "1st. for the restitution of Port Royal, in the state it was in at the time of its capture. 2nd. an order of the said king to his subjects being in Port Royal, for the demolition and abandonment of the place. 3rd. a letter of the chevalier Alexander to captain Amos Forrester, commander at said Port Royal, tending to the same end." Printed in Murdoch, *A history of Nova Scotia*, 1:88–91.

19 "Les melons, concombres, poix, fèves, laitues, pourpier, choufleurs ... Les roses, framboises, grozeilles, petites Cerises, fraises y viennent naturellement ... La mer y est pavé de Turbots ..." This document has been published in facsimile as part of Hivert-Le Faucheux, "La vie quotidienne en Acadie." The source given is BN, fonds fr. 14323. D'Entremont cites another source: BN, Collection Clairambault, vol.864, f.60v.

20 "Jamais le pain de froment, le Vin de trois sortes, le boeuf, lait, beurre, huile, Vinaigre, Espiceries, ris, Sucres et confitures ne luy ont manqué, et

maintenant le laitage, beurre frais, Volailles, et oeufs leur sont communs."
Hivert-Le Faucheux, "La vie quotidienne en Acadie," 123.

21 Ibid., 122.

22 Archeologists have uncovered the remains of a fort and out-buildings, including a store and chapel, at La Hève: Erskine: *The French period in Nova Scotia.*

23 "j'avois douze hommes avec moy, les uns laboureurs, les autres faiseurs de
mairrain ou douves pour barriques, charpentiers, & d'autres pour la chasse,
j'étois muny de toutes sortes de provisions, nous faisions bonne chere car le
gibier ne nous manquoit point ...": Ganong, ed., *Description,* English: 149–50;
French: 482.

24 Ibid., English: 154; French: 484.

25 The historiographical debate has been explored by d'Entremont in *Histoire
du Cap-Sable,* 2:645–7.

26 Ganong, ed., *Description,* English: 154; French: 484.

27 Choquette has estimated that, over the two centuries that France was involved
with Canada, there were "at least 30,000 temporary emigrants for Quebec ...
[and perhaps] 7,000 others embarked for the Maritimes ..." *Frenchmen into
peasants,* 279.

28 AN, Minutier central, 16:69, minutes de Remond, cited in d'Entremont, "Le
350ième anniversaire de La Hève," 18.

29 Ibid.

30 "à Une seule fois plus de 500. François en ce port": Hivert-Le Faucheux, "La
vie quotidienne en Acadie," 123.

31 On this side of Razilly's character, see Bamford, *Fighting ships and prisons,* 19.

32 Le Blant, "Les compagnies du Cap-Breton."

33 *Le Mercure françois,* 19, 806s, cited in Trudel, HNF, 3, I: 62.

34 An account of these years, focusing on the struggle between New England
and Acadia, is Rawlyk, *Nova Scotia's Massachusetts,* 4ff. The best analysis of
comparative colonial development is that of Reid, *Acadia, Maine and New Scotland.*

35 Isaac Allerton was one of the leading figures in the Plymouth venture: see
Reid, *Acadia, Maine and New Scotland,* 84–5.

36 Winthrop, *Journal,* 1:145.

37 Collins, *The state in early modern France,* 4.

38 Macdonald, *Fortune and La Tour,* 30–2.

39 Ibid., 48. The incident is reported in full in *Coll. Man. N.F.,* 1:354ff.

40 René Baudry, "Charles de Menou d'Aulnay," DCB, 1:502–6. D'Aulnay played a
major part in the development of the de Launay-Razilly-Cordonnier company
and after 1634 restricted his dealings in France to this association.

41 D'Entremont, *Histoire du Cap-Sable,* 2:522ff., has summarized the debate at
considerable length and does not believe d'Aulnay's claim.

42 For the original document, see ADCM, La Rochelle, B 5654, pièce 105; it was
published in full, with a commentary by Père Godbout, in SGCF, January 1944,
1:19–30. An English edition of the text was published in the FCAGR, 1 (1968):
55–73.

43 See Massignon, *Les parlers français*, 1:20; Delafosse, "La Rochelle et le Cana-
     da," lists six ships sailing between 1633 and 1636 out of that port alone.
44 D'Entremont, *Denys*, 27.
45 See White, *Dictionnaire généalogique*, 2:1125–6.
46 For an analysis of the comparative agricultural potential of the two areas, see
     Clark, *Acadia*, 95, 102–3.
47 The recent work of Wicken, "Encounters with tall sails," is an invaluable
     source. See also Trigger, *Natives and newcomers*; and Martijn, ed., *Les Micmacs et
     la mer*. The classic study remains Bailey, *The conflict of European and eastern
     Algonkian cultures*.
48 See in particular Martin, *Keepers of the game*, and his critics.
49 Wicken, "Encounters with tall sails," 307; see also chapter 4 of the present
     book.
50 The historiography on these matters is extensive. A place to begin for New
     England is Greene and Pole, ed., *Colonial British America*; for New France,
     Rouillard, *Guide d'histoire du Québec*. See also Taylor, ed., *Canadian history*,
     vol.1, *Beginnings to Confederation*.
51 *SHA*, 28, 2–3 (June/Sept. 1997), is devoted to questions of religious life with-
     in Acadia.
52 Macdonald, *Fortune and La Tour*, 69. Macdonald suggests that her dowry may
     have been shares in the Launay-Razilly-Cordonnier company.
53 *Denys*, English: 151; French: 483.
54 NAC, AC, C11D, 1, f.9, order issued by Louis XIII, 10 Feb. 1638; printed in
     Mém. des Com. du roi, 2:495–6.
55 On this, see d'Entremont, *Histoire du Cap-Sable*, 2:567–93.
56 Winthrop, *Journal*, 1:97–9.
57 Rawlyk, *Nova Scotia's Massachusetts*, 7–9.
58 Winthrop, *Journal*, 2:88.
59 J.-Roger Comeau, "Nicolas Gargot de la Rochette," DCB, 1:323–4. There seems
     to be some confusion as to whether he converted to Catholicism or not; see
     d'Entremont, *Histoire du Cap-Sable*, 2:573–4.
60 Winthrop, *Journal*, 2:88.
61 Ibid., 2:107.
62 George MacBeath: "Françoise-Marie Jacquelin," DCB, 1:383; the wedding con-
     tracts are printed in Macdonald, *Fortune and La Tour*, 184–93.
63 Winthrop, *Journal*, 2:107.
64 Ibid., 2:109, 111.
65 Ibid., 2:111.
66 Ibid., 2:114.
67 Ibid., 2:125.
68 Rawlyk, *Nova Scotia's Massachusetts*, 9.
69 Winthrop, *Journal*, 2:127; Rawlyk, *Nova Scotia's Massachusetts*, 10.
70 Winthrop, *Journal*, 2:135.
71 Ibid., 2:134.
72 Mémoire des Capucins, 20 Oct. 1643, *Coll. Man N.F.*, 1:117.

73 NAC, MG 3, 1, f.7, arrêt de 6 mars 1644, arrêts du Conseil d'État du Roi, conseils du gouvernement des finances.

74. Winthrop, *Journal*, 2:178.

75 Ibid., 2:180.

76 MA, 2, ff. 478–81, D'Aulnay to magistrates of Massachusetts, 21 Oct. 1644.

77 Reid, *Acadia, Maine and New Scotland*, 98.

78 J.-Roger Comeau, "Ignace de Paris," *DCB*, 1:379–80.

79 Reid, *Acadia, Maine and New Scotland*, 98.

80 Winthrop, *Journal*, 2:203; a useful selection of d'Aulnay correspondence with the Council of Massachusetts is "Letters relating to the Acadian–Masachusetts relations in 1644," in MHS *Collections*, sixth series, vol.48 (1915).

81 Winthrop, *Journal*, 2:244ff.

82 MacBeath,"Françoise-Marie Jacquelin," 383.

83 For an exhaustive account of this, see d'Entremont, *Histoire du Cap-Sable*, 2:580–7; an authoritative account is found in Macdonald, *Fortune and La Tour*, 155–71.

84 Queen to Menou d'Aulnay, 27 Sept. 1645, *Coll. Man. N.F.*, 1:119.

85 Baudry, "Charles Menou d'Aulnay."

86 Letters patent, February 1647, naming d'Aulnay "Gouverneur et nostre Lieutenant Général representant nostre personne, en tous les dits païs, costes et confins de la Cadie," *Coll. Man. N.F.*, 1:120.

87 Baudry, "Charles d'Aulnay et la Compagnie de la Nouvelle-France."

88 MacBeath, "Nicolas Denys"; see also Le Blant, "La première compagnie de Miscou."

89 MacBeath, "Nicolas Denys," 256.

90 For a lengthy analysis of these charges, see Baudry, "Charles Menou d'Aulnay"; see also d'Entremont, *Histoire du Cap-Sable*, vol.2, chapter 15.

91 Le Blant, "Les Compagnies du Cap-Breton."

92 Notarial contract, 16 Jan. 1642; see Baudry, "Charles Menou d'Aulnay," 504.

93 Memoir of 1700, *Coll. Man. N.F.*, 2:357.

94 ADCM, La Rochelle, ff. 8–10, Lettres patentes, 25 Feb. 1651; reproduced in full in Couillard Després, *Charles de Saint-Étienne de La Tour*, 401–4.

95 "touttes les habitations ... de la Hève, du Port Royal, Pentagouët, la rivière de St. Jean, celle de Miscou du Cap Breton, et generalement tout ce quy leur apartient": Le Borgne to the king, 1658, printed in *Coll. Man. N.F.*, 1:154.

96 Memoir of 1700, *Coll. Man. N.F.*, 2:357; see also the letter of Ignace (Marie) de Paris, 6 Aug. 1653, ibid., 1:140.

97 Reproduced in full in Couillard Després, *Charles de Saint-Étienne de la Tour*, 408–12.

98 George MacBeath "Jeanne Motin," *DCB*, 1:514.

99 The best biography of this important player in the development of Acadia is found in Couillard Després, *Charles de Saint-Étienne de La Tour*, 418. The nobility of the robe were families whose titles came from service to the French crown, primarily as officials of the state, rather than through military service; see also Mason Wade, "Emmanuel Le Borgne," *DCB*, 1:433–5.

100 D'Entremont, *Denys*, 277nn.9–19.
101 Memoir of 1700, *Coll. Man. N.F.*, 2:358.
102 Concessions, 3 Dec. 1653 and 30 Jan. 1654, printed in d'Entremont, *Denys*, 57–67; but for a clear account of the legal steps, see Trudel, *HNF*, 3, I: 87–8.
103 For more about this raid, see chapter 4.
104 Some of the evidence has been brought together by Debien in "Engagés pour le Canada."
105 The classic study of this industry is Innis, *The fur trade in Canada*. See also Eccles, "A belated review of Harold Adam Innis"; Grant, "One step forward, two steps back"; and Eccles, "A response to Hugh M. Grant."
106 ADCM, Armurier, menusier, Registre de Me Charbonnier, 1637–1640, ff.68–9.
107 "cloutier et forgeron, scieur de bois, boulanger et macon": ADCM, Registre de Me Charbonnier, 1641, ff.14, 17, 26.
108 Contracts listed in Massignon, *Les parlers français*, 1:38.
109 Based on reports of Father Pacifique du Provins, head of the Capucin effort in Acadia, December 1641; cited in *RHAF*, 11 (1957): 235.
110 Estimates of Trudel in *HNF*, 3, I: 102.
111 Clark, *Acadia*, 100.
112 Reid, "Styles of Colonization," 108.
113 Trudel, *HNF*, 3, II: 92.
114 Reid, *Maine, Charles II and Massachusetts*, 49.
115 D'Entremont, *Histoire du Cap-Sable*, 2:658; Larin, *La contribution du Haut-Poitou*, 98–9.
116 Choquette, *Frenchmen into peasants*, 367.
117 White, "La généalogie des trente-sept familles."
118 Clark, *Acadia*, 114.
119 Campbell, "The Seigneurs of Acadie," 303.
120 D'Entremont, *Histoire du Cap-Sable*, 2, chapters 15 and 16, passim; Trudel, *HNF*, 3, II: 102n.9.
121 ADCM, Notaire Teueleron, Registre, 1679–1680, ff.272.3 et verso, cited in d'Entremont, *Histoire du Cap-Sable*, 2:368–71.
122 This has been the subject of extensive archeological work; see Faulkner and Faulkner, *The French at Pentagoet*.
123 Ibid., 20.
124 "un beau & bon Fort"; "Il y a une grande étenduë de prairies que la marée couvroit & que le sieur d'Aunay fit desecher: elle porte à present de beau & bon froment": Ganong, ed., *Description*, English: 123; French: 474.
125 In what follows I have found the work of Clout, *Themes in the historical geography of France*, of great value. But see also Leonard, "The origin and dispersal of dykeland technology."
126 Clout, *The historical geography of France*, 194.
127 Ibid., 198.
128 ADCM, La Rochelle, Minutes Jupin, ff.207–8.
129 The most recent study of dyke construction is that of Milligan, *Maritime*

dykelands. See also Cormier, *Les aboiteaux en Acadie*; Cormier, "Nos aboiteaux"; and LeBlanc, "Les aboiteaux de Barachois" and "Entrevues sur les aboiteaux."

130 Price, "The transatlantic economy," in Greene and Pole, ed., *Colonial British America*, 23.

131 Massignon, *Les parlers français*, 1:34.

132 Trudel, *HNF*, 3, II: 82.

133 "deux cens hommes, tants soldats, laboureurs, que autres artisans, sans compter les hommes et les enfans, ni les Capucins ni les enfans sauvages. Il y a en outre vingt menages francois qui sont passes avec leurs familles ...": BN, Nouv. acq. fr., Ms. 9281.

134 "les tenans toujours esclaves sans leur y laisser faire aucun profit": *Denys*, English: 151; French: 483.

135 See Reid, "Styles of colonization," 111. His evidence is taken from documents in the legal proceedings of the Le Borgne family in 1675 (NAC, C11D, 1, f.68).

136 ADCM, Minutes Jupin, ff.207–8.

137 Johnston, *A history of the Catholic Church in eastern Nova Scotia*, 1:8–18; see also Dragon, *L'Âcadie et ses 40 robes noires*, 69ff.

138 Accounts of this are found in *JR*, vols.4–9, passim.

CHAPTER FOUR

1 See Braudel and Labrousse, ed., *Histoire économique et sociale de la France*, vol.1, in particular Richard Gascon, "La France du mouvement: les commerces et les villes," 229–394.

2 Population figures are debatable. The figure for France is that of Goubert, *Louis XIV and twenty million Frenchmen*; for the St Lawrence, it is that of Trudel, *HNF*, 2:92; for Acadia, it is my own.

3 Hill, *Reformation to industrial revolution*, 61.

4 See Brenner, *Merchants and revolution.*

5 Population statistics for the seventeenth century are most unreliable. On the reasons why this is so, see Cassedy, *Demography in early America.*

6 Bailyn, *The New England merchants*, 86.

7 See Ashley, *Financial and commercial policy.*

8 The policy of the English government was put forward in *A declaration of the Parliament ... relating to the affairs and proceedings between this Commonwealth and the States General of the United Provinces* (London, 1652) and *The case stated between England and the United Provinces* (London, 1652). Both pamphlets are available in the British Library.

9 Davies, *The early Stuarts*, 220.

10 William I. Roberts, 3rd, "Robert Sedgwick," *DCB*, 1:604–5; Bailyn, *The New England merchants*, 79–80.

11 Bond dated 20 Feb. 1646, cited in Bailyn, *The New England merchants*, 79.

12 Published in Leverett Papers, MHS *Collections*, series 4, 2:230–2.

13 Leverett to Cromwell, 4 July 1654, PAC *Report*, 1923, app. D, 90.

14 C. Bruce Fergusson: "John Leverett," *DCB*, 1:474–5.

15 Robert Sedgwick to Oliver Cromwell, 1 July 1654, in Birch, ed., *A collection of the state papers of John Thurloe*, 2:418–19.

16 Mark Harrison to the navy commissioners, 1 July 1654, cited in Reid, *Acadia, Maine and New Scotland*, 135.

17 Document of 1654 partially printed in *Coll. Man. N.F.*, 1:144.

18 Ganong, ed., *Description*, 99.

19 The actual strength of the garrisons and their equipment is debatable. These figures are approximate and come from reports, after the event, by Leverett, who was not part of the expedition.

20 Roberts, "Robert Sedgwick"; see also Dennis Charles Brian Doherty, "Oliver Cromwell, Robert Sedgewick, John Leverett and the Acadian adventure of 1654."

21 NAC, AC, C11D, 1, f.2, "Deposition before the French court ... 1701," passim.

22 "Letter from Major Robert Sedgwick, September 24th, 1654," cited in Faulkner and Faulkner, *The French at Pentagoet*, 20.

23 Reference to a series of documents in a court case, "Peter Crushett vs. Robert Sedgwick, April 11th, 1657," cited in Faulkner and Faulkner, *The French at Pentagoet*, 32n.78.

24 Articles of capitulation printed in *Coll Man. N.F.*, 1:145–9.

25 Trudel, *HNF*, 3, I:89.

26 Ganong, ed. *Description*, 104. Jeanne Motin had at least eight children with d'Aulnay, and she had another five with La Tour. See Campbell, "The seigneurs of Acadie," 89; d'Entremont, *Histoire du Cap-Sable*, 3:858; George MacBeath, "Jeanne Motin," *DCB*, 1:514.

27 *Coll Man. N.F.*, 1:145–9; Ignace de Paris, "Acadia," PAC *Report*, 1904, app. H, 337, gives the English version.

28 White, "La généalogie des trente-sept familles," 83; "Familles éstablies a l'Acadie, 1671," PAC *Report*, 1905, app. A.

29 "a titre de sundic des habitants, Guillaume Trahan signe l'acte de capitulation de Port Royal": NAC, AC, C11D, 1, f.99, 16 Aug. 1654.

30 Zeller, *Les institutions de la France*, 37.

31 "Syndics de village ... n'avaient rien d'agréeable ni de profitable": Marion, *Dictionnaire des institutions de la France*, 523.

32 Trudel, *HNF*, 3, II:255.

33 NAC, MG 18 (Leverett Papers), f.4, Leverett to Cromwell, 8 Sept. 1654; published in Birch, ed., *A collection of the state papers of John Thurloe*, 2:489.

34 Massachusetts General Court to Sedgwick, cited in Rawlyk, *Nova Scotia's Massachusetts*, 24.

35 MHS *Collections*, series 3, vol.7, John Endecott, governor, to Madam D'Aulnay, 12 April 1651, 117.

36 "devoirs seigneuriaux, auxquels ils sont obligés par leurs concessions."

37 Harris, *The seigneurial system in early Canada*, presents a fine analysis of these charges in chapter 5, 63ff.

38 This estimate is based on working back from the 1671 census, about which more later.

39 Reid, *Acadia, Maine and New Scotland*, 117.

40 Brebner, *New England's outpost*, 15.

41 AN, AAE, Correspondance politique, Angleterre, 64, f.298, Bordeaux to Mazarin, 31 Dec. 1654.

42 "le Gouverneur des forts que les Anglois ont pris."

43 See Davis, *The rise of the Atlantic economies*, 127–9; Cassedy, *Demography in early America*, 37–40.

44 Bailyn, *The New England merchants*, 94.

45 Sachse, "Migrations of New Englanders to England."

46 Cited in Rawlyk, *Nova Scotia's Massachusetts*, 26; Fergusson, "John Leverett," *DCB*, 1:475. Leverett returned to Boston in 1663 and was major-general of Massachusetts from 1663 to 1673. He became governor of that colony in 1671 and remained so until his death in 1678/9.

47 Commission to Captain John Leverett, 23 Nov. 1655, partially printed in Murdoch, *A history of Nova Scotia*, 1:133.

48 Rawlyk, *Nova Scotia's Massachusetts*, 26; see also Bailyn, *The New England merchants*, 92.

49 Accounts of 13 May 1654, recorded in December of that year: "Papers of d'Aulnay and La Tour," MHS *Collections*, series 3, 7:118–19. See also Boston Public Library, Rare Book Department, Joshua Scottow, account books. Scottow, who immigrated to Massachusetts in the 1630s, had risen to a prominent position over the years: Bailyn, *The New England merchants*, 122.

50 Rawlyk, *Nova Scotia's Massachusetts*, 26; see also Huia Ryder [in collaboration with], "Sir Thomas Temple," *DCB*, 1:636–7.

51 Huia G. Ryder [in collaboration with], "William Crowne, *DCB*, 1:241–2.

52 Leverett Papers, 1655, MHS *Collections*, series 4, 2:22.

53 AN, AAE, Correspondance politique, Angleterre, 66, ff.40–1, Petit to Bertheret, 5 April 1655; Reid, *Acadia, Maine and New England*, 136.

54 PRO, CO 1, 13, f.11, patent, 9 Aug. 1656; the most detailed account of the arrangements is found in d'Entremont, *Histoire du Cap-Sable*, 2:722–5.

55 *Mem. des Com. du Roi*, vol.2, pt.2, 290–1.

56 Concessions of Îles-aux-Loups-marins (Seal Island) and Îles de la baie de Tousquet (Tusket Island) and perhaps land at Cap Nègre were made, probably in 1653, to Amand Lalloue by Charles de La Tour: d'Entremont, *Histoire du Cap-Sable*, 2:693ff.

57 Indenture, 20 Sept. 1656, in Trask et al., *Suffolk Deeds*, vol.3 (Boston, 1885), 325–30.

58 Boston Public Library, Rare Books Department, Joshua Scottow account books, f.1+.

59 Ibid., f.2+.

60 "en lacquelle j'ay apprins la mort de Monsieur de la Tour jadis lieutenant pour le Roy en ses pais": cited in d'Entremont, *Histoire du Cap-Sable*, 2:727.

61 On the development of Amerindian relationships with the newcomers during the first half of the seventeenth century, see Thorp, "Equals of the king"; and Bourque, "Ethnicity on the Maritime peninsula."

62 20 Nov. 1657: *Coll. Man. N.F.*, 1:151; see also Mason Wade, "Emmanuel Le Borgne," *DCB*, 1:433–5.

63 The St George is a tiny river, roughly half-way between the Kennebec and the Penobscot.

64 PRO, *Cal. St. Papers*, Colonial, 13, ff.53, 54, "Complaint of the ambassador of France ..."; see also NAC, NS/A,1:53.

65 NAC, NS/A, 1:77, "Interregnum"; see also Thomas Lake to John Leverett, 2 Sept. 1658, MHS *Collections*, series 3, 7:120.

66 Arthur Howard Buffington, "Sir Thomas Temple in Boston," Colonial Society of Massachusetts, *Transactions*, 27:311–12.

67 It is always difficult to assess the value of money across time periods. Further, the use of the *livre* for coinage by both England and France complicates matters. These figures are based on a number of sources, in particular the work of Trudel and Braudel.

68 See Debien, "Engagés pour le Canada"; and Ryder, "William Crowne."

69 "Pour un passager ordinaire ...": Trudel, *HNF*, 3, II:298.

70 Ibid., 3, I:282.

71 Wicken, "Encounters with tall sails, " 182.

72 Clément Cormier, "Alexandre Le Borgne de Belle-Isle," *DCB*, 1:435–6; Bosher, *Négociants et navires*, 90–1.

73 MA, 2, f.209, Order of Massachusetts Council on complaint of Thomas Temple, 4 March 1662.

74 Ganong, *Denys*, 101–2.

75 Reid, *Acadia, Maine and New Scotland*, 139.

76 The yearly details of Temple's finances can be found in papers scattered through various archives: see Reid, *Acadia, Maine and New Scotland*, 247n.68.

77 Rawlyk, *Nova Scotia's Massachusetts*, 30.

78 Bailyn, *The New England merchants*, 110–11.

79 This man was a favourite of the then lord chancellor, Clarendon: Rawlyk, *Nova Scotia's Massachusetts*, 29.

80 PRO, CO 1, 14, f.21, petition of Thomas Elliott, 19 July 1660.

81 All this has been disentangled by Reid in *Acadia, Maine and New Scotland*, 139; see also, in the same work, 247nn.69–71.

82 PRO, SP, Colonial, 16, f.86, "Bounds of Sir Thomas Temple's patent of Novia [sic] Scotia," July 1662; PRO, SP 44/7, f.148, warrant to the attorney general, 7 July 1662.

83 NAC, AC, C11D, 1, f.118, Memorandum of Le Borgne du Coudray complaining of this activity, 23 Nov. 1665.

84 Letters patent issued 30 Jan. 1654: Ganong, *Denys*, 61–7.

85 Ibid., 38.

86 Ibid., 158.

87 George MacBeath, "Nicolas Denys," *DCB*, 1:256–9; d'Entremont, *Histoire du Cap-Sable*, 2:700.

88 F. Grenier, "François Doublet," *DCB*, 1:277; d'Entremont, *Denys*, 343.

89 D'Entremont, *Denys*, 29.

90 D'Entremont, *Denys*, 14; Alfred G. Bailey, "Richard Denys de Fronsac," *DCB*, 1:259–61.

91 Bailey, "Richard Denys de Fronsac," 260.

92 Breda, 1 July 1667: AN, Joly de Fleury, 2514, Art. VI, *Status quo ante* for colonial possessions (photocopy in Library of Congress). For an account of the short war and the way it entangled England with France, see Ogg, *England in the reign of Charles II*, 1:307–13.

93 From the sixteenth century until 1752, France used the Gregorian calendar and the British Isles used the Julian system; the difference between the two calendars was ten days during the seventeenth century and eleven days for the eighteenth century. In this book, where the difference in dates is important for the interpretation of documents, both calendars are noted: "N.S." (New Style) for dates in the Gregorian calendar and "O.S." (Old Style) for dates in the Julian calendar. Also, during the same period, the British Isles and the continent differed in the dating of the years: most countries in Europe began the year on 1 January but Britain's year began on 25 March. From the mid-seventeenth century, therefore, official government documents in Britain frequently cited the overlap in years for the months of January to March: e.g., January 1700/01. I have followed the same convention.

94 *Mem. Eng. and Fr. Com.*, 1:580, 587.

95 Edward Rawson to Lord Arlington, 20 May 1669, PRO, *Cal. St. Papers*, Colonial, 1669–1674, 25.

96 PRO, CO 23, f.86, Temple to Privy Council, 24 Nov. 1668.

97 See Reid, *Acadia, Maine and New Scotland*, 156–7.

98 *Mem. Eng. and Fr. Com.*, 1:601.

99 NAC, AC, series B, 1, f.158, Royal authorization to the Sieur de Grand-fontaine, 22 July 1669.

100 Walker had immigrated to Massachusetts sometime in the 1630s and by 1640 was a member of the General Court. See C. Bruce Fergusson, "Richard Walker," *DCB*, 1:666–7.

101 *Mem. Eng. and Fr. Com.*, 1:604–6.

102 AN, AAE, Mémoires et documents, Amérique, 5, ff.277–8, Treaty between the Sieur de Grandfontaine and Temple, 7 July 1670.

103 René Baudry, "Hector d'Andigné de Grandfontaine," *DCB*, 1:61–3.

104 See the description in *Mem. Eng. and Fr. Com.*, 1:611–12. See also the fine account of this fort and its history in Faulkner and Faulkner, *The French at Pentagoet*, 273–81.

105 George MacBeath, "Pierre de Joybert de Soulanges et de Marson," *DCB*, 1:398–400.

106 *Mem. Eng. and Fr. Com.*, 1:612; partially printed in Murdoch, *A history of Nova Scotia*, 1:147.

107 *Mem. Eng. and Fr. Com.*, 1:613; Murdoch, *A history of Nova Scotia*, 1:148.

108 "Instructions pour le Chevalier de Grand Fontaine," 5 March 1670, *Mon. N.F.*, 1:193–4.

109 For an introduction to this topic, see Mousnier, *La plume, la faucille et le marteau.*

110 NAC, G1–466, 2–13. There have been numerous publications of this census. These include *Census of Canada, 1870–71* (Ottawa, 1876), vol.4, 10ff.; see also, PAC *Report*, 1905 (Ottawa, 1905).

111 William F.E. Morley, "Hugues Randin," *DCB*, 1:565.

112 Clark, *Acadia*, 121; Rumilly: *L'Acadie française*, 110–11.

113 "Pierre Melanson a refusé de donner son aage et Le nombre de ses bestiaux et de terres et sa femme ma respondu si jestois si fou de courir les rues pour des choses de mesme": PAC *Report*, 1905, app. A, "Familles establies à l'Acadie," 6.

114 Massignon, *Les parlers français*, 1:42.

115 Clémont Cormier, "Philippe Mius d'Entremont," *DCB*, 1:510; d'Entremont, *Histoire du Cap-Sable*, 3:816ff.

116 Goubert, *Louis XIV and twenty million Frenchmen*, 21.

117 A sophisticated analysis of the living standards of the Acadians in the last three decades of the seventeenth century is that of LeBlanc and Vanderlinden, "Pauvre en France, riche en Acadie?" Vanderlinden has constructed a scale of wealth which takes into consideration family size, land cleared, and animals kept.

118 Anderson, "King Phillip's herds," 603.

119 Jameson, ed., *Johnson's wonder working providence*, 68–9.

120 Anderson, "King Phillip's herds," 604.

121 "Tant en France qu'ailleurs": PAC *Report*, 1905, 5.

122 Dupont, *Histoire populaire de l'Acadie*, 40ff.

123 Thompson, *The making of the English working class*, 18.

124 Hubka, "Farm family mutuality," 13, 15.

125 Wrightson, *English society*, 53–4.

126 Rutman, "Assessing the little communities of early America."

127 On the issue of the number of livestock and the amount of cleared land needed for subsistence farming, as opposed to commercial farming, see Clark, *Acadia*, 170.

128 On the genealogy of this most prolific Acadian family, see White, "La généalogie des trente-sept familles."

129 Cited in Reid, "Styles of colonization," 110–11.

130 See chapter 5.

131 "Depuis que le sieur de Menou s'est veu seul proprietaire de l'accadie il a faict bastir au port Royal le fort qui supciste, une Eglize, et un Convent ...": cited in Reid, "Styles of colonization," 110.

132 Ganong, *Denys*, 123.

133 It is possible that he might have been either a woodworker or a stonemason. The word *tailleur* is often used as part of a double noun: *tailleur de bois*

(woodworker) and *tailleur de pierre* (stonecutter). See Massignon, *Les parlers français*, 1:232.

CHAPTER FIVE

1 Governors received their appointments from France, sometimes on the recommendation of the authorities in Quebec; commanders were most often directly named by the governor in Quebec. Hector d'Andigné de Grandfontaine held his appointment from 1670 to 1673. He was followed by Jacques de Chambly, 1673–78; Pierre de Joybert de Soulanges et de Marson, as commander, 1676–78; and Michel Leneuf de La Vallière et de Beaubassin, as commander and then governor, 1678–84. All the following were, sooner or later, named governor: François-Marie Perrot, 1684–87; Louis-Alexandre des Friches de Meneval, 1687–90; Joseph Robinau de Villebon, 1691–1700; Claude-Sébastien de Villieu, 1700–01; Jacques-François de Monbeton de Brouillan, 1701–05; Simon-Pierre Denys de Bonaventure, 1705–06; and Daniel d'Auger de Subercase, 1706–10.

2 "quand j'aurai besoin de vos avis je vous ferai appeler ... ne déliveront pas une seule expédition je dis jusqu'à un passeport ... sans avoir reçu préalavlement mes ordres": Dinfreville, *Louis XIV*, 157; Wolf, *Louis XIV*, 133.

3 All ministers, even Colbert, were kept very much in a subordinate place: see ibid., 132.

4 Dreyss, ed., *Mémoires de Louis XIV*.

5 *Historical statistics of the United States*, pt. 2, table 1, 1168.

6 On this, see Pierre Léon and et Charles Carrière, "L'appel des marchés," in Braudel and Labrousse, ed., *Histoire économique et sociale de la France*, 2:161–97.

7 A short account of Colbert's policy, and its particular importance for Canada, is that of Jaenen, "Le Colbertisme."

8 See Rothkrug, *Opposition to Louis XIV*.

9 The best introduction to the maze of government institutions is Mousnier, *La vénalité des offices sous Henri IV et Louis XIII*. Colbert's father had been as much a tax-collector as a businessman, capable of funding the advancement of his children into the labyrinthine paths of royal service. Bourgeon, *Les Colbert avant Colbert*, 224, 240.

10 One of his cousins was Jean-Baptiste Colbert de Saint-Pouange, who had reached a high rank in the Department de la Guerre by 1636 and married the sister of François-Michel Le Tellier, its then head. Bourgeon, *Les Colbert avant Colbert*, 216, 225.

11 Murat, *Colbert*, 9.

12 On the twenty-five years of litigation that followed these actions, see Trudel, *HNF*, 3, I:370–4. See also Trudel's introductory essay, "New France, 1524–1713," in *DCB*, 1:26–38. Zoltvany, ed., *The government of New France*, is a useful summary.

13 Young and Dickinson, *A short history of Quebec*, 40.

14 Based upon tables in Proulx, *Between France and New France*, 55–8.

15 The *Saint-Sébastien* in 1665 took 117 days: Camu, *Le Saint-Laurent et les Grands Lacs*, 60.

16 "intendant de la justice, police et finances en nos pays de Canada, Acadie, et Isle de Terreneuve et autres pays de la France Septentrionale": *EO*, 3:33–5.

17 NAC, AN, F 4, Collection Moreau de St. Mery, Canada, 2, ff.61–4, Colbert to Grandfontaine, 11 March 1671; printed in part in *Coll. Man. N.F.*, 1:208–10.

18 AN, F 185, 21, Accounts for colonial expenditures, 1671.

19 Eccles, *Canada under Louis XIV*, 30.

20 Grandfontaine's original instructions on the positioning of his main force at Pentagöuet had been drawn up by the intendant of Rochefort, Colbert de Terron. See René Baudry, "Hector d'Andigné de Grandfontaine," *DCB*, 1:61–3.

21 The full expression of Talon's views is found in his letter to Colbert, 4 Oct. 1665, *RAPQ*, 1930–31, 32–7.

22 "Le principal point surtout auquel vous devrez vous appliquer est de travailler par touttes sortes de moyens à l'establissement des soldats et des familles dans les postes de Port Royal, rivière St Jean et dans toutte l'estendue de la Coste qui appartient à Sa Majesté, en les aydant de tous les secours qui sont en vos mains et en les maintenant en paix et en repos, en sorte que se voyant bien traittés et à leurs ayses, d'autres François soyent conviez d'aller habiter en ce païs là": NAC, Collection Moreau de St Mery, ff.61–5 (also *Coll. Man. N.F.* 1:209), Colbert to Grandfontaine, 11 March 1671.

23 "le plus considérable bien que vous puisiez faire à l'un et l'autre de cerdeux päis": Colbert to Talon, 11 Jan. 1671, *RAPQ*, 1930–31, 47.

24 "et ses soigns à faire une liason et correspondance avec Boston pour en tirer ses besoings": Talon to Colbert, 10 Nov. 1670, ibid., 131.

25 NAC, AC, C11D, 2, f.139, "Mémoire concernant l'Acadie par le chevalier de Grandfontaine," 1671.

26 Daigle, "Nos amis, les ennemis," 81. See also Baudry, "Hector d'Andigné de Grandfontaine."

27 Talon to Colbert, 11 Nov. 1671, *RAPQ*, 1930–31, 161.

28 "Mémoire de Grandfontaine à Colbert."

29 Ibid.

30 "une joie sensible de voir Pentagouet ... entre les mains dy Roy"; "un effect de la crainte quils ont du voisinage des Francois ou d'une veritable passion de passer sous la domination de Sa Majesté": Talon to Colbert, 11 Sept. 1671, *RAPQ*, 1930–31, 165.

31 "Mémoire de Grandfontaine à Colbert."

32 Reid, *Acadia, Maine and New Scotland*, 154.

33 The commission of appointment has not survived, but numerous documents bearing his signature and attesting to his position exist. See Clément Cormier, "Philippe Mius d'Entremont," *DCB*, 1:510–11.

34 Colbert to Talon, 3 July 1669, *RAPQ*, 1930–31, 114.

35 "Mémoire de Grandfontaine à Colbert."

36 For example, it was stated at the trial of Jean Campagna, who was charged, in 1685, with having practised sorcery in Beaubassin, that he and the witness Renault *dit* Bordonnaut arrived at Pentagöeut and were later sent to Port Royal by Grandfontaine. Archives Nationales de Québec, Prévôté de Quebec, registres 11, 24. Part of the proceedings are printed in Rameau de Saint-Père, *Une colonie féodale*, 2:304–7.

37 See Moogk, "Reluctant exiles."

38 Colbert to Grandfontaine, 11 March 1671, *Coll. Man. N.F.*, 1:209.

39 "Concession en faveur de Martin D'Arpentigny," printed in *Pièces et documents*, 1:254–5.

40 "récit de la bonté des terres qui bornent la Rivière St. Jean et qu'elles sont capable de produire abondamment des grains de toutte espece ... pesches sédentaires de morues au autres poissons": Concession en faveur du Sr. Pottier de St Denis, ibid., 1:255–6.

41 "... un nombre de tenanciers suffisans pour former une bourgade ou communauté": ibid., 1:256.

42 George MacBeath, "Pierre de Joybert de Soulanges et de Marson," *DCB*, 1:398–400. Their daughter, Louise-Élisabeth, would marry Philippe de Rigaud de Vaudreuil, the governor of New France from 1703 to 1725.

43 A league was roughly three miles.

44 The act of concession is in *Pièces et documents*, 1:254, 258–9.

45 Harris, *The seigneurial system*. Nor was seigneurial control in France ever a uniform system from Normandy to Provence: see Mandrou, *Classes et luttes de classe en France*; Beik, *Absolutism and society*.

46 Much of the case of Agathe de La Tour, settled in 1733, is printed in Lanctot, Johnston, and Shortt, *Documents*, 190ff.

47 Faulkner and Faulkner, *The French at Pentagoet*, 20.

48 "le garde y subsiste, d'autant plus aisement qu'elle est fort assistée de la pesche et du coquillage que le Voisinage de la mer luy donne abondamment ... tous les ans quantité de viande en eschange de quelques droguets et autres étoffes de la fabrique de Baston": NAC, AC, C11, 3, f.172, "Mémoire de M. Talon au Ministre" (printed in *RAPQ*, 1930–31, 163–4).

49 "L'état misérable où M le chevalier de Grandfontaine ... se trouvait ...en lui envoyant ... les provisions": Frontenac to minister, 2 Nov. 1672, printed in full in *RAPQ*, 1926–27, 10–23.

50 "Si le roi voulait seulement faire pour la conservation de ce pays, ce qu'il fait pour la moindre des villes qu'il a prises sur les Hollandais, et envoyer pour le Canada et l'Acadie ce qu'il y a de garrison dans la plus petite de ces places, nous serions à couvert de toutes sortes d'insultes et en état de faire des choses très avantageuses pour l'augmentation d'un pays qui peur devenir un jour un royaume très considérables": ibid., 15.

51 See Colbert to Talon, 4 June 1672, *RAPQ*, 1930–31, 169.

52 *Pièces et documents*, 267–8.

53 The listing of armaments is printed in full in *Mem. Eng. and Fr. Com.*, 1:606–10.

54 The question of the amount of powder and shot necessary for the guns is discussed in Duffy, *Fire and stone*, 85.

55 Charlevoix, *History and general description of New France*, 3:188, gives a complement of thirty.

56 See account in Faulkner and Faulkner, *The French at Pentagoet*, 29.

57 Webster, *Cornelius Steenwyck*, 3.

58 "Plea and answer of Peter Rodrigo and others," *Doc. Hist. St. Maine*, 6:54.

59 See Henri Brunet's account of this episode: BN, Collection Clairambault, 864, pt.2, f.57, Brunet to Jacques Godefroy, 7 Nov. 1674.

60 Rawlyk, *Nova Scotia's Massachusetts*, 38.

61 "Boucaniers qui venoient de St Domingue et qui avoient passé à Baston": Frontenac to the minister, 14 Nov. 1674, *Coll. Man. N.F.*, 1:230.

62 Colbert to Frontenac, 15 March 1675, ibid., 1:232.

63 Accounts given in *Cal. St. Papers, 1675–76*, 469.

64 A detailed description of Rhoades's actions is found in Rawlyk, *Nova Scotia's Masschusetts*, 38–9. For a full account of the trial, see MA, 61, ff.60–122.

65 Frontenac to Colbert, 17 March 1674, *Coll. Man. N.F.*, 1:230.

66 See Georges Cerbelaud Salagnac, "Jean-Vincent Abbadie de Saint-Castin," *DCB*, 2:4–7, and Le Blant, *Une figure légendaire*. The latter work contains an appendix of primary documents relating to Saint-Castin and his family.

67 Leach, *The northern colonial frontier*, 56.

68 For a brief account, and bibliography, see Leach, *Arms for empire*, 59–69, 517ff.

69 Ibid., 65.

70 Leach, *Flintlock and tomahawk*, 242–50.

71 See Rawlyk, *Nova Scotia's Massachusetts*, 41–2.

72 Jennings, *The invasion of America*, 323–6; Leach, *Arms for empire*, 65–6.

73 Reid, *Maine, Charles II, and Massachusetts*, 55–62, and *Acadia, Maine and New Scotland*, 167.

74 Reid, *Acadia, Maine and New Scotland*, 167.

75 Kennebec sachems to Massachusetts governor, 1 July 1677, cited in Reid, *Acadia, Maine and New Scotland*, 169.

76 Ibid., 174.

77 Quoted in Rawlyk, *Nova Scotia's Massachusetts*, 40.

78 Noble, ed., *Courts of assistance*, 2:86–8.

79 Shurtleff, ed., *Records of ... Massachusetts Bay*, 5:168.

80 Colbert to Frontenac, 15 March 1675, *Coll. Man. N.F.*, 1:232.

81 Macbeath, "Pierre de Joybert de Soulanges et de Marson."

82 Daigle, "Nos amis, les ennemis," 87.

83 J.-Roger Comeau, "Michel Leneuf de La Vallière de Beaubassin, *DCB*, 2: 409–11.

84 Trudel, *HNF*, 4:222.

85 On the question of the value of Cape Breton coal at this early stage, see Clark, *Acadia*, 267; Trudel, *HNF*, 4:447.

86 Comeau, "Michel Leneuf de La Vallière de Beaubassin."

87 "y a de fort belles, & grandes prairies à perte de veuë ... Le pays [serait] ... de grande fertilité s'il estoit cultiué": *JR*, 3: English, 249, 251; French, 248, 250.

88 See Ruth A. Whitehead, "Navigation des Micmacs le long de la côté est de l'Atlantique," in Martijn, *Les Micmacs et la mer*, 224–32.

89 The evidence for this is the numerous reports that date from 1685. See, besides this chapter, Campbell, "The seigneurs of Acadie," 23.

90 "les habitants de la province qui se trouveraient en possession de terres et héritages qu'ils cultivent, habitent et font valoir et font cultiver": Lanctôt, *L'Acadie des origines*, 66.

91 *Mém. des Com.* du Roi, 2:578.

92 See Léopold Lamontagne, "Jacques Duchesneau de la Doussinière et d'Ambault," *DCB*, 1:287–90.

93 BN, Nouv. acq. fr., vol.9281, f.152, Collection Margry, Ordre du Duchesneau, intendant de la Nouvelle-France, 21 Aug. 1677 (précis in d'Entremont, *Denys*, 45–6).

94 Jean Daigle, "Michel Le Neuf de La Vallière," 44.

95 In ibid., Jean Daigle presents an excellent summary of Frontenac's letters on this matter, using the *RAPQ* publication of the correspondence (1926–27:11, 128) as well as the correspondence of Frontenac with Seignalay (NAC, AC, C11, 5, ff.274, 304, 322). La Vallière's commission is reported in NAC, AC, series B, 10, ff.1–7; partially printed in *Coll. Man. N.F.*, 1:310–11.

96 NAC, AC, C11A, 5, f.307, Duchesneau to the minister, 13 Nov. 1681. For an analysis of the relationship between Frontenac and Duchesneau, see Daigle, "Michel Le Neuf de La Vallière," 47. On Duchesneau, see Léopold Lamontagne, "Jacques Duchesneau de la Doussinière et d'Ambault," *DCB*, 1:287–90.

97 See also Campbell, "The seigneurs of Acadie," 311–12.

98 "Ms^r de La Vallière ... m'a fait savoir qu'il avoit esté à Porte Royal, où les habitans avoient temoigné quelque peine de recevoir ses ordres, soit par l'accoutumance où ils estoient d'avoir esté quelques années sans commandant, soit par les divisions qu'il y avoit entre eux, soit enfin par quelque inclination angloise et parlementaries, que leur inspirent la frequentation et le commerce qu'ils ont avec ceux de Baston ....": Frontenac to Louis XIV, 6 Nov. 1679, *RAPQ*, 1926–27, 111.

99 "ayant fait prester un nouveau serment de fidélité à tous les habitans, et fair faire des réjouissances publiques, pour les glorieuses conquestes que Vostre Majesté fit l'année dernière": ibid.

100 See Vanderlinden, *À la rencontre de l'histoire*, 92–7.

101 "Une pièce de terre et de prairie par eux mise en culture et sur laquelle ils habitent, bornée d'un côté: à l'est, par la grande prairie, à l'ouest, par le ruisseau Domanchin [Saint-Père reads this as du Moulin, which makes sense], au midi, par la rivière Dauphin ... et au nord, par la montagne": Rameau de Saint-Père, *Une colonie féodale*, 2:318; English version printed in Murdoch, *A history of Nova Scotia*, 1:156–7.

102 "un denier tournois de rente foncière, un chapon et un boisseau d'avoine ...": ibid.

103 NAC, MG 9, B 9–2, "Assignation par Michel Le Neuf de La Vallière," 20 March 1682.

104 Innis, *The cod fisheries*, 116.

105 Innis reports a warehouse in that area in 1686: Innis, *Select documents*, 55–6.

106 McCully, "The New England-Acadia fishery dispute," 278.

107 Innis, *The cod fisheries*, 122; La Morandière, *Histoire de la pêche française*, 1:428ff.

108 La Morandière, *Histoire de la pêche française*, 1:354; Ganong, ed., *Description*, 338; Innis, *Select documents*, 47.

109 BN, Company records, *Manuscripts de la collection des Cinq Cents de Colbert*, no.204ff., 194v–200v; see also Louis-André Vignereau, "Letters of an Acadian trader."

110 Frontenac to minister of the Marine, 2 Nov. 1681, *Coll. Man. N.F.* 1:284; *RAPQ*, 1926–27, 131–8.

111 Donald F. Chard, "John Nelson," *DCB*, 2:493–4; for a full biography of Nelson, see Johnson, *John Nelson*.

112 Rawlyk, *Nova Scotia's Massachusetts*, 35–6.

113 Reid, *Acadia, Maine and New Scotland*, 173.

114 *Mass. Records*, 5:373–4.

115 Rawlyk, *Nova Scotia's Massachusetts*, 45.

116 NAC, MG 11, 55, f.188, "Autorisation de La Vallière a John Nelson," 22 Oct. 1682.

117 The king to Frontenac, 9 May 1682, *RAPQ*, 1926–27, 141.

118 On the political background of this matter, see Quéniart, *La révocation de l'édit de Nantes*.

119 Bosher, *Négociants et navires*, 41; Bailyn, *The New England merchants*, 147–8.

120 BN, Collection Clairambault, 1016, f.306, Nicolas Denys to Richard Denys, 5 Nov. 1680; English translation printed in Ganong, "Historical and geographical documents relating to Nova Scotia," 15.

121 Partially printed in *Coll. Man. N.F.*, 1:279–80. See also Archives du Séminaire du Québec, Lettre N, no.61.

122 NAC, AC, C11D, 1, ff.150–1.

123 C. Bruce Fergusson: "Charles Duret de Chevry de La Boulaye," *DCB*, 1:298–9.

124 "Il est important de ne point donner d'atteinte à l'édict qui deffend aux Huguenots de s'éstablir en Canada, et surtout de ne les point souffrir en Acadie" (19 Nov. 1682): *Coll. Man. N.F.*, 1:291.

125 NAC, AC, C11D,1, ff.150–70, documents relating to Bergier; partially printed in *Coll. Man. N.F.*, 1:290. See also the account in Webster, *Acadia*, 206.

126 "Mémoire sur l'Acadie," 1682, *Coll. Man. N.F.*, 1:292.

127 Ibid., 293; NAC, AC, C11D, 1, f.163, Bergier to Seigneley, 1682; Daigle, "Nos amis, les ennemis," 98, argues, convincingly, that this has to be 1683.

128 "Les vaisseaux estrangers, qui seroient trouvez faisant le commerce de pelleteries ou la pesche le long de la dite coste, seroient pris et amenez dans

les ports de son Royaume pour y estre confisquez": "Mémoire de l'ambasadeur de France sur l'Acadie," 1684, *Coll. Man. N.F.*, 1:329.

129 Augustin-Thierry, ed., *Un colonial au temps de Colbert*, 262. I think it is possible that Challes is the author of the anonymous "Mémoire de l'ambasadeur
de France sur l'Acadie," 1684, printed in *Coll. Man. N.F.*, 1:291ff.

130 Augustin-Thierry, ed., *Un colonial au temps de Colbert*, 262–5.

131 NAC, AC, series B, 2, f.16, "Register relating to Canada and the islands."

132 "Il a paru extraordinaire ... que Berger ayt entrepris cet establissement sans
que nous en ayons esté informez. Le Sieur de la Vallière n'a pu connoistre
un particulier dans le lieu où il commande ...": De Meulles to the minister,
4 Nov. 1683, printed in *Coll. Man. N.F.*. 1:298.

133 La Barre to minister, 4 Nov. 1683, printed in *Coll. Man. N.F.* 1:312–13.

134 "Il est important, Monseigneur, de ne pas permettre que les Huguenots
françois viennent former un establissement sy prosche des Anglois de la
Nouvelle Angleterre, qui sont aussy de la religion qu'on appelle réformée;
et en un païs où il ne vient point de navires de France pour y faire le commerce et qui ne subsiste que par celuy qu'il faict avec les Bastonnais": ibid.,
1:313.

135 Bishop Laval to the king, 10 Nov. 1683, *Coll. Man. N.F.*, 1:314.

136 *Coll. Man. N.F.*, 1:320.

137 ADCM, La Rochelle, B 5903, pièces 14, 15, 16, 24, 25, 26, 28, 33; "Answer to
the French concerning the fishing at Acadia," 16 Jan. 1686, *Cal. St. Papers,
1685–1688*, 142.

138 "Account of the voyage of Monsieur de Meulles to Acadie, Oct. 11,
1685–July 6, 1686," in Morse, ed., *Acadiensis Nova*, 1:118.

139 Comeau, "Michel Leneuf de La Vallière de Beaubassin"; Murdoch, *A history
of Nova Scotia*, 1:164–5.

140 Fergusson, "Charles Duret de Chevry de la Boulaye."

141 The bishop's full name was Jean-Baptiste de la Croix de Chevrières de Saint-
Vallier. See his biography, written by Alfred Rambaud, in DCB, 2:328–34.

142 Much of de Meulles report is printed in Morse, ed., *Acadiensis Nova*,
1:91–124. The actual census data was submitted by Perrot and assembled by
de Meulles.

143 "Lettre de Monseigneur l'évêque de Québec ...," in Têtu and Gagnon, ed.,
Mandements, 1:191–265.

144 Clark provides an analysis of all the census material in *Acadia*, 123–8.

145 Gysa Hynes, "Some aspects of the demography of Port Royal, 1650–1755,"
in Buckner and Frank, ed., *Atlantic Canada before Confederation*, 1:11–25.

146 Jim Potter, "Demographic development and family structure," in Greene
and Pole, ed., *Colonial British America*, 142.

147 Goubert, *Louis XIV and twenty million Frenchmen*, 21.

148 Héroux, Lahaise, and Vallerand, *La Nouvelle-France*, 222; *Historical statistics of
the United States*, table 1, 1168.

149 The copy of the census used is that of de Meulles, printed in full in Rameau
de Saint-Père, *Une colonie féodale*, 2:394–402. As Clark has pointed out, dis-

crepancies occur, both within a particular census and between differing accounts, but the variations are small. Clark, *Acadia*, 125–6.

150 Têtu et Gagnon, ed., *Mandements*, 216.

151 The actual route has been much discussed: see Caron, "De Québec en Acadie."

152 "la dernière habitation du Canada ... un pays où l'hiver durait encore": Têtu et Gagnon, ed., *Mandements*, 212.

153 "un petit fort de quatre bastions formé de pieux, et dans ce fort une maison": ibid., 214.

154 Ibid., 216.

155 His birth date is unknown: he was married in 1674 and died in 1703. W.J. Eccles, "Jacques de Meulles," *DCB*, 2:470–3.

156 Morse, ed., *Acadiensis Nova*, 1:104.

157 Ibid., 1:109.

158 Têtu et Gagnon, ed., *Mandements*, 216. See also Johnson, *A history of the Catholic Church in eastern Nova Scotia*, 1:25.

159 "l'ay esté trois jours dans cet endroit pour y rendres quelque ordonnances et remédier quelques aux abus qui glissoient parmy ces nouveaux convertis qui continuoient a faire leurs prieres publiques suivans leurs premiere religion, je les obligés dentendre la messe feste et dimanche et de ne travailler que dans les jour permis": DUA, W.I. Morse Collection, de Meulles, "Relation du voyage que j'ay fait dans l'Acadie." English translation: Morse, *Acadiensis Nova*, 1:117.

160 Consideration of the nature of inequalities in rural communities is to be found in Dessureault, "L'égalitarisme paysan." There will be a fuller discussion of economic and social divisions within the colony in later chapters.

161 Russell, *A long deep furrow*, 52.

162 Ibid.

163 Potter, "Demographic development and family structure," 134; Beauregard et al., "Famille, parenté et colonisation en Nouvelle-France"; Jarnoux, "La colonisation de la seigneurie de Batiscan."

164 Nominal version of 1686 census, printed in Rameau de Saint-Père, *Une colonie féodale*, 2:395–402. See also Lanctôt, *Familles Acadiennes*, 1:96.

164 See the excellent, if brief, study by Dunn, *Les Acadiens des Minas*.

166 De Meulles census, partially printed in Murdoch, *A history of Nova Scotia*, 1:170.

167 Saint-Vallier suggested that the inhabitants of Beaubassin had obtained some of their stock from Cap Sable, but no other primary evidence exists for this claim.

168 "les terres labourables étaient inondées de la marée, il a fallu les garantir de l'inondation par des digues qu'on a élevées à force de travail et de dépense": Têtu et Gagnon, ed., *Mandements*, 217.

169 "dessécher leurs marais": ibid., 218.

170 "la nécessité leur a donné l'industrie de se faire quelques toiles et quelques étoffes grossières, mais ils ne peuvent en fabriquer assez pour se vêtir tous": ibid., 217.

171 "Chaque particulier qui avait quelqu'idée d'un métier se lessant commu-
niqué l'un a l'autre ... pour le conserver et maintenir jusqu'à present ... tis-
serans, massons, charpentiers, meunuisiers, taillandiers .... font des baste-
mens pour aller le long des costes ... Des bas, des gants et des bonnets":
"Mémoire sur l'Île Percée et Bonaventure ... [et] Beaubassin," NAC, AC,
C11D, 2, ff.43–8.

172 "... ils cueillent un peu de grain, il s'anime à la pêche, soit celle du saumon
... soit celle de la morue ... [ils] seraient tout-à-fait irréprochables, s'ils
avaient été plus réservés à traiter de l'eau-de-vie avec les Sauvages": Têtu et
Gagnon, ed., *Mandements*, 217.

173 "L'estendue des terres concedez ... ne leur servent que pour s'eloigner des
lieux habitez, afin de s'entretenir plus facilement dans la débauche avec les
Sauvagesses": NAC, AC, C11D, 2, ff.12–24, Sieur Perrot to the minister, 9 Aug.
1686, partially printed in *Coll. Man. N.F.*, 1:365.

174 "[j'ay] publier deux ordonnances ... L'une touchant la traitte des pelletries
... La seconde concernoit les moeurs et les moyens de remedier au libertinage de plusieurs Sujets de Sa Majesté qui on des Sauvagesses chez eux et
d'autre qui les suivent dans les bois abbandonants pere et mere: DUA, W.I.
Morse Collection, de Meulles, "Relation du voyage que j'ay fait dans l'A-
cadie ...." English translation: Morse, *Acadiensis Nova*, 1:110.

175 Gérard Desjardins, "Louis Petit," DCB, 2:521–2.

176 "gens d'un naturel doux, et porté à la piété; on ne voit parmi eux ni jure-
ments, ni débauches de femmes, ni ivrognerie": Têtu et Gagnon, *Mandements*, 219.

177 Evidence from Têtu et Gagnon, *Mandements*, 1:218–21.

178 The social relationships between Mi'kmaq and Acadian will be examined in
more detail in the next chapter.

179 "Il y vient tous les printemps trois ou quatre barque anglois chargés de tout
ce qui leur est nécessaire et traittent en Echange avec leurs peltries et autres
denrées": "Mémoire ... sur la Baie de Chedabouctou"; Mémoire ... sur le
commerce de Chibouctou": NAC, AC, C11D, 2, ff.43–77, de Meulles to the
Marquis de Seignelay, 18 July 1686.

180 Information on this is contradictory. Some writers consider that the Bourgeois family imported lumber from Boston when establishing Beaubassin:
Campbell, "The seigneurs of Acadie," 24.

181 NAC, AC, C11D, 2, f.40, Perrot to the minister, 9 Aug. 1686.

182 Hemp had been mentioned as early as 1670: NAC, AC, C11D, 3, f.77, Talon
to Colbert, 10 Nov. 1670.

183 Barth writes: "I would thus expect to find, in any population of co-mingling
persons, that transactions about support, rallying, and alliance become sys-
tematically related to each other so that these forms of prestation or social
goods constitute a political system in their distribution and circulation. This
would seem to arise regardless of actors' intent or even recognition." Barth,
ed., *Scale and social organization*, 268.

CHAPTER SIX

1 On the similarity between the French and English experience, see Black, *Convergence or divergence?* especially 133ff.

2 Ibid., 138.

3 The Lords of Trade and Plantations was the name given to those responsible for the development of the colonies in the seventeenth century. In 1696 the Board of Trade was created and it endured until 1782. Thus, the official name for the members of the government responsible for colonial matters during this period was the Board of Trade. However, the body was referred to variously until 1696, in both official and private correspondence, as "Lords Commissioners for Trade and Plantations," "Council of Trade," and "Lords of Trade." Also, collections of documents, such as Akins's *Acadia*, as well as the works of historians use the terms almost interchangeably. Further, correspondence with the Board of Trade from officials in the colonies was generally addressed to "Their Lordships," a convention that most modern-day archival calendars have preserved. In this book I use "Board of Trade" except when quoting a primary source or when commenting on such a source; in these cases, the term "Board of Trade" would merely induce confusion.

4 Recent scholarship has underlined the extent to which English settlement in Newfoundland was established well before the eighteenth century; see Handcock, *So longe as there comes noe women*, 33–72.

5 See Andrews, *The colonial period*, vol.4, *England's commercial and colonial policy*, 372ff.

6 On this engaging scamp, see W.J. Eccles, "François-Marie Perrot," *DCB*, 1:540–2.

7 Mémoire de Perrot, 1685, summarized in *Coll. Man. N.F.*, 1:348; précis in Murdoch, *A history of Nova Scotia*, 1:165.

8 Meneval to the minister, 1 Dec. 1687, *Coll. Man. N.F.*, 1:410. It is interesting that Perrot is accused of sending wine and brandy *to* Boston: trade records usually show such goods going the other way. I think it more probable that he sent furs there *for* the items listed.

9 NAC, AC, C11D, 2, f.26; partially printed in *Coll. Man. N.F.*, 1:365–6.

10 "... un grand abus touchant l'estendue des terres concedez ... afin de s'entretenir plus facilement dans la débauche avec les Sauvagesses": ibid.

11 The third son of Emmanuel Le Borgne: see chapters 4 and 5.

12 "un homme extresmement adonné au vin, qui donne des concessions au premier venue ...": NAC, AC, C11D, 2, f.26.

13 Treaty printed in *EO*, 1:258.

14 "que de regler les Limites des Terres que chacune des deux nations doit posseder": Memorandum of the French commissioners to James II, 7 Nov. 1687, cited in Reid, *Acadia, Maine and New Scotland*, 180.

15 The question of London's colonial policy is effectively analysed in W.A. Speck, "The international and imperial context," in Greene and Pole, ed.,

Colonial British America, 384–407, especially 395; and that of Versailles in Cole, *Colbert and a century of French mercantilism*, 2:1–131.

16 Proulx, *Between France and New France*, 57.

17 Rawlyk, *Nova Scotia's Massachusetts*, 49.

18 Kennedy, *The rise and fall of British naval mastery*, 76–7.

19 McCully, "The England-Acadia fishery dispute," 277; see also report by Villebon, "Memoir on the coast fisheries of Acadia and the method of conducting them," 27 Oct. 1699, in Webster, *Acadia*, 138. The original, in almost indecipherable French, is in NBM, Webster Collection, Villebon Papers. A quintal is a hundred-weight.

20 Innis, *The cod fisheries*, 118.

21 Morrison, *The embattled northeast*, 111.

22 Dean R. Snow, "Eastern Abenaki," in Sturtevant, ed., *Handbook of North American Indians*, vol.15, Bruce G. Trigger, ed., *The Northeast*, 137–48.

23 Bailey, *The conflict of European and eastern Algonkian cultures*, 88.

24 Morrison, *The embattled northeast*, 26.

25 Ibid., 90–7, 118.

26 On problems in the period up to 1650, see, in particular, Reid, "Styles of colonization," 105–17.

27 Morrison, *The embattled northeast*, 113.

28 Perrot to Dongan, 29 Aug. 1696, *Coll. Man. N.F.*, 1:366.

29 Georges Cerbelaud Salagnac, "Jean-Vincent d'Abbadie de Saint Castin," DCB, 2:4–7 at 5.

30 Printed in full in *Coll. Man. N.F.*, 2:369.

31 "... Nelson ... qui a faict beaucoup de bien aux habitans par les grands prests qu'il leur a faict dans leur plus grande nécessité": NAC, AC, C11D, f.12, Perrot to the minister, 29 Aug. 1686; partially printed in *Coll. Man. N.F.*, 1:367.

32 NAC, AC, C11D, f.238, Denonville to the minister, 16 Nov. 1686; partially printed in *Coll. Man. N.F.*, 1:369–71.

33 René Baudry, "Louis-Alexandre Des Friches de Meneval," DCB, 2:182–4.

34 NAC, AC, C11D, 2, f.78, 10 April 1687; partially printed in *Coll. Man. N.F.* 1:396–9.

35 For example, Rawlyk, *Nova Scotia's Massachusetts*, 53.

36 Baudry, "Louis-Alexandre Des Friches de Meneval," 182.

37 W.J. Eccles, "Jacques-René de Brisay de Denonville," DCB, 2:98–105 at 98.

38 Gargas, "Mon séjour de (sic) l'Acadie": DUA, W.I. Morse Collection; published in Morse, *Acadiensis Nova*, 1:166.

39 NAC, AC, series B, 13, f.42, "Instruction du Roy au Sieur de Beauregard," 30 March 1687.

40 "prétendent avoir les concessions exclusives sur de vastes estendues dudit païs, mesme avec la faculté d'accorder des concessions à d'aultres, ne se sont employez jusques'à présent, ny à la culture des terres, la nourriture des bestiaux, ny à faire aulcune pesche, et qu'ils sont uniquement occupez à la traitte dans les bois, et dans une débauche scandaleuse, et exercent aussy des vio-

lences contres les François soubs prétextes desdites concessions": ibid.; printed in *Coll. Man. N.F.*, 1:396.

41 Harris, *The seigneurial system*, 26–31.

42 Ibid., 31.

43 De Castin to Denonville, 2 July 1687, *Coll. Man. N.F.*, 1:399.

44 Andros to Sunderland, 30 March 1687, *Cal. St. Papers, 1685–88*, 7:352–3.

45 Toppan and Goodrich, ed., *Edward Randolph*, 6:216.

46 The best short account of this incident is found in McCulley, "The New England-Acadia fishery dispute," 277–90.

47 MA, 2, Council Records, 1686–87, 132.

48 Edmund Andros, "Instructions for Captain Nicholson on his voyage to Port Royal," 6 Aug. 1687, cited in McCulley, "The New England-Acadia fishery dispute," 284.

49 "[Il y a] trente hommes ... vingt bons pescheurs ... Le reste ... charpentiers, tonneliers, serruriers, massons et chirurgiens": de Chevry, "Mémoire sur la pêche sédentaire de l'Acadie," 24 Sept. 1687, *Coll. Man. N.F.*, 1:403.

50 A census was taken by Gargas in the winter of 1687–88, "Recensement de l'Acadie 1687–88," DUA; published in full in Morse, *Acadiensis Nova*, 1:144–55. Its shortcomings are discussed in Clark, *Acadia*, 124.

51 "ne contient que neuf ou dix maisons, la reste essant des granges"; "toutes sont basses, construites par des pieces de bois les uns par les autres, et couuertes de chaume, celle ou loge M. Le Gouverneur essant la seule couuerte de planches": DUA, W.I. Morse Collection, Gargas, "Mon séjour"; English translation: Morse, *Acadiensis Nova*, 1:179.

52 McCully, "The New England-Acadia fishery dispute, 288–9.

53 "nous fûmes obligez de loger dans une cuisine de M.Perrot, qui nous à servez à tous les deux de chambres, de anti-chambres, de cabines, de cuisines, de cave": DUA, W.I. Morse Collection, Gargas, "Mon séjour": English translation: Morse, *Acadiensis Nova*, 1:172.

54 NAC, AC, C11D, 2, f.67, Meneval to the minister, 1 Dec. 1687; partially printed in *Coll. Man. N.F.*, 1:410.

55 "Les dits inhabitants ... tout ce qu'ils ont faict jusques à present n'ayant esté pour payer ce qu'ils doivent aux dits Anglois qui leur ont vendu fort chèrement tout ce dont ils avoient besoing pour se restablir après l'invasion des dits Anglois": *Coll. Man. N.F.*, 1:411.

56 NAC, AC, C11D, 2, f.96, "Mémoire de Monsieur de Meneval sur l'Acadie," 10 Sept. 1688, *Coll. Man. N.F.*, 1:411–12.

57 "La trop grande connaissance que j'avais de toutes ce qui se passoit à l'Acadie": DUA, W.I. Morse Collection, Gargas, "Mon séjour"; English translation: Morse, *Acadiensis Nova*, 1:195–7.

58 Émery LeBlanc [in collaboration with], "Joseph Robinau de Villebon," DCB, 1:576–8.

59 "La verité m'oblige de dire que le d. Vilbon est Capable de destruire la Colonie la mieux Establie es que son sejour est un obstacle invincible pour

son Establissement": DUA, W.I. Morse Collection; English translation: Morse, *Acadiensis Nova*, 1:192ff.

60 "Sr De Villbon, qui parlons Espirit malin inspiroit à la plus part des habitans de me les refuser, jusques a ce point mesme qu'il leur conseilloit de m'envoyer promener lorsque je leur le demanderons: DUA, W.I. Morse Collection, Gargas, "Mon séjour"; English translation: Morse, *Acadiensis Nova*, 1:194.

61 AC, G1, 466, 58–9; printed in Rameau de Saint-Père, *Une colonie féodale*, 2:403.

62 The detailed analysis of this growth in Clark, *Acadia*, 132–76, is a meticulous interpretation of the available data.

63 Ibid., 170.

64 DUA, W.I. Morse Collection, Gargas, "Mon séjour"; English translation: Morse, *Acadiensis Nova*, 1:153.

65 DUA, W.I. Morse Collection, Gargas, "Mon séjour"; English translation: Morse, *Acadiensis Nova*, 1:198.

66 "Il seroit aussy bon de les obliger au défrichement des terres hautes, la Plupart des habitans au port Royal aux Minas ne s'amusant que faire des levées dans les marais ou ils serment leur Bled ... Leurs travaux des marais estant desja fais ils ne veu pas en commancer d'autres, et ce pays restens toujours de mesmes, particulierement M. Le Gouverneur permettant aux jeunes hommes fils des habitans de s'aller establir dans d'autres lieux de la Coste ou ils ne font Que courir et chasser ou traitter avec les sauvages": DUA, W.I. Morse Collection, Gargas, "Mon séjour"; English translation: Morse, *Acadiensis Nova*, 1:177–8.

67 Perrot: NAC, AC, C11D, 2, f.39, 1686; Webster, *Acadia*, 172.

68 Wicken, "Encounters with tall sails and tall tales," 70.

69 DUA, W.I. Morse Collection, Gargas, "Mon séjour"; English translation: Morse, *Acadiensis Nova*, 1:149, 151.

70 Brebner, *New England's outpost*, 48.

71 As published in the *Census of Canada*, 1870–71, 4:10–50.

72 Brebner, *New England's outpost*, 45–6.

73 Ibid.

74 Particularly in the light of the last published volume of Trudel, *HNF*; the biographies of Acadian officials published in the *DCB*; and the articles published by the SHA since its inception in 1961.

75 One of the best short introductions to this point of view is Steele, *Guerillas and grenadiers*.

76 Kennedy, *The rise and fall of the great powers*, 73; italics in the original.

77 Anderson, *War and society*, 83, 100.

78 Ibid., 86.

79 Ibid., 83.

80 Late-seventeenth-century figures for troops in place are as unreliable as the contemporary census figures: counting people became an obsession only in the early eighteenth century. It was in the interest of both those who sold, and those who bought, supplies for the military to inflate the numbers on the rolls. The Acadian figures are based on lists of the complements of soldiers

sent, those for New France on governor's reports, including those of Denonville and Frontenac. Disease has almost always been as deadly to both the army and the navy as enemy action.

81 Anderson, *War and society*, 96.

82 For a full discussion of the reasons behind this action, see Eccles, *Frontenac: The courtier governor*, and Lanctot, *A history of Canada*, 2:113ff.

83 NAC, AC, series B, 15, f.68, "Instruction à Mons. De Frontenac sur l'entreprise contre les Anglois, 7 juin. 1689"; published in full in *Coll. Man. N.F.*, 1:455–61.

84 NAC, AC, series B, 15, f.34, "Lettre du ministere à Mons. De Meneval," 10 April 1688; partially printed in *Coll. Man. N.F.*, 1:422.

85 "Mémoire pour servir d'instruction au sieur Pasquine, ingénieur," 10 April 1688; partially printed in *Coll. Man. N.F.*, 1:420–1. His work was overtaken by events but a short report from him exists: "Mémoire sur l'Acadie de Monsieur Pasquine," 14 Dec. 1688, *Coll. Man. N.F.*, 1:445–6.

86 Bernard Pothier, "Mathieu de Goutin," *DCB*, 2:257–8.

87 These were privately owned vessels, one step removed from private ships, that were equipped with government licences to prey on enemy shipping. Their actions could be challenged in the courts if there were grounds to consider that they had taken place in times of peace.

88 "Mémoire sur l'Acadie," 1689, *Coll. Man. N.F.*, 1:469, but see also an account of the raid in Webster, *Acadia*, 207.

89 Cited in Johnson, *John Nelson*, 47.

90 Cotton Mather, *Decennium Luctuosum* (Boston, 1690), cited in Rawlyk, *Nova Scotia's Massachusetts*, 57.

91 Morrison, *The embattled northeast*, 121; and Le Blant, *Une figure légendaire*, 75.

92 NAC, AC, C11D, 2, f.96, Meneval to Seignely, 10 Sept. 1688; partially printed in *Coll. Man. N.F*, 1:433–6.

93 "Cela a un peu fasché les habitans qui en tiroient des secours; mais ils s'en consoleront aysément sy la compagnie continue à leur faire apporter les mesmes secours comme elle a desjà faict": *Coll. Man. N.F.*, 1:436.

94 Hutchinson, *The history of the colony and province of Massachusetts-Bay* (1764), 2:65.

95 Rawlyk, *Nova Scotia's Massachusetts*, 58.

96 "Salem Petition, 1689," cited in ibid., 60.

97 Steele, *The English Atlantic world*, 94–110.

98 For a recent analysis of this, see Baker and Reid, *The New England knight*, 73, 82–3. At almost the same moment, the Iroquois devastated Lachine.

99 *Doc. Hist. St. Maine*, 5:16.

100 Baker and Reid, *The New England knight*, 83–4.

101 For accounts of infighting in Boston over the leadership, see Johnson, *John Nelson*, 58–62, and Baker and Reid, *The New England knight*, 83–7.

102 See Baker and Reid, *The New England knight*, as well as C.P. Stacey, "Sir William Phips," *DCB*, 1:544–6.

103 "Payment of soldiers ... March 20th, 1690," *Doc. Hist. St. Maine*, 6:60–1.

104 A listing of the ships, captains, and soldiers is given in [Phips], *A journal of the proceedings in the late expedition to Port Royal* (hereafter *Journal*), PAC *Report*, 1912, app. E, 63.

105 An excellent summary of events is provided by Baker and Reid in *The New England knight*, 86ff.

106 [Phips], *Journal*, 56.

107 *Mémoire* of Petit, Trouvé, and Dubreuil, 27 May 1690, *Coll. Man. N.F.* 2:7.

108 [Phips], *Journal*, 56.

109 De Goutin, *Account of the capture of Port Royal*, PAC *Report*, 1912, app. F, 67.

110 "... fut fasché de l'honneste compromis qu'il avoit accordé ...": *Mémoire* of Petit, Trouvé, Dubreuil, de Meneval, etc., *Coll. Man. N.F.*, 2:8.

111 Baker and Reid, *The New England knight*, 90.

112 [Phips], *Journal*, 156.

113 A table listing the livestock reported for Port Royal from 1671 to 1797 is found in Clark, *Acadia*, 167, based on data in NAC, AC, C11D, 2, f.1.

114 Anderson, *War and society*, 54.

115 Two years previously, Louis XIV had waged one of the more barbaric campaigns in the Rhineland, something that even his most laudatory biographer regretted. See Voltaire, *Le siècle de Louis XIV*, 146.

116 [Phips], *Journal*, 56.

117 MA, 36, 123–4a, 1690, Inventory.

118 Rawlyk, *Nova Scotia's Massachusetts*, 69; James Lloyd to the Board of Trade, 8 Jan. 1691, *Cal. St. Papers*, *1689–1692*, 376.

119 Murdoch, *A history of Nova Scotia*, 1:195.

120 "Relation de qui s'est passés de plus remarquable en Canada, depuis le départ des vaisseaux, au mois de novembre, 1689, jusqu'au mois de novembre, 1690": *Coll. Man. N.F.*, 1:507.

121 Southack to his parents, 18 June 1690, *Doc. Hist. St. Maine*, 5:128–9.

122 La Morandière, *Histoire de la pêche française*, 1:360. The relationship of the *écu*, an actual gold coin, to the *livre*, an accounting device, was by this time at least five to one in favour of the *écu*. See Innis, *The cod fisheries*, 28–9.

123 Clark, *Acadia*, table 5.5, 150.

124 1689: NAC, G1-466, 58–9: printed in Rameau de Saint-Père, *Une colonie féodale*, 2:402; 1693: NAC, G1-466, 66–102.

125 Durand, "L'Acadie et les phénomènes de solidarité et fidelité au XVIIIième siècle," 82.

126 "Coronation Oath, 1689": Stephenson and Marcham, *Sources of English constitutional history*, 606.

127 "Prestation de serments pour Messieurs les Ecclésiastiques ... pour la noblesse ... pour messieurs les officiers de la justice" (early 1670s): *Coll. Man. N.F.*, 1:226–7.

128 See chapter 5, and also Griffiths, "Subjects and citizens in the eighteenth century: The question of the Acadian oaths of allegiance," in Mouliasson, Comeau, and Langille, ed., *Les Abeilles*, 23–34.

129 Evans, *Oaths of allegiance in New England*, 10.

130 Ibid., 408.

131 Gipson, *The British empire before the American Revolution*, vol.6, *The great war for empire*, 244.

132 [Phips], *Journal*, 60. This source's account of the oaths administered to the Acadians is replete with apparently random italic type, which is dispensed with here,

133 Ibid., 56.

134 Ibid., 57.

135 "Account of my voyage to Acadia in the ship *Union* and all that took place in the country during my visit": NBM, Webster Collection, Villebon Papers, Villebon to the Marquis de Chevry, 1690; English translation: Webster, *Acadia*, 24.

136 The spelling and orthography is as given in PAC, *Report*, 1912, 60.

137 Ibid.

138 Ibid., 62.

139 Gérard Desjardins, "Louis Petit," *DCB*, 2:521–2.

140 NAC, AC, series B,16, f.28, "Instruction au Sieur de Villebon commandant à l'Acadie," 7 April 1691; printed in *Coll. Man. N.F.*, 2:45–6.

141 De Goutin, *Account of the capture of Port Royal*, 70.

142 "qu'ils avoinet faict par force ... qu'ils supplioient Sa majesté de ne les pas abandonner et qu'ils estoient prests d'exposer leurs vies pour leurs chere patrie Et ne les pas obliger a renoncer a leur religion et embrasser l'anglicane": ibid.

143 On the matter of the militia in colonial America, see S.F. Wise, "The antecedents of the military clauses in the U.S. constitution," in Paschall, ed., *The constitution and the U.S. army*, 1–14.

144 Webster, *Acadia*, 8; LeBlanc, "Joseph Robinau de Villebon."

145 NBM, Webster Collection, Villebon Papers, Villebon to the Marquis de Chevry, 1690; English translation: Webster, *Acadia*, 24.

146 "Qu'on rammasseroit le debris de la garnison du Port royal qu sestoit sauvée de la prison des anglois ...": de Goutin, *Account of the capture of Port Royal*, 70; see also NBM, Webster Collection, Villebon Papers, Villebon to the Marquis de Chevry, 1690; English translation: Webster, *Acadia*, 24.

147 Ganong, *A monograph of historic sites*, 274.

148 "il feroit venir des Sauvages de Naxchouet, Medotecq Et Richibouctou, qui couviroient Jemsec, qu'on les incitiroit à continuer la guerre contre les Anglois": de Goutin, *Account of the capture of Port Royal*, 70.

149 "... Le Sieur de gouttin dressa lacte de Protestation contre le serment ... Et le dit Sr de Vilbon se chargea d'envoyer une copie a la Cour ...": de Goutin, *Account of the capture of Port Royal*, 71.

150 NBM, Webster Collection, Villebon Papers, Villebon to the Marquis de Chevry, 1690; English translation: Webster, *Acadia*, 26–7.

151 NAC, AC, series B, 16, ff.46, 28c, "Mémoire pour servir de l'instruction au Sieur Villebon," 7 April 1691; printed in *Coll. Man. N.F.*, 2:45–7.

152 Daigle: "Nos amis, les ennemis."

153 Charles Bruce Fergusson, "John Alden," *DCB*, 2:14–15.

154 General Court to John Alden, 6 Nov. 1690, MHS *Collections*, 2nd series, 5:159.

155 Saint-Aubin had arrived in Canada sometime around 1660 and settled on Île d'Orléans; he killed a man in self-defence there. Sometime in 1676 he moved to the Passamaquoddy area, and in June 1684 he was given an extensive land grant close to present-day St Andrews. His career reflected the same frontier tensions as those evident in the lives of John Nelson and Saint-Castin. Like the latter, he ended his life in service to France, dying in Acadia in 1705, at the age of eight-four. Clarence J. d'Entremont, "Jean Serreau de Saint-Aubin," *DCB*, 2:604–5.

156 Petition of Jean Martel and Abraham Boudrot, 6 May 1691, cited in Baker and Reid, *New England knight*, 160.

157 D'Entremont, "Du nouveau sur les Melanson," 347.

158 Daigle, "Nos amis, les ennemis," 126; petition of Jean Martel and Abraham Boudrot. See also Bosher, "Huguenot merchants and the Protestant International." On Faneuil, who was also a Huguenot, see Bosher, *Négociants et navires*, 70.

159 Baker and Reid, *The New England knight*, 95–104.

160 For a full account of the politics of this enterprise, see Johnson, *John Nelson*, 66ff.

161 NBM, Webster Collection, Villebon Papers, "Journal de ce qui sest passé a l'acadie depuis le 13ᵉ octobre 1691 jusquau 8 octᵉ 1692" (hereinafter "Journal"); English translation: Webster, *Acadia*, 34. Martel may have been Villebon's son-in-law: Bernard Pothier: "Jean Martel de Magos," *DCB*, 2:459–60.

162 Saint-Castin to Frontenac, 3 Sept. 1691, published in full in Le Blant, *Saint-Castin*, 132–3.

163 For a full analysis of these events, see Baker and Reid, *The New England knight*, 122ff.

164 Ibid., 110–33; Charter of Massachusetts: PRO, CO 5, 905, f.322; order-in-council, 27 Nov. 1691: PRO, CO 5, 856, f.364.

165 "le commandement du Port royal ... a esté mon sergeant, et qui ne la accepté que son mon agrement ...": NBM, Webster Collection, Villebon Papers, "Journal," 4 July 1691; English translation: Webster, *Acadia*, 41; printed in French in Cyr, "Le difficile maintien de la puissance française en Acadie," 16.

166 This man was Louis Phelypeaux, Comte de Pontchartrain, the grandson of Paul Phelypeaux, who was made intendant of finance in 1687 and controller general in 1689. He had succeeded Seignelay in 1690.

167 "Estant impossible sans garder des Menagemens dans un Pays ou je me trouve sans forces, et avec les secours aussy esloignés que ces pauvres gens nessuiassent quelque facheuse Camisade": NBM, Webster Collection, Villebon Papers, "Journal," 12 July 1692; English translation: Webster, *Acadia*, 41; Cyr, "Le difficile maintien de la puissance française," 5. It is clear that Webster translated the original French very freely.

168 "Quaunt au surplus ils tirassent tous les secours qu'ils pourroient Des
      anglois Jusques a nouvel ordre": NBM, Webster Collection, Villebon Papers,
      "Journal," 14 Aug. 1692; English translation: Webster, *Acadia*, 44; Cyr, "Le
      difficile maintien de la puissance française," 18.

169 For an overview of the place of gifts and subsidies in European-Amerindian
      relations, see Cornelius Jaenen, "The role of presents in French-Amerindian
      trade," in Cameron, *Explorations in Canadian economic history*, 231–50.

170 Rawlyk, *Nova Scotia's Massachusetts*, 72–3.

171 "Treize canoes Sauvages MicMacs de Nation": NBM, Webster Collection,
      Villebon Papers, "Journal," 19 Oct. 1691; English translation: Webster, *Aca-
      dia*, 32–3; Cyr, "Le difficile maintien de la puissance française," 3.

172 "Je leur fis festin, leur donné ensuite de La Poudre et des Balles et un peu
      de tabac pour se rendre au rendez-vous": NBM, Webster Collection, Villebon
      Papers, "Journal," 25 May 1692; English translation: Webster, *Acadia*, 38;
      Cyr, "Le difficile maintien de la puissance française," 12.

173 "a prendre les armes contre tout ce qui viendroit de L'europe ...": ibid.

174 "Quil ne pouvoit que Leur en couter la vie ...": ibid.

175 "Mais que ce quils Prometroient, est quils ne se mesteroient de rien, et quils
      seroient les biens venus quand ils ne viendront pas dans le dessein de leur
      nuire, qu sils vouloient estasblir une Garnison comme ils leurs prometroient
      il y avoit longtemps, qu'ils pouroient faire sur tous les batimens francois ce
      quil leur Plaisoit, que pour eux ils seroient Neutres": NBM, Webster Collec-
      tion, Villebon Papers, "Journal," 4 July 1692; English translation: Webster,
      Acadia, 40; Cyr, "Le difficile maintien de la puissance française," 16.

176 "Ils [les Anglais] voulurent ly obliger a signer une seureté en y etablissant
      garnison pour Leurs gens a legard de nos Sauvages, mais les habitans Leurs
      repondirent Comme Je leur avois dit de faire, que bien esloigné den pou-
      voir repondre quils seroient les premiers exposés aussitost que les Sauvages
      les regarderoient comme leurs amis ...": ibid.

177 "Je leurs fis dire ... que Jestois content Deux qu'ils fissent toujours bonne
      Garde, et quils eussent a l'ordinaire de quils avoient de meilleurs effets
      Dans les Bois, Crainte De Surprise ...": NBM, Webster Collection, Villebon
      Papers, "Journal," 14 Aug. 1692; English translation: Webster, *Acadia*, 42;
      Cyr, "Le difficile maintien de la puissance française," 18–19.

178 For a fuller discussion of this issue, see chapter 7.

179 Baker and Reid, *The New England knight*, 160.

180 Jean Daigle pieced together, with meticulous scholarship, much of these
      activities in his doctoral thesis, "Nos amis, les ennemis"; see, in particular,
      131–48.

181 NBM, Webster Collection, Villebon Papers, "Journal," 7 Aug. 1693; English
      translation: Webster, *Acadia*, 46–7.

182 Rawlyk, *Nova Scotia's Massachusetts*, 76.

183 These figures are from Clark, *Acadia*, 150, compiled from the census in the
      NAC, G1-446 series.

184 See chapter 7 for a fuller analysis of settlement growth during the 1690s.

185 NBM, Webster Collection, Villebon Papers, "Journal," 4 July 1692. English translation: Webster, *Acadia*, 41.

186 NAC, AC, C11D, 3, f.2, 437–53, "Mémoire sur les établissements et havres qui sont depuis les Mines ...," October 1699.

187 NBM, Webster Collection, Villebon Papers, "Journal," 7 Aug. 1693 and 28 July 1694; English translation: Webster, *Acadia*, 46 and 56.

188 NBM, Webster Collection, Villebon Papers, "Journal," 24 April 1793. English translation: Webster, *Acadia*, 47.

189 W. Austin Squires, "François Guion," *DCB*, 2:271.

190 W. Austin Squires, "Pierre Maisonnat, *dit* Baptiste," *DCB*, 2:449–50.

191 NBM, Webster Collection, Villebon Papers, "Journal," 7 Oct. 1695; English translation: Webster, *Acadia*, 82.

192 Stoughton to the governor of New York, 11 Nov. 1695, cited in Rawlyk, *Nova Scotia's Massachusetts*, 161.

193 For which Frontenac was awarded the Order of Saint-Louis. On the question of Frontenac's Iroquois policy, see W.J. Eccles, "Louis de Buade de Frontenac et de Palluau," *DCB*, 1:133–42 at 139–40, and *Frontenac: The courtier governor.*

194 See NAC, series B, 16 and 17. Also: "Mémoire sur l'Acadie et la Nouvelle Angleterre ... par Monsieur de Lagny," 1692, *Coll. Man. N.F.*, 2:97–100; "Instructions au Sieur de Villebon ...," 14 Feb. 1693, *Coll. Man. N.F.*, 2:106–8; "Nouvelle de l'Acadie," 1693, *Coll. Man. N.F.*, 2:127.

195 For lists of these gifts, and their cost, see "Estat des presens à envoyer aux chefs Abénaquis à l'Acadie, 1693," *Coll. Man. N.F.*, 2:111; "Aux Micmaks," 1693, *Coll. Man. N.F.*, 2:129–30; "Estat des presens ordinaires pour les sauvages de l'Acadie," 1696, *Coll. Man. N.F.*, 2:206.

196 See in particular "Relation du voyage faict par le sieur de Villieu ...," 1694, *Coll. Man. N.F.*, 2:135–48. Webster, in *Acadia*, 57–65, provides an account in English of this expedition, with Villebon's commentary. Claude-Sébastien de Villieu came to Acadia in 1690 and by 1693 had been given command of a company. Étienne Taillemite, "Claude Sébastien de Villieu," *DCB*, 2:654–5.

197 Bernard Pothier, "Pierre Le Moyne d'Iberville et d'Ardillières," *DCB*, 2:390–401 at 394.

198 "Journal de ... Baudoin," in Gosselin, *Les Normands au Canada*, 36; see also Murdoch, *A history of Nova Scotia*, 1:217–21.

199 Rawlyk, *Nova Scotia's Massachusetts*, 81; also, Howard H. Peckham, "Benjamin Church," *DCB*, 2:145–6.

200 NBM, Webster Collection, Villebon Papers, "Journal," 29 Oct. 1696; English translation: Webster, *Acadia*, 94.

201 Murdoch, *A history of Nova Scotia*, 1:227.

202 Cited in ibid., 1:217.

203 " tout ce monde eust mis pied à terre chacun pris le parti a se sauver et d'emporter ce qu'il avoit de meillieur": NBM, Webster Collection, Villebon Papers, "Journal," 29 Oct. 1696; English translation: Webster, *Acadia*, 95.

204 Cited in Rawlyk, *Nova Scotia's Massachusetts*, 82.

205 NBM, Webster Collection, Villebon Papers, "Nouvelles de l'Acadie depuis le départ des Anglais," October 1696; English translation: Webster, *Acadia*, 96.

206 Villebon's account, "Relation du siège de Natchouak par les Anglois de Baston," is in *Coll. Man. N.F.*, 2:241–6. Short accounts of this event are found in Rawlyk, *Nova Scotia's Massachusetts*, 83; Rumilly, *Histoire des Acadiens*, 1:150–1; Murdoch, *A history of Nova Scotia*, 1:228–30.

207 Pierre Goubert, "Le 'tragique' xvii siècle," in Braudel and Labrousse, ed., *Histoire économique et sociale de la France*, 2:360.

208 Wolf, *Louis XIV*, 476.

209 Collins, *The state in early modern France*, 129.

CHAPTER SEVEN

1 Pierre Goubert, "Recent theories and research on the population of France between 1500 and 1700," in Glass and Eversley, ed., *Population in history*, 469.

2 D.V. Glass, "Population and population movements in England and Wales," in ibid., 240; see also Brown, *Society and economy in modern Britain*, 33.

3 Article 7 of the treaty. Printed versions are to be found in Vast, ed., *Les grands traités du règne de Louis XIV*, vol.3, and Davenport, *European treaties bearing on the history of the United States*, vol.3.

4 Vast, ed., *Les grands traités du règne de Louis XIV*, 3:207–8.

5 Miquelon, *New France, 1701–1744*, 20.

6 Ibid., 18–31, has a clear, and brief, account of the impact of the Treaty of Ryswick on North America.

7 "les bornes de l'Acadie ... à present ... la rivière Quinibéqui ... empescher les Anglois de faire le commerce, ny la pesche dans nos colonies ...": *Coll. Man. N.F.*, 2:295–6.

8 Villebon to Stoughton, 5 Sept. 1698, *Cal. St. Papers, 1697–98*, 501–2.

9 See short memorandum to this effect: *Coll. Man. N.F.*, 2:283.

10 Massachusetts General Court to King William, 19 Nov. 1698: *Acts and resolves public and private ... of Massachusetts Bay*, 7:195.

11 NAC, AC, C11D, 3, ff.150–1, "Mémoire sur l'Acadie," 9 Dec. 1698.

12 "Petition of the fishermen to Lord Bellomont," 23 May 1699, *Cal. St. Papers, Colonial, 1699*, 105.

13 *Acts and resolves public and private ... of Massachusetts Bay*, 7:194–5.

14 Rawlyk, *Nova Scotia's Massachusetts*, 87.

15 Based on Clark, *Acadia*, 124–5.

16 Based on ibid., 124–51.

17 The 1703 census records the population of the colony as 1,244; see also Clark, *Acadia*, 135, 143, 156, which offers a somewhat lower estimate for 1715.

18 This view has been expressed by Melvin Gallant, the Acadian scholar who recently edited Dièreville's work for the SHA. Gallant writes: "... il parle d'eux comme d'une collectivité qui s'est totalement detachée de la France." Dièreville, *Relations du voyage*, SHA *Cahiers* 16, 3–4 (1985): 19. Dièreville, a some-

what enigmatic character, arrived at Port Royal on 13 October 1699, after a voyage of fifty days out of La Rochelle. He was commissioned not only to act as an agent for his backers but also to write a report for them on the state of the colony.

As well as Melvin Gallant's edition of Dièreville's account for the SHA, there is also a Champlain Society version edited by J.C. Webster: *Relation of the voyage to Port Royal in Acadia or New France*. The original edition, published in Rouen in 1708, is available on microfilm. All references that follow are to the Champlain edition.

19 Fernand Ouellet has offered a major and important criticism of this attitude in "L'accroissement naturel de la population catholique québécoise avant 1850."

20 James N. Spuhler, "Behavior and mating patterns in human populations," in Harrison and Boyce, ed., *The structure of human populations*, 178.

21 Vanderlinden, *Se marier en Acadie*, 39–42. His work is based on Arsenault, *Histoire et généalogie des Acadiens*.

22 Massignon, *Les parlers français*, 1:32–9.

23 White, "La généalogie des trente-sept familles."

24 Hynes, "Some aspects of the demography in Port Royal," in Buckner and Frank, ed., *The Acadiensis reader, Vol. I: Atlantic Canada before Confederation*, 15. This article was first published in *Acadiensis*, 3, 1 (autumn 1973): 3–17.

25 Clark, *Acadia*, 204. See also chapter 9 of the present work.

26 Massignon, *Les parlers français*, 1:69, and Saint-Père, *Une colonie féodale*, 2:348.

27 Vanderlinden, *Se marier en Acadie*, 45–8.

28 On this issue see H. Charbonneau et al., *Naissance d'une population*, and Cassedy, *Demography in early America*.

29 See *Inventaire général des sources documentaires sur les Acadiens*, 1:379–423.

30 See Hynes's caveat in "Some aspects of the demography in Port Royal," 11–25.

31 Courtwright, "New England families in historical perspective," 14–15.

32 I should confess that Charbonneau et al., from whose work, *Naissance d'une population*, 90, these figures are taken, give the numbers as 8.1 and 5.7 respectively. I dislike ascribing a fraction of a child to a family.

33 Hynes, "Some aspects of the demography in Port Royal," 22.

34 My italics; calculations are based on Charbonneau et al., *Naissance d'une population*, 111–14, and also Livi-Bacci, *A concise history of world population*, 9.

35 White, "La généalogie des trente-sept familles," 83; Lanctôt: *Familles acadiennes*, 1:93–9.

36 Lanctôt, *Familles acadiennes*, 2:121.

37 Ibid., 2:123; Arsenault, *Histoire et généalogie des Acadiens*, 2:823.

38 Ibid., 1:44, 2:669.

39 Pierre Goubert, "Recent theories and research on the population of France between 1500 and 1700," 468.

40 Hynes, "Some aspects of the demography in Port Royal," 18–19.

41 NAC, G1-466, 66–102.

42 On the first point, see Dumont et al., *L'histoire des femmes au Québec depuis quatre siècles.* 20–5.

43 As well as Courtwright's "New England families in historical perspective," see Smith, "The study of the family in early America."

44 The work published on this is now legion; one of the best introductions to the subject is that of Hufton, *The prospect before her,* chapter 4, passim.

45 Brouillan to the minister, 1701, partially printed in Rameau de Saint-Père, *Une colonie féodale,* 2:338.

46 Dièreville, *Relation du voyage,* 90.

47 See, in particular, NAC, AC, C11D, 3, f.199, Villebon to the minister, 27 Oct. 1699; printed in part in *Coll. Man. N.F.,,* 2:330–1; trans. in Webster, *Acadia,* 128.

48 Dièreville, *Relation du voyage,* 95.

49 Ibid., 109.

50 Ibid., 116.

51 NBM, Webster Collection, Villebon Papers, "Mémoire de Villebon ...," 27 Oct. 1699; English translation: Webster, *Acadia,* 128.

52 " ... nous ne saurions trop vanter/ Leurs adresse et leur industrie.": Dièreville, *Relation of the voyage,* 94; French: 258.

53 "fait que de la bière avec des sommités de sapin ... une forte décoction ...": ibid., 91; French: 256.

54 " plus de trente milliers de poisson ...": ibid., 96; French: 260.

55 NBM, Webster Collection, Villebon Papers, "Mémoire sur les establissemens et havres qui sont depuis les Mines dans le fond de la Baye française, jusques à l'Isle de Cap Breton," 27 Oct. 1699; English translation: Webster, *Acadia,* 133.

56 Brenda Dunn, "Certains aspects de la vie des femmes dans l'ancienne Acadie," in Conrad ed., *Un regard sur l'Acadie,* 33.

57 It is tempting to enter into a discussion on the durability of traditional recipes. Instead, I suggest that those who are interested in the subject start by using the work of Boudreau and Gallant, *Le guide de la cuisine traditionnelle acadienne.*

58 The inventory of goods that Phips took from Port Royal is a good source for such details but see also Dunn, "L'inventaire de la veuve Plemarais, 1705."

59 Charles Melanson to William Stoughton, 5 Feb. 1696, cited in Daigle, "Nos amis, les ennemis,"150.

60 Dièreville, *Relation of the voyage,* 103; French: 263.

61 Ibid., 117–18 and 271.

62 This was one of the five sons of the more famous Charles de La Tour and Jeanne Motin d'Aulnay. See George MacBeath, "Charles de Saint-Étienne de la Tour," *DCB,* 2:591–2.

63 "Quand ils [les enfants] sont en état de travailler, ce qu'ils font de bonne heure; ils épargnent à leurs Peres des journées d'hommes qui coûtent là vingt-cinq & trente sols ...": Dièreville, *Relation of the voyage,* 94; French: 258.

64 John Demos, "Demography and psychology in the historical study of family life: A personal report," in Laslett, ed., *Household and family,* 561–9.

65 Ibid., 562–3; Dunn, "Certains aspects de la vie des femmes," 33.

66 Dièreville, *Relation du voyage*, 84; French: 251.

67 Dupont, *Héritage d'Acadie*, 161.

68 "Cache-cache et attrape qui peut": Massignon, *Les parlers français*, 2:700–19.

69 A critical look at this issue in New England is that of Wall, *Fierce communion*.

70 Dunn, "Certains aspects de la vie des femmes," 40. See also Christianson, *Belleisle 1983*.

71 For example, White, "La généalogie des trente-sept familles."

72 Vanderlinden, *Se marier en Acadie*, 19–92.

73 Ibid., 95.

74 "Hasard des migrations, hasards des rencontres, hasard de la fertilité des couples, qu'il s'agisse du nombre des enfants ou de leur sexe": Vanderlinden, "Alliance entre familles acadiennes," 146.

75 On the Boudrot, Bourg, and Dugas families, see Lanctôt, *Familles acadiennes*, 1:74, 85–6. On the Melanson family, see Arsenault, *Histoire et généalogie*, 1:463–4.

76 Bernard Pothier, "Mathieu de Goutin," DCB, 2:257–8. See also lengthy correspondence in NAC, C11D, 4, and NAC, AC, series B, 23, the minister to Brouillan, 22 March 1702, regarding the problem of de Goutin's many relatives.

77 Extracts from report in the Library of the National Assembly, Quebec, Rameau de Saint-Père, *Une colonie féodale*, 2:304–7.

78 Arsenault, *Histoire et généalogie*, 2:631.

79 D'Entremont, "Du nouveau sur les Melanson," SHA, *Cahiers*, 28 (July/September 1970): 339–53, 370–2.

80 "Recensement de l'Acadie en 1686," printed in full in Rameau de Saint-Père, *Une colonie féodale*, 2:402.

81 Clark, *Acadia*, 135.

82 Ganong, ed., "The Cadillac Memoir of 1692," 81.

83 Clark, *Acadia*, 166.

84 NBM, Webster Collection, Villebon Papers, "Mémoire sur l'estat présent du Port royal de sa situation et les raisons pour le fortified," 27 Oct. 1699; English translation: Webster, *Acadia*, 129.

85 Extract of baptismal role printed in Lanctôt, *Familles acadiennes*, 1:68.

86 White, "La généalogie des trente-sept familles," 79.

87 Basque, *Des hommes de pouvoir*, 29ff.

88 NAC, G1-466, Census of 1701, 169; see also Rameau de Saint-Père, *Une colonie féodale*, 1:205–6.

89 Rutman, "Assessing the little communities of early America," 173.

90 This is not to say that status and rank did not exist or that they did not carry *any* weight. Maurice Basque has demonstrated the way in such factors facilitated the rise to prominence of one family in particular, the Robichauds. See Basque, *Des hommes de pouvoir*, 19–57.

91 On this issue, see, in particular, the Le Borgne and La Tour family claims; the

best source with which to start is probably the material in the *Mem. des com. du Roi* ... vol.1, but see also Couillard Després, *Charles de Saint-Étienne de La Tour.*

92 Clark, *Acadia*, 145.

93 Jean Bourque Campbell has studied those with such claims, and a selection of her work has been published in a series of articles in the SHA *Cahiers.* The excerpt published in 26,1 (January-March 1995), 35–8, 43–6, contains a list of seigneurial grants in chronological order as well as a listing of fifty-five names of those considered as seigneurs.

94 "On voit de même aussi par la foy Conjugale / Une Fille de qualité, / Plutôt de rester Vestale / Avec un Rturier perdre sa dignité: / Malgré l'Alliance inégale, / On veut avoir posterité": Dièreville, *Relation of the voyage*, 93; French: 258.

95 Gaudette, "Famille élargie et copropriété dans l'ancienne Acadie," 16.

96 On the Beaubassin and Shepody disputes, see Clark, *Acadia*, 145–6; on those of the Saint John, see Émery LeBlanc [in collaboration with], "Joseph Robinau de Villebon," *DCB*, 1:576–8. See also PANS, Nova Scotia documents relating to Acadia, de Goutin to the minister, no.3, 5 Nov. 1699.

97 "il faudrait pour cela que les habitants y fussent moins accoutumés au libertinage, qu'on fût plus autorisé et qu'on eût plus de moyens pour les en châtier": Frontenac to Colbert, 14 Nov. 1674, *RAPQ*, 1926–27, 67.

98 A short and entertaining introduction to this question is that of Lewis, *The splendid century*; for a detailed analysis of social mobility in France at the close of the seventeenth century, see Hampson, *Social history of the French revolution.*

99 For a clear background on what this meant, see Dickinson, *Law in New France.*

100 Vanderlinden, "A la rencontre de l'histoire."

101 "Le Sieur Des Cosme Curé des Mines mescrivoi ... me Prioit daprouver la choix que Ces habitans avoient fait de trois déntreu pour acomoder les differents qui survenoient tous les jours au sujet de leurs terres, ou autres demeslés": NBM, Webster Collection, Villebon Papers, Villebon, 12 Jan. 1691/2; printed in Cyr, "Le difficile maintien de la puissance française," 6; English translation: Webster, *Acadia*, 35.

102 "Le Sieur Dubreuil Pourvue de la charge De Procureur du Roy a Portroyal, arriva pour me rendre compte de tout ce qui eoite passé au Port royal et que les habitans craignoient davoir fait quelque demarches qui mauroient peut estre pas plu ...": NBM, Webster Collection, Villebon Papers, Villebon, 11, 14 Aug. 1692; printed in Cyr, "Le difficile maintien de la puissance française," 42.

103 Dièreville, *Relation of the voyage*, 83; French: 251.

104 NAC, AC, C11D, 3, f.208, Villebon to Pontchartrain, 27 Oct. 1699; Webster, *Acadia*, 122–3.

105 NAC, AC, C11D, 3, f.211, Villebon to Pontchartrain, 1693; Webster, *Acadia*, 49–52.

106 Ibid., 51.

107 A more sympathetic picture of Baudoin is given in Casgrain, *Les Sulpiciens*, 111–211.

108 Greene and Pole, *Colonial British America*, provides a superb introduction to this area of inquiry, but see also Canny, ed., *The origins of empire*.

109 There is a vast literature on this question for the English colonies and New France. An excellent place to begin is Taylor, *Canadian history: A reader's guide*, vol.1. For Acadian history, the field is in its infancy. However, articles and short monographs are appearing on the development of political institutions among the Acadians during the French period, most of which are referenced, if not published, in the SHA *Cahiers*.

110 NAC, AC, C11D, 3, ff.244–57, Villebon to Ponchartrain, 1 Oct. 1695; Webster, *Acadia*, 86.

111 George MacBeath, "Mathieu Damours de Freneuse," *DCB*, 1:245–6.

112 See Étienne Taillemite, "Daniel Robinau de Neuvillette" and "René Robinau de Portneuf," *DCB*, 2:579–80.

113 He certainly had a daughter, whether or not she was illegitimate. This was Marie-Anne Robinau. She married Jean Martel, who had arrived in Acadia in the 1680s and was granted land in 1694 near Nashwaak. Martel was also involved in trade with New England and had been arrested by Villebon in 1692 for smuggling. Bernard Pothier, "Jean Martel de Magos," *DCB*, 2:459–60.

114 Webster, *Acadia*, 6.

115 "a faict consommer cent douze livres de poudre à canon au feu de joye pour la paix, en buvant les santez de ses maistresses, et que luy et le Sieur Martel son gendre s'y en yvrèrnt": "Plaintes contre Monsieur de Villebon," *Coll. Man. N.F.*, 2:308.

116 Tibierge to the Marquis de Chevry, 21 June 1699, Murdoch, *A history of Nova Scotia*, 1:244; see also Webster, *Acadia*, 152–5.

117 The surviving documentation is voluminous, some of which is found in NAC, AC, C11D, 1 and 2 and has been printed in the *Coll. Man. N.F.*, 2:352–77. A good examination of the issues and of the impact of the award on other Acadians is in d'Entremont, *Histoire du Cap-Sable*, 3:1282ff.

118 For an overview of this expansion, see Surette, *Atlas de l'établissement des Acadiens*. On Shepody in particular, see ibid., 49–51.

119 NAC, AC, series B, 20–2, f.93, Pontchartrain to Fontenu, 8 April 1699; printed in *Pièces et documents*, 343.

120 Pontchartrain to Fontenu, 15 April 1699, ibid.

121 "Le pays de l'Acadie a esté cy devant devisé en plusieurs concessions qui ont esté faites à des particuliers dont quelques-uns sont encore dans le pays, et les autres l'ont abandonné, ces différentes concessions ont causé plusieurs contestations entre ces particuliers et ont empesché l'establissement de cette colonie. Sa Majesté est informée que ces contestations ne sont pas encore finies et qu'elles nuisent aux desseins qu'Elle a d'establir solidement ce pays, que mesme quelques-uns de ceux qui représentent les premiers

concessionnaires font commerce avec les Anglois et leur donnent des permissions de venir trafiquer à l'Acadie. Et comme Sa Majesté est bien aise de faire cesser ce désordre et de remettre ces concessionnaires dans les bornes de leurs concessions, Elle a rendu l'Arret qu'il trouvera cy-joint pour les obliger de reprendre leurs titres. Il aura soin non seulement de le faire publier et afficher dans les principaux endroits de cette Colonie, mais mesme de les faire signifier à ceux qui sont sur les lieux." NAC, AC, series B, 20–2, f.114; printed in Gaudet, "Les Seigneuries de l'ancienne Acadie," 343.

122 "que plusieurs particuliers qui se disent propriétiares des terres de l'Acadie ... ont non seulement negligé de remplir les obligations qui leur ont esté imposées ... mais ont mesme entretenu commerce avec les Anglois de Baston ... Sa [Majesté] estant en son Conseil a ordonné ... que tous les concessionnaires des terres ... à titre de succession, vente, cession ou autrement remettront à Sa Majesté dans le cours de la presente année les concessions et titres ... ou des coppies autentiques ... à peine d'estre decheus desdites concessions ...": "Arrest qui ordonné ne aux concessionaires de l'Acadie ..." (8 April 1699): NAC, AC, series B, 20–2, f.93; printed in Gaudet, "Les Seigneuries de l'ancienne Acadie," 343.

123 " ... ils avoient leurs titres à Quebec et qu'il leur estoit impossible de les pouvoir produire dans le temps porté par led. Arrest ...": "Arrest qui proroge le temps pour la représentation des titres ..." (9 March 1700): NAC, AC, series B, 22–1, f.92; printed in Gaudet, "Les Seigneuries de l'ancienne Acadie," 344–5.

124 Clarence d'Entremont identifies this man as being the jurist who later became chancellor of France: *Histoire du Cap-Sable*, 3:1318–19. His associates on the committee were Michel Amelot de Chaillou, Marquis de Gournay, a jurist from the law courts of Paris and a minister of the crown, and Nicolas-Antoine Deshaguis, a leading figure in the body that dealt with all forms of indirect taxes, and Nicolas-Prosper, Bauyn d'Angervilliers, another jurist from the Paris law courts. Ibid., 3:1319–20.

125 "la province de l'Acadie en la Nouvelle-France, quoyque tres fertile, et tres heureusement scituée pour procurer un Commerce considerable à ses sujets et devenir puissante à l'exemple de celle des Anglois qui l'avoisine, est presque deserte et ne peut soutenir le Commerce d'un seul Vaisseau par an ... l'estat fascheux de cette Colonie vient ... des concessions vagues ... cela a donné lieu ... à des guerres civilles ... et a esloigné les habitans qui auroient pu s'establir dans ce pays, si ces concessionaires ne leur avoient pas imposé des conditions trop onéreuses et s'ils avoient satisfait eux mesme aux obligations auxquelles ces Concessions leur avoient esté faites" (23 March 1701): Gaudet, "Les seigneuries de l'ancienne Acadie," 346.

126 AN, Nouv. acq. fr., 9281, ff.168–79.

127 Daigle, "Nos amis, les ennemis,"155.

128 "et la crainte qu'ils ont destre surprise par les Anglois": NBM, Webster Collection, F28, Tibierge, "Mémoire sur l'estat present de la province de la Cadie"; English translation: Webster, *Acadia*, 154–5.

129 "[Saint-Castin qui] acheta beaucoup de marchandises ... [en exchange] de tout ce qu'ils avaient de pelleteries": NAC, C11D, 3, f.105, Villebon to the minister, 3 Oct. 1698.

130 "il ny a pas un de ses habitans qui n'ait manqué de vivres l'hiver dernier es comme ils ont fait peu de semances, et qu'ils n'ont pourvu de moulin pour moudre le bled qu'ils pouvons recuillir, ils courens risque de passer encore fort mal l'hiver prochain": NBM, Webster Collection, F28, Tibierge, "Mémoire sur l'estat present de la province de la Cadie"; English translation: Webster, *Acadia*, 154.

131 "... les Sauvages ont jeuné cet hiver. Et ont été obligez de manger les peaux des orginaux qu'ils ont tuez": ibid.

132 MA, 2, 591; partially printed in Daigle, "Nos amis, les ennemis," 218.

133 NAC, AC, C11D, 3, f.165, Villebon to the minister, 27 June 1699.

134 "Estat des dépenses à faire pendant l'année présente pour les 60 soldats d'augmentation pour l'Acadie et les 40 soldats qui sont à l'Acadie": *Coll. Man. N.F.*, 3:207–8.

135 Calculation based on Clark's figures in *Acadia*, 128–9; see also Rameau de Saint-Père, *Une colonie féodale*, 2:205–6.

136 "Il doit y avoir au greffe de Port Royal des pièces qui en peuvent donner des éclaircissemens, et il y a plusieurs personnes sur les lieux qui ont vu ou appris de leurs pères l'origine de l'establissement des Anglois. Vous auriez pu prendre leurs déclarations": NAC, AC, series B, 19, ff.160 1/2, the minister to Villebon, 15 April 1699; printed in *Coll. Man. N.F.*, 2:315.

137 "Il n'y a aulcun acte dans le greffe du Port Royal qui parle des limittes, les Anglois ont eu la précaution de tout enlever dans le temps quils en estoient aultrefois maistres": NAC, AC, C11D, 3, f.68, Villebon to the minister, 27 Oct. 1699; partially printed *in Coll. Man. N.F.*, 2:330–1.

138 NAC, C11D, 3, f.205, Villebon, "Mémoire sur la pêche aux côtes de l'Acadie et de la manière de la faire," 27 Oct. 1699; English translation: Webster, *Acadia*, 138–40.

139 "Mémoire du roy au sieur de Brouillan," 23 March 1700," *Coll. Man. N.F.*, 2:332–3.

140 There is some confusion about this man. I have followed the information given by Étienne Taillemite in "Claude-Sébastien de Villieu," *DCB*, 2:653–4, with the addition of some details from Webster, *Acadia*, 200–2.

141 René Baudry, "Jacques-François de Mombeton de Brouillan," *DCB*, 2:479–81.

142 Coleman, *Acadian history in the isthmus of Chignecto*, 4.

143 Lanctôt, *Familles acadiennes*, 1:290. There are a number of different ways of spelling "Thibodeau"; many of the contemporary sources have it as Tibadau or Tibaudeau. The spelling I have used is that most commonly in print today.

144 Clément Cormier, "Pierre Tibaudeau," *DCB*, 2:629–30.

145 Published in PAC *Report,*1905, 2, app. A, 3.

146 White, *Dictionnaire généalogique*, 1:756; see also Lanctôt, *Familles acadiennes*, 2:288–9.

147 NAC, AC, C11D, 3, f.220, de Goutin to the minister, 29 Oct. 1699; see also NAC, AC, series B, 22, f.167, the minister to de Goutin, 30 March 1701; and NAC, AC, series B, 22–2, f.84, "Arrest [du Conseil concernant les concessions] des terres de l'Acadie"; printed in Gaudet, "Les Seigneuries de l'ancienne Acadie," 347.

148 Census printed in full in Rameau de Saint-Père, *Une colonie féodale*, 2:394–402.

149 Maud Hody, "Guillaume Blanchard," *DCB*, 2:71.

150 Lanctôt, *L'Acadie des origines*, 78; see also Surette, *Atlas de l'établissement des Acadiens*, 98–101.

151 Webster, *Acadia*, 201.

152 NAC, AM, series A, liasse 39, Conseil d'État, 30 March 1703; see also NAC, AC, series B, 27, f.16, "Decree re … grant to Michel de Le Neuf," 2 June 1705.

153 "Sans toutefois que ledit sieur de La Vallière puisse déposséder les habitants de ladite province, qui se trouverent en possession des terres et héritages qu'ils occupent en ce territoire, et qu'ils cultivent, habitent, et font valoir, ou font cultiver … à la charge seulement des censives et droits seigneuriaux envers ledit seigneur de La Vallière pour les terres qu'ils possèdent en ce territoire": NA, AM, series A, liasse 39, Conseil d'Etat, 2 June 1705; partially printed in Rameau de Saint-Père, *Une colonie féodale*, 2:337.

154 Harris, *The seigneurial system in early Canada*, 196–7.

155 NAC, AC, G1-466, 169; see also Clark, *Acadia*, 149.

156 Roy, *Inventaire des concessions*, 4:38–9; partially printed in Rameau de Saint-Père, *Une colonie féodale*, 2:323.

157 Clark, *Acadia*, 149.

CHAPTER EIGHT

1 Anderson, *War and society*, 87.

2 See Lewis, *The splendid century*, chapter 9.

3 There is a considerable debate over population statistics for this era. Kennedy, *The rise and fall of the great powers*, estimates France's population as twenty million, that of the British Isles as nine million, that of the Hapsburg empire as eight million, that of Prussia as two million, and that of the United Provinces as 1.8 million. My estimate of France's population is drawn from Goubert, *Louis XIV and twenty million Frenchmen*, 20.

4 On the rural and agricultural nature of England, see Brown, *Society and economy in modern Britain*, 10–27; on France, see Pierre Goubert: "La force du nombre," in Braudel and Labrousse, ed., *Histoire économique et sociale de la France*, 2:12–13.

5 Pierre Léon, "L'élan industriel et commercial," in ibid., 505.

6 Brown *Society and economy in modern Britain*, 161.

7 Black, *Convergence or divergence?* 142.

8 On this, see Hampson, *A social history of the French revolution*, 1–65; Neale, *Class in English history*, 168; Grassby, *The business community of seventeenth century England*.

9 *Historical statistics of the United States*, series Z:1–19, 756; Brown, *Society and economy in modern Britain*, 33.

10 PAC, *Census of Canada, 1870–71*; see also Gemery, "European emigration to North America," 14.

11 *Frenchmen into peasants*, 279.

12 NAC, Collection Moreau de St. Mery, ff.249–52, 31 May 1701.

13 Eccles, *The ordeal of New France*, 87.

14 On this, see, among other sources, Lacour-Gayet, *Histoire du Canada*, 151.

15 Waller, *Samuel Vetch*, ix; on the importance of the connection between Massachusetts and England, see Baker and Reid, *The New England knight*, chapter 6.

16 Collins, *The state in early modern France*, 159.

17 Clark, *The later Stuarts 1660–1714*, 208.

18 Collins, *The state in early modern France*, 160.

19 Eggenberger, *Encyclopaedia of battles*, 54–5.

20 René Baudry, "Jacques-François de Mombeton de Brouillan," *DCB*, 2:478–2.

21 NAC, AC, C11D, 4, f.37, Pontchartrain to Sieur Brouillan, 28 March 1701; partially printed, but wrongly dated as 23 March 1701, in *Coll. Man. N.F.*, 2:332.

22 NAC, AC, C11D, 4, f.45ff., Brouillan to Pontchartrain, 6 Oct. 1701; lengthy quotations from this document are given in by Murdoch, *A history of Nova Scotia*, 1:247–52.

23 The description is that of Sister Chausson of the Filles de la Croix: "Notre eglise est dans une pauvreté affreuse. Elle n'est couverte que de paille ... les vitres ne sont que de papier." It is cited by Rumilly, *Histoire des Acadiens*, 1:160, and by Casgrain, *Les Sulpiciens*, 124–5.

24 "Le bétail y est tres-abondant ... pres de 800 barriques de bled qu'on Tire Touttes les Années sans rien otter du nécessaire aux habitans": NAC, AC, C11D, 4, f.70, 7 Oct. 1701.

25 "les habitants sont a demi des républicains, tres independents de caractere, et habitués a décider de tout par eux-memes": ibid.

26 "Il les trouva d'abord opposés ... croyant que c'étoit un joug qu'on vouloit leur imposer, lui ayant dit très librement qu'ils n'y vouloient point contribuer si c'étoit pour une compagnie, disant hautement qu'ils aimeroient mieux être aux Anglois": NAC, AC, C11D, 4, f.115, Brouillan to Pontchartrain, 30 Oct. 1701; partially printed in *Coll. Man. N.F.*, 2:385.

27 NAC, AC, C11D, 4, f.45, Brouillan to the minister, 6 Oct. 1701; English translation published in Murdoch, *A history of Nova Scotia*, 1:248–9. A copy of a contemporary map of the fort and its site, dated 20 Oct. 1700, is printed in Ganong, "A monograph of historic sites," 278–9.

28 Duffy, *The military experience*, 289.

29 NAC, AC, C11D, 4, f.115, Brouillan to the minister, 6 Oct. and 22 Oct. 1701, the latter printed in part in *Coll. Man. N.F.*, 2:387–92.

30 NBM, Webster Collection, Villebon Papers, Villebon to Count Pontchartrain, 17 April 1693; Webster, *Acadia*, 46.

31 Charles Melanson to Governor Stoughton, 5 Feb. 1696, cited in Daigle, "Nos amis, les ennemis," 150.

32 On the question of Acadians as seamen, see W. Austin Squires, "Pierre Maissonat, *dit* Baptiste, " *DCB*, 2:449–50.

33 On the militia in Acadia, see Brouillan to the minister, 6 Oct. 1701, and NAC, AC, C11D, 4, f.167, the king to Brouillan, 15 March 1702.

34 Marion, *Dictionnaire des institutions de la France*, 376–80; Duffy, *The military experience*, 93.

35 NAC, AC, C11D, 4, f.37, "Mémoire du Roi au Sieur Brouillan," 28 March 1701; printed in part in *Coll. Man. N.F.*, 2:332–4.

36 "un traité d'union et de bonne correspondance ... en cas qu'il y ait guerre en Europe ... toutes les choses restant en l'état où elles sont, sous aucun prétexte on puisse rompre cette bonne correspondance, qu'en avertissant une année à l'avance": ibid., 333.

37 NAC, AC, C11D, 4, f.40, Brouillan to Lord Bellamont, 22 Aug. 1701.

38 Rawlyk, *Nova Scotia's Massachusetts*, 88–9.

39 Massachusetts Council to Brouillan, 22 Aug. 1701, *Cal. St. Papers, 1701*, 470–1.

40 NAC, AC, C11D, 4, f.107, Brouillan to the minister, 30 Oct. 1701.

41 NAC, AC, AC, C11D, 4, f.148, Louis XIV to Brouillan, 1 Feb. 1702.

42 Minutes of the Massachusetts Council, 30 June 1702, *Cal. St. Papers, 1702*, 434.

43 Dudley to the Lords of Trade and Plantations, 17 Sept. 1702, *Cal. St. Papers, 1702*, 592–5.

44 La Morandière, *Histoire de la pêche française*, 1:361–3.

45 "la réunion de la province de l'Acadie au domaine de Sa Majesté": Conseil Souverain, 30 March 1703, NAC, AM, liasse 39; partially printed in translation in Murdoch, *A history of Nova Scotia*, 1:261ff.

46 NAC, AC, C11D, 4, f.204, Brouillan to the minister, 29 Nov. 1703; a précis is given in Murdoch, *A history of Nova Scotia*, 1:267. A small part of the document is printed in *Coll. Man. N.F.*, 2:408.

47 NAC, AC, C11D, 4, f.222, Brouillan to the minister, 21 Oct. 1702.

48 On the issue of the supplies for the garrison, see NAC, AC, C11D, 4, f.272, Brouillan to the minister, 25 Nov. 1703. See also Desbarats, "The cost of early Canada's native alliances."

49 NAC, AC, C11D, f.294, Brouillan to the minister, 30 Nov. 1703.

50 NAC, AC, C11D, 4, f.272, Brouillan to the minister, 25 Nov. 1703.

51 NAC, AC, C11D, ff.176–272, 2 Oct. 1702–25 Nov. 1703.

52 NAC, AC, C11D, 4, f.191, de Goutin to the minister, 29 Nov. 1702; ibid., f.322, Chacornac to the minister, 1703.

53 Baudry, "Jacques-François de Mombeton de Brouillan," 481.

54 René Baudry, "Claude Barrat," *DCB*, 2:45.

55 René Baudry, "Louise Guyon," *DCB*, 3:681.

56 NAC, AC, C11D, 4, f.316, Bishop Saint-Vallier of Quebec to the minister, 1703.

57 Morrison, *The embattled northeast*, 154.

58 NAC, AC, C11D, 4, f.209, Brouillan to the minister, 30 Dec. 1702.

59 Wrong, *The rise and fall of New France*, 563. For a full account, see Penhallow, *The history of the wars of New England with the eastern Indians*, 4–7.

60 J.-Roger Comeau, "Michel Leneuf de La Vallière de Beaubassin," *DCB*, 2:411–12.

61 Massachusetts Council minutes, 3 Sept. 1703, *Cal. St. Papers, 1702–1703*, 665.

62 "On ne leur parle point ny d'Impots ny de Taille/ ils ne payent quoy que ce soit": Dièreville, *Relation of the voyage*, 90; French: 256.

63 NAC, AC, C11D, 4, f.272, Brouillan to the minister, 25 Nov. 1703.

64 For similar attitudes along the St Lawrence, see Séguin, *La civilisation traditionnelle de l'"habitant,"* 76–80.

65 At this time the difference between the Julian calendar (O.S.) and the Gregorian calendar (N.S.) becomes of great importance in reading the documents, since Massachusetts used the former and the French the latter. For the difference between the two calendars, see chapter 4, n.93.

66 Massachusetts Council minutes, 20 March 1704, cited in Rawlyk, *Nova Scotia's Massachusetts*, 96.

67 Howard H. Peckham, "Benjamin Church, *DCB*, 2:145–6.

68 Rawlyk, *Nova Scotia's Massachusetts*, 97.

69 Benjamin Church, *The history of the eastern expeditions*, 251.

70 Hutchinson, *The history of the colony and province of Massachusetts-Bay*, 2:109.

71 Maud H. Hody, "Michel Chartier," *DCB*, 3:111–12; Roy, *Inventaire des concessions*, 4:116.

72 Church, *The history of the eastern expeditions*, 112.

73 Ibid., 113.

74 Labat, "Invasion des Anglois de Baston," 1 July 1704, *Coll. Man. N.F.*, 2:416.

75 Church, *The history of the eastern expeditions*, 114–15.

76 Ibid., 116.

77 Ibid., 118.

78 Labat, "Invasion des Anglois," 424.

79 Anon., *The deplorable state of New England*, cited in Rawlyk, *Nova Scotia's Massachusetts*, 99.

80 Penhallow, *The history of the wars of New England with the eastern Indians*, 18.

81 Labat, "Invasion des Anglois," 424.

82 Clark, *Acadia*, 150.

83 Ibid., 145.

84 Cormier, *Les aboiteaux en Acadie*, 37–69.

85 NAC, AC, C11D, 5, f.229, de Goutin to the minister, 23 Dec. 1705.

86 NAC, AC, C11D, 4, f.176, de Goutin to the minister, 20 Oct 1703.

87 Louis XIV to Marchin, 13 Sept. 1704, cited in Wolf, *Louis XIV*, 539.

88 May 1705, cited in ibid., 540.

89 For a short account of the war, see Kennedy, *The rise and fall of British naval mastery*, 82–6.

90 Baudry, "Jacques-François de Mombeton de Brouillan," 481.

91 NAC, AC, C11D, 5, ff.103–26, Bonaventure to the minister, 30 Nov. 1705.

92 It was the usual practice for the military at this time to allow soldiers to supplement their irregular labours with work for profit in their off-duty hours. Duffy, *The military experience*, 127.

93 NAC, AC, C11D, 5, f.197, Frère Justinien Durand to the minister, 1705.

94 NAC, AC, C11D, 5, ff. 127–52.

95 René Baudry, "Jean-Chrysostome Loppinot," *DCB*, 2:445.

96 NAC, AC, C11D, 5, f.95, 15 July 1705; f.221, Lettre des Acadiens à Sa Majesté, 15 July 1705.

97 NAC, AC, series B, f.12 1/2, the minister to Bonaventure, 22 May 1706.

98 See Foursans-Bourdette, *Économie et finances en Bearn.*

99 NAC, AC, C11D, 5, f.222, the king to Subercase, 22 May 1706; see also NAC, AC, series B, 27, f.4 1/2, the king to Subercase, 23 May 1706.

100 There is some ambiguity about the dates of these reports, which are calendared as C11D, 5, ff.248 and 259, the first being dated as 26 December. They are also in this order in folio. In the *Coll. Man. N.F.*, 2:460–1, the second letter is printed in part and dated 25 *October*, three days before Subercase arrived.

101 NAC, AC, series B, f.4 1/2, the king to Subercase, 22 May 1706.

102 "fort peu actifs et peu capables d'entreprendre quelques chose par eux-memes; il n'ont point l'air français, quoique bien faits et bien tournés. Ils n'aiment que les procès, et jamais cette colonie ne s'établira bien si l'on ne trouvent le moyen de leur ôter l'esprit de chicane et d'établir la paix et l'union": NAC, AC, C11D, 5, f.259ff., Subercase to the minister, 1706.

103 NAC, AC, C11D, 5, f.229, de Goutin to the minister, 22 Dec. 1706.

104 Lanctot, *A history of Canada*, 2:99.

105 On the matter of coinage, see Griffiths, "The Golden Age," 29.

106 NAC, AC, C11D, 5, f.241, Bonaventure to the minister, 24 Dec. 1706.

107 *Cal. St. Papers, 1706–1708*, 278; *Acts and resolves public and private ... of Massachusetts Bay*, 8:134.

108 Vaudreuil to Pontchartrain, 19 Oct. 1705, printed in Richard, ed., *Supplement to Dr. Brymner's report on the Canadian Archives, 1899*, 389.

109 Cited in Waller, *Samuel Vetch*, 83.

110 John Winthrop to Fitz-John Winthrop, 17 June 1706, cited in ibid.

111 Ibid., 84.

112 Ashurst, *The deplorable state of New England*, 19.

113 Queen in council, 24 Sept. 1707, cited in Murdoch, *A history of Nova Scotia*, 1:283.

114 *Cal. St. Papers, 1706–1708*, 278.

115 Waller, *Samuel Vetch*, 95.

116 Kelley, "Louis Aubert Duforillon in Acadia," 150.

117 Bosher, *Négociants et navires*, 36.

118 Duforillon to Dudley, 8 Jan. 1707, printed in Kelley, "Louis Aubert Duforillon," 156.

119 Dudley to Sampson Sheafe, 15 Jan. 1707 (O.S.), printed in ibid., 158.

120 Rawlyk, *Nova Scotia's Massachusetts*, 100.

121 Dudley to Winthrop, 10 Feb. 1707, MHS *Collections*, 6th series, 3:367.

122 *Acts and resolves public and private ... of Massachusetts Bay*, 8:683.

123 MHS *Proceedings*, 1884–88, 2nd series, 1:159. For an analysis of the general

mood of Massachusetts, see Rawlyk, *Nova Scotia's Massachusetts*, 101–2; and, for an alternative view, see Plank, *An unsettled conquest*, 37–9.

124 *Acts and resolves public and private ... of Massachusetts Bay*, 8:686–7.

125 There are a variety of estimates of the manpower employed. These are approximate figures and are recorded in the autobiography of the Reverend John Barnard, who had been appointed chaplain to the army by Governor Dudley in 1707. MHS *Collections*, 3rd series, 5:189.

126 Ibid., 190–1.

127 John David Krugler, "John March," DCB, 2:452–3.

128 Brebner, *New England's outpost*, 50.

129 Georges Cerbelaud Salagnac, "Bernard-Anselme d'Abbadie de Saint-Castin," DCB, 2:3–4.

130 Bernard Pothier and Donald J. Horton, "Louis Denys de La Ronde," DCB, 3:176.

131 NAC, AC, C11D, 6, f.89, Subercase to the minister, 26 June 1707, printed in *Coll. Man. N.F.*, 2:467–70; anon. (perhaps Bonaventure), "Entreprise des Anglois contre l'Acadie," 26 June 1707, printed in *Coll. Man. N.F.*, 2:464–7. On 6 July the engineer Labat dispatched his version, "Entreprise des Bastonnais sur l'Acadie," printed in *Coll. Man. N.F.*, 2:477–81.

132 *Acts and resolves public and private ... of Massachusetts Bay*, 8:686–729.

133 A number of these are to be found in MHS *Collections* and *Proceedings*: John Marshall's Diary, MHS *Proceedings, 1884–88*, 2nd series, vol.1; "Bernard autobiography," MHS *Collections*, 3rd series, vol.5.

134 These dates are N.S. Among the earliest accounts by historians are those of Charlevoix, *History and general description of New France*, 5:191ff., and Hutchinson, *The history of the colony and province of Massachusetts-Bay*, 2:150ff. See, too, Reid et al., *The conquest of Acadia*.

135 NAC, AC, C11D, 6, f.89, Subercase to the minister, 26 June 1707: *Coll. Man. N.F.*, 2:467–70.

136 Rawlyk, *Nova Scotia's Massachusetts*, 103.

137 Lanctôt, *L'Acadie des origines*, 86.

138 There seems to be a consensus among historians that Brouillon had started the construction of this eighteen- to twenty-gun vessel at Port Royal in late 1705 and completed it in late 1706. See Pothier and Horton, "Louis Denys de La Ronde," 177.

139 While there is not detailed report available on the exact state of affairs within the fort, the presence of cannon and mortars is mentioned in Labat's report to the minister, 6 July 1707, partially printed in *Coll. Man. N.F.*, 2:477–81.

140 Rawlyk, *Nova Scotia's Massachusetts*, 103; Charlevoix, *History and general description of New France*, 5:192; Murdoch, *A history of Nova Scotia*, 1:287–8.

141 Charlevoix, *History and general description of New France*, 5:192–3; Murdoch, *Nova Scotia*, 1:288.

142 Baudry, "Daniel d'Auger de Subercase," 37.

143 Cited in Rawlyk, *Nova Scotia's Massachusetts*, 103.

144 Hutchinson, *The history of the colony and province of Massachusetts-Bay*, 2:124.

145 Murdoch, *A history of Nova Scotia*, 1:288–9; Hutchinson, *The history of the colony and province of Massachusetts-Bay*, 2:123–5; Charlevoix, *History and general description of New France*, 5:192–4.

146 John Winthrop to Fitz-John Winthrop, July 1707, MHS *Collections*, 6th series, 3:389.

147 Hutchinson, *The history of the colony and province of Massachusetts-Bay*, 2:124.

148 "Barnard Autobiography," 194.

149 "Placet présenté par 50 filibustiers du bateau *l'intrepide* à Monseigneur le Comte de Choiseul, gouverneur de La Tortue, Isle et Coste de Saint Domingue": cited in in Le Blant, "Un corsaire de Saint-Domingue en Acadie," 194.

150 NAC, AC, C11D, 6, f.72, Subercase to the minister, 20 Dec. 1707.

151 Hutchinson, *The history of the colony and province of Massachusetts-Bay*, 2:169.

152 *Cal. St. Papers, 1706–1708*, Dudley to the Board of Trade, 590–1.

153 NAC, AC, C11D, 6, f.15, Subercase to the minister, 26 June 1706, partially printed *in Coll. Man. N.F.*, 2:467–70.

154 NAC, AC, C11D, 6, f.72, Subercase to the minister, 20 and 25 Dec. 1707; and f.40, de Goutin to the minister, 23 Dec. 1707.

155 Charlevoix, *History and general description of New France*, 5:201.

156 "Entreprise des Anglois contre l'Acadie"; Subercase to the minister, 26 June 1707, *Coll. Man. N.F.* 2:469; Labat, 6 July 1707, *Coll. Man. N.F.*, 2:480, 481.

157 "La colonie ... se voyait a la veille d'être a son aise par ... le nombre de leurs bestiaux et surtout de moutons ... Ceux des Mines ont plus amasse de lin ... Leurs besoins actuels est de couvertes, de grosses étoffes de laines, de marmites de fer ... il n'y avoit ni marmites, ni faulx, ni faucilles, ni couteaux ... ni haches ni chaudières pour les sauvages ...": NAC, AC, C11D, f.40, de Goutin to the minister, 23 Dec.1707; translation printed in Murdoch, *A history of Nova Scotia*, 1:295–6.

158 "le roi abandonnera le pays s'il continue d'être aussi à charge": NAC, AC, series B, 29, f.4, the minister to Subercase, 6 June 1708.

159 An account of the French military action at this time is found in Wolf, *Louis XIV*, 544–54.

160 Army and navy combined. See Kennedy, *The rise and fall of the great powers*, 104.

161 The request, more tactfully phrased, is in NAC, AC, C11D, 7, f.72, Subercase to the minister, 25 Dec. 1707.

162 Pothier and Horton, "Louis Denys de La Ronde," 177.

163 NAC, AC, C11D, 6, f.70, Subercase to the minister, 20 Dec. 1708.

164 NAC, AC, C11D, 7, f.32, Subercase to the minister, 3 Jan. 1710; and f.81, same to same, 4 Jan.1710.

165 "Le cruel hiver de 1709 acheva de désespéres la nation": Voltaire, *Le siècle de Louis XIV*, 218.

166   Emmanuel Le Roy Ladurie, "De la crise ultime à la vrai croissance, 1660–1789," in Duby and Wallon, *Histoire de la France rurale*, 2:363; Pierre Goubert, "Le 'tragique' XVIIe siècle," in Braudel and Labrouuse, ed., *Histoire économique et sociale de la France*, 2:360.

167   Knapton, *France: An interpretative history*, 218.

168   Marshall, *A digest of all the accounts*, cited in Stevenson, *Popular disturbances*, 115.

169   NAC, AC, series B, 29, f.22, the minister to de Goutin, 6 June 1708.

170   Her father had held a seigneury near Jemseg.

171   Pothier and Horton, "Louis Denys de La Ronde," 177.

172   NAC, AC, C11D, 6, f.219, Subercase to the minister, 25 Dec. 1708; see the précis of this document, with lengthy citations from it, in Murdoch, *A history of Nova Scotia*, 1:300–4.

173   Pothier and Horton, "Louis Denys de La Ronde," 177.

174   NAC, AC, C11D, 6, f.211, Subercase to Pontchartrain, 20 Dec. 1708.

175   NAC, AC, C11D, 6, f.219, Subercase to Pontchartrain, 25–30 Dec. 1708.

176   Ibid.

177   "Tous les habitans qui ont été employez à reparer le fort ont travailler avec beaucoup de joye et ce travail a esté fait avec extrême diligence": NAC, AC, C11D, f.226, Subercase to Pontchartrain, 20 Dec. 1708.

178   NAC, AC, C11D, 6, f.219, Subercase to Pontchartrain, 25–30 Dec. 1708; partially printed in *Coll. Man. N.F.* 2:499–501.

179   NAC, AC, C11D, 7, f.279, de Goutin to the minister, 20 Dec. 1708.

180   Cited in Wolf, *Louis XIV*, 558.

181   Ibid., 559.

182   On these negotiations, see Goubert, *Louis XIV and twenty million Frenchmen*, 259ff.; Wolf, *Louis XIV*, 558ff.

183   Cited in Goubert, *Louis XIV and twenty million Frenchmen*, 259.

184   See ibid., 260–1.

185   Anderson, *War and society*,136; Collins, *The state in modern France*, 162.

186   Subercase to Vaudreuil, 23 July 1709, *Coll. Man. N.F.*, 2:504–6; Subercase to the minister, 19 Oct. 1709, *Coll. Man. N.F.*, 2:507; Subercase to the minister, 7 Nov. 1709, *Coll. Man. N.F.*, 2:508–9.

187   Daigle, "Nos amis, les ennemis," 187.

188   "Il ne manquoit rien pour la défense du fort, ayant des munitions de guerre, du pain et de la viande ... L'Acadie n'a jamais été dans une plus grande abondance de vivres et de marchandises": *Coll. Man. N.F.*, 2:507.

189   *Acts and resolves public and private ... of Massachusetts Bay*, 8:747–8; Rawlyk, *Nova's Scotia's Massachusetts*, 106.

190   *Cal. St. Papers, 1706–1708*, Dudley to the Board of Trade, 590–1.

191   The full plan is to be found in the Letter Book of Samuel Vetch, 1709–11, Museum of the City of New York, and PRO, CO324, 9, 221–46. It is partially printed in *Cal. St. Papers, 1708–1709*, 60. Waller presents a full analysis of it in *Samuel Vetch*, 106–9.

CHAPTER NINE

1 Reid, "'Another Dunkirk,'" 1.

2 Bill of Rights, printed in Stephenson and Marcham, *Sources of English constitutional history*, 604.

3 Jarrett, *Britain 1688 to 1815*, 4. The historiography in the field of English political and constitutional history is immense. I suggest that the interested reader consult, in particular, Brown, *Society and economy*, and Cain and Hopkins, *British imperialism*.

4 Coleman, "Mercantilism revisited," 790.

5 Jarrett, *Britain 1688 to 1815*, 21.

6 On this see Richard S. Dunn, "The Glorious Revolution and America," in Canny, ed., *The Oxford history of the British empire*, 1:445–66.

7 Craven, *The colonies in transition*, 233.

8 See P.J. Marshall's "Introduction" to vol.2 of the *Oxford history of the British empire*, 1–27.

9 For one view of the extent to which this policy was pursued, see Webb, *The governors general*. See also the review of this work by Stephen Baxter in *WMQ*, 3rd series, 37 (October 1980): 658–61.

10 W.A. Speck, "The international and imperial context," in Greene and Pole, *Colonial British North America*. See also Steele, *Politics of colonial policy*, 15–28.

11 See Barrow, *Trade and empire*.

12 Jim Potter, "Demographic development and family structure," in Greene and Pole, *Colonial British North America*, 135.

13 See Wise, "Liberal consensus or ideological battleground."

14 Steele, *The English Atlantic*, 196ff. and appendices 4.3, 4.5, and 4.6.

15 Davis, *The rise of the English shipping industry* and *A commercial revolution*. See also Canny, ed., *Oxford history of the British empire*, vol.1.

16 I am much indebted here to Steele, *The English Atlantic*, 229–50.

17 British political life in the seventeenth and eighteenth centuries has been the subject of a voluminous literature. A good place to begin is Jones, *Country and court*, 8–44. See also Cannon, *Aristocratic century*, and Brown, *Society and economy*.

18 Ian K. Steele, "The anointed, the appointed and the elected: Governance of the British empire, 1689–1784," in Marshall, ed., *The Oxford history of the British empire*, 2:105.

19 Jones, *Country and court*, 16.

20 Steele, *The English Atlantic*, 245.

21 Ibid., 237.

22 Ibid., 238.

23 Alsop, "The age of the projectors," 30n.1.

24 Dudley to the Board of Trade, "Memorial referring to the French settlements in North America," *Cal. St. Papers, 1706–1708*, 590–2.

25 William Blathwayt had recently left his position at the Board of Trade and the

Earl of Nottingham had resigned as secretary of state. Both these men were strong supporters of Dudley. See Waller, *Samuel Vetch*, 95.

26 Rawlyk, *Nova Scotia's Massachusetts*, 106.

27 These biographical details are from Waller, *Samuel Vetch*, chapter 1, and from the same author's "Samuel Vetch" in *DCB*, 2:650–2.

28 See Burton, ed., *The Darien papers*, and Insh, ed., *Papers relating to the ships and voyages*, vi.

29 Clark, "War trade and trade war," 263.

30 Waller, *Samuel Vetch*, 108.

31 *Journals B.T.*, 1–4:530–2; *Cal. St. Papers, 1708–1709*, 71.

32 Waller has provided a full account of the way in which Vetch worked for the success of his proposal: *Samuel Vetch*, 110–12. See also *Journals B.T.*, 1:556–7.

33 Massachusetts General Court to the queen, 20 Oct. 1708, *Cal. St. Papers, 1708–1709*, 314–16.

34 Webb, "The strange career of Francis Nicholson," 525.

35 Bruce T. McCully, "Francis Nicholson," *DCB*, 2:496–9.

36 Webb, *The governors general*, passim.

37 Webb, "Francis Nicholson," 541.

38 Queen Anne's instructions to Vetch, 28 Feb. 1709, *Cal. St. Papers, 1708–1709*, 387.

39 Waller, *Samuel Vetch*, 118.

40 Ibid., 133, 180.

41 On the details of this support, see ibid., 127–32.

42 Dudley, Nicholson, Vetch, and Moody to Sunderland, 24 Oct. 1709, *Cal. St. Papers 1708–1709*, 488.

43 A short account of these events is found in Waller, *Samuel Vetch*, 125–57. See also Bond, *Queen Anne's American kings*, 114–15.

44 An account of the sequence of events is to be found in Jones, *Country and court*, 292–4.

45 NAC, AC, C11D, 7, f.32, Subercase to the minister, 3 Jan. 1710.

46 Chard, "The impact of French privateering," 160.

47 Account of charges, 12 Oct. 1709, *Cal. St. Papers, 1710–11*, 29–30.

48 Waller, *Samuel Vetch*, 151–4.

49 "Address of the principal inhabitants and merchants at Boston," 24 Oct. 1709, enclosed in Vetch, Dudley, Nicholson, and Moody to Sunderland, *Cal. St. Papers. 1708–1709*, 492–3.

50 Memorial of Colonel John Higginson, 1709, *Cal. St. Papers, 1708–1709*, 407–8.

51 Vetch, Dudley, and Moody to Board of Trade, 25 Oct. 1709, *Cal. St. Papers, 1708–1709*, 794, 798; NBM, Webster Collection, Dudley and Moody to Board of Trade, 25 Oct., 18 Nov. 1709 (also cited in Waller, *Samuel Vetch*, 167).

52 Commission, 18 March 1710, printed in NSHS *Collections*, 1 (1878):59–60.

53 MA, 71, House of Representatives order, 21 July 1710.

54 Nicholson to Dartmouth, 16 Sept. 1710, *Cal. St. Papers, 1710–1711*, 174.

55 "Journal of Colonel Nicholson at the capture of Annapolis, 1710," NSHS *Collections*, 1 (1878):64–5.

56 The actual numbers are approximate; the various primary sources give slightly differing figures for Rhode Island. See Rawlyk, *Nova Scotia's Massachusetts*, 119, and Waller, *Samuel Vetch*, 180. Murdoch estimates the force at 3,400 men, "besides the sea forces": *Nova Scotia*, 1:313. Lanctôt, *L'Acadie des origines*, 101, and Rumilly, *Histoire des Acadiens*, 1:189, give the total as about 3,500, including the crews.

57 "Journal of Colonel Nicholson," 65.

58 Charlevoix, *History and general description of New France*, 5:226.

59 Cazaux, *L'Acadie*, 251–3.

60 NAC, AC, C11D, 7, f.90, Subercase to the minister, 1 Oct. 1710; partially printed in translation in Murdoch, *A history of Nova Scotia*, 1:309–10.

61 Charlevoix, *History and general description of New France*, 5:228.

62 "Journal of Colonel Nicholson," 67.

63 Ibid., 68.

64 Ibid., 60; Charlevoix, *History and general description of New France*, 5:229; Murdoch, *A history of Nova Scotia*, 1:314.

65 "Les habitants et les soldats en furent si intimidez qu'ils vinrent lui donner une requête pour lui représenter le pitoyable état auquel tout était réduit, ce qui n'était que trop véritable, et plusiers des uns et des autres désertèrent": NAC, AC, C11D, 7, f.90, Subercase to the minister, 13 Oct. 1710; partially printed in *Coll. Man. N.F.*, 2:529, but incorrectly dated.

66 Nicholson to Subercase, 30 Sept. 1710: "Journal of Colonel Nicholson," 71–2. The exchange of letters between Subercase and Nicholson as to the niceties of negotiation is published in ibid., 71–5, 78–85.

67 Articles of capitulation in English are found in "Journal of Colonel Nicholson," 82–3; a description of the articles in French is in "Résumé d'une lettre de monsieur de Subercase au ministre, Port Royal le 26ᵉ Oct.": *Coll. Man. N.F.*, 2:529. The articles that were sent to France are found in NAC, AC, C11D, 7, f.94, Subercase to the minister, 13 Oct. 1710.

68 "Journal of Colonel Nicholson," 85–6.

69 Ibid., 94–6.

70 Ibid., 88; René Baudry, "Daniel d'Auger de Subercase," *DCB*, 2:35–9.

71 "Journal of Colonel Nicholson," 96–7.

72 John David Krugler, "John Livingston," *DCB*, 2:436–8.

73 Georges Cerbelaud de Salagnac, "Bernard-Anselme d'Abbadie de Saint-Castin," *DCB*, 2:3–4.

74 "... ni gouverneur, ni officiers, ni troupes, ni artillerie, ni administration de la France": Sauvageau, *Acadie*, 152. Sauvageau's work has raised considerable controversy: his background is that of a historian of twentieth-century Europe and he sees little difference between the nationalism of the eighteenth century and that of the twentieth. For a major review of Sauvageau's book, see d'Entremont, "Compte rendu"; and for Sauvageau' s reply, see "Réponse à un

'Compte rendu.'" Anselme Chiasson has in turn commented on Sauvageau's reply to d'Entremont in 'Tout doux, monsieur Sauvageau!'

75 PRO, A&WI, vol.58, no.131, "The present state of the ffort of Annapolis Royal, formerly Port Royal in Nova Scotia, signed by A. Forbes ...," 15 Jan. 1711; printed in Patterson, ed., "Papers connected with the administration of Governor Vetch," 99. All subsequent quotations on the state of the fort are from Patterson.

76 This particular approach is found in the works of Francis Parkman, the nineteenth-century American historian, and, more recently, in Lauvrière, *La tragédie d'un peuple*; Roy, *L'Acadie perdue;* and Sauvageau, *Acadie*.

77 See, in particular, Armitage, ed., *Theories of empire*, vol.20 of Russell, *An expanding world*.

78 For a general introduction, see Said, *Culture and imperialism*. And see also Cazaux, *L'Acadie*.

79 Reid, "'Another Dunkirk,'" 19.

80 These changes in the colony's status were as a result of the Argall raid in 1613 and the Kirke brothers' interventions in 1628–32; the colony's return by the Treaty of Saint-Germain-en-Laye in 1632; its capture by Sedgwick in 1654 and subsequent return by the Treaty of Breda in 1667; its capture by Phips in 1690; and, again, its return by the Treaty of Ryswick in 1697.

81 BL, "Memorial by Mascarene to Nicholson, Annapolis Royal, Nov. 1813"; BM, Add. Mss. 19070, vol.2, Mascarene, "A narrative of events at Annapolis Royal from the capture in Oct. 1710 till Sept. 1711" (hereafter Mascarene, "Narrative"). The latter is printed in Patterson, ed., "Papers connected with the administration of Governor Vetch," 74.

82 Mascarene, "Narrative."

83 Moody, "'A just and disinterested man,'" 11–13. I am much indebted to the author for providing me with a copy of this thesis, thus saving an old friend the chore of reading an excellent work on microfilm.

84 Ibid., 19; Maxwell Sutherland, "Paul Mascarene," *DCB*, 3:436.

85 Mascarene, "Narrative," 70.

86 Ibid., 86.

87 Anderson, *War and society*, 56. See also Eames, "Rustic warriors."

88 Mascarene, "Narrative," 86.

89 Ibid., 71.

90 Mascarene, "Commission to sundries at Minas," in Patterson, ed., "Papers connected with the administration of Governor Vetch," 88.

91 Syndics were discussed in chapter 6.

92 Mascarene, "Narrative," 72.

93 "In Bills ... drawn formerly by Mr. Subercase accepted by Colo. Vetch – by his name being endorsed of the sd Bills – the sums due by Colo Vetch to Mr. Subercase must have considerable since there was an abundance of those Bills." Ibid., 73. Whether these bills were related to the cannon that Vetch bought from Subercase, or to some other trading transaction, is unknown. It is possible that they originated in the trade Vetch plied in Acadia before 1697.

94   "Mascarene's commission to sundries at Minas," 88.
95   NAC, NS/A, 4, Mascarene to Nicholson, 6 Nov. 1713.
96   Mascarene, "Narrative," 73.
97   NAC, AC, C11D, 7, f.98, "Letter of the principal inhabitants of Port Royal to Vaudreuil," 13 Nov. 1710. A full English version of this letter is given in Murdoch, *A history of Nova Scotia*, 1:321–2.
98   He had been in Acadia since 1684, settling first along the Saint John River and moving to Port Royal in 1698 (see chapter 7). The letter is mentioned in George MacBeath, "René Damours de Clignancour," *DCB*, 2:167–8. It would be interesting to know how Vetch used the money. Did he use it for his own personal needs or to pay the soldiers? Or pay it back to the Acadians for the supplies that he bought from them over the next months? Unfortunately, no records of any transactions seem to have survived.
99   Le Blant, *Une figure légendaire*, 104.
100 NAC, series B, 32, f.73, minister to Subercase, Versailles, 20 May 1710.
101 "Depuis que j'ai appris la perte de l'Acadie, je ne cesse de songer aux moyens de recouvrer ce poste important avant que les Anglais n'y soient solidement établis. La conservation de toute l'Amérique septentrionale et le commerce des pêcheries le demandent également. Ce sont deux objets qui me touchent vivement": NAC, AC, C11D, 7, f.100, Pontchartrain to Beauharnois, 24 Dec. 1710.
102 Georges Cerbelaud de Salagnac, "Philippe Pastour de Costebelle," *DCB*, 2:509–13.
103 See, in particular, NAC, AC, C11D, 31, f.3, Vaudreuil to the minister, June 1710. See also Lanctot, *A History of Canada*, 2:152ff., and Miquelon, *New France, 1701–1744*, 38ff.
104 NAC, AC, C11D, 7, f.129, "Instruction pour le sieur baron de St-Castin," 18 Jan. 1711; printed in part in *Coll. Man. N.F.*, 2:534–6.
105 "Qui ne tâchent d'envahir ce continent que pour les réduire eux-mêmes dans l'escavage, en les privant, s'ils venoient à bout de nous, des secours que nous leur donnons, comme les vêtements, la poudre, le plomb et les armes": idid., 534–5.
106 Mascarene, "Narrative," 74.
107 Ibid., 74–5, 76.
108 Ibid., 76.
109 Ibid.
110 Waller, *Samuel Vetch*, 197.
111 Mascarene, "Narrative," 77.
112 PRO, CO 5, f.133, "List of masters of families, inhabitants ... who took the oath of allegiance to Her Majesty," 20 Jan. 1711.
113 Alison Olson, "Sir Charles Hobby," *DCB*, 2:288–90.
114 Mascarene, "Narrative," 78.
115 Ibid., 76.
116 Ibid.
117 Ibid., 78.

118 "Sir Charles Hobby's orders to Major Mascarene," in Patterson, ed.," Papers connected with the administration of Governor Vetch," 79. Emphasis in original.

119 Mascarene, "Narrative," 80.

120 Waller, *Samuel* Vetch, 198-200.

121 Mascarene, "Narrative," 81.

122 PRO, CO 5, f.144, Samuel Vetch to Lord Dartmouth, 14 June 1711.

123 NAC, CO 218, 1, Samual Vetch to Lords of Trade, 15 June 1711; see also "Postscript," 24 June 1711, in Patterson, ed., "Papers connected with the administration of Governor Vetch," 94.

124 Vetch did not date his account of the occurrence but his letter to Governor Dudley was written in the week of 24 June 1711 (O.S.). The account of Father Antoine Gaulin, written at the opening of September, was dated 10 June (N.S.). See NAC, AC, C11D, 7, f.177.

125 "Orders for Capt. Pidgeon," 9 June 1711 (O.S.), Patterson, ed., "Papers connected with the administration of Governor Vetch," 81-2.

126 Vetch wrote two accounts of this action, both of which are published in ibid., 95-7 and 103-4.

127 "Governor Vetch to governor of Massachusetts," n.d., ibid., 96. Costebelle, in a letter to Pontchartrain on 24 July 1711, gives the number of "Indians" as forty; cited in Charlevoix, *History and general description of New France*, 5:288n.1. See also NAC, AC, C11D, 7, f.173, Cahouet to the minister, 20 July 1711, and NAC, AC, C11D, 8, f.177, Antoine Gaulin to the minister, 5 Sept. 1711.

128 René Baudry, "Louise Guyon," *DCB*, 3:681-2.

129 Mascarene, "Narrative," 82.

130 Haliburton, *An historical and statistical account of Nova Scotia*, 1:91.

131 "Proceedings of Council of War, Annapolis Royal, June 15th, 1711," in Patterson, ed., "Papers connected with the administration of Governor Vetch," 98.

132 PRO, CO 5, 9, ff.103, 82, 82a, Vetch to Hill, 11 Sept. 1711; printed as "a skeame of ane establishment for the garison of Annapolis Royal in Nova Scotia," 16 April 1711, in Patterson, ed., "Papers connected with the administration of Governor Vetch," 93-4.

133 Mascarene, "Narrative," 82.

134 Ibid.

135 "Governor Vetch to governor of Massachusetts, n.d.," printed in Patterson, ed., "Papers connected with the administration of Governor Vetch," 95-7.

136 David Lee, "Antoine Gaulin," *DCB*, 2:238.

137 NAC, AC, C11D, 7, f.177, Gaulin to Vaudreuil, 5 Sept. 1711.

138 Mascarene, "Narrative," 83.

139 "Après avoir signifié au Gouverneur anglois qu'ayant contravenu à leur égard aux articles de la Capitulation ils étoient dispensez du serment qu'ils avoient fait de ne point prendre les armes ...": NAC, AC, C11D, 7, f.179, Gaulin to the minister, 5 Sept. 1711.

140 "Instructions to Sir Charles Hobby," 105.

141 The Acadian population in the region of Annapolis Royal is given as 481 in a census taken in 1710 and sent to London on 20 October of that year: NAC, CO 5, 9. Males capable of bearing arms would have numbered less than fifty. For the Acadian population as a whole, the number would have been less than five hundred.

142 Mascarene, "Narrative," 83.

143 NAC, AC, C11D, 7, f.177, Gaulin to Vaudreuil, 5 Sept. 1711.

144 In the following paragraphs I have tried to keep the chronology straight by using phrases that indicate the impact of calendar differences – and imprecise dates – in the contemporary documents.

145 Bruce T. McCully, "Francis Nicholson," 497.

146 *Cal. St. Papers, 1710–1711*, 893.

147 Waller, *Samuel Vetch*, 211.

148 Daigle, "Nos amis, les ennemis," 193.

149 Murdoch, *A history of Nova Scotia*, 1:325. Waller, *Samuel Vetch*, 207–34, recounts in full the preparations for, and fortunes of, this expedition.

150 Le Blant, *Philippe de Pastour de Costebelle*, 157.

151 Murdoch, *A history of Nova Scotia*, 1:325.

152 Letter of Durand La Garenne, 18 Oct. 1711, cited in Le Blant, "Un corsaire de Saint-Domingue," *Nova Francia*, 6 (1931): 203.

153 Gerald S. Graham, "Sir Hovenden Walker," *DCB*, 2:658–62. Waller, *Samuel Vetch*, 225, puts the figures at eight transports and one provision ship.

154 Waller, *Samuel Vetch*, 229.

155 Ibid., 229–30; Charles Bruce Fergusson, "Thomas Caulfield," *DCB*, 2:122–3; F.J. Thorpe, "George Vane," *DCB*, 2:643–4.

156 The date of return, 20 October, is written in the margin of the journal he wrote describing the Quebec expedition. PRO, CO 5, 9.

157 PANS, Vetch Letter Book, 1711–13, 62–3, Vetch to Douglas, 10 Feb. 1712; Waller, *Samuel Vetch*, 235–6.

158 PANS, NS/8, 33–6, 68, Vetch's orders to Captain Rous, 18 Oct. and 12 Nov. 1711.

159 *Cal. St. Papers, 1711–1712*, Vetch to the secretary of state, 3 and 5 Jan. 1712, 253, 303.

160 "qui ne veulent aucun accommodement avec ces Messieurs": "Lettre de Monsieur de St.-Castin aux habitants de la banlieue du Port-Royal," printed in *Coll. Man. N.F.*, 2:543.

161 "Et dans le temps que vous croirez qu'il en aura point au Port-Royal, et que vous vous croirez en sureté pour accommoder ces Messieurs des pièces qu'ils vous demandent, vous vous trouverez saisis par les Sauvages qui tueront vos bestiaux et vous prendront prisonniers comme enemis du Roi": ibid.

162 NAC, AC, C11D, 32, f.99, Felix Le Pain to the minister, 8 Sept. 1711.

163 NAC, CO 217, 31, f.3, Caulfield to the secretary of state, 6 Dec. 1711.

164 Miquelon, *New France, 1701–1744*, 46.

165 Wolf, *Louis XIV*, 581.

166 All dates N.S.: Miquelon, *New France, 1701–1744*, 51.

167 PANS, NS/A, 8:70, 71, 75, Instructions to Livingstone, 12 Nov. 1711, Vetch to Caulfield, 12 March 1711, Vetch to William Alden, 1 March 1711.

168 Charles Bruce Fergusson, "William Winniett," DCB, 3:665–6.

169 Daigle, "Nos amis, les ennemis," 194.

170 Mascarene, "Narrative," 74.

171 Boudrot, in fact, captained *The Three Friends* for Capon in 1713: MA, 7, 475, "Register of ship, July 20, 1713,"; and Daigle, "Nos amis, les ennemis," 194.

172 Waller, *Samuel Vetch*, 251.

CHAPTER TEN

1 NAC, CO 218, 1, Utrecht, circular, "Lords of Trade to Nicholson, with proclamation of peace and copy of Treaty of Utrecht, May 8th, Whitehall, 1713." Also: NAC, NS/A, 4.

2 Wolf, *Louis XIV*, 588–96.

3 NAC, MG 40, D, "Louis aux plénipotentiaires," 20 March 1712.

4 It is from these negotiations that the phrase "la perfide Albion" arises, particularly because of the British treatment of its former allies the Dutch and the Catalans. The best argument in defence of British actions is found in Clark, *The later Stuarts*, 234–7.

5 Lloyd, *The British empire*, 60.

6 The clauses relating to Canada are printed in a number of works, including Lanctot, *A History of Canada*, 2:215–17, and Murdoch, *A History of Nova Scotia*, 1:332.

7 Miquelon, *New France, 1701–1744*, 50; a summary of the early discussions are found in NAC, MG 5, A-1, 18: 88.

8 The Treaty of Utrecht, article 13. On this issue, see Frederic F. Thompson, *The French shore*, 7–9.

9 NAC, CO 218, 1, circular with proclamation and copy of the Treaty of Utrecht, 8 May 1713. Also: NAC, NS/A, 4.

10 NAC, NS/A, 4:97, warrant from the queen; printed in full in Murdoch, *A History of Nova Scotia*, 1:333.

11 NAC, NS/E, 7:3, commission, 20 Oct. 1712.

12 Davies, *Europe and the world*, vol.4, *The north Atlantic*, 308.

13 Gipson, *The British empire before the American Revolution*, 5:80.

14 Lanctot, *A history of Canada*, 2:228.

15 Clark, *Acadia*, 276, puts the figure at 498; McLennan, *Louisbourg*, 371, has a slightly higher figure, 510.

16 Clark, *Acadia*, 276.

17 PRO, BTNS, 1, Vetch to the Lords of Trade, 9 March 1715. See also NAC, NS/A, 6.

18 "Ces peuples sont naturellement adroits et industrieux au dela de ce qu on voit en Europe. Ils reuississent en tout ce qu'ils entreprennent, ils ne devi-

nent qu'a la Nature la Connaissance qu'il sont de plusiers arts. Ils naissent forgerons, menusiers, tonneliers, Charpentiers ...": NAC, AC, C11D, 8, f.40, Saint-Ovide to Comte de Toulouse, 1717.

19 NAC, AC, C11D, 7 and 8, passim, Correspondence of Pastour de Costebelle, Saint-Ovide, Father Gaulin, etc. But see in particular vol.7, f.177, Antoine Gaulin, 5 Sept. 1711.

20 Many English officials frequently received their training in Ireland before moving on to North America. Webb has noted that "between 1689 and 1727 fifteen or more veterans of William III's Irish wars also served as royal governors in Virginia, Gibraltar, Minorca, Jamaica, Barbados, the Leeward Islands, Nova Scotia and Newfoundland, New York and Pennsylvania." See Webb, "Army and empire," 15.

21 In much of what follows I am greatly indebted to Dummet and Nicol, *Subjects, citizens, aliens.*

22 Speck, *Stability and strife,* 16.

23 Reid, "Nova Scotia, 1715," 15.

24 NAC, AC, C, 1, G6, "Mémoires," 30 Nov. 1706 and 20 Aug. 1708. See also C11B, 1, f.277. For a full discussion of these plans, see La Morandière, *Histoire de la pêche française,* 2:643–4.

25 See Camu, *Le Saint-Laurent et les Grands Lacs,* 25ff.

26 NAC, C11B, 1, f.17, Pontchartrain to Vaudreuil and Michel Bégon.

27 NAC, AC, series B, 35, f.2 1/2, Pontchartrain to Vaudreuil, 24 Feb. 1713.

28 Ibid., f.11, Pontchartrain to Saint-Ovide, 20 March 1713.

29 Ibid., f.25, Pontchartrain to Vaudreuil, 29 March 1713.

30 The variation in spelling is common enough for eighteenth-century France. See Bernard Pothier, "Joseph de Monbeton de Brouillan, *dit* Saint-Ovide," DCB, 3:454–7; and René Baudry, "Jacques-François de Mombeton de Brouillan," DCB, 2:478–82.

31 McLennan, *Louisbourg,* 11.

32 Georges Cerbelaud Salagnac, "Philippe Pastour de Costebelle," DCB, 2:509–13.

33 F.J. Thorpe, "Jacques L'Hermitte," DCB, 2:433–5.

34 Bernard Pothier and Donald J. Horton, "Louis Denys de La Ronde," DCB, 3:176–80.

35 J.-Roger Comeau, "Michel Leneuf de La Vallière de Beaubassin," DCB, 2:411–12.

36 "n'avoir trouvé sur ladite isle qu'un habitant francois et 25 a 30 familles de sauvages ...": NAC, AC, C11B, 1, f.11.

37 Clark, *Acadia,* 269.

38 All but four or five of the inhabitants of Plaisance had left for France or Île Royale. See La Morandière, *Histoire de la pêche française,* 2:649. See also NAC, AC, C11B, 1, f.108.

39 On this particular point, see Dickason, *Louisbourg and the Indians,* 9–11, and Reid, "Nova Scotia, 1715," 15–16.

40 Reid, "Nova Scotia, 1715," 15.

41 Wicken, "Encounters with tall sails," 96; Reid, "Nova Scotia, 1715," 15.

42 Upton, *Micmacs and colonists*, 32 ; see also, for a general account of the Mi'k-maq experience on Île Royale, Dickason, *Louisbourg and the Indians.*

43 "Ces sauvages sont peu de choses estant nos allies et pourraient devenir quelque chose de considerable estant nos ennemis": Gaulin to Saint-Ovide, 17 Nov. 1719, cited in Upton, *Micmacs and colonists*, 36.

44 Wicken, "Encounters with tall sails," 253–5.

45 Ibid., 291.

46 NAC, CO 217, 1, Nicholson to the Lords of Trade, 14 Dec. 1713.

47 Brebner, *New England's outpost*, 60.

48 NAC, CO 217, 1, f.83, Nicholson to the Board of Trade, 11 Dec. 1713.

49 McLennan, *Louisbourg*, 14.

50 Ibid., 17.

51 Ibid., *Louisbourg*, 16.

52 See NAC, A, 43, "Papers of various dates laid before the Lords of Trade," 10 Jan. 1715; and CO 217, 1, "Letters of various dates laid before the Lords of Trade," December 1713–August 1714.

53 Pontchartrain to d'Iberville, 7 Nov. 1714, partially printed in Akins, *Acadia*, 4; see also NAC, AC, series B, f.426, Pontchartrain to Costebelle, 28 Feb. 1714.

54 Accounts of this meeting and of subsequent meetings at Minas and Cobequid are found in NAC, CO 217, 1, ff.193–6, "Copies of several papers relating to the French inhabitants, with lists of those who embark for Cape Breton, 10 Feb. 1714/15.

55 "En ce jour, fête de Saint Louis, nous soussignés, avec toute la joie et la satis-faction dont nous sommes capables, donnons par la presente la preuve éter-nelle que nous voulons vivre et mourir fidelles sujets de sa Majesté tres Chré-tienne en nous engageant de nous aller establir à l'Isle Royalle ou autres terres de la domination françoise supposons que nous ne puissions establir a la ditte Isle, nous et nos enfans, en foy de quoy nous avons signé ce present ...": NAC, CO 217, f.226. These declarations are the same for all settlements, but that for Cobequid is the best preserved and the most read.

56 NAC, CO 217, 1, f.193, August 1714.

57 NAC, CO 217, 1, f.218, 27 Aug. 1714.

58 "Je vous faire a scavoir que je signe pour notre bon Roy essant a l'impossible d'y aller a cause de grain qui est en perdition. pierre terriot": NAC, CO 217, 1, f.226, 27 Aug. 1714.

59 Brebner, *New England's outpost*, 69.

60 Charles Bruce Fergusson, "Thomas Caulfeild," *DCB*, 2: 122–3. Evidence of let-ter, Nicholson to Caulfeild, 24 Nov. 1714.

61 "douze moutons, Trois Jeune Boeufs, Une Vache, Un Veau et quatre Bar-riques de Grains": NAC, CO 217, 1, f.224, "List of the inhabitants that have shipt themselves and their effects in the sloop *Marie-Joseph*.

62 Bernard Pothier, "Acadian emigration to Île Royale," 123–4.

63 Doucett to the Board of Trade, 6 Feb. 1717, cited in McLennan, *Louisbourg*, 18.

64 NAC, AC, series B, 37, f.1, Pontchartrain to Desmaretz, 4 Jan. 1714/15.

65 Ibid.

66 See Speck, *Stability and strife,* 160–85.

67 NAC, CO 217, 1, ff.83–99; partially printed in Akins, *Acadia,* 5–7.

68 Clark, *Acadia,* 234.

69 Many of these have been partially printed in Akins, *Acadia,* 7–16.

70 NAC, CO 217, 2, Caulfeild to the Board of Trade, 1 Nov. 1715; printed in full in MacMechan, *Nova Scotia Archives II,* 24–7.

71 Basque, *Des hommes de pouvoir,* 62.

72 NAC, CO 217, f.220, report of Mascarene, 13 Sept. 1714.

73 Cited in Clark, *Acadia,* 257.

74 Chard, "The Impact of Île Royale on New England," xii.

75 Clark, *Acadia,* 319.

76 NAC, AC, C11B, 7:140; see also Clark, *Acadia,* 317.

77 Chard, "The Impact of Île Royale on New England," xiii.

78 Governor Philipps to Mr Popple, secretary of Board of Trade, n.d. but MacMechan, *Nova Scotia Archives II,* 71–2, places it after 28 Dec. 1720.

79 Reid, "Acadia and the Acadians," 26–31.

80 See N.E.S. Griffiths, "Subjects and citizens in the eighteenth century," in Moulaison, Comeau, and Langille, ed., *Les abeilles,* 23–34.

81 See chapter 11.

82 Caulfeild to the Board of Trade, 24 Dec. 1714 and 13 May 1715, in MacMechan, *Nova Scotia Archives II,* 13.

83 NAC, CO 324, 10, draft for the proclamation of King George, 6 Aug. 1714, Caulfeild to the Lords of Trade, 12 Jan.1714/15, instructions to Peter Capoon, n.d.; printed in Akins, *Acadia,* 3.

84 Doucett to the secretary of state, 5 Nov. 1717, in MacMechan, *Nova Scotia Archives II,* 51–3; oath also printed in Akins, *Acadia,* 14.

85 See *Coll. Doc. Inédits,* 1:110–13; and NAC, NS/A, 5:155–8.

86 "Moy je promes sincerrement Et jure que je veut Estre fidelle Et tenir vne veritable alegence a sa majeste Le roy George tan que je sere a Lacadie et nouuel Escosse Et qu'il me sera permy de me retiré La ou je jugeré a propos auec tous mais Bien meuble Et Effet quant je Le jugeré a propos san que nulle persone puise man Enpesche" (22 Jan. 1715): *Coll. Doc. Inédits,* 1:110. This oath is not included in Akins, *Acadia.*

87 On the importance of this individual, see Basque, *Des hommes de pouvoir,* 55, 61–2.

88 "Bontee que le Roy George que nous reconnaissons Estre Legitime souverain de la Grande Bretagne veut bien avour pour nous": NAC, NS/A, 6.

89 "Et sous La Domination duquel nous nous fussions une véritable joie de Restaer, Etant ainsi bon Prince comme il Est, si nous n'avons pas pris ... des l'Eté dernier ... [la résolution] de retourner Sous la Domination de Prince Le Roy de France ... nous nous obligeons avec plaisir et par reconnaissons pendant que nous Resterons ici, a la Cadie, De ne Rien faire n'y entreprende contre Sa Majesté Britannique Le Roy George ..." (12 March 1715): ibid.

90 NAC, CO 217, 2, Caulfeild to the Board of Trade, 1 Nov. 1715.

91 Pothier, "Acadian emigration to Île Royale," 122, 125–6.

92 NAC, AC, C11B, 1, f.265, Costebelle to the minister, 12 Jan. 1714/15.

93 Le Blant, *Philippe de Pastour de Costebelle*, 192n.1.

94 Harvey, *The French regime in Prince Edward Island*, 34.

95 NAC, CO 217, 16, Caulfeild to the Board of Trade, 1 Nov. 1715; printed in MacMechan, *Nova Scotia Archives II*, 24–7.

96 NAC, AC, C11, IR, f.198, Saint-Ovide to the minister, 10 Sept. 1715.

97 NAC, AC, C11, IR, f.232, La Ronde to the minister, 2 Dec. 1715.

98 Caulfeild to the secretary of war, 24 Oct. 1716, MacMechan, *Nova Scotia Archives II*, 44–6.

99 NAC, AC, C11, IR, f.404, unaddressed letter of Costebelle, 8 Oct. 1715.

100 Charles Bruce Fergusson, "John Doucett," *DCB*, 2:198–9.

101 NAC, CO 217, 2, Doucette to the secretary of state, 5 Nov. 1717; printed in MacMechan, *Nova Scotia Archives II*, 51–3.

102 Chard, "Canso, 1710–1721," 56; see also NAC, CO 217, 1, pt.3, f.303, "Estimate of charges of victualling the garrison from 1 May to 31 May 1715."

103 Philipps to customs commissioners, 24 Nov. 1720, MacMechan, *Nova Scotia Archives II*, 69.

104 Chard, "Canso, 1710–1721," 60–2.

105 Wicken, "Encounters with tall sails," 293. Wicken goes on to point out that, according to shipping records, all but two of the vessels returning to Boston from Annapolis Royal between August 1718 and July 1719 carried furs or skins.

106 Brebner, *New England's outpost*, 255.

107 Philipps to Cragg, July 1720, MacMechan *Nova Scotia Archives II*, 63.

108 "En cas qu'on ne put pas trouver d'autres Moyens, Nous Smmes prets de prester Serment comme quoy Nous ne prendrons point les armes ny contre Sa Majeste Britannique ny contre la France, ny contre aucun de leurs Sujets ou de leurs Alliez": included in NAC, NS/A, 8:183ff., Doucett to the secretary of state, 5 Nov. 1717; printed in MacMechan, *Nova Scotia Archives II*, 52–3.

109 "les offres et les advantages qui nous ont étez fais par le Roy George Roy de la grande Bretagne": NAC, NS/A, 6; printed in *Coll. Doc. Inédits*, 1:170–1.

110 "aux d'Esespoir de ne pouvoir y répondre comme vous l'auriez Souhaitté": ibid.

111 "nos ancestres ont étés sous la Domination angloise on ne leur a Jamais Exigé de pareille Serments": ibid.

112 Parkman: *Montcalm and Wolfe*, vol.1, chapter 4; Haliburton: *An historical and statistical account of Nova Scotia*, 156.

113 Cited in Bernard, *Le drame acadien depuis 1604*, 254.

114 See the extensive correspondence on this subject in dispatches sent to the officials on Île Royale during the years 1713–17: NAC, AC, C11, 1–2.

115 Rumilly, *Histoire des Acadiens*, 1:219–21. It is interesting that Brebner, in *New England's outpost*, does not refer to these efforts at all.

116 See Dumont-Johnson, *Apôtres ou agitateurs.*

117 See, in particular, Basque, *Des hommes de pouvoir.*

118 On dyke agriculture and its impact on group solidarity, see Bertrand, "La culture de marais endigués." On the issue of communal fields, see a 1738 document on the apportionment of a meadow between three farmers: PANS, Grant Book 1738 (I am indebted to Régis Brun for this document). And, on the question of Acadian agriculture as a whole, see chapter 11.

119 The rate of illiteracy among the Acadians was not particularly high for rural Catholic populations of the time. The work most often used for estimating Acadian literacy is Le Gresley, *L'enseignement du français en Acadie.* Also valuable is Dugas, "L'alphabétisation des Acadiens."

120 Maxwell Sutherland, "Richard Philipps," DCB, 3:515–18.

121 Commissions in NAC, NS/E, 7:5, 7. See also NAC, CO 218, 1, Lords of Trade to Lord Justices, 19 June 1719.

122 NAC, NS/E, 7:7.

123 Brebner, *New England's outpost,* 135. Brebner's analysis of what this meant is well worth reading in full.

124 Published in MacMechan, ed., *Original minutes of His Majesty's Council,* and *Nova Scotia Archives III,* 28–9.

125 Godfrey, *Pursuit of profit,* 3.

126 Moody, "'A Just and Disinterested Man,'" 54. Mascarene had been a brevet-major in his former regiment.

127 Ibid., 56.

128 NAC, CO 218, 1, Philipps to the Board of Trade, 11 March 1718; NAC, NS/A, 18.

129 NAC, NS/A, 11, Philipps to the Board of Trade, 3 Jan. 1719; précis in MacMechan, *Nova Scotia Archives II,* 56.

130 Dalton, *George the First's army,* 1:240; Smythies, *Historical records of the 40th,* 3. As it turned out, for the next ten years, there would be no more than four understrength companies of the 40th Foot stationed in Nova Scotia, without either naval support or that of a local militia.

131 A précis, including the quotation, is in MacMechan, *Nova Scotia Archives II,* 53–4.

132 26 May 1720: précis in MacMechan, *Nova Scotia Archives* III; verbatim excerpts in Murdoch, *A History of Nova Scotia,* 1:362.

133 The details are laid out in Philipps to the secretary of war and to the Board of Ordnance; for a summary of this document, see MacMechan, *Nova Scotia Archives II,* 60–2. See also NAC, CO 217, 3, Philipps to the Lords of Trade, 26 May 1720.

134 In what follows I am deeply indebted to the work of T.G. Barnes, especially his "'The dayly cry for justice.'"

135 NAC, CO 217, 2, f.84, Caulfeild to the Board of Trade, 16 May 1716.

136 NAC, CO 217, 3, f.111, Vetch to the Board of Trade, 21 Aug. 1720.

137 MacMechan, *Nova Scotia Archives III,* 1–3; all vessels on arrival and departure were expected to report to this officer.

138 Barnes, "'The dayly cry for justice,'" 23.

139 NAC, CO 218, 1, Lords of Trade to Lord Justices, 19 June 1719 (articles 11–13 of Philipps's instructions, along with his commission).

140 Philipps's account of this is set out in NAC, CO 217, 3, Philipps to Cragg, 26 May 1720; précis in MacMechan, *Nova Scotia Archives II*, 60–1.

141 Micheline D. Johnson, "Justinien Durand," *DCB*, 3: 207–8.

142 These proclamations are printed in MacMechan, *Nova Scotia Archives II*, 57. See also Akins, *Acadia*, 21–2.

143 NAC, AC, series B, 42, f.486 1/2, Ministry of the Marine to the archbishop of Cambrai, 12 Sept. 1720. The archbishop was the ecclesiastical superior of the Recollets.

144 See Keohane, *Philosophy and the state in France.*

145 NAC, AC, series B, IR, 55, f.563, president of Navy Board to de Bourville, 10 July 1731. See also chapter 11.

146 NAC, CO 217, 3, Philipps to Lord Carteret, January 1720; partially printed in Akins, *Acadia*, 18–19.

147 NAC, CO 217, 3:18, Philipps to Lords of Trade, 27 Sept. 1720; partially printed in Akins, *Acadia*, 49–52; see also the précis of the letter to Cragg, n.d., in MacMechan, *Nova Scotia Archives II*, 67–9.

148 NAC, CO 217, 3, Philipps to Cragg, 26 May 1720; précis in MacMechan, *Nova Scotia Archives II*, 60–1; partially printed in Akins, *Acadia*, 31–5.

149 Pothier, "Acadian emigration to Île Royale," 126.

150 "Minutes of the Council ...," 4 May 1720, MacMechan, *Nova Scotia Archives III*, 7. For more on the qualifications required of deputies, see chapter 11.

151 "Letter of the inhabitants of Acadie to Mr. de St. Ovide ...," 6 May 1720, Akins, *Acadia*, 25–6.

152 Philipps to Saint-Ovide, 14 May 1720; précis in MacMechan, *Nova Scotia Archives II*; printed in Akins, *Acadia*, 26–8.

153 NAC, AC, C11, IR, 5, f.189, Sainte-Ovide to the governor of Annapolis Royal, 30 June 1720 (N.S.).

154 NAC, CO 217, 3, Philipps to Board of Trade, 26 May 1720; partially printed in Akins, *Acadia*, 31–5.

155 Dated only by the month, May; printed in full in ibid., 28.

156 NAC, CO 217, 3, Philipps to Board of Trade, 26 May 1720; printed in Akins, *Acadia*, 35. Philipps was mistaken on the matter of rent payments: see chapter 11.

157 Moody, "'A Just and disinterested Man,'" 63–7.

158 David Parker, "The Huguenots in seventeenth century France," in Hepburn, ed., *Minorities in history,* 11–30, gives the present accepted state of knowledge on the matter. See also Quéniart, *La révocation de l'édit de Nantes.*

159 Philipps sent the report to the Board of Trade in one of his dispatches. See NAC, CO 217, 3, f.18, 27 Sept. 1720; printed in full in Akins, *Acadia*, 39–49.

160 Ibid., 43.

161 Moody, "'A just and disinterested man,'" 75–83; Brebner, *New England's outpost,* 81.

CHAPTER ELEVEN

1 The most recent expression of the view that Acadians have no core of self-generated distinctiveness is to be found in Fernand Ouellet, "Démographie, développement économique." His arguments will be examined in more detail in the body of this chapter.

2 Couturier, "'L'Acadie, c'est un détail.'"

3 Wicken, "Encounters with tall sails," 96, table 2.1.

4 All figures and place-name spellings are from ibid.

5 See the remainder of this chapter and also Bertrand, "La culture des marais en digués."

6 Clark, *Acadia*, 35–6.

7 I am indebted for much of what follows to Chard, "Canso 1710–1721."

8 See map in Clark, *Acadia*, 226.

9 Chard, "Canso 1710–1721," 62; NAC, AC, C11B, f.143, Saint-Ovide to the minister, 30 Nov. 1717.

10 Clark, *Acadia*, 227.

11 "Memorial of James Pitt, Oliver Noyes," 9 June 1718, *Cal. St. Papers, 1719–1720*, 103–4.

12 PRO, CO 5, 792, ff.231–2, Minutes of the Massachusetts Assembly, 20 June 1718.

13 Chard, "Canso, 1710–1721," 66. The events of the expedition are recounted in full not only in this article but also in McLennan, *Louisbourg*, chapter 4, and Rawlyk, *Nova Scotia's Massachusetts*, 125–8.

14 *Cal. St. Papers, 1719–1720*, 99.

15 Chard, "Canso, 1710–1721," 71.

16 Clark, *Acadia*, 228.

17 NAC, AC, IR, C11, 3, f.109, Saint-Ovide and de Soubras to the Council, 19 Oct. 1718.

18 Savelle, *The diplomatic history of the Canadian boundary*, 3, 7.

19 Smart to Burchett, 20 Oct. 1719, cited in Douglas, "Nova Scotia and the Royal Navy," 18.

20 NAC, NS/A, 9:151, Captain Christopher Aldridge to Governor Philipps, 24 Dec. 1718.

21 NAC, CO 217, 4, account of Lawrence Armstrong, at this time serving at Annapolis Royal, 20 Nov. 1720; printed in full in McLennan, *Louisbourg*, 68–9. Also: account of three witnesses, dated 29 Aug. 1720 and sent to Governor Philipps at Annapolis Royal, published in Lanctot, Johnston, and Shortt, ed., *Documents*, 133. See, too, NAC, NS/A, 15:3, Armstrong's "Memorial," 18 May 1722.

22 Account of Lawrence Armstrong, 20 Nov. 1720, McLennan, *Louisbourg*, 68.

23 "Plundering of traders at Canso," in Lanctot, Johnston, and Shortt, ed., *Documents*, 133.

24 Account of Lawrence Armstrong, 20 Nov. 1720, McLennan, *Louisbourg*, 68.

25 Murdoch, *A history of Nova Scotia*, 1:375.

26 Governor Philipps to Secretary Cragg, 26 Sept. 1720, MacMechan, *Nova Scotia Archives II*, 67–8; partially printed in Akins, *Acadia*, 49–52.

27 Douglas, "Nova Scotia and the Royal Navy," 20.

28 Philipps to Armstrong, 22, 24 Oct. 1720, MacMechan, *Nova Scotia Archives II*, 69.

29 NAC, NS/A, 12:77–8, John Alden to Governor Philipps; printed in Lanctot, Johnston, and Shortt, ed., *Documents*, 133–4.

30 Governor Philipps to Secretary Cragg, 26 Sept. 1720; précis in MacMechan, *Nova Scotia Archives II*, 67–9; partially printed in Akins, *Acadia*, 51.

31 See Morin, *L'usurpation de la souveraineté autochtone*, especially 17–126.

32 See Dickason, "Amerindians between French and English in Nova Scotia," 33.

33 "cete terre icy que Dieu nous a donné dont nous pouvons conté estre ausy tot que les arbes y sont né ne pouvez nous estre disputé par personne ... Nous sommes Maistre independente de personne et voulons avoyr notre pays libre": CO, 217, 3, ff.155–6, Antoine and Pierre Couaret to Governor Philipps, 2 Oct. 1720. Upton gives a less free translation in *Micmacs and colonists*, 199.

34 MacMechan, *Nova Scotia Archives II*, 67–8; partially printed in Akins, *Acadia*, 49–52.

35 For a brief summary of international relations in this period, see Kennedy, *The rise and fall of the great powers*, 107–8.

36 Philipps to Popple, n.d., Akins, *Acadia*, 54. Similar examples can be found throughout the correspondence between British officials in Nova Scotia and London, and between France, Quebec, and Louisbourg.

37 NAC, AC, series B, 37, f.26 1/2, Pontchartrain to Desmaretz, 10 Feb. 1715. Again, similar concerns are easily found among English documents.

38 NAC, MG 1, C11B, 1, f.129, Costebelle to the minister, 9 Sept. 1715.

39 Dickason, *Louisbourg and the Indians*, 128.

40 Moody, "'A Just and Disinterested Man,'" 71.

41 Charles Bruce Fergusson, "William Winniett," *DCB*, 3:665–6.

42 A superb introduction to the complex financial organization of the British administration of Nova Scotia is given in Lanctot, Johnston, and Shortt, ed., *Documents*, xv–xlix.

43 Ibid., xxix. On the role and structure of the Ordnance Board, see Chester, *The English administrative system*, 46.

44 NAC, NS/A, 13, Washington to George Musgrave, 25 Jan. 1719/20.

45 In the compressed account of this turgid affair that follows, I am greatly indebted to Moody, "'A Just and Disinterested Man,'" 71–82.

46 NAC, NS/A, 13, "Answers to Lieut.Washington's malicious scandalous and vile underhand unjust and unwarrantable representations to Great Brittain and elsewhere against His Excellency Governr Philipps and ye whole garrison," June 1721.

47 Governor Philipps to Secretary Cragg, 26 May 1720; précis in MacMechan, *Nova Scotia Archives II*, 60–1; partially printed in Akins, *Acadia*, 31.

48 Council minutes, 19 April 1721, MacMechan, *Nova Scotia Archives III*, 28–9;

on the use of the Virginia model, see Barnes, "'The dayly cry for justice,'" 17–19.

49 Council Minutes, 4 May 1720, MacMechan, *Nova Scotia Archives, III*, 7.

50 Philipps to the French inhabitants of Annapolis Royal, 20 May 1720, MacMechan, *Nova Scotia Archives II*, 59.

51 I do not find tenable the assertion by Plank, in *An unsettled conquest*, 122, that these deputies were rejected because of their opposition to British rule of the colony, especially given the fact that Robichaud served in this role three years later: Basque, *Des hommes de pouvoir*, 71–2.

52 Prudent Robichaud's commission as justice of the peace, Annapolis Royal, MacMechan, *Nova Scotia Archives II*, 172.

53 Council minutes, 13 Oct. 1731, MacMechan, *Nova Scotia Archives III*, 196; see also Barnes, "'The dayly cry for justice,'" 31.

54 Council minutes, 10 April 1721, MacMechan, *Nova Scotia Archives III*, 26.

55 Murdoch, *A history of Nova Scotia*, 1:388.

56 Armstrong to La Goudalie, 20 Aug. 1733, MacMechan, *Nova Scotia Archives II*, 89.

57 NAC, CO 217, 1, Vetch to the Lords of Trade, 26 Nov. 1711.

58 Bell, *The "foreign Protestants,"* 25, 33–4.

59 Ibid., 44, cites "Proposals from navy commissioners, 12 Feb. 1719," B85, BTNS, 2, PAC *Report*, 1894.

60 Bell, *The "foreign Protestants,"* 43–51.

61 Vol.1: Canny, *The origins of empire*. Vol.2: P.J. Marshall, *The eighteenth century*.

62 Bailyn, "The first British empire."

63 See Turner, *The cabinet council*, vol.2.

64 Parris, *Constitutional bureaucracy*, 23.

65 Bell, *The "foreign Protestants,"* 17.

66 Ibid., 19.

67 Ibid., 20.

68 NAC, CO, 218, 1, Lords of Trade to Philipps, 14 Dec. 1720. The printed excerpt in Akins, *Acadia*, 58, is wrongly dated.

69 Mascarene's report is, as already noted, included in a letter of the Board of Ordnance to the Lords of Trade. It is annotated as received on 25 Feb.1725/26 and read on 16 May 1727, but it must have arrived in London earlier since it was included in Philipps to the Lords of Trade, 27 Sept. 1720. There is no way of discovering who first read Mascarene's report or when. The report is published in full in Akins, *Acadia*, 39–49.

70 Great Britain, *Journal of the Commissioners for Trade and Plantations*, 4:315–20.

71 The impact of this suggestion on the deportation will be discussed fully in chapter 13.

72 Wicken, "26 August 1726," 6.

73 On examples, see Dickason, "La 'guerre navale' des Micmacs contre les Britanniques, 1713–1763," in Martijn, ed., *Les Micmacs et la mer*, 233–48.

74 McLennan, *Louisbourg*, 66.

75 A magnificently illustrated article on the construction and use of this canoe is

that of Ingeborg Marshall, "Le canot de haute mer des Micmacs," in Martijn, *Les Micmacs et la mer*, 29–48.

76 NAC, CO 217, 4, ff.45–8, Philipps to the Lords of Trade, 1 Oct. 1721.

77 NAC, Brown Papers, Mss. 19071, f.15, Philipps to Mascarene, 5 Sept. 1721.

78 NAC, CO 217, 4, ff.154–5, 157–9, Philipps to Lords of Trade, 19 Sept 1722.

79 Dickason, "La 'guerre navale,'" 244.

80 NAC, CO 217, 4, ff.154–5, Philipps to Lords of Trade, 19 Sept. 1722.

81 There are a number of accounts of the events of this summer: for example, Rawlyk, *Nova Scotia's Massachusetts*, 129; Dickason: "La 'guerre navale,'" 244. Francophone historians, such as Rumilly and Roy, pay little attention to these events.

82 NAC, CO 218, 2, ff.14–17, Lords of Trade to Philipps, 6 June 1722.

83 Murdoch, *A history of Nova Scotia*, 1:388–9.

84 NAC, CO 217, 4, Governor Philipps to the Board of Trade, 19 Sept. 1722; partially printed in Akins, *Acadia*, 61.

85 The list is in NAC, CO 217, 4, 23 Sept. 1724.

86 Murdoch, *A history of Nova Scotia*, 1:408.

87 MacMechan, *Nova Scotia Archives III*, 57.

88 These were Mascarene, Adams, Newton, Skene, and Shirreff; not all attended each meeting. Mascarene was always named immediately after the lieutenant governor; in 1722 he was fourth in seniority on the regimental list. See Smythies, *Historical records of the 40th*, 2.

89 Murdoch has him shot on "the spot where serjeant McNeal had been slain." Murdoch, *A history of Nova Scotia*, 1:409.

90 Ibid., 410.

91 See Council minutes, 16 July, 18 July, 22 July, 12 Aug., 29 Aug. 1724, MacMechan, *Nova Scotia Archives III*, 57–74.

92 Council minutes, 29 Aug. 1724, MacMechan, *Nova Scotia Archives III*, 73.

93 See Rawlyk, *Nova Scotia's Massachusetts*, 125–44.

94 Supposedly Philipps's regiment had a complement of 815 but in 1717 he had only 445 men under his command, with one company, of perhaps fifty men, stationed at Placentia. At Annapolis Royal he stationed six companies, none of them more fifty men in size. There was one company stationed at Canso. See Murdoch, *A history of Nova Scotia*, 1:351.

95 Philipps and Council to the king, 27 Sept. 1720, MacMechan, *Nova Scotia Archives II*, 66–8; Philipps to the Board of Ordnance, 28 Dec. 1720, ibid., 70–1.

96 See NAC, AC, series B, 1, minute of 11 Aug. 1725.

97 Dickason, "Amerindians between French and English," 38.

98 The texts of these treaties are in Daughterty, *Maritime Indian treaties*, 75–8.

99 NAC, AC, C11B, 8, ff.25–30, 9, ff.22–9, 10, ff.79–89, Saint-Ovide to the minister, 11 Sept. 1726, 20 Sept. 1727, and 3 Nov. 1728.

100 See in particular Wicken, "26 August 1726." Also: Upton: *Micmacs and colonists*, 44.

101 NAC, CO 217, 37, Armstrong to Newcastle, 5 Sept. 1726; see also NAC, NS/A, 20.

102 NAC, CO 217, 37, Armstrong to Newcastle, 5 Sept. 1726.

103 NAC, CO 217, 38, f.7, Armstrong to the Lords of Trade, 2 Dec. 1725; see also NS/A, 20: 101.

104 Council minutes, 25 Sept. 1726, published in full in MacMechan, *Nova Scotia Archives III*, 128–30.

105 NAC, CO 217, 38, f.13, Armstrong to Newcastle, 24 Nov. 1726.

106 *Coll. Man. N.F.*, 1:110.

107 Council minutes, 23 May 1727, MacMechan, *Nova Scotia Archives III*, 143–4.

108 NAC, CO 217, 38, f.15, Armstrong to the Newcastle, 30 April 1727, with enclosures; partially printed in Akins, *Acadia*, 70–1.

109 Council minutes, 25 and 28 July 1727, MacMechan, *Nova Scotia Archives III*, 148–52.

110 Council minutes, ibid., 142–54.

111 Ibid., 9 Sept.1727, 157.

112 The form of the assurances differed somewhat from region to region. Those of Beaubassin were assured: "1. Qu'ils seront éxempts de prendre Les armes contre qui que se soit, tandis qu'ils seront sous la domination du Roi d'Angleterre. 2. Qu'ils seront Libres de se retirer ou bon leur semblera, et qu'ils seront deschargés du serment qu'ils auront fait aussitost qu'ils seront hors la Domination Du Roy de La grande Bretagne. 3. Qu'ils auront Leur pleine et Entierre Liberté de Leur Religion, et d'auoir des Prêtres catholiques appostoliques & Romaines." Those of Minas were further assured: "Qu'ils demeuront en Une véritable possession de leurs biens qui leur seront accordés a eux et Leurs hoirs dans le même étendûe qu'ils en ont jouÿs cy devant et en payant les mêmes droits accoutumez du Paÿs." NAC, CO 217, 38, f.16, Armstrong to the secretary of state, 17 Nov. 1727, "Report by Ensign Wroth," 143

113 Council minutes, 13 Nov. 1727, MacMechan, *Nova Scotia Archives III*, 168.

114 Brebner, *New England's outpost*, 92. Brebner argues that Armstrong gave "rights and privileges" to all Acadians but Armstrong's account itself refers only to those who had sworn a satisfactory oath.

115 NAC, CO 217, 38, f.16ff., Armstrong to Newcastle, 17 Nov. 1727, with enclosures including Council minutes, 13 May–13 November; Wroth's report on his activities; and written assurances given by Wroth to the inhabitants of Minas, Pisiquid, etc. Some excerpts are printed in Akins, *Acadia*, 79–81.

116 NAC, CO 217, 5, with enclosure containing the replies of the Chignecto inhabitants.

117 NAC, CO 217, 5, Armstrong to the Lords of Trade, 9 July 1728.

118 Barry M. Moody, "Alexander Cosby," *DCB*, 3:143–4.

119 NAC, CO 217, 5, Newcastle to Lords of Trade, 13 March 1727/28 and 22 May 1728.

120 NAC, CO, 217, 23, Lords of Trade to Newcastle, 16 July 1728.

121 CO 218, 2, commissions and instructions.

122 For a clear account, see Bell, *The "foreign Protestants,"* 40–7. Also: NAC, CO 5,
     916, Lords of Trade to Privy Council, 14 May 1729; and NAC, CO 217, 5,
     Popple to Lords of Trade, 16 May 1729.

123 NAC, CO 217, 5, f.170ff., Philipps to secretary of state, 2 Oct. 1729.

124 NAC, CO 217, 5, f.176ff., Philipps to secretary of state, 25 Nov. 1729.

125 Ibid.

126 NAC, CO 217, 39, enclosure, Philipps to the Board of Trade, 3 Jan. 1730;
     NAC, NS/A, 10.

127 Doughty, *The Acadian exiles,* 45.

128 NAC, CO 218, 2, Popple to Philipps, 20 May 1730; partially printed in Akins,
     Acadia, 84–5.

129 The argument was over the employment of what Popple considered the
     dative case for "fidelle" and the use of the accusative for "obéirai" in French.
     These changes, he contended, made the oath no more than an expression of
     fidelity rather than a true oath of allegiance. In fact, the argument arose
     from a fundamental distrust of French Catholics by an English Protestant.

130 BTNS, 6, Phillips to the Board of Trade, 26 Nov. 1730; partially printed in
     Akins, *Acadia,* 87–8. Murdoch, in *A history of Nova Scotia,* 1:465, has some
     interesting observations on the matter.

131 NAC, CO 217, 39; partially printed in Akins, *Acadia,* 86–7.

132 The oath sworn by the inhabitants of the Minas Basin and other settlements
     read as follows: "Nous Promettons et Jurons sincèrement en foi de Chretien
     que nous serons entièrement Fidelle et Nous Soumettrons Véritablement à
     Sa Majesté George Le Second, Roy de la Grand Bretagne, que nous recon-
     noissons pour Le Souverain Seigneur de La Nouvelle Ecosse et de L'Acadie":
     PAC *Report,* 1905, 2, app. D, 77–81. My translation: We promise and Swear
     sincerely on the faith of Christians that we will be entirely faithful and we
     will truly submit to His Majesty George the Second, King of Great
     Britain, whom we recognize as the Sovereign Lord of Nova Scotia and
     of Acadia.

133 NAC, Brown Papers, Mss. 19071, f.110. Antoine Bernard refers to such a
     document, dated 25 April 1730, witnessed by Alexandre Bourg, at that time
     one of the notaries at Minas, as being in the archives of the ministère des
     affaires étrangères. See *Le drame acadien,* 267.

134 See in particular the petitions of those Acadians who were sent to Pennsylva-
     nia: MacKinney, ed., *Votes and proceedings of the House of Representatives of the
     Province of Pennsylvannia,* vol.5, 8th series; "Report of the overseers of the
     poor on Acadian petitions," Pennsylvania Historical Society [Archives], Har-
     risburg; Easterby, *The Journals of the Commons House of Assembly of South Caroli-
     na,* 26 Nov. 1755 (containing a copy of Wroth's oath).

135 Brebner, *New England's outpost,* 97.

136 For a summary of the British experience, see Dummett and Nicol, *Subjects,
     citizens, aliens,* 58, 77; for France, see the essays in Durand, *Hommage à
     Roland Mousnier.*

137 See the summary, both of French political thought on this issue in the eighteenth century and of Acadian ideas, given in Durand, "L'Acadie et les phénomènes de solidarité et de fidelité au XVIIIᵉ siècle."

138 Memorial of the Council of the Marine to the officials of Île Royale, 12 Sept. 1720; NAC, AC, AN, series B, 41, f.486 1/2, 10 July 1721. See also PAC, *Report*, 1905, app. K, 149.

139 See Harvey, *The French regime*, 73–93.

140 Madden and Fieldhouse, *The classical period of the first British empire*, vol.2, *The foundations of a colonial system of government*,173n.4; see also, in the same work, vol.1, "*The empire of the Bretaignes,*" 185.

141 Muriel K. Roy provides a collation of the estimates of various scholars in "Peuplement et croissance démographique en Acadie," in Jean Daigle, ed., *Les Acadiens des Maritimes*, 144.

142 Clark, *Acadia*, 207; based on NAC, AC, G 1, 466, 262. Fernand Ouellet's decision, in "Démographie, développement économique," 3–31, to accept lower figures is based upon the data for 1755 and will be discussed in chapters 12 and 13.

143 Council minutes, 13 Oct. 1731 and 11 Aug. 1733, MacMechan, *Nova Scotia Archives III*, 196, 284–5.

144 Barnes, "'The dayly cry for justice,'" 31–2.

145 "As to the letter [to council] ... and the deputies regarding the difficulty of dividing the land between the Depuis and the Claudes, Armstrong can give no further directions. They should divide it at once": Armstrong to Bourg, 28 March 1732, MacMechan, *Nova Scotia Archives II*, 81.

146 Brebner, *New England's outpost*, 149.

147 Ibid., 75.

148 Barnes, "'The dayly cry for justice,'" 18.

149 Council minutes, 20 April 1726, MacMechan, *Nova Scotia Archives III*, 111–13.

150 Ibid., 113.

151 Barnes, "'The dayly cry for justice,'" 18. Barnes provides an analysis of these cases and the process that was involved.

152 NAC, CO 217, 241, memorandum of Mascarene, 27 May 1740.

153 Barnes, "'The dayly cry for justice,'" 32; Basque, *Des hommes de pouvoir*, 71–2.

154 This assertion is based upon the evidence published by White in *Dictionnaire généalogique.*

155 See Clark, *Acadia*, 204.

156 The surviving registers for Saint-Jean-Baptiste of Port Royal and Saint-Charles of Grand Pré are catalogued in NAC as MG 9, B-8, lots 12(3) and 24(2).

157 Fergusson, "William Winniet."

158 Godfrey, *Pursuit of profit*, passim..

159 Hale, "Journal of a voyage to Nova Scotia," 225–6.

160 I draw here upon Pierre Flatres, "Historical geography of western France," in Clout, ed., *Themes in the historical geography of France*, 300–13.

161 Hale, "Journal of a voyage to Nova Scotia," 231.

162 Ibid., 233–4.

163 Publication of this work is only now taking place. The watercolour paintings by Nova Scotia Museum artist Azor Vienneau, based on the archeological and historical evidence, are an aid to comprehension of this question.

164 Cunningham and Prince, *Tamped Clay*, 11.

165 J.-Rudolphe Bourque, "Social and agricultural aspects of Acadians in New Brunswick," cited in ibid., 11–12.

166 Smith, *Nationalism and modernism*, 191.

167 While this is a generation later than the period under discussion, I know of no major technological change which would have affected the construction of such dykes in the intervening forty years. Those who laboured and directed the work were Acadian, See LeBlanc, "Documents acadiens sur les aboiteaux."

168 Ibid., 40.

169 Bertrand, "La culture des marais endigués."

170 An overview of this issue is found in Dumont-Johnson, *Apôtres ou agitateurs*. See also Léger, "Cent personalités de l'histoire religieuses de l'Acadie."

171 Têtu and Gagnon, ed., *Mandements*, 15–16; some excerpts are printed in de Grâce, Desjardins, and Mallet, *Histoire d'Acadie par les textes*, 1:19.

172 See Casgrain, *Les Sulpiciens*, passim, and Dragon, *L'Acadie et ses 40 robes noires*.

173 Hale, "Journal of a voyage to Nova Scotia," 232.

174 For a list of those that are extant, see "Registres de l'état civil ... A: Registres d'avant la dispersion ...," in *Inventaire général*, 1:380ff.

175 Hale, "Journal of a voyage to Nova Scotia," 225.

176 Ibid., 233.

177 I derive some of the ideas in the following pages from the essays in Barth, ed., *Scale and social organization*.

178 See Dupont, *Héritage d'Acadie* and *Histoire populaire de l'Acadie*.

179 Maillet, *Rabelais et les traditions populaires en Acadie*.

180 Fernand Ouellet places great importance on this in his article "Démographie, développement économique." See, in particular, 21–2.

181 Rutman, "Assessing the little communities of early America."

182 Dugas, "L'alphabétisation des Acadiens," 187.

183 "Assomption en Pigeguit: copie de la requête des habitants de la paroisse de l'Assomption ... à l'évêque de Quebec, se plaignant de ce qu'il n'y a pas de prêtres pour leur administrer les sacrements de la religion" (18 Feb. 1749): NAC, AC, C11D, 8, f.148.

184 PANS, Grant Book 1, 1732–41, "Judgement: Prejean, Doucet et Easson," 15 Jan. 1738. I am much indebted to Régis Brun for bringing my attention to this document.

185 For example, Council minutes, 13 Oct. 1731, MacMechan, *Nova Scotia Archives III*, 196–7.

CHAPTER TWELVE

1 Maxwell Sutherland, "Richard Philipps," *DCB*, 3:515–18 at 517.

2 Murdoch, *A history of Nova Scotia*, 1:470, 471.

3 NAC, CO 217, 39, f.4, Philipps to the Duke of Newcastle, 27 July 1731.

4 NAC, CO 217, 5, Representation by Mascarene and other councillors against Major Cosby, 27 Sept. 1731; see also NAC, NS/A, 20, Mascarene, William Skene, John Adams, and William Sheriff to Lawrence Armstrong, 27 Sept. 1731.

5 Moody, "'A just and disinterested man,'" 95–6.

6 NAC, CO 218, 2, Lords of Trade to Philipps, 2 Nov. 1732; NS/A, 2.

7 Council minutes, 23 Dec. 1732, MacMechan, *Nova Scotia Archives III*, 259.

8 Armstrong to the deputies, Annapolis Royal, 30 Aug. 1731, MacMechan, *Nova Scotia Archives II*, 79; published in Akins, *Acadia*, 88–9.

9 Armstrong to the secretary of war, 5 Feb. 1738/39, cited in Murdoch, *A history of Nova Scotia*, 1:530. It was a common practice for troop commanders at this time to inflate the number of troops under their command in order to receive more provisions than would otherwise be sent. However, given the letter that Armstrong also wrote to Captain James Mitford, then in command at Canso, about this matter, it appears as if Philipps was indeed sending inadequate supplies to the troops. See Armstrong to Mitford, 13 April 1739, MacMechan, *Nova Scotia Archives II*, 122.

10 Sutherland, "Richard Philipps," 518.

11 Philipps reported thirty-one men per company, but the actual strength of the nine companies was probably less. NAC, CO 217, 39, Philipps to the Duke of Newcastle, 5 Sept. 1739.

12 Murdoch, *A history of Nova Scotia*, 1:529.

13 McLennan, *Louisbourg*, 99.

14 NAC, CO 217, 39, Armstrong to the secretary of state, 9 Oct. 1733.

15 This broke out in 1733. One of the claimants, Stanislas Lescynki, was Louis XV's father-in-law.

16 Jonathan Belcher to J.L. Gyse, 6 Oct. 1735, MHS *Collections*, 6th series, 6:329.

17 Rawlyk, *Nova Scotia's Massachusetts*, 131.

18 Freiburg, ed., *Journals of the House of Representatives of Massachusetts, 1724–26*, 88, cited in Rawlyk, *Nova Scotia's Massachusetts*, 131.

19 I am deeply interested in the formation of community identities, my mind having been formed by the impact of the Second World War and reactions to the extreme nationalism that supported the racial policies of the Third Reich. I am also particularly interested in the reality of historical knowledge. See Hobsbawm's arguments in *On history* and Goldman, *Knowledge in a social world* (especially the passages on xenophobia at 7–9).

20 Murdoch, *A history of Nova Scotia*, 1: 497.

21 Muriel K. Roy collates the estimates of various scholars in "Peuplement et croissance démographique en Acadie," in Daigle, ed., *Les Acadiens des Maritimes*, 144.

22 Clark, *Acadia*, 207, based on NAC, AC, G 1, 466, 262.

23 This estimate is in line with the *Census of Canada*, 1931, 4:133–44.

24 NAC, AC, C11D, f.219, Duchambon to the minister, 14 Nov. 1754. This contains a good account of the Acadian settlements in the last named region. See also Ganong, *A monograph of historic sites*, 280–8.

25 Maxwell Sutherland, "Lawrence Armstrong," *DCB*, 2:21–4 at 24.

26 NAC, CO 217, 6, Armstrong to the Lords of Trade, 5 Oct. 1731; partially printed in Akins, *Acadia*, 91.

27 Ibid; printed in Akins, *Acadia*, 92.

28 NAC, CO 18, 2, Lords of Trade to Armstrong, Whitehall, 2 Nov. 1732; précis published in MacMechan, *Nova Scotia Archives II*, 194.

29 Council minutes, 11 Nov. 1731, MacMechan, *Nova Scotia Archives III*, 201.

30 NAC, CO 217, Armstrong to the Lords of Trade, 16 Nov. 1731; partially printed in Akins, *Acadia*, 94.

31 Barnes, "'The dayly cry for justice,'" 16.

32 Council minutes, 21 Sept. 1726, MacMechan, *Nova Scotia Archives III*, 124–5.

33 MacMechan, *Nova Scotia Archives III*, 96–102; for an analysis, see Barnes, "'The dayly cry for justice,'" 19.

34 "Governor's order in relation to sheep," 19 July 1733, MacMechan, *Nova Scotia Archives II*, 194–5.

35 On what that would have meant, given the impossibility of empanelling a jury, see Barnes, "'The dayly cry for justice,'" 27–9.

36 "Order for choosing new deputies, Annapolis, Aug. 26, 1732," NS/A, 21:132–5; published in full in Lanctot, Johnston, and Shortt, ed., *Documents*, 187; see also MacMechan, *Nova Scotia Archives II*, 190.

37 "Order for choosing new deputies, Annapolis, Aug. 30, 1733," MacMechan, *Nova Scotia Archives II*, 196.

38 Ibid., 193.

39 Ibid., 196.

40 Ibid., 200–1.

41 Ibid., 240.

42 Council minutes, 28 June 1732, MacMechan, *Nova Scotia Archives III*, 233.

43 Order to deputies, 2 June 1740, MacMechan, Nova Scotia *Archives II*, 239–40.

44 A short comment on the issue is found in Bell, *The "foreign Protestants,"* 22–3. A more general study is Bond, *The quit-rent system in the American colonies.*

45 NAC, Brown Papers, Mss. 19071, f.55b–56.

46 Murdoch, *A history of Nova Scotia*, 2:496.

47 NAC, CO 218,1, "Instructions to Governor Philipps," 19 June 1719.

48 Printed in Lanctot, Johnston, and Shortt, ed., *Documents*, 177; the source given is Murdoch, *A history of Nova Scotia*, 1:468.

49 Both primary and secondary sources are voluminous. For a brief account, see Clarence J. D'Entremont, "Agathe Saint-Étienne de La Tour," *DCB*, 2:590–1. See also MacMechan, *Nova Scotia Archives III*, 290–362; and Basque, "Seigneuresse, mère et veuve." She was an interesting woman, born in 1690,

who married, first, Edward Bradstreet in 1714. After his death in 1718, she married another British officer, Lieutenant Hugh Campbell, who also died in short order. A detailed account of her life and final days in Ireland is found in Godfrey, *Pursuit of profit*, 3–8, but see also Basque, "Seigneuresse, mère et veuve."

50 NAC, CO 218, 2, Popple to John Scope, 22 March 1733/34; printed in Lanctot, Johnston, and Shortt, ed., *Documents*, 197.

51 NAC, CO 218, 2, 2 Oct. 1734; printed in Lanctot, Johnston, and Shortt, ed., *Documents*, 201.

52 The accounts are included in NAC, CO 217, 39, Armstrong to the secretary of state, 10 May 1734. A summary and sterling equivalents are found in Lanctot, Johnston, and Shortt, ed., *Documents*, xxix, 200.

53 Order, 10 Dec. 1730, MacMechan, *Nova Scotia Archives II*, 180.

54 Order to Prudance Robichau, 1 Dec. 1733, ibid., 197.

55 Council minutes, 19 and 26 Jan.1739/40, cited in *Minutes of His Majesty's Council*, in Fergusson, ed., *Nova Scotia Archives IV*, 22–5. See as well: enclosure, copy of Council minutes, 16 March 1741/42, Mascarene to the Board of Trade; also published in Lanctot, Johnston, and Shortt, ed., *Documents*, 222–3.

56 NAC, Brown Papers, Mss. 19071, ff.138–48, contains Judge Deschamps's accounts of quit-rents from 1753 to 1755.

57 Council minutes, 24 May 1736, MacMechan, *Nova Scotia Archives III*, 346.

58 The number of cases is that given by Barnes in "'The dayly cry for justice," 18.

59 NAC, CO 217, 3, ff.47–8, enclosure, Philipps to Craggs, 26 May 1720.

60 Deputies at "Shickanecto ... to Examine and Enquire into the Partys Right and pretentions": Council minutes, 29 Oct. 1734, MacMechan, *Nova Scotia Archives III*, 308.

61 Council minutes, 17 Aug. 1736, ibid., 361.

62 Barnes, "'The dayly cry for justice,'" 11; authority cited is Chief Justice Edward Coke in *Calvin's Case* (1608) 7 Co. Rep. 17b, 77ER 377 (KB).

63 Smith and Barnes, *The English legal system*. The argument made by some historians that Nova Scotia was, in fact, not a conquered territory but a long-standing possession temporarily alienated until 1710 does not materially alter the situation, since in either case the British authorities had the right to impose the legal system.

64 Case brought by Emmanuel Hebert and the inhabitants of Minas concerning the use of common land. See Council minutes, 8 May 1732, MacMechan, *Nova Scotia Archives III*, 221.

65 Council minutes, 20 July 1732, ibid., 237–8.

66 See the commentary on this in Vanderlinden, *À la rencontre de l'histoire*.

67 Council minutes, 30 Jan. 1732/33, MacMechan, *Nova Scotia Archives III*, 265–6.

68 Council minutes, 25, 27 March 1723, ibid., 218.

69 Council minutes, 4 Sept. 1732, ibid., 252.

70 Council minutes, 2 July 1736, ibid., 358.

71 Order to Alexandre Bourg and [François] Mangeant, 6 May 1738, MacMechan, *Nova Scotia Archives II*, 221; the quotation included in this citation is part of the order recorded.

72 NAC, C 217, 39, Mascarene to the secretary of state, 15 Nov. 1740; partially printed in Akins, *Acadia*, 108–10.

73 Council minutes, 27 March 1732, MacMechan, *Nova Scotia Archives III*, 217.

74 Charles Bruce Fergusson, "William Winniett," *DCB*, 3:665–6; see also White, *Dictionnaire généalogique*, 2:1588–9.

75 NAC, CO 217, 7, Philipps to the Lords of Trade, 3 Aug. 1734; partially printed in Murdoch, *A history of Nova Scotia*, 1:499.

76 NAC, AC, C11D, 59, f.71, Beauharnois to the minister, October 1733.

77 NAC, CO, 217, 7, Philipps, "An account of the situation, commerce etc. ...," 1734. This request produced a number of responses. See also: "Representation to the state of the province in case of war with France," enclosed in NAC, CO 217, 39, Armstrong to Newcastle, 18 July 1734; précis given in MacMechan, *Nova Scotia Archives II*, 91–2.

78 NAC, AC, IR, C11, 15, f.121, Saint-Ovide to the minister, 28 Oct. 1734.

79 These conditions were summarized by Mascarene, with the agreement of Council, in 1742/43: Order Book, Council minutes, 1 March1742/43; printed in full in Akins, *Acadia*, 124–5.

80 PRO, A&WI, 30, f.135, Armstrong to the secretary of state, 16 July 1736, entitled "The humble representastion of Col. ..." and including copies of correspondence between Brouillan and Saint-Ovide and Armstrong and Saint-Ovide.

81 "Il est essentiel pour le bien de la religion que les missionnaires de l'Acadie se conduisent bien avec le gouverneur et les autres officiers de la colonie": NAC, AC, series B, 76, f.73, Maurepas to the bishop of Quebec, 8 May 1743. Maurepas went on to say that he thought that Mascarene would deal justly with the Acadians.

82 NAC, CO 217, 5, Armstrong to the Lords of Trade, 23 June 1729.

83 Mascarene to Jean-Baptiste de Gay Desenclaves, 29 June 1741. Précis given in MacMechan, *Nova Scotia Archives II*, 149–50, and printed in Akins, *Acadia*, 111–12.

84 In her biography of Desenclaves, Micheline Dumont-Johnson assesses the results of this belief. See "Jean-Baptiste de Gay Desenclaves," *DCB*, 3:256–7. Moody offers an elegant and convincing analysis of Mascarene's religious beliefs in "'A just and disinterested man," 158–87.

85 "Ces Mms ... s'immaginent avoir la tiarre sur la teste et veulent absolument etre de petites Eveques [et] veulent dominer le temporel comme dans le Spirituel et si quiesque ose leur resiste cet un crime de majeste divine Le crime capital": NAC, AC, IR, C11, 16, f.165, de Pensens to the minister, 24 Oct. 1734.

86 The best summary is that given by Dumont-Johnson in *Apôtres ou agitateurs*, 136–43.

87 Cited in Johnson, "Jean-Baptiste de Gay Desenclaves," 256.

88 Gérard Finn, "Jean-Louis Le Loutre, *DCB*, 4:453–8.

89 A clear account of the events leading up this war, which puts Jenkins's ear in its proper place, is Speck, *Stability and strife*, 233–4; see also Langford, *A polite and commercial people*, 51–3.

90 NAC, CO 217, 39, Mascarene to Newcastle, 7 June 1740.

91 Murdoch, *A history of Nova Scotia*, 1:529–30.

92 NAC, CO 217, 8, E66, Adams to the Lords of Trade, 8 Dec. 1739. Moody has pointed out that Adams was the only person "who even mentioned the 'Melancholy fitts' to which Armstrong had been subjected for a long time; and did so only after the lieutenant-governor's death." See "'A just and disinterested man,'" 113.

93 Moody, "'A just and disinterested man,'" 116.

94 Barry Moody, "John Adams," *DCB*, 3:3–4; Murdoch, *A history of Nova Scotia*, 2:2–3.

95 NAC, NS/25, commission, Philipps to Mascarene, 21 Aug. 1740.

96 Barry Moody provides a lengthy account of this squabble in "'A just and disinterested man,'" 114–30, and a shorter version in "Alexander Cosby," *DCB*, 3:144–5.

97 Cited in Moody, "'A just and disinterested man,'" 126; NAC, NS/A, Philipps to Mascarene, 21 Aug. 1740.

98 NAC, CO 217, 39, Mascarene to Newcastle, 7 June 1740.

99 Mascarene to the Lords of Trade, 14 March 1740/41, ibid.

100 NAC, NS/A, 25, Mascarene to the Lords of Trade, 15 Nov. 1740; printed in Akins, *Acadia*. 109.

101 Mascarene to the deputies of Minas, 27 May 1740, MacMechan, *Nova Scotia Archives II*, 241–2.

102 Brockliss and Eastwood, *A union of multiple identities*; see also Kearney, *The British Isles*.

103 Mascarene to Bergeau [a deputy at Minas], 1740 (probably August), MacMechan, *Nova Scotia Archives II*, 140.

104 NAC, NS/A, 25, Mascarene to La Goudalie, 10 Nov. 1741; cited in Moody, "'A just and disinterested man,'" 166. See also "Proclamation regarding Romish priests," 3 July 1740, MacMechan, *Nova Scotia Archives II*, 342–3.

105 "Circular letter to the deputys of Mines and places adjacent & to those of Chignigto," January 1740/41, MacMechan, *Nova Scotia Archives II*, 144.

106 Mascarene to the deputies of "Chicanecto," 16 Nov. 1744, Akins, *Acadia*, 139.

107 PRO, A&WI, 30, f.194, Mascarene to the Lords of Trade, 1 Dec.1743; partially printed in Akins, *Acadia*, 128–30.

108 As well as the work by Hobsbawm already cited, there are three other books that I have found particularly helpful: Gellner, *Culture, identity and politics*; Horsman and Marshall, *After the nation-state*; and Smith: *Nationalism and modernism*.

109 Houghton Library, Mascarene Papers, Mascarene to Saint-Poncy, 22 April 1739; cited in Moody, "'A just and disinterested man,'" 158.

110 NAC, NS/A, 27, Mascarene to Newcastle, 28 June 1742; printed in Akins, *Acadia*, 109.

111 Murdoch, *A history of Nova Scotia*, 2:24. For a more recent judgment, see Henretta, *"Salutary neglect."*

112 PRO, E68, BTNS, 8, Philipps to the Lords of Trade, June 1740.

113 NAC, War Office, 1558:2, James Wibault, "Defences of Annapolis," n.d.; cited in Moody, "'A just and disinterested man,'" 195.

114 PRO, A&WI, 454, f.179, Mascarene to the secretary of state, 1 Dec. 1743; partially printed in Akins, *Acadia*, 128–30.

115 NAC, NS/A, 26, Mascarene to King Gould (Philipps's agent), 14 June 1744; cited in Rawlyk, *Yankees at Louisbourg*, 5.

116 NAC, CO 217, 31, Mascarene to the Lords of Trade, 1 Dec. 1743; partially printed in Akins, *Acadia*, 129–30.

117 MHS, Paul Mascarene Papers, vol.1, Mascarene to Gould, 21 May 1744.

118 NAC, Brown Papers, Mss. 19071, f.61, 1752.

119 NAC, Brown Papers, Mss. 19071, f.46b, Mascarene to the Lords of Trade, 9 June 1744.

120 [In collaboration], "Isaac-Louis de Forant," *DCB*, 2:224–6.

121 Blaine Adams, "Jean-Baptiste-Louis Le Prévost Duquesnel," *DCB*, 3:392–3.

122 NAC, AC, IR, B70, f.41 1/2, Maurepas to Duquesnel, 18 Sept 1740.

123 NAC, AC, C11B, 21, ff.72–4, Forant to Maurepas, 14 Nov. 1739.

124 "On a toujours regardé la cession qui fut faite par le traité d'Utrecht a L'Angleterre de l'Acadie et de l'Isle de Terre Neuve, infinimens préjudiciable à la France par rapport a la pesche de la morue ... [par l'établissmens d'Ile Royale et Ile Saint Jean] la préjudice de cette cession se trouve en partie reparé mais malgré tous les avantages de ces établissemens dont les anglais sont extremament jaloux, on a toujours eu en vue de profiter de la première occasion pour reprendre la province de l'Acadie": NAC, AC, C11D, 8, f.83, "Project concernant ... l'Acadie,"

125 Bernard Pothier, "François Du Pont Duvivier," *DCB*, 2:205–6; see also the introduction to Pothier's *Course à l'Accadie*. Marie was the daughter of Jacques Mius d'Entremont de Pobomcoup and Anne de Saint-Étienne de La Tour.

126 Bernard Pothier, "Joseph Du Pont Duvivier,"*DCB*, 3:205–7.

127 "Mémoire sur l'Acadie"; translation in Murdoch, *A history of Nova Scotia*, 1:508–11. The document has not survived in the original but is mentioned in NAC, AC, C11B, 22, ff.98–101, Duquesnel to Maurepas, 1 Dec. 1740.

128 NAC, AC, IR, C11, 21, f.268, "Memoir concerning the work to be done on the fortifications ...," 19 Dec. 1739. See also McLennan, *Louisbourg*, 95–6.

129 NAC, AC, IR, C11, 22, f.93, Duquesnel to the minister, December 1740.

130 McLennan, *Louisbourg*, 222.

131 NAC, CO 217, 31, Hibbert Newton, collector of customs at Canso, to Captain Robert Young, 1 Sept. 1743, enclosed in Lords of Trade to secretary of state, 16 Dec. 1743.

132 McLennan, *Louisbourg*, 107.

133 NAC, AC, IR, C11, 26, f.8, Duquesnel to the minister, 9 May 1744; McLennan, *Louisbourg*, 109.

134 NAC, AC, IR, C11, 25, f.3, Duquesnel to the minister, 12 Aug. 1743.

135 NAC, AC, IR, C11, 26, f.3, Duquesnel and Bigot to the minister, 9 May 1744.

136 NAC, AC, F3, 50, pt.2, Moreau de Saint-Mery Papers, "Description of the Canso armament." See also Rawlyk, *Yankees at Louisbourg*, 166n.26.

137 For accounts of the action, see Rawlyk, *Yankees at Louisbourg*, 4–6; McLennan, *Louisbourg*, 111–12. The capitulation terms are printed in *Coll. Man. N.F.*, 3:201–2.

138 Duquesnel's orders to Duvivier, noted in NAC, AC, C11D, 8, ff.96, 100–1, "Various letters written by Duquesnel ..."; printed in Pothier, *Course à l'Accadie*, 159–61. See also Mascarene to Alexander Bourg, 27 July 1774, Akins, *Acadia*, 130–1.

139 Webster, *The career of the Abbé Le Loutre*, 35.

140 For a full account, see Rawlyk, *Yankees at Louisbourg*, 9–11.

141 NAC, Brown Papers, Mss. 19071, f.51b, Mascarene to Shirley, 28 July 1744; a lengthy précis of this is in PAC *Report*, 1894, 102.

142 " ... les Sauvages ... que je scay qui y font du desordre ... tuent les bestiaux pour vivre, y pillent les habitants": Duquesnel's orders, printed in Pothier, *Course à l'Accadie*, 159.

143 NAC, AC, IR, C11, 21, f.72, Forant to the minister, 14 Nov. 1739.

144 Duvivier's route to Nova Scotia was via Port Lajoie (Charlottetown), Île Saint-Jean. He actually left Louisbourg with only thirty troops, gathering more at Port Lajoie. See Rawlyk, *Yankees at Louisbourg*, 11–12; and Duvivier's journal, in Pothier, *Course à l'Accadie*, 42–4.

145 Pothier, *Course à l'Accadie*, 43.

146 Ibid.

147 "qu'ils scavoient que j'etois Acadien, et que tout ce qui estoit de ce pays me faisoit plaisir": entry for 15 Aug. 1744, ibid., 71.

148 "engager les jeunes gens à venir avec moy pour déffendre leur liberté et la tranquilité de leur religion ... la déclaration de la guerre les privoit de la continuation des droits que Louis Quatorze d'heureuse mémoire leurs avoit conservé en cedant le pays au Roy d'Angleterre ... ils devoient toujours regarder l'Anglois comme leur cruel ennemy, que si ils leur faisoient caresser ce n'étoit que pour mieux les tromper et surprendre leur bonne foy, que les loys d'Angleterre de pouvoient s'accorder avec la religion romaine": entry for 13 Aug. 1744, ibid., 68–70.

149 "Leurs anciens amis ... les seuls avec lesquels ils pourroient jouir de leurs biens et tranquilité de la religion": ibid., 70.

150 "cet ancien cœur français se retrouveroit dans nos Accadiens ...": entry for 16 Aug. 1745, ibid., 72.

151 "Le reste croyant n'être point aperçeu de moy dans la foulle furent trompez": ibid.

152 Based on Clark, *Acadia*, 222, table 6.8.

153 Pothier, *Course à l'Accadie*, 74.

154 Entries for 21–23 Aug. 1745, ibid., 74–5.

155 Ibid., 75–6.

156 "... luy-même se trouvoit bien du sien dans cet endroit où il est comme un petit pape": entry for 23 Aug. 1745, ibid., 76.

157 "Quoique je n'eusse pas intention de les y forcer, je faisois cette démarche pour mieux couvrir au cas d'incident pour faire paroître qu'ils m'avoient résistez ... [et] pour les mettre à l'abry des reproches des Anglois": entry for 24 Aug. 1744, ibid., 77.

158 NAC, AC, C11B, 26, f.196, "Ordre de Duvivier aux habitants des Mines et régions environantes," 27 Aug. 1744; printed in full in Pothier, *Course à l'Accadie*, 161–2.

159 These are approximate figures, based upon Clark's estimates in *Acadia*, 216–19, tables 6.5, 6.6, and 6.7.

160 Bernard Pothier's estimate is just over a dozen: *Course à l'Accadie*, 49.

161 White, *Dictionnaire généalogique*, 2:987–8.

162 "État des sommes dues...pour diverse fournitures ...": NAC, AC, C11D, 8, ff.109–10; printed in full in Pothier, *Course à l'Accadie*, 162–4.

163 Shirley to the Lords of Trade, 25 July 1744, in Lincoln, ed., *The correspondence of William Shirley*, 1:135.

164 Rawlyk, *Yankees at Louisbourg*, 12.

165 Mascarene to Shirley, December 1744, printed in Akins, *Acadia*, 144.

166 NAC, AC, series B, 78, f.24, Maurepas to Duquesnel, 30 April 1744.

167 H. Paul Thibault, "Michel de Gannes de Falaise," *DCB*, 3:235–6.

168 NAC, AC, C11D, 8, ff.112–13, de Gannes to Maurepas, 8 Nov. 1744.

169 Basque, *Des hommes de pouvoir*, 94–6.

170 Ibid., 93. See also Duvivier's journal, 10 Sept. 1744, in Pothier, *Course à l'Accadie*, 91, 174–5.

171 Bernard Pothier, "Joseph-Nicolas Gautier, *dit* Bellair," *DCB*, 3:254–5; Arsenault, *Histoire et généalogie des Acadiens*, 1:410.

172 Clark, *Acadia*, 247.

173 Pothier, *Course à l'Accadie*, 47; Pothier, "Joseph-Nicolas Gautier, *dit* Bellair," 255.

174 "Mr Dupont fut commandé avec six fuzilliers pour aller d'un côté de la paroisse, et le sergent de l'autre où ils feurent obligéz de prendre le pain que les habitants cachoient partout": NAC, AC, C11D, 8, f.115; printed in Pothier, *Course à l'Accadie*, 177.

175 NAC, AC, C11D, 8, ff.109–10, notarial records, Louisbourg, 7 Nov. 1752; printed in Pothier, *Course à l'Accadie*, 173–4.

176 NAC, AC, C11D, 8, ff.87–95, "Unfinished narrative of an expedition against Port Royal, which failed from an error of M. de Gannes, 1711"; see also the final entries in Duvivier's journal, 152–7, in which he accuses de Gannes of making no effort to continue the siege.

177 "... il est impossible d'en fournir cette quantité ... puisque les récoltes n'ont pas étéz aussy bonnes comme l'on l'avoit espéré, ce qui seroit nous mettre

dans un péril visible qu'il ne se pourrroit faire qu'en tuant tous les bestiaux et consommant tous les grains et semances ...": NAC, AC, C11D, 8, ff.114–44, 13 Oct. 1744; printed in Pothier, *Course à l'Accadie*, 176–7.

178 "Nous espérons, messieurs, que vous ne voudréz point nous plonger dans une misère de perte totalle de nous et nos familles, et qu'en cette considération vous ferez retirer les Sauvages et trouppes de nos cantons. Nous sommes sous un gouvernement doux et tranquille et duquel nous avons tous lieu d'être contens": ibid.

179 NAC, AC, C11D, 8, f.92. This marginal note has often been omitted from the copies made of these documents, and there is rarely any reference to it.

180 NAC, Brown Papers, Mss. 19071, f.53, Mascarene to the Lords of Trade, 20 Sept. 1744; printed in Akins, *Acadia*, 131–3.

181 Mascarene to the Lords of Trade, 25 Sept. 1744; printed in Akins, *Acadia*, 133–4.

182 Both these letters are printed in Akins, *Acadia*, 140–6, 146–50.

183 Council minutes, 11 Dec. 1744, Fergusson, *Nova Scotia Archives IV*, 52.

184 See Basque, *Des hommes de pouvoir*, 94–6.

185 On the role of these factors in the emergence of national ideologies, see Smith, *Nationalism and modernism*, 63–70.

186 Council minutes, 4 Jan. 1744/45, Fergusson, *Nova Scotia Archives IV*, 55.

CHAPTER THIRTEEN

1 Council minutes, 12 Oct. 1744 (O.S.), Fergusson, *Nova Scotia Archives IV*, 50.

2 Council meeting, 6 Dec. 1744 (O.S.), ibid.

3 John David Krugler, "John Gorham," *DCB*, 3:260–1; Council minutes, 6 and 8 Dec. 1744, Fergusson, *Nova Scotia Archives IV*, 50–2.

4 Alexandre Bourg, notary and deputy; Joseph Leblanc, *dit* Le Maigre; and Amand Bugaud.

5 "Interrogatorys for Monsr Alex Bourg ...," Fergusson, *Nova Scotia Archives IV*, 58.

6 Council minutes, 4 Jan. 1744/45, ibid., 55–6.

7 Mascarene to [?], 15 March 1744/45, printed in Akins, *Acadia*, 151.

8 NAC, CO 217, 40, Mascarene to the secretary of state, 15 June 1748.

9 NAC, CO 217, 40, Mascarene to the secretary of state, 8 Sept. 1748.

10 Included in NAC, CO 217, 39, Mascarene to the secretary of state, 9 Dec. 1748, printed in Fergusson, *Nova Scotia Archives IV*, 80–4.

11 MHS, Paul Mascarene Papers, Mascarene to Shirley, 7 Dec. 1745; Moodie, "'A just and disinterested man,'" 338–41.

12 82 per cent English, 4.4 per cent Scottish, 3.9 per cent Irish; *Historical statistics of the United States: Colonial times to 1970*, pt.2, 1168.

13 Boston *Evening Post*, 22 Oct. 1744, cited in Plank, *An unsettled conquest*, 10; see also *Journals of the House of Representatives of Massachusetts*, 21:99, 106–7.

14 Council minutes, 4 Jan. 1744/45, Fergusson, *Nova Scotia Archives IV*, 55.

15 "Extrait en forme de journal ...," *Coll. Man. N.F.*, 3:217.

16 The number of men that Marin commanded is uncertain. See NAC, AC, IR, C11, 26, f.90, Duchambon to the minister, 27 Nov. 1755.

17 "Extrait en forme de journal ...," entry for 11 June 1745, *Coll. Man. N.F.,* 3:218.

18 Council minutes, 2 and 10 May 1745 (O.S.), Fergusson, *Nova Scotia Archives IV,* 68–70.

19 Pote wrote a narrative of his capture and imprisonment; see Paltsits, ed., *The journal of Captain William Pote.* This work is the basis of MacMechan's account of Pote's adventures in *Red snow on Grand Pré,* 56–158.

20 Reported in the Boston *Gazette,* 23 Oct. 1744, in Chard, "The impact of Île Royale on New England," 79.

21 Chard, "The impact of Île Royale on New England," 78.

22 NAC, AC, IR, C11B, 27, ff..26–31, "Memorandum on English ships taken at Louisbourg, 1744," 1745.

23 In 1709–10 two French privateers sailing out of Acadia captured thirty-five ships in New England waters: Subercase to the minister, in Chard, "The impact of Île Royale on New England," 73n.18.

24 Biographical details of Shirley's early career are taken from Schutz, *William Shirley.*

25 On the functions of the court itself, see Madden and Fieldhouse, ed., *The classical period of the first British empire,* 2:24–5.

26 Schutz, *William Shirley,* 12.

27 See Moodie, "'A just and disinterested man,'" 206–44.

28 NAC, Admiralty Papers I, 3817, Mascarene to Warren, 22 Oct. 1744.

29 Moodie, "'A just and disinterested man,'" 242.

30 Shirley to Benning Wentworth, 10 Nov. 1744, in Lincoln, ed., *The correspondence of William Shirley,* 1:152.

31 Rawlyk, *Nova Scotia's Massachusetts,* 150–1.

32 Ibid., 163.

33 Ibid.

34 The *Superbe,* sixty guns; the *Launceston,* forty guns; the *Mermaid,* forty guns; and the *Eltham,* also forty guns. It is unclear whether the *Bien Aimé,* forty guns, ever arrived. Rawlyk, *Yankees at Louisbourg,* 55–6.

35 Bower, "Louisbourg: The chimera," *Papers and abstracts for a symposium on Île Royale,* 7.

36 The account given by McLennan in *Louisbourg,* 147–80, conveys the details of the siege with great eloquence.

37 Rawlyk, *Yankees at Louisbourg,* 154.

38 Ibid., 146–51.

39 McLennan, *Louisbourg,* 164–5.

40 MHS *Collections,* 3rd series, 10, 308, T. Hubbard to Pepperell, 7 July 1745.

41 Earl of Chesterfield to Robert Trevor, 13 Aug. 1745, in Rawlyk, *Yankees at Louisbourg,* 155.

42 Britain finally paid up, if not in full, in 1749: Massachusetts was paid £183,649.2.7; New Hampshire, £16,355.13.4; Connecticut, £28,863.19.1; and Rhode Island, £16,322.12.10. See McLennan, *Louisbourg,* 167n.1.

43 See Pritchard, *Anatomy of a naval disaster*, 24–6.

44 Ibid., 33–43.

45 NAC, AC, C11, 83, f.3, Beauharnois and Hocquart to the minister, 12 Sept. 1745; partially printed in Murdoch, *A history of Nova Scotia*, 2:79–82.

46 Pritchard, *Anatomy of a naval disaster*, 4.

47 This is my estimate, based on ibid., 4–5. Pritchard himself has written that "no one knows how many men died during the expedition; some estimates range as high as 8000." His book is a work of meticulous and impressive scholarship and a pleasure to read.

48 Ibid., 112, 176; tables of the dead and sick at 180–3.

49 Archives de la Guerre, Vincennes, A1, 3188, no.313, Autrechaud to Argenson, 4 Nov. 1746, cited in Pritchard, *Anatomy of a naval disaster*, 156.

50 Ibid., 133.

51 Rawlyk, *Yankees at Louisbourg*, 158.

52 McLennan, *Louisbourg*, 165.

53 Warren to Vice-Admiral Isaac Townsend, 16 May 1746, printed in PAC *Report*, 1905, app. C, 42.

54 Bumsted, *Land, settlement, and politics*, 7.

55 NAC, AC, C11, 83, f.3, Beauharnois and Hocquart to the minister, 12 Sept. 1745; partially printed in Murdoch, *A history of Nova Scotia*, 2:79–82.

56 Warren to Thomas Corbett, 3 Oct. 1745, in Moodie, "A just and disinterested man,'" 332n.61.

57 NAC, C11, 83, f.3, Beauharnois and Hocquart to the minister, 12 Sept. 1745; partially printed in Murdoch, *A history of Nova Scotia*, 2:79–82.

58 NAC, AC, C11, 87, f.324, [Daniel-Hyacinthe-Marie Liénard de Beaujeu], "Journal de la campagne du détachement de Canada à l'Acadie et aux Mines, en 1746–47"; printed in full in *Coll. Doc. Inédits*, 2:16–75. Beaujeu was then in his mid-thirties. See Malcolm MacLeod's biography of Beaujeu in DCB, 3:400–2.

59 Beaujeu, "Journal de la campagne," *Coll. Doc. Inédits*, 2:22–3; a short account of the raid is given in Harvey, *The French regime*, 118–19.

60 " ... les députés des Mines s'assemblèrent chez Mr de Ramezay pour luy représenté qu'ils étoient absolument hors d'état de nourrir pendant l'hiver le détachement de Mr Coulon qui devoit y rester ...": Beaujeu, "Journal de la campagne," *Coll. Doc. Inédits*, 2:32.

61 "... qu'ils n'y avoit plus a compter que sur les bœufs de charüe pour avoir de la viande et que pour lors il falloit qu'ils abandonnassent la culture des terres que le séjour de ce détachement, qui au reste décideroit rien, les brouilleroit, plus que jamais avec les Anglois, et qu'ils espéroient que leur juste représentation le porteroit a le retirer": ibid.

62 " ... mais beaucoup moins qu'il nous en falloit": ibid., 2:34.

63 " ... il payera le prix comptant": "Extrait en forme de journal ...," *Coll. Man. N.F.*, 3:310.

64 " ... ils refusoient même aux Canadiens ... qui y doivent hyverner les secours les plus pressans dans la crainte de n'être pas payés de très longtemps de leurs fournitures ...": ibid.

65 Deposition of Joseph Leblanc, *dit* Le Maigre, 1750, printed in Rameau de Saint-Père, *Une colonie féodale*, 2:376–7.

66 Acadian discontent probably increased because of reports from Île Saint-Jean that the British paid for the supplies they requisitioned. See Beaujeu, "Journal de la campagne," 23 July 1746, *Coll. Doc. Inédits*, 2:27,

67 "Le 10 [oct.] ... environ 300 hommes officiers et miliciens et un fort petit nombre de sauvages, la maladies les ayant pour lors presque tout enlevé ...": ibid., 2:40.

68 Ibid., 2:40–8.

69 " ... pas plus de 200 hommes, mangés de vermines et accablés de misère, nus et hors d'état de nous deffendre. Ce tableau désadvantageux ... fut donné aux Anglois par les Acadiens mêmes qui nous paroissoient les plus dévoüés: ibid., 2:52.

70 "Mais assez ordinairement se déclare-ton pour le parti le plus fort; quoiqu'il en soit, les Anglois comptoient nous chasser des Mines et n'y épargné que les habitants qui auroient exactement gardé la neutralité": ibid.

71 Council minutes, 29 Sept. 1746, Fergusson, *Nova Scotia Archives IV*, 90.

72 NAC, CO 5, 42, Newcastle to Shirley, 30 May 1747.

73 Barry M. Moodie, "Arthur Noble, " *DCB*, 3:483–4.

74 Council minutes, 31 Oct. 1746 (O.S.), Fergusson, *Nova Scotia Archives IV*, 92–3; see also Murdoch, *A history of Nova Scotia*, 2:104–5.

75 C. Alexander Pincombe, "Edward How," *DCB*, 3:297–8.

76 William G. Godfrey, "Erasmus James Philipps," *DCB*, 3:514–15.

77 PANS, Edward How Papers, Mascarene to How and Philipps, 8 Dec. 1746; cited in Moody, "'A just and disinterested man," 361–2.

78 Council minutes, 31 Oct. 1746 (O.S.), Fergusson, *Nova Scotia Archives IV*, 93.

79 Council minutes, 20 Nov. 1746 (O.S.)., ibid., 95.

80 Diary kept by La Corne, published in *Coll. Doc. Inédits.*, 2:10–16; see also Beaujeu, "Journal de la campagne," entry for 8 Jan. 1746/47, *Coll. Doc. Inédits*, 2:58.

81 Council minutes, 29 Dec. 1746 (O.S.), Fergusson, *Nova Scotia Archives IV*, 97.

82 PANS, vol.13, Noble to Mascarene, 28 Jan. 1747.

83 Stanley, *New France*, 24.

84 Beaujeu, "Journal de la campagne," entry for 8 Jan. 1747 (N.S.), *Coll. Doc. Inédits*, 2:58.

85 W.J. Eccles, "Nicolas-Antoine Coulon de Villiers," *DCB*, 3:149–150.

86 There have been a number of secondary accounts. See, for example, Stanley, *New France*, 22–5; Lanctot, *A history of New France*, 3:68–9; and, for a lengthy but florid description, MacMechan, *Red snow on Grand Pré*, 11–15.

87 The distance travelled has been calculated, from the Beaujeu account, by Donald Wyllie, a geographer at Mount St Mary's University, Halifax. However, he resolutely refused to walk the trail in winter conditions.

88 "Plusieurs acadiens se joignirent cependant à nous, mais qui ne servirent qu'a figurer. Car quoy qu'ils se fussent enrôlés comme combattant ils ne nous servirent que de guides; et a la vérité nous en avions besoin": Beaujeu, "Journal de la campagne," 10 Feb. 1747 (N.S.), *Coll. Doc. Inédits*, 2:65.

89 Moody, "Arthur Noble," 484; Beaujeu, "Journal de la campagne," 12 Feb. 1747 (N.S.), *Coll. Doc. Inédits*, 2:71. See also the calculations in Murdoch, *A history of Nova Scotia*, 2:107.

90 The dispute over the numbers is examined in Murdoch, *A history of Nova Scotia*, 2:107; see also Moodie, "Arthur Noble," *DCB*, 3:484.

91 " ... avec les honneurs de la guerre, six jours de vivres, l'havre sac, une livre de pourdre, une livre de balles par chaque homme": Beaujeu, "Journal de la campagne," 12 Feb. 1747 (N.S.), *Coll. Doc. Inédits*, 2:69. The terms are printed in full in this source. For an English version, see Murdoch, *A history of Nova Scotia*, 2:114–15.

92 " ... en buvant le ponche": Beaujeu, "Journal de la campagne," 13 Feb. 1747 (N.S.), *Coll. Doc. Inédits*, 2:72.

93 " ... que la grande consommation de vivres que les différents détachements francois et anglois avoient faits depuis plusieurs années les avoit réduits a un état pitoyable ..." (19 Feb. 1747): ibid., 73.

94 " ... quie cependant ils étoient si charmés de nous avoir au milieu d'eux, qu'ils ne pouvoient nous refuser nôtre subsistance, mais qu'il leur étoit bien difficile de nous la fournir": ibid.

95 Coleman, *Acadian history in the isthmus of Chignecto*, 52–3; Brodhead and O'Callaghan, *Documents*, 10:105–11.

96 "... n'ayant pour vivres que de la farine avec du suif a chandelle, dont nous faisions de la colle": Beaujeu, "Journal de la campagne," 10 March 1747 (N.S.), *Coll. Doc. Inédits*, 2:75.

97 Shirley to Newcastle, 27 Feb. 1747, in Parkman, *A half-century of conflict*, app. C.

98 Ibid.

99 "Extrait en forme de journal ...," *Coll. Doc. N.F.*, 3:330.

100 NAC, CO 217, 32, Mascarene to the Lords of Trade.

101 Étienne Taillemite, "Jacques-Pierre de Taffanel de La Jonquière," *DCB*, 3:609–12.

102 NAC, AC, C11, 87, f.87, La Galissonière to Maurepas, 6 Nov. 1747.

103 Étienne Taillemite, "Roland-Michel Barrin de La Galissonière," *DCB*, 3:26–32.

104 NAC, NS/A, 30:182–9, 31 March and 24 April 1747.

105 W.A.B. Douglas, "John Rous," *DCB*, 3:572–4.

106 NAC, NS/A, 30, Mascarene to John Winslow, 25 March 1747.

107 Ibid., Mascarene to Charles Morris, 23 March 1747.

108 He would probably have defended his return to Grand Pré before the term of his six-month absence, required by the articles of capitulation, had ended by referring to the orders received from Mascarene.

109 MHS, Misc. Bound, Mascarene to Governor Shirley, 6 April 1748; cited in Moodie, "A just and disinterested man," 375.

110 NAC, Brown Papers, Mss. 19069, f.41b, Mascarene to Captain Donnell, 26 April 1748. See also NAC, NS/A, 32:64–76; printed in Lanctot, Johnston, and Shortt, ed., *Documents*, 269.

111 Ibid.

112 Mascarene to Captain Askew of the *Port Mahon*, 31 May 1748; printed in Lanctot, Johnston, and Shortt, ed., *Documents*, 271–2.

113 The accounts are published in Lanctot, Johnston, and Shortt, ed., *Documents*, 277–8, and Murdoch, *A history of Nova Scotia*, 2:125–7.

114 Council minutes, 17 Dec.1744, Fergusson, *Nova Scotia Archives IV*, 53; for a summary of his life, see White, *Dictionnaire généalogique*, 2:1009–12.

115 NAC, Brown Papers, Mss. 19069, f.41b, Mascarene to Captain Donnell, 26 April 1748. Also: NAC, NS/A, 32:64–76; printed in Lanctot, Johnston, and Shortt, ed., *Documents*, 271.

116 Declaration of William Shirley, enclosed in letter to Mascarene, 20 Oct. 1747; printed in PAC *Report*, 1905, 2 app. C, 47–8; see also the account in Murdoch, *A history of Nova Scotia*, 2:117.

117 Mascarene to the Acadian deputies, 30 Aug. 1748; printed in full in Akins, *Acadia*, 162–4.

118 Ibid.

119 Rawlyk, *Nova Scotia's Massachusetts*, 190.

120 Dummett and Nicol, *Subjects, citizens, aliens*, 22.

121 See, in particular, Cain and Hopkins, *British imperialism*, and Le Roy Ladurie, *The ancien régime*.

122 NAC, CO 217, 40, Mascarene to the secretary of state, 8 Sept. 1748; partially printed in Akins, *Acadia*, 164.

123 Maxwell Sutherland, "Paul Mascarene," *DCB*, 3:435–40 at 439.

CHAPTER FOURTEEN

1 See the recent monumental work by Anderson, *The crucible of war*.

2 For a brief and clear summary of the diplomatic negotiations, see Kennedy, *The rise and fall of the great powers*, 110–11. Sosin's article, "Louisbourg and the peace of Aix-la-Chapelle, 1748," provides a good overview of the historiography of the treaty, as well as the way in which particular clauses came about.

3 "Le Français désirait la paix ... mais le Français aime la gloire et l'honneur ... tout le public tombé dans la consternation de la médiocrité des conditions ..." 'Quoi!' dit on, on rendons toutes nos conquêtes, toutes sans exception?": Marquis d'Argenson, *Journal et mémoires*, 5:27.

4 Issue of 7 May 1749, cited in Gipson, *The British empire before the American revolution*, 5:178. Emphasis in original.

5 See Cain and Hopkins, *British imperialism*, 72–7.

6 For a brief overview, see Black, *Convergence or divergence?* 152–6.

7 Gibson, *Best of enemies*, 86.

8 Black, *Convergence or divergence?* 156.

9 Abbé Le Blanc, *Lettres d'un français* (1745), cited in Gibson, *Best of enemies*, 89.

10 Breuilly, "Approaches to nationalism," in Balakrishnan, ed., *Mapping the nation*, 146.

11 "Les motifs d'honneur, de gloire et de Religion ne permettent point d'abandonner une Colonie établie, de livrer a eux memes ou plutöt a une Nation

ennemis par goût, par education et principe de Religion les françois qui ont passé [la] ... Enfin de renoncer a un ouvrage aussi salutaire que celui de la conversion des Infideles qui habitent ce vaste continent": NAC, AC, C11, A, 181–2, La Galissonière to Maurepas, 1 Sept. 1748; English translation printed in O'Callaghan, ed., *Documents relative to the colonial history of the state of New York*, 10:222. There is considerable controversy over the dating of the document and whether La Galissonière was the sole author: see Lamontagne, *La Galissonière et le Canada*, 49–58.

12 Stanley, *New France*, 58.

13 John Fortier, "Charles Des Herbiers de La Ralière," DCB, 3:182–4.

14 Akins, *History of Halifax*, 5. See also a lively overview by Fingard, Guildford, and Sutherland, *Halifax*.

15 J. Murray Beck, "Edward Cornwallis," DCB, 4:168–71.

16 Cornwallis's instructions, dated 1 May 1749, are in NAC, CO 219, 30, and are printed in full in Akins, *Acadia*, 497–505.

17 Printed in full in PAC *Report*, 1905, 2, pt.3, app. N, 291–3.

18 " ... les anciens habitans qui avoient toujours conserve le désir et l'esperance de rentrer sous la domination de France, seront obligés de renoncer à l'un et à l'autre, et de se soumettre sérieusement et pour toujours à la domination angloise ...": ibid., 292.

19 " ... puisqu'ils sont en droit de faire à l'Acadie tels établissemens qu'ils jugeront à propos ...": ibid.

20 "... il ne reste qu'à y apporter autant d'obstacles indirects qu'il sera possible sans se compromettre ...": ibid.

21 " ... les Missionaires des uns et des autres ont des ordres et sont disposés à se conduire selon ces vues ...": ibid.

22 McLennan, *Louisbourg*, 188.

23 Clark, *Acadia*, 276–7, table 7.1.

24 McLennan, *Louisbourg*, 188.

25 PAC *Report*, 1905, 2, app. N, 292.

26 Stanley, *New France*, 62.

27 British arguments for immediate action on this issue, made on 1 Sept 1750, are found in CO 323, 12, and cited in Gipson, *The British empire before the American revolution*, 5:304–5.

28 Article 12 of the treaty.

29 Claims and counter-claims are found, in mind-numbing detail, in *Mémoires des commissaires* and *Memorials of the English and French commissaries*. While these volumes include a great deal of specious argument, they also contain an interesting collection of documents on the seventeenth-century history of the colony.

30 The others were La Galissonière and Étienne de Silhouette for France and William Mildmay for Great Britain.

31 Schutz, *William Shirley*, 159–63.

32 La Galissonière to Mascarene, 15 Jan. 1749, cited in Murdoch, *A history of Nova Scotia*, 2:132.

33 NAC, CO 218, 3, Lords of Trade to the Duke of Bedford, 10 Aug. 1749; NAC, C11, 93, f.143, La Galissonière to the minister, 26 June 1749; NAC, C11, 93, f.153, Boishébert to La Galissonière, 26 Aug. 1746.

34 The most politic expression of these views is contained in NAC, NS/A, 33:148–9, Shirley to the Duke of Bedford, 18 Feb. 1748/49. On this, see both Brebner, *New England's outpost*, 118ff., and Gipson, *The British empire before the American revolution*, 5:180.

35 Bell, *The "foreign Protestants,"* 9–10.

36 See, in particular, ibid., 318–35.

37 *The Northcliffe collection*, 68.

38 Cited in Bell, *The "foreign Protestants,"* 337.

39 Ibid., 336n.1. Lord Halifax was then president of the Board of Trade and Plantations.

40 Akins, *History of Halifax*, 4.

41 NAC, CO 218, 2, "Instructions for our trusty and well beloved Edward Cornwallis ...," 29 April 1749; printed in part in PAC *Report*, 1905, 2, pt.3, app. C, 49–52.

42 Raddall, *Halifax, warden of the north*, 22.

43 Ibid., 21.

44 Clark, *Acadia*, 337.

45 NAC, CO, 217, 82, f.82, Cornwallis to the Lords of Trade, 24 July 1749; printed in part in Akins, *Acadia*, 565–7.

46 Report of Des Herbiers on the repossession of Louisbourg, 29 July 1749, printed in full in *Coll. Man. N.F.*, 3:439–49.

47 Akins, *History of Halifax*, 19.

48 Wright, *Planters and pioneers*, 8.

49 Cornwallis to the Lords of Trade, 30 April 1750, printed in full in Akins, *Acadia*, 608–9.

50 Bell, *The "foreign Protestants,"* 287–91.

51 NAC, CO 217, 10, Cornwallis to the Lords of Trade, 24 July 1749; partially printed in Akins, *Acadia*, 565–7.

52 NAC, CO 217, 40, f.61; published in full in Akins, *Acadia*, 561–4.

53 John David Krugler, "John Gorham," *DCB*, 3:260–1; Bates, "John Gorham," 28. John's brother, Joseph, also served in Nova Scotia and by 1752 commanded his own company there: David A. Charters and Stuart R.J. Sutherland, "Joseph Goreham (Gorham)," *DCB*, 4:308–10.

54 NAC, CO 217, 9, Cornwallis to the Lords of Trade, 11 Sept. 1749; printed in full in Akins, *Acadia*, 583–5.

55 PRO, A&WI, 31, f.68, Hugh Davidson to Aldworth, 24 July 1749.

56 "A Journal," printed in full in the *Northcliffe collection*, 68–76; on the accuracy of this account, see Bell, *The "foreign Protestants,"* 328n.22a. As noted earlier, there is a general view that the figures for regimental strength in eighteenth-century records are considerably inflated. It is likely that the Warburton companies consisted of fewer than a hundred men and officers, and that the figure for the Lascelles regiment was probably well under three hundred.

57 "A Journal," *Northcliffe collection*, 76.

58 Cornwallis's instructions, PAC *Report*, 1905, 2, pt.3, app. C, 50.

59 Brebner, *New England's outpost*, 166.

60 Clark, *Acadia*, 339n.24.

61 The records of Nova Scotia Council meetings are available both at PANS and at the NAC; the references that follow are those from the NAC. For the meeting of 14 July 1749, see NAC, MG 11, CO 220, NS (B), 4; partially printed in Akins, *Acadia*, 166–7.

62 Cornwallis's commission: Akins, *Acadia*, 498.

63 The others present at this meeting were John Horseman, Robert Ellison, and James Mercer, all military men from Louisbourg, as well as John Gorham, Benjamin Green (a New Englander who had been in Louisbourg as government secretary from 1745 to 1745), and William Steele (one of the newly arrived immigrants from Great Britain).

64 NAC, MG 11, CO 220, NS (B), 4; Akins, *Acadia*, 166–7.

65 After the deportation, the same thinking saw the French plan Acadian settlements among French villages on Belle-Île-sur-Mer in Brittany.

66 Given in French in original minutes. English translation: "I promise and sincerely swear on the faith of a Christian that I will be entirely faithful and truly obey His Majesty King George the Second whom I acknowledge as the Sovereign Lord of Acadia or Nova Scotia."

67 "A Declaration with relation to the French subjects of His Majesty King George inhabiting Nova Scotia, sent to the Acadian French by Govr. Cornwallis on the formation of the civil government at Halifax in 1749": Cornwallis's Letterbook; printed in full in Akins, *Acadia*, 165.

68 NAC, MG 11, CO 220, NS (B), 4; minutes printed in full in Akins, *Acadia*, 168.

69 NAC, MG 11, CO 220, NS (B), 4, Council minutes, 31 July 1749; printed in Akins, *Acadia*, 169.

70 NAC, MG 11, CO 220, NS (B), 4, Council minutes, 1 Aug. 1749; printed in Akins, *Acadia*, 170.

71 Printed in full in Akins, *Acadia*, 171–2.

72 This is based on an estimated Acadian population of 12,000 in 1750: Jean Daigle, "L'Acadie de 1604–1763," in Daigle, ed., *L'Acadie des Maritimes*, 22. The number of adult males in such a population would be approximately 2,500. As has been noted, I consider this population estimate on the low side and would suggest that the Acadians numbered closer to 14,000 by 1750.

73 NAC, MG 11, CO 220, NS (B), 4, Council minutes, 6 Sept. 1749; partially printed in Akins, *Acadia*, 172–6; for the Acadians' letter, in French, see NAC, MG 11, CO 220, NS (B), 4, 209.

74 "Si Votre Excellence veut nous accorder notre ancien serment avec exemption d'armes à nous et nos hoirs [*sic*], nous l'accepterons: mais si Votre Excellence n'est pas dans la résolution de nous l'accorder ce que prenons la liberté de demander nous sommes tous en général dans la résolution de nous retirer du pays": ibid.

75 "Ce que fait peine à tout le monde c'est d'apprendre que les anglois veulent s'habiter parmi nous": ibid.

76 "[Ca] paroit vous vous croyez indépendent de tous Gouvernement et vous voudrez traites avec le roi sur ce pied à ... : NAC, MG 11, CO 220, N.S. (B), 4, Council minutes, 6 Sept. 1749; English version in Akins, *Acadia*, 174–5.

77 Speck, *Stability and strife*, 62, 16.

78 "Vous vous trompez si vous croyez être en liberté de choiser si vous vous être sujets du roi ou non": NAC, MG 11, CO 220, N.S. (B), 4, Council minutes, 6 Sept. 1749; English version in Akins, *Acadia*, 174–5.

79 "depuis l'année 1714 n'a plus dependu de vous": ibid. On this issue, see particularly Speck, *Stability and strife*, chapter 6. The subject of the political and social disabilities of Catholics and others who were not members of the Church of England has led to considerable partisan debate. Relatively recent writings on the issue of British democracy in this era include Kearney, *The British Isles*, and Brockliss and Eastwood, ed., *A union of multiple identities.*

80 NAC, CO 217, 9, Cornwallis to the Lords of Trade, 11 Sept. 1749; partially printed in Akins, *Acadia*, 175–6.

81 Brebner, *New England's outpost*, 183.

82 NAC, CO 217, 40, Cornwallis to the Lords of Trade, 11 Sept. 1749; printed in full in Akins, *Acadia*, 583–4.

83 Enclosure in Mascarene to Newcastle, 20 Oct. 1747, PAC *Report*, 1905, 2, pt.3, app. C, 47.

84 NAC, CO 220, NS (B), 4, Council minutes, 31 July 1749; printed in Akins, *Acadia*, 169.

85 AM, "Description de l'Acadie avec le nom des paroisses et le nombre des habitants – 1748," *Coll. Doc. Inédits*, 1:44.

86 NAC, Brown Papers, Mss.19071, f.85. At this time Brook Watson was associated with the Nova Scotia merchant Joshua Mauger. In 1752 Watson became secretary to Lieutenant-Colonel Robert Monckton at Fort Lawrence. See L.F.S. Upton, "Sir Brook Watson, *DCB*, 5:842–4.

87 Proclamation of William Shirley, 20 Oct. 1747; printed in full in PAC *Report*, 1905, 2, pt.3, app. C, 48; Harvey, *The French regime*, 134–5.

88 Clark, *Three centuries and the island*, 32.

89 A valuable overview of the history of this region is that of Surette, *Atlas de l'établissment des Acadiens.*

90 "A Breif [*sic*] survey of Nova Scotia," unpublished mss. in the Library of the Royal Artillery Regiment, Woolwich; copy in NAC, AC, MG 18, f.10, and cited in Clark, *Acadia*, 220.

91 Clark, *Acadia*, 236, table 6.11.

92 Ibid., 210–11.

93 AAQ, V.-G., III–51, Abbé de L'Isle Dieu to Pontbriand, 4 April 1750. La Rue had been appointed the administrative head of the Catholic Church in the French dominions in North America in 1734. His letters, with a biographical introduction, are published in RAPQ, *Rapport*, 10 (1935–6). The letter of 4 April 1750 is at 294–306. A further argument for a higher population is to be

found in the reports about the number of refugees from this area, as discussed elsewhere in this chapter.

94 NAC, AC, IR, C11, 28, f.10, Des Herbiers and Prevost to the minister, 15 Aug. 1749; printed in full in PAC *Report*, 1905, 2, pt.3, app. N, 285.

95 " ... je feray mon possible pour rassembler mes Sauvages et comme on ne peut s'opposer ouvertement aux entreprises des anglais, je pense qu'on ne peut mieux faire que d'exciter les Sauvages à continuer de faire la guerre aux anglois, mon dessein est d'engager les Sauvages de faire dire aux anglois qu'ils ne souffriront pas que l'on fasse de nouveaux établissemens dans l'Acadie, qu'ils prétendent qu'elle doit rester où elle était avant la guerre, que si les anglois persistent dans leur dessein les Sauvages ne seront jamais en paix avec eux et leur déclarereont une guerre eternelle": Le Loutre to the minister, 29 Aug. 1749, ibid., 284.

96 " ... Monsieur Bigot lui a donné une augmentation en étoffe, couvertes, poudre et balles au cas qu'ils voulussent inquiéter les Anglois dans leur établissemens à Chiboucto": Des Herbiers and Prevost to the minister, 15 Aug. 1749, ibid., 285.

97 See Upton, *Micmacs and colonists*, 50–1.

98 "cete terre icy que Dieu nous a donné dont nous pouvons conté estre ausy tot que les arbres y sont né ne pouvez estre disputé par personnes ... Nous sommes Maistre independente de personne et voulons avoyr notre pays libre": NAC, CO 217, 3, Antoine and Pierre Couaret to Governor Philipps, 2 Oct. 1720; trans. in Upton, *Micmacs and colonists*, 199n.41.

99 "L'endroit où tu es, où tu fais des habitations, où tu bâtis un fort, où tu veux maintenant comme t'inthroniser, cette terre dont tu veux présentement te rendre maître absolu, cette terre m'appartient, j'en suis certes sorti comme l'herbe, c'est le propre lieu de ma naissance et de ma résidence ...": contained in Maillard to Abbé du Fau, 18 Oct. 1749, Archives du Séminaire de Québec; printed in *Coll. Doc. Inédits*, 1:17.

100 See Plank, "The two majors cope."

101 Dickason, "Amerindians between French and English," 42.

102 NAC, CO 217, 40, ff.142–4, Governor Cornwallis to the Duke of Bedford, 17 Oct. 1749; printed in Akins, *Acadia*, 593–5.

103 Ibid.

104 Calnek, *History of the County of Annapolis*, 114.

105 Murdoch, *A history of Nova Scotia*, 2:150.

106 This project took several years and even in 1760 the road was used only infrequently. See Bell, *The "foreign Protestants,"* 340.

107 NAC, NS/A, 34, "Orders of the savages to the French inhabitants," 12 Dec. 1749. Akins omitted this document from his *Acadia*.

108 NAC, CO 220, NS (B), 4, List presented to Council by Hugh Davidson, 13 Dec. 1749; Akins, *Acadia*, 177.

109 Instructions from Governor Cornwallis to Major Lawrence, 4 April 1750, enclosed in Cornwallis to the Duke of Bedford, 4 June 1750; printed in Webster, *The forts of Chignecto*, app. A, 109.

110 Webster, *The forts of Chignecto*, 110.

111 Major Charles Lawrence, "A journal of the proceedings of the detachment under my command after entering the Basin of Chignecto – 1750," enclosed in NAC, CO 217, 40, Cornwallis to the Lords of Trade, 30 April 1750; printed in PAC *Report*, 1905, 2, app. N, 321.

112 La Corne's report of this affair to Des Herbiers is printed in PAC *Report*, 1905, 2, app. N, 323–4. The only major difference between his account and that of Lawrence is the latter's description of his difficulties with the tides.

113 NAC, AC, IR, C11, 28, f.10, Desherbiers and Prevost to the minister, 15 Aug. 1749; printed in PAC *Report*, 1905, 2, app. N, 285–315.

114 "Le vingt trois Septembre les familles des Planches, Wiskok, Mencan, Nain-pan, les Hébert, Menoudy, dont les habitans étoient déjà à la pointe à Beauséjour, évacuèrent et passèrent sur notre terrain, les sauvages et les accadiens mirent le feu dans toutes les maisons et granges qui étoient pleines de bled et de fourage, ce qui a causé une grande dizette, et obligé de nourrir toutes ces familles aux dépens du Roy, ayant perdu même une grande partye de leurs bestiaux dans cette occasion et le reste pendant l'hyver n'ayant point eu de sel pour saller ce qu'ils avoient pu réchapper, les choses ont continué dans le même etat.": La Valière, "Journal de ce qui s'est passé à Chicnitou .. depuis le 15 septembere 1750 jusqu'au 28 juillet 1751," PAC *Report*, 1905, 2, app. N, 325.

115 La Jonquière and Bigot to the minister, 5 Oct. 1750, PAC *Report*, 1905, 2, app. N, 316.

116 For a detailed account of the settling of the refugees on Île Saint-Jean, see Harvey, *The French regime*, 137–71.

117 "Tour of inspection made by the Sieur de La Rocque; census; 1752," PAC *Report*, 1905, 2, pt.1, app. N, 3–172, is a lengthy nominal census of Île Saint-Jean for 1752 and provides details of where the inhabitants had come from, as well as their immediate situation that year.

118 Ibid., 79.

119 NAC, AC, IR, C11, 30, f.29, Bonaventure to Des Herbiers, 13 June 1751; see also Clark, *Three centuries and the island*, 32–40.

120 NAC, AC, IR, C11, 29, f.174, Prevost to the minister, 25 Nov. 1750.

121 Accounts of their experiences are found in Du Boscq de Beaumont, *Les derniers jours de l'Acadie*, 34–89. The memoirs of Aumasson de Courville exist in a number of versions; the most accessible is that printed as "Mémoires sur le Canada, depuis 1749 jusqu'à 1760," in RAPQ, 1924–25, but see also the version printed by the LHSQ, *Historical documents*, 1st series, 1 (1838), reprinted in 1873.

122 Aumasson de Couville, "Mémoires sur le Canada, depuis 1749 jusqu'à 1760," LHSQ ed., 2–4.

123 NAC, AC, IR, C11, 30, f.7, Des Herbiers to Chevalier Pierre Roch de Saint-Ours, 9 June 1751.

124 There are a number of primary sources for this enterprise. These include NAC, CO 219, 35, f.138, Cornwallis to the Duke of Bedford, 19 Aug. 1750;

NAC, CO 219, 38, Cornwallis to the Lords of Trade, 22 Sept. 1750; and La Valière, "Journal de ce qui s'est passé à Chicnitou ...," PAC *Report*, 1905, 2, pt.1, app. N, 324–30. The actual building of the fort is recounted in an anonymous diary held by the Gates Collections in New York and published by Webster as *The building of Fort Lawrence in Chignecto*. Between these various sources, there is some discrepancy in details – such as the date of the arrival of Lawrence, the number of soldiers under his command, and so on – but nothing substantial.

125 La Valière, "Journal de ce qui s'est passé à Chicnitou," 325.

126 There are three accounts of this incident, two of which lay the blame on Le Loutre. The third, a letter by Abbé Maillard, states that it was a personal matter between How and the Mi'kmaq: Webster, *The forts of Chignecto*, 33.

127 A description and plan of the fort is in Webster, *The forts of Chignecto*, 45–7.

128 Franquet's journals, containing an account of his visit to the two forts and descriptions of them, are in *RAPQ*, 1923–24, 111–40; see also Ganong, *A monograph of historic sites*, 280, 288 (Beauséjour), 291 (Gaspereau).

129 Stanley, *New France*, 74–5.

130 Reid, *Six crucial decades*, 34.

131 " ... marcher contre l'Anglois et se battre en braves contre l'ennemi de l'etat": Le Loutre to the minister, 4 Oct. 1749, PAC *Report*, 1905, 2, pt.3, app. N., 297.

132 AAQ, Vicaire-général, III/51, 4 April 1750; printed in *RAPQ*, 1936, 294–306.

133 " ... j'ay déclaré que tous ceux qui, huit jours après sa publication, n'auront pas prêté ce serment, et ne seront point incorporés dans les compagnies de milices, seront avérés rebelles, et comme tels chassés des terres dont ils sont en possession": La Jonquière to the minister, 1 March 1751, PAC *Report*, 1905, 2, pt.3, app. N., 340. An English version is published in Griffiths, *The Acadian deportation*, 83.

134 From the evidence of Cornwallis's reply, which was dated 19 March 1750, it arrived within less than a month: NAC, CO 219, 13.

135 NAC, CO 218, series B115, Lords of Trade to Cornwallis, 16 Feb. 1749/50; partially printed in Akins, *Acadia*, 601.

136 NAC, CO 219, 10, 3, Lords of Trade to Cornwallis, 22 March 1750/51; partially printed in Akins, *Acadia*, 196.

137 Bell, *The "foreign Protestants,"* 347.

138 Bell provides an exhaustive analysis of their origins in ibid., 304–16.

139 Ibid., 318.

140 Ibid., 372–7.

141 Ibid., 426.

142 NAC, CO 217, 40, Cornwallis to the Lords of Trade; printed in full in Akins, *Acadia*, 591–2.

143 NAC, CO 219, 38, f.189, Lords of Trade to Cornwallis, 16 Feb. 1749/50; partially printed in Akins, *Acadia*, 601–2.

144 It did not help that he had severe arthritis and was frequently confined to

bed with this disease. See Bell, *The "foreign Protestants,"* 346–62; J. Murray Beck, "Edward Cornwallis," DCB, 4:168–71.

145 For a more elaborate analysis of these problems, see chapter 15.

146 In particular, the actions of Captain John Rous: see W.A.B. Douglas, "John Rous," DCB, 3:572–4.

147 See Chard, "The Impact of Île Royale on New England," 201–2; a total of 2,471 vessels entered and cleared Halifax between 19 July 1749 and 31 Dec. 1755.

148 Aumasson de Courville, "Mémoires sur le Canada, depuis 1749 jusqu'à 1760," LHSQ ed., 32.

CHAPTER FIFTEEN

1 Wendy Cameron, "Peregrine Thomas Hopson," DCB, 3: 294–5.

2 T.A. Crowley, "Jean-Louis de Raymond," DCB, 4:655–7.

3 Brebner, *New England's outpost,* 188.

4 Crowley, " Jean-Louis de Raymond," 655.

5 NAC, CO 217, 14, Hopson to the Lords of Trade, 28 March 1752/53; partially printed in Akins, *Acadia,* 681.

6 "His Majesty's commission to His Excellency Governor Cornwallis," printed in full in Akins, *Acadia,* 497–505; on his powers to appoint judges and justice of the peace, see ibid., 501–2. See also commentary in Madden and Fieldhouse, ed., *The classical period of the first British empire,* 181–2.

7 Among the signatories were Joshua Mauger, Vere Rous, and Isaac Deschamps: see NAC, CO, 220, NS (B), 5, ff.245–6, Council minutes, 12 Dec. 1752. An account of this affair is given in Akins, *History of Halifax,* 38ff.

8 Memorial of complaints in NAC, CO 220, NS (B), 6, ff.3–17, Council minutes, 3 Jan. 1753.

9 Proceedings of the inquiry are in NAC, CO 220, NS (B), 6, ff.18–78, Council minutes; the report of decision is in BTNS, 14, Hopson to the Lords of Trade, 28 March 1752/53; see also Akins, *Acadia,* 681.

10 NAC, CO 219, 18, Hopson to the Lords of Trade, 1 Oct. 1753; see also the account given in Murdoch, *A history of Nova Scotia,* 2:217–18.

11 Ibid.

12 A full account of what occurred is found in Bell, *The "foreign Protestants,"* chapter 11.

13 As Bell has pointed out, it is impossible to say exactly how many settlers there were; fifteen hundred is a conservative estimate. See ibid., 418–25.

14 For an analysis of the full bureaucratic idiocy of this decision, see ibid., 363–71.

15 NAC, CO 217, 13, Hopson to the Lords of Trade, 16 Oct. 1752; partially printed in Akins, *Acadia,* 674–9.

16 Marquis Duquesne to Hopson, 30 Sept. 1752, *Northcliffe collection,* 1:5; NAC, CO 219, 16, Hopson to the Lords of Trade, 6 Dec. 1752. See also Bell's discussion of the motives for this agreement in *The "foreign Protestants,"* 377–8.

17 NAC, CO 219, 17, Hopson to the Lords of Trade, 16 Oct. 1752. For a commentary by the French on those who migrated to their territory, see Surlaville's reports in Du Boscq de Beaumont, *Les derniers jours de l'Acadie*, 89ff.; English translation given in Webster, *Forts of Chignecto*, 127–30.

18 NAC, CO 220, NS (B), 6, Council minutes, 10 Aug. 1752.

19 Hopson's reasons for choosing the site can be found in his letters to the Lords of Trade of 26 May 1753, in NAC, CO 219, 17. See Bell's discussion of this in *The "foreign Protestants,"* 401–4.

20 There was a considerable amount of political discussion over this; see Bell, *The "foreign Protestants,"* 405–7.

21 Harvey, ed., *Journal and letters of Colonel Charles Lawrence*.

22 Ibid., 8–9.

23 Lawrence to Cornwallis, 27 June 1753, ibid., 27–8.

24 Plank, "The two majors cope," 34.

25 NAC, CO 220, NS (B), 6, Council minutes, 14 Sept. 1752; a report on the meeting is in NAC, CO 217, 17, Hopson to the Lords of Trade, 14 Sept. 1752; Akins, *Acadia*, 671.

26 NAC, CO 217, 13, Hopson to the Lords of Trade, 6 Dec. 1752. There has been considerable debate over what precisely this treaty meant; for one point of view, see Patterson, "Indian-white relationships in Nova Scotia."

27 NAC, CO 220, NS (B), 6, Council minutes, 24 Nov. 1752; printed in Akins, *Acadia*, 685–6.

28 NSC, CO 217, 13, Hopson to the Lords of Trade, 16 Oct. 1752.

29 NAC, CO 217, 40, Hopson to the secretary of state, 18 Oct. 1752. At this point, Robert D'Arcy, the fourth Earl of Holderness, held the office.

30 NAC, CO, 220, NS (B), 5, f.217, Council minutes, 12 Dec. 1752.

31 Ibid., f.218.

32 Governor's Order Book, printed in Akins, *Acadia*, 197–8.

33 See, in particular, the response made on 19 April 1750 to the deputies of "la Rivière de Canard, Le Grand Pré & Piziquid," who had asked permission to "evacuate the Province and carry off their Effects": NAC, CO 220, NS (B), 6, Council minutes, 19 April 1750; printed in full in Akins, *Acadia*, 185–8.

34 Akins, *Acadia*, 186.

35 NAC, CO 217, 13, Hopson to the Lords of Trade, 10 Dec. 1752.

36 NAC, CO 217, 14, Hopson to the Lords of Trade, 23 July 1753; printed in full in Griffiths, *The Acadian deportation*, 84–5.

37 Petition (in French) of 4 Sept. 1753, and discussion of it, is found in NAC, CO 220, NS (B), 6, ff.225–32, Council minutes, 12 Sept. 1753; an English translation of the petition is in Akins, *Acadia*, 201–3.

38 "Quand nous avons prettés le Serment de Fidelité à Sa Majeste Britannique nous ne l'avons prettés qu'a Condition que l'on nous laisseront Libre L'exercise de notre Religion, et que l'on nous accorderoit des Ministres suffisantes pour la pratiquer": NAC, CO 220, NS (B), 6, f.227, Council minutes, 12 Sept. 1753.

39 "Nous nous voisions privées de L'essentiel que l'on nous a accordés": ibid.

40 Ibid., ff.229–30.

41 NAC, CO 220, NS (B), 6, f.235, Council minutes, 27 Sept. 1753.

42 "... nous avons fait sortir..n'été que par raport d'un nouveau serment que son Excellence Monseigneur Cornwallis a voulû exiger de nous, voulant casser et revoquer celui que nous avoit eté accordé le onzieme Octobre mille sept cents vingt sept ... Ayant appris depuis notre départ que si nous voulions retourner, nous aurions les mêmes faveurs que nous avoient étés accordés": ibid., 236; printed, with the petition given in English, in Akins, *Acadia*, 203–5.

43 Enclosure, in NAC, CO 217, 30, Philipps to the Lords of Trade, 3 Jan. 1730; printed in Akins, *Acadia*, 84 (oath and signatures printed as folded inset). There were minor variations in the oaths administered to the various communities between 1727 and 1730; see chapter 14. The oath chosen for present purposes of comparison was one taken by a large group of Acadians and contains the most detailed collection of provisions.

44 "Etant loges comme nous etions ... il est impossible pour nous d'en signer d'autre, par raport aux Nations Sauvages": NAC, CO 220, NS (B), 6, f.237.

45 Dummett and Nicol, *Subjects, citizens, aliens*, 22. On the implications of the earlier Acadian oath, see Griffiths, "Subjects and citizens," 23–34.

46 "Que nous aurons pleine et entierre Liberté de notre Religion, et des Pretres Catholiques et Romaines autant qu'il nous sera necessaire, sans qu'on exige d'eux aucun Serment de fidelite": NAC, CO 220, NS (B), 6, f.237.

47 "... qu'ils ne seront nullement obligés a prendre les armes contre qui que se soit, et de nulle obligation de ce qui regarde la guerre": ibid.

48 The translation of the 1753 demand is taken from Akins, *Acadia*, 204; the original in the Council minutes reads: "que nous seroit exemptes de prendres les Armes contre qui que se soit qui s'entend contre les Anglois, Francois, Sauvages, ny autre nations, et que nous ne seront, ny aucun de nous, et de nos descendants, pris pour pilloter ny aller ou nous ne voudrions pas aller." See NAC, CO 220, NS (B), 6, f.237.

49 "Nous serons libres et nos descendants de nous retirer ou bon nous semblera, la tête levée et d'emporter nos biens – meubles et immeubles, ou vendre ce que nous ne pouvons pas emporter ...": NAC, CO 220, NS (B), 6, f.238.

50 "et que nous seront dechargés de tout serment aussitot que nous seront hors de la Domination du Roy de la Grande Bretagne": ibid.

51 "Qu'ils seront Libres de se retirer quand il leur semblera, et de pouvoir vendre leurs biens et de transporter Le provenue avec Eux sans aucun trouble, moyennant toute fois que la Vente sera faitte a des Sujets naturelles de La grande Bretagne, et Lorsqu'ils seront hors du Terrain de Sa Majeste ils seront descharges Entierrement de leur signature de serment": ibid.

52 "Qu'ils demeuront en Une Veritable possession de leurs biens qui leur seront accordé a eux et Leurs hoirs dans La meme étendue qu'ils en ont jouys cy devant et en payant Les même droits accoutumes du Pays": ibid.

53 "Que nous auront la Jouissance entiere de nos biens, sans etre inquietés par qui que se soit et que les Terreins occupés pas Messieurs les Anglois seront revenus à qui ils appartient cy devant": ibid.

54 "Les quels articles nous esperons que nous seront accordés par votre Excellence et même ratifies par la court d'Angleterre afin que ceux qui suivront votre Excellence ne prennent pas le pretexte que son Excellence Cornwallis a pris en disant que Monsieur Philips n'avoit aucun pouvoir de la Cour d'Angleterre pour le Serment qu'ils nous avoit accordés": ibid., f.239.

55 "Les demandes que nous faisons nous paroissant justes, nous esperons ... que vous nous les accorderey le plus promptement que faire se poura afin de nous mettre en etat de faire valoir nos biens etant preseque ruiner pas l'abandon que nous en avons fait depuis trois ans ...": ibid.

56 Akins, *Acadia*, 255, note.

57 Donald F. Chard, "Benjamin Green," *DCB*, 4:312–13.

58 "Je Promets ... et Jure Sincerement que Je serai fidelle et que Je porterai une Loyauté parfaite vers sa Majesté Le Roy George le Second. Ainsi que Dieu me soit en aide": NAC, CO 220, NS (B), 6, f.240.

59 Léon, "L'élan industriel et commercial," in Braudel and Labrousse, ed., *Histoire économique et sociale*, 2:503–7.

60 Brewer, *The sinews of power*.

61 Eccles, "Pierre-Joseph Céleron de Blainville," *DCB*, 3:99–101.

62 I am indebted to Tom Barnes for a copy of his paper "From Great Meadow to Grand Pré," which gives a concise overview of the military concerns of the British and French forces in North America during these years.

63 Washington's journal, cited in Parkman, *Montcalm and Wolfe*, 1:139; see also the account in Anderson, *The crucible of war*, 43–5.

64 For Britain's viewpoint, see Langford, *A polite and commercial people*, and for France's, see Riley, *The Seven Years War*. A Canadian perspective is provided in Stanley, *New France*, and Frégault, *La guerre de la Conquête*, while opposing American points of view are found in Jennings, *Empire of fortune*, in particular xv–xxxiii, and Anderson, *Crucible of war*, xviii–xix. Not only are the preceding works valuable in and of themselves, but their bibliographies provide a guide through the material available.

65 For the military preparations, see, especially, the introductory essays in *DCB*, 3: W.J. Eccles, "The French forces in North America during the Seven Years' War," xv–xxiii; and C.P. Stacey, "The British forces in North America during the Seven Years' War," xxiv–xxx.

66 Stanley, *New France*, 91–107; Frégault, *La guerre de la Conquête*, 103–58.

67 Records for the payment of quit-rents by the inhabitants of "Grand Pré, Rivière Canard and Petit Codiac" for the winter of 1752–53 and for the inhabitants of "Pisiquid, Port Babin, and Coegeun, Cannad, Ste. Croix, Cobequid and Minas" for the winter of 1754–55 are found in NAC, Brown Papers, Mss.19071, ff.138–49. The accounts were drawn up by Judge Isaac Deschamps.

68 "fort naturel": La Galissonière, AAQ, GIII, 106, "Mémorandum: Triste situation des Acadiens," 19 May 1752.

69 See the Introduction to this volume; Griffiths, "The formation of a community"; Smith, *Nationalism and modernism*; and *Le Congrès mondial acadian L'Acadie en 2004*, chapter 6, "L'Acadie d'aujourd'hui et l'Acadie de demain."

70 See Brockliss and Eastwood, *A union of multiple identities*; Kearney, *The British Isles*; Elliott, "A Europe of composite monarchies"; and Weber, *Peasants into Frenchmen*.

71 "Les champs, les rangs / les petits les grands / Tout passe / D'autres prennent la place / Et s'en vont à leur tour / Dans le mortel séjour / Tout passe": NAC, Brown Papers, Mss. 19069, ff.56–60.

72 NAC, CO 219, 7, Newcastle to Shirley, 30 May 1747, partially printed in PAC *Report*, 1905, app. B, 46–7; proclamation, enclosed in Shirley to Newcastle, 20 Oct. 1747, published in full in ibid., 47–8.

73 Minutes of instructions to be given to Marquis Duquesne, April 1752, O'Callghan, ed., *Documents relative to the colonial history of the State of New York*, 10:144.

74 Clarke, *Observations on the late and present conduct of the French*, 26.

75 BL, Newcastle Papers, Mss. 32,029, f.96, cited in Jennings, *Empire of fortune*, 118n.26.

76 "un type odieux de cette caste militaire anglaise qui, au xviiie se montra si souvent denuée de scrupule et d'honneur": Lauvrière, *La tragédie d'un peuple*, 1:399.

77 "comme la plupart de ses compatriotes, détestait les Français et voulait à tout prix la ruine de leur puissance en Amérique": ibid., 1:400.

78 "tyran bassement rusé et flatteur accompli ... il écrase outrageusement quiconque n'entre pas dans ses vues": ibid.

79 Doughty, *The Acadian exiles*, 89–90.

80 Brebner, *New England's outpost*, 191–2.

81 Dominick Graham, "Charles Lawrence," DCB, 3:361–6, rightly emphasizes the general situation of the colony as the context in which Lawrence made his administrative choices.

82 Letters and journal of Lawrence in NAC, Brown Papers, Mss. 19072, ff.52–89, f.68.

83 The following believe that Lawrence's mind was already made up when he took office: Brebner, *New England's outpost*, 192; Doughty, *The Acadian exiles*, 90; Gaudet, *Le grand dérangement*, 27; and Rumilly, *Histoire des Acadiens*, 1:413.

84 Plank, *An unsettled conquest*, 141–5.

85 Lauvrière, *La tragédie d'un peuple*, 1:400.

86 Frégault, *La guerre de la Conquête*, 271–2.

87 NAC, NS/A, 54, Lawrence to the Lords of Trade, 5 Dec. 1753.

88 The dispatch is printed only in part in Akins, *Acadia*, 205–6, and this sentence is omitted.

89 Brebner, *New England's outpost*, 207.

90 "*Les habitants qui refusent le serment sans réserve n'ont aucun droit de propriété*": Rumilly, *Histoire des Acadiens* 1:413 (italics in original).

91 A full account is given in Bell, *The "foreign Protestants,"* 450–68; see also I.K. Steele, "Robert Monckton," DCB, 4:540–2.

92 NAC, CO 220, NS (B), 6–7, Council minutes, 18 Dec. 1753–21 June 1754.

93 Webster, *The career of the Abbé Le Loutre*, 47.

94 NAC, CO 217, 15, Lawrence to the Lords of Trade, 1 June and 1 Aug. 1754; partially printed in Akins, *Acadia*, 212–14.

95 La Houssaye to Surlaville, 2 Aug. 1753, Du Boscq de Beaumont, *Les derniers jours de l'Acadie*, 98.

96 NAC, AC, IR, C11, 1754, f.1, "Orders of the king and dispatches," minister to d'Aillebout and Prevost, 5 March 1754; and f.15, minister to Franquet, 12 May 1754.

97 Shirley to the General Court, 28 March 1754, in Freiburg, *Journals of the House of Representatives of Massachusetts*, 1754, 263–6.

98 NAC, CO 217, 15, Lawrence to the Lords of Trade, 1 June 1754.

99 Ibid., Lawrence to the Lords of Trade, 14 June 1754.

100 NAC, CO 218, 5, Lords of Trade to Lawrence, 4 April 1754; partially printed in Akins, *Acadia*, 207–8, where the dispatch is misdated as 4 March 1754.

101 See Tomlins, "The many legalities of colonization," in Tomlins and Mann, ed., *The many legalities of early America*, 1–24.

102 NAC, CO 218, 5, Lords of Trade to Lawrence, 4 April 1754.

103 NAC, CO 220, NS (B), 7, Council minutes, 21 June 1754.

104 NAC, CO 218, 5, Lawrence to the Lords of Trade, 1 Aug. 1754; partially printed in Akins, *Acadia*, 212–14.

105 NAC, CO 220, NS (B), 7, Council minutes, 25 May 1750; printed in full in Akins, *Acadia*, 189–92.

106 Brebner, *New England's outpost*, 209; Doughty, *The Acadian exiles*, 91ff. Gaudet offers a lengthy analysis of the complete dispatch in *Le grand dérangement*, 29ff.

107 Gipson, *The British empire before the American revolution*, 6:248; Lauvrière, *La tragédie d'un peuple*, 1:402.

108 Brebner, *New England's outpost*, 209.

109 Speck, *The butcher*, 180, 181. The classic work on the fate of those imprisoned after the rebellion is that of Seton and Arnot, *The prisoners of the '45*.

110 General Court to Shirley, 9 April 1754, Lincoln, ed., *The correspondence of William Shirley*, 2:47–51.

111 Shirley to Sir Thomas Robinson, 8 May 1754, ibid., 2:62. See Rawlyk, *Nova Scotia's Massachusetts*, 198–203, for an account of the evolution of Shirley's policy.

112 W.J. Eccles, "Louis Coulon de Villiers," *DCB*, 3:148–9.

113 Stanley, *New France*, 56–7.

114 For a clear account of this engagement, see ibid., 54–7.

115 Shirley to Halifax, 20 Aug. 1754, printed in full in Pargellis, ed., *Military affairs in North America*, 22–6.

116 Lawrence to Halifax, 23 Aug. 1754, printed in full in ibid., 26–30. This was a personal communication of Lawrence. It is not calendared in the PAC *Report* of 1894, nor is any part of it printed in Akins, *Acadia*.

117 "Tho' I would be very far from attempting such a step [imposing the unqualified oath] without your Lordships approbation, yet I cannot help

being of the opinion that it would be much better, if they refuse the oaths, that they were away": NAC, CO 217, 15 Lawrence to the Lords of Trade, 1 Aug. 1754; partially printed in Akins, *Acadia*, 212–14.

CHAPTER SIXTEEN

1 *Histoire philosophique et politique de l'établissment des Européennes dans les deux Indes*, 1766 ed., 7 vols.

2 "des jalousies nationales, de cette cupidité des gouvernements qui dévorent les terres et les hommes": ibid., 6:364.

3 "font telles qu'un cœur humain & généreux ne les adopte jamais qu'à regret": William Burck, *Histoire des colonies européennes dans l'Amérique en six parties ...* (Paris: Merlin 1767), 2 vols., 2:319. My translation.

4 For a collection of opinions on the issue, see Griffiths, *The Acadian deportation*.

5 For the nineteenth-century debate, see Parkman, *Montcalm and Wolfe* and *A half-century of conflict*, and Casgrain, *Un pèlerinage au pays d'Évangéline*. The debate was continued in the twentieth century by a great number of writers, most recently by Sauvageau, *Acadie. La guerre de Cents Ans des Français d'Amérique*, Cazaux, *L'Acadie: Histoire des Acadiens*; and Plank, *An unsettled conquest*. The bibliographies produced by the Centre d'Études Acadiennes, at the Université de Moncton, New Brunswick, are the first place to begin a survey of this literature. See, in particular, *Inventaire général*, vol.2, *Bibliographies acadienne ... à 1975* (n.d.), and various supplements. Worthwhile consulting, too, is Griffiths, "The Acadian deportation," which provides a critical survey of what was published before 1956.

6 Wade, ed., *The journals of Francis Parkman*, 2:548.

7 A full account of their actions is found in Dumont-Johnson, *Apôtres ou agitateurs*, 116–28.

8 NAC, CO 220, NS (B), 7, ff.63–73, Council minutes, 9 September 1754; translation of Le Loutre's letter is printed in full in Akins, *Acadia*, 215–19.

9 Lawrence to Hussey, 8 Nov. 1754, printed in Akins, *Acadia*, 37–8.

10 PANS, Pichon Papers, no.B, Pontbriand to Le Loutre, 1754; a full translation is provided in Akins, *Acadia*, 240–1. A discussion of whether the letter might be a forgery is in Webster, *The Career of the Abbé Le Loutre*, 15–17.

11 AAQ, Vic. Gen., III/51, Abbé de L'Isle Dieu, 4 April 1750. It will be remembered that the L'Isle Dieu was the man responsible for the dispatch of priests to French dioceses in North America.

12 See chapter 13, as well as the account in Dumont-Johnson, *Apôtres ou agitateurs*, 116–28.

13 On Le Loutre's independence from secular authority, consider this statement: "L'abbé Le Loutre, sans attendre les ordres de la Cour, a fait préparer tous les matériaux nécessaires pour ses abotos [*sic*] ...": M. Joubert to Surla-ville, 1754, in Du Boscq de Beaumont, *Les derniers jours de l'Acadie*, 114.

14 Micheline D. Johnson, "Henri Daudin," *DCB*, 3:165–6.

15 NAC, CO 220, NS (B), 7, ff.117–19, Council minutes, 9 Oct. 1754; partially printed in Akins, *Acadia*, 228.

16 "La pensée de chaque departement est que le Serment de fidelité que nous avons preté à Sa Majesté Britannique ne nous oblige pas de fournir les garrisons de bois, nous devons seulement estre tranquil sur nous biens ...": NAC, CO 220, NS (B), 7, ff.86–91, Council minutes, 24 Sept. 1754; the excerpts printed in Akins, *Acadia*, 221–7, are severely curtailed.

17 NAC, CO 220, NS (B), 7, ff.97–102, Council minutes, 2 Oct. 1754; partially printed in Akins, *Acadia*, 225–6.

18 NAC, CO 220, NS (B), 7, f.106, Council minutes 2 Oct. 1754.

19 NAC, CO 220, NS (B), 7, ff.107–9, Council minutes, 3 Oct. 1754; printed in Akins, *Acadia*, 226–7.

20 NAC, CO 220, NS (B), 7, f.128, Council minutes, 21 Oct. 1754.

21 Gaudet has attempted to estimate the size and distribution of the population in French-controlled areas, excluding Île Saint-Jean. He believes that this population as a whole numbered 1,541. See "Census of Chignecto and outlying districts in 1754," in Webster, *Forts of Chignecto*, 37; and Surette, *Atlas de l'établissement des Acadiens*, passim.

22 C.J. d'Entremont, "Joseph Brossard," *DCB*, 3:87–8.

23 NAC, CO 220, NS (B), 7, ff.82–3; printed in full in Akins, *Acadia*, 219–20.

24 NAC, CO 220, NS (B), 7, ff.110–16, Council minutes, 5 Oct. 1754. In fact, Lawrence and the councillors, who included on that day Benjamin Green, William Cotterell, Robert Monckton, and John Rous, did not have the authority to pass legislation. The Board of Trade sent the matter to the attorney general and solicitor general for their opinion, which was given on 29 April 1755. They concluded that the governor and Council did not have power to enact laws for Nova Scotia but must act under the authority of commissions and instructions. Laws, it was stated, could not be passed until an assembly was called (NAC, CO 217, 15). This was a matter that would become of major importance with the creation of a House of Assembly in 1758.

25 NAC, AC, C11B, 35, f.310, Bigot to the minister, 14 May 1755.

26 Chard, "The impact of Île Royale on New England," 218. This is a meticulous examination of the subject.

27 Clark, *Acadia*, 234; NAC, G1–466, 215–31.

28 NAC, CO 218, 5, Board of Trade to Lawrence, 29 Oct. 1754.

29 As I have stated, I think the larger number is the more accurate.

30 Albermarle to Robinson, 18 Sept. 1754, Pease, ed., *Anglo-French boundary disputes*, 52–3; see also Savelle, *The diplomatic history of the Canadian boundary*, passim.

31 Newcastle to Robinson, 29 June 1754, cited in Stanley, *New France*, 128. Stanley's account of the diplomatic relations of France and Great Britain at this time is succinct and clear.

32 British politics in this period are complex; it should be remembered, for example, that the office of prime minister and the concept of cabinet government were still evolving and the power of the crown remained a central part

of the government. There is a massive literature on this subject. A good place to begin is Langford, *A polite and commercial people*. On the relationship between the politicians and the emerging civil service, see Anderson, *The crucible of war*, 751–2n.2.

33 See Pargellis, ed., *Military affairs in North America*.

34 Robinson had been secretary to the embassy at Paris from 1723 to 1730 and plenipotentiary at the peace negotiations leading to the Treaty of Aix-la-Chapelle in 1748. He was appointed a member of the Board of Trade in 1748–49. See Valentine, *The British establishment*, 2:743–4.

35 Robinson to Shirley, 5 July 1754, printed in full in Akins, *Acadia*, 382–3.

36 Ibid.

37 Shirley to Robinson, 11 Nov. 1754, partially printed in Akins, *Acadia*, 384–9.

38 NAC, CO 217, 15, Lawrence to the Board of Trade, 12 Jan. 1755. The helpful habit of dating letters on receipt was followed haphazardly. This letter from the Board of Trade was not dated this way but Lawrence's reply of 12 January answers questions it contained.

39 Printed in part in Akins, *Acadia*, 384–9.

40 NAC, Vernon-Wager Papers, instructions to Monckton; printed in full in Akins, *Acadia*, 391–2.

41 Report of the Pepperell committee, in *Doc. Hist. St. Maine*, 12:236–41.

42 On the way in which Shirley persuaded the Court, see Rawlyk, *Nova Scotia's Massachusetts*, 204–9.

43 For Governor Shirley's speech in February 1755, see *Doc. Hist. St. Maine*, 12:350–62.

44 Barry M. Moody, "John Winslow," *DCB*, 4:774–5.

45 John Winslow's journals have been published in the NSHS *Collections*: "Journal of Colonel John Winslow of the provincial troops, while engaged in removing the Acadian French from Grand Pre" and "Journal of Colonel John Winslow of the provincial troops, while engaged in the siege of Beausejour."

46 Anderson, *Crucible of war*, 86–93.

47 The draft of these instructions is found in "Sketch for the operations in North America, Nov. 16th 1754," Pargellis, ed., *Military affairs in North America*, 45.

48 See Rawlyk, *Nova Scotia's Massachusetts*, 108–9.

49 Fifty-four per cent of the volunteers were aged from seventeen to twenty-two, and 84 per cent ranged from seventeen to thirty: Rawlyk, *Nova Scotia's Massachusetts*, 209.

50 I.K. Steele, "Robert Monckton," *DCB*, 4:540–2.

51 See Jennings, *Empire of fortune*, 204–22.

52 Stacey, *New France*, 110.

53 NAC, CO 217, 15, Lawrence to the Board of Trade, 1 Aug. 1754; Akins, *Acadia*, 213.

54 NAC, CO 218, 5, Board of Trade to Lawrence, 29 Oct. 1754; partially printed in Akins, *Acadia*, 235–7.

55 NAC, CO 217, 15, Lawrence to the Board of Trade, 12 Jan. 1755.

56 NAC, CO 220, NS (B), 8, f.126, Council minutes.

57 NAC, CO 218, 5, Board of Trade to Lawrence, 31 Jan. 1755.

58 Ibid., Board of Trade to Lawrence, 7 May 1755.

59 A short corrective to present-day visions of the eighteenth century as a time of highly civilized and compassionate behaviour, epitomized by the glorious music of Bach and Mozart and the paintings of Fragonard, is found in Anderson, *War and society*. See also Palmer, *Age of the democratic revolution*.

60 The best estimate of the number of Huguenots who left France between 1685 and 1690 is 250,000: see Parker, "The Huguenots in seventeenth century France," in Hepburn, ed., *Minorities in history*, 11–30.

61 Smith, *Colonists in bondage*, 148.

62 Ibid., 92.

63 Ibid., 188–95.

64 NAC, Vernon-Wager Papers, printed in Griffiths, *The Acadian deportation*, 108. It is clear from the body of Lawrence's correspondence that he is using the word "extirpate" to mean "to clear away persons from a locality" and not in the sense of "to kill." See *Oxford English Dictionary*.

65 See Stanley, *New France*, 95.

66 Included in a letter of 14 April 1756 from Secretary Fox to the Lords of Trade, printed in PAC *Report*, 1905, app. B, 63–5. As lieutenant governor of Nova Scotia, Belcher displayed a harsh attitude towards the Acadians: see Townsend, "Jonathan Belcher."

67 Susan Buggey, "Jonathan Belcher," *DCB*, 4:50–4.

68 NAC, CO 220, NS (B), 8, ff.2–7, Council minutes.

69 Ibid., ff. 95–6, Council minutes, 29 April 1755.

70 NAC, CO 220, NS (B), 8, ff.69–71, Council minutes, 10 April 1755; see also Bell, *The "foreign Protestants,"* 488–9.

71 See Abbé de L'Isle-Dieu to Pontbriand, 25 March 1755, in "Lettres et mémoires de l'abbé de l'Isle-Dieu," *RAPQ*, 1935–36.

72 Pichon to Surlaville, 12 Nov. 1754, in Du Boscq de Beaumont, *Les derniers jours de l'Acadie*, 130.

73 "legitime souverain": Rumilly, *Histoire des Acadiens*, 1:436.

74 Brebner, "Canadian policy towards the Acadians in 1751," 284. This includes the proclamation of La Jonquière on the subject, as does Griffiths, *The Acadian deportation*, 82–3.

75 Rumilly, *Histoire des Acadiens*, 1:436–7; Webster, *The forts of Chignecto*, 59.

76 Patterson, "Colonial wars and aboriginal peoples," 133, in Buckner and Reid, *The Atlantic region to Confederation*.

77 John Fortier, "Augustin de Boschenry de Drucour," *DCB*, 3:71–4.

78 Bernard Pothier, "Louis Du Pont Duchambon de Vergor," *DCB*, 4:249–51.

79 The sole letter in his own hand that has survived shows that he could write his own language only phonetically: "... je neux sanpeche pas ... de gette ... toute la cargeson ..," for "je ne vous empêche pas ... d'acheter toute la cargaison": Pothier, "Du Pont Duchambon de Vergor," 250. He may well have been dyslexic rather than illiterate.

80 See excerpts and analysis in Webster, *Forts of Chignecto*, 58–60.

81 Aumasson de Courville, *Mémoires sur le Canada, depuis 1749 jusqu'à 1760*, LHSQ ed.

82 For an account of Pichon's career, with references to those of his papers held in PANS, see Webster, *Thomas Pichon*. For a précis of the sort of information that Pichon sent the British, see T.A. Crowley, "Thomas Pichon," *DCB*, 4:630–2.

83 Webster, *Journals of Beauséjour*, 16, 17, and 100.

84 "Extrait du "journal de Beauséjour," in Du Boscq de Beaumont, *Les derniers jours de l'Acadie*, 159.

85 Stanley, *New France*, 111.

86 NAC, AC, IR, C11, 35, f.19, Drucour to the minister, 2 June 1755.

87 Jacau de Fiedmont's account is printed in Webster, *Forts of Chignecto*, 53.

88 Winslow journal is cited in ibid., 50.

89 Vergor to Vaudreuil, 18 Aug. 1754, *The Northcliffe collection*, vol.6, "Document relating to the expedition against the French forces in the Bay of Fundy in 1755, with a French document 'sur la situation actuel' of Fort Beauséjour." A translation is provided in the PAC calendar to the same collection, 39.

90 Murdoch, *A history of Nova Scotia*, 2:262.

91 See Webster, *Forts of Chignecto*, 46–7, based on Franquet's journal.

92 Jacau's account as well as that of Winslow, cited in Webster, *Forts of Chignecto*, 52, 54.

93 In his diary Winslow carefully distinguished between troops from Great Britain and colonial militia. See Webster, *Forts of Chignecto*, 52.

94 Jacau's journal, ibid., 54.

95 Winslow's journal, ibid., 52.

96 Jacau's journal, ibid., 54.

97 "... n'avoient pas voulu venir; qu'ils avoient mis les armes bas et jetté leurs munitions, disant qu'ils ne vouloient pas courir le risque d'être pendus, comme les Anglois les en avoient menacés, s'ils prennoient les armes contre eux": "Journal de Beauséjour," Du Boscq de Beaumont, *Les derniers jours de l'Acadie*, 141.

98 I have followed Stanley's account here; see *New France*, 111–17. Also, see the discursive narrative in Murdoch, *A history of Nova Scotia*, 2:259–73.

99 Webster, ed., *The journals of Beauséjour: The diary of John Thomas*, 16–17.

100 Jacau's journal, Webster, *The Forts of Chignecto*, 55.

101 Webster, ed., *The journals of Beauséjour*, 16–17.

102 NAC, AC, IR, C11, 35, f.156, 7 June 1755.

103 Aumasson de Courville, *Mémoires sur le Canada*, 48.

104 Jacau's journal, Webster, *Forts of Chignecto*, 56.

105 "puisqu'ils n'avoient point espoir de secours, il n'y avoit plus moyen de résister à tant de forces, et qu'ils ne vouloient pas se sacrificier inutilement ...": "Journal de Beauséjour," Du Boscq de Beaumont, *Les derniers jours de l'Acadie*, 143.

106 Jacau's journal, Webster, *Forts of Chignecto*, 56.

107 Webster, *Forts of Chignecto*, 60.

108 Ibid., 64.

109 Preston, Roland, and Wise, *Men in arms*, 144.

110 NAC, AC, series B, IR, 101, IR, f.10.

111 NAC, AC, IR, C11, 100, f.72, the minister to Vaudreuil, 5 Sept 1755.

112 For a forceful presentation of the importance of the Mi'kmaq at this juncture, see Patterson, "Colonial wars and aboriginal peoples."

113 Akins, *Acadia*, 212–14.

114 PAC *Report*, 1905, app. B, 60; a description of the disarming is in *Coll. Doc. Inédits*, 1:138–9.

115 See, in particular, the evidence of Judge Isaac Deschamps in NAC, Brown Papers, Mss. 19073, item 52; and Grace M. Tratt: "Isaac Deschamps," *DCB*, 5:250–2.

116 See NAC, CO 220, NS (B), 8, ff.159–65, Council minutes, 3 July 1755. The French version of this petition is printed in full in PAC *Report*, 1905, app. A, pt.3, app. C, 60–1; the English version, also printed in full, is in Akins, *Acadia*, 248–9.

117 "Les habitans des Mines, de Pisiquid, et de la Rivière-aux-Canards ... pour ... témoigner combien ils sont sensibles à la conduite que le gouvernement tient à leur égard": PAC *Report*, 1905, 2, app.A, pt.3, app.B, 60.

118 "Il parait, monseigneur que votre Excellence doute de la sincérité avec laquelles nous avons promis d'être fidels à Sa Majesté Britanique": ibid.

119 "loin de fausser le serment que nous avons prettés, nous l'avons maintenus dans son entier, malgré les sollicitations et les menaces effrayantes d'une autre puissance": ibid.

120 "tandis que Sa Majesté nous laissera les mêmes libertés qu'elle nous a accordés ...": ibid.

121 "que nous regardons comme nos propres meubles ...": ibid.

122 "ce n'est pas ce fusil que possède un Habitan qui le portera à la Revolte, ni la privation de ce même Fusil qui le rendre plus fidel, mais sa conscience seule le doit engager à maintneir son sermen": ibid.

123 "En dernier lieu, il nous est douloureux, Monseigneur, de nous voir coupable sans le scavoir ... Pierre Melanson a été saisi et arrêté avec le charge de son canot, avant d'avoir entendu aucun Ordre portant deffence de ces sorts de transport": ibid., 161,

124 NAC, CO 220, NS (B), 8, f.167, Council minutes, 3 July 1755.

125 "Signé par quarante-quatre des susdits habitants, au nom de tous": Council minutes, 5 July 1755, ff.166–7, printed in full in French in PAC *Report*, 1905, app.A, pt. 3, and in English in Akins, *Acadia*, 249–50.

126 "si dans la Requette qu'ils ont eu l'honneur de présenter à votre Excellence il se trouvoit quelque faute ou quelque manque de respect envers le gouvernement, que c'est contre leur intention ...": ibid.

127 NAC, Vernon-Wager Papers, Lawrence to Monckton, 25 June 1755; printed in part in Griffiths, *The Acadian deportation*, 109.

128 NAC, CO 217, 15, Lawrence to the Lords of Trade, 28 June 1755.

129 Brebner believes that the British, clearly irritated, attempted to make the Acadians declare themselves unequivocally: *New England's outpost*, 215ff. Gipson maintains that the British judiciously presented their position to the Acadians: *The British empire before the American revolution*, 6:255ff.; Lauvrière is convinced that the meeting was a Machiavellian inquisition, designed to make the Acadians appear guilty: *La tragédie d'un peuple*, 1:428ff.

130 NAC, CO 220, NS (B), 8, Council minutes, 3 July 1755; printed in Akins, *Acadia*, 250.

131 "Permettez-nous, s'il vous plait, d'exposer ici les circonstances genantes dans lesquelles on nous retiens au prejudice de la tranquillité dont nous devons jouir": ibid.

132 The point about the right of Roman Catholics to carry arms was undoubtedly made by Belcher, as a result of his experience in Ireland.

133 NAC, CO 220, NS (B), 8, Council minutes, 4 July 1755; printed in Akins, *Acadia*, 256.

134 See chapter 6 for a discussion of the decision by French jurists that the British crown was justified in demanding an oath of allegiance.

135 Dummett and Nicol, *Subjects, citizens, aliens*, 45.

136 NAC, CO 220, NS (B), 8, Council minutes, 4 July 1755.

137 Ibid., 25 July 1755; printed in Akins, *Acadia*, 261.

138 Ibid., 14 July 1755; printed in Akins, *Acadia*, 257.

139 NAC, CO 218, 5, Secretary of State Robinson's circular to all governors, 15 April 1755.

140 NAC, Vernon-Wager Papers, Lawrence to Monckton, 13 July 1755.

141 NAC, CO 220, NS (B), 8, Council minutes, 15 July 1755; printed in Akins, *Acadia*, 258–9.

142 Douglas, "Nova Scotia and the Royal Navy," 242.

143 NAC, CO 220, NS (B), 8, Council minutes, 15 July 1755; printed in Akins, *Acadia*, 258.

144 CO 5, 211, BL, Mss. 19073, f.42, Robinson to Charles Lawrence, 13 Aug. 1755; printed in full in Griffiths, *The Acadian deportation*, 111.

145 NAC, CO 217, 15, Lawrence to the Lords of Trade, 18 July 1755.

146 In much the same way that officials in France were shaken in 1685 when Protestants chose exile rather than conversion.

147 Brought by one of the ships, the brig *Lily* out of New York. See Macdonald, "The Hon Edward Cornwallis," 42.

148 "nous pouvons bien assurer votre Excellence que plusieurs d'entre nous se sont risqué la vie pour donner connoissance au gouvernement de l'ennemis et aussi lorsqu'il a été nécessaire de travailler pour l'entretient du Fort d'Annapolis ... nous nous y avons porter de tout notre cœur": NAC, CO 220, NS (B), 8 Council minutes, 25 July 1755; PAC *Report*, 2, app. A, pt.3, app. C, 61.

149 "nous leurs enjoignons de ne contracter aucun nouveaux serment": ibid., 61.

150 "nous sommes résons et en volontéz de nous en tenir à celuy que nous avons donnéz ... les Ennemis de Sa Majesté nousont sollicité à prendre les armes contre le gouvernement mais nous n'avons en garde de le faire": ibid.

151 Ibid.

152 This memorial was not sent to the Lords of Trade until 24 Dec. 1755. It was included in a dispatch from Belcher, the main body of which was concerned with the need for an assembly for Nova Scotia: NAC: CO 217,16; printed in full in PAC *Report*, 1905, 2, app.A, pt. 3, app.C, 63–5.

153 Belcher obviously believed that the Catholic hierarchy might proclaim that oaths sworn to a Protestant monarch were not binding. Such a position was extreme, but, when one recalls that Belcher had lived in United Kingdom during the Stuart rebellion of 1745, which had been openly financed by France, it becomes understandable.

154 "depuis un nombre d'Années en jouissant paisiblement de nos droits suivant la Teneur de notre serment en toute sa teneur, et réserve, et nous ayant toujours appuié sur notre serment de fidelité ... et nous sommes résons tous de bon consentement et de foy de ne prendre aucun autre serment": NAC, CO 220, NS (B), 8, Council minutes, 28 July 1755; PAC *Report*, 1905, 2, app. A, pt.3, app. C, 62.

155 "nous ne commetrons jamais l'inconstance de prendre un serment qui change tant soit peut les conditions et les priviléges dans lesquels nos souvereins et nos Perres nous ont placé par le passé": ibid., 62.

156 Dummett and Nicol, *Subjects, citizens, aliens*, 22.

157 For the French view, and their wish to have the Acadians as settlers on Île Royale, see NAC, AC, IR, C11B, 1, f.123, Costebelle to the minister, 1715; for the English view, and their fear that the departure of the Acadians would strip Nova Scotia of its population, see NAC, NS/A, 5:1, Caulfeild to the Lords of Trade, 1715.

158 NAC, CO 217, 15, Lawrence, "Circular letter to the governors of certain colonies," 11 Aug. 1755; printed in PAC *Report*, 1905, 2, app.B, 15–16.

159 See Bernard, *Le drame acadien*, 247–85.

Bibliography

The primary sources for early Acadian history are rich and various. France, England, and Scotland, which sought to establish colonies on the lands that would be known as "Acadie ou la Nouvelle Écosse," "Acadia or Nova Scotia," in international treaties from 1632 to 1763, recorded such efforts in the official correspondence carried on between European governments and colonial officials, as well as between the monarchs granting rights to men eager to explore and exploit the region. Such documentation has been gathered and labelled appropriately in state archives, the French files catalogued in series under "Acadie" at the Archives Nationales (AN) and the Bibliothèque Nationale (BN) in Paris, those of Scotland in files catalogued as "Nova Scotia" in the Scottish Record Office (SRO) in Edinburgh and, similarly labelled, in files in the Public Record Office (PRO) and the British Library (BL) in London. These records, however, are only a small proportion of what is available, for, whether as "Acadie" or as "Nova Scotia," this land formed the southeastern boundary of French claims in North America and the northeastern limits of British interests. Its fortunes were a matter of interest, from the mid-sixteenth century onwards, to both French and British explorers and politicians, traders and settlers, from the moment that contact between North America and Europe became commonplace. So evidence about happenings there is also to be found in the material related primarily to other questions: constitutional and judicial issues raised by colonial developments in general, rights of particular religious authorities over new settlements, and missionary activities. The reaction of New England and New France to this small colony has a documentary history of outstanding importance, one that is recorded not only in European archives but also in those in Quebec, Massachusetts, and Maine. In these circumstances, archival research in Acadian history resembles something of a journey through an ever enticing maze, and there is a continual need for the researcher to remember what particular questions are of immediate importance. Acadian history can easily become a case study for theories concerned with imperial politics, the development of Amerindian relations, the emergence of particular identities, and so on, with the unique nature of Acadian experience drowned in the consideration of broader problems. I have tried to avoid this by concentrating on the growth of Acadian society chronologically and analysing the events that affected the lives of the Europeans who settled the land.

The collections of documents cited below are those I found of particular relevance for this work. There are obviously archival resources that, while consulted, were not of central importance to my purposes. For scholars with questions about other issues of Acadian history, there are three major inventories that are helpful: *The General inventory manuscripts*, vols. 1–3 (Ottawa: Public Archives of Canada 1971–76); *Inventaire général des sources documentaires sur les Acadiens* (Moncton: Centre d'Études Acadiennes de l'Université [CEA] de Moncton 1975); and the *Calendar of state papers, colonial series: America and the West Indies* (London, 1860; repr. Valdez, 1964–). Other major inventories and calendars that I found useful are listed in a later section in this bibliography. In the listing of sources that follows, the European archives of deposit is given, followed, when applicable, by the Canadian archives where a copy may be seen. I had the great good fortune that, when I began my studies for my doctorate in 1964, the Canada Council supported my research in the archives of France and the United Kingdom.

The main archives consulted in France were those in Paris and in the departmental archives of Charente-Maritime in La Rochelle and those of Ille-et-Vilaine, in Rennes. In Paris the collections consulted at the AN included the Archives des Colonies: Série C11, Correspondance générale, Canada; Série C11B, Correspondance générale, Île Royale; Série C11D, Correspondance générale, Acadie; Série F2A, Compagnies de commerce, 1667–1764; Série F2B: Commerce aux colonies, 1714–190; and Serie F3, Collection Moreau de Saint-Méry; Série G3, Notariat, 187–1710. At the Archives de la Marine (AM), I consulted Série A1, Actes de pouvoir souverain, 1610–1714; and Série B2, Ordres et dépêches, 1679–1763. Collections consulted at the Archives du Ministère des Affaires Étrangères were: Correspondance politique Angleterre, various volumes, in particular 43–5, 78–94, 208–9, 448–51, and 640. All these collections are available in the National Archives of Canada (NAC) and have been calendared and inventoried by that body. Copies are also available for most of these series at the CEA. At the BN, the main collections I consulted included the Collection Baluze; the Collection Clairambault; Mélanges Colbert; and the Collection Moreau. Certain, but not all, of these documents are available in the NAC. In Paris, too, I did research at the Bibliothèque de l'Arsenal, where commentaries on the strategic position of Acadia are to be found, in particular Mss. 2786 and 6432. At the Archives de la Charente-Maritime, there are volume after volume consisting of the contracts made between intending emigrants and shipowners. The most useful listings of these contracts for my purposes were: Minutes Cherbonnier, 1638–67; Minutes Teuleron, 1638–80; Minutes Drouyrea, 1652–85; Minutes Demontreau, 1652–73; Minutes Rabusson, 1644–98; and Minutes Groze, 1681–86. Other notarial records of importance for me were: Minutes Jupin, 1632–38 (copies at CEA); Minutes Rivière et Soulard, 1684–1733 (copies at NAC); and Minutes Mongrelon, 1632–35 copies at NAC); Minutes Teuleron, 1632–66; and Minutes Cherbonnier,

1642–1662 (copies at CEA and NAC). These archives also contain the original register of births at Beaubassin, 1712–48, a copy of which is at the CEA. At the Archives de Ille-et-Vilaine, Sèrie E, Dossier de l'affaire Denys, 1657–64, was of particular value.

The British archival holdings of relevance to the Acadian experience are as voluminous and as varied as those of the French and the NAC holds transcripts – handwritten, typed, xeroxed, or microfilmed – of the vast majority of these. So does the Provincial Archives of Nova Scotia (PANS). There are, however, a number of exasperating matters that have to be understood when using this material, whether the researcher is working in Halifax, London, Ottawa, or Moncton. Over the last two hundred years, the British have changed their reference systems for archival holdings, but the invaluable *Calendars of state papers, colonial series, America and the West Indies* for the years before 1801 uses the old system, not the new one. Further, the Canadian archivist who assembled the invaluable NAC guide to the use of the Nova Scotia A series – "a comprehensive body of records dealing with Nova Scotia" – brought together records not only from the British Board of Trade/Nova Scotia and America and West Indies series but also other documents from PRO collections as well as documents held in the British Museum and Lambeth Palace. The way through this morass is to use the guides produced by both the PRO and the NAC as well as that to be found in Charles M. Andrews, *Guide to the materials for American history to 1783, in the Public Record Office of Great Britain*, vol.1, *The state papers* (Washington: Carnegie Institute of Washington 1912.) This work contains an invaluable appendix of tables which gives the new references for the colonial papers for Nova Scotia, the CO 217 and CO 218 series. Finally, the official collections of British papers, those of the Colonial Office, the Admiralty, the Treasury, and the War Office, among others, are not the only British archival holdings that have been copied for the NAC: papers of individuals such as William Pitt, the Earl of Chatham, and the Duke of Newcastle are among the transcriptions available in the NAC.

In the United States, the most crucial collections for me were those relating to the early history of Maine and Massachusetts, both those held in the Library of Congress in Washington and those held in the state archives and libraries. Important series have been published and are listed later in this bibliography. The majority of these have not been copied by the CEA and NAC. The records held by the Massachusetts Historical Society and the Boston Public Library are so voluminous that the scholar needs to visit these institutions in person, to investigate first-hand such collections as the Mascarene Papers, the John Winslow Papers, and many small but illuminating collections of papers left by men who were in Acadia briefly during these years. The records of the fishing fleets, exploited so well by Donald F. Chard, are especially worth studying.

Before turning to archives within Canada, the archives in Italy need consideration. The work of Luca Codignola is a meticulous and magnificent introduction to the Roman archival holdings relating to North America. His guide to the collection of the Propaganda Fide made my research in that institution much more fruitful than it otherwise would have been. There is also a *Calendar of documents relating to*

French and British North America in the Archives of the Sacred Congreation "de Propaganda Fide" in Rome, 1622–1799, in the Research Centre in Religious History of Canada at Saint Paul University in Ottawa. However, my advice is to consult Codignola's work, listed in the next section of this bibliography.

Lastly, we come to the collections of first deposit held in Canada, particularly those at the National Archives in Ottawa, the provincial and episcopal archives in Quebec City, and the provincial archives in Halifax, Moncton, Fredericton, and Saint John. All are voluminous and of great importance for understanding the Acadian experience. The guides to these collections are many and excellent, and, as well, a considerable number of documents have been published. Private papers such as those of J.C. Webster in Saint John should not be overlooked, and the careful researcher would also do well to consult the bibliographies provided in each volume of the *Dictionary of Canadian Biography* (*DCB*).

BIBLIOGRAPHIES, INVENTORIES, AND REFERENCE WORKS

Bibliographie acadienne: liste des volumes, brochures et thèses concernant l'Acadie et les Acadiens des débuts à 1975. Moncton, N.B.: Centre d'Études Acadiennes.

Bosher, J.F. *Négociants et navires du commerce avec le Canada de 1660 à 1760: Dictionnaire biographique.* Ottawa: National Historic Sites, Parks Service, Environment Canada 1992.

Burton, John H., et al. *The register of the Privy Council of Scotland.* Edinburg: Privy Council 1877–1970.

Codignola, Lucia. *Guide to documents relating to the French and British North America in the Archives of the Sacred Congregation "de Propaganda Fide" in Rome, 1622–1799.* Ottawa: National Archives of Canada 1991.

Dictionary of Canadian Biography, 14 vols. Toronto/Quebec City: University of Toronto Press/ Les Presses de l'Université Laval 1966–present.

Eggenberger, David. *Encyclopedia of battles: Accounts of over 1,560 battles from 1479 BC to the present.* Rev. ed. New York: Dover Press 1985.

Harbec, Hélène, and Paulette Lévesque, ed. *Guide bibliographique de l'Acadie, 1976–1987.* Moncton, N.B.: Centre d'Études Acadiennes 1988.

Harris, R. Cole, ed. *Historical Atlas of Canada.* Vol.1: *From the beginning to 1800.* Toronto: University of Toronto Press 1987.

Inventaire général des sources documentaires sur les Acadiens. Moncton: Centre d'Études Acadiennes de l'Université de Moncton 1975.

Marion, Marcel. *Dictionnaire des institutions de la France aux XVIIᵉ et XVIIIᵉ siècles.* Paris: Éditions A. and J. Picard 1969. Originally published 1923.

Quebec. *État général des archives publiques et privées* Quebec: Ministère des Affaires Culturelles 1968.

Roy, Pierre-Georges. *Inventaire des concessions en fief et seigneurie, fois et hommages, et aveux et dénombrements, conservés aux archives de la province de Québec.* 6 vols. Beauceville, Que.: L'Éclaireur 1927–29.

Stephenson, Carl, and F.G. Marcham, ed. and trans. *Sources of English constitutional history: A selection of documents from 600 AD to the present.* London: Harper 1937.

Sturtevant, W.C. *Handbook of North American Indians.* 20 vols. Vol.15, Bruce M. Trigger ed., *The Northeast.* Washington: Smithsonian Institution 1978.

Surette, Paul. *Atlas de l'établissement des Acadiens aux Trois Rivières du Chignectou, 1660–1775.* Moncton: Éditions d'Acadie 1996.

Taillemite, Étienne. *Inventaire analytique de la correspondance générale avec les colonies, départ, série B (déposée aux Archives Nationales), I, registres 1 à 37 (1654–1715).* Paris, 1959.

Taylor, M. Brook. *Canadian history: A reader's guide.* Vol.1: *Beginnings to Confederation.* Toronto: University of Toronto Press 1994.

United States, Bureau of the Census. *Historical Statistics of the United States: Colonial Times to 1970.* 2 vols. Washington: US Government Print Office 1975.

Valentine, Alan. *The British establishment, 1760–1784: An eighteenth century biographical dictionary.* Norman: University of Oklahoma Press 1970.

White, Stephen A. *Dictionnaire généalogique des familles acadiennes: première partie, 1636 à 1714. Elaboré à partir des recherches commencées par Hector-J. Hébert et Patrice Gallant,* 2 vols. Moncton, N.B.: Centre d'Études Acadiennes, Université de Moncton 1999.

PRINTED COLLECTIONS OF DOCUMENTS

Canada

Government of Canada. *Census of Canada, 1870–1871.* Ottawa: Queen's Printer 1876.

Innis, Harold A. *Select documents in Canadian economic history 1497–1783.* Toronto: University of Toronto Press 1929.

Lanctot, Gustave, Victor K. Johnston, and Adam Shortt., ed. *Documents relating to currency, exchange and finance in Nova Soctia, with prefatory documents.* Ottawa, 1933.

Le Blant, Robert, and René Baudry, ed. *Nouveaux documents sur Champlain et son époque.* Vol.1: *1560–1622.* Ottawa, 1967.

The Northcliffe collection: Presented to the government of Canada by Sir Leicester Harmsworth, as a memorial to his brother the Right Honourable Alfred Williams Harmsworth, viscount of Northcliffe. Ottawa: F.A. Acland 1926.

Nova Francia. 7 vols. Paris: Sociétée d'histoire du Canada 1925–32.

Report of the Public Archives of Canada. Various years.

Richard, Édouard, ed. *Supplement to Dr. Brymner's report on the Canadian Archives, 1899.* Ottawa: King's Printer 1901.

France

Bréard, Charles, and Paul Bréard, *Documents relatifs à la marine normande et à ses armements aux XVIe et XVIIe siècles pour le Canada, l'Afrique, les Antilles, le Brésil et les Indes.* Rouen: A. Lestringant 1889.

Du Boscq de Beaumont, Gaston. *Les derniers jours de l'Acadie (1748–1759), corre-spondances et mémoires: extraits du portefeuille de M. le Courtois de Surlaville, lieutenant-général des armées du roi, ancien major des troupes de l'Île Royale, mis en ordre et annotés.* Genève: Slatkine-Megariotis Reprints 1975.

Gosselin, É., ed. *Nouvelles glanes historiques normandes puisées exclusivement dans les documents inédits.* Rouen: H. Boissel 1871–72.

Mémoires de commissaires du roi et de ceux de sa majesté britannique, sur les possessions & les droits respectifs des deux couronnes en Amérique; avec les actes publics & pièces justificatives. 4 vols. Paris: Imprimerie royale 1755.

Vast, Henri, ed. *Les grands traités du règne de Louis XIV.* 3 vols. Paris: A. Picard et fils 1893–99.

Great Britain

Birch, Thomas, ed. *A collection of the state papers of John Thurloe, Esq.,* 7 vols. London, 1742.

Burton, John H., ed. *The Darien papers: Being a selection of original letters and official documents relating to the establishment of a colony at Darien by the Company of Scotland trading to Africa and the Indes, 1675–1700.* Edinburg: Bannatyne Club 1849.

– et al., ed. *The register of the Privy Council of Scotland.* 38 vols., series 1. Edinburgh, 1877–1970.

The Case stated between England and the United Provinces, in this present juncture. Together with a short view of those Netherlanders in their late practices as to religion, liberty, leagues, treaties, amities. Publish'd for the information of, and a warning to England by a Friend to this Commonwealth. London: T. Newcomb 1652.

Colonial Office. *America and West Indies, original correspondence etc., 1606–1807.* Nendeln, Liechtenstein: Kraus-Thomson Organization, in cooperation with Public Record Office and Her Majesty's Stationery Office, London, 1975.

A Declaration of the Parliament of the Commonwealth of England, relating to the affairs and proceedings between this Commonwealth and the States General of the United Provinces of the Low Countreys, and the present differences occasioned on the States' part. London, 1652.

Insh, George Pratt, ed. *Papers relating to the ships and voyages of the Company of Scotland trading to Africa and the Indes, 1696–1707.* 3rd series. Edinburgh: Scottish History Society Publication 1924.

Journal of the Commissioners for Trade and Plantations. 14 vols. London: Public Record Office 1920–38.

Laing, David, ed. *Royal letters, charters and tracts: Relating to the colonization of New Scotland, and the institution of the Order of Knight Baronets of Nova Scotia, 1621–1638.* Edinburg: Bannatyne Club 1867.

Madden, Fredrick, and David Fieldhouse, ed. *The classical period of the first British empire, 1689–1763: The foundations of a colonial system of government.* Vol. 2 in the *Select documents on the constitutional history of the British empire and commonwealth* series. Westport, Conn.: Greenwood Press 1985.

Marshall, J., ed. *A digest of all the accounts diffused through more than 600 volumes of journals, reports and papers, presented to Parliament since 1799.* London: W. Robson 1833.

Memoirs of the English and French commissaries concerning the limits of Nova Scotia or Acadia. London, 1755.

Morse, W.I., ed. *Acadiensis Nova, 1598–1779: New and unpublished documents and other Data relating to Acadia.* London: B. Quaritch 1935.

Pargellis, Stanley, ed. *Military affairs in North America, 1748–1765: Selected documents from the Cumberland collection in Windsor Castle.* Hamden, Conn.: Archon Books 1969.

Sainsbury, W.N., ed. *Calendar of state papers, colonial series,* 44 vols. London: Longman Green, Longman and Roberts 1860–1969.

Smythies, Raymond H.R. *Historical records of the 40th (2nd Somersetshire) Regiment, now 1ˢᵗ Battalion, the Prince of Wales's Volunteers (South Lancashire Regiment): From its formation in 1717 to 1893.* Devonport, U.K.: A.H. Swiss 1894.

New Brunswick

Collections of the New Brunswick Historical Society. Edited by W.F. Ganong.

Cyr, Jean Roch. "Le difficile maintien de la puissance française en Acadie: quelques journaux de Joseph Robineau Villebon." *Le Petit Courier* (Fredericton) 5, 1 (1986): 16.

"Historical and Geographical Documents Relating to Nova Scotia," NBHS, *Papers,* no.7

Webster, John Clarence, ed. *Acadia at the end of the 17ᵗʰ century: Letters, journals and memoirs of Joseph Robineau de Villebon, commandant in Acadia, 1690–1700, and other contemporary documents.* Saint John: New Brunswick Museum 1934. Monograph Series no.1.

– *The Career of Abbé Le Loutre in Nova Scotia: With a translation of his autobiography.* Sediac, N.B.: J.C. Webster 1933.

Nova Scotia

Akins, Thomas Beamish, ed. *Acadia and Nova Scotia: Documents relating to the Acadian French and the first British colonization of the province, 1714–1758.* Cottonport, La.: Polyanthos 1979. Repr. of Halifax: Charles Annand 1869 ed..

Fergusson, Charles Bruce, ed. *Nova Scotia Archives IV: Minutes of His Majesty's Council at Annapolis Royal, 1736–1749.* Halifax: Public Archives of Nova Scotia 1967.

Harvey, D.C. *Journal and letters of Colonel Charles Lawrence: Being a day by day account of the founding of Luneburg by the officer in command of the project, transcribed from the Brown manuscripts in the British Museum.* Halifax, N.S.: Public Archives of Nova Scotia 1953.

"Journal of Colonel John Winslow of the provincial troops, while engaged in removing the Acadian French inhabitants from Grand Pre"; "Journal of Colonel John Winslow of the provincial troops, while engaged in the siege of Beausejour." NSHS *Collections* 3 (1883): 71–196, and 4 (1885): 113–246.

MacMechan, Archibald M., ed. *Nova Scotia Archives II: A calendar of two letter books*

and one commission-book in the possession of the government of Nova Scotia, 1713–1714.
Halifax: Herald Printing House, J. Burgoyne 1900.

– *Nova Scotia Archives III: Original minutes of His Majesty's Council at Annapolis Royal,
1720–1739.* Halifax: McAlpine Publishing Company 1908.

Patterson, Rev. George, ed. "Papers connected with the administration of Governor
Vetch," NSHS *Collections* 4 (1884).

Pothier, Bernard, ed. *Course à l'Accadie; Journal de campagne de François Du Pont
Duvivier en 1744.* Moncton: Éditions d'Acadie 1982.

Webster, J.C., ed. *Journals of Beauséjour: Diary of John Thomas, journal of Louis de
Courville.* Halifax: Public Archives of Nova Scotia 1937.

Quebec

Collection de documents inédits sur le Canada et l'Amérique. 3 vols. Quebec: Le Canada-
français 1888–1890.

*Collection de manuscrits contenant lettres, mémoires, et autres documents historiques docu-
ments relatifs à l'histoire de la Nouvelle-France recueilles aux archives de la province de
Québec, ou copiés à l'étranger.* 4 vols. Quebec: A. Côté 1883–85.

*Édits, ordonnances royaux, déclarations et arrêts du Conseil d'État du roi concernant le
Canada: revus et corrigés d'après les pièces originales déposées aux archives provinciales,* 3
vols. Quebec: Fréchette 1854–56.

Godbout. A., ed. "Rolle de Jehan." *Mémoires de la Société génealogique canadienne
française,* 1, 2 (January 1944).

Literary and Historical Society of Quebec. *Historical Documents,* 1st Series, 1 (1838).

Ordonnances, commissions, etc., des gouverneurs et intendants, 1639–1706. 2 vols.
Beauceville, Que.: Éditions P.-G. Roy 1924.

*Pièces et documents relatifs à la tenure seigneuriale demandés par une adresse de l'Assemblée
legislative.* 2 vols. Quebec: E.R. Fréchette 1852.

Rapport de l'archiviste de la province de Québec. Quebec. Various dates.

Têtu, H., et C.O. Gagnon, ed. *Mandements, lettres pastorales et circulaires des évêques de
Québec.* Quebec: Impr. générale A. Coté 1887–1890.

United States

Collections of the Massachusetts Historical Society. 3rd series, vol.5, "Autobiography of
the Rev. John Barnard," 177–243.

Collections of the Massachusetts Historical Society. 6th series, vol.48 (1905), "Letters
relating to the Acadian-Massachusetts relations in 1644."

Davenport, Frances G. *European treaties bearing on the history of the United States and its
dependencies.* 4 vols. Washington: Carnegie Institute of Washington 1917–37.

Easterby, J.H., ed. *The journals of the Commons House of Assembly of South Carolina,
South Carolina colonial records,* 9 vols.+. Columbia, S.C., 1951–62+.

Freiburg, Malcolm, ed. *Journals of the House of Representatives of Massachusetts.* 37 vols.
Boston: Massachusetts Historical Society 1919–67.

Hale, Robert [of Beverly]. "Journal of a voyage to Nova Scotia made in 1731 ...,"
Historical Collections of the Essex Institute, 42, 3 (July 1906): 217–43.

Lincoln, Charles Henry, ed. *The correspondence of William Shirley, governor of Massachusetts and military commander in America.* 2 vols. New York: Macmillan 1912.

MacKinney, G., ed. *Votes and proceedings of the House of Representatives of the province of Pennsylvania,* vol.5, 8th series. Philadelphia, 1951.

Massachusetts. *Acts and resolves public and private of the province of Massachusetts Bay.* Boston, 1878.

Noble, John, ed. *Courts of assistance of the colony of Massachusetts Bay, 1639–1692.* 3 vols. Boston: Country of Suffolk 1901–28.

O'Callaghan, E.B., ed. *Documents relative to the colonial history of the State of New York, procured in Holland, England and France by James Romeyn Brodhead,* 15 vols. Albany, N.Y.: Weed, Parsons 1853–87.

Pennsylvania Historical Society, Harrisburg [Archives]. "Report of the overseers of the poor on Acadian petitions."

Shurtleff, N.B., ed. *Records of the governor and Company of the Massachusetts Bay in New England, 1628–1686.* 5 vols. Boston: W. White 1853–54.

Thwaites, R.G., ed. *The Jesuit Relations and allied documents: Travels and explorations of the Jesuit missionaries in New France, 1610–1791.* 73 vols. New York: Pageant 1959. Originally published, Cleveland: Burrows 1896–1901.

Toppan, R.N., and A.T.S. Goodrick, ed. *Edward Randolph; including his letters and official papers from the New England, middle, and southern colonies in America, with other documents relating chiefly to the vacating of the royal charter of the colony of Massachusetts Bay, 1898–1909.* Boston: Prince Society 1898–1909.

Transactions of the Colonial Society of Massachusetts.

Trask, William Blake, et al. *Suffolk Deeds.* 14 vols. Boston: Rockwell and Churchill 1880–1906.

Wade, Mason., ed. *The Journals of Francis Parkman.* London: Eyre and Spottiswood *c.*1940–49.

Willis, William Willis, et al., ed. *Documentary history of the state of Maine.* 24 vols. Portland, Me., and Cambridge, Mass.: Maine Historical Society *Collections,* series 2, 1869–1916.

BOOKS PUBLISHED BEFORE 1800

Alexander, Sir William. *Encouragement to Colonies.* London: Stansby 1624.

Ashurst, Sir Henry. *The deplorable state of New England due to the covetous Governor Dydley and an account of the Miscarriages of the late expedition against Port Royal.* London, 1708.

Biggar, H.P., ed. *The works of Samuel de Champlain.* 3 vols. Toronto: Champlain Society 1922.

Charlevoix, P.-F.-X. *History and general description of New France.* Translated with notes by J.G. Shea. Chicago: Loyola University Press 1962. Originally published *c.*1744.

Clarke, William. *Observations on the late and present conduct of the French: with regard to their encroachments upon the British colonies in North America: together with remarks on the importance of these colonies to Great Britain.* Boston 1755.

Courville, Louis-Léonard Aumasson, Sieur de. *Mémoires sur le Canada, depuis*

1749 jusqu'à 1760. LHSQ, series 1, vol.1. Quebec: Imprimerie de T. Cary 1838.

Denys, Nicolas. *Description géographique et historique des costes de l'Amerique septentrionale*. Paris: Chez Claude Babin 1672.

– *Description and natural history of the coasts of North America (Acadia)*. Translated and edited by William F. Ganong. Westport, Conn.: Greenwood *c.*1975. Originally published 1672.

Dièreville, N. de. *Relation du voyage du Port Royal de l'Acadie ou de la Nouvelle France*. Amsterdam: Pierre Humbert 1710. SHA *Cahiers*, 16, 3–4 (September-December 1985), with introduction and notes by Melvin Gallant.

– *Relation of the voyage to Port Royal in Acadia or New France*. Edited by J.C. Webster. New York: Greenwood Press 1968. Repr. of Champlain Society ed. 1933. Originally published 1708.

Dreyss, Charles, ed. *Mémoires de Louis XIV*. 2 vols. Paris, 1860.

Hutchinson, Thomas. *The History of the colony and province of Massachusetts-Bay*. 3 vols. Edited by L.S. Mayo. Cambridge, Mass.: Harvard University Press 1936.

Jameson, J. Franklin, ed. *Johnson's wonder working providence of Sion's saviours in New England*. New York: Barnes and Noble 1937. Originally published 1654.

Le Clercq, Christian. *Premier établissement de la foy*. Paris, 1691.

Lescarbot, Marc. *The history of New France*, 3 vols. Edited and translated by W.L Grant and H.P. Biggar. Toronto: Champlain Society 1914. Originally published *c.*1600.

Malapart, André. *La prise d'un seigneur escossois et de ses gensqui pilloient les navires pescheurs de France par Monsieur Daniel, dèdié a Monsieur Lauzon par le sieur Malapart, parisien, soldier dudit sieur Daniel*. Rouen, 1630.

Penhallow, Samuel. *The history of the wars of New England with the eastern Indians, or a narrative of their continued perfidy and creulty, from the 10th of August, 1703, to the peace renewed 13th of July, 1713. And from the 25th of July, 1722, to their submission 15th December 1725, wich was ratified August 5th, 1726*. Boston, 1726.

Phips, Sir William. *A journal of the proceedings in the late expedition to Port Royal, on board Her Majesties ship, the Six Friends, the Honourable William Phips Knight, commander in chief, etc.: A true copy, attested by Joshua Natstock clerk*. Boston: Benjamin Harris at the London-Coffee House 1690.

Raynal, Abbé Guillaume. *Histoire philosophique et politique des établissements du commerce des Européens dans les deux Indes*. Originally published, La Haye: Gosse 1766; repr. Maspero 1981.

Richelieu, Cardinal, Armand du Plessis. *Testament politique*. Paris: Louis André 1947. Originally published *c.*1640.

Voltaire. *Le siècle de Louis XIV*. Paris: Éditions du Monde, n.d.

BOOKS PUBLISHED BEFORE 1900

Akins, T.B. *History of Halifax city*. Halifax: Nova Scotia Historical Society 1895. Repr. Belleville, Ont.: Mika 1973.

Argenson, René Louis de Voyer, Marquis d'. *Journal et mémoires du marquis d'Argenson*. 9 vols. Paris: Renouard 1859–67.

Calnek, W.A. *History of the County of Annapolis*. Edited and completed by A.W. Savary. Toronto: William Briggs 1897. Facsimile edition, Belleville, Ont.: Mika Studio 1980.

Casgrain, H.R. *Guerre du Canada, 1756–1760: Montcalm et Lévis*. Quebec: L.J. Demers 1891.

– *Un pèlerinage au pays d'Évangiline*. Quebec: Demers 1887.

– *Les Sulpiciens et les prêtres des Missions-Étrangères en Acadie*. Quebec: Pruneau and Kirouac 1897.

Church, Benjamin. *The history of the eastern expeditions of 1689, 1692, 1696, and 1704, against the Indians and French*. Introduction and notes by H.M. Dexter. Boston: Wiggin and Lunt 1867.

Deschamps, Léon. *Un colonisateur du temps de Richelieu, Issac de Razilly: biographie – mémoire inédit*. Paris: Institut Geographique de Paris 1980. Originally published Paris: Ch. Delagrave 1887.

Drake, S.G. *The history of Philip's War, commonly called the Great Indian War, of 1675 and 1676. Also, of the French and Indian wars at the eastward in 1689, 1690, 1692, 1696, and 1704*. Edited by Thomas Church. Boston, 1917.

Félix, J., ed. *Voyage à la Nouvelle France du capitaine Charles Daniel de Dieppe, 1629*. Société des Bibliophiles Normands, no.39. Rouen: H. Boissel 1881.

Fraser, William. *The Red Book of Monteith*. 2 vols. Edinburgh, 1880.

Gosselin, Auguste. *Les Normands au Canada* [1892?].

Gosselin, É., ed. *Précis analytique des travaux de l'Académie de Rouen, 1871–2*. Rouen: H. Boissel 1871–72.

Haliburton, Thomas Chandler. *An historical and statistical account of Nova Scotia*. 2 vols. Halifax: J. Howe 1829.

Hannay, James. *The history of Acadia from its first discovery to its surrender to England by the Treaty of Paris*. Saint John, N.B.: Macmillan 1879.

Le Tac, Sixte. *Histoire chronologique de la Nouvelle France ou Canada depuis sa découverte (mil cinq cents quatre) jusques en l'an mil six cents trent deux. Publiée pour la première fois d'après le manuscrit original de 1689 et accompagnée de notes et d'un appendice tout compôsé de documents originaux et inédits, par Eug. Réveillaud*. Paris: Fischbacher 1888.

Maurault, J A. *Histoire des Abénakis depuis 1605 jusqu'à nos jours*. Quebec: Sorel 1866.

Murdoch, Beamish. *A history of Nova Scotia, or Acadie*, 3 vols. Halifax: J. Barnes 1865–67.

Paltsits, V.H., ed. *The journal of Captain William Pote, Jr., during his captivity in the French and Indian War from May 1745 to August 1747*. New York, 1896.

Parkman, Francis. *A half-century of conflict*. 2 vols. Boston: Little 1897

– *Montcalm and Wolfe*. 2 vols. Boston: Little, Brown 1884.

Poirier, Pascal. *Origine des Acadiens*. Montreal: Senecal 1874.

Rameau de Saint-Père, François-Edme. *Une colonie féodale en Amérique: l'Acadie (1604–1881)*. 2 vols. Paris: E. Plon, Nourrit 1889.

Sagard, Gabriel. *Histoire du Canada et voyage: que les Frères mineurs Recollets y ont faicts pour la conversion des infidelles*. Paris: Tross 1866.

BOOKS PUBLISHED AFTER 1900

Adams, James Thurslow. *The founding of New England.* Boston: Atlantic Monthly Press 1949.

Anderson, Fred. *The crucible of war: The Seven Years' War and the fate of Europe in British North America, 1754–1766.* New York: Alfred Knopf 2000.

Anderson, M.S. *War and society in Europe of the old regime, 1618–1789.* Montreal and Kingston, Ont.: McGill-Queen's University Press 1998.

Andrews, Charles M. *The colonial period of American history.* 4 vols. New Haven, Conn.: Yale University Press 1964.

Angus, Ian. *A border within national identity, cultural plurality, and wilderness.* Montreal and Kingston, Ont.: McGill-Queen's University Press 1997.

Armitage, David, ed. *Theories of empire, 1450–1800.* Vol.20, *An expanding world: The European in world history.* General editor, A.J.R. Russell. Aldershot Hampshire, U.K.: Ashgate Variorum 1998.

Arsenault, Bona. *Histoire et généalogie des Acadiens.* 2 vols. Quebec: Quebec Le Conseil de la Vie Française en Amérique 1965.

Ashley, Maurice. *Financial and commercial policy under the Cromwellian protectorate.* London: F. Cass 1962.

Augustin-Thierry, A., ed. *Un colonial au temps de Colbert: mémoires de Robert Challes, écrivain du roi.* Librairie Plon 1931.

Axtell, James. *The European and the Indian: Essays in the ethnohistory of colonial North America.* New York: Oxford University Press 1981.

Bailey, A.G. *The conflict of European and eastern Algonkian cultures, 1504–1700. A study in Canadian civilization,* 2nd ed. Toronto: University of Toronto Press 1969.

Bailyn, Bernard. *The New England merchants in the seventeenth century.* New York: Torchbook 1964.

Baker, Emerson W., and John G. Reid. *The New England knight: Sir William Phips, 1651–1695.* Toronto: University of Toronto Press 1998.

Bamford, Paul W. *Fighting ships and prisons: The Meditarranean galleys of France in the age of Louis XIV.* Minneapolis: University of Minnesota Press 1973.

Barbiche, B. *Sully.* Paris: A. Michel 1978.

Barrow, Thomas C. *Trade and empire: The British customs service in colonial America, 1660–1775.* Cambridge, Mass.: Harvard University Press 1967.

Barth, Fredrik, ed. *Scale and social organization.* Oslo: Universitetsforl 1978.

Basque, Maurice. *Des hommes de pouvoir: histoire d'Otho Robichaud et de sa famille, notables acadiens de Port Royal et de Néguac.* Neguac, N.B.: Société Historique de Néguac 1996.

Beik, William. *Absolutism and society in seventeenth-century France: State power and provincial aristocracy in Languedoc.* Cambridge, U.K.: Cambridge University Press 1985.

Bell, Winthrop Pickard. *The "foreign Protestants" and the settlement of Nova Scotia: The history of a piece of arrested British colonial policy in the eighteenth century.* Toronto: University of Toronto Press 1961.

Bernard, Antoine. *Le drame acadien depuis 1604.* Montreal: Clercs de Saint Viateur 1936.

Biggar, H.P. *The early trading companies of New France: A contribution to the history of commerce and discovery in North America.* Toronto: University of Toronto Library 1901.

Bishop, Morris. *Champlain: The life of fortitude.* Toronto: McClelland and Stewart 1963.

Bitton, Davis. *The French nobility in crisis, 1560–1640.* Stanford, Calif.: Stanford University Press 1969.

Black, Jeremy. *Convergence or divergence?: Britain and the continent.* London: Macmillan 1994.

Bond, Beverly W. *The quit-rent system in the American colonies.* Gloucester, Mass.: Peter Smith 1965. Originally published in 1919.

Bond, Richard P. *Queen Anne's American kings.* Oxford, U.K.: Clarendon Press 1952.

Bosher, J.F. *The Canadian merchants, 1713–1763.* Oxford, U.K.: Clarendon Press 1987.

Boudreau, Marielle, and Melvin Gallant. *Le guide de la cuisine traditionnelle acadienne.* Montreal: Stanké 1980.

Bourgeon, Jean-Louis. *Les Colbert avant Colbert: destin d'une famille marchande.* Paris: Presses Universitaires de France 1971.

Braudel, Fernand. *Capitalism and material life, 1400–1800.* Translated by Miriam Kochan. New York: Harper and Row 1973.

– and Camille Ernest Labrousse, ed. *Histoire économique et sociale de la France.* 4 vols. in 7 pts. Paris: Presses Universitaires de France 1970–80.

Brebner, John Bartlet. *New England's outpost: Acadia before the conquest of Canada.* Hamden: Archon 1927.

Brenner, Robert. *Merchants and revolution: Commercial change, political conflict, and London's oversea's traders, 1550–1653.* Cambridge, U.K.: Cambridge University Press 1993.

Brewer, John. *The sinews of power: War, money and the English state, 1688–1783.* London: Unwin Hyman 1989.

Brockliss, Lawrence, and David Eastwood, ed. *A union of multiple identities: The British Isles, c. 1750–c.1850.* Manchester, U.K.: Manchester University Press 1997.

Brown, Richard. *Society and economy in modern Britain, 1700–1850.* London: Routledge 1991.

Bulter, Jon. *The Huguenots in America: A refugee people in New World society.* Cambridge, Mass.: Harvard University Press 1983.

Bumsted, J.M. *Land, settlement, and politics in eighteenth-century Prince Edward Island.* Montreal and Kingston: McGill-Queen's University Press 1987.

Cain, P.J., and A.G. Hopkins. *British imperialism: Innovation and expansion, 1688–1914.* London: Longman 1993.

Cameron, Duncan, ed. *Explorations in Canadian economic history: Essays in honour of Irene Spry.* Ottawa: University of Ottawa Press 1985.

Campeau, Lucien. *Monumenta Novæ Franciæ*, 5 vols. Quebec: Les Presses de l'Université Laval 1967–1990.

Camu, Pierre. *Le Saint-Laurent et les Grands Lacs au temps de la voile, 1608–1850*. Vol. 1. La Salle, Que.: Hurtubise HMH 1996.

Cannon, John. *Aristocratic century: The peerage of eighteenth century England*. Cambridge, U.K.: Cambridge University Press 1998.

Canny, Nicholas. *Europeans on the move: Studies on European migration, 1500–1800*. Oxford, U.K.: Clarendon Press 1994.

– ed. *The Oxford history of the British empire*. Vol.1, *The origins of empire*. Oxford, U.K.: Oxford University Press 1998.

Cassedy, James H. *Demography in early America: Beginnings of the statistical mind*. Cambridge, Mass.: Harvard University Press 1969.

Cazaux, Yves. *L'Acadie: histoire des Acadiens du XVIIe siecle à nos jours*. Paris: Albin Michel 1992.

Cell, Gillian. *English enterprise in Newfoundland, 1577–1660*. Toronto: University of Toronto Press 1969.

Charbonneau, H., et al. *Naissance d'une population: les français établis au Canada au XVIIe siècle*. Institut National d'Études Démographiques, travaux et documents, Cahiers no.118. Montreal: Presses de l'Université de Montreal 1987.

Chester, Norman. *The English administrative system, 1780–1870*. Oxford, U.K.: Clarendon Press 1981.

Christianson, David J. *Belleisle 1983: Excavations at a pre-expulsion Acadian site*. Report no.48. Halifax: Nova Scotia Museum 1984.

Coleman, Margaret. *Acadian history in the isthmus of Chignecto*. National Historic Sites Service, Manuscript no.29. Ottawa: NHSS, Department of Indian Affairs and Northern Development 1968.

Clark, A.H. *Acadia: The geography of early Nova Scotia to 1760*. Madison: University of Wisconsin Press 1968.

– *Three centuries and the island: A historical geography of settlement and agriculture in Prince Edward Island, Canada*. Toronto: University of Toronto Press 1959.

Clark, Sir George. *The later Stuarts, 1660–1714*. 2nd ed. Oxford, U.K.: Clarendon Press 1956.

Clout, Hugh D., ed. *Themes in the historical geography of France*. New York: Academic Press 1977.

Cohen, A., ed. *Belonging: Identity and social organization in British rural cultures*. St John's, Nfld.: Institute of Social and Economic Research 1982.

Cole, C.W. *Colbert and a century of French mercantalism*. 2 vols. Hamden, Conn.: Archon Books 1964.

Collins, James B. *Fiscal limits of absolutism: Direct taxation in early seventeenth century France*. Berkeley: University of California Press 1988.

– *The state in early modern France*. Cambridge, UK.: Cambridge University Press 1995.

Conrad, Margaret, ed. *Un regard sur l'Acadie: trois discours illustrés*. Halifax: Musée de la Nouvelle-Écosse 1998.

Cormier, Yves. *Les aboiteaux en Acadie: hier et aujourd'hui*. Moncton, N.B.: Chaire d'Études Acadiennes 1990.

Coulliard Després, Azarie. *Charles de Saint Étienne de La Tour, gouverneur, lieutenant-general en Acadie, et son temps, 1593–1666.* Quebec: Arthabasca 1930.

Craven, Wesley Frank. *The colonies in transition, 1660–1713.* New York: Harper and Row 1968.

Crepaux, André, and Brenda Dunn. *The Melanson settlement: An Acadian farming community (c. 1664–1755).* Ottawa: Parks Canada 1986.

Cunningham, Robert, and Prince, John B. *Tamped clay and saltmarsh hay (artifacts of New Brunswick).* Fredericton: Brunswick Press 1976.

Daigle, Jean. *Les Acadiens des Maritimes: Études thématiques.* Moncton, N.B.: Centre d'Études Acadiennes, 1980.

– *L'Acadie des Maritimes: Études thématiques des débuts à nos jours.* Moncton, N.B.: Université de Moncton 1993.

Dalton, Charles. *George the First's army, 1714–1727.* 2 vols. London: Eyre and Spottiswoode 1910–1912.

Dardel, Pierre. *Navires et marchandises dans les ports de Rouen au XVIIe siècle.* Paris: S.E.V.P.E.N. 1963.

Daughtery, William. *Maritime Indian treaties in perspective.* Ottawa: Indian and Northern Affairs Canada 1983.

Davies, Godfrey. *The early Stuarts, 1603–1660.* 2nd ed. Oxford, U.K.: Oxford University Press, 1987.

Davies, K.G. *Europe and the world in the age of expansion.* Vol.4, *The North Atlantic world in the seventeenth century.* Minneapolis: University of Minnesota Press 1974.

Davis, Ralph K. *A commercial revolution: English overseas trade in the seventeenth and eighteenth centuries.* London: Historical Association 1967.

– *The rise of the Atlantic economies.* London: Weidenfeld and Nicholson 1973.

– *The rise of the English shipping industry in the seventeenth and eighteenth centuries.* New York: St Martin's Press 1962.

De Grâce, Éloi. *Noms géographiques de l'Acadie.* Moncton, N.B.: Société Historique Acadienne 1974.

– G. Desjardins, and R.A. Mallet. *Histoire d'Acadie par les textes.* 4 vols. Fredericton: Ministère de l'éducation du Nouveau-Brunswick 1976.

Delumeau, Jean. *Le mouvement du port de Saint-Malo (1681–1720): bilan statistique.* Paris: Institut de recherches historiques de Rennes 1966.

Diamond, Jared. *Guns, germs, and steel: The fates of human society.* New York: W.W. Norton Company 1997.

Dickason, Olive Patricia. *Louisbourg and the Indians: A study in imperial race relations, 1713–1760.* Ottawa: Government of Canada, National Historical Parks and Sites Branch 1976.

– *The myth of the savage and the beginnings of French colonialism in the Americas.* Edmonton: University of Alberta Press 1984. Originally published 1977.

Dickinson, John A. *Law in New France.* Canadian Legal History Project, Working Paper no.92/5. Winnipeg: University of Manitoba Faculty of Law, c.1992.

Dillon, Francis. *A place for habitation: The Pilgrim fathers and their quest.* London: Hutchinson 1973.

Dinfreville, Jacques. *Louis XIX: les saisons d'un grand règne.* Paris: Éditions Albatros 1977.

Doughty, Arthur G. *The Acadian exiles: A chronicle of the land of Evangeline.* Toronto: Glasgow, Brook 1916.

Dragon, Antonio. *L'Acadie et ses 40 robes noires.* Montreal: Bellarmin 1973.

Duby, Georges, et Armand Wallon. *Histoire de la France rurale.* Paris: Seuil 1975.

Duffy, Christopher. *Fire and stone: The science of fortress warfare, 1600–1860.* Newton Abbot, U.K.: David and Charles 1975.

– *The military experience in the age of reason.* Ware, Hertfordshire, U.K.: Woodsworth Editions 998.

Dummett, Anne, and Andrew Nicol. *Subjects, citizens, aliens and others: Nationality and immigration law.* London: Wiedenfeld and Nicolson 1990.

Dumont, Micheline, et al. *L'histoire des femmes au Québec depuis quatre siècles.* Montreal: Quinze 1982.

Dumont-Johnson, Micheline. *Apôtres ou agitateurs: la France missionnaire en Acadie.* Trois-Rivières, Que.: Boréal Express 1970.

Dupont, Jean-Claude. *Héritage d'Acadie.* Montreal: Lemeac 1977.

– *Histoire populaire de l'Acadie.* Montreal: Leméac 1978.

Dunn, Brenda. *Les Acadiens des Minas.* Ottawa: Parks Canada 1985.

Durand, Yves, ed. *Hommage à Roland Mousnier: clientèles et fidélités en Europe à l'époque moderne.* Paris, Presses Universitaires de France 1981.

Eccles, W.J. *Canada under Louis XIV, 1663–1701.* Toronto: McClelland and Stewart 1964.

– *France in North America.* New York: Harper and Row 1972.

– *Frontenac: The courtier governor.* Toronto: McClelland and Stewart 1959.

– *The ordeal of New France.* Toronto: CBC International Service 1966.

Entremont, Clarence-Joseph d'. *Histoire du Cap-Sable, de l'an mil au Traité de Paris, 1763.* 5 vols. Eunice, La.: Hébert Publications 1981.

– *Nicolas Denys, sa vie et son œuvre.* Yarmouth, N.S.: Imp. Lescarbot 1982.

Erskine, John. *The French period in Nova Scotia, 1500–1758 AD and present remains: Historical, archeological, and botanical survey.* Wolfville, N.S.: privately printed 1975.

Evans, Charles. *Oaths of allegiance in New England.* Baltimore, Md.: Clearfield 1998. Repr. of Worcester, Mass.: American Antiquarian Society 1921.

Faulkner, Alaric, and Gretchen Pearson Faulkner. *The French at Pentagoet (1635–1674): An archeological portrait of the Acadian frontier.* Augusta. Me., and Saint John, N.B.: Maine Historical Preservation Commission and the New Brunswick Museum 1987.

Fingard, Judith, Janet Guildford, and David Sutherland. *Halifax: The first 250 years.* Halifax: Formac Publishing 1999.

Foursans-Bourdette, Marie-Pierrette. *Économie et finances en Béarn au XVIIIᵉ siecle.* Bordeaux: Éditions Bière 1965.

Frégault, Guy. *La guerre de la Conquête.* Montreal: Fides 1955.

Games, Alison. *Migration and the origins of the English Atlantic world.* Cambridge, Mass.: Harvard University Press 1999.

Gaudet, Placide. *Le grand dérangement: sur qui retombe la responsibilité de l'explusion des Acadiens?* Ottawa: Ottawa Print 1922.

Gellner, Ernest. *Culture, identity and politics.* Cambridge, U.K.: Cambridge University Press 1987.

Glass, D.V., and D.E.C. Eversley. *Population in history: Essays in historical demography.* London: E. Arnold 1965.

Gibson, Robert. *Best of enemies: Anglo-French relations since the Norman conquest.* London: Sinclair-Stevenson 1995.

Gipson, L.H. *The British empire before the American revolution.* Vol. 5, *Zones of international friction: The Great Lakes frontier, Canada, the West Indies, 1748–1754.* New York: Alfred A. Knopf 1942.

– *The British empire before the American revolution.* Vol. 6, *The great war for empire: The years of defeat, 1754–1757.* New York: Alfred A. Knopf 1946.

Girard, Philip, and Jim Phillips, ed. *Essays in the history of Canadian law.* Vol.3, *Nova Scotia.* Toronto: Osgoode Society for Canadian Legal History/University of Toronto Press 1990.

Godfrey, William G. *Pursuit of profit and preferment in colonial North America: John Bradstreet's quest.* Waterloo, Ont.: Wilfrid Laurier University Press 1982.

Goldman, Alvin I. *Knowledge in a social world.* Oxford, U.K.: Clarendon Press 1999.

Goubert, Pierre. *L'Ancien régime.* 2 vols. Vol.1, *La Société.* Paris: A. Colin 1969.

– *Louis XIV and twenty million Frenchmen.* London: Lane 1970.

Grassby, Richard. *The business community of seventeenth century England.* Cambridge, U.K.: Cambridge University Press 1995.

Green, L.C., and Olive P. Dickason. *The law of nations and the New World.* Edmonton: University of Alberta Press 1989.

Greene, Jack P., and J.R. Pole, ed. *Colonial British North America: Essays in the new history of the early modern era.* Baltimore, Md.: Johns Hopkins University Press 1984.

Griffiths, N.E.S. *The Acadian deportation: Deliberate perfidy or cruel necessity?* Toronto: Copp Clark 1969.

– *The context of Acadian history, 1686–1784.* Montreal and Kingston: McGill-Queen's University Press 1993. Trans. Kathryn Hamer, *L'Acadie de 1686 à 1784: contexte d'une histoire.* Moncton, N.B.: Éditions d'Acadie 1997.

Hampson, Norman. *A social history of the French revolution.* Toronto: University of Toronto Press 1963.

Handcock, W. Gordon. *So longe as there comes noe women: Origins of English settlement in Newfoundland.* St John's: Breakwater 1989.

Harris, R.C. *The seigneurial system in early Canada: A geographical study.* Madison, Wis., and Quebec: University of Wisconsin Press and Les Presses de l'Université de Laval 1968.

Harrison, G.A., and A.J. Boyce, ed. *The structure of human populations.* Oxford, U.K.: Clarendon Press 1972.

Harvey, D.C. *The French regime in Prince Edward Island.* New York: AMS Press 1970. Repr. of New Haven, Conn: Yale University Press 1926.

Henretta, James A. *"Salutary neglect": Colonial administration under the Duke of Newcastle.* Princeton, N.J.: Princeton University Press 1972.

Héroux, Denis, Robert Lahaise, and Noël Vallerand. *La Nouvelle-France*. Montreal: Centre de Psychologie et de Pédagogie 1967.

Hill, Christopher. *Reformation to industrial revolution: 1530–1780*. Harmondsworth, U.K.: Penguin Books 1969.

Hobsbawm, Eric J. *On history*. London: Weidenfeld and Nicolson 1997.

Horsman, Matthew, and Andrew Marshall. *After the nation-state: Citizens, tribalism and the New World disorder*. London: HarperCollins 1994.

Hosmer, J.K., ed. *Winthrop's journal: A history of New England, 1630–49*. New York: Barnes 1908.

Hufton, Olwen. *The prospect before her: A history of women in western Europe*. New York: Alfred Knopf 1995.

Hugolin, R.P. *Les Récollets de la province de l'Immaculée Conception en Aquitaine, missionnaires en Acadie, 1619–1633*. Quebec: Lévis 1912.

Huguet, A. *Jean de Poutrincourt, fondateur de Port-Royal en Acadie, vice-roi du Canada, 1557–1615: campagnes, voyages et aventures d'un colonisateur sous Henri IV*. Amiens: Société des Antiquaires de Picardie 1932.

Hutchinson, John. *Modern nationalism*. London: Fontana Press 1994.

Innis, Harold A. *The cod fisheries: The history of an international economy*. Toronto: University of Toronto Press 1978.

– *The fur trade in Canada: An introduction to Canadian economic history*. Rev. ed. Toronto: University of Toronto Press 1970.

Insh, George Pratt. *Scottish colonial schemes, 1620–1686*. Glasgow: Maclehose, Jackson 1922.

Jaenen, Cornelius J. *The role of the church in New France*. Toronto: McGraw-Hill Ryerson 1976.

Jarrett, Derek. *Britain, 1688 to 1815*. London: Longman 1965.

Jennings, Francis. *Empire of fortune: Crowns, colonies, and tribes in the Seven Years War in America*. New York: Norton 1988.

– *The invasion of America: Indians, colonialism, and the cant of conquest*. New York: Norton 1976.

Jernegan, M.W. *The American colonies, 1492–1750: A study of their political, economic and social development*. New York: F. Ungar 1963.

Johnson, Richard R. *John Nelson: Merchant adventurer. A life between empires*. New York: Oxford University Press 1991.

Johnston, A.A. *A history of the Catholic Church in eastern Nova Scotia*. Antigonish, N.S.: St Francis Xavier University Press 1960.

Jones, Elizabeth. *Gentlemen and Jesuits: Quests for glory and adventure in the early days of New France*. Toronto: University of Toronto Press 1986.

Jones, J.R. *Country and court: England, 1658–1714*. London: E. Arnold 1978.

Kearney, Hugh. *The British Isles: A history of four nations*. Cambridge, U.K.: Cambridge University Press 1989.

Kennedy, Paul M. *The rise and fall of British naval mastery*. London: Ashfield Press 1976.

– *The rise and fall of the great powers: Economic change and military conflict from 1500–2000*. New York: Random House 1987.

Keohane, Nannerl O. *Philosophy and the state in France from the Renaissance to the Enlightenment*. Princeton, N. J.: Princeton University Press 1980.

Knapton, Ernest John. *France: An Interpretive History*. New York: Scribner and Son 1971.

Lacour-Gayet, Robert. *Histoire du Canada*. Paris: Fayard 1966.

Lamontagne, Roland. *La Galissonière et le Canada*. Montreal: Les Presses de l'université de Montréal 1962.

La Morandière, Charles de. *Histoire de la pêche française de la morue dans l'Amérique septentrionale*. 3 vols. Paris: Maisonneuve et Larose 1962–66.

Lanctot, Gustave. *A history of Canada*, 3 vols. Translated by Josphine Hambleton and Margaret Cameron. Cambridge, Mass.: Harvard University Press 1963.

Lanctôt, Léopold. *L'Acadie des origines, 1603–1771*. Montreal: Éditions du Fleuve 1988.

– *Familles acadiennes*. 2 vols. Sainte-Julie, Que.: Éditions du Libre-Échange 1994.

Langford, Paul. *A polite and commercial people: England, 1727–1783*. Oxford, U.K.: Clarendon Press 1989.

Larin, Robert. *La contribution du Haut-Poitou au peuplement de la Nouvelle-France*. Moncton, N.B.: Éditions d'Acadie 1994.

Laslett, Peter, ed. *Household and family in past time: Comparative studies in the size and structure of the domestic group over the last three centuries in England, France, Serbia, Japan and colonial North America, with further materials from western Europe*. Cambridge, U.K.: Cambridge University Press 1972.

Lauvrière, Émile. *La tragédie d'un peuple: histoire du peuple acadien de ses origines à nos jours*. 2 vols. Paris: Éditions Brossard 1922.

Leach, Edward Douglas. *Arms for empire: A military history of the British colonies in North America, 1607–1763*. New York: Macmillan 1973.

– *Flintlock and tomahawk: New England in King Phillip's War*. New York: Macmillan 1958.

– *The northern colonial frontier, 1607–1763*. New York: Holt, Rhinehart and Winston 1966.

Le Blant, Robert. *Un colonial sous Louis XIV: Philippe de Pastour de Costebelle: governeur de Terre-Neuve puis de l'Ile Royale*. Paris: Dax 1935.

– *Une figure légendaire de l'histoire acadienne: le Baron de St-Castin*. Dax: Éditions P. Pradeu 1934.

Le Gresley, Omer. *L'enseignement du français en Acadie, 1604–1926*. Mamers, France: G. Enault 1926.

Le Roy Ladurie, Emmanuel. *The ancien regime: A history of France, 1610–1774*. Oxford, U.K.: Blackwell 1996.

Lewis, W.H. *The splendid century: Life in the France of Louis XIV*. London: Doubleday Anchor Books 1957.

Linebaugh, Peter, and Marcus Rideker. *The many-headed hydra: Sailors, slaves, commoners, and the hidden history of the revolutionary Atlantic*. New York: Verso 2000.

Livi-Bacci, Massimo. *A concise history of world population*. 2nd ed. Translated by Carl Ipsen. Cambridge, Mass.: Blackwell 1997.

Lloyd, T.O. *The British empire, 1558–1983*. New York: Oxford University Press 1984.

Lough, John. *An introduction to seventeenth century France.* London: Longmans 1966.

Macdonald, Marjorie A. *Fortune and La Tour: The civil war in Acadia.* Toronto: Methuen 1983.

MacMechan, Archibald. *Red snow on Grand Pré.* Toronto: McClelland 1931.

Maillet, Antonine. *Rabelais et les traditions populaires en Acadie.* Quebec: Les Presses de l'Université de Laval 1971.

Mandrou, Robert. *Classes et luttes de classe en France au début du XVIIe siècle.* Messina: G. D'Anna 1965.

Marshall, P.J., ed. *The Oxford history of the British empire.* Vol. 2, *The eighteenth century.* Oxford, U.K.: Oxford University Press 1998.

Martijn, Charles A. *Les Micmacs et la mer.* Quebec: Researches amérindiennes au Québec 1986.

Martin, Calvin. *Keepers of the game: Indian-animal relationships and the fur trade.* Berkeley: University of California Press 1978.

Massignon, Geneviève. *Les parlers français d'Acadie – enquête linguistique.* 2 vols. Paris: C. Klincksieck 1962.

McCrone, David. *Understanding Scotland: The sociology of a stateless nation.* London: Routledge 1992.

McLennan, J.S. *Louisbourg, from its foundation to its fall, 1713–1758.* London: Macmillan 1918.

Meinig, D.W. *The shaping of America: A geographical perspective on 500 years of history.* Vol.1, *Atlantic America, 1492–1800.* New Haven, Conn.: Yale University Press 1986.

Milligan, D.C.. *Maritime dykelands: The 350 year struggle.* Halifax: Province of Nova Scotia, Dept. of Agriculture and Marketing 1987.

Miquelon, Dale. *New France, 1701–1744: "A supplement to Europe."* Toronto: McClelland and Stewart 1987.

Morin, Michel. *L'ursurpation de souveraineté autochtone: le cas des peuples de la Nouvelle-France et des colonies anglaises de l'Amérique du Nord.* Montreal: Boréal 1997.

Morrison, Kenneth M. *The embattled northeast: The elusive ideal of alliance in Abenaki-Euroamerican relations.* Berkeley: University of California Press 1984.

Morrison, Samuel Eliot. *Samuel de Champlain: Father of New France.* Toronto: Little Brown 1972.

Mousnier, Roland. *La plume, la faucille et le marteau: institutions et société en France du Moyen Âge à la Révolution.* Paris: Presses Universitaires de France 1970.

– *La vénalité des offices sous Henri IV et Louis XIII.* 2nd ed. Paris: Presses Universitaires de France 1971.

– et al. *Comment les Francais voyaient la France au XVIIe siècle.* Bulletin de la Société d'Étude du XVIIe siècle, 25–6 (1955).

Murat, Ines. *Colbert.* Translated by Robert Francis Cook and Jeannie Van Asselt. Charlottesville: University of Virginia Press 1984.

Nant, Candide de. *Pages glorieuses de l'épopée canadienne: une mission capucine en Acadie.* Montreal: *Le Devoir* 1927.

Neale, R.S. *Class in English history.* Oxford, U.K.: Blackwell 1981.

Ogg, David. *England in the reign of Charles II.* 2nd ed. London: Oxford University Press 1963.

Palmer, R.R. *Age of democratic revolution: A political history of Europe and America 1760–1800.* 2 vols. Princeton, N.J.: Princeton University Press 1964.

Parris, Henry. *Constitutional bureaucracy: The development of British central administration since the eighteenth century.* London: Allen and Unwin 1969.

Parry, J.H. *The discovery of the sea.* Berkeley: University of California Press 1981.

Paschall, Rod, ed. *The constitution and the US army.* Carlisle Barracks, Penn.: US Army War College and US Army Military History Institute 1988.

Pease, Theodore Calvin, ed. *Anglo-French boundary disputes in the west, 1749–1763.* Springfield, Ill.: Trustees of the Illinois State Historical Library 1936.

Perroy, Édouard, et al. *Histoire de la France pour tous les Français.* 2 vols. Paris: Hachette 1950.

Plank, Geoffrey Gilbert. *An unsettled conquest: The British campaign against the peoples of Acadia.* Philadelphia: University of Pennsylvania Press 2001.

Pothier, Bernard. *Course à l'Accadie: journal de campagne de François Du Pont Duvivier en 1744.* Moncton: Éditions d'Acadie 1982.

Preston, Richard A. *Gorges of Plymouth Fort: A life of Sir Ferdinando Gorges, captain of Plymouth Fort, and lord of the province of Maine.* Toronto: University of Toronto Press 1953.

– Alex Roland, and Sydney F. Wise. *Men in arms: A history of warfare and its interrelationships with western society.* 5th ed. Fort Worth, Tex.: Holt, Rinehart and Winston 1991.

Pritchard, James. *Anatomy of a naval disaster: The 1746 French naval expedition to North America.* Montreal and Kingston: McGill-Queen's University Press 1995.

Proulx, Gilles. *Between France and New France: Life aboard the tall sailing ships.* Toronto: Dundurn Press/Parks Canada, 1984.

Purchas, Samuel. *Hakluytus Posthumus or Purchas: His piligrimes.* 20 vols. Glascow: McLehose 1905–07.

Quéniart, Jean. *La révocation de l'édit de Nantes: protestants et catholiques en France de 1598 à 1685.* Paris: Desclée de Brouwer 1985.

Quinn, David B., with Alison Quinn, ed. *The English New England voyages, 1602–1608.* London: Hakluyt Society 1983.

Raddall, T.H. *Halifax, warden of the north.* Rev. ed. Toronto: McClelland and Stewart 1971.

Rawlyk, George A. *Nova Scotia's Massachusetts: A study of Massachusetts-Nova Scotia relations, 1630 to 1784.* Montreal and Kingston: McGill-Queen's University Press 1973.

– *Yankees at Louisbourg: The story of the first siege, 1745.* Wreck Cove, N.S.: Breton Books 1999.

Reid, John. G. *Acadia, Maine and New Scotland: Marginal colonies in the seventeenth century.* Toronto: University of Toronto Press, in association with Huronia Historical Parks and the Ontario Ministry of Culture, 1981.

– *Maine, Charles II and Massachusetts: Governmental relationships in early northern New England.* Portland: Maine Historical Society 1977.

– *Six crucial decades: Times of change in the history of the Maritimes.* Halifax: Nimbus Publishing 1987.

Rich, E.E., and C.H. Wilson, ed. *The Cambridge economic history of Europe*. Vol.4, *The economy of expanding Europe in the sixteenth century*. Cambridge, U.K.: Cambridge University Press 1967.

Riley, J.C. *The Seven Years War and the old regime in France: The economic and financial toll*. Princeton, N.J.: Princeton University Press 1986.

Rothkrug, Lionel. *Opposition to Louis XIV: The social and political origins of the French Enlightenment*. Princeton, N.J.: Princeton University Press 1965.

Rouillard, Jacques. *Guide d'histoire du Québec, du régime français à nos jours: bibliographie commentée*. Montreal: Méridien 1991.

Roy, M. *L'Acadie, des origines à nos jours*. Montreal:Québec/Amérique 1981.

– *L'Acadie perdue*. Montreal: Éditions Québec/Amérique 1978.

Rumilly, R. *L'Acadie française, 1497–1713*. Montreal: Fides 1981.

– *Histoire des Acadiens*. 2 vols. Montreal: Fides 1955.

Russell, Howard S. *A long, deep furrow: Three centuries of farming in New England*. Abridged with a foreword by Mark Lapping. Hanover, N.H.: University of New England Press 1982.

Said, Edward W. *Culture and imperialism*. New York: Knopf 1993.

Sauvageau, Robert. *Acadie: La guerre de Cent Ans des Français d'Amérique aux Maritimes et en Louisiane, 1678–1769*. Paris: Berger-Levrault 1987.

Savelle, Max. *The diplomatic history of the Canadian boundary, 1749–1763*. New Haven. Conn.: Yale University Press 1940.

Schulze, Hagen. *States, nations and nationalism*. Oxford, U.K.: Basil Blackwell 1996.

Schutz, John A. *William Shirley: King's governor of Massachusetts*. Chapel Hill: University of North Carolina Press 1961.

Séguin, R.-L. *La civilisation traditionnelle de l'"habitant" au 17ᵉ et 18ᵉ siècles*. Montreal: Fides 1967.

Seton, Sir Bruce, and Jean Gordon Arnot. *The Prisoners of the '45*. 3 vols. Edinburgh: Scottish Historical Society 1928.

Smith, Abbott Emerson. *Colonists in bondage: White servitude and convict labor in America, 1607–1776*. New York: W.W. Norton 1971.

Smith, Anthony D. *Nationalism and modernism: A critical survey of recent theories of nations and nationalism*. London and New York: Routledge 1998.

Speck, W.A. *The butcher: The Duke of Cumberland and the suppression of the 45*. Oxford, U.K.: Blackwell 1981.

– *Stability and strife: England, 1714–1760*. London: Edward Arnold 1977.

Sprott, Walter. *Human groups*. Harmondsworth, U.K.: Penguin Books 1958.

Stanley, George F. *New France: The Last Phase, 1744–1760*. Toronto: McClelland and Stewart 1968.

Steele, Ian K. *The English Atlantic, 1675–1740: An exploration of communication and community*. New York: Oxford University Press 1986.

– *Guerillas and grenadiers: The struggle for Canada, 1689–1790*. Toronto: Ryerson Press 1969.

– *The politics of colonial policy: The Board of Trade in colonial administration, 1696–1720*. Oxford, U.K.: Clarendon Press, 1968.

– *Warpaths: Invasions of North America*. New York: Oxford University Press 1994.

Stevenson, John. *Popular disturbances in England, 1700–1832.* New York: Longman 1992.

Thompson, E.P. *The making of the English working class.* New York: Pantheon Books 1963.

Thompson, Frederic F. *The French shore problem in Newfoundland: An imperial study.* Vol.2, Canadian Studies in History and Government. Toronto: University of Toronto Press 1961.

Trigger, Bruce G. *Natives and newcomers: Canada's heroic age reconsidered.* Montreal and Kingston: McGill-Queen's University Press 1985.

– and Wilcomb E. Washburn, ed. *The Cambridge history of the native peoples of the Americas.* Vol.1, pt.1, *North America.* Cambridge, U.K.: Cambridge University Press 1996.

Trudel, Marcel. *Histoire de la Nouvelle-France.* Vol.2, *Le Comptoir 1604–1627.* Montreal: Fides 1966.

– *Histoire de la Nouvelle-France.* Vol.3, *La seigneurie des Cent-Associés, 1627–1663.* In 2 pts. Montreal: Fides 1979.

Turner, Edmund Raymond. *The cabinet council of England in the seventeenth and eighteenth centuries, 1622–1784.* New York: Russell and Russell 1970.

Upton, L.F.S. *Micmacs and colonists: Indian-white relations in the Maritimes, 1713–1867.* Vancouver: University of British Columbia Press 1979.

Vanderlinden, Jacques. *Se marier en Acadie française XVIIe et VIIIe siècles.* Moncton, N.B.: Chaire d'Études acadiennes, Université de Moncton 1998.

– *À la rencontre de l'histoire du droit en Acadie avant le dérangement; premières impressions d'un nouveau-venu.* Canadian Legal History Project, Working Paper, no.92/2. Winnipeg: University of Manitoba, Faculty of Law 1993.

Van Doren, Mark, ed. *Anthology of world poetry.* London: Literary Guild of America 1928.

Van Kirk, Sylvia. *"Many tender ties": Women in fur-trade society in western Canada, 1670–1870.* Winnipeg: Watson and Dwyer 1980.

Wall, Helena M. *Fierce communion: Family and community in early America.* Cambridge, Mass.: Harvard University Press 1995.

Waller, G.M. *Samuel Vetch: Colonial enterpriser.* Chapel Hill, N.C.: University of North Carolina Press 1960.

Webb, Steven Saunders. *The governors general: The English army and the definition of empire, 1569–1681.* Chapel Hill: Published for the Institute of Early American History and Culture, Williamsburg, Va., by the University of North Carolina Press 1979.

Weber, Eugen. *Peasants into Frenchmen: The modernization of rural France, 1870–1914.* London: Chatto and Windus 1977.

Webster, J C. *The building of Fort Lawrence in Chignecto.* Historic Studies no.3. Saint John: New Brunswick Museum 1941.

– *The Career of the Abbé Le Loutre in Nova Scotia, with a translation of his autobiography.* Shediac, N.B., 1933.

– *Cornelius Steenwyck: Dutch governor of Acadie.* Shediac, N.B., 1929.

– *The forts of Chignecto: A study of the eighteenth century conflict between France and Great Britain in Acadia.* Shediac, 1930.

– *Thomas Pichon, "the Spy of Beausejour," an Account of his career in Europe and America.* Sackville, N.B.: Tribune Press 1937.

Winthrop, John. *Winthrop's journal, "History of New England," 1630–1649.* Edited by James Kendall Hosmer. New York: Barnes and Noble 1966. Originally published *c.*1908.

White, John Manchip. *Marshal of France: The life and times of Maurice, Comte de Saxe [1696–1750].* London: Hamish Hamilton 1962.

Williams, Robert. *The American Indian in western legal thought: The discourses of conquest.* New York: Oxford University Press 1990.

Wolf, John B. *Louis XIV.* New York: Norton 1968.

Wright, Ester Clark. *Planters and pioneers: Nova Scotia, 1749 to 1775.* Wolfville, N.S.: E.C. Wright 1978.

Wrightson, Keith. *English society, 1580–1680.* London: Hutchinson 1982.

Wrong, George, M. *The rise and fall of New France.* New York: Macmillan 1928.

Young, Brian, and John A. Dickinson. *A short history of Quebec: A socio-economic perspective.* Toronto: Copp Clark Pitman 1988.

Zeller, Gaston. *Les institutions de la France au XVI* siecle.* Paris: Les Presses Universitaires de France 1948.

Zoltvany, Yves F. *The government of New France: Royal, clerical or class rule?* Scarborough, Ont.: Prentice-Hall of Canada 1971.

ARTICLES, ESSAYS, AND PAPERS

"L'Acadie d'aujourd'hui et l'Acadie de demain." In *Le Congrès mondial acadien: L'Acadie en 2004: Actes des conférences et des table rondes.* Moncton, 1996.

Alsop, James D. "The age of the projectors: British imperial strategy in the North Atlantic in the War of Spanish Succession." *Acadiensis* 21, 1 (1991): 30–53.

– "Samuel Vetch's 'Canada Survey'd': The formation of a colonial strategy, 1706–1710." *Acadiensis* 12, 1 (1982): 39–58.

Anderson, Virginia Dejohn. "King Phillip's herds: Indians, colonists and the problem of livestock in early New England." *WMQ* 3, 2 (1994): 601–14.

Bailyn, Bernard. "The British empire." *WMQ* 62, 3 (2000): 647–59.

Barnes, Thomas G. "'The dayly cry for justice': The juridical failure of the Annapolis Royal regime, 1713–1749." In Philip Girard and Jim Phillips, ed., *Essays in the history of Canadian law,* vol 3, *Nova Scotia.* Toronto: Osgoode Society for Canadian Legal History/ University of Toronto Press 1990. 10–41.

– "From Great Meadow to Grand Pré: Western Pennsylvania and *le grand dérangement,* 1749–1755." Unpublished paper, delivered at the ACSUS conference, Pittsburgh, November 2000.

– and Joseph H. Smith. "The English legal system: Carryover to the colonies. Paper read at a Clark Library seminar, November 3, 1973." Los Angles: William Andrews Clark Memorial Library, University of California 1975.

Basque, Maurice. "Seigneuresse, mère et veuve: analyse d'une identité féminine en Acadie coloniale au XVIIIe siècle." *Dalhousie French Studies,* 62 (spring 2003): 73–80.

Baudry, René. "Charles d'Aulnay et la Compagnie de la Nouvelle-France." *RHAF* 11, 2 (1957): 218–41.

Baxter, Stephen. Review of Steven Saunders Webb's *The governors general: The English army and the definition of empire, 1569–1681*. *WMQ*, 3rd series, 37 (October 1980): 658–61.

Beauregard, Yves, et al. "Famille, parenté et colonisation en Nouvelle-France." *RHAF* 39, 3 (1986): 391–405.

Bertrand, G. "La culture des marais endigués et le développement de la solidarité militante en Acadie entre 1710 et 1755." SHA *Cahiers* 24, 4 (1993): 238–49.

Bosher, J.F. "Huguenot merchants and the Protestant International in the seventeenth century." *WMQ*, 3rd series, 52, 1 (1995): 77–103.

Bourinot, John G. "Builders of Nova Scotia." *Proceedings and Transactions of the Royal Society of Canada*, 2nd series, 5 (1899), s.2: 104–21.

Bourque, Bruce C. "Ethnicity on the Maritime peninsula, 1600–1759." *Ethnohistory* 36 (1989): 257–84.

Bower, P. "Louisbourg: The chimera, 1745–1748." In *Papers and abstracts for a symposium on Île Royale during the French regime*. Ottawa: History Division, National Museum of Canada April 1972.

Breuilly, John. "Approaches to Nationalism." In Gopal Balakrishnan, ed., *Mapping the nation*. London and New York: Verso 1996.

Buffington, Arthur Howard. "Sir Thomas Temple in Boston: A case of benevolent assimilation." *TCSM* 27 (1932): 311–12.

Campbell, Joan Bourque. "The seigneurs of Acadie: History and genealogy." SHA *Cahiers* 25, 4 (1994): 285–313; 26, 1 (1995): 23–55; 26, 3/4 (1995): 136–80.

Caron, Adrien. "De Québec en Acadie: sur les pas de Mgr. De Saint Vallier, avril-août, 1686." *Cahiers d'Histoire*, no.15. Quebec: A.T. Caron 1975.

Chard, D.F. "Canso, 1710–1721: Focal point of New England-Cape Breton rivalry," NSHS, *Collections* 53 (1977): 49–77.

– "The impact of French privateering on New England, 1689–1713." *American Neptune* 35 (1975): 153–65.

Chiasson, Anselme. "Tout doux, monsieur Sauvageau!" SHA *Cahiers* 21, 1 (1990): 49–50.

Choquette, Leslie. "French and British emigration to the North American colonies: A comparative view." In Dublin Seminar for New England Folklife, *Annual Proceedings*, 1989 (Boston, 1992), *New England/New France 1600–1850*.

Clark, G.N. "War and trade war, 1701–1713." *Economic History Review* 1 (1927–28): 262–80.

Coleman, D.C. "Mercantalism Revisited." *Historical Journal* 23 (1980): 773–91.

Coornaert, E.L.J. "European economic institutions and the New World: The chartered companies." In E.E. Rich and C.H. Wilson, ed., *The economic history of Europe*, vol.4, *The economy of expanding Europe in the sixteenth and seventeenth century*. Cambridge, U.K.: Cambridge University Press 1967.

Cormier, Yves. "Nos aboiteaux." SHA *Cahiers* 19, 1–2 (1988): 5–17.

Couturier, Jacques Paul. "'L'Acadie, c'est un détail': Les représentations de l'Acadie dans le récit national canadien." *Acadiensis* 29, 2 (2000): 102–19.

Courtwright, David T. "New England families in historical perspective." In *Families and children*, Dublin Seminar for New England Folklife, *Annual Proceedings*, 1985.

Daigle, Jean. "L'Acadie de 1604–1763." In *L'Acadie des Maritimes: Études thématiques des débuts à nos jours*. Moncton, N.B.: Université de Moncton, Chaire d'Études Canadiens 1993.

Dawson, Joan. "L'Acadie en 1632: la carte d'Issac de Razilly." SHA *Cahiers* 15, 4 (1984): 127–37.

Debien, G. "Engagés pour le Canada au XVIIᵉ vus de La Rochelle." *RHAF* 6, 2 (1952): 177–233.

Delafosse, M. "La Rochelle et le Canada au XVIIᵉ siècle." *RHAF* 4, 5 (1951): 469–511.

Desbarats, Catherine M. "The cost of early Canada's native alliances: Reality and scarcity rhetoric." *WMQ*, 3ʳᵈ series, 52 (October 1995): 609–30.

Dessureault, Christian. "L'Égalitarisme paysan dans l'ancienne société rurale de la vallée du Saint-Laurent: éléments pour une ré-interprétation." *RHAF* 40, 3 (1987): 373–407.

Dickason, Olive P. "Amerindians between French and English in Nova Scotia, 1713–1763." *American Indian Culture and Research Journal* 10, 4 (1986): 33.

Dunn, Brenda. "L'inventaire de la veuve Plemarais, 1705." SHA *Cahiers* 25, 1 (1994): 27–37.

Durand, Regis. "L'Acadie et les phénomènes de solidarité et fidelité au XVIIIième siècle." *Études canadiennes/Canadian Studies* 13 (1983): 81–4.

Eccles, W.J. "A belated review of Harold Adams Innis, 'The fur trade in Canada.'" *CHR* 60, 4 (1979): 419–41.

– "A response to Hugh M. Grant on Innis." *CHR* 62, 3 (1981): 323–9.

Elliott, J.H. "A Europe of composite monarchies." *Past and Present* 137 (1992): 48–71.

Entremont, Clarence-J. d'. "Compte rendu." SHA *Cahiers* 19, 4 (1988): 162–7.

– "Du nouveau sur les Melanson." SHA *Cahier* 28, 8 (1970): 339–52; 29, 9 (1970): 363–9.

– "Premier enfant né en Acadie, 1620." SHA *Cahier* 19, 9 (1968): 350–6.

– "Le 350ⁱᵉᵐᵉ anniversaire de La Hève." SHA *Cahiers* 13, 1 (1982): 9–35.

Gallant, Melvin, ed. Dièreville, "Voyage à l'Acadie, 1699–1700." SHA *Cahiers* 16, 3–4 (1985).

Ganong, William F. "The Cadillac memoir of 1692." NBHS *Collections* 13 (1930).

– "A monograph of historic sites in the province of New Brunswick." *Transactions of the Royal Society of Canada*, s.2 (1899): 80–97.

Gaudet, Placide. "Les seigneuries de l'ancienne Acadie." *Bulletin des Recherches Historiques* 33 (1927): 313–47.

Gaudette, Jean. "Famille élargie et copropriété dans l'ancienne Acadie." SHA *Cahiers* 25, 1, (1994): 15–26.

Gemery, Henry. "European emigration to North America, 1700–1820: Numbers and quasi-numbers." *Perspectives in American History* 1, new series (1984): 283–333.

Grant, Hugh M. "One step forward, two steps back: Innis, Eccles and the Canadian fur trade." *CHR* 62, 3 (1981): 304–23.

Gravit, Francis W. "Observations de Peiresc sur les curiositiés rapportée d'Acadie par Pierre du Gua, sieur de Mons." *La Revue de l'université Laval* 1, 4 (1946): 282–8.

Greene, Jack P., et al. "Albions' seed: Four British folkways in America: A symposium." *William and Mary Quarterly,* 3rd series, 48, 2 (1991): 224–309.

Griffiths, N.E.S. "The formation of a community and the interpretation of identity: The Acadians, 1664–1997." *British Journal of Canadian Studies* 13, 1 (1998): 32–46.

– "Fur, fish and folk," in *The Atlantic region to Confederation: A history.* Edited by P.A. Buckner and John G. Reid. Toronto: University of Toronto Press 1994. 40–60.

– "The golden age: Acadian life, 1713–1748." *Histoire Sociale/Social History,* 17, 33 (1984): 21–34.

– "Mating and marriage in early Acadia." *Renaissance and Modern Studies* 35 (1992):109–27.

– "Subjects and citizens in the eighteenth century: The question of Acadian oaths of allegiance." In Glenn Moulaison, Muriel Comeau, and Édouard Langille, ed., *Les abeilles pillotent-mélanges offerts à René Leblanc.* Pointe-de-l'Église: Revue de l'U-niversité de Sainte-Anne 1998. 23–33.

– and John G. Reid. "New evidence on New Scotland." *WMQ,* 3rd series, 49 (July 1992): 492–508.

Henige, David. "Primary source by primary source? On the role of epidemics in New World depopulation." *Ethnohistory* 33, 3 (1986): 293–312.

Hivert-Le Faucheux, Monique. "La vie quotidienne en Acadie au temps de Razilly: Le témoignage d'un document manuscript." SHA *Cahiers* 26, 2 (1995): 116–29.

Hubka, Thomas, C. "Farm family mutuality: The mid-nineteenth century Maine farm neighbourhood." Dublin Seminar for New England Folklife, *Annual Proceedings,* 1986. Boston, 1988.

Hynes, Gysa. "Some aspects of demography in Port Royal." In P.A. Buckner and David Frank, ed., *Atlantic Canada before Confederation: The Acadiensis reader,* vol.1. Fredericton: Acadiensis Press 1985. 11–25.

Jaenen, C. "L'autre' en Nouvelle-France/The 'other' in early Canada." Presidential address, Canadian Historical Association, *Historical Papers/Communications historiques,* 1989.

– "Le Colbertisme." *RHAF* 18, 1 (1964): 64–84.

Jarnoux, Philippe. "La colonisation de la seigneurie de Batiscan aux 17e et 18e siècles: l'espace et les hommes." *RHAF* 40, 2 (1986): 163–91.

Kelly, Gerald M. "Louis Aubert Duforillon in Acadia." SHA *Cahiers* 5, 4 (1974): 150–60.

LeBlanc, R.-Gilles. "Les aboiteaux"/"Entrevues sur les aboiteaux." SHA *Cahiers,* 19, 1–2 (1988): 18–67.

– "Documents acadiens sur les aboiteaux." SHA *Cahiers* 19, 1–2 (1988): 39–46.

LeBlanc, Stephane, and Jacques Vanderlinden. "Pauvre en France, riche en Acadie?" SHA *Cahiers* 29, 1–2 (1998): 10–33.

Le Blant, Robert. "Le compagnie de la Nouvelle France et la restitution de l'Acadie, 1627–1636." *Revue d'histoire des colonies* 42 (1955): 69–91.

- "Les compagnies du Cap-Breton, 1629–1647." *RHAF* 16, 1 (1962): 81–94.
- "Un corsaire de Saint-Domingue en Acadie: Pierre Morpain, 1707–1711." *Nova Francia* 6 (1931): 194.
- "La premières compagnie de Miscou, 1635–1645." *RHAF* 17, 3 (1963): 363–70.
- "Le ravitaillment du Port Royal d'Acadie par Charles de Biencourt et les marchands rochelais, 1615–1618." *Revue d'histoire des colonies* 44 (1958): 138–64.

Leger, Maurice A. "Cent personalités de l'histoire religieuse de l'Acadie." SHA *Cahiers* 31, 2 (2000): 100–46.

Leonard, Kevin. "The origin and dispersal of dykeland technology." SHA *Cahiers* 22, 1 (1991): 31–59.

Massignon, Geneviève. "Les Trahans." SHA *Cinquième Cahier* (1964): 10–23.

McCully, B.T. "The New England-Acadia fishery dispute and the Nicholson mission of August 1680." *Essex Institute Historical Collections*, 96 (1966).

Miller, V.P. "The decline of the Nova Scotia Micmac population, A.D. 1600–1850." *Culture* 2, 3 (1982): 107–20.

Moogk, Peter N. "Reluctant exiles: The problem of colonization in French North America." *WMQ* 46, 5 (1989): 463–505.

Norton, Susan L. "Population growth in colonial America: A study of Ipswich, Massachusetts." *Population Studies* 25 (1971): 433–52.

Ouellet, F. "L'accroissement naturel de la population catholique québécoise avant 1850: apercus historiques et quantitatifs." *L'Actualité économique. Revue d'analyse économique* 59, 3 (1983): 402–22.

- "Démographie, développement économique, fréquentation scolaire et alphabétisation dans les populations acadiennes des Maritimes avant 1911: une perspective régionale et comparative." *Acadiensis* 26, 1 (1996): 3–31.

Parker, David. "The Huguenots in seventeenth century France." In A.C. Hepburn, ed. *Minorities in history: Papers read before the Thirteenth Irish Conference of Historians at the University of Ulster, 1978*. London: E. Arnold 1977.

Pastore, Ralph. "Native history in the Atlantic region during the colonial period." *Acadiensis* 20, 1 (1990): 209–13.

Patterson, Stephen E. "Indian-white relationships in Nova Scotia, 1749–1761: A study in political interaction." *Acadiensis* 23, 1 (1993): 23–59.

Plank, Geoffrey. "The two majors cope: The boundaries of nationality in mid-eighteenth century Nova Scotia." *Acadiensis* 25, 2 (1996): 18–41.

Pothier, Bernard. "Acadian emigration to Île Royale after the conquest of Acadia." *Histoire Sociale/Social History* 6 (November 1970): 123–6.

Potter, Jim. "Demographic development and family structure." In Jack P. Greene and J.R. Pole, ed., *Colonial British North America: Essays in the new history of the early modern era*. Baltimore, Md.: Johns Hopkins University Press 1984.

Quinn, David B. "Colonies in the beginning: Examples from North America." In Stanley H. Palmer and Denis Reinhartz, ed. *Essays on the history of North American discovery and exploration.* Walter Prescott Erbb Memorial Lectures, no.21. College Station, Texas. A&M University Press 1988.

Reid, John G. "Acadian and the Acadians: In the shadow of Quebec." *The Beaver* 67, 5 (1987): 26–31.

– "'Another Dunkirk': The historiography of the conquest of Acadia." Presented at the Atlantic Studies Conference, St John's, Nlfd., 21 May 1992.

– "Nova Scotia, 1715: Mission to the Micmac." *The Beaver,* 70, 5 (1990): 15–22.

– "The Scots crown and the restitution of Port Royal, 1629–1632." *Acadiensis* 6 (spring 1977): 39–63.

– "Styles of colonization and social disorders in early Acadia and Maine: A comparative approach." SHA *Cahiers* 7, 3 (1976): 105–17.

Rutman, Darrett B. "Assessing the little communities of early America." *WMQ,* 3rd series, 43, 2 (1986): 163–78.

Sachse, W.L. "The migration of New Englanders to England, 1640–1660." *American Historical Review,* 53, 2 (1948): 251–78.

Sauvageau, Robert. "Réponse à un 'Compte rendu' en forme de massacre." SHA *Cahiers* 20, 4 (1989): 196–207.

Smith, Daniel Blake. "The study of the family in early America: Trends, problems and prospects." *WMQ,* 3rd series, 39, 1 (1982): 384–407.

Snow, Dean R., and Kim M. Lanphear. "European contact and Indian depopulation in the northeast: The timing of the first epidemics." *Ethnohistory* 35, 1 (1988): 15–33.

Sosin, Jack M. "Louisbourg and the Peace of Aix-la-Chapelle, 1748." *WMQ,* 3rd series, 14 (October 1957): 516–35.

Speck, W.A.. "The international and imperial context." In Jack P. Greene and J.R. Pole, ed., *Colonial British North America: Essays in the new history of the early modern era.* Baltimore, Md.: Johns Hopkins University Press, 1984. 384–407.

Throp, Daniel B. "Equals of the king: The balance of power in early Acadia." *Acadiensis* 25, 2 (1996): 3–17.

Tomlins, Christopher. "The many legalities of colonization: A manifest of destiny for early American legal history." In Christopher Tomlins and Bruce H. Mann, ed., *The many legalities of early America.* Chapel Hill: University of North Carolina Press 2001. 1–23.

Vanderlinden, Jacques. "Alliances entre familles acadiennes pendant la période française." SHA *Cahiers* 27, 2–3 (1996): 125–48.

– "À la recontre de l'histoire du droit en Acadie avant le dérangement." *Revue de l'Unversité de Moncton* 28, 1 (1995).

Vignereau, Louis-André. "Letters of an Acadian trader, 1674–76." *New England Quarterly* 13 (January 1940): 98–110.

Webb, Stephen Saunders. "Army and empire: English garrison government in Britain and America, 1596–1763." *WMQ,* 3rd series, 34 (1977): 1–31.

– "The strange career of Francis Nicholson." *WMQ,* 3rd series, 23 (1966): 513–48.

White, Stephen A. "La généalogie des trente-sept familles hotesses des 'Retrouvailles 94.'" *La Société historique acadienne* 25, 2–3 (1994).

Wicken, Bill. "26 August 1726: A case study in Mi'kmaq-New England relations in the early 18th century." *Acadiensis* 23, 1 (1993): 6.

Wilkins, E.H. "Arcadia in America." *Proceedings of the American Philosophical Society*, 101, 1 (1957): 4–20.

Wise, S.F. "Liberal consensus or ideological background: Some reflections on the Hartz thesis." Presidential address, Canadian Historical Association, *Historical Papers/Communications Historiques*, 1974, 1–14.

THESES

Belada, Mario. "Les migrations au Canada sous le regime français." PhD thesis, Université de Montréal 1983.

Chard, Donald F. "The Impact of Île Royale on New England." PhD thesis, University of Ottawa Ottawa 1977.

Choquette, Leslie. "Frenchmen into peasants: Modernity and tradition in the peopling of French Canada (17th– 18th centuries)." PhD thesis, Harvard University 1994.

Daigle, Jean. "Michel Le Neuf de La Vallière: seigneur de Beaubassin et gouverneur d'Acadie." MA thesis, Université de Montréal 1970.

– "Nos amis, les ennemis: relations commerciales de l'Acadie avec le Massachusetts, 1670–1711." PhD thesis, University of Maine 1975.

Doherty, Dennis Charles Brian. "Oliver Cromwell, Robert Sedgewick, John Leverett and the Acadian adventure of 1654." MA thesis, Queen's University 1969.

Douglas, W.A.B. "Nova Scotia and the Royal Navy, 1713–1766." PhD thesis, Queen's University 1973.

Dugas, L.J. "L'alphabétisation des Acadiens, 1700–1850." MA thesis, University of Ottawa 1992.

Eames, Stephen Charles. "Rustic warriors: Warfare and the provincial soldier on the northern frontier, 1669–1748." PhD thesis, University of New Hampshire 1989.

Griffiths, N.E.S. "The Acadian deportation: A study in historiography and literature." MA thesis, University of New Brunswick 1957.

Moody, Barry. "'A just and disinterested man': The Nova Scotia career of Paul Mascarene, 1710–1752." PhD thesis, Queen's University 1976.

Plank, Geoffrey Gilbert. "The culture of conquest: The British colonists and Nova Scotia, 1600–1750." PhD thesis, Princeton University 1994.

Roy, Raymond. "La croissance démographique en Acadie de 1671 à 1763." Memoire de Maîtrise, Université de Montréal 1975.

Wicken, William, C. "Encounters with tall sails and tall tales: Mi'kmaq society, 1500–1760." PhD thesis, McGill University 1994.

Index

—